NISSAN PICK-UPS 1970-88 REPAIR MANUAL

CEO	Rick Van Dalen
President	Dean F. Morgantini, S.A.E.
Vice President–Finance	Barry L. Beck
Vice President–Sales	Glenn D. Potere
Executive Editor	Kevin M. G. Maher, A.S.E.
Manager–Consumer Automotive	Richard Schwartz, A.S.E.
Manager–Professional Automotive	Richard J. Rivele
Manager–Marine/Recreation	James R. Marotta, A.S.E.
Production Specialists	Brian Hollingsworth, Melinda Possinger
Project Managers	Thomas A. Mellon, A.S.E., S.A.E., Eric Michael Mihalyi, A.S.E., S.T.S., S.A.E., Christine L. Sheeky, S.A.E., Richard T. Smith, Ron Webb
Schematics Editors	Christopher G. Ritchie, A.S.E., S.A.E., S.T.S., Stephanie A. Spunt
Editor	Tony Tortorici, A.S.E., S.A.E.

CHILTON Automotive Books

PUBLISHED BY **W. G. NICHOLS, INC.**

Manufactured in USA
© 1994 W. G. Nichols, Inc.
1025 Andrew Drive
West Chester, PA 19380
ISBN 0-8019-8585-4
Library of Congress Catalog Card No. 98-071957
11 12 13 14 15 9 8 7 6 5 4 3 2 1 0

Chilton is a registered trademark of Cahners Business Information, a division of Reed Elsevier, Inc., and has been licensed to W. G. Nichols, Inc.

www.chiltononline.com

Contents

1 GENERAL INFORMATION AND MAINTENANCE

- 1-2 HOW TO USE THIS BOOK
- 1-2 TOOLS AND EQUIPMENT
- 1-4 SERVICING YOUR VEHICLE SAFELY
- 1-5 FASTENERS, MEASUREMENTS AND CONVERSIONS
- 1-7 SERIAL NUMBER IDENTIFICATION
- 1-10 ROUTINE MAINTENANCE AND TUNE-UP
- 1-23 FLUIDS AND LUBRICANTS
- 1-36 TRAILER TOWING
- 1-37 JUMP STARTING A DEAD BATTERY
- 1-37 JACKING
- 1-39 MAINTENANCE INTERVALS

2 ENGINE PERFORMANCE AND TUNE-UP

- 2-2 TUNE-UP PROCEDURES
- 2-5 FIRING ORDERS
- 2-5 POINT TYPE IGNITION
- 2-7 ELECTRONIC IGNITION
- 2-11 IGNITION TIMING
- 2-13 VALVE LASH
- 2-16 IDLE SPEED AND MIXTURE ADJUSTMENTS

3 ENGINE AND ENGINE REBUILDING

- 3-2 ENGINE ELECTRICAL
- 3-9 ENGINE MECHANICAL
- 3-50 EXHAUST SYSTEM

4 EMISSION CONTROLS

- 4-2 EMISSION CONTROLS
- 4-15 ELECTRONIC ENGINE CONTROLS
- 4-21 VACUUM DIAGRAMS AND SYSTEM COMPONENTS

5 FUEL SYSTEM

- 5-2 CARBURETED FUEL SYSTEM
- 5-10 FUEL INJECTION SYSTEM
- 5-14 FUEL TANK

6 CHASSIS ELECTRICAL

- 6-2 UNDERSTANDING AND TROUBLESHOOTING ELECTRICAL SYSTEMS
- 6-8 HEATING AND AIR CONDITIONING
- 6-12 RADIO
- 6-12 WINDSHIELD WIPERS
- 6-15 INSTRUMENTS AND SWITCHES
- 6-17 LIGHTING
- 6-19 TRAILER WIRING
- 6-19 CIRCUIT PROTECTION
- 6-28 WIRING DIAGRAMS

Contents

7 DRIVE TRAIN
- 7-2 MANUAL TRANSMISSION
- 7-5 CLUTCH
- 7-10 AUTOMATIC TRANSMISSION
- 7-12 TRANSFER CASE
- 7-13 DRIVELINE
- 7-18 REAR DRIVE AXLE
- 7-21 FRONT DRIVE AXLE

8 SUSPENSION AND STEERING
- 8-2 FRONT SUSPENSION
- 8-16 REAR SUSPENSION
- 8-20 STEERING

9 BRAKES
- 9-2 BRAKE OPERATING SYSTEM
- 9-3 BRAKE SYSTEM
- 9-10 FRONT DRUM BRAKES
- 9-12 FRONT DISC BRAKES
- 9-16 REAR DRUM BRAKES
- 9-21 REAR DISC BRAKES
- 9-22 PARKING BRAKE

10 BODY AND TRIM
- 10-2 EXTERIOR
- 10-5 INTERIOR

GLOSSARY
- 10-8 GLOSSARY

MASTER INDEX
- 10-13 MASTER INDEX

See last page for information on additional titles

SAFETY NOTICE

Proper service and repair procedures are vital to the safe, reliable operation of all motor vehicles, as well as the personal safety of those performing repairs. This manual outlines procedures for servicing and repairing vehicles using safe, effective methods. The procedures contain many NOTES, CAUTIONS and WARNINGS which should be followed, along with standard procedures to eliminate the possibility of personal injury or improper service which could damage the vehicle or compromise its safety.

It is important to note that repair procedures and techniques, tools and parts for servicing motor vehicles, as well as the skill and experience of the individual performing the work vary widely. It is not possible to anticipate all of the conceivable ways or conditions under which vehicles may be serviced, or to provide cautions as to all possible hazards that may result. Standard and accepted safety precautions and equipment should be used when handling toxic or flammable fluids, and safety goggles or other protection should be used during cutting, grinding, chiseling, prying, or any other process that can cause material removal or projectiles.

Some procedures require the use of tools specially designed for a specific purpose. Before substituting another tool or procedure, you must be completely satisfied that neither your personal safety, nor the performance of the vehicle will be endangered.

Although information in this manual is based on industry sources and is complete as possible at the time of publication, the possibility exists that some car manufacturers made later changes which could not be included here. While striving for total accuracy, Nichols Publishing cannot assume responsibility for any errors, changes or omissions that may occur in the compilation of this data.

PART NUMBERS

Part numbers listed in this reference are not recommendations by Nichols Publishing for any product brand name. They are references that can be used with interchange manuals and aftermarket supplier catalogs to locate each brand supplier's discrete part number.

SPECIAL TOOLS

Special tools are recommended by the vehicle manufacturer to perform their specific job. Use has been kept to a minimum, but where absolutely necessary, they are referred to in the text by the part number of the tool manufacturer. These tools can be purchased, under the appropriate part number, from your local dealer or regional distributor, or an equivalent tool can be purchased locally from a tool supplier or parts outlet. Before substituting any tool for the one recommended, read the SAFETY NOTICE at the top of this page.

ACKNOWLEDGMENTS

Nichols Publishing expresses appreciation to Nissan Motor Company for their generous assistance.

Nichols Publishing would like to express thanks to all of the fine companies who participate in the production of our books:
- Hand tools supplied by Craftsman are used during all phases of our vehicle teardown and photography.
- Many of the fine specialty tools used in our procedures were provided courtesy of Lisle Corporation.
- Lincoln Automotive Products (1 Lincoln Way, St. Louis, MO 63120) has provided their industrial shop equipment, including jacks (engine, transmission and floor), engine stands, fluid and lubrication tools, as well as shop presses.
- Rotary Lifts (1-800-640-5438 or www.Rotary-Lift.com), the largest automobile lift manufacturer in the world, offering the biggest variety of surface and in-ground lifts available, has fulfilled our shop's lift needs.
- Much of our shop's electronic testing equipment was supplied by Universal Enterprises Inc. (UEI).
- Safety-Kleen Systems Inc. has provided parts cleaning stations and assistance with environmentally sound disposal of residual wastes.
- United Gilsonite Laboratories (UGL), manufacturer of Drylok® concrete floor paint, has provided materials and expertise for the coating and protection of our shop floor.

No part of this publication may be reproduced, transmitted or stored in any form or by any means, electronic or mechanical, including photocopy, recording, or by information storage or retrieval system, without prior written permission from the publisher.

1 GENERAL INFORMATION AND MAINTENANCE

HOW TO USE THIS BOOK 1-2
WHERE TO BEGIN 1-2
AVOIDING TROUBLE 1-2
MAINTENANCE OR REPAIR? 1-2
AVOIDING THE MOST COMMON
  MISTAKES 1-2
TOOLS AND EQUIPMENT 1-2
SPECIAL TOOLS 1-4
SERVICING YOUR VEHICLE SAFELY 1-4
DO'S 1-4
DON'TS 1-5
**FASTENERS, MEASUREMENTS AND
  CONVERSIONS 1-5**
BOLTS, NUTS AND OTHER THREADED
  RETAINERS 1-5
TORQUE 1-6
  TORQUE WRENCHES 1-6
  TORQUE ANGLE METERS 1-7
STANDARD AND METRIC
  MEASUREMENTS 1-7
SERIAL NUMBER IDENTIFICATION 1-7
VEHICLE IDENTIFICATION NUMBER 1-7
ENGINE SERIAL NUMBER 1-8
  L16, L18 AND L20B ENGINES 1-9
  Z20, Z22, Z24 AND Z24I ENGINES 1-9
  VG30I ENGINES 1-9
TRANSMISSION 1-9
**ROUTINE MAINTENANCE AND
  TUNE-UP 1-10**
AIR CLEANER 1-10
  REMOVAL & INSTALLATION 1-10
FUEL FILTER 1-11
  REMOVAL & INSTALLATION 1-11
PCV VALVE 1-12
  REMOVAL, TESTING & INSTALLATION 1-13
AIR INJECTION/INDUCTION VALVE FILTER 1-13
  REMOVAL & INSTALLATION 1-13
EVAPORATIVE CANISTER 1-13
  SERVICING 1-13
HEAT RISER 1-14
  SERVICING 1-14
BATTERY 1-14
  PRECAUTIONS 1-14
  GENERAL MAINTENANCE 1-14
  BATTERY FLUID 1-14
  CABLES 1-15
  CHARGING 1-15
  REPLACEMENT 1-16
DRIVE BELTS 1-16
  INSPECTION 1-16
  ADJUSTMENT 1-16
HOSES 1-18
  REPLACEMENT 1-18
AIR CONDITIONING SYSTEM 1-19
  SYSTEM SERVICE & REPAIR 1-19
  PREVENTIVE MAINTENANCE 1-19
  SYSTEM INSPECTION 1-20
  ISOLATING THE COMPRESSOR 1-20
WINDSHIELD WIPERS 1-20
  ELEMENT (REFILL) CARE &
    REPLACEMENT 1-20
TIRES AND WHEELS 1-21
  TIRE ROTATION 1-21
  TIRE DESIGN 1-21
  TIRE STORAGE 1-21
  INFLATION & INSPECTION 1-22
FLUIDS AND LUBRICANTS 1-23
OIL AND FUEL RECOMMENDATIONS 1-23
  OIL 1-23
  FUEL 1-24
  OPERATION IN FOREIGN COUNTRIES 1-24
ENGINE 1-24
  OIL LEVEL CHECK 1-24
  OIL AND FILTER CHANGE 1-24
MANUAL TRANSMISSION 1-26
  FLUID RECOMMENDATIONS 1-26
  FLUID LEVEL CHECK 1-26
  DRAIN AND REFILL 1-26
  CHECKING WATER ENTRY 1-27
AUTOMATIC TRANSMISSION 1-27
  FLUID RECOMMENDATIONS 1-27
  FLUID LEVEL CHECK 1-27
  DRAIN AND REFILL 1-28
TRANSFER CASE 1-28
  FLUID RECOMMENDATIONS 1-28
  FLUID LEVEL CHECK 1-28
  DRAIN AND REFILL 1-28
DRIVE AXLES (DIFFERENTIALS) 1-29
  FLUID RECOMMENDATIONS 1-29
  FLUID LEVEL CHECK 1-29
  DRAIN AND REFILL 1-30
COOLING SYSTEM 1-30
  FLUID RECOMMENDATIONS 1-30
  FLUID LEVEL CHECK 1-30
  DRAIN AND REFILL 1-31
  SYSTEM INSPECTION 1-31
  CHECKING SYSTEM PROTECTION 1-31
MASTER CYLINDERS 1-31
  FLUID RECOMMENDATIONS 1-32
  FLUID LEVEL CHECK 1-32
POWER STEERING PUMP 1-32
  FLUID RECOMMENDATIONS 1-32
  FLUID LEVEL CHECK 1-33
STEERING GEAR 1-33
  FLUID RECOMMENDATIONS 1-33
  FLUID LEVEL CHECK 1-33
BATTERY 1-33
CHASSIS GREASING 1-33
  MANUAL TRANSMISSION AND CLUTCH
    LINKAGE 1-34
  AUTOMATIC TRANSMISSION LINKAGE 1-34
  PARKING BRAKE LINKAGE 1-34
WHEEL BEARINGS 1-34
  ADJUSTMENT AND LUBRICATION 1-34
TRAILER TOWING 1-36
GENERAL RECOMMENDATIONS 1-36
TRAILER WEIGHT 1-36
HITCH (TONGUE) WEIGHT 1-36
COOLING 1-36
  ENGINE 1-36
TRANSMISSION 1-36
JUMP STARTING A DEAD BATTERY 1-37
JUMP STARTING PRECAUTIONS 1-37
JUMP STARTING PROCEDURE 1-37
JACKING 1-37
JACKING PRECAUTIONS 1-38
MAINTENANCE INTERVALS 1-39
SPECIFICATIONS CHARTS
  ENGINE IDENTIFICATION 1-9
  MAINTENANCE INTERVALS 1-39
  CAPACITIES 1-40

HOW TO USE THIS BOOK 1-2
TOOLS AND EQUIPMENT 1-2
SERVICING YOUR VEHICLE SAFELY 1-4
FASTENERS, MEASUREMENTS
  AND CONVERSIONS 1-5
SERIAL NUMBER IDENTIFICATION 1-7
ROUTINE MAINTENANCE
  AND TUNE-UP 1-10
FLUIDS AND LUBRICANTS 1-23
TRAILER TOWING 1-36
JUMP STARTING A DEAD BATTERY 1-37
JACKING 1-37
MAINTENANCE INTERVALS 1-39

1-2 GENERAL INFORMATION AND MAINTENANCE

HOW TO USE THIS BOOK

This Chilton's Total Car Care manual for Nissan Trucks is intended to help you learn more about the inner workings of your vehicle while saving you money on its upkeep and operation.

The beginning of the book will likely be referred to the most, since that is where you will find information for maintenance and tune-up. The other sections deal with the more complex systems of your vehicle. Systems (from engine through brakes) are covered to the extent that the average do-it-yourselfer can attempt. This book will not explain such things as rebuilding a differential because the expertise required and the special tools necessary make this uneconomical. It will, however, give you detailed instructions to help you change your own brake pads and shoes, replace spark plugs, and perform many more jobs that can save you money and help avoid expensive problems.

A secondary purpose of this book is a reference for owners who want to understand their vehicle and/or their mechanics better.

Where to Begin

Before removing any bolts, read through the entire procedure. This will give you the overall view of what tools and supplies will be required. So read ahead and plan ahead. Each operation should be approached logically and all procedures thoroughly understood before attempting any work.

If repair of a component is not considered practical, we tell you how to remove the part and then how to install the new or rebuilt replacement. In this way, you at least save labor costs.

Avoiding Trouble

Many procedures in this book require you to "label and disconnect . . ." a group of lines, hoses or wires. Don't be think you can remember where everything goes—you won't. If you hook up vacuum or fuel lines incorrectly, the vehicle may run poorly, if at all. If you hook up electrical wiring incorrectly, you may instantly learn a very expensive lesson.

You don't need to know the proper name for each hose or line. A piece of masking tape on the hose and a piece on its fitting will allow you to assign your own label. As long as you remember your own code, the lines can be reconnected by matching your tags. Remember that tape will dissolve in gasoline or solvents; if a part is to be washed or cleaned, use another method of identification. A permanent felt-tipped marker or a metal scribe can be very handy for marking metal parts. Remove any tape or paper labels after assembly.

Maintenance or Repair?

Maintenance includes routine inspections, adjustments, and replacement of parts which show signs of normal wear. Maintenance compensates for wear or deterioration. Repair implies that something has broken or is not working. A need for a repair is often caused by lack of maintenance. for example: draining and refilling automatic transmission fluid is maintenance recommended at specific intervals. Failure to do this can shorten the life of the transmission/transaxle, requiring very expensive repairs. While no maintenance program can prevent items from eventually breaking or wearing out, a general rule is true: MAINTENANCE IS CHEAPER THAN REPAIR.

TOOLS AND EQUIPMENT

▶ See Figures 1 thru 15

Without the proper tools and equipment it is impossible to properly service your vehicle. It would be virtually impossible to catalog every tool that you would need to perform all of the operations in this book. It would be unwise for the amateur to rush out and buy an expensive set of tools on the theory that he/she may need one or more of them at some time.

The best approach is to proceed slowly, gathering a good quality set of those tools that are used most frequently. Don't be misled by the low cost of bargain tools. It is far better to spend a little more for better quality. Forged wrenches, 6 or 12-point sockets and fine tooth ratchets are by far preferable to their less expensive counterparts. As any good mechanic can tell you, there are few worse experiences than trying to work on a vehicle with bad tools. Your monetary savings will be far outweighed by frustration and mangled knuckles.

Two basic mechanic's rules should be mentioned here. First, whenever the left side of the vehicle or engine is referred to, it means the driver's side. Conversely, the right side of the vehicle means the passenger's side. Second, screws and bolts are removed by turning counterclockwise, and tightened by turning clockwise unless specifically noted.

Safety is always the most important rule. Constantly be aware of the dangers involved in working on an automobile and take the proper precautions. Please refer to the information in this section regarding SERVICING YOUR VEHICLE SAFELY and the SAFETY NOTICE on the acknowledgment page.

Avoiding the Most Common Mistakes

Pay attention to the instructions provided. There are 3 common mistakes in mechanical work:

1. Incorrect order of assembly, disassembly or adjustment. When taking something apart or putting it together, performing steps in the wrong order usually just costs you extra time; however, it CAN break something. Read the entire procedure before beginning. Perform everything in the order in which the instructions say you should, even if you can't see a reason for it. When you're taking apart something that is very intricate, you might want to draw a picture of how it looks when assembled in order to make sure you get everything back in its proper position. When making adjustments, perform them in the proper order. One adjustment possibly will affect another.

2. Overtorquing (or undertorquing). While it is more common for overtorquing to cause damage, undertorquing may allow a fastener to vibrate loose causing serious damage. Especially when dealing with aluminum parts, pay attention to torque specifications and utilize a torque wrench in assembly. If a torque figure is not available, remember that if you are using the right tool to perform the job, you will probably not have to strain yourself to get a fastener tight enough. The pitch of most threads is so slight that the tension you put on the wrench will be multiplied many times in actual force on what you are tightening.

There are many commercial products available for ensuring that fasteners won't come loose, even if they are not torqued just right (a very common brand is Loctite®). If you're worried about getting something together tight enough to hold, but loose enough to avoid mechanical damage during assembly, one of these products might offer substantial insurance. Before choosing a threadlocking compound, read the label on the package and make sure the product is compatible with the materials, fluids, etc. involved.

3. Crossthreading. This occurs when a part such as a bolt is screwed into a nut or casting at the wrong angle and forced. Crossthreading is more likely to occur if access is difficult. It helps to clean and lubricate fasteners, then to start threading the bolt, spark plug, etc. with your fingers. If you encounter resistance, unscrew the part and start over again at a different angle until it can be inserted and turned several times without much effort. Keep in mind that many parts have tapered threads, so that gentle turning will automatically bring the part you're threading to the proper angle. Don't put a wrench on the part until it's been tightened a couple of turns by hand. If you suddenly encounter resistance, and the part has not seated fully, don't force it. Pull it back out to make sure it's clean and threading properly.

Be sure to take your time and be patient, and always plan ahead. Allow yourself ample time to perform repairs and maintenance.

Begin accumulating those tools that are used most frequently: those associated with routine maintenance and tune-up. In addition to the normal assortment of screwdrivers and pliers, you should have the following tools:

• Wrenches/sockets and combination open end/box end wrenches in sizes 1/8–3/4 in. and/or 3mm–19mm 13/16 in. or 5/8 in. spark plug socket (depending on plug type).

➥ If possible, buy various length socket drive extensions. Universal-joint and wobble extensions can be extremely useful, but be careful when using them, as they can change the amount of torque applied to the socket.

• Jackstands for support.
• Oil filter wrench.

GENERAL INFORMATION AND MAINTENANCE

Fig. 1 All but the most basic procedures will require an assortment of ratchets and sockets

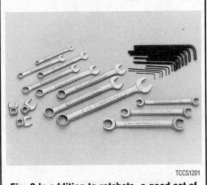
Fig. 2 In addition to ratchets, a good set of wrenches and hex keys will be necessary

Fig. 3 A hydraulic floor jack and a set of jackstands are essential for lifting and supporting the vehicle

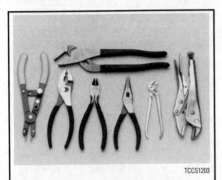
Fig. 4 An assortment of pliers, grippers and cutters will be handy for old rusted parts and stripped bolt heads

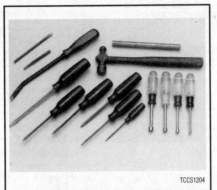
Fig. 5 Various drivers, chisels and prybars are great tools to have in your toolbox

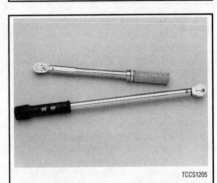
Fig. 6 Many repairs will require the use of a torque wrench to assure the components are properly fastened

Fig. 7 Although not always necessary, using specialized brake tools will save time

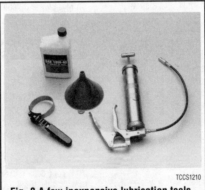
Fig. 8 A few inexpensive lubrication tools will make maintenance easier

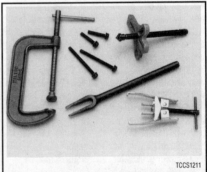
Fig. 9 Various pullers, clamps and separator tools are needed for many larger, more complicated repairs

Fig. 10 A variety of tools and gauges should be used for spark plug gapping and installation

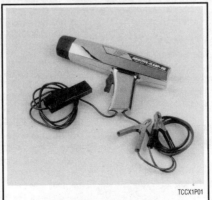
Fig. 11 Inductive type timing light

Fig. 12 A screw-in type compression gauge is recommended for compression testing

1-4 GENERAL INFORMATION AND MAINTENANCE

Fig. 13 A vacuum/pressure tester is necessary for many testing procedures

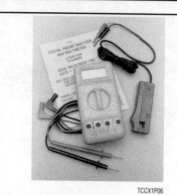

Fig. 14 Most modern automotive multimeters incorporate many helpful features

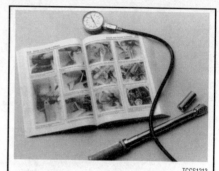

Fig. 15 Proper information is vital, so always have a Chilton Total Car Care manual handy

- Spout or funnel for pouring fluids.
- Grease gun for chassis lubrication (unless your vehicle is not equipped with any grease fittings)
- Hydrometer for checking the battery (unless equipped with a sealed, maintenance-free battery).
- A container for draining oil and other fluids.
- Rags for wiping up the inevitable mess.

In addition to the above items there are several others that are not absolutely necessary, but handy to have around. These include an equivalent oil absorbent gravel, like cat litter, and the usual supply of lubricants, antifreeze and fluids. This is a basic list for routine maintenance, but only your personal needs and desire can accurately determine your list of tools.

After performing a few projects on the vehicle, you'll be amazed at the other tools and non-tools on your workbench. Some useful household items are: a large turkey baster or siphon, empty coffee cans and ice trays (to store parts), a ball of twine, electrical tape for wiring, small rolls of colored tape for tagging lines or hoses, markers and pens, a note pad, golf tees (for plugging vacuum lines), metal coat hangers or a roll of mechanic's wire (to hold things out of the way), dental pick or similar long, pointed probe, a strong magnet, and a small mirror (to see into recesses and under manifolds).

A more advanced set of tools, suitable for tune-up work, can be drawn up easily. While the tools are slightly more sophisticated, they need not be outrageously expensive. There are several inexpensive tach/dwell meters on the market that are every bit as good for the average mechanic as a professional model. Just be sure that it goes to a least 1200–1500 rpm on the tach scale and that it works on 4, 6 and 8-cylinder engines. The key to these purchases is to make them with an eye towards adaptability and wide range. A basic list of tune-up tools could include:

- Tach/dwell meter.
- Spark plug wrench and gapping tool.
- Feeler gauges for valve adjustment.
- Timing light.

The choice of a timing light should be made carefully. A light which works on the DC current supplied by the vehicle's battery is the best choice; it should have a xenon tube for brightness. On any vehicle with an electronic ignition system, a timing light with an inductive pickup that clamps around the No. 1 spark plug cable is preferred.

In addition to these basic tools, there are several other tools and gauges you may find useful. These include:

- Compression gauge. The screw-in type is slower to use, but eliminates the possibility of a faulty reading due to escaping pressure.
- Manifold vacuum gauge.
- 12V test light.
- A combination volt/ohmmeter
- Induction Ammeter. This is used for determining whether or not there is current in a wire. These are handy for use if a wire is broken somewhere in a wiring harness.

As a final note, you will probably find a torque wrench necessary for all but the most basic work. The beam type models are perfectly adequate, although the newer click types (breakaway) are easier to use. The click type torque wrenches tend to be more expensive. Also keep in mind that all types of torque wrenches should be periodically checked and/or recalibrated. You will have to decide for yourself which better fits your pocketbook, and purpose.

Special Tools

Normally, the use of special factory tools is avoided for repair procedures, since these are not readily available for the do-it-yourself mechanic. When it is possible to perform the job with more commonly available tools, it will be pointed out, but occasionally, a special tool was designed to perform a specific function and should be used. Before substituting another tool, you should be convinced that neither your safety nor the performance of the vehicle will be compromised.

Special tools can usually be purchased from an automotive parts store or from your dealer. In some cases special tools may be available directly from the tool manufacturer.

SERVICING YOUR VEHICLE SAFELY

▶ See Figures 16, 17 and 18

It is virtually impossible to anticipate all of the hazards involved with automotive maintenance and service, but care and common sense will prevent most accidents.

The rules of safety for mechanics range from "don't smoke around gasoline," to "use the proper tool(s) for the job." The trick to avoiding injuries is to develop safe work habits and to take every possible precaution.

Do's

- Do keep a fire extinguisher and first aid kit handy.
- Do wear safety glasses or goggles when cutting, drilling, grinding or prying, even if you have 20–20 vision. If you wear glasses for the sake of vision, wear safety goggles over your regular glasses.
- Do shield your eyes whenever you work around the battery. Batteries contain sulfuric acid. In case of contact with, flush the area with water or a mixture of water and baking soda, then seek immediate medical attention.
- Do use safety stands (jackstands) for any undervehicle service. Jacks are for raising vehicles; jackstands are for making sure the vehicle stays raised until you want it to come down.
- Do use adequate ventilation when working with any chemicals or hazardous materials. Like carbon monoxide, the asbestos dust resulting from some brake lining wear can be hazardous in sufficient quantities.
- Do disconnect the negative battery cable when working on the electrical system. The secondary ignition system contains EXTREMELY HIGH VOLTAGE. In some cases it can even exceed 50,000 volts.
- Do follow manufacturer's directions whenever working with potentially hazardous materials. Most chemicals and fluids are poisonous.
- Do properly maintain your tools. Loose hammerheads, mushroomed

GENERAL INFORMATION AND MAINTENANCE 1-5

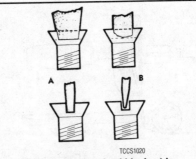

Fig. 16 Screwdrivers should be kept in good condition to prevent injury or damage which could result if the blade slips from the screw

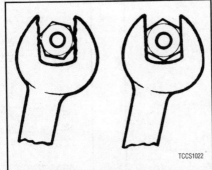

Fig. 17 Using the correct size wrench will help prevent the possibility of rounding off a nut

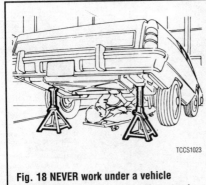

Fig. 18 NEVER work under a vehicle unless it is supported using safety stands (jackstands)

punches and chisels, frayed or poorly grounded electrical cords, excessively worn screwdrivers, spread wrenches (open end), cracked sockets, slipping ratchets, or faulty droplight sockets can cause accidents.

- Likewise, keep your tools clean; a greasy wrench can slip off a bolt head, ruining the bolt and often harming your knuckles in the process.
- Do use the proper size and type of tool for the job at hand. Do select a wrench or socket that fits the nut or bolt. The wrench or socket should sit straight, not cocked.
- Do, when possible, pull on a wrench handle rather than push on it, and adjust your stance to prevent a fall.
- Do be sure that adjustable wrenches are tightly closed on the nut or bolt and pulled so that the force is on the side of the fixed jaw.
- Do strike squarely with a hammer; avoid glancing blows.
- Do set the parking brake and block the drive wheels if the work requires a running engine.

Don'ts

- Don't run the engine in a garage or anywhere else without proper ventilation—EVER! Carbon monoxide is poisonous; it takes a long time to leave the human body and you can build up a deadly supply of it in your system by simply breathing in a little at a time. You may not realize you are slowly poisoning yourself. Always use power vents, windows, fans and/or open the garage door.
- Don't work around moving parts while wearing loose clothing. Short sleeves are much safer than long, loose sleeves. Hard-toed shoes with neoprene soles protect your toes and give a better grip on slippery surfaces. Watches and jewelry is not safe working around a vehicle. Long hair should be tied back under a hat or cap.
- Don't use pockets for toolboxes. A fall or bump can drive a screwdriver deep into your body. Even a rag hanging from your back pocket can wrap around a spinning shaft or fan.
- Don't smoke when working around gasoline, cleaning solvent or other flammable material.
- Don't smoke when working around the battery. When the battery is being charged, it gives off explosive hydrogen gas.
- Don't use gasoline to wash your hands; there are excellent soaps available. Gasoline contains dangerous additives which can enter the body through a cut or through your pores. Gasoline also removes all the natural oils from the skin so that bone dry hands will suck up oil and grease.
- Don't service the air conditioning system unless you are equipped with the necessary tools and training. When liquid or compressed gas refrigerant is released to atmospheric pressure it will absorb heat from whatever it contacts. This will chill or freeze anything it touches.
- Don't use screwdrivers for anything other than driving screws! A screwdriver used as an prying tool can snap when you least expect it, causing injuries. At the very least, you'll ruin a good screwdriver.
- Don't use an emergency jack (that little ratchet, scissors, or pantograph jack supplied with the vehicle) for anything other than changing a flat! These jacks are only intended for emergency use out on the road; they are NOT designed as a maintenance tool. If you are serious about maintaining your vehicle yourself, invest in a hydraulic floor jack of at least a 1½ ton capacity, and at least two sturdy jackstands.

FASTENERS, MEASUREMENTS AND CONVERSIONS

Bolts, Nuts and Other Threaded Retainers

♦ See Figures 19 and 20

Although there are a great variety of fasteners found in the modern car or truck, the most commonly used retainer is the threaded fastener (nuts, bolts, screws, studs, etc.). Most threaded retainers may be reused, provided that they are not damaged in use or during the repair. Some retainers (such as stretch bolts or torque prevailing nuts) are designed to deform when tightened or in use and should not be reinstalled.

Whenever possible, we will note any special retainers which should be replaced during a procedure. But you should always inspect the condition of a retainer when it is removed and replace any that show signs of damage. Check all threads for rust or corrosion which can increase the torque necessary to achieve the desired clamp load for which that fastener was originally selected. Additionally, be sure that the driver surface of the fastener has not been compromised by rounding or other damage. In some cases a driver surface may become only partially rounded, allowing the driver to catch in only one direction. In many of these occurrences, a fastener may be installed and tightened, but the driver would not be able to grip and loosen the fastener again.

If you must replace a fastener, whether due to design or damage, you must ALWAYS be sure to use the proper replacement. In all cases, a retainer of the same design, material and strength should be used. Markings on the heads of

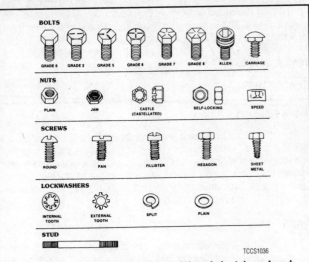

Fig. 19 There are many different types of threaded retainers found on vehicles

1-6 GENERAL INFORMATION AND MAINTENANCE

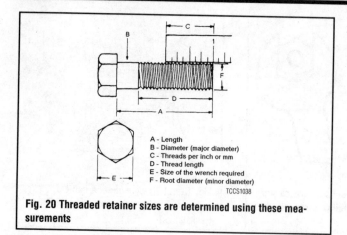

Fig. 20 Threaded retainer sizes are determined using these measurements

A - Length
B - Diameter (major diameter)
C - Threads per inch or mm
D - Thread length
E - Size of the wrench required
F - Root diameter (minor diameter)

most bolts will help determine the proper strength of the fastener. The same material, thread and pitch must be selected to assure proper installation and safe operation of the vehicle afterwards.

Thread gauges are available to help measure a bolt or stud's thread. Most automotive and hardware stores keep gauges available to help you select the proper size. In a pinch, you can use another nut or bolt for a thread gauge. If the bolt you are replacing is not too badly damaged, you can select a match by finding another bolt which will thread in its place. If you find a nut which threads properly onto the damaged bolt, then use that nut to help select the replacement bolt.

※※ WARNING

Be aware that when you find a bolt with damaged threads, you may also find the nut or drilled hole it was threaded into has also been damaged. If this is the case, you may have to drill and tap the hole, replace the nut or otherwise repair the threads. NEVER try to force a replacement bolt to fit into the damaged threads.

Torque

Torque is defined as the measurement of resistance to turning or rotating. It tends to twist a body about an axis of rotation. A common example of this would be tightening a threaded retainer such as a nut, bolt or screw. Measuring torque is one of the most common ways to help assure that a threaded retainer has been properly fastened.

When tightening a threaded fastener, torque is applied in three distinct areas, the head, the bearing surface and the clamp load. About 50 percent of the measured torque is used in overcoming bearing friction. This is the friction between the bearing surface of the bolt head, screw head or nut face and the base material or washer (the surface on which the fastener is rotating). Approximately 40 percent of the applied torque is used in overcoming thread friction. This leaves only about 10 percent of the applied torque to develop a useful clamp load (the force which holds a joint together). This means that friction can account for as much as 90 percent of the applied torque on a fastener.

TORQUE WRENCHES

♦ See Figure 21

In most applications, a torque wrench can be used to assure proper installation of a fastener. Torque wrenches come in various designs and most automotive supply stores will carry a variety to suit your needs. A torque wrench should be used any time we supply a specific torque value for a fastener. Again, the general rule of "if you are using the right tool for the job, you should not have to strain to tighten a fastener" applies here.

Beam Type

The beam type torque wrench is one of the most popular types. It consists of a pointer attached to the head that runs the length of the flexible beam (shaft) to a scale located near the handle. As the wrench is pulled, the beam bends and the pointer indicates the torque using the scale.

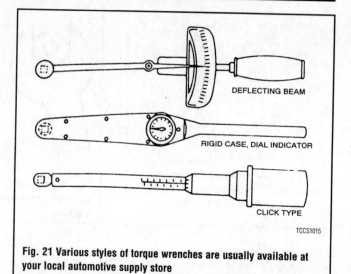

Fig. 21 Various styles of torque wrenches are usually available at your local automotive supply store

Click (Breakaway) Type

Another popular design of torque wrench is the click type. To use the click type wrench you pre-adjust it to a torque setting. Once the torque is reached, the wrench has a reflex signaling feature that causes a momentary breakaway of the torque wrench body, sending an impulse to the operator's hand.

Pivot Head Type

♦ See Figure 22

Some torque wrenches (usually of the click type) may be equipped with a pivot head which can allow it to be used in areas of limited access. BUT, it must be used properly. To hold a pivot head wrench, grasp the handle lightly, and as you pull on the handle, it should be floated on the pivot point. If the handle comes in contact with the yoke extension during the process of pulling, there is a very good chance the torque readings will be inaccurate because this could alter the wrench loading point. The design of the handle is usually such as to make it inconvenient to deliberately misuse the wrench.

➥It should be mentioned that the use of any U-joint, wobble or extension will have an effect on the torque readings, no matter what type of wrench you are using. For the most accurate readings, install the socket directly on the wrench driver. If necessary, straight extensions (which hold a socket directly under the wrench driver) will have the least effect on the torque reading. Avoid any extension that alters the length of the wrench from the handle to the head/driving point (such as a crow's foot). U-joint or wobble extensions can greatly affect the readings; avoid their use at all times.

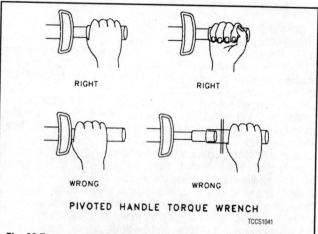

Fig. 22 Torque wrenches with pivoting heads must be grasped and used properly to prevent an incorrect reading

GENERAL INFORMATION AND MAINTENANCE   1-7

Rigid Case (Direct Reading)

A rigid case or direct reading torque wrench is equipped with a dial indicator to show torque values. One advantage of these wrenches is that they can be held at any position on the wrench without affecting accuracy. These wrenches are often preferred because they tend to be compact, easy to read and have a great degree of accuracy.

TORQUE ANGLE METERS

Because the frictional characteristics of each fastener or threaded hole will vary, clamp loads which are based strictly on torque will vary as well. In most applications, this variance is not significant enough to cause worry. But, in certain applications, a manufacturer's engineers may determine that more precise clamp loads are necessary (such is the case with many aluminum cylinder heads). In these cases, a torque angle method of installation would be specified. When installing fasteners which are torque angle tightened, a predetermined seating torque and standard torque wrench are usually used first to remove any compliance from the joint. The fastener is then tightened the specified additional portion of a turn measured in degrees. A torque angle gauge (mechanical protractor) is used for these applications.

Standard and Metric Measurements

▶ See Figure 23

Throughout this manual, specifications are given to help you determine the condition of various components on your vehicle, or to assist you in their installation. Some of the most common measurements include length (in. or cm/mm), torque (ft. lbs., inch lbs. or Nm) and pressure (psi, in. Hg, kPa or mm Hg). In most cases, we strive to provide the proper measurement as determined by the manufacturer's engineers.

Though, in some cases, that value may not be conveniently measured with what is available in your toolbox. Luckily, many of the measuring devices which are available today will have two scales so the Standard or Metric measurements may easily be taken. If any of the various measuring tools which are available to you do not contain the same scale as listed in the specifications, use the accompanying conversion factors to determine the proper value.

The conversion factor chart is used by taking the given specification and multiplying it by the necessary conversion factor. For instance, looking at the first line, if you have a measurement in inches such as "free-play should be 2 in." but your ruler reads only in millimeters, multiply 2 in. by the conversion factor of 25.4 to get the metric equivalent of 50.8mm. Likewise, if the specification was given only in a Metric measurement, for example in Newton Meters (Nm), then look at the center column first. If the measurement is 100 Nm, multiply it by the conversion factor of 0.738 to get 73.8 ft. lbs.

CONVERSION FACTORS

LENGTH-DISTANCE

Inches (in.)	x 25.4	= Millimeters (mm)	x .0394	= Inches
Feet (ft.)	x .305	= Meters (m)	x 3.281	= Feet
Miles	x 1.609	= Kilometers (km)	x .0621	= Miles

VOLUME

Cubic Inches (in3)	x 16.387	= Cubic Centimeters	x .061	= in3
IMP Pints (IMP pt.)	x .568	= Liters (L)	x 1.76	= IMP pt.
IMP Quarts (IMP qt.)	x 1.137	= Liters (L)	x .88	= IMP qt.
IMP Gallons (IMP gal.)	x 4.546	= Liters (L)	x .22	= IMP gal.
IMP Quarts (IMP qt.)	x 1.201	= US Quarts (US qt.)	x .833	= IMP qt.
IMP Gallons (IMP gal.)	x 1.201	= US Gallons (US gal.)	x .833	= IMP gal.
Fl. Ounces	x 29.573	= Milliliters	x .034	= Ounces
US Pints (US pt.)	x .473	= Liters (L)	x 2.113	= Pints
US Quarts (US qt.)	x .946	= Liters (L)	x 1.057	= Quarts
US Gallons (US gal.)	x 3.785	= Liters (L)	x .264	= Gallons

MASS-WEIGHT

Ounces (oz.)	x 28.35	= Grams (g)	x .035	= Ounces
Pounds (lb.)	x .454	= Kilograms (kg)	x 2.205	= Pounds

PRESSURE

Pounds Per Sq. In. (psi)	x 6.895	= Kilopascals (kPa)	x .145	= psi
Inches of Mercury (Hg)	x .4912	= psi	x 2.036	= Hg
Inches of Mercury (Hg)	x 3.377	= Kilopascals (kPa)	x .2961	= Hg
Inches of Water (H_2O)	x .07355	= Inches of Mercury	x 13.783	= H_2O
Inches of Water (H_2O)	x .03613	= psi	x 27.684	= H_2O
Inches of Water (H_2O)	x .248	= Kilopascals (kPa)	x 4.026	= H_2O

TORQUE

Pounds-Force Inches (in-lb)	x .113	= Newton Meters (N·m)	x 8.85	= in-lb
Pounds-Force Feet (ft-lb)	x 1.356	= Newton Meters (N·m)	x .738	= ft-lb

VELOCITY

Miles Per Hour (MPH)	x 1.609	= Kilometers Per Hour (KPH)	x .621	= MPH

POWER

Horsepower (Hp)	x .745	= Kilowatts	x 1.34	= Horsepower

FUEL CONSUMPTION*

Miles Per Gallon IMP (MPG)	x .354	= Kilometers Per Liter (Km/L)		
Kilometers Per Liter (Km/L)	x 2.352	= IMP MPG		
Miles Per Gallon US (MPG)	x .425	= Kilometers Per Liter (Km/L)		
Kilometers Per Liter (Km/L)	x 2.352	= US MPG		

*It is common to covert from miles per gallon (mpg) to liters/100 kilometers (1/100 km), where mpg (IMP) x 1/100 km = 282 and mpg (US) x 1/100 km = 235.

TEMPERATURE

Degree Fahrenheit (°F)	= (°C x 1.8) + 32
Degree Celsius (°C)	= (°F − 32) x .56

TCCS1044

Fig. 23 Standard and metric conversion factors chart

SERIAL NUMBER IDENTIFICATION

Vehicle Identification Number

▶ See Figures 24 thru 30

The vehicle serial number is stamped on a plate found in the upper center portion of the firewall on 1970–78 models. It can also be found stamped on a metal tag, fastened to the driver's side door pillar (all models).

On 1979–88 models, the number is located on the right front fender apron in the engine compartment (behind the wheel arch). All 1979–88 models also have the vehicle identification number stamped on a plate attached to the left side of the instrument panel. The plate is visible through the windshield.

The vehicle identification (model variation codes) may be interpreted as follows:

• 1970–71: All models are marked PL521TU. The first letter, P, indicates the L16 engine. The second letter, L, means left hand drive, 521 is the model number. The first suffix letter, T, indicates a floor shift. The second suffix letter, U, indicates a U.S. and Canada specification model.

• 1972: All models are marked PL620TU. The only change from 1970–71 is the model number, 620.

• 1973–74: The prefix letters remain the same, PL, with P indicating the 1600cc engine through mid 1973, or the 1800cc engine thereafter. The next three numbers, 620 are the model number. Four suffix letters are used. The first is either a K or a blank; K indicates an automatic transmission. The second and third suffix letter are T and U, with the same meaning as in earlier year. The fourth suffix letter is an H or blank; H indicates that no heater is installed.

• 1975–76: Three prefix letters and four suffix letters are used. The first letter is an H, for the L20B engine. The second letter is L, for left hand drive. The third letter is either a G or a blank; G is for long wheelbase (long bed) trucks. The next three numbers, 620, are the model number. The four suffix letters remain the same as in 1973–74, with the exception of the last letter in 1976, which may be a V or a blank; V indicates a California model.

• 1977–79: Four prefix and four suffix letter are used. The first letter is a K or a blank; K indicates a king cab model. The second, third, and fourth letters are the same as those used in 1975–76. The next three numbers are the model number, 620. The first suffix letter is either a K, an F, or a blank; K indicates automatic transmission, F indicates a 5-speed, a blank indicates a 4-speed. The second and third suffix letter, T and U, have the same meaning as in earlier years. The last letter is either a V, an N, or a blank; V indicates a California model, N indicates a Canada model, a blank indicates a 49 States model.

• 1980–81: A four letter prefix for 2-wheel drive models and a five letter prefix for 4-wheel drive models followed by a three digit code denoting the truck series is used. The suffix for these years is either four letters for 2-wheel drive or two letters for 4-wheel drive.

• 1982–83: All truck models use a five letter prefix followed by the model designation, then a four letter suffix explained in the illustration.

• 1984–86 (720 Series): All truck models use a five letter prefix followed by the model designation, then a five letter suffix; the last two letters separated by a slash, explained in the illustration.

• 1986–88 (D21 Series): All truck models use a four letter prefix followed by the model designation, then a five letter suffix explained in the illustration.

1-8 GENERAL INFORMATION AND MAINTENANCE

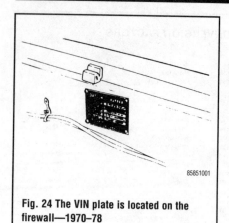

Fig. 24 The VIN plate is located on the firewall—1970–78

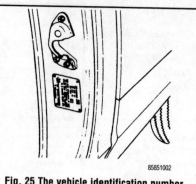

Fig. 25 The vehicle identification number is also found on the driver's side door pillar—1970–78

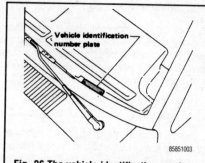

Fig. 26 The vehicle identification number can be found on the left side of the instrument panel, visible through the windshield—1979–88

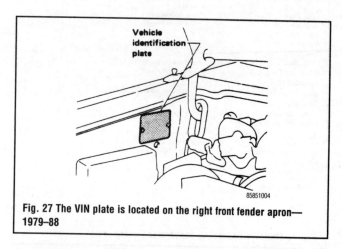

Fig. 27 The VIN plate is located on the right front fender apron—1979–88

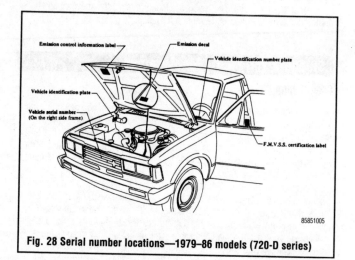

Fig. 28 Serial number locations—1979–86 models (720-D series)

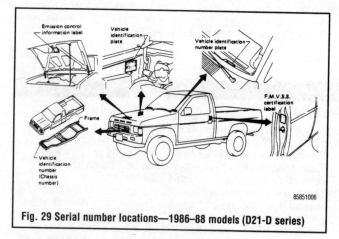

Fig. 29 Serial number locations—1986–88 models (D21-D series)

The serial number on all 1970–80 models consists of a series identification (see chart) followed by a six digit production number. The serial number on all 1981–88 models has been changed to the 17-digit format. The first three digits are the World Manufacturer Identification number. The next five digits are the Vehicle Description Section (same as the series identification number above). The remaining nine digits are the production numbers.

Engine Serial Number

The engine serial number consists of an engine series identification number followed by a six digit production number.

Vehicle Identification

Model/Type	Year	Identification Number
Pick-Up/L16	1970–72	PL521
Pick-Up/L18 L20B	1973–74 1975–78	PL620
Pick-Up/L20B Z20 Z22 Z24 SD22 SD25	1979–86	720-D
Pick-Up & Pathfinder/ Z24 Z24i VG30i SD25	1986½– 1988	D21-D

Fig. 30 Vehicle Identification chart

GENERAL INFORMATION AND MAINTENANCE

ENGINE IDENTIFICATION

Year	Model	Engine Displacement cu. in. (cc)	Engine Series Identification	No. of Cylinders	Engine Type
1970-72	Pick-Up	97.3 (1595)	L16	4	SOHC
1973-74	Pick-Up	108.0 (1770)	L18	4	SOHC
1975-80	Pick-Up	119.1 (1952)	L20B	4	SOHC
1981-83	Pick-Up	133.5 (2187)	Z22	4	SOHC
		132.0 (2164)	SD22	4	Diesel/SOHC
1984-86	Pick-Up	119.8 (1952)	Z20	4	SOHC
		146.8 (2389)	Z24	4	SOHC
		152.0 (2488)	SD25	4	Diesel/SOHC
1986½-88	Pick-Up/Pathfinder	146.8 (2389)	Z24	4	SOHC
		146.8 (2389)	Z24i	4	SOHC
		181.0 (2960)	VG30i	6	SOHC
		152.0 (2488)	SD25	4	Diesel/SOHC

SOHC—Single Overhead Camshaft

85851R021

L16, L18 and L20B Engines

♦ See Figure 31

The serial number is stamped on the right side of the cylinder block, just below No. 4 spark plug.

Z20, Z22, Z24 and Z24i Engines

♦ See Figures 32 and 33

The serial number is stamped on the left side of the cylinder block, below the No. 3 and No. 4 spark plugs.

VG30i Engines

♦ See Figure 34

The serial number is stamped on the cylinder block, below the rear of the right side cylinder head.

Transmission

♦ See Figures 35, 36, 37, 38 and 39

The transmission serial number is stamped on the front upper face of the transmission case on manual transmissions, or on the right side of the transmission case on automatic transmissions.

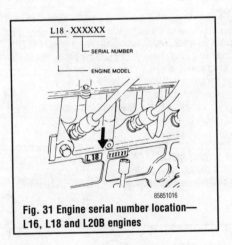

Fig. 31 Engine serial number location—L16, L18 and L20B engines

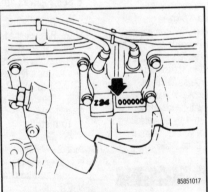

Fig. 32 Engine serial number location—Z20, Z22 and Z24 engines

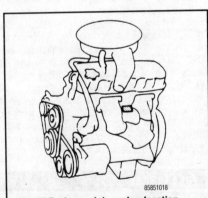

Fig. 33 Engine serial number location—Z24i engine

1-10 GENERAL INFORMATION AND MAINTENANCE

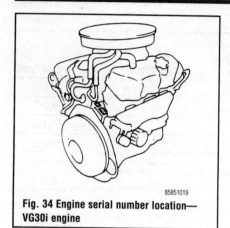

Fig. 34 Engine serial number location—VG30i engine

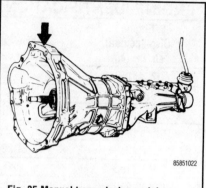

Fig. 35 Manual transmission serial number location—1970–86

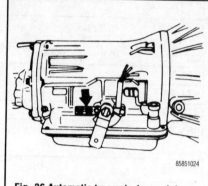

Fig. 36 Automatic transmission serial number location—1974–86

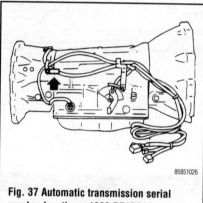

Fig. 37 Automatic transmission serial number location—1988 RE4R01A

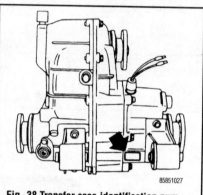

Fig. 38 Transfer case identification number location—all except D21 series

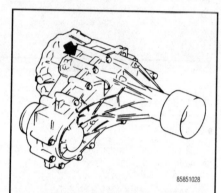

Fig. 39 Transfer case identification number location—D21 series

ROUTINE MAINTENANCE AND TUNE-UP

Proper maintenance and tune-up is the key to long and trouble-free vehicle life. Studies have shown that a properly tuned and maintained vehicle can achieve better gas mileage than an out-of-tune vehicle. As a conscientious owner and driver, set aside a Saturday morning, say once a month, to check or replace items which could cause major problems later. Keep your own personal log to jot down which services you performed, how much the parts cost you, the date, and the exact odometer reading at the time. Keep all receipts for such items as engine oil and filters, so that they may be referred to in case of related problems or to determine operating expenses. As a do-it-yourselfer, these receipts are the only proof you have that the required maintenance was performed. In the event of a warranty problem, these receipts will be invaluable.

The literature provided with your vehicle when it was originally delivered includes the factory recommended maintenance schedule. If you no longer have this literature, replacement copies are usually available from the dealer.

Air Cleaner

REMOVAL & INSTALLATION

The element should be replaced at the recommended intervals shown in the Maintenance Intervals charts. If your truck is operated under severely dusty conditions or severe operating conditions, more frequent changes will certainly be necessary. Inspect the element at least twice a year. Early spring and early fall are always good times for inspection. Remove the element and check for any perforations or tears in the filter. Check the cleaner housing for signs of dirt or dust that may have leaked through the filter element or in through the snorkel tube. Position a droplight on one side of the element and look through the filter at the light. If no glow of light can be seen through the element material, replace the filter. If holes in the filter element are apparent or signs of dirt seepage through the filter are evident, replace the filter.

Air Cleaner Assembly (Housing)

♦ See Figures 40 and 41

1. Disconnect all hoses, ducts and vacuum tubes from the air cleaner assembly.
2. Remove the top cover wing nut (two on later models) and grommet (if equipped). Most models will also utilize three or four side clips to further secure the top of the assembly, simply pull the wire tab and release the clip; in fact air cleaners on a few engines are secured solely by means of clips (air box-to-cleaner housing). Remove the cover and lift out the filter element.
3. Remove any side mount brackets and/or retaining bolts and lift off the air cleaner assembly.

To install:

4. Clean or replace the filter element as detailed previously. Wipe clean all surfaces of the air cleaner housing and cover. Check the condition of the mounting gasket and replace it if it appears worn or broken.
5. Reposition the air cleaner assembly and install the mounting bracket and/or bolts.

Fig. 40 Sometimes the air filter can be cleaned with low pressure compressed air

GENERAL INFORMATION AND MAINTENANCE

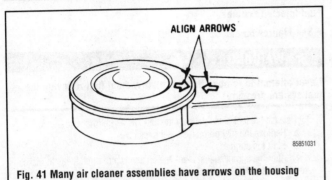

Fig. 41 Many air cleaner assemblies have arrows on the housing and lid—always make sure they align

6. Reposition the filter element in the case and install the cover being careful not to overtighten the wingnut(s). On round-style cleaners, be certain that the arrows on the cover lid and the snorkel match up properly.

➡ Filter elements on many engines have a TOP and BOTTOM side, be sure they are inserted correctly.

7. Reconnect all hoses, ductwork and vacuum lines.

➡ Never operate the engine without the air filter element in place.

Air Cleaner Element

♦ See Figures 42 thru 47

The element can, in most cases be replaced by removing the wingnut(s) and side clips as already detailed.

Crankcase Ventilation Filter

Certain models may also utilize a cleaner-mounted crankcase ventilation filter, if so, it should also be cleaned or replaced at the same time as the regular filter element. To replace the filter, remove the air cleaner top cover and pull the filter from its housing on the side of the cleaner assembly. Push a new filter into the housing and reinstall the cover. If the filter and plastic holder are in need of replacement, remove the clip mounting the feeder tube to the cleaner housing and then remove the assembly from the air cleaner.

Air Induction/Injection Valve Filter

1981–86 CARBURETED ENGINES

♦ See Figure 48

These models utilize an additional filter in the air cleaner housing and it is easily replaced. Unscrew the mounting bolts and remove the valve filter case. Pull the valve out and remove the filter that lies underneath it. Install the new filter and then the valve. Pay particular attention to which way the valve is facing so that the exhaust gases will not flow backward through the system. Install the valve case.

Fuel Filter

REMOVAL & INSTALLATION

✱✱ CAUTION

NEVER SMOKE WHEN WORKING AROUND OR NEAR GASOLINE! MAKE SURE THAT THERE IS NO ACTIVE IGNITION SOURCE NEAR YOUR WORK AREA!

Fig. 42 View of a common air cleaner assembly

Fig. 43 Use a ratchet wrench to loosen the top nut on the air cleaner lid

Fig. 44 Release the side clamp on the air cleaner assembly

Fig. 45 Lift the air cleaner element from the housing

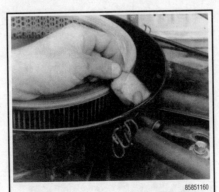

Fig. 46 Removing the crankcase filter, if so equipped

Fig. 47 During installation, make sure the air filter is correctly positioned

1-12 GENERAL INFORMATION AND MAINTENANCE

1970–83 Carbureted Engines

♦ See Figures 49 and 50

The fuel filter is located on the right inner fender in the engine compartment. It is a disposable cartridge type.

1. Using a pair of pliers, expand the hose clamp on one side of the filter, and slide the clamp further down the hose, past the point to which the filter pipe extends. Remove the other clamp in the same manner.
2. Grasp the hoses near the ends and twist them gently to pull them free from the filter pipes.
3. Pull the filter from the clip and discard.
4. Install the new filter into the clip. Push the hoses onto the filter pipes, and slide the clamps back into position. Start the engine and check for leaks.

1984–86 Carbureted Engines

♦ See Figures 51, 52, 53 and 54

The fuel filter is located on the inside of the frame above the left rear spring front shackle.

Changing the filter is VERY awkward. Since it is in-line and below tank level, fuel will pour from the fuel lines when they are disconnected from the filter. The only way of preventing this, is to siphon all of the gasoline from the tank before replacing the filter. Another possible method is to clamp and plug the fuel line, but this is not recommended because of the danger of leaking fuel or damage which could occur to the fuel line when clamped. It would, therefore, be a good idea to run the tank almost dry before changing the filter. Once the tank is dry, disconnect the fuel lines at the filter, unbolt the old filter and install a new one. Reconnect the fuel lines, fill the tank, start the engine and check for leaks.

Fuel Injected Engines

♦ See Figures 55 and 56

※ WARNING

Never attempt to remove the fuel filter without first relieving the fuel system pressure!

1. Release the fuel pressure from the fuel line as follows:
   a. Remove the fuel pump fuse at the fuse box.
   b. Start the engine.
   c. After the engine stalls, crank the engine two or three times to make sure that the fuel pressure is released.
   d. Turn the ignition switch **OFF** and reinstall the fuel pump fuse.
2. Loosen the hose clamps at the fuel inlet and outlet lines then slide each line off the filter nipples.
3. Remove the fuel filter.
4. Replace the fuel filter. Always be sure to use new hose clamps.

PCV Valve

♦ See Figure 57

The PCV valve regulates crankcase ventilation during various engine operating conditions. At high vacuum (idle speed and partial load range) it will open slightly and at low vacuum (full throttle) it will open fully. This causes vapor to be removed from the crankcase by the engine vacuum and then sucked into the combustion chamber where it is burned.

➡ The PCV system will not function properly unless the oil filler cap is tightly sealed. Check the gasket on the cap and be certain it is not leaking. Replace the cap, gasket or both to ensure proper sealing.

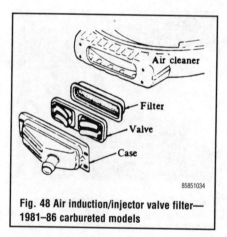

Fig. 48 Air induction/injector valve filter—1981–86 carbureted models

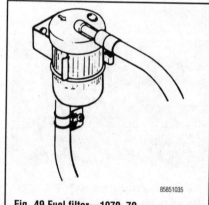

Fig. 49 Fuel filter—1970–79

Fig. 50 Fuel filter—1980–83

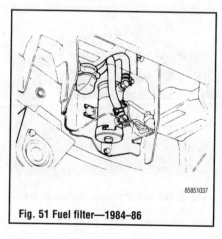

Fig. 51 Fuel filter—1984–86

Fig. 52 Remove the shield mounting bolts

Fig. 53 Remove the shield, if necessary for fuel filter removal

GENERAL INFORMATION AND MAINTENANCE 1-13

Fig. 54 Removing fuel filter—always replace fuel line clamps

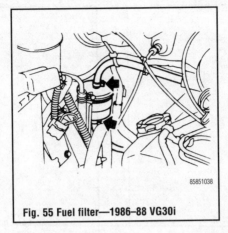

Fig. 55 Fuel filter—1986–88 VG30i

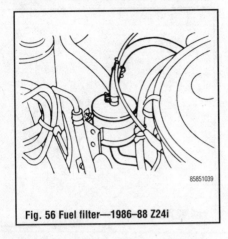

Fig. 56 Fuel filter—1986–88 Z24i

REMOVAL, TESTING & INSTALLATION

1. Check the ventilation hoses and lines for leaks or clogging. Clean or replace as necessary.
2. With the engine running at idle, locate the PCV valve then remove the ventilation hose from the valve; a strong hissing sound should be heard as air passes through the valve.
3. With the engine still idling, place your finger over the valve; a strong vacuum should be felt.
4. If the PCV valve failed either of the preceding two checks, it will require replacement.
5. Locate the PCV valve in the cylinder head cover or intake manifold and remove it by unscrewing it and then pulling it upward.

To install:

6. Slip the hose back onto the proper end of the PCV valve and then press it into the retaining grommet or screw it back in.
7. An additional check without removing the valve could be: with the engine running, remove the ventilator hose from the PCV valve. If the valve is working, a hissing noise will be heard as air passes through the valve and a strong vacuum should be felt immediately when the valve inlet is blocked with a finger. If the valve is suspected of being plugged, it should be replaced.
8. For further information on the PCV system, please refer to Section 4.

Air Injection/Induction Valve Filter

◆ See Figures 58 and 59

REMOVAL & INSTALLATION

1975–80 Carbureted Engines 1986–88 Fuel Injected Engines

Regular maintenance for this component includes a check of the drive belt tension at the specified interval, and replacement of the air pump filter every 24,000 miles (40,000 km). The air filter case is located in the left front of the engine compartment on most models. To replace the air filter, simply unscrew the wing nut(s) securing the cover to the case, withdraw the old filter, install the new one, and reinstall the case. More information on the air pump system can be found in Section 4.

1981–86 Carbureted Engines

These models utilize an air cleaner-mounted valve and filter. Removal and installation procedures are detailed in the Air Cleaner section.

Evaporative Canister

SERVICING

◆ See Figures 60 and 61

Check the evaporation control system every 15,000 miles (24,000 km). Check the fuel and vapor lines/hoses for proper connections and correct routing, as well as condition. Replace damaged or deteriorated parts as necessary. Remove and check the operation of the check valve on 1970–75 models in the following manner:

1. With all the hoses disconnected from the valve, apply air pressure to the fuel tank side of the valve. The air should flow through the valve and exit the crankcase side of the valve. If the valve does not behave in the above manner, replace it.
2. Apply air pressure to the crankcase side of the valve. Air should not pass to either of the other two outlets.
3. When air pressure is applied to the carburetor side of the valve, the air should pass through to exit out the fuel tank and/or the crankcase side of the valve.

On 1975–88 models, the flow guide valve is replaced with a carbon filled canister which stores fuel vapors until the engine is started, the vapors are then drawn into the combustion chambers and burned.

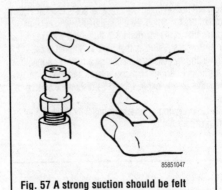

Fig. 57 A strong suction should be felt when a finger is placed over the PCV valve with the engine idling

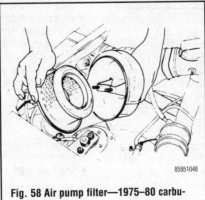

Fig. 58 Air pump filter—1975–80 carbureted engines

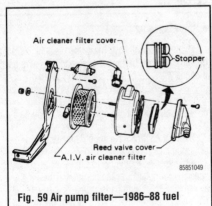

Fig. 59 Air pump filter—1986–88 fuel injected engines

1-14 GENERAL INFORMATION AND MAINTENANCE

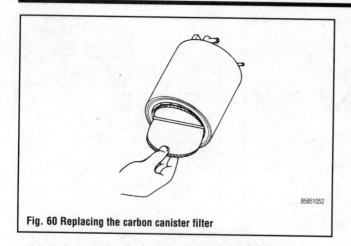

Fig. 60 Replacing the carbon canister filter

Fig. 61 View of the carbon canister assembly

To check the operation of the carbon canister purge control valve, disconnect the rubber hose between the canister control valve and the T-fitting (at the T-fitting). Apply vacuum to the hose leading to the control valve. The vacuum condition should be held indefinitely. If the control valve leaks, remove the top cover of the valve and check for a dislocated or cracked diaphragm. If the diaphragm is damaged, a repair kit containing a new diaphragm, retainer, and spring is available and should be installed.

The carbon canister has an air filter in the bottom of the canister. Most filters are replaceable. The filter element should be checked once a year or every 15,000 miles (24,000 km); more frequently if the truck is operated in dusty areas. Replace the filter by pulling it out of the bottom of the canister and installing a new one.

Heat Riser

SERVICING

♦ See Figure 62

The heat control valve (heat riser) is a thermostatically operated valve used on some engines (in the exhaust manifold). It is used only on 1975–77 trucks. It opens when the engine is warming up, to direct hot exhaust gases to the intake manifold. The gases preheat the incoming air/fuel mixture. If it sticks shut, the result will be frequent stalling during warm-up, especially in cold or damp weather. If it sticks open, the result will be a rough idle after the engine is warm.

The heat control valve should be checked for free operation every six months or 6000 miles (9600 km). Simply give the counterweight a twirl (engine cold) to ascertain that no binding exists. If the valve sticks, apply a heat control solvent specially formulated for the purpose to the ends of the shaft. This solvent is available at most auto parts stores. Sometimes lightly rapping the end of the shaft with a plastic mallet (engine hot) will break it loose. If this fails, the components will have to be removed from the truck for further repairs.

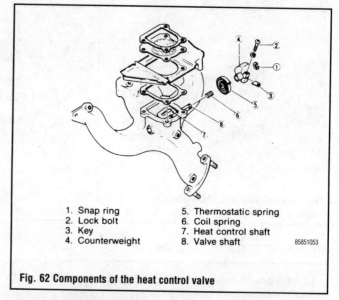

1. Snap ring
2. Lock bolt
3. Key
4. Counterweight
5. Thermostatic spring
6. Coil spring
7. Heat control shaft
8. Valve shaft

Fig. 62 Components of the heat control valve

Battery

PRECAUTIONS

Always use caution when working on or near the battery. Never allow a tool to bridge the gap between the negative and positive battery terminals. Also, be careful not to allow a tool to provide a ground between the positive cable/terminal and any metal component on the vehicle. Either of these conditions will cause a short circuit, leading to sparks and possible personal injury.

Do not smoke or all open flames/sparks near a battery; the gases contained in the battery are very explosive and, if ignited, could cause severe injury or death.

All batteries, regardless of type, should be carefully secured by a battery hold-down device. If not, the terminals or casing may crack from stress during vehicle operation. A battery which is not secured may allow acid to leak, making it discharge faster. The acid can also eat away at components under the hood.

Always inspect the battery case for cracks, leakage and corrosion. A white corrosive substance on the battery case or on nearby components would indicate a leaking or cracked battery. If the battery is cracked, it should be replaced immediately.

GENERAL MAINTENANCE

Always keep the battery cables and terminals free of corrosion. Check and clean these components about once a year.

Keep the top of the battery clean, as a film of dirt can help discharge a battery that is not used for long periods. A solution of baking soda and water may be used for cleaning, but be careful to flush this off with clear water. DO NOT let any of the solution into the filler holes. Baking soda neutralizes battery acid and will de-activate a battery cell.

Batteries in vehicles which are not operated on a regular basis can fall victim to parasitic loads (small current drains which are constantly drawing current from the battery). Normal parasitic loads may drain a battery on a vehicle that is in storage and not used for 6–8 weeks. Vehicles that have additional accessories such as a phone or an alarm system may discharge a battery sooner. If the vehicle is to be stored for longer periods in a secure area and the alarm system is not necessary, the negative battery cable should be disconnected to protect the battery.

Remember that constantly deep cycling a battery (completely discharging and recharging it) will shorten battery life.

BATTERY FLUID

♦ See Figure 63

Check the battery electrolyte level at least once a month, or more often in hot weather or during periods of extended vehicle operation. On non-sealed batter-

GENERAL INFORMATION AND MAINTENANCE 1-15

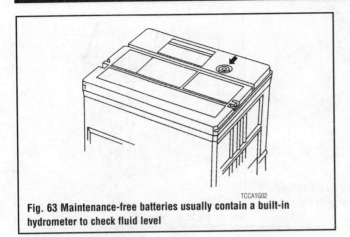

Fig. 63 Maintenance-free batteries usually contain a built-in hydrometer to check fluid level

ies, the level can be checked either through the case (if translucent) or by removing the cell caps. The electrolyte level in each cell should be kept filled to the split ring inside each cell, or the line marked on the outside of the case.

If the level is low, add only distilled water through the opening until the level is correct. Each cell must be checked and filled individually. Distilled water should be used, because the chemicals and minerals found in most drinking water are harmful to the battery and could significantly shorten its life.

If water is added in freezing weather, the vehicle should be driven several miles to allow the water to mix with the electrolyte. Otherwise, the battery could freeze.

Although some maintenance-free batteries have removable cell caps, the electrolyte condition and level on all sealed maintenance-free batteries must be checked using the built-in hydrometer "eye." The exact type of eye will vary. But, most battery manufacturers, apply a sticker to the battery itself explaining the readings.

➡ Although the readings from built-in hydrometers will vary, a green eye usually indicates a properly charged battery with sufficient fluid level. A dark eye is normally an indicator of a battery with sufficient fluid, but which is low in charge. A light or yellow eye usually indicates that electrolyte has dropped below the necessary level. In this last case, sealed batteries with an insufficient electrolyte must usually be discarded.

Checking the Specific Gravity

▶ See Figures 64, 65 and 66

A hydrometer is required to check the specific gravity on all batteries that are not maintenance-free. On batteries that are maintenance-free, the specific gravity is checked by observing the built-in hydrometer "eye" on the top of the battery case.

✶✶ CAUTION

Battery electrolyte contains sulfuric acid. If you should splash any on your skin or in your eyes, flush the affected area with plenty of clear water. If it lands in your eyes, get medical help immediately.

The fluid (sulfuric acid solution) contained in the battery cells will tell you many things about the condition of the battery. Because the cell plates must be kept submerged below the fluid level in order to operate, the fluid level is extremely important. And, because the specific gravity of the acid is an indication of electrical charge, testing the fluid can be an aid in determining if the battery must be replaced. A battery in a vehicle with a properly operating charging system should require little maintenance, but careful, periodic inspection should reveal problems before they leave you stranded.

At least once a year, check the specific gravity of the battery. It should be between 1.20 and 1.26 on the gravity scale. Most auto stores carry a variety of inexpensive battery hydrometers. These can be used on any non-sealed battery to test the specific gravity in each cell.

The battery testing hydrometer has a squeeze bulb at one end and a nozzle at the other. Battery electrolyte is sucked into the hydrometer until the float is lifted from its seat. The specific gravity is then read by noting the position of the float. If gravity is low in one or more cells, the battery should be slowly charged and checked again to see if the gravity has come up. Generally, if after charging, the specific gravity between any two cells varies more than 50 points (0.50), the battery should be replaced, as it can no longer produce sufficient voltage to guarantee proper operation.

CABLES

▶ See Figures 67, 68, 69 and 70

Once a year (or as necessary), the battery terminals and the cable clamps should be cleaned. Loosen the clamps and remove the cables, negative cable first. On top post batteries, the use of a puller specially made for this purpose is recommended. These are inexpensive and available in most parts stores. Side terminal battery cables are secured with a small bolt.

Clean the cable clamps and the battery terminal with a wire brush, until all corrosion, grease, etc., is removed and the metal is shiny. It is especially important to clean the inside of the clamp thoroughly (an old knife is useful here), since a small deposit of oxidation there will prevent a sound connection and inhibit starting or charging. Special tools are available for cleaning these parts, one type for conventional top post batteries and another type for side terminal batteries. It is also a good idea to apply some dielectric grease to the terminal, as this will aid in the prevention of corrosion.

After the clamps and terminals are clean, reinstall the cables, negative cable last; DO NOT hammer the clamps onto battery posts. Tighten the clamps securely, but do not distort them. Give the clamps and terminals a thin external coating of grease after installation, to retard corrosion.

Check the cables at the same time that the terminals are cleaned. If the cable insulation is cracked or broken, or if the ends are frayed, the cable should be replaced with a new cable of the same length and gauge.

CHARGING

✶✶ CAUTION

The chemical reaction which takes place in all batteries generates explosive hydrogen gas. A spark can cause the battery to explode

Fig. 64 On non-sealed batteries, the fluid level can be checked by removing the cell caps

Fig. 65 If the fluid level is low, add only distilled water until the level is correct

Fig. 66 Check the specific gravity of the battery's electrolyte with a hydrometer

1-16 GENERAL INFORMATION AND MAINTENANCE

Fig. 67 The underside of this special battery tool has a wire brush to clean post terminals

Fig. 68 Place the tool over the battery posts and twist to clean until the metal is shiny

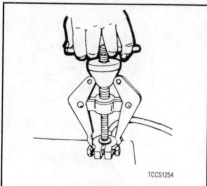
Fig. 69 A special tool is available to pull the clamp from the post

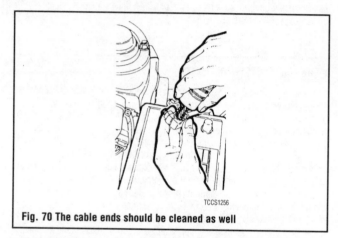
Fig. 70 The cable ends should be cleaned as well

and splash acid. To avoid personal injury, be sure there is proper ventilation and take appropriate fire safety precautions when working with or near a battery.

A battery should be charged at a slow rate to keep the plates inside from getting too hot. However, if some maintenance-free batteries are allowed to discharge until they are almost "dead," they may have to be charged at a high rate to bring them back to "life." Always follow the charger manufacturer's instructions on charging the battery.

REPLACEMENT

When it becomes necessary to replace the battery, select one with an amperage rating equal to or greater than the battery originally installed. Deterioration and just plain aging of the battery cables, starter motor, and associated wires makes the battery's job harder in successive years. This makes it prudent to install a new battery with a greater capacity than the old.

Drive Belts

INSPECTION

♦ See Figures 71, 72, 73, 74 and 75

Inspect the belts for signs of glazing or cracking. A glazed belt will be perfectly smooth from slippage, while a good belt will have a slight texture of fabric visible. Cracks will usually start at the inner edge of the belt and run outward. All worn or damaged drive belts should be replaced immediately. It is best to replace all drive belts at one time, as a preventive maintenance measure, during this service operation.

ADJUSTMENT

♦ See Figures 76 thru 87

Alternator

To adjust the tension of the alternator drive belt, loosen the pivot and mounting bolts on the alternator. Using a wooden hammer handle or a broomstick, or even your hand if you're strong enough, move the alternator one way or the other until the tension is within acceptable limits.

✻✻ CAUTION

Never use a screwdriver or any other metal device such as a prybar, as a lever when adjusting the alternator belt tension!

Tighten the mounting bolts securely. If a new belt has been installed, always recheck the tension after a few hundred miles of driving.

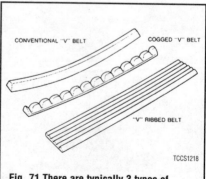
Fig. 71 There are typically 3 types of accessory drive belts found on vehicles today

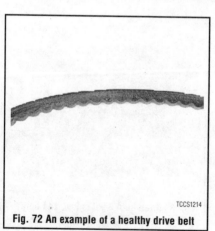
Fig. 72 An example of a healthy drive belt

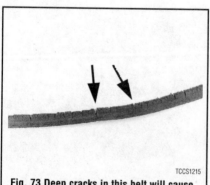
Fig. 73 Deep cracks in this belt will cause flex, building up heat that will eventually lead to belt failure

GENERAL INFORMATION AND MAINTENANCE   1-17

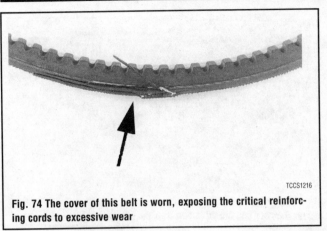

Fig. 74 The cover of this belt is worn, exposing the critical reinforcing cords to excessive wear

Fig. 75 Installing too wide a belt can result in serious belt wear and/or breakage

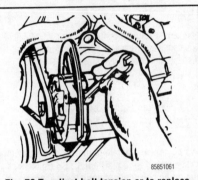

Fig. 76 To adjust belt tension or to replace a belt—first loosen the component mounting and adjusting bolt slightly

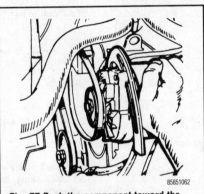

Fig. 77 Push the component toward the engine and slip off the belt

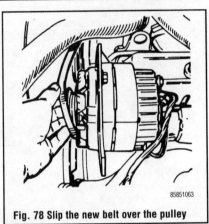

Fig. 78 Slip the new belt over the pulley

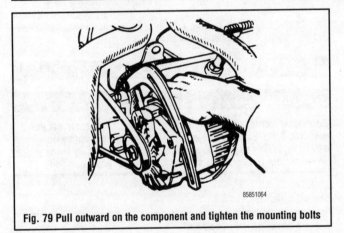

Fig. 79 Pull outward on the component and tighten the mounting bolts

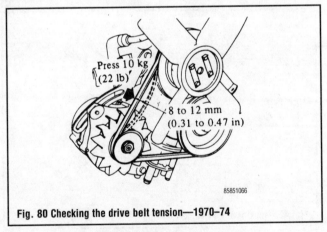

Fig. 80 Checking the drive belt tension—1970–74

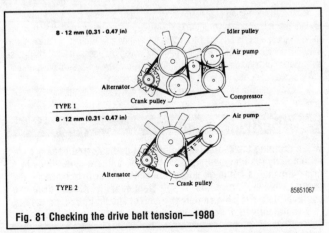

Fig. 81 Checking the drive belt tension—1980

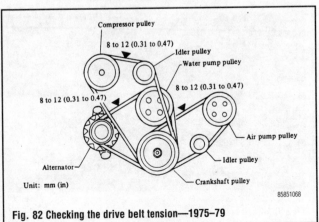

Fig. 82 Checking the drive belt tension—1975–79

1-18 GENERAL INFORMATION AND MAINTENANCE

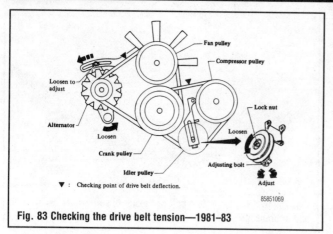

Fig. 83 Checking the drive belt tension—1981–83

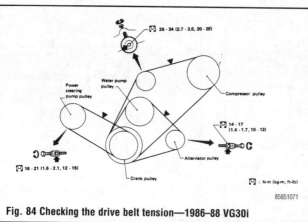

Fig. 84 Checking the drive belt tension—1986–88 VG30i

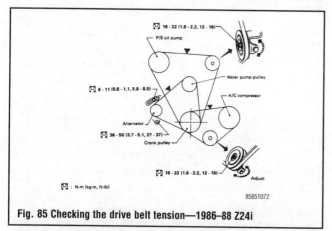

Fig. 85 Checking the drive belt tension—1986–88 Z24i

Fig. 86 Adjusting the drive belt

Fig. 87 Installing the drive belt over the pulley

Air Conditioning Compressor

A/C compressor belt tension can be adjusted by turning the tension adjusting bolt which is located on the compressor tensioner bracket. Turn the bolt clockwise to tighten the belt and counterclockwise to loosen it.

Air Pump

To adjust the tension of the air pump drive belt, loosen the adjusting lever bolt and then the pivot bolt. Move the pump in or out until the desired tension is achieved.

➥The tension should always be checked between the air pump and the crankshaft pulley on all trucks without air conditioning. On trucks with air conditioning, tension should be checked between the A/C compressor and the crankshaft pulley.

Power Steering Pump

Tension on the power steering belt is adjusted by means of an idler pulley. Turn the adjusting bolt on the idler pulley until the desired tension is achieved and the retighten the idler pulley lockbolt.

Hoses

✱✱ CAUTION

On models equipped with an electric cooling fan, disconnect the negative battery cable, or fan motor wiring harness connector before replacing any radiator/heater hose. The fan may come on, under certain circumstances, even though the ignition is OFF.

REPLACEMENT

♦ See Figures 88, 89, 90 and 91

Inspect the condition of the radiator and heater hoses periodically. Early spring and at the beginning of the fall or winter, when you are performing other maintenance, are good times. Make sure the engine and cooling system are cold. Visually inspect for cracking, rotting or collapsed hoses, replace as necessary. Run your hand along the length of the hose. If a weak or swollen spot is noted when squeezing the hose wall, replace the hose.

1. Drain the cooling system into a suitable container (if the coolant is to be reused).

✱✱ CAUTION

When draining the coolant, keep in mind that cats and dogs are attracted by the ethylene glycol antifreeze, and are quite likely to drink any that is left in an uncovered container or in puddles on the ground. This will prove fatal in sufficient quantity. Always drain the coolant into a sealable container. Coolant should be reused unless it is contaminated or several years old.

GENERAL INFORMATION AND MAINTENANCE

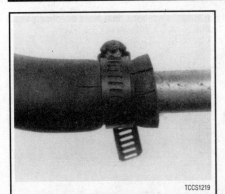

Fig. 88 The cracks developing along this hose are a result of age-related hardening

Fig. 89 A hose clamp that is too tight can cause older hoses to separate and tear on either side of the clamp

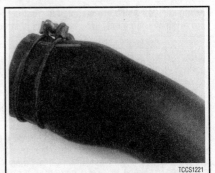

Fig. 90 A soft spongy hose (identifiable by the swollen section) will eventually burst and should be replaced

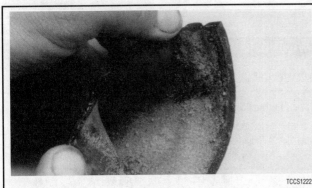

Fig. 91 Hoses are likely to deteriorate from the inside if the cooling system is not periodically flushed

2. Loosen the hose clamps at each end of the hose that requires replacement.
3. Twist, pull and slide the hose off the radiator, water pump, thermostat or heater connection.

To install:

4. Clean the hose mounting connections. Position the hose clamps on the new hose.
5. Coat the connection surfaces with a water resistant sealer and slide the hose into position. Make sure the hose clamps are located beyond the raised bead of the connector (if equipped) and centered in the clamping area of the connection.
6. Tighten the clamps. Do not overtighten.
7. Fill the cooling system.
8. Start the engine and allow it to reach normal operating temperature. Check for leaks.

Air Conditioning System

SYSTEM SERVICE & REPAIR

➡ It is recommended that the A/C system be serviced by an EPA Section 609 certified automotive technician utilizing a refrigerant recovery/recycling machine.

The do-it-yourselfer should not service his/her own vehicle's A/C system for many reasons, including legal concerns, personal injury, environmental damage and cost.

According to the U.S. Clean Air Act, it is a federal crime to service or repair (involving the refrigerant) a Motor Vehicle Air Conditioning (MVAC) system for money without being EPA certified. It is also illegal to vent R-12 and R-134a refrigerants into the atmosphere. State and/or local laws may be more strict than the federal regulations, so be sure to check with your state and/or local authorities for further information.

➡ Federal law dictates that a fine of up to $25,000 may be levied on people convicted of venting refrigerant into the atmosphere.

When servicing an A/C system you run the risk of handling or coming in contact with refrigerant, which may result in skin or eye irritation or frostbite. Although low in toxicity (due to chemical stability), inhalation of concentrated refrigerant fumes is dangerous and can result in death; cases of fatal cardiac arrhythmia have been reported in people accidentally subjected to high levels of refrigerant. Some early symptoms include loss of concentration and drowsiness.

➡ Generally, the limit for exposure is lower for R-134a than it is for R-12. Exceptional care must be practiced when handling R-134a.

Also, some refrigerants can decompose at high temperatures (near gas heaters or open flame), which may result in hydrofluoric acid, hydrochloric acid and phosgene (a fatal nerve gas).

It is usually more economically feasible to have a certified MVAC automotive technician perform A/C system service on your vehicle.

R-12 Refrigerant Conversion

If your vehicle still uses R-12 refrigerant, one way to save A/C system costs down the road is to investigate the possibility of having your system converted to R-134a. The older R-12 systems can be easily converted to R-134a refrigerant by a certified automotive technician by installing a few new components and changing the system oil.

The cost of R-12 is steadily rising and will continue to increase, because it is no longer imported or manufactured in the United States. Therefore, it is often possible to have an R-12 system converted to R-134a and recharged for less than it would cost to just charge the system with R-12.

If you are interested in having your system converted, contact local automotive service stations for more details and information.

PREVENTIVE MAINTENANCE

Although the A/C system should not be serviced by the do-it-yourselfer, preventive maintenance should be practiced to help maintain the efficiency of the vehicle's A/C system. Be sure to perform the following:

• The easiest and most important preventive maintenance for your A/C system is to be sure that it is used on a regular basis. Running the system for five minutes each month (no matter what the season) will help ensure that the seals and all internal components remain lubricated.

➡ Some vehicles automatically operate the A/C system compressor whenever the windshield defroster is activated. Therefore, the A/C system would not need to be operated each month if the defroster was used.

• In order to prevent heater core freeze-up during A/C operation, it is necessary to maintain proper antifreeze protection. Be sure to properly maintain the engine cooling system.
• Any obstruction of or damage to the condenser configuration will restrict air flow which is essential to its efficient operation. Keep this unit clean and in proper physical shape.

1-20 GENERAL INFORMATION AND MAINTENANCE

➡Bug screens which are mounted in front of the condenser (unless they are original equipment) are regarded as obstructions.

• The condensation drain tube expels any water which accumulates on the bottom of the evaporator housing into the engine compartment. If this tube is obstructed, the air conditioning performance can be restricted and condensation buildup can spill over onto the vehicle's floor.

SYSTEM INSPECTION

Although the A/C system should not be serviced by the do-it-yourselfer, system inspections should be performed to help maintain the efficiency of the vehicle's A/C system. Be sure to perform the following:

The easiest and often most important check for the air conditioning system consists of a visual inspection of the system components. Visually inspect the system for refrigerant leaks, damaged compressor clutch, abnormal compressor drive belt tension and/or condition, plugged evaporator drain tube, blocked condenser fins, disconnected or broken wires, blown fuses, corroded connections and poor insulation.

A refrigerant leak will usually appear as an oily residue at the leakage point in the system. The oily residue soon picks up dust or dirt particles from the surrounding air and appears greasy. Through time, this will build up and appear to be a heavy dirt impregnated grease.

For a thorough visual and operational inspection, check the following:
• Check the surface of the radiator and condenser for dirt, leaves or other material which might block air flow.
• Check for kinks in hoses and lines. Check the system for leaks.
• Make sure the drive belt is properly tensioned. During operation, make sure the belt is free of noise or slippage.
• Make sure the blower motor operates at all appropriate positions, then check for distribution of the air from all outlets.

➡**Remember that in high humidity, air discharged from the vents may not feel as cold as expected, even if the system is working properly.**

This is because moisture in humid air retains heat more effectively than dry air, thereby making humid air more difficult to cool.

ISOLATING THE COMPRESSOR

▶ See Figure 92

It is not necessary to discharge the system for compressor removal. The compressor can be isolated from the rest of the system, eliminating the need for recharging.

1. Connect a manifold gauge set.
2. Close both gauge hand valves and mid-position (crack) both compressor service valves.
3. Start the engine and turn on the air conditioning.
4. Turn the compressor suction valve slowly clockwise towards the front-seated position. When the suction pressure drops to zero, stop the engine and turn off the air conditioning. Quickly front-seat the valve completely.
5. Front-seat the discharge service valve.
6. Loosen the oil level check plug to remove any internal pressure.

The compressor is now isolated and the service valves can now be removed.

Windshield Wipers

ELEMENT (REFILL) CARE & REPLACEMENT

▶ See Figures 93, 94 and 95

For maximum effectiveness and longest element life, the windshield and wiper blades should be kept clean. Dirt, tree sap, road tar and so on will cause streaking, smearing and blade deterioration if left on the glass. It is advisable to wash the windshield carefully with a commercial glass cleaner at least once a month. Wipe off the rubber blades with the wet rag afterwards. Do not attempt to move wipers across the windshield by hand; damage to the motor and drive mechanism will result.

To inspect and/or replace the wiper blade elements, place the wiper switch in the **LOW** speed position and the ignition switch in the **ACC** position. When the wiper blades are approximately vertical on the windshield, turn the ignition switch to **OFF**.

Examine the wiper blade elements. If they are found to be cracked, broken or torn, they should be replaced immediately. Replacement intervals will vary with usage, although ozone deterioration usually limits element life to about one year. If the wiper pattern is smeared or streaked, or if the blade chatters across the glass, the elements should be replaced. It is easiest and most sensible to replace the elements in pairs.

If your vehicle is equipped with aftermarket blades, there are several different types of refills and your vehicle might have any kind. Aftermarket blades and arms rarely use the exact same type blade or refill as the original equipment.

Regardless of the type of refill used, be sure to follow the part manufacturer's instructions closely. Make sure that all of the frame jaws are engaged as the refill is pushed into place and locked. If the metal blade holder and frame are allowed to touch the glass during wiper operation, the glass will be scratched.

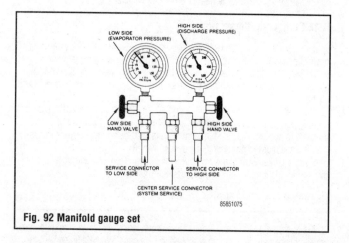

Fig. 92 Manifold gauge set

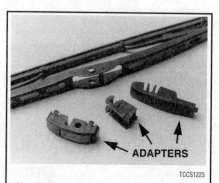

Fig. 93 Most aftermarket blades are available with multiple adapters to fit different vehicles

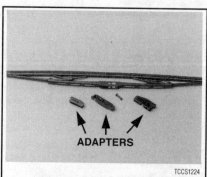

Fig. 94 Choose a blade which will fit your vehicle, and that will be readily available next time you need blades

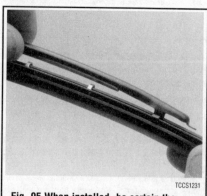

Fig. 95 When installed, be certain the blade is fully inserted into the backing

GENERAL INFORMATION AND MAINTENANCE

Tires and Wheels

Common sense and good driving habits will afford maximum tire life. Make sure that you don't overload the vehicle or run with incorrect pressure in the tires. Either of these will increase tread wear. Fast starts, sudden stops and sharp cornering are hard on tires and will shorten their useful life span.

➡For optimum tire life, keep the tires properly inflated, rotate them often and have the wheel alignment checked periodically.

Inspect your tires frequently. Be especially careful to watch for bubbles in the tread or sidewall, deep cuts or underinflation. Replace any tires with bubbles in the sidewall. If cuts are so deep that they penetrate to the cords, discard the tire. Any cut in the sidewall of a radial tire renders it unsafe. Also look for uneven tread wear patterns that may indicate the front end is out of alignment or that the tires are out of balance.

TIRE ROTATION

♦ See Figure 96

Tires must be rotated periodically to equalize wear patterns that vary with a tire's position on the vehicle. Tires will also wear in an uneven way as the front steering/suspension system wears to the point where the alignment should be reset.

Rotating the tires will ensure maximum life for the tires as a set, so you will not have to discard a tire early due to wear on only part of the tread. Regular rotation is required to equalize wear.

When rotating "unidirectional tires," make sure that they always roll in the same direction. This means that a tire used on the left side of the vehicle must not be switched to the right side and vice-versa. Such tires should only be rotated front-to-rear or rear-to-front, while always remaining on the same side of the vehicle. These tires are marked on the sidewall as to the direction of rotation; observe the marks when reinstalling the tire(s).

Some styled or "mag" wheels may have different offsets front to rear. In these cases, the rear wheels must not be used up front and vice-versa. Furthermore, if these wheels are equipped with unidirectional tires, they cannot be rotated unless the tire is remounted for the proper direction of rotation.

➡The compact or space-saver spare is strictly for emergency use. It must never be included in the tire rotation or placed on the vehicle for everyday use.

TIRE DESIGN

♦ See Figure 97

For maximum satisfaction, tires should be used in sets of four. Mixing of different brands or types (radial, bias-belted, fiberglass belted) should be avoided. In most cases, the vehicle manufacturer has designated a type of tire on which the vehicle will perform best. Your first choice when replacing tires should be to use the same type of tire that the manufacturer recommends.

When radial tires are used, tire sizes and wheel diameters should be selected to maintain ground clearance and tire load capacity equivalent to the original specified tire. Radial tires should always be used in sets of four.

✱✱ CAUTION

Radial tires should never be used on only the front axle.

When selecting tires, pay attention to the original size as marked on the tire. Most tires are described using an industry size code sometimes referred to as P-Metric. This allows the exact identification of the tire specifications, regardless of the manufacturer. If selecting a different tire size or brand, remember to check the installed tire for any sign of interference with the body or suspension while the vehicle is stopping, turning sharply or heavily loaded.

Snow Tires

Good radial tires can produce a big advantage in slippery weather, but in snow, a street radial tire does not have sufficient tread to provide traction and control. The small grooves of a street tire quickly pack with snow and the tire behaves like a billiard ball on a marble floor. The more open, chunky tread of a snow tire will self-clean as the tire turns, providing much better grip on snowy surfaces.

To satisfy municipalities requiring snow tires during weather emergencies, most snow tires carry either an M + S designation after the tire size stamped on the sidewall, or the designation "all-season." In general, no change in tire size is necessary when buying snow tires.

Most manufacturers strongly recommend the use of 4 snow tires on their vehicles for reasons of stability. If snow tires are fitted only to the drive wheels, the opposite end of the vehicle may become very unstable when braking or turning on slippery surfaces. This instability can lead to unpleasant endings if the driver can't counteract the slide in time.

Note that snow tires, whether 2 or 4, will affect vehicle handling in all non-snow situations. The stiffer, heavier snow tires will noticeably change the turning and braking characteristics of the vehicle. Once the snow tires are installed, you must re-learn the behavior of the vehicle and drive accordingly.

➡Consider buying extra wheels on which to mount the snow tires. Once done, the "snow wheels" can be installed and removed as needed. This eliminates the potential damage to tires or wheels from seasonal removal and installation. Even if your vehicle has styled wheels, see if inexpensive steel wheels are available. Although the look of the vehicle will change, the expensive wheels will be protected from salt, curb hits and pothole damage.

TIRE STORAGE

If they are mounted on wheels, store the tires at proper inflation pressure. All tires should be kept in a cool, dry place. If they are stored in the garage or basement, do not let them stand on a concrete floor; set them on strips of wood, a mat or a large stack of newspaper. Keeping them away from direct moisture is of paramount importance. Tires should not be stored upright, but in a flat position.

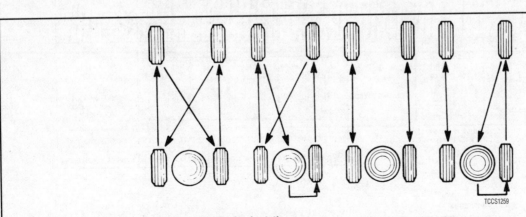

Fig. 96 Common tire rotation patterns for 4 and 5-wheel rotations

1-22 GENERAL INFORMATION AND MAINTENANCE

INFLATION & INSPECTION

♦ See Figures 98 thru 103

The importance of proper tire inflation cannot be overemphasized. A tire employs air as part of its structure. It is designed around the supporting strength of the air at a specified pressure. For this reason, improper inflation drastically reduces the tire's ability to perform as intended. A tire will lose some air in day-to-day use; having to add a few pounds of air periodically is not necessarily a sign of a leaking tire.

Two items should be a permanent fixture in every glove compartment: an accurate tire pressure gauge and a tread depth gauge. Check the tire pressure (including the spare) regularly with a pocket type gauge. Too often, the gauge on the end of the air hose at your corner garage is not accurate because it suffers too much abuse. Always check tire pressure when the tires are cold, as pressure increases with temperature. If you must move the vehicle to check the tire inflation, do not drive more than a mile before checking. A cold tire is generally one that has not been driven for more than three hours.

A plate or sticker is normally provided somewhere in the vehicle (door post, hood, tailgate or trunk lid) which shows the proper pressure for the tires. Never counteract excessive pressure build-up by bleeding off air pressure (letting some air out). This will cause the tire to run hotter and wear quicker.

✲✲ CAUTION

Never exceed the maximum tire pressure embossed on the tire! This is the pressure to be used when the tire is at maximum load-ing, but it is rarely the correct pressure for everyday driving. Consult the owner's manual or the tire pressure sticker for the correct tire pressure.

Once you've maintained the correct tire pressures for several weeks, you'll be familiar with the vehicle's braking and handling personality. Slight adjustments in tire pressures can fine-tune these characteristics, but never change the cold pressure specification by more than 2 psi. A slightly softer tire pressure will give a softer ride but also yield lower fuel mileage. A slightly harder tire will give crisper dry road handling but can cause skidding on wet surfaces. Unless you're fully attuned to the vehicle, stick to the recommended inflation pressures.

All automotive tires have built-in tread wear indicator bars that show up as ½ in. (13mm) wide smooth bands across the tire when 1/16 in. (1.5mm) of tread remains. The appearance of tread wear indicators means that the tires should be replaced. In fact, many states have laws prohibiting the use of tires with less than this amount of tread.

You can check your own tread depth with an inexpensive gauge or by using a Lincoln head penny. Slip the Lincoln penny (with Lincoln's head upside-down) into several tread grooves. If you can see the top of Lincoln's head in 2 adjacent grooves, the tire has less than 1/16 in. (1.5mm) tread left and should be replaced. You can measure snow tires in the same manner by using the "tails" side of the Lincoln penny. If you can see the top of the Lincoln memorial, it's time to replace the snow tire(s).

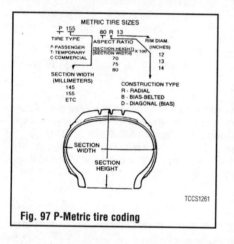

Fig. 97 P-Metric tire coding

Fig. 98 Tires with deep cuts, or cuts which

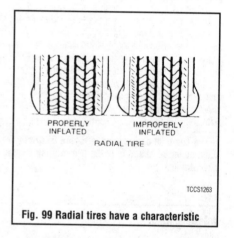

Fig. 99 Radial tires have a characteristic

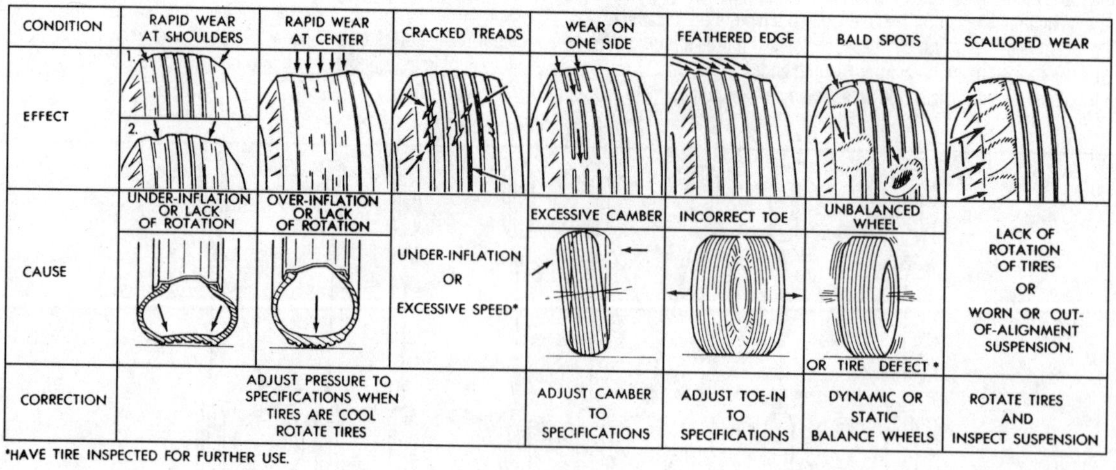

Fig. 100 Common tire wear patterns and causes

GENERAL INFORMATION AND MAINTENANCE

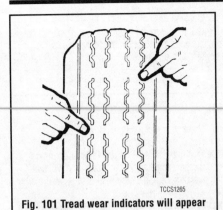

Fig. 101 Tread wear indicators will appear when the tire is worn

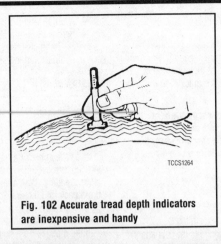

Fig. 102 Accurate tread depth indicators are inexpensive and handy

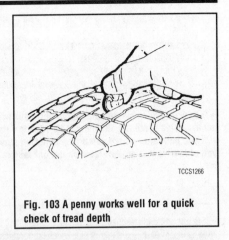

Fig. 103 A penny works well for a quick check of tread depth

FLUIDS AND LUBRICANTS

Oil and Fuel Recommendations

OIL

▶ See Figures 104 and 105

The SAE (Society of Automotive Engineers) grade number indicates the viscosity of the engine oil; its resistance to flow at a given temperature. The lower the SAE grade number, the lighter the oil. For example, the mono-grade oils begin with SAE 5 weight, which is a thin light oil, and continue in viscosity up to SAE 80 or 90 weight, which are heavy gear lubricants. These oils are also known as straight weight, meaning they are of a single viscosity, and do not vary with engine temperature.

Multi-viscosity oils offer the important advantage of being adaptable to temperature extremes. These oils have designations such as 10W-40, 20W-50, etc. The 10W-40 means that in winter (the W in the designation) the oil acts like a thin 10 weight oil, allowing the engine to spin easily when cold and offering rapid lubrication. Once the engine has warmed up, however, the oil acts like a straight 40 weight, maintaining good lubrication and protection for the engine's internal components. A 20W-50 oil would therefore be slightly heavier than and not as ideal in cold weather as the 10W-40, but would offer better protection at higher rpm and temperatures because when warm it acts like a 50 weight oil. Whichever oil viscosity you choose when changing the oil, make sure you are anticipating the temperatures your engine will be operating in until the oil is changed again. Refer to the oil viscosity chart for oil recommendations according to temperature.

The API (American Petroleum Institute) designation indicates the classification of engine oil used under certain given operating conditions. Only oils designated for use Service SF should be used. Oils of the SF type perform a variety of functions inside the engine in addition to the basic function as a lubricant. Through a balanced system of metallic detergents and polymeric dispersants, the oil prevents the formation of high and low temperature deposits and also keeps sludge and particles of dirt in suspension. Acids, particularly sulfuric acid, as well as other by-products of combustion, are neutralized. Both the SAE grade number and the APE designation can be found on top of the oil can.

For recommended oil viscosities, refer to the chart. Note that 10W-30 and 10W-40 grade oils are not recommended for sustained high speed driving when the temperature rises above the indicated limit.

Synthetic Oil

There are many excellent synthetic and fuel-efficient oils currently available that can provide better gas mileage, longer service life, and in some cases better engine protection. These benefits do not come without a few hitches, however; the main one being the price of synthetic oils, which can be three or four times the price per quart of conventional oil.

Synthetic oil is not for every truck and every type of driving, so you should consider your engine's condition and your type of driving. Also, check your truck's warranty conditions regarding the use of synthetic oils.

Both brand new engines and older, high mileage engines are the wrong candidates for synthetic oil. The synthetic oils are so slippery that they can prevent the proper break-in of new engines; most manufacturers recommend that you wait until the engine is properly broken in at least (3000 miles) before using synthetic oil. Older engines with wear have a different problem with synthetics: they use (consume during operation) more oil as they age. Slippery synthetic oils get past these worn parts easily. If your engine is using conventional oil, it will use synthetics much faster. Also, if your truck is leaking oil past old seals you'll probably have a much greater leak problem with synthetics.

Consider your type of driving. If most of your accumulated mileage is high speed, highway type driving, the more expensive synthetic oils may be a benefit. Extended highway driving gives the engine a chance to warm up, accumulating less acids in the oil and putting less stress on the engine over the long run. Under these conditions, the oil change interval can be extended (assuming your oil filter can last the extended life of the oil) up to the advertised mileage claims of the synthetics. Trucks with synthetic oils may show increased fuel economy in highway driving, due to less internal friction. However, many automotive

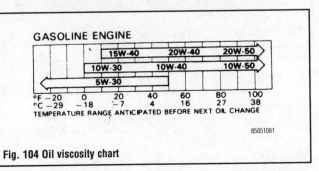

Fig. 104 Oil viscosity chart

Recommended Lubricants	
Component	Lubricant
Engine Oil	API SF/CC
Manual Transmission	API GL-4, SAE 75W-90 or 80W-90 ①
Automatic Transmission	ATF DEXTRON® II
Transfer Case	API GL-4, SAE 75W-90 or 80W-90
Differentials	API GL-5, SAE 80W-90
Brake Master Cylinder	DOT 3, SAE J1703
Clutch Master Cylinder	DOT 3, SAE J1703
Power Steering	ATF DEXTRON® II
Steering Gear	API GL-4, SAE 75W-90 or 80W-90
Steering Knuckle	NLGI #2
Ball Joints	NLGI #1 or #2
Wheel Bearings	NLGI #2
Coolant	Ethylene Glycol-Based Antifreeze

① Diesel Engines: API GL-3 or GL-4 90W or 140W

Fig. 105 Recommended Lubricants Chart

1-24 GENERAL INFORMATION AND MAINTENANCE

experts agree that 50,000 miles (80,000 km) is far too long to keep any oil in your engine.

Trucks used under harder circumstances, such as stop-and-go, city type driving, short trips, or extended idling, should be serviced more frequently. For the engines in these trucks, the much greater cost of synthetic or fuel-efficient oils may not be worth the investment. Internal wear increase much quicker on these trucks, causing greater oil consumption and leakage.

➡ **The mixing of conventional and synthetic oils is not recommended. If you are using synthetic oil, it might be wise to carry two or three quarts with you no matter where you drive, as not all service stations carry this type of lubricant. Non-detergent or straight mineral oils must never be used.**

FUEL

It is important to use fuel of the proper octane rating in your truck. Octane rating is based on the quantity of anti-knock compounds added to the fuel and it determines the speed at which the gas will burn. The lower the octane rating, the faster it burns. The higher the octane, the slower the fuel will burn and a greater percentage of compounds in the fuel prevent spark ping (knock), detonation and preignition (dieseling).

As the temperature of the engine increases, the air/fuel mixture exhibits a tendency to ignite before the spark plug is fired. If fuel of an octane rating too low for the engine is used, this will allow combustion to occur before the piston has completed its compression stroke, thereby creating a very high pressure very rapidly.

Fuel of the proper octane rating, for the compression ratio and ignition timing of your truck, will slow the combustion process sufficiently to allow the spark plug enough time to ignite the mixture completely and smoothly. Many non-catalyst models are designed to run on regular fuel. The use of some super-premium fuel is no substitution for a properly tuned and maintained engine. Chances are that if your engine exhibits any signs of spark ping, detonation or pre-ignition when using regular fuel, the ignition timing should be checked against specifications.

Vehicles equipped with catalytic converters must use UNLEADED GASOLINE ONLY. Most converter equipped models are designed to operate using unleaded gasoline with a minimum rating of 87 octane. Use of unleaded gas with octane ratings lower than 87 can cause persistent spark knock which could lead to engine damage.

Light spark knock may be noticed when accelerating or driving up hills. The slight knocking may be considered normal (with 87 octane) because the maximum fuel economy is obtained under condition of occasional light spark knock. Gasoline with an octane rating higher than 87 may be used, but it is not necessary (in most cases) for proper operation.

If spark knock is constant, when using 87 octane, at cruising speeds on level ground, ignition timing adjustment may be required.

➡ **Your engine's fuel requirement can change with time, mainly due to carbon buildup, which changes the compression ratio. If your engine pings, knocks or runs on, switch to a higher grade of fuel. Sometimes just changing brands will cure the problem. If it becomes necessary to retard the timing from specifications, don't change it more than a few degrees. Retarded timing will reduce power output and fuel mileage and will increase the engine temperature.**

OPERATION IN FOREIGN COUNTRIES

If you plan to drive your truck outside the United States or Canada, there is a possibility that fuels will be too low in anti-knock quality and could produce engine damage. It is wise to consult with local authorities upon arrival in a foreign country to determine the best fuels available.

Engine

✱✱ CAUTION

Prolonged and repeated skin contact with used engine oil, with no effort to remove the oil, may be harmful. Always follow these simple precautions when handling used motor oil:

- Avoid prolonged skin contact with used motor oil.
- Remove oil from skin by washing thoroughly with soap and water or waterless hand cleaner. Do not use gasoline, thinners or other solvents.
- Avoid prolonged skin contact with oil-soaked clothing.

OIL LEVEL CHECK

▶ See Figures 106 and 107

Every time you stop for fuel, check the engine oil as follows:
1. Park the truck on level ground.
2. When checking the oil level it is best for the engine to be at operating temperature, although checking the oil immediately after a stopping will lead to a false reading. Wait a few minutes after turning off the engine to allow the oil to drain back into the crankcase.
3. Open the hood and locate the dipstick which is on the left side (L16, L18 and L20B engines) or the right side (Z20, Z22, Z24, Z24i and VG30i engines). Pull the dipstick from its tube, wipe it clean and reinsert it.
4. Pull the dipstick out again and, holding it horizontally, read the oil level. The oil should be between the **H** and **L** marks on the dipstick. If the oil is below the **L** mark, add oil of the proper viscosity through the capped opening on the top of the cylinder head cover. See the Oil and Fuel Recommendations chart in this section for the proper viscosity ad rating of oil to use.
5. Replace the dipstick and check the oil level again after adding any oil. Be careful not to overfill the crankcase. Approximately one quart of oil will raise the level from the **L** to the **H**. Excess oil will generally be consumed at an accelerated rate.

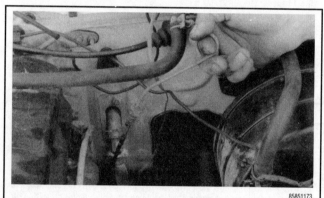

Fig. 106 Removing the oil dipstick from the engine

Fig. 107 The oil level indicated on the dipstick should never be below the L line or above the H line

OIL AND FILTER CHANGE

▶ See Figures 108 thru 119

The oil should be changed every 6000 miles (9600 km) on models built between 1970–77. All 1978–88 models should have the oil changed every 7500 miles (12,000 km).

GENERAL INFORMATION AND MAINTENANCE 1-25

> ⚠️ **CAUTION**
>
> Prolonged and repeated skin contact with used engine oil, with no effort to remove the oil, may be harmful. Always follow these simple precautions when handling used motor oil.

- Avoid prolonged skin contact with oil-soaked clothing.

The oil drain plug is located on the bottom, rear of the oil pan (bottom of the engine, underneath the truck). The oil filter is located on the right side of the engine on all models.

The mileage figures given are the Nissan recommended intervals assuming normal driving and conditions. If your truck is being used under dusty, polluted or off-road conditions, change the oil and filter more frequently than specified. The same goes for trucks driven in stop-and-go traffic or only for short distances. Always drain the oil after the engine has been running long enough to bring it to normal operating temperature. Hot oil will flow easier and more contaminants will be removed along with the oil than if it were drained cold. To change the oil and filter:

> ⚠️ **CAUTION**
>
> The EPA warns that prolonged contact with used engine oil may cause a number of skin disorders, including cancer! You should make every effort to minimize your exposure to used engine oil. Protective gloves should be worn when changing the oil. Wash your hands and any other exposed skin areas as soon as possible after exposure to used engine oil. Soap and water, or waterless hand cleaner should be used.

1. Run the engine until it reaches normal operating temperature.
2. Jack up the front of the truck and support it on safety stands.
3. Slide a drain pan of at least 6 quarts capacity under the oil pan.

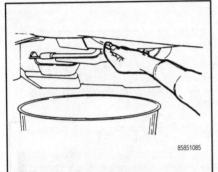

Fig. 108 By keeping an inward pressure on the drain plug as you unscrew it, the oil won't escape past the threads

Fig. 109 Remove the oil filter with a strap wrench

Fig. 110 Lubricate the gasket on the new oil filter with clean engine oil—a dry gasket may not make a good seal and will allow the filter to leak

Fig. 111 Install the new oil filter by hand

Fig. 112 Add oil through the cylinder head (valve cover) only

Fig. 113 Use a cap-type oil filter removal tool on fuel injected engines

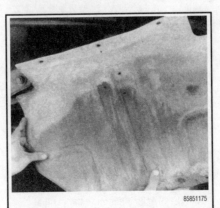

Fig. 114 Removing the under carriage pan retaining bolts

Fig. 115 Removing the under carriage pan

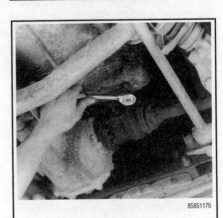

Fig. 116 Removing the oil plug

1-26 GENERAL INFORMATION AND MAINTENANCE

Fig. 117 Draining the oil from the engine

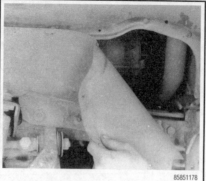

Fig. 118 Removing the dirt shield for oil filter removal-on some models

Fig. 119 View of the oil filler cap-make sure the cap fits properly

4. Loosen the drain plug. Turn the plug out by hand. By keeping an inward pressure on the plug as you unscrew it, oil won't escape past the threads and you can remove it without being burned by hot oil.

5. Allow the oil to drain completely and then install the drain plug(s). Don't overtighten the plug(s), or you'll be buying a new pan or a trick replacement plug for stripped threads.

6. Using a strap wrench, remove the oil filter; on Z24i and VG30i engines, use a cap-type filter removal tool. Keep in mind that it's holding about one quart of dirty, hot oil.

7. Empty the old filter into the drain pan and dispose of the filter.

8. Using a clean rag, wipe off the filter adapter on the engine block. Be sure that the rag doesn't leave any lint which could clog an oil passage.

9. Coat the rubber gasket on the filter with fresh oil. Spin it onto the engine by hand; when the gasket touches the adapter surface give it another ½–¾ turn. No more, or you'll squash the gasket and it may leak.

10. Refill the engine with the correct amount of fresh oil. See the Capacities chart.

11. Check the oil level on the dipstick. It is normal for the level to be a bit above the full mark. Start the engine and allow it to idle for a few minutes.

✲✲ CAUTION

Do not run the engine above idle speed until it has built up oil pressure, indicated when the oil light goes out.

12. Shut off the engine, allow the oil to drain for a few minutes, and check the oil level. Check around the filter and drain plug for any leaks, and correct as necessary.

Manual Transmission

FLUID RECOMMENDATIONS

- Pick-Ups and Pathfinders: multipurpose gear oil API GL-4; SAE 75W-90 or 80W-90

FLUID LEVEL CHECK

▶ See Figures 120 and 121

The oil in the manual transmission should be checked at least every 7500 miles (12,000 km) for 1970–78 vehicles, or 15,000 miles (24,000 km) for 1979–88 vehicles and replaced every 25,000–30,000 miles (40,000–48,000 km), even more frequently if driven through deep water.

1. With the truck parked on a level surface, remove the filler plug (square head on some models, Allen head on others) from the left side of the transmission housing.

2. If the lubricant begins to trickle out of the hole, there is enough. Otherwise, carefully insert your finger (watch out for sharp threads!) and check to see if the oil is up to the edge of the hole.

3. If not, add oil through the hole until the level is at the edge of the hole. Most gear lubricants come in a plastic squeeze bottle with a nozzle; making additions simple. You can also use a common everyday kitchen baster.

4. Replace the filler plug, run the engine and check for leaks.

DRAIN AND REFILL

▶ See Figure 122

Once every 24,000 miles (40,000 km) for 1970–78 vehicles, or once every 30,000 miles (48,000 km) for 1979–88 vehicles, the oil in the manual transmission should be changed.

1. The transmission oil should be hot before it is drained. If the engine is at normal operating temperature, the transmission oil should be hot enough.

2. Raise the truck and support it properly on jackstands so that you can safely work underneath. You will probably not have enough room to work if the truck is not raised.

3. The drain plug is located on the bottom of the transmission. Place a pan under the drain plug and remove it. Keep a slight upward pressure on the plug while unscrewing it, this will keep the oil from pouring out until the plug is removed.

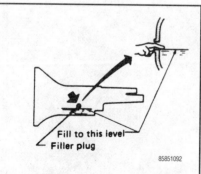

Fig. 120 The oil level in the manual transmission should be up to the bottom of the filler (upper) plug

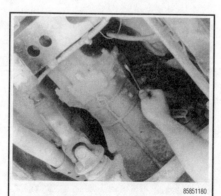

Fig. 121 Checking the oil in the manual transmission

Fig. 122 Draining the oil from the manual transmission

GENERAL INFORMATION AND MAINTENANCE   1-27

✽✽ CAUTION

The oil will be HOT! Be careful when you remove the plug so that you don't take a bath in hot gear oil.

4. Allow the oil to drain completely. Clean off the plug and replace it, tightening it until it is just snug.

5. Remove the filler plug from the side of the transmission case. It is on the driver's (left) side. There is usually a gasket underneath this plug. Replace it if damaged.

6. Fill the transmission with gear oil through the filler plug hole as detailed previously. Refer to the Capacities Chart for the approximate amount of oil needed to refill your transmission.

7. The oil level should come right up to the edge of the hole. You can stick your finger in to verify this. Watch out for sharp threads!

8. Replace the filler plug and gasket, lower the truck, and check for leaks. Dispose of the old oil in the proper manner.

CHECKING WATER ENTRY

▶ See Figure 123

1986–88 4WD Models Only

After having driven in deep water or mud, the clutch housing should always be checked for water entry. There is a small rubber gasket at the bottom of the left side leading edge of the transmission case where it mates with the rear of the engine block, carefully pry it out and let any water that has collected in the clutch housing seep out.

Automatic Transmission

FLUID RECOMMENDATIONS

- All models: DEXRON®II ATF

FLUID LEVEL CHECK

▶ See Figures 124, 125, 126 and 127

Check the automatic transmission fluid level at least every 6000 miles (9600 km) for 1973–79 vehicles; 15,000 miles (24,000 km) for 1980–88 vehicles. The dipstick is in the right rear of the engine compartment. The fluid level should be checked only when the transmission is hot (normal operating temperature). The transmission is considered hot after about 20 miles of highway driving.

1. Park the truck on a level surface with the engine idling. Shift the transmission into **P** and set the parking brake.

2. Remove the dipstick, wipe it clean and reinsert if firmly. Be sure that it has been pushed all the way in. Remove the dipstick and check the fluid level while holding it horizontally. With the engine running, the fluid level should be between the **H** and **L** marks on 1973–87 models. 1988–88 models have a HOT and a COLD side to the dipstick. On 2wd models, the fluid level should be between the two hash marks on the HOT side or between the two notches on the COLD side. On 4wd models, the fluid level should be within the cross-hatched area on the HOT or COLD sides.

3. If the fluid level is below the **L** mark on 1973–87 models, below the lower hash mark (HOT) or lower notch (COLD) on 1988–88 2wd models, or not within the cross-hatched area on either side of the dipstick on 1988 4wd mod-

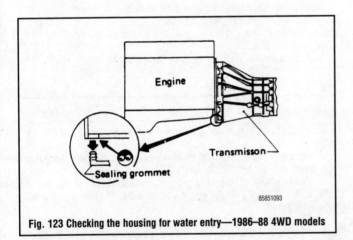

Fig. 123 Checking the housing for water entry—1986–88 4WD models

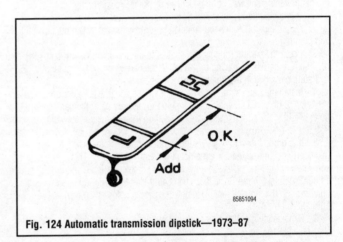

Fig. 124 Automatic transmission dipstick—1973–87

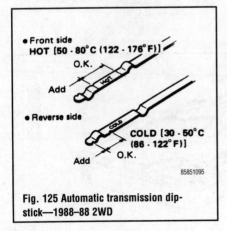

Fig. 125 Automatic transmission dipstick—1988–88 2WD

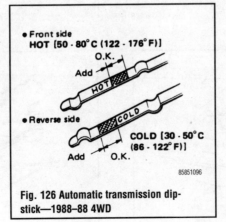

Fig. 126 Automatic transmission dipstick—1988–88 4WD

Fig. 127 Add automatic transmission fluid through the dipstick tube with a funnel

1-28 GENERAL INFORMATION AND MAINTENANCE

els, pour DEXRON®II ATF into the dipstick tube. This is easily done with the aid of a funnel. Check the level often as you are filling the transmission. Be extremely careful not to overfill it. Overfilling will cause slippage, seal damage and overheating. Approximately one pint of ATF will raise the level from one notch to the other.

➥Always use the proper transmission fluid when filling your truck's transmission. All models use DEXRON®II. Always check with the owner's manual to be sure. NEVER use Type F in a transmission requiring DEXRON®or vice versa, as severe damage will result.

✸✸ CAUTION

The fluid on the dipstick should always be a bright red color. It if is discolored (brown or black), or smells burnt, serious transmission troubles, probably due to overheating, should be suspected.

DRAIN AND REFILL

The automatic transmission fluid should be changed at least every 25,000–30,000 miles (40,000–48,000 km). If the truck is normally used in severe service, such as stop-and-go driving, trailer towing or the like, the interval should be halved. The fluid should be hot before it is drained; a 20 minute drive will accomplish this.

Pan and Filter Service

◆ See Figures 128 and 129

1. There is no drain plug; the fluid pan must be removed. Partially loosen the pan retaining screws until the pan can be pulled down at one corner. Lower a corner of the pan and allow all fluid to drain out.
2. After the pan has drained completely, remove the pan retaining screws and then remove the pan and gasket.
3. Clean the pan thoroughly and allow it to air dry. If you wipe it out with a rag you run the risk of leaving bits of lint in the pan which will clog the tiny hydraulic passages in the transmission.
4. Install the pan using a new gasket. If you decide to use sealer on the gasket, apply it only in a very thin bead running to the outside of the pan screw holes. Tighten the pan screws evenly in rotation from the center outwards, to 3–5 ft. lbs. (4–7 Nm).
5. It is a good idea to measure the amount of fluid drained from the transmission to determine the correct amount of fresh fluid to add. This is because some parts of the transmission may not drain completely and using the dry refill amount specified in the Capacities chart could lead to overfilling. Fluid is added only through the dipstick tube. Use only the proper automatic transmission fluid; do not overfill.
6. Replace the dipstick after filling. Start the engine and allow it to idle. DO NOT race the engine.
7. After the engine has idled for a few minutes, shift the transmission slowly through the gears and then return it to **P**. With the engine still idling, check the fluid level on the dipstick. If necessary, add more fluid to raise the level to where it is supposed to be.

✸✸ CAUTION

Check the fluid in the drain pan, it should always be a bright red color. It if is discolored (brown or black), or smells burnt, serious transmission troubles, probably due to overheating, should be suspected. The transmission should be inspected by a qualified service technician to locate the cause of the burnt fluid.

Transfer Case

FLUID RECOMMENDATIONS

• Pick-Ups and Pathfinder: multipurpose gear oil API GL-4; SAE 75W-90 or 80W-90

FLUID LEVEL CHECK

◆ See Figures 130, 131 and 132

The oil in the transfer case should be checked at least every 15,000 miles (24,000 km) and replaced every 25,000–30,000 miles (40,000–48,000 km), or more frequently if driven through deep water or mud.

1. With the truck parked on a level surface, remove the filler plug from the side of the transfer case housing on 1980–86 models (720 series), or the rear of the housing on 1986–88 models (D21 series).
2. If the lubricant begins to trickle out of the hole, there is enough. Otherwise, carefully insert your finger (watch out for sharp threads!) and check to see if the oil is up to the edge of the hole.
3. If not, add oil through the hole until the level is at the edge of the hole. Most gear lubricants come in a plastic squeeze bottle with a nozzle; making additions simple. You can also use a common everyday kitchen baster.
4. Replace the filler plug, run the engine and check for leaks.

DRAIN AND REFILL

◆ See Figure 133

Once every 30,000 miles (48,000 km), the oil in the transfer case should be changed.

1. The transfer case oil should be hot before it is drained. If the engine is at normal operating temperature, the oil should be hot enough.
2. Raise the truck and support it properly on jackstands so that you can safely work underneath. You will probably not have enough room to work if the truck is not raised.
3. The drain plug is located on the bottom of the transfer case. Place a pan under the drain plug and remove it. Keep a slight upward pressure on the plug while unscrewing it, this will keep the oil from pouring out until the plug is removed.

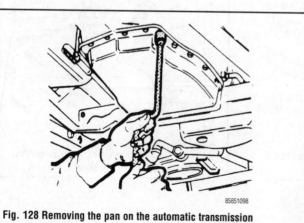

Fig. 128 Removing the pan on the automatic transmission

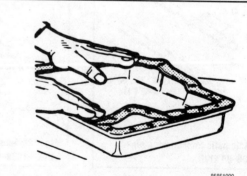

Fig. 129 Always replace the gasket when installing the transmission oil pan

GENERAL INFORMATION AND MAINTENANCE

Fig. 130 Removing the transfer case shield mounting bolts

Fig. 131 Removing the transfer case shield

Fig. 132 Checking the oil in the transfer case

✱✱ CAUTION

The oil will be HOT. Be careful when you remove the plug so that you don't take a bath in hot gear oil.

4. Allow the oil to drain completely. Clean off the plug and replace it, tightening it until it is just snug.
5. Remove the filler plug from the side of the case. There will be a gasket underneath this plug. Replace it if damaged.
6. Fill the transfer case with gear oil through the filler plug hole as detailed previously. Refer to the Capacities Chart for the approximate amount of oil needed to refill your transfer case.
7. The oil level should come right up to the edge of the hole. You can stick your finger in to verify this. Watch out for sharp threads.
8. Replace the filler plug and gasket, lower the truck, and check for leaks. Dispose of the old oil in the proper manner.

Drive Axles (Differentials)

FLUID RECOMMENDATIONS

- All models: Hypoid gear oil API GL-5; below 0°F (−18°C): SAE 90W, above 0°F (−18°C): SAE 80W or 80W-90.

FLUID LEVEL CHECK

▶ See Figures 134, 135, 136, 137 and 138

The oil in the front and/or rear differential should be checked at least every 15,000 miles (24,000 km) and replaced every 25,000–30,000 miles (40,000–48,000 km). If driven through deep water it should be replaced immediately.

Fig. 133 Removing the transfer case drain plug

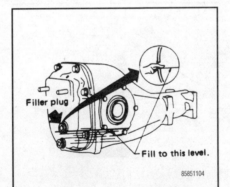
Fig. 134 Checking the fluid level in the front differential

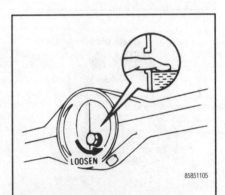
Fig. 135 Checking the fluid level in the rear differential

Fig. 136 Removing the plug in the rear differential

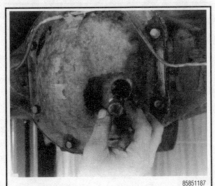
Fig. 137 Checking the oil in the rear differential

Fig. 138 Adding oil in the rear differential

1-30 GENERAL INFORMATION AND MAINTENANCE

1. With the truck parked on a level surface, remove the filler plug from the back of the differential.

➡ The plug on the bottom is the drain plug on rear differentials. The lower of the two plugs on the back of the housing is the drain plug on front differentials.

2. If the oil begins to trickle out of the hole, there is enough. Otherwise, carefully insert your finger (watch out for sharp threads!) into the hole and check to see if the oil is up to the bottom edge of the filler hole.

3. If not, add oil through the hole until the level is at the edge of the hole. Most gear oils come in a plastic squeeze bottle with a nozzle, making additions simple. You can also use a common kitchen baster. Use standard GL-5 hypoid type gear oil; SAE 90 or SAE 80 if you live in a particularly cold area.

4. Replace the filler plug and drive the truck for a while. Stop the truck and check for leaks.

DRAIN AND REFILL

♦ See Figures 139, 140 and 141

The gear oil in the front or rear axle should be changed at least every 25,000–30,000 miles (40,000–48,000 km); immediately if driven in deep water. To drain and fill the differential, proceed as follows:

1. Park the vehicle on a level surface. Set the parking brake.
2. Remove the filler (upper) plug. Place a container which is large enough to catch all of the differential oil, under the drain plug.
3. Remove the drain (lower) plug and gasket, if so equipped. Allow all of the oil to drain into the container.
4. Install the drain plug. Tighten it so that it will not leak, but do not overtighten.

➡ Its usually a good idea to replace the drain plug gasket at this time.

5. Refill with the proper grade and viscosity of axle lubricant (see Recommended Lubricants chart). Be sure that the level reaches the bottom of the filler plug. DO NOT overfill.
6. Install the filler plug and check for leakage.

Cooling System

FLUID RECOMMENDATIONS

When additional coolant is required to maintain the proper level, always add a 50/50 mixture of ethylene glycol antifreeze (coolant) and water.

FLUID LEVEL CHECK

♦ See Figures 142, 143, 144, 145 and 146

Dealing with the cooling system can be a tricky matter unless the proper precautions are observed. It is best to check the coolant level in the radiator when the engine is cold. This is done by removing the radiator cap and seeing that the coolant is within ¾ inch; of the bottom of the filler neck. On later models, the cooling system has, as one of its components, an expansion tank. If coolant is visible above the **Low** or **Min** mark on the tank, the level is satisfactory. Always be certain that the filler caps on both the radiator and the reservoir are tightly closed.

In the event that the coolant level must be checked when the engine is warm or on engines without the expansion tank, place a thick rag over the radiator cap and slowly turn the cap counterclockwise until it reaches the first detent. Allow all the hot steam to escape. This will allow the pressure in the system to drop gradually, preventing an explosion of hot coolant. When the hissing noise stops, remove the cap the rest of the way.

It's a good idea to check the coolant every time that you stop for fuel. If the coolant level is low, add equal amounts of ethylene glycol based antifreeze and clean water. On models without an expansion tank, add coolant through the radiator filler neck. Fill the expansion tank to the **Full** or **Max** level on trucks with that system.

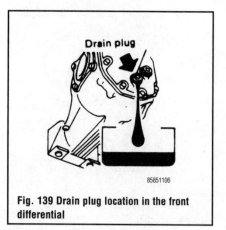

Fig. 139 Drain plug location in the front differential

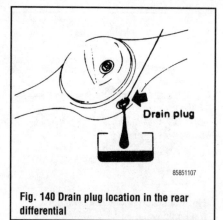

Fig. 140 Drain plug location in the rear differential

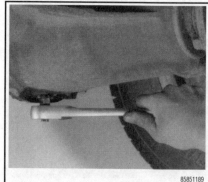

Fig. 141 Removing the drain plug in the rear differential

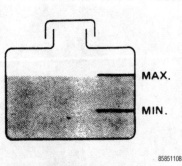

Fig. 142 The coolant level should never fall below the MIN mark on models with expansion tank

Fig. 143 Removing the radiator cap—always remove cap when engine is COLD

Fig. 144 Adding coolant—always add coolant when engine is COLD

GENERAL INFORMATION AND MAINTENANCE 1-31

> ※※ **CAUTION**
>
> Never add cold coolant to a hot engine unless the engine is running, to avoid cracking the engine block.

Avoid using water that is known to have a high alkaline content or is very hard (except in emergency situations). Drain and flush the cooling system as soon as possible after using such water.

The radiator hoses and clamps and the radiator cap should be checked at the same time as the coolant level. Hoses which are brittle, cracked, or swollen should be replaced. Clamps should be checked for tightness (screwdriver tight only! Do not allow the clamp to cut into the hose or crush the fitting). The radiator cap gasket should be checked for any obvious tears, cracks or swelling, or any signs of incorrect seating in the radiator neck.

DRAIN AND REFILL

> ※※ **CAUTION**
>
> When draining the coolant, keep in mind that cats and dogs are attracted by the ethylene glycol antifreeze, and are quite likely to drink any that is left in an uncovered container or in puddles on the ground. This will prove fatal in sufficient quantity. Always drain the coolant into a sealable container. Coolant should be reused unless it is contaminated or several years old.

Completely draining and refilling the cooling system every two years at least will remove accumulated rust, scale and other deposits.

➥Use a good quality antifreeze with water pump lubricants, rust inhibitors and other corrosion inhibitors along with acid neutralizers. Use a permanent type coolant that meets specification ESE–M97B44A or the equivalent.

1. Drain the existing antifreeze and coolant. Open the radiator and engine drain petcocks (models equipped), or disconnect the bottom radiator hose, at the radiator outlet. Set the heater temperature controls to the full HOT position.

➥Before opening the radiator petcock, spray it with some penetrating lubricant.

2. Close the petcock or reconnect the lower hose and fill the system with water.
3. Add a can of quality radiator flush. Be sure the flush is safe to use in engines having aluminum components.
4. Idle the engine until the upper radiator hose gets hot.
5. Drain the system again.
6. Repeat this process until the drained water is clear and free of scale.
7. Close all petcocks and connect all the hoses.
8. If equipped with a coolant recovery system, flush the reservoir with water and leave empty.
9. Determine the capacity of your cooling system (see Capacities specifications). Add a 50/50 mix of quality antifreeze (ethylene glycol) and water to provide the desired protection.

SYSTEM INSPECTION

Most permanent antifreeze/coolant have a colored dye added which makes the solution an excellent leak detector. When servicing the cooling system, check for leakage at:
- All hoses and hose connections.
- Radiator seams, radiator core, and radiator draincock.
- All engine block and cylinder head freeze (core) plugs, and drain plugs.
- Edges of all cooling system gaskets (head gaskets, thermostat gasket).
- Transmission fluid cooler.
- Heating system components, water pump.
- Check the engine oil dipstick for signs of coolant in the engine oil.
- Check the coolant in the radiator for signs of oil in the coolant.

Investigate and correct any indication of coolant leakage.

Check the Radiator Cap

♦ See Figure 147

While you are checking the coolant level, check the radiator cap for a worn or cracked gasket. If the cap doesn't seal properly, fluid will be lost and the engine will overheat.

A worn cap should be replaced with a new one.

Clean Radiator of Debris

♦ See Figure 148

Periodically clean any debris such as leaves, paper, insects, etc., from the radiator fins. Pick the large pieces off by hand. The smaller pieces can be washed away with water pressure from a hose.

Carefully straighten any bent radiator fins with a pair of needle nose pliers. Be careful, the fins are very soft. Don't wiggle the fins back and forth too much. Straighten them once and try not to move them again.

CHECKING SYSTEM PROTECTION

♦ See Figure 149

A 50/50 mix of coolant concentrate and water will usually provide protection to −35°F (−37°C). Freeze protection may be checked by using a cooling system hydrometer. Inexpensive hydrometers (floating ball types) may be obtained from a local department store (automotive section) or an auto supply store. Follow the directions packaged with the coolant hydrometer when checking protection.

Master Cylinders

All models utilize both a brake and a clutch master cylinder. Both are located above the brake booster unit at the driver's side firewall.

1972–80 models utilize two (2) brake master cylinder reservoirs.

Fig. 145 View of the coolant expansion tank

Fig. 146 Adding coolant to the expansion tank always—add coolant when engine is COLD

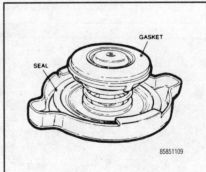

Fig. 147 Check the radiator cap seal and gasket condition

1-32 GENERAL INFORMATION AND MAINTENANCE

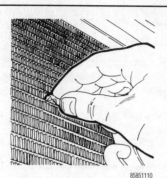

Fig. 148 Clean the radiator fins of any debris which impedes air flow

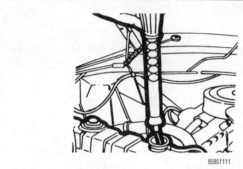

Fig. 149 The freezing protection rating can be checked with an antifreeze tester

FLUID RECOMMENDATIONS

Use only Heavy Duty Brake fluid meeting DOT 3 or SAE J1703 specifications.

FLUID LEVEL CHECK

▶ See Figures 150, 151, 152, 153 and 154

The fluid in the brake and/or clutch master cylinders should be checked every 6 months or 6000 miles (9600 km).

➡It is normal for the fluid level to fall as the disc brake pads wear. However, if the master cylinder requires filling frequently, you should check the system for leaks in the hoses, master cylinder, or wheel cylinders or calipers.

Check the fluid level on the side of the reservoir. If fluid is required, remove the screw (if so equipped) on the cap, then remove the filler cap and gasket from the master cylinder. Fill the reservoir to the full line in the reservoir. Install the filler cap, making sure the gasket is properly seated in the cap.

➡Brake fluid dissolves paint. It also absorbs moisture from the air; never leave a container or the master cylinder or the clutch cylinder uncovered any longer than necessary. The clutch master cylinder uses the same fluid as the brakes, and should be checked at the same time as the brake master cylinder.

Power Steering Pump

FLUID RECOMMENDATIONS

- Use only DEXRON®II ATF in the power steering system.

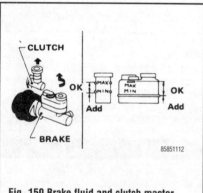

Fig. 150 Brake fluid and clutch master cylinder

Fig. 151 Checking the brake master cylinder

Fig. 152 Adding brake fluid in the master cylinder

Fig. 153 Checking the clutch master cylinder

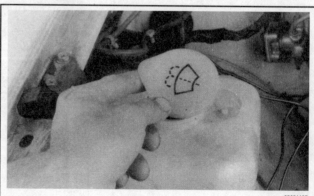

Fig. 154 Adding windshield washer fluid

GENERAL INFORMATION AND MAINTENANCE   1-33

FLUID LEVEL CHECK

▶ See Figures 155, 156, 157, 158 and 159

Check the power steering fluid level every 6 months or 6000 miles (9600 km).

1. Park the vehicle on a level surface. Run the engine until normal operating temperature is reached.
2. Turn the steering all the way to the left and then all the way to the right several times. Center the steering wheel and shut off the engine.
3. Open the hood and check the power steering reservoir fluid level.
4. Remove the filler cap and wipe the dipstick attached clean.
5. Re-insert the dipstick and tighten the cap. Remove the dipstick and note the fluid level indicated on the dipstick.
6. The level should be at any point below the upper hash mark, but not below the lower hash mark (in the HOT or COLD ranges).
7. Add fluid as necessary. Do not overfill.

Steering Gear

FLUID RECOMMENDATIONS

Use standard hypoid-type gear oil GL-4, SAE 90W when refilling the steering gear.

FLUID LEVEL CHECK

▶ See Figure 160

Every year or 15,000 miles (24,000 km) you should check the steering gear housing lubricating oil. The filler plug is on top of the housing and requires a 14mm wrench for removal. The level should be at or near the top of the housing.

Battery

▶ See Figure 161

At every fuel stop the level of the battery electrolyte should be checked. The level should be maintained between the upper and lower levels marked on the battery case or the bottom of the vent well in each cell.

Except on maintenance free batteries, if the electrolyte level is low, distilled water should be added until the proper level is reached. Each cell is completely separate from the others, so each must be filled individually. It is a good idea to add the distilled water with a squeeze bulb to avoid having electrolyte splash out. If water is frequently needed, the most likely cause is overcharging, caused by a faulty voltage regulator. If any acid solution should escape, it can be neutralized with a baking soda and water solution, but don't let the stuff get in the battery. In winter, add water only before driving to prevent the battery from freezing and cracking. When replacing a battery, it is important that the replacement have an output rating equal to or greater than original equipment. See Section 3 for details on battery replacement.

✳✳ CAUTION

If you get acid on you skin or in your eyes, rinse it off immediately with lots of water. Go to a doctor if it gets in you eyes. The gases formed inside the battery cells are highly explosive. Never check the level of the electrolyte in the presence of flame or while smoking.

Chassis Greasing

▶ See Figures 162 and 163

Complete chassis greasing should include an inspection of all rubber suspension bushings, lubrication of all body hinges, as well as proper greasing of

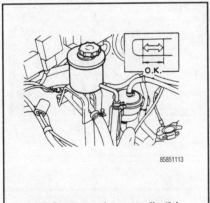
Fig. 155 Power steering pump dipstick

Fig. 156 Removing the power steering pump cap cover

Fig. 157 Removing the power steering pump dipstick

Fig. 158 Checking the power steering fluid level

Fig. 159 View of the power steering pump cap—note service information

1-34 GENERAL INFORMATION AND MAINTENANCE

Fig. 160 Checking the steering gear fluid level

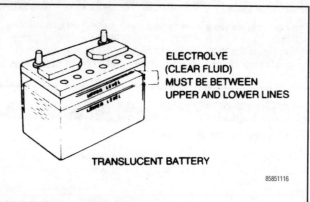

Fig. 161 Some batteries have level indicator lines on their sides

Fig. 162 View of grease fitting on tie rod end

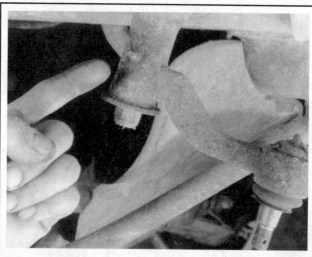

Fig. 163 View of grease fitting on idler arm

the front suspension upper and lower ball joints and control arm bushings. To provide correct operation, the chassis should be greased every 6 months or 6000 miles (9600 km) on 1970–78 trucks. The 1979–88 trucks should be greased every 7500 miles (12,000 km).

If you wish to perform this operation yourself you should purchase a cartridge type grease gun and several cartridges of multipurpose lithium base grease. You will also need to purchase grease fittings from your Nissan dealer, as certain front end components are fitted with screw-in plugs to prevent entry of foreign material.

Remove the plug and install the grease fitting (if necessary). Push the nozzle of the grease gun down firmly onto the fitting and while applying pressure, force the new grease into the boot. Force sufficient grease into the fitting to cause the old grease to be expelled. When this has been accomplished, remove the fitting and replace the plug. Follow this procedure on each front suspension lubrication point.

Certain models have a two piece driveshaft which must be greased at the same 6 month/7,500 mile interval. The driveshaft is equipped with a grease fitting, located on the shaft just behind the center support bearing. Simply wipe off the fitting and pump in two or three shots of grease. There is no built in escape hole for the old grease to exit, so don't keep pumping in grease until the seal gives way.

MANUAL TRANSMISSION AND CLUTCH LINKAGE

On models so equipped, apply a small amount of chassis grease to the pivot points of the transmission and clutch linkage as per the chassis lubrication diagram.

AUTOMATIC TRANSMISSION LINKAGE

On models so equipped, apply a small amount of 10W engine oil to the kickdown and shift linkage at the pivot points.

PARKING BRAKE LINKAGE

At yearly intervals or whenever binding is noticeable in the parking brake linkage, lubricate the cable guides, levers and linkage with a suitable chassis grease.

Wheel Bearings

➡ The following procedures are for 2wd only. For wheel bearing procedures on 4wd vehicles, please refer to the Front Drive Axle section in Section 7 of this manual.

ADJUSTMENT AND LUBRICATION

♦ See Figures 164, 165, 166 and 167

Only the front wheel bearings require periodic service. The lubricant to use is high temperature disc brake wheel bearing grease meeting NLGI No. 2 specifications. (This grease should be used even if the truck is equipped with drum brakes; it has superior protection characteristics.) This service is recommended at the specified period in the Maintenance Intervals chart or whenever the truck has been driven in water up to the hub.

GENERAL INFORMATION AND MAINTENANCE

Before handling the bearings there are a few things that you should remember:

Remember to DO the following:
1. Remove all outside dirt from the housing before exposing the bearing.
2. Treat a used bearing as gently as you would a new one.
3. Work with clean tools in clean surroundings.
4. Use clean, dry canvas gloves, or at least clean, dry hands.
5. Clean solvents and flushing fluids are a must.
6. Use clean paper when laying out the bearings to dry.
7. Protect disassembled bearings from rust and dirt. Cover them up.
8. Use clean rags to wipe bearings
9. Keep the bearings in oil-proof paper when they are to be stored or are not in use.
10. Clean the inside of the housing before replacing the bearings.

Do NOT do the following:
11. Don't work in dirty surroundings.
12. Don't use dirty, chipped, or damaged tools.
13. Try not to work on wooden work benches or use wooden mallets.
14. Don't handle bearings with dirty or moist hands.
15. Do not use gasoline for cleaning; use a safe solvent.
16. Do not spin dry bearings with compressed air. They will be damaged.
17. Do not spin unclean bearings.
18. Avoid using cotton waste or dirty cloths to wipe bearings.
19. Try not to scratch or nick bearing surfaces.
20. Do not allow the bearing to come in contact with dirt or rust at any time.

2-Wheel Drive

If your truck has drum brakes you will need a special claw type puller to remove the inner bearing and the steering knuckle grease retainer.

Procedures are basically the same for either disc or drum brakes.
1. Remove the bake drum or brake caliper, following the procedure outlined in Section 9 of this manual.
2. It is not necessary to remove the drum or disc from the hub. The outer wheel bearing will come off with the hub. Simply pull the hub and disc or drum assembly towards you off the spindle. Be sure to catch the bearing before it falls to the ground.
3. Drum brakes: The inner bearing and grease retainer must be pulled from the spindle with the claw puller. Be sure that the fingers of the tool pull on the seal, and not on the bearing itself. Discard the grease retainer.
   Disc brakes: The inner bearing will have to be driven from the hub along with the oil seal. Use a brass rod as a drift and carefully drive the inner bearing cone out. Remove the bearing and the oil seal. Discard the seal.
4. Clean the bearings in solvent and allow to air dry. You risk leaving bits of lint in the races if you dry them with a rag. Clean the bearing cups in the hub.
5. Inspect the bearings carefully. If they are worn, pitted, burned, or scored, they should be replaced, along with the bearing cups in which they run.
6. You can use a brass rod as a drift, or a large socket or piece of pipe to drive the inner and outer bearing cups out of the hub.
7. Install the new inner cup, and then the outer cup, in that order, into the hub, using either the brass drift or socket method outlined earlier.

➡ Use care not to cock the bearing cups in the hub. If they are not fully seated, the bearings will be impossible to adjust properly.

8. Drum brakes: Press a new grease retainer onto the spindle. Place a large glob of grease into one palm and force the edge of the inner bearing into it so that the grease fills the bearing. Do this until the whole bearing is packed. Press the inner bearing into the spindle, seating it firmly against the grease retainer.
   Disc brakes: Coat the inner bearing cup with grease. Pack the inner bearing with grease as outlined for drum brakes, and press the inner bearing into the

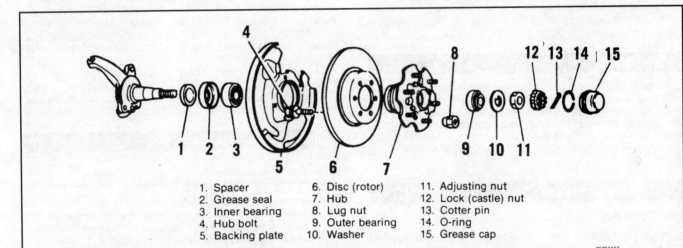

Fig. 164 Exploded view of the 2wd hub and bearing with disc brakes—drum brakes are similar

1. Spacer
2. Grease seal
3. Inner bearing
4. Hub bolt
5. Backing plate
6. Disc (rotor)
7. Hub
8. Lug nut
9. Outer bearing
10. Washer
11. Adjusting nut
12. Lock (castle) nut
13. Cotter pin
14. O-ring
15. Grease cap

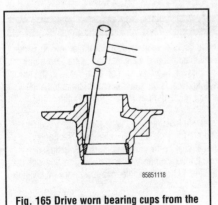

Fig. 165 Drive worn bearing cups from the hub with a soft drift and a hammer

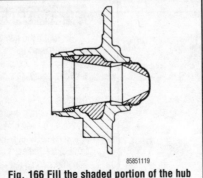

Fig. 166 Fill the shaded portion of the hub and grease cap with grease—also coat the cups with grease

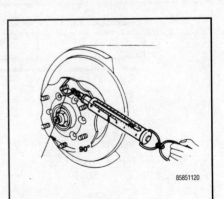

Fig. 167 Checking the wheel bearing preload

1-36 GENERAL INFORMATION AND MAINTENANCE

cup. Press a new oil seal into place on top of the bearing. You may have to give the seal a few gentle raps with a soft drift to get it to seat properly.

9. Install the hub and drum or disc assembly onto the spindle. With drum brakes, first thoroughly coat the inner cup with grease.

10. Coat the outer bearing cup with grease. Pack the outer bearing with grease and install into the cup.

11. Pack the grease cap with grease and set it aside. It will be replaced last, after the preload adjustment. You can put the grease away now.

12. Install the lock washer, and castellated nut (lock washer, nut, and adjusting castle nut with disc brakes) loosely, and proceed to the preload adjustment following.

BEARING PRELOAD ADJUSTMENT

1. While turning the hub forward, tighten the castellated nut (plain nut on disc brakes) to 25–29 ft. lbs. (34–39 Nm).
2. Rotate the hub a few more times to snug down the bearings.
3. Retighten the nut to the above specification. Unscrew it 1/8 of a turn and lock it in place with a new cotter pin. On disc brakes, snug the adjusting nut up against the washer and then back it off the required distance to insert a new cotter pin. You should not have to back it off more than 1/8 of a turn.
4. Install the grease cap, and wipe off any grease that oozes out.
5. Install the front wheel and a couple of lug nuts. Check the axial play of the wheel by shaking it back and forth; the bearing free-play should feel close to zero, but the wheel should spin freely. With drum brakes, be sure that the shoes are not dragging against the drum.

6. If the bearing play is correct with drum brakes you can install the rest of the lug nuts. With disc brakes, remove the wheel, replace the caliper, then install the wheel.

4-Wheel Drive

For wheel bearing procedures on 4wd vehicles, please refer to the Front Drive Axle section in @SUB2:External Vehicle Components

For lock cylinders, apply graphite lubricant sparingly thought the key slot. Insert the key and operate the lock several times to be sure that the lubricant is worked into the lock cylinder.

Hinges should be sprayed with a silicone lubricant on the hinge pivot points to eliminate any binding conditions. Open and close the door several times to be sure that the lubricant is evenly and thoroughly distributed.

On tailgates, spray a silicone lubricant on all of the pivot and friction surfaces to eliminate any squeaks or binds. Work the tailgate to distribute the lubricant

Be sure that the body drain holes in the doors and rocker panels are cleared of obstruction. A small screwdriver can be used to clear them of any debris.

TRAILER TOWING

General Recommendations

Your vehicle was primarily designed to carry passengers and cargo. It is important to remember that towing a trailer will place additional loads on your vehicles engine, drive train, steering, braking and other systems. However, if you decide to tow a trailer, using the prior equipment is a must.

Local laws may require specific equipment such as trailer brakes or fender mounted mirrors. Check your local laws.

Trailer Weight

The weight of the trailer is the most important factor. A good weight-to-horsepower ratio is about 35:1, 35 lbs. of Gross Combined Weight (GCW) for every horsepower your engine develops. Multiply the engine's rated horsepower by 35 and subtract the weight of the vehicle passengers and luggage. The number remaining is the approximate ideal maximum weight you should tow, although a numerically higher axle ratio can help compensate for heavier weight.

Hitch (Tongue) Weight

▶ See Figure 168

Calculate the hitch weight in order to select a proper hitch. The weight of the hitch is usually 9–11% of the trailer gross weight and should be measured with the trailer loaded. Hitches fall into various categories: those that mount on the frame and rear bumper, the bolt-on type, or the weld-on distribution type used for larger trailers. Axle mounted or clamp-on bumper hitches should never be used.

Check the gross weight rating of your trailer. Tongue weight is usually figured as 10% of gross trailer weight. Therefore, a trailer with a maximum gross weight of 2000 lbs. will have a maximum tongue weight of 200 lbs. Class I trailers fall into this category. Class II trailers are those with a gross weight rating of 2000–3000 lbs., while Class III trailers fall into the 3500–6000 lbs. category. Class IV trailers are those over 6000 lbs. and are for use with fifth wheel trucks, only.

When you've determined the hitch that you'll need, follow the manufacturer's installation instructions, exactly, especially when it comes to fastener torques. The hitch will subjected to a lot of stress and good hitches come with hardened bolts. Never substitute an inferior bolt for a hardened bolt.

Cooling

ENGINE

Aftermarket engine oil coolers are helpful for prolonging engine oil life and reducing overall engine temperatures. Both of these factors increase engine life. While not absolutely necessary in towing Class I and some Class II trailers, they are recommended for heavier Class II and all Class III towing. Engine oil cooler systems usually consist of an adapter, screwed on in place of the oil filter, a remote filter mounting and a multi-tube, finned heat exchanger, which is mounted in front of the radiator or air conditioning condenser.

Transmission

An automatic transmission is usually recommended for trailer towing. Modern automatics have proven reliable and, of course, easy to operate, in trailer towing. The increased load of a trailer, however, causes an increase in the temperature of the transmission fluid. Heat is the worst enemy of an automatic transmission. As the temperature of the fluid increases, the life of the fluid decreases.

It is essential, therefore, that you install an automatic transmission cooler and that you pay close attention to transmission fluid changes. The cooler, which consists of a multi-tube, finned heat exchanger, is usually installed in front of the radiator or air conditioning compressor, and hooked in-line with the transmission cooler tank inlet line. Follow the cooler manufacturer's installation instructions.

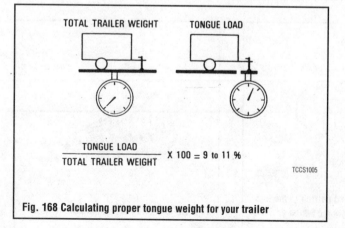

Fig. 168 Calculating proper tongue weight for your trailer

GENERAL INFORMATION AND MAINTENANCE

JUMP STARTING A DEAD BATTERY

◆ See Figure 169

Whenever a vehicle is jump started, precautions must be followed in order to prevent the possibility of personal injury. Remember that batteries contain a small amount of explosive hydrogen gas which is a by-product of battery charging. Sparks should always be avoided when working around batteries, especially when attaching jumper cables. To minimize the possibility of accidental sparks, follow the procedure carefully.

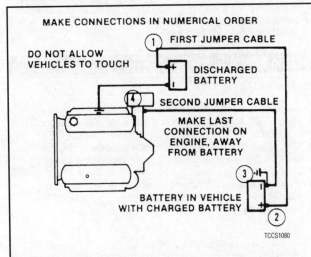

Fig. 169 Connect the jumper cables to the batteries and engine in the order shown

✱✱ CAUTION

NEVER hook the batteries up in a series circuit or the entire electrical system will go up in smoke, including the starter!

Vehicles equipped with a diesel engine may utilize two 12 volt batteries. If so, the batteries are connected in a parallel circuit (positive terminal to positive terminal, negative terminal to negative terminal). Hooking the batteries up in parallel circuit increases battery cranking power without increasing total battery voltage output. Output remains at 12 volts. On the other hand, hooking two 12 volt batteries up in a series circuit (positive terminal to negative terminal, positive terminal to negative terminal) increases total battery output to 24 volts (12 volts plus 12 volts).

Jump Starting Precautions

- Be sure that both batteries are of the same polarity (have the same terminal, in most cases NEGATIVE grounded).
- Be sure that the vehicles are not touching or a short could occur.
- On non-sealed batteries, be sure the vent cap holes are not obstructed.
- Do not smoke or allow sparks anywhere near the batteries.
- In cold weather, make sure the battery electrolyte is not frozen. This can occur more readily in a battery that has been in a state of discharge.
- Do not allow electrolyte to contact your skin or clothing.

JACKING

◆ See Figures 170 and 171

Your vehicle was supplied with a jack for emergency road repairs. This jack is fine for changing a flat tire or other short term procedures not requiring you to go beneath the vehicle. If it is used in an emergency situation, carefully follow the instructions provided either with the jack or in your owner's manual. Do not attempt to use the jack on any portions of the vehicle other than specified by the vehicle manufacturer. Always block the diagonally opposite wheel when using a jack.

Jump Starting Procedure

1. Make sure that the voltages of the 2 batteries are the same. Most batteries and charging systems are of the 12 volt variety.
2. Pull the jumping vehicle (with the good battery) into a position so the jumper cables can reach the dead battery and that vehicle's engine. Make sure that the vehicles do NOT touch.
3. Place the transmissions/transaxles of both vehicles in **Neutral** (MT) or **P**(AT), as applicable, then firmly set their parking brakes.

➡ **If necessary for safety reasons, the hazard lights on both vehicles may be operated throughout the entire procedure without significantly increasing the difficulty of jumping the dead battery.**

4. Turn all lights and accessories OFF on both vehicles. Make sure the ignition switches on both vehicles are turned to the **OFF** position.
5. Cover the battery cell caps with a rag, but do not cover the terminals.
6. Make sure the terminals on both batteries are clean and free of corrosion for good electrical contact.
7. Identify the positive (+) and negative (–) terminals on both batteries.
8. Connect the first jumper cable to the positive (+) terminal of the dead battery, then connect the other end of that cable to the positive (+) terminal of the booster (good) battery.
9. Connect one end of the other jumper cable to the negative (–) terminal on the booster battery and the final cable clamp to an engine bolt head, alternator bracket or other solid, metallic point on the engine with the dead battery. Try to pick a ground on the engine that is positioned away from the battery in order to minimize the possibility of the 2 clamps touching should one loosen during the procedure. DO NOT connect this clamp to the negative (–) terminal of the bad battery.

✱✱ CAUTION

Be very careful to keep the jumper cables away from moving parts (cooling fan, belts, etc.) on both engines.

10. Check to make sure that the cables are routed away from any moving parts, then start the donor vehicle's engine. Run the engine at moderate speed for several minutes to allow the dead battery a chance to receive some initial charge.
11. With the donor vehicle's engine still running slightly above idle, try to start the vehicle with the dead battery. Crank the engine for no more than 10 seconds at a time and let the starter cool for at least 20 seconds between tries. If the vehicle does not start in 3 tries, it is likely that something else is also wrong or that the battery needs additional time to charge.
12. Once the vehicle is started, allow it to run at idle for a few seconds to make sure that it is operating properly.
13. Turn ON the headlights, heater blower and, if equipped, the rear defroster of both vehicles in order to reduce the severity of voltage spikes and subsequent risk of damage to the vehicles' electrical systems when the cables are disconnected. This step is especially important to any vehicle equipped with computer control modules.
14. Carefully disconnect the cables in the reverse order of connection. Start with the negative cable that is attached to the engine ground, then the negative cable on the donor battery. Disconnect the positive cable from the donor battery and finally, disconnect the positive cable from the formerly dead battery. Be careful when disconnecting the cables from the positive terminals not to allow the alligator clips to touch any metal on either vehicle or a short and sparks will occur.

A more convenient way of jacking is the use of a garage or floor jack. You may use the floor jack on the frame points shown. You can also lift the rear of the vehicle by placing the jack under the center of the rear axle.

Never place the jack under the radiator, engine or transmission components. Severe and expensive damage will result when the jack is raised. Additionally, never jack under the floorpan or bodywork; the metal will deform.

Whenever you plan to work under the vehicle, you must support it on jack-

1-38 GENERAL INFORMATION AND MAINTENANCE

Fig. 170 Vehicle lift positions—Front

Fig. 171 Vehicle lift positions—Rear

stands or ramps. Never use cinder blocks or stacks of wood to support the vehicle, even if you're only going to be under it for a few minutes. Never crawl under the vehicle when it is supported only by the tire-changing jack or other floor jack.

➡**Always position a block of wood or small rubber pad on top of the jack or jackstand to protect the lifting point's finish when lifting or supporting the vehicle.**

Small hydraulic, screw, or scissors jacks are satisfactory for raising the vehicle. Drive-on trestles or ramps are also a handy and safe way to both raise and support the vehicle. Be careful though, some ramps may be too steep to drive your vehicle onto without scraping the front bottom panels. Never support the vehicle on any suspension member (unless specifically instructed to do so by a repair manual) or by an underbody panel.

Jacking Precautions

♦ See Figures 172 and 173

The following safety points cannot be overemphasized:
- Always block the opposite wheel or wheels to keep the vehicle from rolling off the jack.
- When raising the front of the vehicle, firmly apply the parking brake.
- When the drive wheels are to remain on the ground, leave the vehicle in gear to help prevent it from rolling.
- Always use jackstands to support the vehicle when you are working underneath. Place the stands beneath the vehicle's jacking brackets. Before climbing underneath, rock the vehicle a bit to make sure it is firmly supported.

GENERAL INFORMATION AND MAINTENANCE 1-39

MAINTENANCE INTERVALS

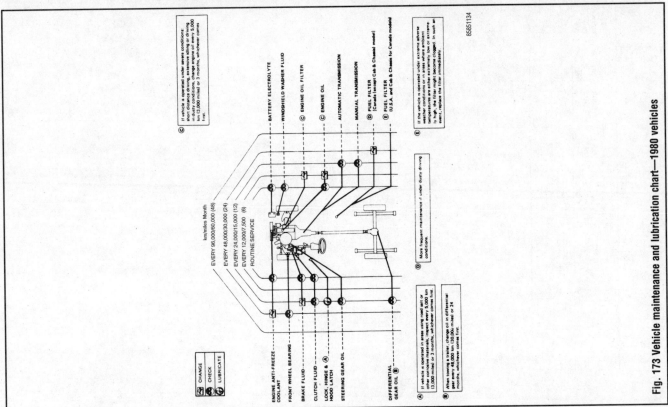

Fig. 173 Vehicle maintenance and lubrication chart—1980 vehicles

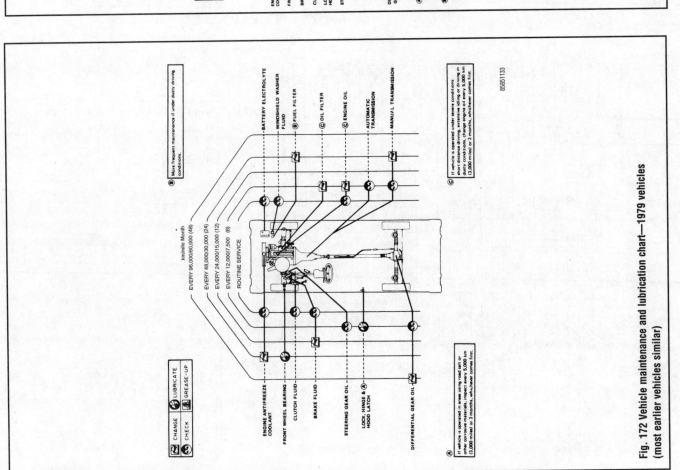

Fig. 172 Vehicle maintenance and lubrication chart—1979 vehicles (most earlier vehicles similar)

1-40 GENERAL INFORMATION AND MAINTENANCE

CAPACITIES

Year	Model	Engine	Engine Displacement Cu. In. (cc)	Engine Crankcase (qts.) With Filter	Engine Crankcase (qts.) Without Filter	Transmission (pts.) Manual 4-spd	Transmission (pts.) Manual 5-spd	Transmission (pts.) Auto.	Transfer Case (qts.)	Drive Axle (qts.) Front	Drive Axle (qts.) Rear	Gasoline Tank (gals.)	Cooling System (qts.)
1970	Pick-Up	L16	97.3 (1595)	4.4	3.6	4.2	—	—	—	—	1.7	11	7.2
1971	Pick-Up	L16	97.3 (1595)	4.4	3.6	4.2	—	—	—	—	1.7	11	7.2
1972	Pick-Up	L16	97.3 (1595)	4.4	3.6	4.2	—	—	—	—	2.1	12	6.3
1973	Pick-Up	L18	108.0 (1770)	5.0	4.5	4.5	—	—	—	—	2.1	12	6.3
1974	Pick-Up	L18	108.0 (1770)	5.0	4.5	3.6	—	11.7	—	—	2.1	12	6.3
1975	Pick-Up	L20B	119.1 (1952)	5.0	4.5	3.6	—	—	—	—	2.1	12	6.3
1976	Pick-Up	L20B	119.1 (1952)	5.0	4.5	3.6	4.2	11.7	—	—	2.1	12	8.5
1977	Pick-Up	L20B	119.1 (1952)	5.0	4.5	3.6	4.2	11.7	—	—	2.1	12	8.5
1978	Pick-Up	L20B	119.1 (1952)	5.0	4.5	3.6	4.2	11.7	—	—	2.1	12	8.5
1979	Pick-Up	L20B	119.1 (1952)	4.5	4.0	3.6	4.2	11.7	—	—	2.1	12	9.3
1980	Pick-Up	L20B	119.1 (1952)	4.5	4.0	3.6	4.2	11.7	—	—	2.1	13①	9.3
1981	Pick-Up	Z22	133.5 (2187)	4.6	4.0	3.6	4.2	11.7	3.0	2.1	2.6	13.2②	9.3
		SD22	132.0 (2164)	5.8	5.0	—	4.2	—	—	—	2.6	15.8②	10.5
1982	Pick-Up	Z22	133.5 (2187)	4.6	4.0	3.6	4.2	11.7	3.0	2.1	2.6	15.8②	10.75
		SD22	132.0 (2164)	6.4	5.9	—	4.2	—	—	—	2.6	15.8②	10.5
1983	Pick-Up	Z22	133.5 (2187)	4.6	4.0	3.6	4.2	11.7	3.0	2.1	2.6	15.8②	10.75
		SD22	132.0 (2164)	5.3	4.8	—	4.2	—	—	—	2.6	15.8②	10.5
1984	Pick-Up (2WD)	Z22	119.0 (1952)	4.4	3.9	—	4.2	11.7	—	—	2.6	②	10.75
		Z24	146.8 (2389)	4.4	3.9	—	4.2	11.7	—	—	2.6④	②	10.75
		SD25	152.0 (2488)	5.4	4.9	—	4.2	—	—	—	2.6	②	11.2
	Pick-Up (4WD)	Z24	146.8 (2389)	4.5	4.0	—	4.2	11.7	3.0	2.1	2.6	②	10.75
1985	Pick-Up (2WD)	Z20	119.0 (1952)	3.9	3.4	—	4.2	11.7	—	—	2.6④	②	10.75
		Z24	146.8 (2389)	3.9	3.4	—	4.2	11.7	—	—	2.6④	②	10.75
		SD25	152.0 (2488)	5.75	4.9	—	4.2	—	—	—	2.6	②	11.2
	Pick-Up (4WD)	Z24	146.8 (2389)	4.25	3.75	—	4.2	11.7	3.0	2.1	2.6	②	10.75
1986	Pick-Up (2WD)	Z20	119.0 (1952)	3.9	3.4	—	4.2	11.7	—	—	2.6④	②	10.75
		Z24	146.8 (2389)	3.9	3.4	—	4.2	11.7	—	—	2.6④	②	11.2
	Pick-Up (4WD)	Z24	146.8 (2389)	4.0	3.5	—	4.2	14.7	3.0	2.1	2.6	15.9③	8.6
		VG30i	181.0 (2960)	4.2	3.8	—	5.0	14.7	4.6	—	②	15.9③	10.5
		SD25	152.0 (2488)	4.25	3.75	—	4.2	—	—	—	②	15.9③	11.2
1987	Pick-Up (2WD)	Z24	146.8 (2389)	4.5	4.0	—	7.6	14.7	—	—	2.1	15.9③	10.5
		VG30i	181.0 (2960)	3.9	3.5	—	5.0	15.6	—	—	②	15.9③	8.6
		SD25	152.0 (2488)	3.8	3.2	—	4.2	11.7	—	—	2.6	15.9③	12.9
	Pick-Up (4WD)⑥	Z24i	146.8 (2389)	4.5	4.0	—	8.5	14.7	4.6	②	②	15.9③	8.6
		VG30i	181.0 (2960)	3.9	3.2	—	8.5	15.6	4.6	②	②	15.9③	10.5
1988	Pick-Up (2WD)	Z24i	146.8 (2389)	4.0	3.5	NA	4.2	14.7	—	—	②	15.9	8.6
		VG30i	181.0 (2960)	4.2	3.8	—	5.1	14.7	—	—	②	21.1②	10.5
	Pick-Up (4WD)⑥	Z24i	146.8 (2389)	4.5	4.0	—	8.5	16.0	4.6	②	②	15.9	8.6
		VG30i	181.0 (2960)	3.9	3.2	—	7.9	16.0	4.6	②	②	21.1②	10.5

NA—Not available
① Long Bed: 17
② 2WD Std. Wheelbase: 13.2
   4WD Std. Wheelbase: 15.8
   2WD Long Wheelbase: 16.8
   4WD Long Wheelbase: 19.8
③ Long Wheelbase: 16.8
④ Dual Rear Wheels: 2.75
⑤ R180A: 2.7
   R200A: 3.1
   C200: 2.7
   H190A: 3.1
   H233B: 5.8
⑥ King Cab & Heavy Duty: 21.2
   2WD SE & 4WD Regular Cab SE: 15.9
⑦ Includes Pathfinder

GENERAL INFORMATION AND MAINTENANCE

ENGLISH TO METRIC CONVERSION: MASS (WEIGHT)

Current mass measurement is expressed in pounds and ounces (lbs. & ozs.). The metric unit of mass (or weight) is the kilogram (kg). Even although this table does not show conversion of masses (weights) larger than 15 lbs, it is easy to calculate larger units by following the data immediately below.

To convert ounces (oz.) to grams (g): multiply th number of ozs. by 28
To convert grams (g) to ounces (oz.): multiply the number of grams by .035

To convert pounds (lbs.) to kilograms (kg): multiply the number of lbs. by .45
To convert kilograms (kg) to pounds (lbs.): multiply the number of kilograms by 2.2

lbs	kg	lbs	kg	oz	kg	oz	kg
0.1	0.04	0.9	0.41	0.1	0.003	0.9	0.024
0.2	0.09	1	0.4	0.2	0.005	1	0.03
0.3	0.14	2	0.9	0.3	0.008	2	0.06
0.4	0.18	3	1.4	0.4	0.011	3	0.08
0.5	0.23	4	1.8	0.5	0.014	4	0.11
0.6	0.27	5	2.3	0.6	0.017	5	0.14
0.7	0.32	10	4.5	0.7	0.020	10	0.28
0.8	0.36	15	6.8	0.8	0.023	15	0.42

ENGLISH TO METRIC CONVERSION: TEMPERATURE

To convert Fahrenheit (°F) to Celsius (°C): take number of °F and subtract 32; multiply result by 5; divide result by 9
To convert Celsius (°C) to Fahrenheit (°F): take number of °C and multiply by 9; divide result by 5; add 32 to total

Fahrenheit (F)		Celsius (C)		Fahrenheit (F)		Celsius (C)		Fahrenheit (F)		Celsius (C)	
°F	°C	°C	°F	°F	°C	°C	°F	°F	°C	°C	°F
−40	−40	−38	−36.4	80	26.7	18	64.4	215	101.7	80	176
−35	−37.2	−36	−32.8	85	29.4	20	68	220	104.4	85	185
−30	−34.4	−34	−29.2	90	32.2	22	71.6	225	107.2	90	194
−25	−31.7	−32	−25.6	95	35.0	24	75.2	230	110.0	95	202
−20	−28.9	−30	−22	100	37.8	26	78.8	235	112.8	100	212
−15	−26.1	−28	−18.4	105	40.6	28	82.4	240	115.6	105	221
−10	−23.3	−26	−14.8	110	43.3	30	86	245	118.3	110	230
−5	−20.6	−24	−11.2	115	46.1	32	89.6	250	121.1	115	239
0	−17.8	−22	−7.6	120	48.9	34	93.2	255	123.9	-120	248
1	−17.2	−20	−4	125	51.7	36	96.8	260	126.6	125	257
2	−16.7	−18	−0.4	130	54.4	38	100.4	265	129.4	130	266
3	−16.1	−16	3.2	135	57.2	40	104	270	132.2	135	275
4	−15.6	−14	6.8	140	60.0	42	107.6	275	135.0	140	284
5	−15.0	−12	10.4	145	62.8	44	112.2	280	137.8	145	293
10	−12.2	−10	14	150	65.6	46	114.8	285	140.6	150	302
15	−9.4	−8	17.6	155	68.3	48	118.4	290	143.3	155	311
20	−6.7	−6	21.2	160	71.1	50	122	295	146.1	160	320
25	−3.9	−4	24.8	165	73.9	52	125.6	300	148.9	165	329
30	−1.1	−2	28.4	170	76.7	54	129.2	305	151.7	170	338
35	1.7	0	32	175	79.4	56	132.8	310	154.4	175	347
40	4.4	2	35.6	180	82.2	58	136.4	315	157.2	180	356
45	7.2	4	39.2	185	85.0	60	140	320	160.0	185	365
50	10.0	6	42.8	190	87.8	62	143.6	325	162.8	190	374
55	12.8	8	46.4	195	90.6	64	147.2	330	165.6	195	383
60	15.6	10	50	200	93.3	66	150.8	335	168.3	200	392
65	18.3	12	53.6	205	96.1	68	154.4	340	171.1	205	401
70	21.1	14	57.2	210	98.9	70	158	345	173.9	210	410
75	23.9	16	60.8	212	100.0	75	167	350	176.7	215	414

ENGLISH TO METRIC CONVERSION: LENGTH

To convert inches (ins.) to millimeters (mm): multiply number of inches by 25.4
To convert millimeters (mm) to inches (ins.): multiply number of millimeters by .04

Inches			Decimals	Milli-meters	Inches to millimeters		Inches			Decimals	Milli-meters	Inches to millimeters	
					inches	mm						inches	mm
		1/64	0.051625	0.3969	0.0001	0.00254			33/64	0.515625	13.0969	0.6	15.24
	1/32		0.03125	0.7937	0.0002	0.00508		17/32		0.53125	13.4937	0.7	17.78
		3/64	0.046875	1.1906	0.0003	0.00762			35/64	0.546875	13.8906	0.8	20.32
1/16			0.0625	1.5875	0.0004	0.01016	9/16			0.5625	14.2875	0.9	22.86
		5/64	0.078125	1.9844	0.0005	0.01270			37/64	0.578125	14.6844	1	25.4
	3/32		0.09375	2.3812	0.0006	0.01524		19/32		0.59375	15.0812	2	50.8
		7/64	0.109375	2.7781	0.0007	0.01778			39/64	0.609375	15.4781	3	76.2
1/8			0.125	3.1750	0.0008	0.02032	5/8			0.625	15.8750	4	101.6
		9/64	0.140625	3.5719	0.0009	0.02286			41/64	0.640625	16.2719	5	127.0
	5/32		0.15625	3.9687	0.001	0.0254		21/32		0.65625	16.6687	6	152.4
		11/64	0.171875	4.3656	0.002	0.0508			43/64	0.671875	17.0656	7	177.8
3/16			0.1875	4.7625	0.003	0.0762	11/16			0.6875	17.4625	8	203.2
		13/64	0.203125	5.1594	0.004	0.1016			45/64	0.703125	17.8594	9	228.6
	7/32		0.21875	5.5562	0.005	0.1270		23/32		0.71875	18.2562	10	254.0
		15/64	0.234375	5.9531	0.006	0.1524			47/64	0.734375	18.6531	11	279.4
1/4			0.25	6.3500	0.007	0.1778	3/4			0.75	19.0500	12	304.8
		17/64	0.265625	6.7469	0.008	0.2032			49/64	0.765625	19.4469	13	330.2
	9/32		0.28125	7.1437	0.009	0.2286		25/32		0.78125	19.8437	14	355.6
		19/64	0.296875	7.5406	0.01	0.254			51/64	0.796875	20.2406	15	381.0
5/16			0.3125	7.9375	0.02	0.508	13/16			0.8125	20.6375	16	406.4
		21/64	0.328125	8.3344	0.03	0.762			53/64	0.828125	21.0344	17	431.8
	11/32		0.34375	8.7312	0.04	1.016		27/32		0.84375	21.4312	18	457.2
		23/64	0.359375	9.1281	0.05	1.270			55/64	0.859375	21.8281	19	482.6
3/8			0.375	9.5250	0.06	1.524	7/8			0.875	22.2250	20	508.0
		25/64	0.390625	9.9219	0.07	1.778			57/64	0.890625	22.6219	21	533.4
	13/32		0.40625	10.3187	0.08	2.032		29/32		0.90625	23.0187	22	558.8
		27/64	0.421875	10.7156	0.09	2.286			59/64	0.921875	23.4156	23	584.2
7/16			0.4375	11.1125	0.1	2.54	15/16			0.9375	23.8125	24	609.6
		29/64	0.453125	11.5094	0.2	5.08			61/64	0.953125	24.2094	25	635.0
	15/32		0.46875	11.9062	0.3	7.62		31/32		0.96875	24.6062	26	660.4
		31/64	0.484375	12.3031	0.4	10.16			63/64	0.984375	25.0031	27	690.6
1/2			0.5	12.7000	0.5	12.70							

ENGLISH TO METRIC CONVERSION: TORQUE

To convert foot-pounds (ft. lbs.) to Newton-meters: multiply the number of ft. lbs. by 1.3
To convert inch-pounds (in. lbs.) to Newton-meters: multiply the number of in. lbs. by .11

in lbs	N-m	in lbs	N-m	in lbs	N-m	in lbs	N-m	in lbs	N-m
0.1	0.01	1	0.11	10	1.13	19	2.15	28	3.16
0.2	0.02	2	0.23	11	1.24	20	2.26	29	3.28
0.3	0.03	3	0.34	12	1.36	21	2.37	30	3.39
0.4	0.04	4	0.45	13	1.47	22	2.49	31	3.50
0.5	0.06	5	0.56	14	1.58	23	2.60	32	3.62
0.6	0.07	6	0.68	15	1.70	24	2.71	33	3.73
0.7	0.08	7	0.78	16	1.81	25	2.82	34	3.84
0.8	0.09	8	0.90	17	1.92	26	2.94	35	3.95
0.9	0.10	9	1.02	18	2.03	27	3.05	36	4.0

TUNE-UP PROCEDURES 2-2
SPARK PLUGS 2-2
    REMOVAL 2-3
    INSPECTION & GAPPING 2-3
    INSTALLATION 2-4
SPARK PLUG WIRES 2-4
    CHECKING AND REPLACEMENT 2-4
FIRING ORDERS 2-5
POINT TYPE IGNITION 2-5
    INSPECTION AND CLEANING 2-5
    REMOVAL & INSTALLATION 2-6
    ADJUSTMENT OF THE BREAKER POINTS 2-6
ELECTRONIC IGNITION 2-7
CARBURETED ENGINES 2-7
FUEL INJECTED ENGINES 2-8
DISTRIBUTOR SERVICE 2-8
    CARBURETED ENGINES 2-8
    PICK-UP COIL AND RELUCTOR REPLACEMENT 2-9
    RELUCTOR AND IC IGNITION UNIT 2-10
    FUEL INJECTED ENGINES 2-10
TROUBLESHOOTING 2-10
    CARBURETED ENGINES 2-10
IGNITION TIMING 2-11
CHECKING AND ADJUSTMENT 2-13
    1970–86 CARBURETED ENGINES 2-13
    1986–88 FUEL INJECTED ENGINES 2-13
VALVE LASH 2-13
ADJUSTMENTS 2-14
    L16, L18 AND L20B ENGINES 2-14
    1981–82 Z22 ENGINES 2-14
    Z20, Z22 (EXCEPT 1981–82), Z24 & Z24i ENGINES 2-15
    VG30i ENGINES 2-16
IDLE SPEED AND MIXTURE ADJUSTMENTS 2-16
CARBURETOR 2-16
    ADJUSTMENT PROCEDURES 2-16
ELECTRONIC FUEL INJECTION (EFI) 2-17
    IDLE SPEED ADJUSTMENT PROCEDURE 2-17
SPECIFICATIONS CHART
GASOLINE ENGINE TUNE-UP SPECIFICATIONS 2-18
TROUBLESHOOTING CHARTS
BASIC STARTING SYSTEM PROBLEMS 2-19
BASIC CHARGING SYSTEM PROBLEMS 2-20

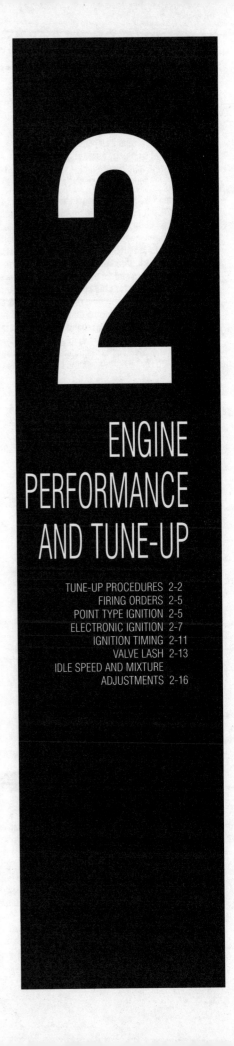

2

ENGINE PERFORMANCE AND TUNE-UP

TUNE-UP PROCEDURES 2-2
FIRING ORDERS 2-5
POINT TYPE IGNITION 2-5
ELECTRONIC IGNITION 2-7
IGNITION TIMING 2-11
VALVE LASH 2-13
IDLE SPEED AND MIXTURE ADJUSTMENTS 2-16

2-2 ENGINE PERFORMANCE AND TUNE-UP

TUNE-UP PROCEDURES

▶ See Figures 1 and 2

In order to extract the best performance and economy from your engine it is essential that it be properly tuned at regular intervals. A regular tune-up will keep your engine running smoothly and will prevent the annoying minor breakdowns and poor performance associated with an untuned engine.

➡ All Nissan Pick-Ups use a conventional breaker points ignition system through 1975. All 1970–73 models utilize a dual points system for emission control purposes. In 1976 Nissan switched to a transistorized ignition system. This system was much like the previous system with one basic difference; instead of the breaker points switching the primary current to the coil on and off, they triggered an igniter which did it for them. This igniter contains two transistors and an assortment of resistors which together serve as a switching device to turn the coil primary current on and off. The advantage of this type of circuitry is a reduced current through the distributor breaker points, thus prolonging their expected life and reducing scheduled maintenance. In 1976, a few models sold in California came equipped with a fully transistorized electronic ignition system. Most 1976–77 49 States and Canada models use the single breaker points system used in all models in 1974–75. In 1978, this system became standard on all models.

A complete tune-up should be performed every 15,000 miles (24,000 km) or twelve months, whichever comes first. This interval should be halved if the truck is operated under severe conditions, such as trailer towing, prolonged idling, continual stop and start driving, or if starting or running problems are noticed. It is assumed that the routine maintenance described in Section 1 has been kept up, as this will have a decided affect on the results of a tune-up. All of the applicable steps of a tune-up should be followed in order, as the result is a cumulative one.

If the specifications on the tune-up sticker in the engine compartment of your Nissan disagree with the Tune-Up Specifications chart in this section, the figures on the sticker must be used. The sticker often reflects changes made during the production run.

normal. Any other color, or abnormal amounts of deposit, indicates that there is something amiss in the engine.

The gap between the center electrode and the side or ground electrode can be expected to increase not more than 0.001 in. (0.025mm) every 1,000 miles (1600 km) under normal conditions.

When a spark plug is functioning normally or, more accurately, when the plug is installed in an engine that is functioning properly, the plugs can be taken out, cleaned, regapped, and reinstalled without harming the engine.

If a plug fouls and begins to misfire, you will have to investigate, correct the cause of the fouling, and either clean or replace the plug.

Spark plugs suitable for use in your Nissan's engine are offered in a number of different heat ranges. The amount of heat which the plug absorbs is determined by the length of the lower insulator. The longer the insulator the hotter the plug will operate; the shorter the insulator, the cooler it will operate. A spark plug that absorbs (retains) little heat and remains too cool will accumulate deposits of lead, oil, and carbon, because it is not hot enough to burn them off. This leads to fouling and consequent misfiring. A spark plug that absorbs too much heat will have no deposits, but the electrodes will burn away quickly and, in some cases, preignition may result. Preignition occurs when the spark plug tips get so hot that they ignite the air/fuel mixture before the actual spark fires. This premature ignition will usually cause a pinging sound under conditions of low speed and heavy load. In severe cases, the heat may become high enough to start the air/fuel mixture burning throughout the combustion chamber rather than just to the front of the plug. In this case, the resultant explosion will be strong enough to damage pistons, rings, and valves.

In most cases the factory recommended heat range is correct; it is chosen to perform well under a wide range of operating conditions. However, if most of your driving is long distance, high speed travel, you may want to install a spark plug one step colder than standard. If most of your driving is of the short trip variety, when the engine may not always reach operating temperature, a hotter plug may help burn off the deposits normally accumulated under those conditions.

Fig. 1 Vehicle Emission Control Information (VECI) label

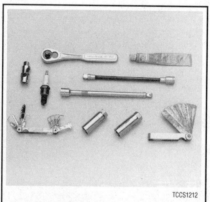

Fig. 2 Spark plug service tools and gauges

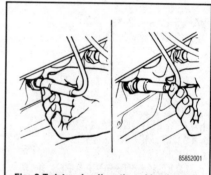

Fig. 3 Twist and pull on the rubber boot to remove the spark plug wires; NEVER pull on the wire itself

Spark Plugs

▶ See Figures 3 and 4

Spark plugs ignite the air and fuel mixture in the cylinder as the piston reaches the top of the compression stroke. The controlled explosion that results forces the piston down, turning the crankshaft and the rest of the drive train.

The average life of a spark plug is 15,000 miles (24,000 km), although manufacturers are now claiming spark plug lives of up to 30,000 miles (48,000 km) or more with the new platinum tipped plugs. This is, however, dependent on a number of factors: the mechanical condition of the engine; the type of fuel; the driving conditions; and the driver.

When you remove the spark plugs, check their condition. They are a good indicator of the condition of the engine. It is a good idea to remove the spark plugs every 6000 miles (9600 km) or so to keep an eye on the mechanical state of the engine.

A small deposit of light tan or gray material (or rust red with unleaded fuel) on a spark plug that has been used for any period of time is to be considered

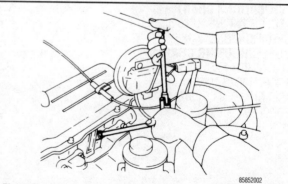

Fig. 4 Plugs are removed using the proper combination of socket wrench, universals and extensions

ENGINE PERFORMANCE AND TUNE-UP

REMOVAL

1. Number the wires so that you won't cross them during installation.
2. Remove the wire from the end of the spark lug by grasping the wire by the rubber boot. If the boot sticks to the plug, remove it by twisting and pulling at the same time. Do not pull wire itself or you will damage the core.
3. Use a correct spark plug socket to loosen all of the plugs about two turns.

➡ The cylinder head is cast from aluminum. Remove the spark plugs when the engine is cold, if possible, to prevent damage to the threads. If removal of the plugs is difficult, apply a few drops of penetrating oil or silicone spray to the area around the base of the plug, and allow it a few minutes to work.

4. If compressed air is available, apply it to the area around the spark plug holes. Otherwise, use a rag or a brush to clean the area. Be careful not to allow any foreign material to drop into the spark plug holes.
5. Remove the plugs by unscrewing them the rest of the way from the engine.

INSPECTION & GAPPING

♦ See Figures 5, 6, 7 and 8

Check the plugs for deposits and wear. If they are not going to be replaced, clean the plugs thoroughly. Remember that any kind of deposit will decrease the efficiency of the plug. Plugs can be cleaned on a spark plug cleaning machine, which can sometimes be found in service stations, or you can do an acceptable job of cleaning with a stiff brush. If the plugs are cleaned, the electrodes must be filed flat. Use an ignition points file, not an emery board or the like, which will leave deposits. The electrodes must be filed perfectly flat with sharp edges; rounded edges reduce the spark plug voltage by as much as 50%.

Check spark plug gap before installation. The ground electrode (the L-shaped one connected to the body of the plug) must be parallel to the center electrode and the specified size wire gauge (please refer to the Tune-Up Specifications chart for details) must pass between the electrodes with a slight drag.

➡ NEVER adjust the gap on a used platinum type spark plug.

A **normally worn** spark plug should have light tan or gray deposits on the firing tip.

A **carbon fouled** plug, identified by soft, sooty, black deposits, may indicate an improperly tuned vehicle. Check the air cleaner, ignition components and engine control system.

This spark plug has been **left in the engine too long**, as evidenced by the extreme gap- Plugs with such an extreme gap can cause misfiring and stumbling accompanied by a noticeable lack of power.

An **oil fouled** spark plug indicates an engine with worn poston rings and/or bad valve seals allowing excessive oil to enter the chamber.

A **physically damaged** spark plug may be evidence of severe detonation in that cylinder. Watch that cylinder carefully between services, as a continued detonation will not only damage the plug, but could also damage the engine.

A **bridged or almost bridged** spark plug, identified by a build-up between the electrodes caused by excessive carbon or oil build-up on the plug.

Fig. 5 Inspect the spark plug to determine engine running conditions

2-4 ENGINE PERFORMANCE AND TUNE-UP

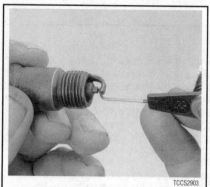
Fig. 6 Checking the spark plug gap with a feeler gauge

Fig. 7 Adjusting the spark plug gap

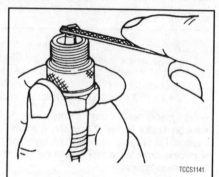
Fig. 8 If the standard plug is in good condition, the electrode may be filed flat—WARNING: do not file platinum plugs

Always check the gap on new plugs as they are not always set correctly at the factory. Do not use a flat feeler gauge when measuring the gap on a used plug, because the reading may be inaccurate. A round-wire type gapping tool is the best way to check the gap. The correct gauge should pass through the electrode gap with a slight drag. If you're in doubt, try one size smaller and one larger. The smaller gauge should go through easily, while the larger one shouldn't go through at all. Wire gapping tools usually have a bending tool attached. Use that to adjust the side electrode until the proper distance is obtained. Absolutely never attempt to bend the center electrode. Also, be careful not to bend the side electrode too far or too often as it may weaken and break off within the engine, requiring removal of the cylinder head to retrieve it.

INSTALLATION

♦ See Figures 9, 10 and 11

1. Lubricate the threads of the spark plugs with a drop of oil. Install the plugs and tighten them hand-tight. Take care not to cross-thread them.

2. Tighten the spark plugs with the socket. Do not apply the same amount of force you would use for a bolt; just snug them in. If a torque wrench is available, tighten to 11–15 ft. lbs. (15–20 Nm).

3. Install the wires on their respective plugs. Make sure the wires are firmly connected. You will be able to feel them click into place.

Spark Plug Wires

CHECKING AND REPLACEMENT

♦ See Figures 12, 13 and 14

At every tune-up, visually inspect the spark plug cables for burns cuts, or breaks in the insulation. Check the boots and the nipples on the distributor cap and coil. Replace any damaged wiring.

Every 36,000 miles (58,000 km) or so, the resistance of the wires should be checked with an ohmmeter. Wires with excessive resistance will cause misfiring,

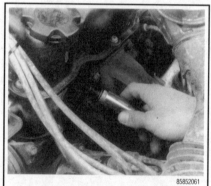
Fig. 9 Always install the spark plug by hand before tightening with a tool

Fig. 10 Once it is properly threaded, tighten the spark plug with a socket wrench

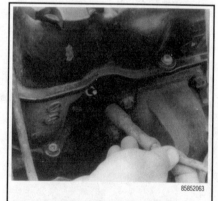
Fig. 11 Installing the spark plug wire

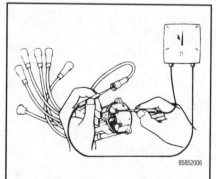
Fig. 12 Checking plug wire resistance with an ohmmeter

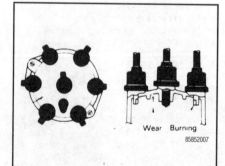
Fig. 13 Check the distributor cap for cracks; check the cable ends for wear

Fig. 14 Removing the spark plug wire from the distributor cap—always mark it first, for correct installation

ENGINE PERFORMANCE AND TUNE-UP   2-5

and may make the engine difficult to start in damp weather. Generally, the useful life of the cables is 36,000–50,000 miles (58,000–80,000 km).

To check resistance, remove the distributor cap, leaving the wires attached. Connect one lead of an ohmmeter to an electrode within the cap; connect the other lead to the corresponding spark plug terminal (remove it from the plug for this test). Replace any wire which shows a resistance over 30,000 Ω. Test the high tension lead from the coil by connecting the ohmmeter between the center contact in the distributor cap and either of the primary terminals of the coil. If resistance is more than 25,000 Ω, remove the cable from the coil and check the resistance of the cable alone. Anything over 15,000 Ω is cause for replacement. It should be remembered that resistance is also a function of length; the longer the cable, the greater the resistance. Thus, if the cables on your truck are longer than the factory originals, resistance will be higher, quite possibly outside these limits.

When installing new cables, replace them one at a time to avoid mix-ups. Start by replacing the longest one first. Install the boot firmly over the spark plug. Route the wire over the same path as the original. Insert the nipple firmly into the tower on the cap or the coil.

FIRING ORDERS

▶ See Figures 15, 16, 17, 18 and 19

➡ To avoid confusion, remove and tag the spark plug wires one at a time, for replacement.

If a distributor is not keyed for installation with only one orientation, it could have been removed previously and rewired. The resultant wiring would hold the correct firing order, but could change the relative placement of the plug towers in relation to the engine. For this reason it is imperative that you label all wires before disconnecting any of them. Also, before removal, compare the current wiring with the accompanying illustrations. If the current wiring does not match, make notes in your book to reflect how your engine is wired.

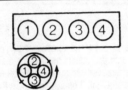

Fig. 15 1970–73 L16 and L18 Engines
Engine firing order: 1–3–4–2
Distributor rotation: counterclockwise

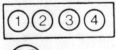

Fig. 16 1974 L18 Engines
Engine firing order: 1–3–4–2
Distributor rotation: counterclockwise

Fig. 17 1975–80 L20B Engines
Engine firing order: 1–3–4–2
Distributor rotation: counterclockwise

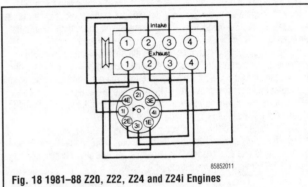

Fig. 18 1981–88 Z20, Z22, Z24 and Z24i Engines
Engine firing order: 1–3–4–2
Distributor rotation: counterclockwise

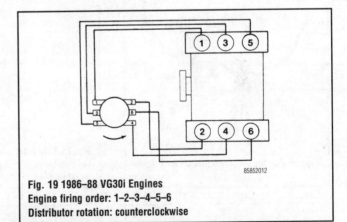

Fig. 19 1986–88 VG30i Engines
Engine firing order: 1–2–3–4–5–6
Distributor rotation: counterclockwise

POINT TYPE IGNITION

INSPECTION AND CLEANING

▶ See Figure 20

The breaker points should be inspected and cleaned at 6000 mile (9600 km) intervals. To do so, perform the following steps:
1. Disconnect the high tension lead from the coil.
2. Unsnap the two distributor cap retaining clips and lift the cap straight up. Leave the leads connected to the cap and position it out of the way.
3. Remove the rotor and dust cover by pulling them straight up.
4. Place a screwdriver against the breaker points and gently pry them open. Examine their condition. If they are excessively worn, burned, or pitted, they should be replaced.
5. Polish the points with a point file. Do not use emery cloth or sandpaper; these may leave particles on the points causing them to arc.
6. Clean the distributor cap and rotor with alcohol. Inspect the cap terminals for looseness and corrosion. Check the rotor tip for excessive burning. Inspect both the cap and rotor for cracks. Replace either if they show any of the above signs of wear or damage.
7. Check the operation of the centrifugal advance mechanism by turning the rotor clockwise. Release the rotor; it should return to its original position. If it doesn't, check for binding parts.

ENGINE PERFORMANCE AND TUNE-UP

8. Check the vacuum advance unit, but removing the plastic cap and pressing on the octane selector. It should return to its original position. Check for binding if it doesn't.

9. If the points do not require replacement, proceed with the adjustment section below. Otherwise perform the point and condenser replacement procedures.

REMOVAL & INSTALLATION

1. Mark or tag then remove the coil high tension wire from the top of the distributor cap. Remove the distributor cap and place it out of the way. Remove the rotor from the distributor shaft by pulling up.

2. On single point distributors, remove the condenser from the distributor body. On early dual point distributors, you will find that one condenser is virtually impossible to reach without removing the distributor from the engine. To do this, first note and mark the position of the distributor on the small timing scale on the front of the distributor. Then mark the position of the rotor in relation to the distributor body. Do this by simply replacing the rotor on the distributor shaft and marking the spot on the distributor body where the rotor is pointing. Be careful not to turn the engine over while performing this operation.

3. Remove the distributor on dual point models by removing the small bolt at the rear of the distributor. Lift the distributor out of the block. It is now possible to remove the rear condenser. Do not crank the engine with the distributor removed.

4. On single point distributors, remove the points assembly attaching screws and then remove the points. A magnetic screwdriver or one with a holding mechanism will come in handy here, so that you don't drop a screw into the distributor and have to remove the entire distributor to retrieve it. After the points are removed, wipe off the cam and apply new cam lubricant. If you don't, the points may wear out in a few thousand miles.

5. On dual point distributors, you will probably find it easier to simply remove the points assemblies while the distributor is out of the engine. Install the new points and condensers. You can either set the point gap now or later after you have reinstalled the distributor.

To install:

6. On dual point models, install the distributor, making sure the marks made earlier are lined up. Note that the slot for the oil pump drive is tapered and will only fit one way.

7. On single point distributors, slip the new set of points onto the locating dowel and install the screws that hold the assembly onto the plate. Don't tighten them all the way yet, since you'll only have to loosen them to set the point gap.

8. Install the new condenser on single point models and attach the condenser lead to the points.

9. Set the point gap or dwell (see the following sections).

ADJUSTMENT OF THE BREAKER POINTS

With A Feeler Gauge

SINGLE POINT DISTRIBUTOR

▶ See Figures 21, 22, 23, 24 and 25

1. If the contact points of the assembly are not parallel, bend the stationary contact so that the points make contact across the entire contact surface. Bend only the stationary bracket part of the point assembly; not the movable contact.

2. Turn the engine until the rubbing block of the points is on one of the high points of the distributor cam. You can do this by either turning the ignition switch to the start position and releasing it quickly (bumping the engine) or by using a wrench on the center bolt which holds the crankshaft pulley to the crankshaft.

3. Place the correct size feeler gauge between the contacts (see the Tune-Up Specifications chart). Make sure that it is parallel with the contact surfaces.

4. With your free hand, insert a screwdriver into the eccentric adjusting screw, then twist the screwdriver to either increase or decrease the gap to the proper setting.

5. Tighten the adjustment lockscrew and recheck the contact gap to make sure that didn't change when the lockscrew was tightened.

6. Replace the rotor and distributor cap, then connect the high tension wire which connects the top of the distributor and the coil. Make sure that the rotor

Fig. 20 Pull the rotor straight up to remove it

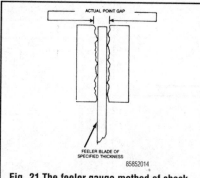

Fig. 21 The feeler gauge method of checking point gap is less accurate than the dwell method

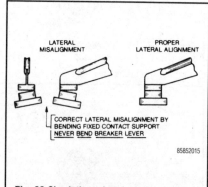

Fig. 22 Check the points for proper alignment after installation

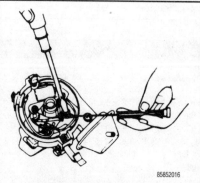

Fig. 23 All single point distributor gaps are adjusted with the eccentric screw

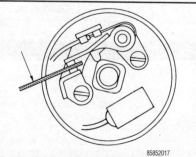

Fig. 24 The arrow indicates the flat feeler gauge used to measure the point gap—be sure that the rubbing block rests on the high spot of the camshaft as shown

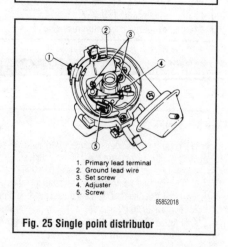

1. Primary lead terminal
2. Ground lead wire
3. Set screw
4. Adjuster
5. Screw

Fig. 25 Single point distributor

ENGINE PERFORMANCE AND TUNE-UP 2-7

is firmly seated all the way onto the distributor shaft and that the tab of the rotor is aligned with notch in the shaft. Align the tab in the base of the distributor cap with the notch in the distributor body. Make sure that the cap is firmly seated on the distributor and that the retainer clips are in place. Make sure that the end of the high tension wire is firmly placed in the top of the distributor and the coil.

DUAL POINT DISTRIBUTOR

▶ See Figures 26 and 27

The two sets of breaker points are adjusted with a feeler gauge in the same manner as those in a single point distributor, except that you do the actual adjusting by twisting a screwdriver in the point set notch. Check the Tune-up Specifications chart for the correct setting. Both are set to the same opening.

DWELL ANGLE

▶ See Figure 28

The dwell angle or cam angle is the number of degrees that the distributor cam rotates while the points are closed. There is an inverse relationship between dwell angle and point gap. Increasing the point gap will decrease the dwell angle and vice versa. Checking the dwell angle with a meter is a far more accurate method of measuring point opening than the feeler gauge method.

After setting the point gap to specification with a feeler gauge as described above, check the dwell angle with a meter. Attach the dwell meter according to the manufacturer's instruction sheet. The negative lead is normally grounded while the positive lead is connected to the primary wire terminal which runs from the coil to the distributor. Start the engine, let it idle and reach operating temperature, then observe the dwell on the meter. The reading should fall within the allowable range. If it does not, the gap will have to be reset or the breaker points will have to be replaced.

Using A Dwell Meter

Dwell can be checked with the engine running or cranking. Decrease dwell by increasing the point gap; increase by decreasing the gap. Dwell angle is simply the number of degrees of distributor shaft rotation during which the points stay closed. Theoretically, if the point gap is correct, the dwell should also be correct or nearly so. Adjustment with a dwell meter produces more exact, consistent results since it is a dynamic adjustment. If dwell varies more than 3° between idle speed and 1,750 engine rpm, the distributor is worn.

SINGLE POINT DISTRIBUTOR

1. Adjust the points with a feeler gauge as previously described.
2. Connect the dwell meter to the ignition circuit as according to the manufacturer's instructions. One lead of the meter is usually connected to a ground and the other lead is connected to the distributor post on the coil. An adapter is usually provided for this purpose.
3. If the dwell meter has a set line on it, adjust the meter to zero the indicator.
4. Start the engine.

➡ Be careful when working on any vehicle while the engine is running. Make sure that the transmission is in Neutral and that the parking brake is applied. Keep hands, clothing, tools and the wires of the test instruments clear of the rotating fan blades.

5. Observe the reading on the dwell meter. If the reading is within the specified range, turn off the engine and remove the dwell meter.

➡ If the meter does not have a scale for 4 cylinder engines, multiply the 8 cylinder reading by two.

6. If the reading is above the specified range, the breaker point gap is too small. If the reading is below the specified range, the gap is too large. In either case, the engine must be stopped and the gap adjusted in the manner previously covered. After making the adjustment, start the engine and check the reading on the dwell meter. When the correct reading is obtained, disconnect the dwell meter.
7. Check the adjustment of the ignition timing.

DUAL POINT DISTRIBUTOR

Adjust the point gap of a dual point distributor with a dwell meter as follows:
1. Mark and disconnect the wiring harness of the distributor from the engine wiring harness.
2. Using a jumper wire, connect the black wire of the engine side of the harness to the black wire of the distributor side of the harness (advance points).
3. Start the engine and observe the reading on the dwell meter. Shut the engine off and adjust the points accordingly as previously outlined for single point distributors.
4. Disconnect the jumper wire from the black wire of the distributor side of the wiring harness and connect it to the yellow wire (retard points).
5. Adjust the point gap as necessary.
6. After the dwell of both sets of points is correct, remove the jumper wire and connect the engine-to-distributor wiring harness securely.

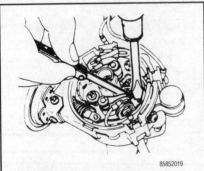

Fig. 26 Point gap on the dual point distributor is adjusted by twisting a screwdriver in the notch

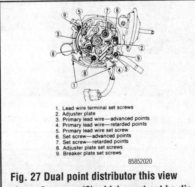

Fig. 27 Dual point distributor this view shows 2 screws (8) which must not be disturbed when adjusting or replacing points

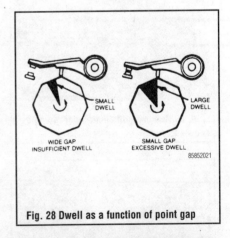

Fig. 28 Dwell as a function of point gap

ELECTRONIC IGNITION

Carbureted Engines

Datsun/Nissan pick-ups sold in California beginning in 1976 are equipped with electronic ignition. All 1978 and later trucks are also equipped with the system. The 1978 system differs somewhat from the earlier system and 1979 and later system is markedly different.

The electronic ignition differs from its conventional counterpart only in the distributor component area. The secondary side of the ignition system is the same as a conventional breaker points system.

Located in the distributor, in addition to the normal ignition rotor, is a four spoke rotor (reluctor) which rests on the distributor shaft where the breaker points cam is found on earlier systems. A pick-up coil, consisting of

2-8 ENGINE PERFORMANCE AND TUNE-UP

a magnet, coil, and wiring, rests on the breaker plate next to the reluctor. The system also uses a transistor ignition unit, located on the right side of the firewall in the passenger compartment, through 1978. All 1979–80 models have an integrated circuit (IC) ignition unit, which is mounted on the side of the distributor. In addition, 1979–80 models use a ring-type pick-up coil, which surrounds the reluctor, rather than the arm-type coil used through 1978.

When a reluctor spoke is not aligned with the pick-up coil, it generates large lines of flux between itself, the magnet, and the pick-up coil. This large flux variation results in high generated voltage in the pick-up coil, preventing current from flowing to the pick-up coil. When a reluctor spoke lines up with the pick-up coil, the flux variation is low, thus, zero voltage is generated, allowing current to flow to the pick-up coil. Ignition primary current is then cut off by the electronic unit, allowing the field in the ignition coil to collapse, inducing high secondary voltage in the conventional manner. The high voltage then flows through the distributor to the spark plug, as usual.

Because no points or condenser are used, and because dwell is determined by the electronic unit, no adjustments are necessary. Ignition timing is checked in the usual way, but unless the distributor is disturbed it is not likely to ever change very much.

All 1981 and later models are equipped with a different ignition system and do not utilize a pick-up coil. This system uses two ignition coils and each cylinder has two spark plugs which fire simultaneously. In this manner the engine is able to consume large quantities of recirculated exhaust gas which would cause a single spark plug cylinder to misfire and idle roughly.

Fuel Injected Engines

The Electronic Concentrated engine Control System (ECCS) is used on these engines. This system employs a microcomputer which controls fuel injection, spark timing, Exhaust Gas Recirculation (EGR), idle speed, fuel pump operation and mixture ratio feedback. Electrical signals from each sensor are fed into the computer and each actuator is controlled by an electrical pulse with a duration that is computed in the microcomputer. There are some basic tests that may be performed to check the ignition system as outlined under Troubleshooting later in this section, however, when engine malfunctions occur, the use of an ECCS analyzer is necessary to accurately diagnose the problem.

The ECCS analyzer monitors several input and output signals that are emitted in response to various engine operating and stopped conditions. Input signals are compared to computerized signal values stored in the Central Electronic Control Unit (CECU) while output signals are monitored to ensure they are properly attuned before they are emitted from the CECU unit to the actuators. In other words, this analyzer examines all electrical signals that are transmitted to and from the CECU unit.

Since this analyzer would be very expensive to purchase, any suspected malfunction of the engine cannot be corrected by an obvious visual inspection, that should be left to a qualified repair shop that contains this equipment.

Distributor Service

♦ See Figures 29, 30, 31, 32 and 33

Service consists of inspection of the distributor cap, rotor, and ignition wires, replacing when necessary. These parts can be expected to last for at least 40,000 miles (52,000 km). In addition, the reluctor air gap should be checked periodically.

CARBURETED ENGINES

1976–80 Models

♦ See Figures 34 and 35

1. The distributor cap is held on by two clips. Release them with a screwdriver and lift the cap straight up and off, with the wires attached. Inspect the cap for cracks, carbon tracks, or a worn center contact. Replace it if necessary, transferring the wires one at a time from the old cap to the new.

2. Pull the ignition rotor (not the spoked reluctor) straight up to remove. Replace it if its contacts are worn, burned, or pitted. Do not file the contacts. To replace, press it firmly onto the shaft. It only goes on one way, so be sure it is fully seated.

Fig. 29 Removing the distributor cap hold-down screws

Fig. 30 Removing the distributor cap

Fig. 31 View of the coil wire installed

Fig. 32 Removing the coil wire

Fig. 33 Removing the coil dust boot cover

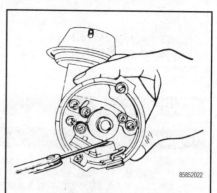

Fig. 34 Air gap adjustment—1976–77 Calif. and 1978 vehicles

ENGINE PERFORMANCE AND TUNE-UP 2-9

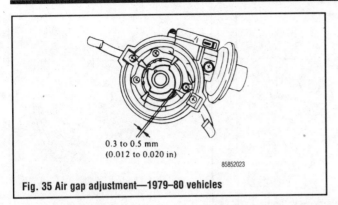

Fig. 35 Air gap adjustment—1979–80 vehicles

3. Before replacing the ignition rotor, check the reluctor air gap. Use a non-magnetic feeler gauge. Rotate the engine until a reluctor spoke is aligned with the pick-up coil (either bump the engine around with the starter, or turn it with a wrench on the crankshaft pulley bolt). The gap should measure 0.008–0.16 in. (0.20–0.40mm) through 1978 vehicles, or 0.012–0.020 in. (0.30–0.50mm) for 1979–80 vehicles. Adjustment, if necessary, is made by loosening the pick-up coil mounting screws and shifting its position on the breaker plate either closer to or farther from the reluctor. On 1979–80 models, center the pick-up coil (ring) around the reluctor. Tighten the screws and recheck the gap.

4. Inspect the wires for cracks or brittleness. Replace them one at a time to prevent crosswiring, carefully pressing the replacement wires into place. The cores of electronic wires are more susceptible to breakage than those of standard wires, so treat them gently.

1981–86 Vehicles

♦ See Figure 36

1. Remove the distributor cap then remove the rotor retaining screw.
2. Adjust the air gap between the reluctor and stator. The air gap should be 0.012–0.020 in. (0.30–0.50mm).
3. Inspect the wires, cap and rotor as outlined in the earlier procedure.

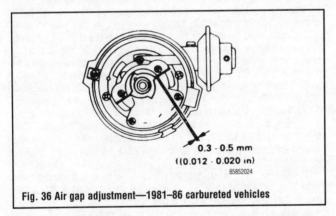

Fig. 36 Air gap adjustment—1981–86 carbureted vehicles

PICK-UP COIL AND RELUCTOR REPLACEMENT

Carbureted Engines

1976–78 VEHICLES

♦ See Figures 37, 38 and 39

The reluctor cannot be removed on some early models. It is an integral part of the distributor shaft. Non-removable reluctors can be distinguished by the absence of a roll pin (retaining pin) which locks the reluctor in place on the shaft.

1. To replace the pick-up coil on all 1976–78 models:
   a. Remove the distributor cap by releasing the two spring clips. Remove the ignition rotor by pulling it straight up and off the shaft.
   b. Disconnect the distributor wiring harness at the terminal block.
   c. Remove the two pick-up coil mounting screws. Remove the screws retaining the wiring harness to the distributor.
   d. Remove the pick-up coil. When replacing the pick-up coil leave the mounting screws slightly loose to facilitate air gap adjustment.
2. To replace the reluctor on models with a roll pin:
   a. Remove the distributor cap, ignition rotor and the pick-up coil.
   b. Use two pry bars or equivalent to pry the reluctor from the distributor shaft. Be extremely careful not to damage the reluctor teeth. Remove the roll pin.
   c. To install; press the reluctor firmly onto the shaft. Install a new roll pin with the slit facing away from the distributor shaft. Do not re-use the old roll pin.

1979–86 VEHICLES

♦ See Figures 40, 41 and 42

1. Remove the distributor cap. Remove the ignition rotor by pulling the rotor straight up and off the shaft.
2. Use a pair of needle nose pliers to disconnect the pick-up coil spade connectors from the ignition unit. Do not pull on the pick-up coil wires themselves.
3. Remove the toothed stator and the ring magnet underneath it by removing the three mounting screws.
4. Remove the reluctor by prying it from the distributor shaft with two small pry bars or a small puller. Be careful not to damage any of the reluctor teeth. Remove the roll pin.
5. Remove the screw retaining the pick-up coil wiring harness to the distributor. Remove the pick-up coil.

To install:

6. Install the pick-up coil into place in the distributor body. Replace the wiring harness retainer.
7. Press the reluctor firmly into place on the shaft. Install a new roll pin with the slit in the pin parallel to the flat on the shaft.
8. Install the magnet and stator, and center the stator around the reluctor. Check the air gap.
9. Press the pick-up coil spade connectors onto the ignition unit terminals with your fingers. The proper connections can be determined from the color code marked on the grommet. Replace the ignition rotor and the distributor cap.

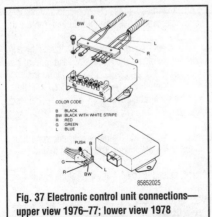

Fig. 37 Electronic control unit connections—upper view 1976–77; lower view 1978

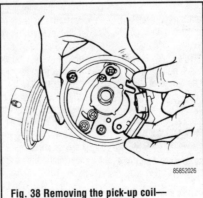

Fig. 38 Removing the pick-up coil—1976–78

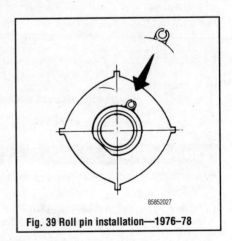

Fig. 39 Roll pin installation—1976–78

2-10 ENGINE PERFORMANCE AND TUNE-UP

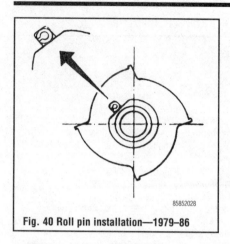

Fig. 40 Roll pin installation—1979–86

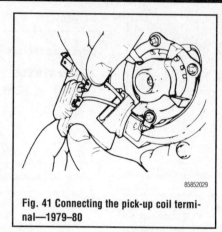

Fig. 41 Connecting the pick-up coil terminal—1979–80

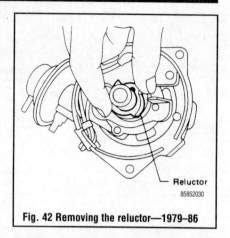

Fig. 42 Removing the reluctor—1979–86

RELUCTOR AND IC IGNITION UNIT

Carbureted Engines

➡On all fuel injected models (VG30i and Z24i) a crank angle sensor in the distributor is used.

1. Remove the distributor cap and rotor. The rotor is held to the distributor shaft by a retaining screw, which must be removed.
2. Remove the wiring harness and the vacuum controller from the housing.
3. Using 2 flat bladed screwdrivers, place one on each side of the reluctor and pry it from the distributor shaft.

➡When removing the reluctor, be careful not to damage or distort the teeth.

4. Remove the roll pin from the reluctor.

➡To remove the IC unit, mark and remove the breaker plate assembly then separate the IC unit from it. Be careful not to loose the spacers when you remove the IC unit.

To install:

5. Install the IC unit to the breaker plate assembly.
6. Install the wiring harness and the vacuum controller to the distributor housing. When you install the roll pin into the reluctor position the cutout direction of the roll pin in parallel with the notch in the reluctor. Make sure that the harness to the IC ignition unit is tightly secured, then adjust the air gap between the reluctor and the stator.

FUEL INJECTED ENGINES

All fuel injected models (VG30i and Z24i) utilize a crank angle sensor in the distributor. The only service that is possible is to replace the distributor cap and rotor, as necessary. Removal and installation of the distributor assembly is covered in Section 3 of this manual.

1. The distributor cap is held on by two screws. Release them with a screwdriver and lift the cap straight up and off, with the wires attached. Inspect the cap for cracks, carbon tracks, or a worn center contact.
2. Pull the ignition rotor straight up to remove. Replace it if its contacts are worn, burned, or pitted. Do not file the contacts. To replace, press it firmly onto the shaft. It only goes on one way, so be sure it is fully seated.
3. Inspect the wires for cracks or brittleness. Replace them one at a time to prevent crosswiring, carefully pressing the replacement wires into place. The cores of electronic wires are more susceptible to breakage than those of standard wires, so treat them gently.
4. Install the distributor cap and tighten the two screws.

Troubleshooting

➡For troubleshooting on fuel injected engines, please refer to Section 4 of this manual.

➡All fuel injected models (VG30i and Z24i) utilize a crank angle sensor in the distributor. This sensor controls ignition timing and has other engine control functions. There is no vacuum or centrifugal advance. All timing settings are controlled by the Electronic Control Unit (ECU).

CARBURETED ENGINES

1976–78 Vehicles

The main differences between the 1976–77 and 1978 systems are: (1) the 1976–77 system uses an external ballast resistor located next to the ignition coil, and (2) the earlier system uses a wiring harness with individual eyelet connectors to the electronic unit, while the later system uses a multiple plug connector. You will need an accurate voltmeter and ohmmeter for these test, which must be performed in the order given.

1. Check all connections for corrosion, looseness, breaks, etc., and correct if necessary. Clean and gap the spark plugs.
2. Disconnect the harness (connector or plug) from the electronic unit. Turn the ignition switch **ON**. Set the voltmeter to the DC 50v range. Connect the positive (+) voltmeter lead to the black/white wire terminal, and the negative (−) lead to the black wire terminal. Battery voltage should be obtained. If not, check the black/white and black wires for continuity; check the battery terminals for corrosion; check the battery state of charge.
3. Next, connect the voltmeter (+) lead to the blue wire and the (−) lead to the black wire. Battery voltage should be obtained. If not, check the blue wire for continuity; check the ignition coil terminals for corrosion or looseness; check the coil for continuity. On 1976–77 models, also check the external ballast resistor.
4. Disconnect the distributor harness wires from the ignition coil ballast resistor on 1976–77 models, leaving the ballast resistor-to-coil wires attached. On 1978 models, disconnect the ignition coil wires. Connect the leads of an ohmmeter to the ballast resistor outside terminals (at each end) through 1977; resistance should be 1.6–2.0Ω. In 1978, connect the ohmmeter to the coil terminals: resistance should be 0Ω. If more than 2.0Ω, 1976–77, or 1.8Ω, 1978, replace the coil.
5. Disconnect the harness from the electronic control unit. Connect an ohmmeter to the red and the green wire terminals. Resistance should be 720Ω. If far more or far less, replace the distributor pick-up coil.
6. Disconnect the anti-dieseling solenoid connector (see Section 4). Connect a voltmeter to the red and green terminals of the electronic control harness. When the starter is cranked, the needle should deflect slightly. If not, replace the distributor pick-up coil.
7. Reconnect the ignition coil and the electronic control unit. Leave the anti-dieseling solenoid wire disconnected. Unplug the high tension lead (coil-to-distributor) from the distributor and hold it 0.012–0.24 in. (3–6mm) from the cylinder head with a pair of insulated pliers and a heavy glove. BE CAREFUL! When the engine is cranked, a spark should be observed. If not, check the lead, and replace the electronic control unit.
8. Reconnect all wires.

- 1976–77: connect the voltmeter (+) lead to the blue electronic control harness connector and the (−) lead to the black wire. The harness should be attached to the control unit.
- 1978: connect the voltmeter (+) lead to the (−) terminal of the ignition coil and the (−) lead to the ground.

As soon as the ignition switch is turned **ON**, the meter should indicate battery voltage. If not, replace the electronic control unit.

ENGINE PERFORMANCE AND TUNE-UP

1979–80 Vehicles

1. Make a check of the power supply circuit. Turn the ignition **OFF**. Disconnect the connector from the top of the IC unit. Turn the ignition **ON**. Measure the voltage at each terminal of the connector in turn by touching the probe of the positive lead of the voltmeter to one of the terminals, and touching the probe of the negative lead of the voltmeter to a ground, such as the engine. In each case, battery voltage should be indicated. If not, check all wiring, the ignition switch, and all connectors for breaks, corrosion, discontinuity, etc., and repair as necessary.

2. Check the primary windings of the ignition coil. Turn the ignition **OFF**. Disconnect the harness connector from the negative coil terminals. Use an ohmmeter to measure the resistance between the positive and negative terminals on the coil. If resistance is 0.84–1.02Ω, the coil is OK. Replace if far from this range. If the power supply, circuits, wiring, and coil are in good shape, check the IC unit and pick-up coil, as follows:
   a. Turn the ignition **OFF**.
   b. Remove the distributor cap and ignition rotor.
   c. Use an ohmmeter to measure the resistance between the two terminals of the pick-up coil, where they attach to the IC unit. Measure the resistance by reversing the polarity of the probes. If approximately 400Ω are indicated, the pick-up coil is OK, but the IC unit is bad and must be replaced. If other than 400Ω are measured, go to the next step.
   d. Be certain the 2-pin connector to the IC unit is secure. Turn the ignition **ON**. Measure the voltage at the ignition coil negative terminal. Turn the ignition **OFF**.

✽✽ WARNING

Remove the tester probe from the coil negative terminal before switching the ignition OFF, to prevent burning out the tester.

If zero voltage is indicated, the IC unit is bad and must be replaced. If battery voltage is indicated, proceed.

3. Remove the IC unit from the distributor:
   a. Disconnect the battery ground (negative) cable.
   b. Remove the distributor cap and ignition rotor.
   c. Disconnect the harness connector at the top of the IC unit.
   d. Remove the two screws securing the IC unit to the distributor.
   e. Disconnect the two pick-up coil wires from the IC unit.

➡ **Pull the connectors free with a pair of needlenosed pliers. Do not pull on the wires to detach the connectors.**

   f. Remove the IC unit.

4. Measure the resistance between the terminals of the pick-up coil. It should be approximately 400Ω. If so, the pick-up coil is OK, and the IC unit is bad. If not approximately 400Ω, the pick-up coil is bad and must be replaced.

5. With a new pick-up coil installed, install the IC unit. Check for a spark at one of the spark plugs. If a good spark is obtained, the IC unit is OK. If not, replace the IC unit.

1981–86 Vehicles

BATTERY VOLTAGE (NO LOAD)

With the ignition key in the **OFF** position, connect a voltmeter to the positive and negative terminals of the battery. The reading should not be below 11.5 volts. A lower reading indicates a faulty battery, charging or starting system.

BATTERY CRANKING VOLTAGE

1. Connect a voltmeter to the battery and set to the appropriate scale.
2. Remove the coil wire from the distributor cap and ground it.
3. Crank the engine for approximately 15 seconds. The voltage reading should not be less than 9.6 volts while cranking. A lower reading indicates a faulty battery, charging or starting system.

SECONDARY WIRING TEST

With the distributor cap removed, connect an ohmmeter to each end of the spark plug cables. The resistance readings should be less than 30,000Ω. If the resistance readings are greater than 30,000Ω, replace the distributor cap and/or plug wires.

IGNITION COIL SECONDARY CIRCUIT

With the ignition key in the **OFF** position, and the coil wire removed from the coil, connect an ohmmeter with one probe to the coil wire socket and the other to the negative terminal. Check both coils. The resistance reading should be between 7,000–11,000Ω. If not, replace the ignition coil.

POWER SUPPLY CIRCUIT

1. Connect a voltmeter with the positive probe to the **B** terminal (power source) and the negative probe to the distributor housing.
2. Turn the ignition key to the **ON** position.
3. The reading should be between 11.5–12.5 volts. If below 11.5 volts, check the wiring between the ignition switch and the I.C. unit.

POWER SUPPLY CIRCUIT (CRANKING)

1. Connect a voltmeter as in Step 1 above.
2. Pull the coil wire from the distributor cap and ground it.
3. Turn the key to the **START** position and observe the voltmeter while the engine is cranking.
4. If the voltage reading is more than 1 volt below battery cranking voltage and/or is below 8.6 volts, check the ignition switch and wiring from the switch to the I.C. unit.

IGNITION PRIMARY CIRCUIT

1. Connect a voltmeter negative probe to the **I** terminal and the negative voltmeter probe to the distributor housing.
2. Turn the ignition key to the **ON** position. If the reading is between 11.5–12.5 volts proceed to Step 3. If the reading is below 11.5 volts proceed to the Ignition Coil Primary Circuit test.
3. Connect the voltmeter positive probe to the **E** terminal and the negative voltmeter probe the distributor housing.
4. Turn the ignition key to the **ON** position. If the reading is between 11.5–12.5 volts proceed to the I.C. Unit Ground Circuit test. If the reading is below 11.5 volts proceed to the Ignition Coil Primary Circuit test.

IGNITION COIL PRIMARY CIRCUIT

1. Place the ignition key in the **OFF** position.
2. Remove the coil wire from the coil.
3. Measure the resistance between the two terminals of the coil. The resistance should be between 1.04–1.27Ω. If not the ignition coil is defective and should be replaced.

I.C. UNIT GROUND CIRCUIT

1. Connect the positive probe of a voltmeter to the housing of the distributor.
2. Connect the negative probe of a voltmeter to the negative terminal of the battery.
3. Pull out the coil wire from the distributor cap and ground it.
4. Turn the key to the **START** position and observe the voltmeter while cranking.
5. If the voltmeter reading is 0.05 volts or less, replace the IC ignition unit assembly.
6. If the voltmeter reading is more than 0.5 volts, check the distributor ground, wiring from the chassis ground to the battery including battery cable connections.

IGNITION TIMING

▶ See Figures 43 thru 48

Ignition timing is the measurement in degrees of crankshaft rotation of the instant the spark plugs in the cylinders fire, in relation to the location of the piston, while the piston is on its compression stroke.

Ignition timing is adjusted by loosening the distributor locking device and turning the distributor in the engine.

Ideally, the air/fuel mixture in the cylinder will be ignited (by the spark plug) and just beginning its rapid expansion as the piston passes top dead center (TDC) of the compression stroke. If this happens, the piston will be beginning the power stroke just as the compressed (by the movement of the piston) air/fuel mixture starts to expand. The expansion of the air/fuel mixture will then force the piston down on the power stroke and turn the crankshaft.

2-12 ENGINE PERFORMANCE AND TUNE-UP

It takes a fraction of a second for the spark from the plug to completely ignite the mixture in the cylinder. Because of this, the spark plug must fire before the piston reaches TDC, if the mixture is to be completely ignited as the piston passes TDC. This measurement is given in degrees (of crankshaft rotation) before the piston reaches top dead center (BTDC). If the ignition timing setting for your engine is seven 7°BTDC, this means that the spark plug must fire at a time when the piston for that cylinder is 7°before top dead center of its compression stroke. However, this only holds true while your engine is at idle speed.

As you accelerate from idle, the speed of your engine (rpm) increases. The increase in rpm means that the pistons are now traveling up and down much faster. Because of this, the spark plugs will have to fire even sooner if the mixture is to be completely ignited as the piston passes TDC. To accomplish this, the distributor incorporates various means to advance the timing of the spark as engine speed increases.

The distributor in your Nissan has two means of advancing the ignition timing. One is called centrifugal advance and is actuated by weights in the distributor. The other is called vacuum advance and is controlled by that larger circular housing on the side of the distributor.

In addition, some distributors have a vacuum retard mechanism which is contained in the same housing on the side of the distributor as the vacuum advance. The function of this mechanism is to retard the timing of the ignition spark under certain engine conditions. This causes more complete burning of the air/fuel mixture in the cylinder and consequently lowers exhaust emissions.

Because these mechanisms change ignition timing, it is necessary to disconnect and plug the one or two vacuum lines from the distributor when setting the basic ignition timing.

➡ON ALL FUEL INJECTED MODELS (VG30i AND Z24i) A CRANK ANGLE SENSOR IN THE DISTRIBUTOR IS USED. THIS SENSOR HELP CONTROL IGNITION TIMING AND IS USED FOR OTHER ENGINE CONTROL FUNCTIONS. THERE IS NO VACUUM OR CENTRIFUGAL ADVANCE ALL TIMING SETTINGS ARE CONTROLLED BY THE ECU unit.

If ignition timing is set too far advanced (BTDC), the ignition and expansion of the air/fuel mixture in the cylinder will try to force the piston down the cylinder while it is still traveling upward. This causes engine ping, a sound which resembles marbles being dropped into an empty tin can. If the ignition timing is too far retarded (after, or ATDC), the piston will have already started down on the power stroke when the air/fuel mixture ignites and expands. This will cause the piston to be forced down only a portion of its travel. This will result in poor engine performance and lack of power.

Ignition timing adjustment is checked with a timing light. This instrument is connected to the number one (No. 1) spark plug of the engine. The timing light flashes every time an electrical current is sent from the distributor, through the No. 1 spark plug wire, to the spark plug. The crankshaft pulley and the front cover of the engine are marked with a timing pointer and a timing scale. When the timing pointer is aligned with the **0** mark on the timing scale, the piston is the No. 1 cylinder is at TDC of its compression stroke. With the engine running, and the timing light aimed at the timing pointer and timing scale, the stroboscopic flashes from the timing light will allow you to check the ignition timing setting of the engine. The timing light flashes every time the spark plug in the No. 1 cylinder of the engine fires. Since the flash from the timing light makes the crankshaft pulley seem stationary for a moment you will be able to read the exact position of the piston in the No. 1 cylinder on the timing scale on the front of the engine.

There are three basic types of timing lights available. The first is a simple neon bulb with two wire connections (one for the spark plug and one for the plug wire, connecting the light in series). This type of light is quite dim, and must be held closely to the marks to be seen, but it is inexpensive. The second type of light operates from the battery. Two alligator clips connect to the battery terminals, while a third wire connects to the spark plug with an adapter. This type of light is more expensive, but the xenon bulb provides a nice bright flash which can even be seen in sunlight. The third type replaces the battery source with 110 volt house current. Some timing lights have other functions built into them, such as dwell meters, tachometers, or remote starting switches. These are convenient, in that they reduce the tangle of wires under the hood, but may duplicate the functions of tools you already have.

If your Nissan has electronic ignition, you should use a timing light with an inductive pickup. This pickup simply clamps onto the No. 1 plug wire, eliminating the adapter. It is not susceptible to crossfiring or false triggering, which may occur with a conventional light, due to the greater voltages produced by electronic ignition.

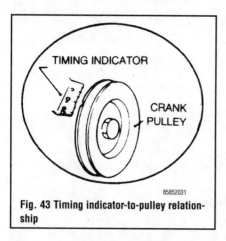

Fig. 43 Timing indicator-to-pulley relationship

Fig. 44 Timing marks

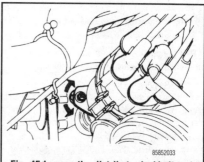

Fig. 45 Loosen the distributor lockbolt and turn the distributor slightly to advance (upper arrow) or retard (lower arrow) the timing—1970–80

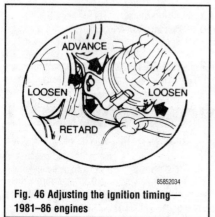

Fig. 46 Adjusting the ignition timing—1981–86 engines

Fig. 47 View of the timing scale and timing mark (white mark on crankshaft pulley)

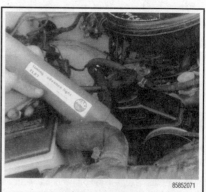

Fig. 48 Aim the timing light at the marks (but be careful of the fan blades)

ENGINE PERFORMANCE AND TUNE-UP

Checking and Adjustment

1970–86 CARBURETED ENGINES

➡ Refer to Section 4 to check and adjust the phase timing of the two sets of points in 1970–73 models. If the underhood emissions decal differs from the information given in this manual, always use the information on the decal as this reflects the latest changes made during production.

1. Set the dwell of the breaker points to the proper specification, on those trucks so equipped.
2. Locate the timing marks on the crankshaft pulley and the front of the engine.
3. Clean off the timing marks, so that you can see them.
4. Use chalk or white paint to color the mark on the crankshaft pulley and the mark on the scale which will indicate the correct timing when aligned with the notch on the crankshaft pulley.
5. Attach a tachometer to the engine.
6. Attach a timing light to the engine, according to the manufacturer's instructions. If the timing light has three wires, one, usually green or blue, is attached to the No. 1 spark plug with an adapter. The other wires are connected to the battery. The red wire goes to the positive side of the battery and the black wire is connected to the negative terminal of the battery. If the truck has electronic ignition use an inductive timing light as described above.
7. Leave the vacuum line connected to the distributor vacuum diaphragm on models through 1980. On 1982–86 models disconnect the distributor vacuum hose from the vacuum controller and plug the hose. Also on Canadian Z24 engines disconnect the air injection hoses and cap the injection pipes.

❈❈ CAUTION

Keep fingers, clothes, tools, hair, and leads clear of the spinning engine fan. Be sure that you are running the engine in a well ventilated area!

8. Allow the engine to run at the specified idle speed with the gearshift in Neutral with manual transmission and Drive (D) with automatic transmission.

❈❈ CAUTION

Be sure that the parking brake is firmly set and that the front wheels are blocked to prevent the truck from rolling forward, especially when Drive is selected with an automatic!

9. Point the timing light at the marks indicated in the chart and illustrations. With the engine at idle, timing should be at the specification given on the Tune-Up Specifications chart in this section.
10. If the timing is not at the specification, loosen the pinch bolt (hold-down bolt) at the base of the distributor just enough so that the distributor can be turned. Turn the distributor to advance or retard the timing, as required. Once the proper marks are aligned, timing is correct.
11. Stop the engine and tighten the pinch bolt. Start the engine and recheck the timing to assure it did not change while tightening the bolt. Stop the engine; disconnect the tachometer and timing light.
12. Tighten the distributor lockbolt and recheck the timing.

1986–88 FUEL INJECTED ENGINES

➡ When checking ignition timing on air conditioner equipped trucks, make sure that the air conditioner is OFF when proceeding with the check. Refer to Idle Speed And Mixture Adjustments.

❈❈ CAUTION

Automatic transmission equipped models should be shifted into D for idle speed checks. When in Drive, the parking brake must be fully applied with both front and rear wheels chocked. When racing the engine on automatic transmission equipped models, make sure that the shift lever is in the N or P position.

1. Run the engine until it reaches normal operating temperature.
2. Open the hood, and race the engine at 2000 rpm for about 2 minutes under no-load (all accessories **OFF**).
3. Run the engine at idle speed.
4. Race the engine two or three times under no-load, then run the engine for one minute at idle.
5. Check the idle speed. Adjust the idle speed to specifications by turning the idle speed adjusting screw. Refer to the Tune Up Specifications Chart.
6. Connect a timing light according to the light manufacturer's instructions. Adjust the timing by loosening the distributor hold-down bolts and turning the distributor clockwise to advance and counterclockwise to retard.
7. Recheck timing after tightening the hold-down bolt to assure it did not change while tightening the bolt.

VALVE LASH

▸ **See Figures 49 thru 55**

As part of every major tune-up or once every 6000 miles (1970–74) 12,500 miles (1975–78) or 15,000 miles (1979–88) the valve clearance should be checked and adjusted, if necessary.

Valve lash is one factor which determines how far the intake and exhaust valves will open into the cylinder.

If the valve clearance is too large, part of the lift of the camshaft will be used up in removing the excessive clearance, thus the valves will not be opened far enough. This condition has two effects, the valve train components will emit a tapping noise as they take up the excessive clearance, and the engine will perform poorly, since the less the intake valves open, the smaller the amount of air/fuel mixture admitted to the cylinders. The less the exhaust valves open, the

Fig. 49 Removing the air cleaner assembly—mark all necessary lines

Fig. 50 Removing valve cover retaining bolts

Fig. 51 Removing valve cover

2-14 ENGINE PERFORMANCE AND TUNE-UP

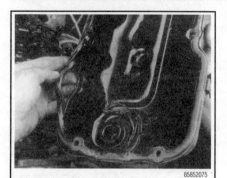

Fig. 52 Removing valve cover gasket—always replace this gasket when the valve cover is removed

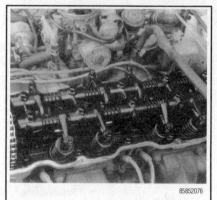

Fig. 53 View of the rocker arm assembly

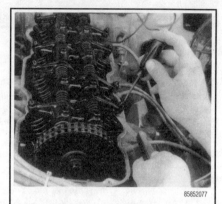

Fig. 54 Adjust the valve clearance

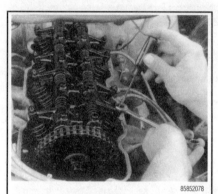

Fig. 55 Tighten the locknut after valve clearance adjustment

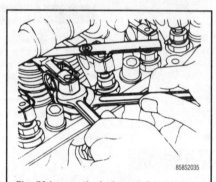

Fig. 56 Loosen the locknut and turn the pivot adjuster to adjust the valve clearance—L16, L18 and L20B engines

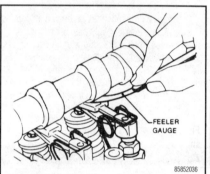

Fig. 57 Checking the valve clearance with a flat feeler gauge—L16, L18 and L20B engines

greater the back-pressure in the cylinder which prevents the air/fuel mixture from entering the cylinder.

If the valve clearance is too small, the intake and exhaust valves will not fully seat on the cylinder head when they close. When a valve seats on the cylinder head it does two things; it seals the combustion chamber so none of the gases in the cylinder can escape and it cools itself by transferring some of the heat it absorbed from the combustion process through the cylinder head and into the engine cooling system. Therefore, if the valve clearance is too small, the engine will run poorly (due to gases escaping from the combustion chamber), and the valves will overheat and warp (since they cannot transfer heat unless they are touching the seat in the cylinder head).

➡Although Nissan recommends that the valve lash on certain models be set while the engine is running, we feel that for the average owner/mechanic it is more convenient to adjust the valves statically (engine off). Thus, running valve lash and adjustment procedures have been omitted from the manual. While all valve adjustments must be as accurate as possible, it is better to have the valve adjustment slightly loose than slightly tight, as burnt valves may result from overly tight adjustments.

Adjustments

L16, L18 AND L20B ENGINES

♦ See Figures 56 and 57

1. The valves are adjusted with the engine at normal operating temperature. Oil temperature, and the resultant parts expansion, is much more important than water temperature. Run the engine for at least fifteen minutes to ensure that all the parts have reached their full expansion. After the engine is warmed up, shut it off.
2. Purchase either a new gasket or some silicone gasket seal before removing the cylinder head cover. Note the location of any wires and hoses which may interfere with cover removal, disconnect them and move them aside. Then remove the bolts which hold the cylinder head cover in place and remove the cover.

3. Place a wrench on the crankshaft pulley bolt and turn the engine over until the valves for the No. 1 cylinder are closed. When both camshaft lobes are pointing up, the valves are closed. If you have not done this before, it is a good idea to turn the engine over slowly several times and watch the valve action until you have a clear idea of just when the valve is closed.
4. Check the clearance of the intake and exhaust valves. You can differentiate between them by lining them up with the tubes of the intake and exhaust manifolds. The correct size feeler gauge should pass between the base circle of the camshaft and the rocker arm with just a slight drag. Be sure the feeler gauge is inserted straight and not on an angle.
5. If the valves need adjustment, loosen the locking nut and then adjust the clearance with the adjusting screw. You will probably find it necessary to hold the locking nut while you turn the adjuster. After you have the correct clearance, tighten the locking nut and recheck the clearance. Remember, its better to have them too loose than too tight, especially exhaust valves.
6. Repeat this procedure until you have checked and/or adjusted all the valves. Keep in mind that all that is necessary is to have the valves closed and the camshaft lobes pointing up. It is not particularly important what stroke the engine is on.
7. Install the cam cover gasket, the cam cover, and any wires and hoses which were removed.

1981–82 Z22 ENGINES

♦ See Figures 58, 59, 60 and 61

1. The valves must be adjusted with the engine warm, so start the truck and run the engine until the needle on the temperature gauges reaches the middle of the gauge indicating normal operating temperature. After the engine is warm, shut it off.
2. Purchase either a new gasket or some silicone gasket sealer before removing the cylinder head cover. Counting on the old gasket to be in good shape is a losing proposition; always use new gaskets. Note the location of any wires and hoses which may interfere with cylinder head cover removal, disconnect them and move them to one side. Remove the bolts holding the cover in place and remove the cover. Remember, the engine will be hot, so be careful!

ENGINE PERFORMANCE AND TUNE-UP 2-15

3. Place a wrench on the crankshaft pulley bolt and turn the engine over until the first cam lobe behind the camshaft timing chain sprocket is pointing straight down.

→If you decide to turn the engine by bumping it with the starter, be sure to disconnect the high tension wire from the coil(s) to prevent the engine from accidentally starting and spewing oil all over the engine compartment.

✳✳ CAUTION

Never attempt to turn the engine by using a wrench on the camshaft sprocket bolt; there is a one to two turning ratio between the camshaft and the crankshaft which will put a tremendous strain on the timing chain.

the gauge indicating normal operating temperature. After the engine is warm, shut it off.

2. Purchase either a new gasket or some silicone gasket sealer before removing the cylinder head cover. Counting on the old gasket to be in good shape is a losing proposition; always use new gaskets. Note the location of any wires and hoses which may interfere with cylinder head cover removal, disconnect them and move them to one side. Remove the bolts holding the cover in place and remove the cover. Remember, the engine will be hot, so be careful!

3. Rotate the crankshaft until the timing marks indicate that the No. 1 piston is at TDC of the compression stroke. If you're not sure of which stroke you're on, remove the No. 1 spark plug and hold your thumb over the hole. Pressure will be felt as the piston starts up on the compression stroke.

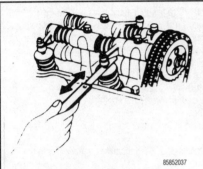

Fig. 58 The proper size feeler gauge should pass with a slight drag—1981–82 Z22 engines

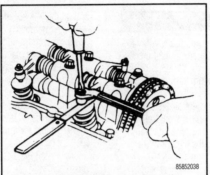

Fig. 59 Loosen the locknut and turn the adjusting screw to adjust the valve clearance—1981–82 Z22 engines

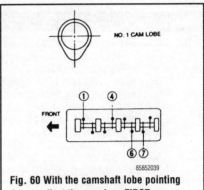

Fig. 60 With the camshaft lobe pointing down, adjust these valves FIRST—1981–82 Z22 engines

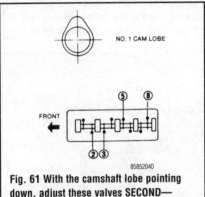

Fig. 61 With the camshaft lobe pointing down, adjust these valves SECOND—1981–82 Z22 engines

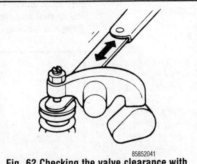

Fig. 62 Checking the valve clearance with a flat feeler gauge (a slight drag should be felt)—Z20, Z22 (except 1981–82), Z24 and Z24i engines

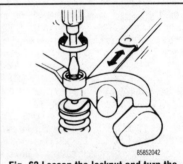

Fig. 63 Loosen the locknut and turn the adjusting screw to adjust the valve clearance—Z20, Z22 (except 1981–82), Z24 and Z24i engines

4. See the illustration marked FIRST, and check valves (1), (4), (6) and (7) using a 0.012 in. (0.3mm) flat bladed feeler gauge. The feeler gauge should pass between the valve stem end and the rocker arm screw with a very slight drag. Insert the feeler gauge straight, not at an angle.

5. If the clearance is not within specified value, loosen the rocker arm locknut and turn the rocker arm screw to obtain the proper clearance. After correct clearance is obtained, tighten the locknut.

6. Turn the engine over so that the first cam lobe behind the camshaft timing chain sprocket is pointing straight up and check the valves marked (2), (3), (5) and (8) in the SECOND illustration. They, too, should have a clearance of 0.012 in. (0.3mm). Adjust as necessary.

7. Install the cylinder head cover gasket, the cover itself and any wires and hoses which were removed.

Z20, Z22 (EXCEPT 1981–82), Z24 & Z24i ENGINES

♦ See Figures 62, 63 and 64

1. The valves must be adjusted with the engine warm, so start the truck and run the engine until the needle on the temperature gauge reaches the middle of

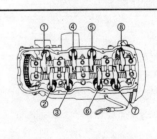
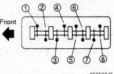

Fig. 64 With the No. 1 piston at TDC, adjust the top set of valves FIRST; with the No. 4 piston at TDC, adjust the bottom set of valves SECOND—Z20, Z22 (except 1981–82), Z24 and Z24i engines

2-16 ENGINE PERFORMANCE AND TUNE-UP

4. See the proper illustration marked FIRST, and check valves (1), (2), (4) and (6) using a flat bladed feeler gauge. The feeler gauge should pass between the valve stem end and the rocker arm screw with a very slight drag. Insert the feeler gauge straight, not at an angle.

5. If the clearance is not within specified value, loosen the rocker arm locknut and turn the rocker arm screw to obtain the proper clearance. After correct clearance is obtained, tighten the locknut.

6. Rotate the crankshaft until the timing marks indicate that the No. 4 piston is at TDC of the compression stroke. If you're not sure of which stroke you're on, remove the No. 4 spark plug and hold your thumb over the hole. Pressure will be felt as the piston starts up on the compression stroke.

7. See the appropriate illustration marked SECOND, and check valves (3), (5), (7) and (8). Check and adjust valve clearance as detailed in Steps 4–5.

8. Install the cylinder head cover gasket, the cover itself and any wires and hoses which were removed.

VG30i ENGINES

These models utilize hydraulic valve lifters. Periodic adjustment is neither necessary or possible.

IDLE SPEED AND MIXTURE ADJUSTMENTS

Carburetor

This section contains only carburetor adjustments as they normally apply to engine tune-up. Descriptions of the carburetor and complete adjustment procedures can be found in Section 5 of this manual.

When the engine in your Nissan is running, air/fuel mixture from the carburetor is being drawn into the engine by a partial vacuum which is created by the downward movement of the pistons on the intake stroke of the 4-stroke cycle of the engine. The amount of air/fuel mixture that enters the engine is controlled by throttle plates in the bottom of the carburetor. When the engine is not running, the throttle plates are closed, completely blocking off the bottom of the carburetor from the inside of the engine. The throttle plates are connected, through the throttle linkage, to the gas pedal in the passenger compartment of the truck. After you start the engine and put the transmission in gear, you depress the gas pedal to start the truck moving. What you actually are doing when you depress the gas pedal is opening the throttle plate in the carburetor to admit more of the air/fuel mixture to the engine. The further you open the throttle plates in the carburetor, the higher the engine speed becomes.

As previously stated, when the engine is not running, the throttle plates in the carburetor are closed. When the engine is idling, it is necessary to open the throttle plates slightly. To prevent having to keep your foot on the gas pedal when the engine is idling, an idle speed adjusting screw was added to the carburetor. This screw has the same affect as keeping your foot slightly depressed on the gas pedal. The idle speed adjusting screw contacts the throttle lever on the outside of the carburetor. When the screw is turned in, it opens the throttle plate on the carburetor, raising the idle speed of the engine. This screw is called the curb idle adjusting screw, and the procedures in this section tell you how to adjust it.

Since it is difficult for the engine to draw the air/fuel mixture from the carburetor with the small amount of throttle plate opening that is present when the engine is idling, an idle mixture passage is provided in the carburetor. This passage delivers air/fuel mixture to the engine from a hole which is located in the bottom of the carburetor below the throttle plates. This idle mixture passage contains an adjusting screw which restricts the amount of air/fuel mixture that enters the engine at idle.

ADJUSTMENT PROCEDURES

1970–81 Vehicles

▶ See Figures 65 and 66

1. Start the engine and run it until it reaches operating temperature.
2. Allow the engine idle speed to stabilize by running the engine at idle for at least 1 minute.
3. If it hasn't already been done, check and adjust the ignition timing to the proper setting.
4. Turn OFF the engine and connect a tachometer to the engine.
5. Disconnect and plug the air hose between the three way connector and check valve, if equipped. Start the engine. With the transmission in **N**, check the idle speed on the tachometer. If the reading on the tachometer is correct, turn the idle adjusting screw clockwise to increase the idle speed and counterclockwise to decrease it.
6. With an automatic transmission in **D**(wheels chocked and parking brake applied) or a manual transmission in **N**, turn the mixture screw out until the engine rpm starts to drop due to an overly rich mixture.
7. Turn the screw in past the starting point until the engine rpm start to drop because of a too lean mixture. On 1975–77 models, turn the mixture screw in until the idle speed drops 60–70 rpm with manual transmission, or 15–25 rpm with automatic transmission (in **D**). On 1978 models, the rpm drop should be 45–55 rpm for all trucks. For 1979–81 models the rpm drop should be 45–55 rpm with manual transmission, or 25–35 rpm with automatic transmission (in **D**). If the mixture limiter cap will not allow this adjustment, remove it, make the adjustment, and reinstall it. Go on to Step 10 for 1975–81 trucks.
8. On 1970–74 models, turn the mixture screw back out to the point midway between the two extreme positions where the engine began losing rpm to achieve the fastest and smoothest idle.
9. Adjust the curb idle speed to the proper specification on 1970–74 models.
10. Install the air hose. If the engine speed increases, reduce it with the idle speed screw.

➡ **To be sure that the vehicle is complying with emission laws, have the exhaust checked with a CO meter. The percentages of CO should be 3% for 1970–71, 2% 1972, 1.5% 1973–74, 2% 1975–77, and 1% 1978–81 at idle speed. Idle limiter caps are installed on the mixture adjusting screws so that an incorrect adjustment cannot be made. If a satisfactory idle cannot be obtained within the range of the limiter caps, remove them and make the adjustment as outlined above. Reinstall the limiter**

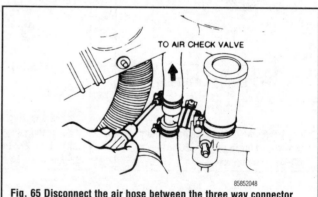

Fig. 65 Disconnect the air hose between the three way connector and the check valve—1970–81

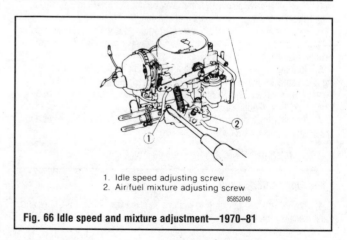

1. Idle speed adjusting screw
2. Air/fuel mixture adjusting screw

Fig. 66 Idle speed and mixture adjustment—1970–81

ENGINE PERFORMANCE AND TUNE-UP 2-17

caps so that the cap can be turned only 1/8 of a turn counterclockwise before it reaches the stop. Have the engine checked with a CO meter after making the adjustment.

1982–86 Vehicles

▶ See Figures 67 and 68

➡ These models require the use of a CO meter to adjust their mixture ratios, therefore only idle speed adjustments are given.

1. Connect a tachometer according to the manufacturer's instructions.
2. Turn all the accessories and lights **OFF**. Make sure that the wheels are straight ahead on models with power steering.
3. Run the engine at 2000 rpm for 2 minutes with the transmission in **P** or **N**.
4. Run the engine at normal idle speed for 1 minute in **P** or **N**.
5. Check the idle speed with the automatic transmission in **D**, wheel blocked and the parking brake on, use the figures provided on your underhood sticker. If the indicated idle speed does not agree with the specified speed, adjust the idle by turning the throttle adjusting screw at the carburetor.

Electronic Fuel Injection (EFI)

These trucks use a rather complex electronic fuel injection system which is controlled by a series of temperature, altitude (for California) and air flow sensors which feed information into a central control unit. The control unit then relays an electronic signal to the injector nozzle, which allows a predetermined amount of fuel into the combustion chamber. There is no mixture adjustment possible on these models.

IDLE SPEED ADJUSTMENT PROCEDURE

▶ See Figures 69, 70 and 71

1. Turn off the: headlights, heater blower, air conditioning, and rear window defogger. If the truck has power steering, make sure the wheel is in the straight ahead position. The ignition timing must be correct to get an effective idle speed adjustment. Connect a tachometer (a special adapter harness may be needed, SST# EG11170000) according to the instrument manufacturer's directions.
2. Start the engine and idle until it reaches normal operating temperature. The water temperature indicator should be in the middle of the gauge.
3. Run engine at 2000 rpm for about 2 minutes under no load.
4. Race the engine to 2000–3000 rpm a few times under no load and then allow it to return to idle speed.
5. Apply the parking brake securely and then put the transmission into **D**, (if the truck has an automatic). Adjust the idle speed to the figure shown in the Tune-Up Specifications Chart by turning the idle speed adjusting screw.
6. Turn the engine OFF and remove the tachometer. Road test for proper operation.

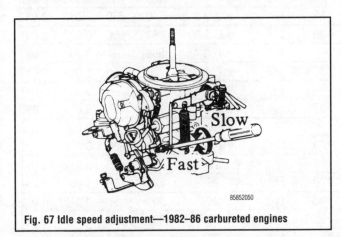

Fig. 67 Idle speed adjustment—1982–86 carbureted engines

Fig. 68 Idle speed adjustment

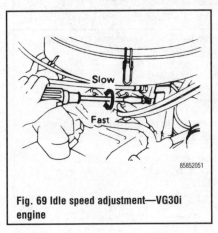

Fig. 69 Idle speed adjustment—VG30i engine

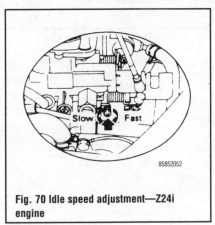

Fig. 70 Idle speed adjustment—Z24i engine

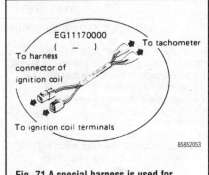

Fig. 71 A special harness is used for tachometer connection on fuel injected engines

2-18 ENGINE PERFORMANCE AND TUNE-UP

GASOLINE ENGINE TUNE-UP SPECIFICATIONS

Year	Engine Type	Spark Plugs Type	Spark Plugs Gap (in.)	Distributor Point Dwell (deg.)	Distributor Point Gap (in.)	Ignition Timing (deg.)▲ MT	Ignition Timing (deg.)▲ AT	Compression Pressure (psi)**	Fuel Pump Pressure (psi)	Idle Speed (rpm)▲ MT	Idle Speed (rpm)▲ AT	Valve Clearance (in.)‡ In.	Valve Clearance (in.)‡ Ex.
1970	L16	B6ES	0.033	52	0.020	10B	—	171	2.6–3.4	700	—	0.010	0.012
1971	L16	B6ES	0.033	52	0.020	10B	—	171	2.6–3.4	700	—	0.010	0.012
1972	L16	B6ES	0.032	52	0.020	7B	—	171	2.6–3.4	700	—	0.010	0.012
1973	L16	B6ES	0.030	52	0.020	8B	—	171	2.6–3.4	800	—	0.010	0.012
	L18	B6ES	0.030	52	0.020	5B	5B	171	2.6–3.4	800	650	0.010	0.012
1974	L18	B6ES	0.030	52	0.020	12B	12B	171	2.6–3.4	800	650	0.010	0.012
1975	L20B	BP6ES	0.034	52	0.020	12B①	12B	171	2.8–3.8	750	650	0.010	0.012
1976	L20B	②	③	④	④⑤	12B①	12B	171	2.8–3.8	750	650	0.010	0.012
1977	L20B	②	③	④	④⑤	12B①	12B	171	2.8–3.8	750	650	0.010	0.012
1978	L20B	BP6ES-11	0.041	—	⑤	12B	12B	171	3.0–3.9⑦	600	600	0.010	0.012
1979	L20B	BP6ES-11	0.041	—	⑥	12B	12B	171	3.0–3.9⑦	650	630	0.010	0.012
1980	L20B	BP6ES-11	0.041	—	⑥	12B①	12B	171	3.0–3.9⑦	600	600	0.010	0.012
1981	Z22	BP6ES⑧	0.033	—	⑥	5B	5B	171	3.0–3.9	650⑨	650	0.012	0.012
1982	Z22	⑩	0.033	—	⑥	3B	3B	171	3.0–3.9	650⑨	650	0.012	0.012
1983	Z22	⑩	0.033	—	⑥	3B	3B	171	3.0–3.9	650⑨	650	0.012	0.012
1984	Z20	⑩	0.033	—	⑥	5B	—	171	2.7–3.4	600	—	0.012	0.012
	Z24	⑩	0.033	—	⑥	3B	3B	171	2.7–3.4	700⑪	650	0.012	0.012
1985	Z20	⑩	0.033	—	⑥	5B	—	171	2.7–3.4	600	—	0.012	0.012
	Z24	⑩	0.033	—	⑥	3B	3B	171	2.7–3.4	700⑪	650	0.012	0.012
1986	Z20	⑩	0.033	—	⑥	5B	—	171	2.7–3.4	600	—	0.012	0.012
	Z24	⑩	0.033	—	⑥	3B	3B	171	2.7–3.4	700⑪	650	0.012	0.012
	Z24i	BPR5ES	0.033	—	—	5B	5B	173	36	900	650	0.012	0.012
	VG30i	BCPR5ES-11	0.041	—	—	12B	12B	173	36	800	700	Hyd.	Hyd.
1987	Z24i	BPR5ES	0.033	—	—	10B	10B	173	36	800	750	0.012	0.012
	VG30i	BCPR5ES-11	0.041	—	—	12B	12B	173	36	800	700	Hyd.	Hyd.
1988	Z24i	BPR5ES	0.033	—	—	10B	10B	173	36	800	650	0.012	0.012
	VG30i	BCPR5ES-11	0.041	—	—	12B	12B	173	36	800	700	Hyd.	Hyd.

NOTE: The underhood specifications sticker often reflects tune-up specification changes made while the car is in production. Sticker figures must be used if they disagree with those in this chart.

▲ With the manual transmission in Neutral and the automatic transmission in Drive (D)
** Lowest reading must be at least 80% of highest
‡ Valve clearances checked with the engine HOT
MT—Manual Transmission
AT—Automatic Transmission
B—Before Top Dead Center
In.—Intake
Ex.—Exhaust

① 1975–77 Calif. & 1980 Calif. Heavy Duty: 10B
② Point-type (exc. 1977 Canada): BP6ES
   1977 Canada: BPR6ES
   Transistorized: BP6ES-11
③ Point-type: 0.033
   Transistor-type: 0.041
④ Point-type; Dwell—52; Gap—0.020
⑤ Air gap: 0.008–0.016
⑥ Air gap: 0.012–0.020
⑦ W/electric fuel pump (A/C models): 4.6 or less
⑧ Canada: BPR6ES
⑨ 4WD: 800
⑩ Intake: BPR6ES
   Exhaust: BPR5ES
⑪ 4WD: 800
   2WD Canada: 650

ENGINE PERFORMANCE AND TUNE-UP

Troubleshooting Basic Starting System Problems

Problem	Cause	Solution
Starter motor rotates engine slowly	• Battery charge low or battery defective	• Charge or replace battery
	• Defective circuit between battery and starter motor	• Clean and tighten, or replace cables
	• Low load current	• Bench-test starter motor. Inspect for worn brushes and weak brush springs.
	• High load current	• Bench-test starter motor. Check engine for friction, drag or coolant in cylinders. Check ring gear-to-pinion gear clearance.
Starter motor will not rotate engine	• Battery charge low or battery defective	• Charge or replace battery
	• Faulty solenoid	• Check solenoid ground. Repair or replace as necessary.
	• Damaged drive pinion gear or ring gear	• Replace damaged gear(s)
	• Starter motor engagement weak	• Bench-test starter motor
	• Starter motor rotates slowly with high load current	• Inspect drive yoke pull-down and point gap, check for worn end bushings, check ring gear clearance
	• Engine seized	• Repair engine
Starter motor drive will not engage (solenoid known to be good)	• Defective contact point assembly	• Repair or replace contact point assembly
	• Inadequate contact point assembly ground	• Repair connection at ground screw
	• Defective hold-in coil	• Replace field winding assembly
Starter motor drive will not disengage	• Starter motor loose on flywheel housing	• Tighten mounting bolts
	• Worn drive end busing	• Replace bushing
	• Damaged ring gear teeth	• Replace ring gear or driveplate
	• Drive yoke return spring broken or missing	• Replace spring
Starter motor drive disengages prematurely	• Weak drive assembly thrust spring	• Replace drive mechanism
	• Hold-in coil defective	• Replace field winding assembly
Low load current	• Worn brushes	• Replace brushes
	• Weak brush springs	• Replace springs

ENGINE PERFORMANCE AND TUNE-UP

Troubleshooting Basic Charging System Problems

Problem	Cause	Solution
Noisy alternator	• Loose mountings • Loose drive pulley • Worn bearings • Brush noise • Internal circuits shorted (High pitched whine)	• Tighten mounting bolts • Tighten pulley • Replace alternator • Replace alternator • Replace alternator
Squeal when starting engine or accelerating	• Glazed or loose belt	• Replace or adjust belt
Indicator light remains on or ammeter indicates discharge (engine running)	• Broken belt • Broken or disconnected wires • Internal alternator problems • Defective voltage regulator	• Install belt • Repair or connect wiring • Replace alternator • Replace voltage regulator/alternator
Car light bulbs continually burn out—battery needs water continually	• Alternator/regulator overcharging	• Replace voltage regulator/alternator
Car lights flare on acceleration	• Battery low • Internal alternator/regulator problems	• Charge or replace battery • Replace alternator/regulator
Low voltage output (alternator light flickers continually or ammeter needle wanders)	• Loose or worn belt • Dirty or corroded connections • Internal alternator/regulator problems	• Replace or adjust belt • Clean or replace connections • Replace alternator/regulator

ENGINE ELECTRICAL 3-2
IGNITION COIL 3-2
    TESTING 3-2
    REMOVAL & INSTALLATION 3-2
DISTRIBUTOR 3-3
    REMOVAL 3-3
    INSTALLATION 3-3
ALTERNATOR 3-5
    ALTERNATOR PRECAUTIONS 3-5
    REMOVAL & INSTALLATION 3-5
REGULATOR 3-5
    REMOVAL & INSTALLATION 3-5
    ADJUSTMENT 3-6
STARTER 3-8
    REMOVAL & INSTALLATION 3-8
    OVERHAUL 3-8
BATTERY 3-9
    REMOVAL & INSTALLATION 3-9
ENGINE MECHANICAL 3-9
ENGINE OVERHAUL TIPS 3-9
    TOOLS 3-9
    INSPECTION TECHNIQUES 3-9
    OVERHAUL TIPS 3-9
    REPAIRING DAMAGED THREADS 3-9
CHECKING ENGINE COMPRESSION 3-10
ENGINE 3-10
    REMOVAL & INSTALLATION 3-10
CYLINDER HEAD COVER 3-13
    REMOVAL & INSTALLATION 3-13
ROCKER ARMS AND ROCKER PIVOTS 3-13
    REMOVAL & INSTALLATION 3-13
ROCKER ARM/SHAFT ASSEMBLY 3-13
    REMOVAL & INSTALLATION 3-13
    INSPECTION 3-15
THERMOSTAT 3-15
    REMOVAL & INSTALLATION 3-15
INTAKE MANIFOLD 3-16
    REMOVAL & INSTALLATION 3-16
EXHAUST MANIFOLD 3-18
    REMOVAL & INSTALLATION 3-18
AIR CONDITIONING COMPRESSOR 3-19
    REMOVAL & INSTALLATION 3-19
AIR CONDITIONING CONDENSER 3-20
    REMOVAL & INSTALLATION 3-20
RADIATOR 3-20
    REMOVAL & INSTALLATION 3-20
WATER PUMP 3-21
    REMOVAL & INSTALLATION 3-21
CYLINDER HEAD 3-22
    REMOVAL & INSTALLATION 3-22
    CLEANING AND INSPECTION 3-26
    RESURFACING 3-26
    CYLINDER BLOCK CLEANING 3-26
VALVES AND SPRINGS 3-27
    ADJUSTMENT (AFTER ENGINE
      SERVICE) 3-27
    REMOVAL & INSTALLATION 3-27
    INSPECTION 3-28
    REFACING 3-29
VALVE SPRINGS 3-29
    INSPECTION 3-29
VALVE GUIDES 3-29
    INSPECTION 3-29
    REMOVAL & INSTALLATION 3-29
OIL PAN 3-30
    REMOVAL & INSTALLATION 3-30
OIL PUMP 3-31
    REMOVAL & INSTALLATION 3-31
TIMING CHAIN COVER 3-32
    REMOVAL & INSTALLATION 3-32
TIMING BELT COVER 3-34
    REMOVAL & INSTALLATION 3-34
FRONT OIL SEAL 3-34
    REMOVAL & INSTALLATION 3-34
TIMING CHAIN AND TENSIONER 3-35
    REMOVAL & INSTALLATION 3-35
    TIMING CHAIN ADJUSTMENT 3-37
TIMING BELT 3-37
    REMOVAL & INSTALLATION 3-37
CAMSHAFT SPROCKET/PULLEYS 3-39
    REMOVAL & INSTALLATION 3-39
CAMSHAFT 3-39
    REMOVAL & INSTALLATION 3-39
    CHECKING CAMSHAFT RUNOUT 3-40
    CHECKING CAMSHAFT LOBE
      HEIGHT 3-41
    CHECKING CAMSHAFT JOURNALS AND
      CAMSHAFT BEARING SADDLES 3-41
    CHECKING CAMSHAFT ENDPLAY 3-41
PISTONS AND CONNECTING RODS 3-41
    REMOVAL & INSTALLATION 3-41
    IDENTIFICATION AND POSITIONING 3-42
    PISTON RING REPLACEMENT 3-43
    WRIST PIN REMOVAL &
      INSTALLATION 3-44
    CLEANING AND INSPECTION 3-44
    CYLINDER BORE INSPECTION 3-45
    CONNECTING ROD INSPECTION AND
      BEARING REPLACEMENT 3-45
REAR MAIN OIL SEAL 3-46
    REPLACEMENT 3-46
CRANKSHAFT AND MAIN BEARING 3-47
    REMOVAL & INSTALLATION 3-47
    INSPECTION 3-47
    MAIN BEARING CLEARANCE
      CHECK 3-48
    MAIN BEARING REPLACEMENT 3-48
FLYWHEEL AND RING GEAR 3-49
    REMOVAL & INSTALLATION 3-49
EXHAUST SYSTEM 3-50
    INSPECTION 3-50
FRONT PIPE 3-50
    REMOVAL & INSTALLATION 3-50
CATALYTIC CONVERTER 3-51
    REMOVAL & INSTALLATION 3-51
TAILPIPE AND MUFFLER 3-51
    REMOVAL & INSTALLATION 3-51
SPECIFICATIONS CHARTS
    ALTERNATOR AND REGULATOR
      SPECIFICATIONS 3-7
    BATTERY AND STARTER
      SPECIFICATIONS 3-7
    GENERAL ENGINE
      SPECIFICATIONS 3-52
    VALVE SPECIFICATIONS 3-52
    CAMSHAFT SPECIFICATIONS 3-53
    CRANKSHAFT AND CONNECTING RODS
      SPECIFICATIONS 3-54
    PISTON AND RING
      SPECIFICATIONS 3-55
    TORQUE SPECIFICATIONS 3-56
TROUBLESHOOTING CHARTS 3-58
    ENGINE MECHANICAL PROBLEMS 3-59
    ENGINE PERFORMANCE 3-60

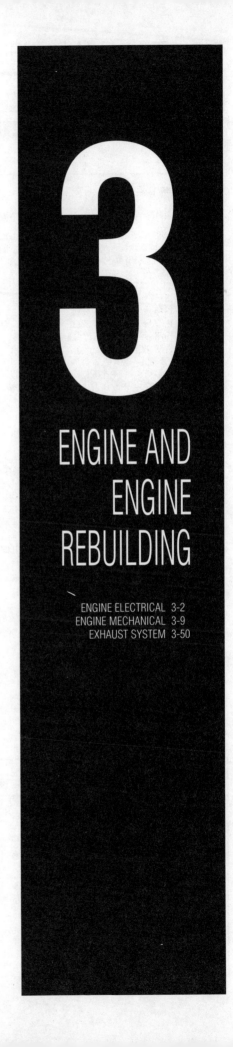

3

ENGINE AND ENGINE REBUILDING

ENGINE ELECTRICAL 3-2
ENGINE MECHANICAL 3-9
EXHAUST SYSTEM 3-50

ENGINE AND ENGINE REBUILDING

ENGINE ELECTRICAL

Ignition Coil

TESTING

♦ See Figures 1, 2, 3 and 4

Primary Resistance Check

In order to check the coil primary resistance, you must first disconnect all wires from the ignition coil terminals. Using an ohmmeter, check the resistance between the positive (15) and the negative (1) terminals on the coil. The resistance should be:

- L16 and L18—1.17–1.43Ω;
- L20B (1975)—1.17–1.43Ω;
- L20B (1976 Fed.)—1.17–1.43Ω;
- L20B (1977 Fed.)—1.08–1.32Ω;
- L20B (1976–77 Calif.)—0.45–0.55Ω;
- L20B (1978–80)—0.84–1.02Ω;
- Z22 (1981–83)—1.04–1.27Ω;
- Z20 (1984–86)—0.84–1.02Ω;
- Z24 (1984–87)—1.05–1.27Ω;
- Z24i (1986–88)—0.80–1.00Ω;
- VG30i (1986–88)—0.80–1.00Ω;

➡Remember that all Z20, Z22, Z24 and Z24i engines have 2 ignition coils; check them both!

If the resistance is not within these tolerances, the coil will require replacement.

Secondary Resistance Check

In order to check the coil secondary resistance, you must first disconnect all wires from the ignition coil terminals. Using an ohmmeter, check the resistance between the positive (15) terminal and the coil wire (4) terminal. The resistance should be:

- L16 and L18—11,200–16,800Ω;
- L20B (1975)—11,200–16,800Ω;
- L20B (1976 Fed.)—11,200–16,800Ω;
- L20B (1977 Fed.)—8,240–12,400Ω;
- L20B (1976–77 Calif.)—8,500–12,700Ω;
- L20B (1978–80)—8,200–12,400Ω;
- Z22 (1981–83)—7,300–11,000Ω;
- Z20 (1984–86)—8,300–12,600Ω;
- Z24 (1984–87)—8,400–12,600Ω;
- Z24i (1986–88)—7,600–11,400Ω;
- VG30i (1986–88)—7,600–11,400Ω;

➡Remember that all Z20, Z22, Z24 and Z24i engines have 2 ignition coils; check them both!

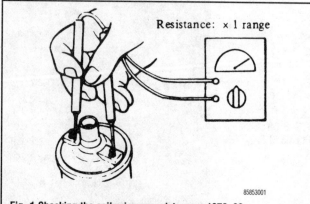

Fig. 1 Checking the coil primary resistance—1970–86

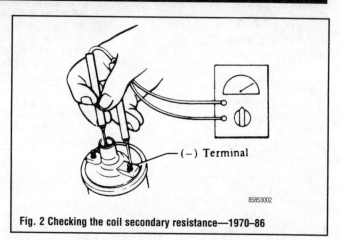

Fig. 2 Checking the coil secondary resistance—1970–86

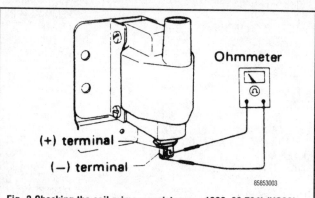

Fig. 3 Checking the coil primary resistance—1986–88 Z24i (VG30i similar)

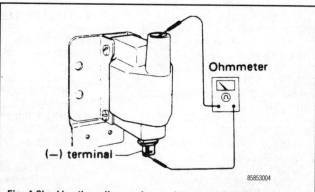

Fig. 4 Checking the coil secondary resistance—1986–88 Z24i (VG30i similar)

If the resistance is not within these tolerances, the coil will require replacement.

REMOVAL & INSTALLATION

1. Disconnect the negative battery cable.
2. Tag and disconnect all electrical leads at the coil.
3. Remove the mounting bolts and lift off the ignition coil.

To install:

4. Install the coil in position and tighten the mounting bolts.
5. Connect all wires.
6. Connect the negative battery cable.

ENGINE AND ENGINE REBUILDING   3-3

Distributor

▶ See Figures 5 thru 14

REMOVAL

To remove the distributor, proceed in the following order:
1. Unfasten the retaining clips and lift the distributor cap straight off. It will be easier to install the distributor if the wiring is left connected to the cap. If the wires must be removed from the cap, mark their positions to aid in installation.
2. Remove the dust cover and mark the position of the rotor relative to the distributor body; then mark the position of the body relative to the block.
3. Disconnect the coil primary wire and the vacuum lines, mark which is which for installation.
4. Remove the pinch-bolt and lift the distributor straight out, away from the engine. The rotor and body are marked so that they can be returned to the position from which they were removed. Do not turn or disturb the engine (unless absolutely necessary, such as for engine rebuilding), after the distributor has been removed.

INSTALLATION

Timing Not Disturbed

1. Insert the distributor in the block and align the matchmarks made during removal.

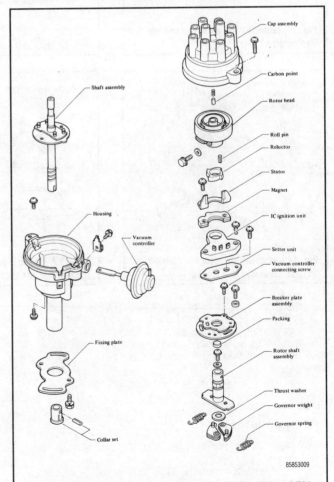

Fig. 6 Exploded view of the distributor—1979–80

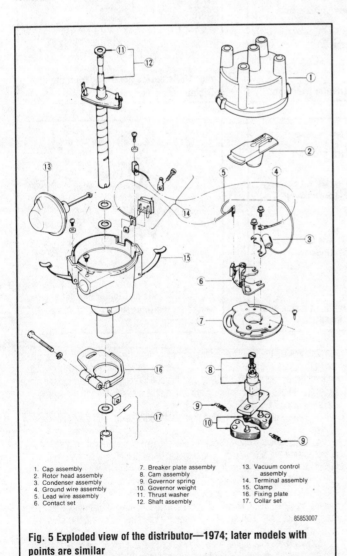

Fig. 5 Exploded view of the distributor—1974; later models with points are similar

Fig. 7 Exploded view of the distributor—1981–86 Z20, Z22 and Z24 engines

3-4 ENGINE AND ENGINE REBUILDING

Fig. 8 Matchmark the distributor rotor to distributor body

Fig. 9 Matchmark the distributor body to engine block

Fig. 10 Removing the distributor hold-down

Fig. 11 Removing the electrical connection on distributor

Fig. 12 View of the distributor assembly

Fig. 13 Removing the O-ring from the distributor assembly

Fig. 14 Removing the rotor after the distributor assembly is removed

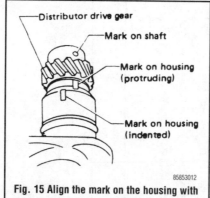

Fig. 15 Align the mark on the housing with the mark on the shaft—VG30i

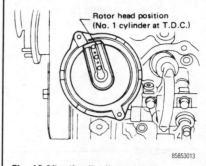

Fig. 16 After the distributor has been installed, the rotor should be in this position—VG30i

2. Engage the distributor driven gear with the distributor drive.
3. Install the distributor clamp and secure it with the pinch-bolt.
4. Install the cap, primary wire, and vacuum line(s).
5. Install the spark plug leads. Consult the marks made during removal to be sure that the proper lead goes to each plug. Install the high tension wire if it was removed.
6. Start the engine. Check the timing and adjust it if necessary.

Timing Lost

◆ See Figures 15 and 16

If the engine has been cranked, dismantled, or the timing otherwise lost, proceed as follows:

1. It is necessary to place the No. 1 cylinder in the firing position to correctly install the distributor. To locate this position, the ignition timing marks on the crankshaft front pulley are used.

2. Remove the No. 1 cylinder spark plug. Turn the crankshaft until the piston in the No. 1 cylinder is moving up on the compression stroke. This can be determined by placing your thumb over the spark plug hole and feeling the air being forced out of the cylinder. Stop turning the crankshaft when the timing marks indicate **TDC** or **0**.

3. Oil the distributor housing lightly where the distributor bears on the cylinder block.

4. Install the distributor so that the rotor, which is mounted on the shaft, points toward the No. 1 spark plug terminal tower position when the cap is installed. Of course you won't be able to see the direction in which the rotor is pointing if the cap is on the distributor. Lay the cap on the top of the distributor and make a mark on the side of the housing just below the No.1 spark plug terminal plug terminal. Make sure that the rotor points toward that mark when you install the distributor. On the VG30i, align the mark on the distributor shaft with the **protruding** mark on the housing.

5. When the distributor shaft has reached the bottom of the hole, move the rotor back and forth slightly until the driving lug on the end of the shaft enter

ENGINE AND ENGINE REBUILDING 3-5

the slots cut in the end of the oil pump shaft and the distributor assembly slides down into place.

6. When the distributor is correctly installed, the breaker points should be in such a position that they are just ready to break contact with each other or a lobe of the reluctor is aligned with the stator contact. This is accomplished by rotating the distributor body after it has been installed in the engine. Once again, line up the marks that you made before the distributor was removed from the engine. On the VG30i, the distributor rotor should be in the 11:25 o'clock position (between 11 and 12 o'clock).

7. Install the distributor hold-down bolt.
8. Install the spark plugs.
9. Install the cap, primary wire, and vacuum line(s).
10. Install the spark plug leads. Consult the marks made during removal to be sure that the proper lead goes to each plug. Install the high tension wire if it was removed.
11. Start the engine. Check the timing and adjust it if necessary.

Alternator

The alternator converts the mechanical energy supplied by the drive belt into electrical energy by a process of electromagnetic induction. When the ignition switch is turned ON, current flows from the battery through the charging system light (or ammeter) to the voltage regulator, and finally to the alternator. When the engine is started, the drive belt turns the rotating field (rotor) in the stationary windings (stator), inducing alternating current. This alternating current is converted into usable direct current by the diode rectifier. Most of this current is used to charge the battery and to supply power for the vehicle's electrical accessories. A small part of this current is returned to the field windings of the alternator enabling it to increase its power output. When the current in the field windings reaches a predetermined level, the voltage regulator grounds the circuit preventing any further increase. The cycle is continued so that the voltage supply remains constant.

All models use a 12 volt alternator. Amperage ratings vary according to the year and model. 1970–77 models utilize a separate, adjustable regulator, while 1978–88 models have a transistorized, nonadjustable regulator, integral with the alternator.

ALTERNATOR PRECAUTIONS

To prevent damage to the alternator and regulator, the following precautionary measures must be taken when working with the electrical system.
- Never reverse the battery connections. Always check the battery polarity visually. This is to be done before any connections are made to ensure that all of the connections correspond to the battery ground polarity of the truck
- Booster batteries must be connected properly. Make sure the positive cable of the booster battery is connected to the positive terminal of the battery which is getting the boost
- Disconnect the battery cables before using a fast charger; the charger has a tendency to force current through the diodes in the opposite direction for which they were designed
- Never use a fast charger as a booster for starting the truck
- Never disconnect the voltage regulator while the engine is running, unless as noted for testing purposes
- Do not ground the alternator output terminal
- Do not operate the alternator on an open circuit with the field energized
- Do not attempt to polarize the alternator
- Disconnect the battery cables and remove the alternator before using an electric arc welder on the truck
- Protect the alternator from excessive moisture. If the engine is to be steam cleaned, cover or remove the alternator

REMOVAL & INSTALLATION

♦ See Figures 17 and 18

➡ On some models, the alternator is mounted very low on the engine. On these models, it may be necessary to remove the gravel shield and work from beneath the truck in order to gain access to the alternator.

1. Disconnect the negative battery cable.
2. Remove the alternator pivot bolt. Push the alternator in and remove the drive belt.
3. Pull back the rubber boots and disconnect the wiring from the back of the alternator.

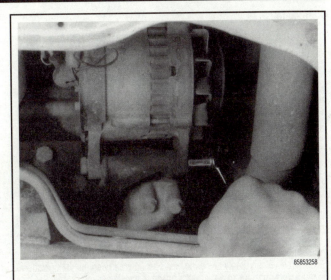

Fig. 17 Removing the alternator lower mounting bolt

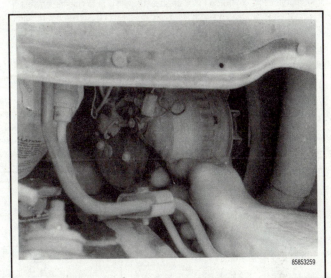

Fig. 18 Removing the alternator electrical connection

4. Remove the alternator mounting bolt and then withdraw the alternator from its bracket.

To install:

5. Position the alternator in its mounting bracket and lightly tighten the mounting and adjusting bolts.
6. Connect the electrical leads at the rear of the alternator.
7. Adjust the belt tension as detailed in Section 1.

Regulator

All 1970–77 models are equipped with a separate, adjustable regulator. All 1978–88 models are equipped with a transistorized regulator which is attached to the brush assembly on the side of the alternator housing. If faulty, it must be replaced; there are no adjustments which can be made.

REMOVAL & INSTALLATION

1970–77

1. Disconnect the negative battery cable.
2. Disconnect the wiring harness connector at the back of the regulator.
3. Remove the regulator mounting bolts.
4. Remove the regulator.

3-6 ENGINE AND ENGINE REBUILDING

To install:

5. Install the regulator and tighten the mounting bolts.
6. Connect the wiring harness and the negative battery cable.

1978–88

The transistorized regulator is soldered to the brush assembly inside the alternator. It is non-adjustable, and must be replaced together with the brush assembly if faulty.

1. Remove the alternator.
2. Remove the thru-bolts and separate the front cover from the stator housing.
3. Unsolder the wire connecting the diode plate to brush at the brush terminal.
4. Remove the bolt retaining the diode plate to the rear cover.
5. Remove the nut securing the battery terminal bolt.
6. Lift the stator slightly, together with the diode plate, to gain access to the diode plate screw. Remove the screw.
7. Separate the stator and diode, then remove the brush and regulator assembly.
8. On assembly, apply soldering heat sparingly, carrying out the operation as quickly as possible, to avoid heat damage to transistors and diodes. Before assembling the alternator halves, bend a piece of wire into an L-shape and slip it through the rear cover next to the brushes. Use the wire to hold the brushes in a retracted position until the case halves are assembled. Remove the wire carefully, to prevent damage to the slip rings.

ADJUSTMENT

1970–72

♦ See Figures 19, 20 and 21

1. Operate the alternator long enough to raise the temperature of the regulator to normal operating temperature.
2. Adjust the back gap of the voltage regulator coil by loosening the armature set screw and sliding the armature. The gap should be 0.035–0.039 in. (0.89–1.00mm).
3. Adjust the air gap of the voltage regulator coil by bending the primary contact support to the right or left with a pair of needlenose pliers. The gap should be 0.032–0.047 in. (0.80–1.20mm).
4. Adjust the point gap by bending the secondary contact support to the right or left with pliers. The gap should be 0.016–0.020 in. (0.40–0.50mm).
5. Adjust the pilot lamp relay coil yoke gap by loosening the armature set screw, adjusting the gap and retightening the set screw. The gap should be 0.008 in. (0.20mm).
6. Adjust the pilot lamp relay coil air gap by loosening the contact set screw and inserting a screwdriver in the hole provided and moving the points up or down. The gap should be 0.020–0.024 in. (0.50–0.60mm).
7. Adjust the pilot lamp relay coil point gap by loosening the contact point retaining screw and inserting a screwdriver in the hole provided and moving the point contact either up or down. The gap should be between 0.016–0.020 in. (0.40–0.50mm).
8. Adjust the voltage valve by bending the stopper on the voltage regulator coil. The regulated voltage should be between 14–15 volts at 4000 alternator rpm.

1973–77

♦ See Figures 22, 23 and 24

1. Adjust the voltage regulator core gap by loosening the screw which is used to secure the contact set on the yoke, and move the contact up or down as necessary. Retighten the screw. The gap should be 0.024–0.039 in. (0.60–1.00mm).
2. Adjust the point gap of the voltage regulator coil by loosening the screw used to secure the upper contact and move the upper contact up or down. The gap should be 0.012–0.016 in. (0.30–0.40mm) for 1973–75 models or 0.014–0.018 in. (0.35–0.45mm) for 1976–77 models.
3. The core gap and point gap on the charge relay coil is or are adjusted in the same manner as previously outlined for the voltage regulator coil. The core

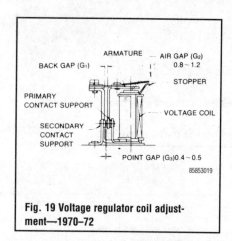

Fig. 19 Voltage regulator coil adjustment—1970–72

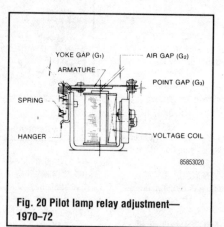

Fig. 20 Pilot lamp relay adjustment—1970–72

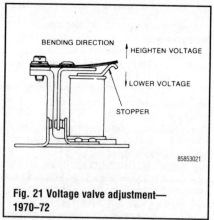

Fig. 21 Voltage valve adjustment—1970–72

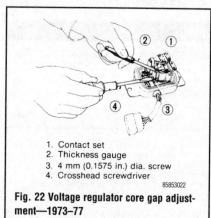

Fig. 22 Voltage regulator core gap adjustment—1973–77

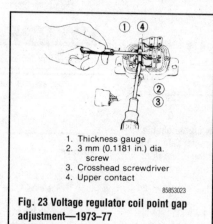

Fig. 23 Voltage regulator coil point gap adjustment—1973–77

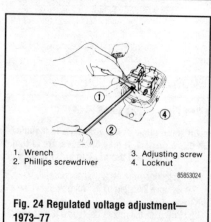

Fig. 24 Regulated voltage adjustment—1973–77

ENGINE AND ENGINE REBUILDING 3-7

Alternator and Regulator Specifications

Year	Alternator Manufacturer and/or Part Number	Output @ Generator rpm	Charge Indicator Relay Back Gap (in.)	Charge Indicator Relay Air Gap (in.)	Charge Indicator Relay Point Gap (in.)	Voltage Regulator Back Gap (in.)	Voltage Regulator Air Gap (in.)	Voltage Regulator Point Gap (in.)	Regulated Voltage
1970–72	Hitachi LT130–41	22 Amp @ 2500 (14 volts)	0.007	0.022	0.018	0.037	0.039	0.014	14–15
1973	Hitachi LT135–13B	28 Amp @ 2500 (14 volts)	—	0.035	0.020	—	0.032	0.014	14–15
1974	Hitachi LT135–13B	28 Amp @ 2500 (14 volts)	—	0.035	0.020	—	0.032	0.014	14–15
1975	Hitachi LT135–13B LT135–19B ①	28 Amp @ 2500 (14 volts)	—	0.035	0.020	—	0.032	0.014	14–15
1976	Hitachi LT135–13B LT135–19B ①	28 @ 2500	—	0.035	0.020	—	0.032	0.016	14.3–15.3
1977	Hitachi LT135–36B LT138–01B ①	28 @ 2500 30 @ 2500	—	0.035	0.020	—	0.032	0.016	14.3–15.3
1978–80	Hitachi LR135–44 LR138–01 ①	27.5 @ 2500 30.0 @ 2500	—Transistorized Non-Adjustable Relay—						14.4–15.0
1981–84	Hitachi LR150–98 LR160–98 LR150–52 LR160–78	50 @ 5000 60 @ 5000 50 @ 5000 60 @ 5000	—Transistorized Non-Adjustable Relay—						14.4–15.0
1985–88	Hitachi LR150–98B LR150–197B LR160–78B LR160–140B LR150–177 LR150–194B LR160–120 LR160–151 LR160–154 LR160–422B LR150–403 LR155–401	50 @ 5000 50 @ 5000 60 @ 5000 60 @ 5000 50 @ 5000 60 @ 5000 60 @ 5000 60 @ 5000 60 @ 5000 60 @ 5000 50 @ 5000 55 @ 5000	—Transistorized Non-Adjustable Relay—						14.4–15.0 ②

① With air conditioning — Non applicable
② LR160–151: 14.1–14.7

Battery and Starter Specifications

Year	Engine	Battery Amp Hour Capacity	Battery Volts	Battery Ground	Starter Lock Test Amps	Starter Lock Test Volts	Starter Lock Test Torque (ft. lbs.)	Starter No Load Test Amps	Starter No Load Test Volts	Starter No Load Test RPM	Starter Brush Spring Tension (oz)
1970–72	L16	①	12	Neg	350	10.5	7.95	60	12	7000+ ②	28
1973	L16	①	12	Neg	Not Recommended			60	12	7000+ ②	56
1973–74	L18	①	12	Neg	Not Recommended			60	12	7000+ ②	56
1975–80	L20B	①	12	Neg	Not Recommended			60	12	7000+ ②	56
1981–83	Z20, 22, 24	④	12	Neg	Not Recommended			60 ③	11.5 ④	6000–7000	56
1984–86	SD22, 25	①	12	Neg	800	5.0	21.0	55	12	6500	123.2
1984–86	Z20, Z24 SD25 (720 series)	⑤	12	Neg	Not Recommended			⑥	⑦	⑧	⑧
1986–88	Z24i, VG30i, SD25 (D21 series)	⑩	12	Neg	Not Recommended			⑪	⑫	⑬	⑭

① 40, 50, or 69 amp hour batteries were available
② 6000+ if equipped with automatic transmission
③ Canada: 100
④ Canada: 11.0
⑤ U.S.A.: 60 amp., (65 optional)
  Canada: 65 amp.
  Diesel: 80 amp.
⑥ U.S.A.: 60 amp.
  Canada: 100 amp.
  Diesel: 150 amp.
⑦ U.S.A.: 11.5 volt
  Canada: 11 volt
  Diesel: 12 volt
⑧ U.S.A. w/A.T.: 6,000 rpm
  U.S.A. w/M.T.: 7,000 rpm
  Diesel: 3,500 rpm
⑨ U.S.A.: 72 oz.
  Canada: 64 oz.
  Diesel: 128 oz.
⑩ U.S.A.: 60 amp
  Canada: Z24i—65 amp.
  VG30i—70 amp.,
  Diesel—65 amp.
⑪ VG30i eng: 90 amp.
  2WD (4 cyl.): 60 amp.
  4WD (4 cyl.): 100 amp.
  Diesel: 160 amp.
⑫ VG30i eng: 11.0
  2WD (4 cyl.): 11.5
  4WD (4 cyl.): 11.0
  Diesel: 11.0
⑬ VG30i: 2,650 rpm
  2WD w/A.T.: 7,000 rpm
  2WD w/M.T.: 6,000 rpm
  4WD: 3,900 rpm
  Diesel: 3,900 rpm
⑭ 2WD: 72 oz.
  4WD: 64 oz.
  Diesel: 104 oz.

3-8 ENGINE AND ENGINE REBUILDING

gap is to be set at 0.032–0.039 in. (0.80–1.00mm) and the point gap adjusted to 0.016–0.024 in. (0.40–0.60mm).

4. The regulated voltage is adjusted by loosening the lock-nut and turning the adjusting screw clockwise to increase, or counterclockwise to decrease the regulated voltage. The voltage should be between 14.3–15.3 volts at 68°F (20°C).

1978–88

Regulators on these models are not adjustable.

Starter

REMOVAL & INSTALLATION

◆ See Figures 25 and 26

➡On some models with automatic transmission, it may be necessary to disconnect the throttle rod.

1. Disconnect the negative (–) battery cable at the battery, then disconnect the positive (+) battery cable at the starter.
2. Disconnect the remaining electrical connections at the starter solenoid.

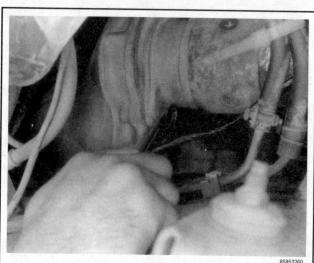

Fig. 25 Removing the starter mounting bolts

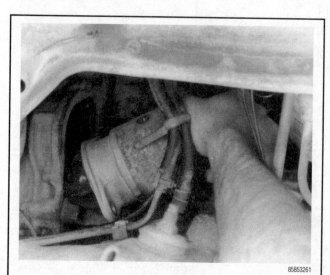

Fig. 26 Removing the starter assembly

3. Remove the two nuts holding the starter to the bell housing and pull the starter toward the front of the vehicle.
4. To install the unit, insert the starter into the bell housing being sure that the starter drive is not jammed against the flywheel. Tighten the attaching nuts EVENLY and replace all electrical connections making the battery connection the last.

OVERHAUL

Solenoid Replacement

1. Remove the starter.
2. Unscrew the two solenoid switch (magnetic switch) retaining screws.
3. Remove the solenoid. In order to unhook the solenoid from the starter drive lever, lift it up at the same time that you are pulling it out of the starter housing.
4. Installation is in the reverse order of removal. Make sure that the solenoid switch is properly engaged with the drive lever before tightening the mounting screws.

Brush Replacement

NON-REDUCTION GEAR TYPE

1. Remove the starter.
2. Remove the solenoid (magnetic switch).
3. Remove the two end frame cap mounting bolts and remove the end frame cap.
4. Remove the O-ring and lock plate from the armature shaft groove and then slide the shims off the shaft.
5. Unscrew the two long housing screws (they are found at the front of the starter) and carefully pull off the end plate.
6. Using a screwdriver, separate the brushes from the brush holder.
7. Slide the brush holder off of the armature shaft.
8. Crush the old brushes off of the copper braid and file away any remaining solder.
9. Fit the new brushes to the braid and spread the braid slightly.

➡Use a soldering iron of at least 250 watts.

10. Solder the brush to the braid using a radio-grade solder. Grip the copper braid with flat pliers to prevent the solder from flowing down its length.
11. File off any extra solder and then repeat the procedure for the remaining three brushes.
12. Installation is in the reverse order of removal.

➡When installing the brush holder, make sure that the brushes line up properly.

REDUCTION GEAR TYPE

1. Remove the starter. Remove the solenoid.
2. Remove the thru-bolts and the rear cover. The rear cover can be pried off with a small prybar, but be careful not to damage the O-ring.
3. Remove the starter housing, armature, and brush holder from the center housing. They can be removed as an assembly.
4. Remove the positive side brush from its holder. The positive brush is insulated from the brush holder, and its lead wire is connected to the field coil.
5. Carefully lift the negative brush from the commutator and remove it form the holder.
6. Installation is in the reverse order of removal.

Starter Drive Replacement

NON-REDUCTION GEAR TYPE

1. With the starter motor removed from the vehicle, remove the solenoid from the starter.
2. Remove the two through-bolts and separate the gear case from the yoke housing.
3. Remove the pinion stopper clip and the pinion stopper.
4. Slide the starter drive off the armature shaft.
5. Install the starter drive and reassemble the starter in the reverse order of removal.

ENGINE AND ENGINE REBUILDING 3-9

REDUCTION GEAR TYPE

1. Remove the starter.
2. Remove the solenoid and the shift lever.
3. Remove the bolts securing the center housing to the front cover and separate the parts.
4. Remove the gears and starter drive.
5. Installation is in the reverse order of removal.

Battery

Refer to Section 1 for details on battery maintenance.

REMOVAL & INSTALLATION

1. Disconnect the negative battery cable from the terminal, then disconnect the positive cable. Special pullers are available to remove post clamps.

➡ To avoid sparks, always disconnect the negative cable first and reconnect it last.

2. Unscrew and remove the battery hold-down clamp.
3. Remove the battery, being careful not to spill any of the acid.

➡ Spilled acid can be neutralized with a baking soda and water solution. If you somehow get acid into your eyes, flush it out with lots of clean water and get to a doctor as quickly as possible.

To install:

4. Clean the battery terminals thoroughly before reinstalling or when installing a new one.
5. Clean the cable clamps using the special tools or a wire brush, both inside and out.
6. Install the battery, and the hold-down clamp. Connect the positive and then the negative cable. Do not hammer post clamps into place. The terminals should be coated with grease to prevent corrosion.

✳✳ CAUTION

Make absolutely sure that the battery is connected properly before you turn on the ignition switch. Reversed polarity can burn out our alternator and regulator in a matter of seconds.

ENGINE MECHANICAL

Engine Overhaul Tips

Most engine overhaul procedures are fairly standard. In addition to specific parts replacement procedures and complete specifications for your individual engine, this section also is a guide to accept rebuilding procedures. Examples of standard rebuilding practice are shown and should be used along with specific details concerning your particular engine.

Competent and accurate machine shop services will ensure maximum performance, reliability and engine life. Certain procedures marked with the symbol shown above should be performed by a competent machine shop, and are provided so that you will be familiar with the procedures necessary for a successful overhaul.

In most instances it is more profitable for the do-it-yourself mechanic to remove, clean and inspect the component, buy the necessary parts and deliver these to a shop for actual machine work.

On the other hand, much of the rebuilding work (crankshaft, block, bearings, piston rods, and other components) is well within the scope of the do-it-yourself mechanic.

TOOLS

The tools required for an engine overhaul or parts replacement will depend on the depth of your involvement. With a few exceptions, they will be the tools found in a mechanic's tool kit (see Section 1). More in-depth work will require any or all of the following:

- a dial indicator (reading in thousandths) mounted on a universal base
- micrometers and telescope gauges
- jaw and screw type pullers
- scraper
- valve spring compressor
- ring groove cleaner
- piston ring expander and compressor
- ridge reamer
- cylinder hone or glaze breaker
- Plastigage®
- engine stand

Use of most of these tools is covered in this section. Many can be rented for a one-time use from a local parts jobber or tool supply house specializing in automotive work.

Occasionally, the use of special tools is recommended. See the information on Special Tools and Safety Notice in the front of this book before substituting another tool.

INSPECTION TECHNIQUES

Procedures and specifications are given in this section for inspecting, cleaning and assessing the wear limits of most major components. Other procedures such as Magnaflux® and Zyglo® can be used to locate material flaws and stress cracks. Magnaflux® is a magnetic process applicable only to ferrous materials. The Zyglo® process coats the material with a fluorescent dye penetrant and can be used on any material Check for suspected surface cracks can be more readily made using spot check dye. The dye is sprayed onto the suspected area, wiped off and the area sprayed with a developer. Cracks will show up brightly.

OVERHAUL TIPS

Aluminum has become extremely popular for use in engines, due to its low weight. Observe the following precautions when handling aluminum parts:

- Never hot tank aluminum parts (the caustic hot-tank solution will eat the aluminum.
- Remove all aluminum parts (identification tag, etc.) from engine parts prior to the tanking.
- Always coat threads lightly with engine oil or anti-seize compounds before installation, to prevent seizure.
- Never overtorque bolts or spark plugs especially in aluminum threads.

Stripped threads in any component can be repaired using any of several commercial repair kits (Heli-Coil®, Microdot®, Keenserts®, etc.).

When assembling the engine, any parts that will be subject to frictional contact must be prelubed to provide lubrication at initial start up. Any product specifically formulated for this purpose can be used, but engine oil is not recommended as a prelube.

When semi-permanent (locked, but removable) installation of bolts or nuts is desired, threads should be cleaned and coated with Loctite® or other similar, commercial non-hardening sealant.

REPAIRING DAMAGED THREADS

▶ See Figures 27, 28, 29, 30 and 31

Several methods of repairing damaged threads are available. Heli-Coil® (shown here), Keenserts® and Microdot® are among the most widely used. All involve basically the same principle, drilling out stripped threads, tapping the hole and installing a prewound insert, making welding, plugging and oversize fasteners unnecessary.

Two types of thread repair inserts are usually supplied: a standard type for most Inch Coarse, Inch Fine, Metric Course and Metric Fine thread sizes and a spark lug type to fit most spark plug port sizes. Consult the individual manufacturer's catalog to determine exact applications. Typical thread repair kits will contain a selection of prewound threaded inserts, a tap (corresponding to the outside diameter threads of the insert) and an installation tool. Spark plug inserts usually differ because they require a tap equipped with pilot threads and a combined reamer/tap section. Most manufacturers also supply blister packed thread repair inserts separately in addition to a master kit containing a variety of taps and inserts plus installation tools.

Before attempting to repair a threaded hole, remove any snapped, broken or

3-10 ENGINE AND ENGINE REBUILDING

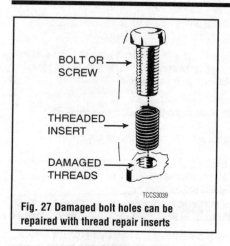

Fig. 27 Damaged bolt holes can be repaired with thread repair inserts

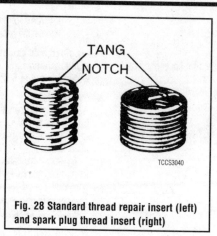

Fig. 28 Standard thread repair insert (left) and spark plug thread insert (right)

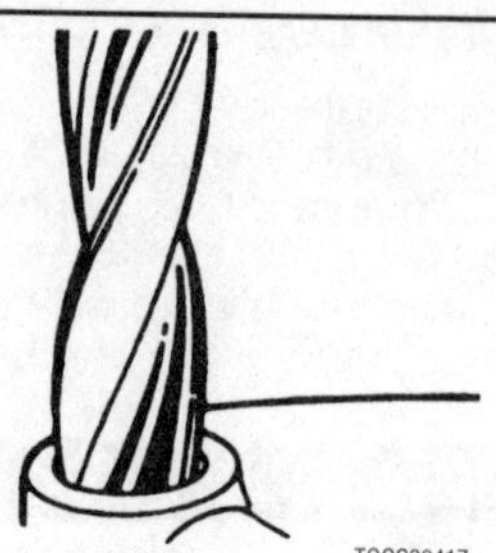

Fig. 29 Drill out the damaged threads with specified drill bit—Be sure to drill completely through the hole or to the bottom of a blind hole

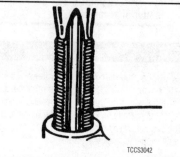

Fig. 30 With the tap supplied, tap the hole to receive the thread insert—Keep the tap well oiled and back it out frequently to avoid clogging the threads

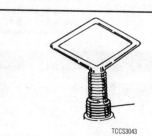

Fig. 31 Screw the threaded insert onto the installation tool until the tang engages the slot—Screw the insert into the tapped hole until it is 1/4–1/2 turn below the top surface. After installation break off the tang with a hammer and punch

Fig. 32 The screw-in type compression gauge is more accurate

damaged bolts or studs. Penetrating oil can be used to free frozen threads; the offending item can be removed with locking pliers or with a screw or stud extractor. After the hole is clear, the thread can be repaired as shown in the series of illustrations or the kit manufacturer's instructions.

Checking Engine Compression

▶ See Figure 32

A noticeable lack of engine power, excessive oil consumption and/or poor fuel mileage measured over an extended period are all indicators of internal engine wear. Worn piston rings, scored or worn cylinder bores, blown head gaskets, sticking or burnt valves and worn valve seats are all possible culprits. A check of each cylinder's compression will help you locate the problems.

As mentioned in the Tools and Equipment Section 1, a screw-in type compression gauge is more accurate than the type you simply hold against the spark plug hole, although it takes slightly longer to use. It's worth it to obtain a more accurate reading.

1. Warm up the engine to normal operating temperature.
2. Remove all spark plugs.
3. Disconnect the high tension lead from the ignition coil.
4. On carbureted trucks, fully open the throttle either by operating the carburetor throttle linkage by hand or by having an assistant floor the accelerator pedal. On fuel injected trucks, disconnect the cold start valve and all injector connections.
5. Screw the compression gauge into the No. 1 spark plug hole until the fitting is snug.

➥Be careful not to crossthread the plug hole. On aluminum cylinder heads use extra care, as the threads in these heads are easily ruined.

6. Ask an assistant to depress the accelerator pedal fully on both carbureted and fuel injected trucks. Then, while you read the compression gauge, ask the assistant to crank the engine two or three times in short bursts using the ignition switch.

7. Read the compression gauge at the end of each series of cranks, and record the highest of these readings. Repeat this procedure for each of the engine's cylinders. Compare the highest reading of each cylinder to the compression pressure specification in the Tune-Up Specifications chart in Section 2. The specifications in this chart are maximum values.

A cylinders compression pressure is usually acceptable if it is not less than 80% of maximum. The difference between each cylinder should be no more than about 12–14 lbs.

8. If a cylinder is unusually low, pour a tablespoon of clean engine oil into the cylinder through the spark plug hole and repeat the compression test. If the compression comes up after adding the oil, it appears that the cylinder's piston rings or bore are damaged or worn. If the pressure remains low, the valves may not be seating properly (a valve job is needed), or the head gasket may be blown near that cylinder. If compression in any two adjacent cylinders is low, and if the addition of oil doesn't help the compression, there is leakage past the head gasket. Oil and coolant water in the combustion chamber can result from this problem. There may be evidence of water droplets on the engine dipstick when a head gasket has blown.

Engine

REMOVAL & INSTALLATION

1970–83 Vehicles

▶ See Figures 33, 34 and 35

It is much easier to remove the engine and the transmission together as an assembly than to remove only the engine from the engine compartment. After the engine and transmission are removed from the vehicle, the two can be separated.

1. Disconnect the battery ground cable. Remove the battery.
2. Mark the location of the hood hinges on the body in order to facilitate installation and remove the hood.

ENGINE AND ENGINE REBUILDING

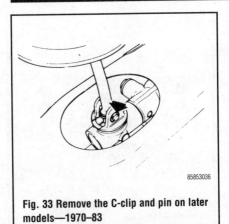

Fig. 33 Remove the C-clip and pin on later models—1970–83

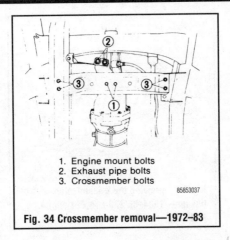

1. Engine mount bolts
2. Exhaust pipe bolts
3. Crossmember bolts

Fig. 34 Crossmember removal—1972–83

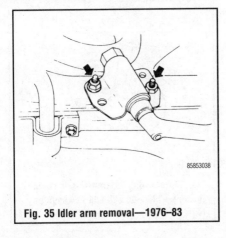

Fig. 35 Idler arm removal—1976–83

3. Remove the air cleaner after disconnecting the PCV hose from the rocker cover.
4. Drain the radiator of coolant and the engine crankcase of oil.

✽✽ CAUTION

When draining the coolant, keep in mind that cats and dogs are attracted by the ethylene glycol antifreeze, and are quite likely to drink any that is left in an uncovered container or in puddles on the ground. This will prove fatal in sufficient quantity. Always drain the coolant into a sealable container. Coolant should be reused unless it is contaminated or several years old.

5. Disconnect the upper and lower radiator hoses from the engine. Disconnect and plug the automatic transmission cooler lines at the radiator, if so equipped. Use a flare nut wrench if one is available.
6. Remove the four bolts securing the radiator and remove the radiator from the vehicle.
7. Disconnect the engine ground cable at the cylinder head.
8. Disconnect the electrical leads at the starter, alternator, distributor, the high tension ignition coil cable, and the oil pressure and temperature sending units' wires.
9. Disconnect the fuel line at the fuel pump (or filter on electric pump models), the heater hose at the engine side, and the choke wire and accelerator cable at the carburetor. Disconnect the emission hoses or wires to the carbon canister, air pump, B.C.D.D. solenoid, and fuel cut solenoid; the vacuum hose to the brake booster (on models so equipped), and any other wires or hoses running to the engine. Tag all wires as they are disconnected for assembly.
10. Remove the transmission control linkage from the transmission; in the case of an automatic transmission, remove the cross-shaft assembly from the transmission. Remove the selector rod from the selector lever on the automatic transmission. On manual transmissions, lift the rubber boot and remove the nut or C-clip from the shift lever and detach the shift lever from the transmission.
11. Remove the two bolts securing the clutch slave cylinder. Disconnect the clutch slave cylinder and the flexible tubing as an assembly.
12. Disconnect the speedometer cable and the back-up light wiring (and neutral switch, if equipped) from the rear section of the transmission.
13. Disconnect the exhaust pipe from the exhaust manifold.
14. Disconnect the driveshaft center bearing bracket from the third crossmember of the frame. Disconnect the driveshaft at the differential housing. Remove the driveshaft assembly from the vehicle and plug the rear end of the transmission extension housing to prevent loss of transmission lubricant.
15. Attach a suitable lifting device to the engine and lift the engine slightly.
16. Remove the front engine mount bolts on both sides of the engine.
17. Place a jack under the transmission and lift it slightly.
18. Loosen the two combination engine rear mounting/transmission mounting bolts. On models with a catalytic converter, loosen the two exhaust pipe hanger bolts.
19. On 1972 and later models, remove the four bolts (two on each side) securing the engine rear mounting/transmission support side member and detach the support from the frame.
20. On 1976 and later models, remove the bolts securing the idler arm to the frame, and push down the tie rod.

21. Pull the engine toward the front as far as possible and carefully raise the engine with the transmission up and out of the vehicle.
22. Install the engine in the reverse order of removal, taking note of the following:
  • Do not connect any parts of the engine or transmission until the engine and transmission are in place on the engine/transmission mounts and secured by the mounting bolts.
  • Secure the rear support first and then the front engine mounts, using the upper bolt hole as a guide.

1984–86 720-D Series

▶ See Figures 36, 37, 38, 39 and 40

1. Disconnect the negative battery cable.
2. Remove the engine undercover.
3. Disconnect the windshield washer hose and then remove the hood. Scribe matchmarks around the hinges for easy installation.
4. Drain the engine oil. Drain the engine coolant from the radiator and the cylinder block.
5. Drain the automatic transmission fluid on models so equipped.
6. Disconnect the air cleaner hose and then remove the air cleaner.
7. Remove the radiator and shroud as detailed later in this section. On models with automatic transmission oil coolers, disconnect and plug the oil lines at the radiator
8. Remove the coupling fan.
9. Disconnect the two heater hoses at the engine.
10. Remove the drive belts.
11. Remove the power steering pump from its bracket (if equipped). Disconnect the ground strap from the bracket.
12. On models with air conditioning, loosen the drive belt and remove the air conditioning compressor. Position it out of the way with the refrigerant lines still attached.
13. Remove the transmission control linkage.
14. Disconnect the speedometer cable. Tag and disconnect any electrical leads at the transmission.
15. On models with manual transmission, remove the clutch release cylinder and its bracket from the transmission. Position it aside without disconnecting the hydraulic lines.
16. Remove the bolts and disconnect the exhaust pipe at the manifold.
17. Disconnect and remove the parking brake cable at the brake lever side.
18. Matchmark the rear driveshaft to the transmission flange, then remove the driveshaft. Be sure to plug the hole in the extension housing.
19. Matchmark the front driveshaft (4wd models) to the transfer case flange, then remove the front driveshaft.
20. Attach an engine hoist chain to the lifting brackets on the engine, then raise the engine just enough to ease the weight on the front and rear engine mount insulators.
21. On models with 4wd, carefully slide a floor jack underneath the front differential carrier and remove the front mounting bolt. Remove the rear mounting bolts and crossmember, then slowly lower the carrier.
22. On models with automatic transmission, remove the rear engine mount support-to-body bolts.

3-12 ENGINE AND ENGINE REBUILDING

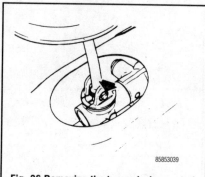

Fig. 36 Removing the transmission control linkage—1984–86 Z20 and Z24 engines (with M/T)

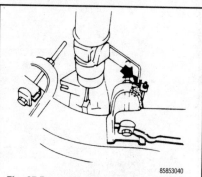

Fig. 37 Removing the transmission control linkage—1984–86 Z20 and Z24 engines (with A/T)

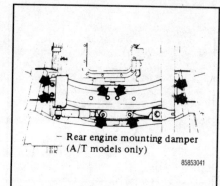

Fig. 38 Removing the rear engine mount support—1984–86

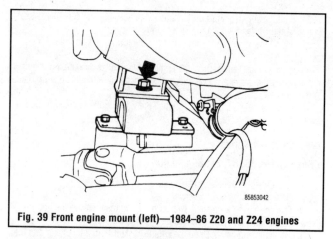

Fig. 39 Front engine mount (left)—1984–86 Z20 and Z24 engines

Fig. 40 Front engine mount (right)—1984–86 Z20 and Z24 engines

23. Remove the mounting bolts for the front engine mount.
24. Tighten the engine hoist chain, then carefully lift the engine/transmission assembly up and out of the truck. Be very careful not to bump into anything as the engine comes out of the engine compartment.

To install:
25. Slowly lower the engine/transmission assembly into the engine compartment.
26. Raise the transmission onto the crossmember with a floor jack.
27. Align the holes in the engine mounts and the frame, install the bolts and then remove the engine hoist chain.
28. On models with automatic transmission, install the rear engine mount support-to-body bolts.
29. On models with 4wd, carefully raise the floor jack underneath the front differential carrier, then install the rear mounting bolts and crossmember. Install the front mounting bolt.
30. Install the front driveshaft (4wd models) to the transfer case flange.
31. Remove the plug in the extension housing and the connect the rear driveshaft to the transmission flange.
32. Connect and install the parking brake cable.
33. Install the exhaust pipe at the manifold.
34. Install the clutch release cylinder and its bracket at the transmission.
35. Connect the speedometer cable. Reconnect any electrical leads at the transmission (check the tags you made in Step 14).
36. Install the transmission control linkage.
37. Install the air conditioning compressor and drive belt.
38. Install the power steering pump and its bracket (if equipped). Be sure to connect the ground strap to the bracket.
39. Install the drive belts.
40. Connect the heater hoses.
41. Install the coupling fan.
42. Install the radiator and shroud. Unplug the automatic transmission oil cooler lines and connect them (if equipped).
43. Install the air cleaner.
44. Refill the engine and automatic transmission with fluid.
45. Install and adjust the hood.
46. Install the engine undercover.
47. Connect the negative battery cable, start the truck and road test it.

1986–88 D21-D Series

1. Disconnect the negative battery cable.
2. Remove the engine undercover.
3. Disconnect the windshield washer hose, then remove the hood. Scribe matchmarks around the hinges for easy installation.
4. Drain the engine oil. Drain the engine coolant from the radiator and the cylinder block.
5. Drain the automatic transmission fluid on models so equipped.
6. Disconnect the air cleaner hose and then remove the air cleaner.
7. Remove the radiator and shroud as detailed later in this section. On models with automatic transmission oil coolers, disconnect and plug the oil lines at the radiator.
8. Remove the coupling fan.
9. Disconnect the two heater hoses at the engine.
10. Remove the drive belts.
11. Remove the power steering pump from its bracket (if equipped). Disconnect the ground strap from the bracket.
12. On models with air conditioning, loosen the drive belt and remove the air conditioning compressor. Position it out of the way with the refrigerant lines still attached.
13. Remove the transmission control linkage.
14. On 4wd models, disconnect the starter leads and remove the starter. On 2wd models disconnect the starter motor leads.
15. Disconnect the speedometer cable. Tag and disconnect any electrical leads at the transmission.
16. On models with manual transmission, remove the clutch release cylinder and its bracket from the transmission. Position it aside without disconnecting the hydraulic lines.
17. Remove the bolts and disconnect the exhaust pipe at the manifold.
18. On 4wd models:

ENGINE AND ENGINE REBUILDING

a. Matchmark the front driveshaft (4wd models) to the transfer case flange and then remove the front driveshaft.

b. Carefully slide a floor jack underneath the front differential carrier and remove the front mounting bolt. Remove the rear mounting bolts and crossmember and then slowly lower the carrier.

c. Remove the transmission-to-engine bracket mounting nuts.

d. Remove the mounting bolts for the front engine mounts.

19. Attach an engine hoist chain to the lifting brackets on the engine and then raise the engine just enough to ease the weight on the front and rear engine mount insulators.

20. On 4wd models, remove the front differential carrier.

21. On 2wd models:

a. Matchmark the rear driveshaft to the transmission flange and then remove the driveshaft. Be sure to plug the hole in the extension housing.

b. Remove the transmission-to-rear engine mount bracket bolts.

c. Remove the transmission member.

22. On 4wd models, remove the transmission-to-engine mounting bolts.

23. Tighten the engine hoist chain and carefully lift the engine (4wd) or engine/transmission (2wd) assembly up and out of the truck. Be very careful not to bump into anything as the engine comes out of the engine compartment.

To install:

24. Slowly lower the engine/transmission assembly into the engine compartment.

25. Raise the transmission onto the crossmember with a floor jack.

26. Align the holes in the engine mounts and the frame, install the bolts and then remove the engine hoist chain.

27. On 4wd models, install the transmission-to-engine mounting bolts. Tighten the 16mm and 25mm bolts to 22–29 ft. lbs. (29–39 Nm).

28. On 2wd models:

a. Install the transmission member.

b. Install the transmission-to-rear engine mount bracket bolts and tighten to 30–38 ft. lbs. (41–52 Nm).

c. Install the rear driveshaft to the transmission flange.

29. On 4wd models:

a. Install the front differential carrier.

b. Install the mounting bolts for the front engine mounts and tighten to 23–31 ft. lbs. (31–42 Nm).

c. Install the transmission-to-engine bracket mounting nuts and tighten to 30–38 ft. lbs. (41–52 Nm).

d. Align the matchmarks on the front driveshaft to those on the transfer case flange and then install the front driveshaft.

30. Connect the exhaust pipe to the manifold.

31. Install the clutch release cylinder and its bracket to the transmission.

32. Connect the speedometer cable. Connect any electrical leads at the transmission.

33. On 4wd models, connect the starter leads and install the starter. On 2wd models, connect the starter motor leads.

34. Install the air conditioning compressor and drive belt.

35. Install the power steering pump and its bracket (if equipped). Be sure to connect the ground strap to the bracket.

36. Install the drive belts.

37. Connect the heater hoses.

38. Install the coupling fan.

39. Install the radiator and shroud. Unplug the automatic transmission oil cooler lines and connect them (if equipped).

40. Refill the engine and automatic transmission with fluid.

41. Install and adjust the hood.

42. Install the engine undercover.

43. Connect the negative battery cable, start the truck and road test it.

Cylinder Head Cover

REMOVAL & INSTALLATION

1. Remove the air cleaner assembly.
2. Disconnect the PCV hose(s) from the cylinder head cover.
3. Remove the nuts and washers. Lift the cover off the cylinder head. Cover the oil return hole in the head to prevent dirt or objects from falling in. Remove the gasket.

To install:

4. Replace the cover gasket if it shows any signs of damage, breaks or cracking. Tighten the nuts evenly, reconnect the PCV hose and install the air cleaner assembly.

Rocker Arms and Rocker Pivots

REMOVAL & INSTALLATION

♦ See Figure 41

L16, L18 and L20B Engines

1. Remove the cylinder head cover.
2. Loosen the rocker pivot lock-nut. Lower the pivot by screwing it down into the cylinder head.
3. Remove the rocker arm by pressing down on the valve spring.
4. To remove the rocker pivots, loosen the lock-nut, then unscrew the pivot from the cylinder head.

To install:

5. Install the pivots and screw them into the cylinder head. Tighten the lock-nut.
6. Press down on the valve spring and install the rocker arm.
7. Refer to Section 2 for valve lash adjustment.
8. Install the cylinder head cover.

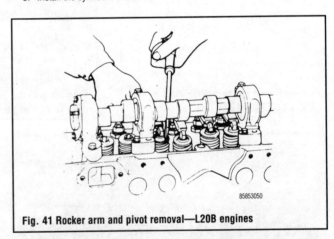

Fig. 41 Rocker arm and pivot removal—L20B engines

Rocker Arm/Shaft Assembly

REMOVAL & INSTALLATION

Z20, Z22, Z24 and Z24i Engines

♦ See Figures 42 thru 49

1. Remove the cylinder head cover. The rocker shaft assembly is removed by simply unthreading the retaining bolts.

➡ **When removing the bolts, DO NOT REMOVE THE NO.1 AND NO. 5 BRACKET BOLTS SINCE THE ROCKER SHAFT BRACKET AND ROCKER ARM WILL SPRING OUT!**

2. Remove the rocker shaft bracket, then slide the valve rockers and springs off of the rocker shaft. Be absolutely sure to keep all parts in the order in which they were removed; they must be reassembled in the same order.
3. Inspect the rocker arms and shaft for damage, replace as necessary.

To install:

4. Slide the springs and rockers onto the shafts in the order that they were removed.
5. The intake rocker shaft has a slit on its leading edge, but the exhaust shaft does not. Additionally, each shaft has a punch mark on its leading edge.

3-14 ENGINE AND ENGINE REBUILDING

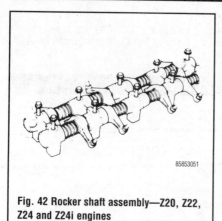

Fig. 42 Rocker shaft assembly—Z20, Z22, Z24 and Z24i engines

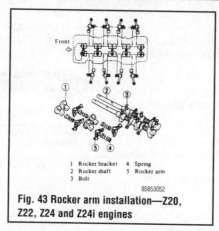

1 Rocker bracket
2 Rocker shaft
3 Bolt
4 Spring
5 Rocker arm

Fig. 43 Rocker arm installation—Z20, Z22, Z24 and Z24i engines

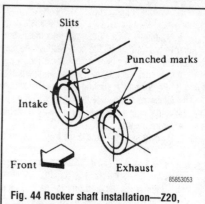

Fig. 44 Rocker shaft installation—Z20, Z22, Z24 and Z24i engines

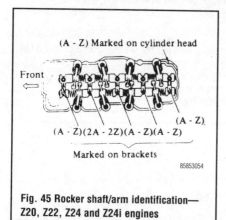

Fig. 45 Rocker shaft/arm identification—Z20, Z22, Z24 and Z24i engines

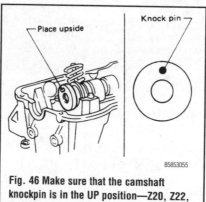

Fig. 46 Make sure that the camshaft knockpin is in the UP position—Z20, Z22, Z24 and Z24i engines

Fig. 47 Removing the rocker arm/shaft assembly bolts

Fig. 48 Removing the rocker arm/shaft assembly

Fig. 49 View of the rocker arm/shaft—keep all bolts in order for correct installation

The shafts should be assembled with these marks facing upward as they are used for oil hole identification.

6. The intake and exhaust rockers for the Nos. 1 and 3 cylinders are the same and are identified by the mark **1**. The same holds true for the rockers on Nos. 2 and 4 cylinders; they are identified with a **2**.

7. The rocker shaft brackets are also marked as to their original location; simply match them to the like marks on the cylinder head.

8. At this point, reinsert a bracket bolt into holes for the No. 1 and No. 5 brackets (any bolt is fine). This will insure that the assembly stays together while you mount it on the head.

9. Mount the rocker shaft assembly on the cylinder head in a manner that accommodates the camshaft knock pin and then tighten the retaining bolts gradually, in two or three stages to 11–18 ft. lbs. (15–25 Nm).

10. Refer to Section 2 for valve lash adjustment.

VG30i Engines

♦ See Figure 50

1. Remove the cylinder head covers.
2. Remove the rocker arm shaft-to-cylinder head bolts and lift the rocker arm/shaft assembly from the cylinder head.
3. Separate the rocker arms from the shaft.

ENGINE AND ENGINE REBUILDING   3-15

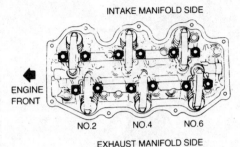

Fig. 50 Rocker shaft installation direction—VG30i engine

➡ When separating the rocker arms from the rocker arm shafts, be sure to keep the parts in order for reinstallation purposes.

4. Check the rocker arms, the shafts, the valves and the valve lifter for damage. If necessary, replace the damaged components.

✴✴ CAUTION

When installing the rocker arm shafts, be certain that they are installed in their original positions.

To install:

5. Slide the rocker arms onto the shafts and then install the shaft/arm assemblies onto the cylinder head in the proper positions.

6. Make sure the camshaft knock pin is at the top of the camshaft and that the lobe is not in the lifted position. Set the No. 1 piston at TDC of its compression stroke and then tighten the rocker shaft bolts for the Nos. 2, 4 and 6 cylinders. Set the No. 4 piston at TDC of its compression stroke and tighten the Nos. 1, 3 and 5 cylinder rocker shaft bolts. Tighten all bolts gradually, in two or three stages to 13–16 ft. lbs. (18–22 Nm).

7. Refer to Section 2 for valve lash adjustment.
8. Install the cylinder head cover.

INSPECTION

▶ See Figures 51, 52 and 53

The oil clearance between the rocker arm and shaft is measured in two steps. Measure the outside diameter of the rocker shaft with a micrometer. Measure the inside diameter of the rocker arms with a dial indicator. The difference between the rocker arm inner diameter and the shaft outer diameter is the oil clearance. Clearance specifications are as follows:

- Z20: 0.0003–0.0019 in. (0.008–0.050mm)
- Z22: 0.0003–0.0019 in. (0.008–0.050mm)
- Z24: 0.0003–0.0019 in. (0.008–0.050mm)
- Z24i: 0.0003–0.0019 in. (0.008–0.050mm)
- VG30i: 0.0003–0.0019 in. (0.008–0.050mm)

If specifications are not within these ranges, replace either the rocker shaft or rocker arm. Clearance can also be checked by moving the rocker arm laterally on the shaft when assembled. **There should be little or no movement.**

While disassembled, check the cam follower end (the flat end that contacts the camshaft) of the rocker arm for excess wear. The surface should be smooth and shiny. If excess wear is evident, also check the lobe of the camshaft, it may also be worn.

Reassemble the rocker shaft assemblies in the exact opposite order or removal. Accelerated camshaft wear and/or sloppy valve action will result if rocker arms are mixed and end up operating against the wrong cam lobes.

Thermostat

REMOVAL & INSTALLATION

▶ See Figures 54 thru 60

1. Drain the engine coolant into a clean container so that the level is below the thermostat housing.

✴✴ CAUTION

When draining the coolant, keep in mind that cats and dogs are attracted by the ethylene glycol antifreeze, and are quite likely to drink any that is left in an uncovered container or in puddles on the ground. This will prove fatal in sufficient quantity. Always drain the coolant into a sealable container. Coolant should be reused unless it is contaminated or several years old.

2. Disconnect the upper radiator hose at the water outlet.
3. Loosen the two securing nuts and remove the water outlet, gasket, and the thermostat from the thermostat housing.
4. When installing the thermostat always use a new gasket with sealer and make sure the thermostat spring is facing the inside of the engine. The factory installed thermostat opening temperature is 180°F (82°C) for trucks sold in the U.S., 190°F (88°C) for trucks sold in Canada.

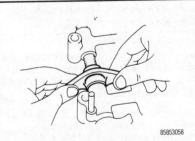

Fig. 51 Check the rocker arm-to-shaft wear by wiggling the arm laterally on the shaft—Little or no movement should be felt

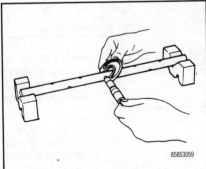

Fig. 52 Measure the outside diameter of the rocker shaft with a outside micrometer

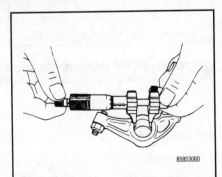

Fig. 53 Measure the inside diameter of the rocker shaft with a inside micrometer

3-16 ENGINE AND ENGINE REBUILDING

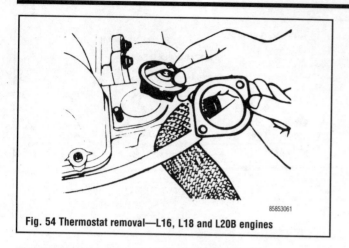
Fig. 54 Thermostat removal—L16, L18 and L20B engines

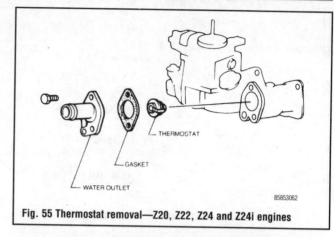
Fig. 55 Thermostat removal—Z20, Z22, Z24 and Z24i engines

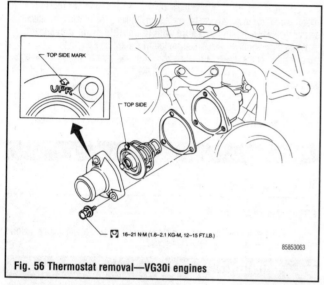
Fig. 56 Thermostat removal—VG30i engines

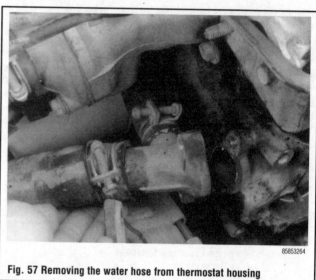
Fig. 57 Removing the water hose from thermostat housing

Fig. 58 Removing the thermostat housing

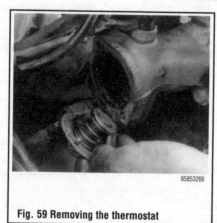
Fig. 59 Removing the thermostat

Fig. 60 View of the electrical connection for water temperature sending unit

Intake Manifold

REMOVAL & INSTALLATION

L16, L18 and L20B Engines

▶ See Figure 61

1. Remove the air cleaner assembly together with all of the attending hoses. Remove the EGR tube on 1974–80 models.
2. Drain the cooling system and disconnect the battery.

➥It is important to replace the gasket whenever the intake manifold is removed. Because the intake and exhaust manifolds share a common gasket, whenever the intake manifold is removed, the exhaust manifold must also be removed, so that the gasket can be replaced.

3. Disconnect the throttle linkage, fuel, and vacuum lines from the carburetor. Label all wires and hoses as they are removed to simplify installation.
4. The carburetor can be removed from the manifold at this point or can be removed as an assembly with the intake manifold.
5. Loosen the intake manifold attaching nuts, working from the two ends toward the center, and then remove them.
6. Remove the intake manifold from the engine.

ENGINE AND ENGINE REBUILDING   3-17

Fig. 61 Intake manifold—L16, L18 and L20B engines

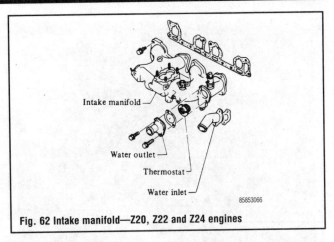

Fig. 62 Intake manifold—Z20, Z22 and Z24 engines

To install:

7. Cover the cylinder head ports with shop cloths to keep anything from falling into the cylinder head or block.

8. When installing the intake manifold, always use a new gasket. Tighten the manifold bolts from the center outwards, in two progressive steps, to 9–12 ft. lbs. (12–16 Nm).

9. Install the carburetor (if removed), then connect all hoses and lines. Install the air cleaner and fill the cooling system.

Z20, Z22, Z24 and Z24i Engines

▶ See Figures 62 thru 67

➡ Always release the fuel pressure on fuel injected engines before removing any fuel system component.

1. Drain the coolant and disconnect the battery cable.

※※ CAUTION

When draining the coolant, keep in mind that cats and dogs are attracted by the ethylene glycol antifreeze, and are quite likely to drink any that is left in an uncovered container or in puddles on the ground. This will prove fatal in sufficient quantity. Always drain the coolant into a sealable container. Coolant should be reused unless it is contaminated or several years old.

2. On the Z24i, remove the air cleaner hoses. On the Z20, Z22 and Z24, remove the air cleaner.

3. Remove the radiator hoses from the manifold.

4. On the Z20, Z22 and Z24, remove the fuel, air and vacuum hoses from the carburetor. Remove the throttle linkage and remove the carburetor.

5. Remove the throttle cable and disconnect the fuel pipe and the return fuel line on the Z24i. Plug the fuel pipe to prevent spilling fuel.

➡ When unplugging wires and hoses, mark each hose and its connection with a piece of masking tape, then mark the two pieces of tape with the numbers 1, 2, 3, etc. When assembling, simply match the pieces of tape.

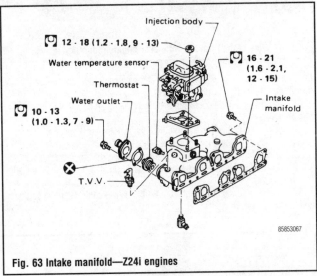

Fig. 63 Intake manifold—Z24i engines

6. Remove all remaining wires, tubes, the air cleaner bracket (Z20, Z22 and Z24) and the EGR and PCV tubes from the rear of the intake manifold. Remove the air induction pipe from the front of the engine (Z20, Z22 and Z24). Remove the manifold supports on the Z24i.

7. Unbolt and remove the intake manifold. On the Z24i, remove the manifold with injectors, EGR valve, fuel tubes, etc., still attached.

To install:

8. Clean the gasket mounting surfaces then install the intake manifold on the engine. Always use a new intake manifold gasket. Tighten the mounting bolts from the center, out, to 12–15 ft. lbs. (16–21 Nm)

9. Connect all electrical connections, tubes, the air cleaner bracket (Z20, Z22 and Z24) and the EGR and PCV tubes to the rear of the intake manifold.

Fig. 64 Removing the intake manifold bolts

Fig. 65 Removing the fuel line for intake manifold removal

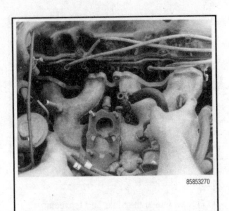

Fig. 66 Removing the intake manifold

3-18 ENGINE AND ENGINE REBUILDING

Fig. 67 View of the intake manifold-to-engine mounting

Install the air induction pipe to the front of the engine (Z20, Z22 and Z24). Install the manifold supports on the Z24i.

10. Install the throttle cable and reconnect the fuel pipe and the return fuel line on the Z24i.
11. Install the carburetor and throttle linkage. Reconnect the fuel, air and vacuum hoses to the carburetor on these models.
12. Install the radiator hoses to the intake manifold.
13. On the Z24i, install the air cleaner hoses. On all other engines, install the air cleaner.
14. Refill the coolant level and connect the battery cable. Start the engine and check for leaks.

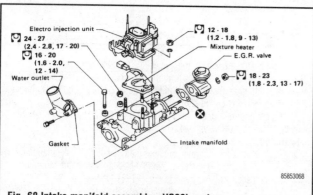

Fig. 68 Intake manifold assembly—VG30i engine

VG30i Engines

♦ See Figures 68, 69 and 70

1. Release the fuel system pressure (Section 1) and disconnect the battery cables.
2. Drain coolant by removing the drain plug on the left side of the cylinder block.

❋❋ CAUTION

When draining the coolant, keep in mind that cats and dogs are attracted by the ethylene glycol antifreeze, and are quite likely to drink any that is left in an uncovered container or in puddles on the ground. This will prove fatal in sufficient quantity. Always drain the coolant into a sealable container. Coolant should be reused unless it is contaminated or several years old.

3. Disconnect all valves, lines, hoses, cables and or brackets to gain access to the collector cover and collector assembly retaining bolts.
4. Remove the collector cover. Remove the collector-to-intake manifold bolts in numerical order.
5. Remove the intake manifold and injection unit assembly. Loosen intake manifold bolts in the sequence shown.

To install:

6. Install the intake manifold and injection unit assembly with a new gasket to the engine. Tighten the manifold bolts and nuts in two or three stages, to 12–14 ft. lbs. (16–20 Nm) in the order shown.
7. Install the collector and collector cover with new gaskets. Tighten collector-to-intake manifold bolts in two or three stages, in the reverse order of removal.
8. Connect all valves, lines, hoses, cables and or brackets to the collector cover and collector assembly.
9. Refill the cooling system. Reconnect the battery cables.
10. Check fluid levels, start the engine and check for leaks.

Exhaust Manifold

REMOVAL & INSTALLATION

All Except VG30i Engines

♦ See Figures 71, 72, 73, 74 and 75

➡You may find that removing the intake manifold will provide better access to the exhaust manifold on some early models.

1. Remove the air cleaner assembly. Remove the heat shield.
2. Tag and disconnect the high tension wires from the spark plugs on the exhaust side of the engine.
3. Disconnect the exhaust pipe from the exhaust manifold.

➡If necessary, soak the exhaust pipe retaining bolts with penetrating oil to loosen them.

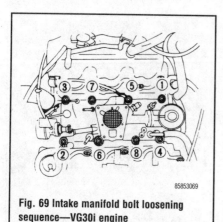

Fig. 69 Intake manifold bolt loosening sequence—VG30i engine

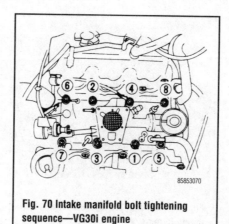

Fig. 70 Intake manifold bolt tightening sequence—VG30i engine

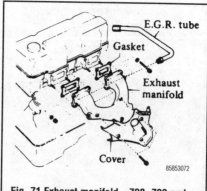

Fig. 71 Exhaust manifold—Z20, Z22 and Z24 engines

ENGINE AND ENGINE REBUILDING 3-19

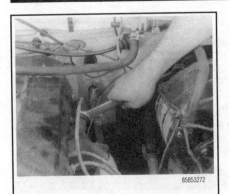
Fig. 72 Removing exhaust manifold connections

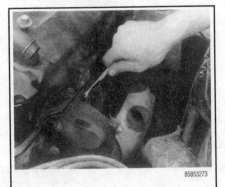
Fig. 73 Removing exhaust manifold mounting bolts

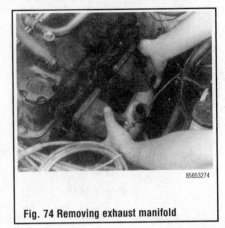
Fig. 74 Removing exhaust manifold

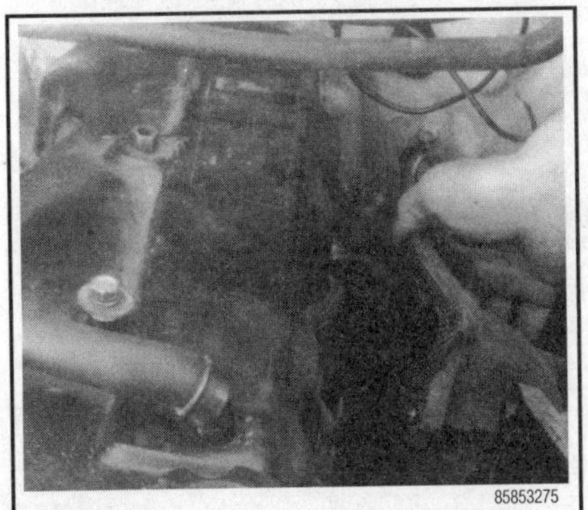

Fig. 75 View of exhaust manifold mounting and gasket

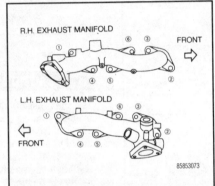
Fig. 76 Exhaust manifold bolt loosening sequence—VG30i engines

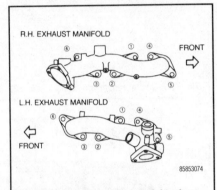
Fig. 77 Exhaust manifold bolt tightening sequence—VG30i engines

4. On the carbureted models, remove the air induction and/or the EGR tubes from the exhaust manifold. On the Z24i, disconnect the exhaust gas sensor electrical connector.
5. Remove the exhaust manifold mounting nuts and then remove the manifold from the cylinder head.

To install:

6. Using a putty knife, clean the gasket mounting surfaces.
7. Install the manifold onto the engine, use new gaskets and, from the center working to the end, tighten the exhaust manifold nuts/bolts to 12–15 ft. lbs. (16–21 Nm)
8. Install the air induction and/or the EGR tubes to the exhaust manifold or the exhaust gas sensor electrical connector.
9. Reconnect exhaust pipe to the manifold.
10. Connect spark plug wires and air cleaner and any related hoses.
11. Start engine and check for exhaust leaks.

VG30i Engines

◆ See Figures 76 and 77

1. Remove the exhaust manifold sub-cover and manifold cover. Remove the EGR tube from the right side exhaust manifold. Remove the exhaust manifold stay.
2. Disconnect the left side exhaust manifold at the exhaust pipe by removing retaining nuts and then disconnect the right side manifold from the connecting pipe.

➡ Soak the exhaust pipe retaining bolts with penetrating oil if necessary to loosen them.

3. Remove bolts for each manifold in the order shown.

To install:

4. Clean all gasket surfaces. Install new gaskets.
5. Install the manifold to the engine, tightening the mounting bolts alternately, using two stages of the order shown. Tighten the left side bolts to 13–16 ft. lbs. (18–22 Nm); tighten the right side bolts to 16–20 ft. lbs. (22–27 Nm).

6. Reconnect the exhaust pipe and the connecting pipe. Be careful not break these bolts.
7. Install the exhaust manifold stay and the EGR tube to the right side manifold.
8. Install the exhaust manifold covers. Start the engine and check for exhaust leaks.

Air Conditioning Compressor

Please refer to Section 1 for all Charging and Discharging procedures.

➡ It may be illegal in certain areas to service air conditioning components unless you are certified. Consult with your local authorities.

REMOVAL & INSTALLATION

All Models

◆ See Figures 78 and 79

** CAUTION

The compressed refrigerant used in the air conditioning system expands into the atmosphere at a temperature of −2°F or lower. This will freeze any surface, including your eyes, that it contacts. In addition, the refrigerant decomposes into a poisonous gas in the presence of a flame. Do not open or disconnect any part of the air conditioning system until you have read the SAFETY WARNINGS section in Section 1.

1. Disconnect the negative battery cables.
2. Remove all the necessary equipment in order to gain access to the compressor mounting bolts.
3. Remove the compressor drive belt.

3-20 ENGINE AND ENGINE REBUILDING

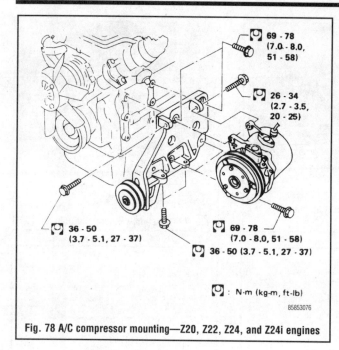

Fig. 78 A/C compressor mounting—Z20, Z22, Z24, and Z24i engines

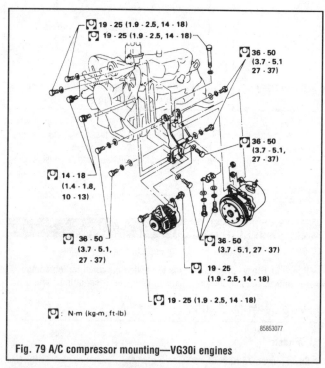

Fig. 79 A/C compressor mounting—VG30i engines

➡ To facilitate removal of the compressor belt, remove the idler pulley and bracket as an assembly beforehand from the underside of the truck.

4. Discharge and recover the air conditioning refrigerant.
5. Disconnect and plug the refrigerant lines with a clean shop towel.

➡ Be sure to use 2 wrenches (one to loosen fitting—one to hold fitting in place) when disconnecting the refrigerant lines.

6. Tag and disconnect all electrical connections.
7. Remove the compressor mounting bolts. Remove the compressor from the vehicle.

To install:
8. Install the compressor on the engine and evenly tighten all the mounting bolts equally.

9. Connect all the electrical connections and unplug and reconnect all refrigerant lines.
10. Install all the necessary equipment in order to gain access to the compressor mounting bolts.
11. Install and adjust the drive belt.
12. Connect the negative battery cable.
13. Evacuate and charge the system as required. Make sure the oil level is correct for the compressor.

➡ Do not attempt to the leave the compressor on its side or upside down for more than a couple minutes, as the oil in the compressor will enter the low pressure chambers. Always be sure to replace the O-rings.

Air Conditioning Condenser

Please refer to Section 1 for all Charging and Discharging procedures.

➡ It may be illegal in certain areas to service air conditioning components unless you are certified. Consult with your local authorities.

REMOVAL & INSTALLATION

All Models

✱✱ CAUTION

The compressed refrigerant used in the air conditioning system expands into the atmosphere at a temperature of −2°F or lower. This will freeze any surface, including your eyes, that it contacts. In addition, the refrigerant decomposes into a poisonous gas in the presence of a flame. Do not open or disconnect any part of the air conditioning system until you have read the SAFTEY WARNINGS section in Section 1.

1. Disconnect the negative battery cables.
2. Remove the necessary components in order to gain access to the condenser retaining bolts. If equipped, remove the condenser fan motor, as necessary.
3. Discharge the system. Remove the condenser refrigerant lines and plug them with a clean shop towel.

➡ On some models the receiver/drier assembly should be removed before removing the condenser.

4. Remove the condenser retaining bolts. Remove the condenser from the vehicle.

To install:
5. Install the condenser in the vehicle and evenly tighten all the mounting bolts.

➡ Always use new O-rings in all refrigerant lines.

6. Reconnect all the refrigerant lines.
7. Install all equipment removed in order to gain access to the condenser mounting bolts. Install the condenser fan motor if removed.
8. Connect the negative battery cable.
9. Evacuate and charge the system as required.

Radiator

REMOVAL & INSTALLATION

▶ See Figures 80 thru 87

➡ On some models, it may be necessary to remove the grille before removing the radiator. The cooling system can be drained by opening the drain cock at the bottom of the radiator or by removing the lower radiator hose. Be careful not to damage the fins or core tubes when removing and installing the radiator. NEVER OPEN THE RADIATOR CAP WHEN HOT!

1. Drain the engine coolant into a clean container. On fuel injected models, remove the air cleaner inlet pipe.

ENGINE AND ENGINE REBUILDING 3-21

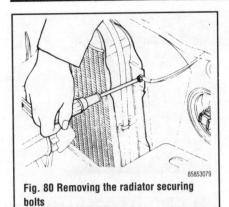
Fig. 80 Removing the radiator securing bolts

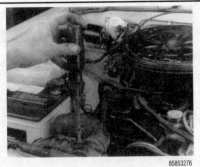
Fig. 81 Removing the upper radiator hose clamp

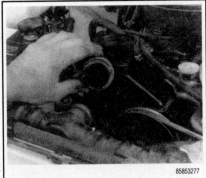
Fig. 82 Removing the upper radiator hose

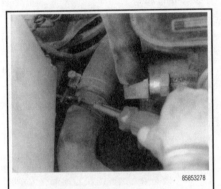
Fig. 83 Removing the lower radiator hose clamp

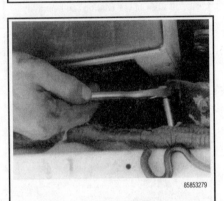
Fig. 84 Removing the radiator mounting bolts

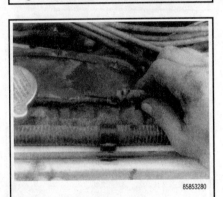
Fig. 85 Removing the radiator overflow hose

Fig. 86 Removing the radiator

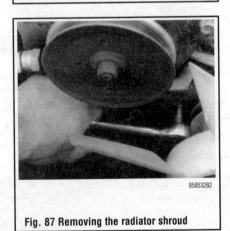
Fig. 87 Removing the radiator shroud

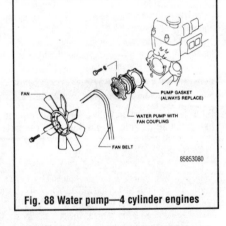
Fig. 88 Water pump—4 cylinder engines

✽✽ CAUTION

When draining the coolant, keep in mind that cats and dogs are attracted by the ethylene glycol antifreeze, and are quite likely to drink any that is left in an uncovered container or in puddles on the ground. This will prove fatal in sufficient quantity. Always drain the coolant into a sealable container. Coolant should be reused unless it is contaminated or several years old.

2. Disconnect the upper and lower radiator hoses and the coolant reserve tank hose.
3. Disconnect the automatic transmission oil cooler lines if so equipped. Plug the lines to keep dirt from entering them.
4. If the radiator has a fan shroud, unbolt the shroud and move it back. Hang it over the fan.
5. Remove the radiator mounting bolts and the radiator.

To install:

6. Install the radiator in the vehicle and tighten the mounting bolts evenly.
7. If equipped with an automatic transmission, connect the cooling lines at the radiator.
8. Connect the upper and lower hoses, along with the coolant reserve tank hose.
9. Refill the cooling system (refer to Section 1) and automatic transmission if necessary, operate the engine until warm and then check the coolant level. Check also for any leaks.

Water Pump

REMOVAL & INSTALLATION

▶ See Figures 88 thru 94

1. Drain the cooling system.
2. Unfasten the fan shroud securing bolts and remove the fan shroud, if so equipped.
3. Loosen the alternator adjusting link bolt and remove the drive belt.

3-22 ENGINE AND ENGINE REBUILDING

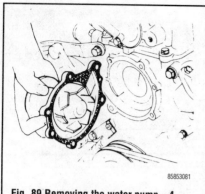
Fig. 89 Removing the water pump—4 cylinder engines

Fig. 90 View of the cooling fan assembly

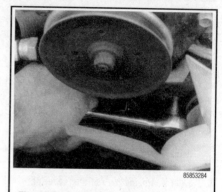
Fig. 91 Removing water pump lower mounting bolt

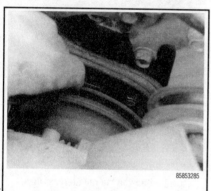
Fig. 92 Removing the water pump upper mounting bolt

Fig. 93 Removing the water pump assembly—note location of bolts for correct installation

Fig. 94 View of the water pump mounting surface

4. Repeat Step 3 for the air and/or power steering pump drive belt, if so equipped.

5. Unfasten the water pump retaining bolts (note the different size bolts on the VG30i), then remove the water pump and fan assembly, using care not to damage the radiator with the fan.

✱✱ CAUTION

If the fan is equipped with a fluid coupling, do not tip the fan/pump assembly on its side, as the fluid will run out.

To install:

6. Remove all traces of gasket and/or sealant from the pump-to-cover mounting surfaces. Install the water pump. Tighten the M6 mounting bolts to 3–7 ft. lbs. (4–10 Nm) and the M8 bolts to 7–12 ft. lbs. (10–16 Nm) on 4 cylinder engines; the M8 bolts to 12–15 ft. lbs. (16–21 Nm) on the VG30i. Always use a new gasket between the pump body and its mounting.

7. Install the drive belt and adjust the tension.

8. Refill the cooling system, start the engine and check for leaks.

Cylinder Head

REMOVAL & INSTALLATION

◆ See Figures 95, 96, 97 and 98

L16, L18 and L20B Engines

◆ See Figures 99, 100 and 101

1. Crank the engine until the No. 1 piston is at TDC of the compression stroke and disconnect the negative battery cable, drain the cooling system, and remove the air cleaner and attending hoses.

2. Remove the alternator.

3. If equipped with air conditioning, unbolt the compressor and move it aside onto the fender. Do not detach any of the compressor lines; the escaping refrigerant will freeze any surface it contacts, including your skin.

4. Disconnect the carburetor throttle linkage, the fuel line and any other vacuum lines or electrical leads, and remove the carburetor.

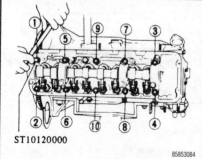
Fig. 95 Cylinder head bolt loosening sequence—L16, L18 and L20B engines

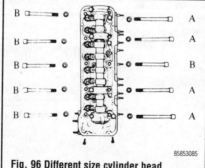
Fig. 96 Different size cylinder head bolts—L16, L18 and L20B engines

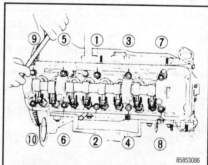
Fig. 97 Cylinder head bolt tightening sequence—L16, L18 and L20B engines

ENGINE AND ENGINE REBUILDING 3-23

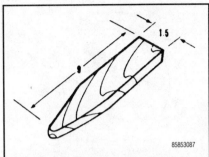

Fig. 98 Dimensions for fabricating the wooden wedge used in support for the timing chain—L16, L18 and L20B engines (Z-series engine similar)

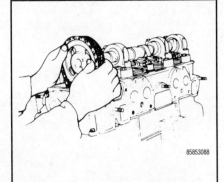

Fig. 99 Removing the camshaft sprocket and chain—L16, L18 and L20B engines

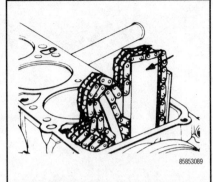

Fig. 100 Support the timing chain with a wedge—L16, L18 and L20B engines

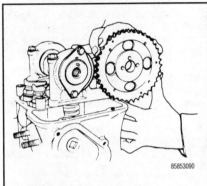

Fig. 101 Installing the camshaft sprocket—L16, L18 and L20B engines

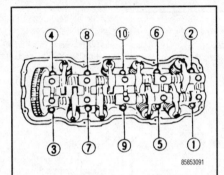

Fig. 102 Cylinder head bolt loosening sequence—Z20, Z22, Z24 and Z24i engines

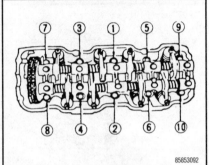

Fig. 103 Cylinder head bolt tightening sequence—Z20, Z22, Z24 and Z24i engines

5. Disconnect the exhaust pipe from the exhaust manifold.
6. Remove the fan and fan pulley.
7. Remove the spark plugs to protect them from damage. Lay the spark plugs aside and out of the way.
8. Remove the cylinder head cover.
9. Remove the water pump.
10. On models with a mechanical fuel pump, remove the pump from the cylinder head.
11. Remove the fuel pump drive cam.
12. Mark the relationship of the camshaft sprocket to the timing chain with paint or chalk. If this is done, it will not be necessary to locate the factory timing marks. Before removing the camshaft sprocket, it will be necessary to wedge the chain in place so that it will not fall down into the front cover. The factory procedure is to wedge the timing chain in place with the wooden wedge. The problem with this is that it may allow the chain tensioner to move out far enough to cock itself against the chain. If this happens, you'll find that the chain won't go back over the sprocket after you've put the sprocket back on. In this case, you'll have to remove the front cover and push the tensioner back. After installing the wedge, unbolt and remove the camshaft sprocket.
13. Loosen and remove the cylinder head bolts, gradually and in the order shown. You will need a 10mm Allen wrench to remove the head bolts. Keep the bolts in order, because they are different sizes. Lift the cylinder head assembly from the engine. Remove the intake and exhaust manifolds as necessary.

To install:
14. Thoroughly clean the cylinder block and head mating surfaces. Check the block and head for flatness before installing the head. Install a new cylinder head gasket. Do not use sealer on the cylinder head gasket of 1973–80 models. Use sealer on all other models.
15. With the crankshaft turned so that the No. 1 piston is at TDC of the compression stroke (if not already done so as mentioned in Step 1), make sure that the camshaft sprocket timing mark and the oblong groove in the camshaft retaining plate are aligned.
16. Place the cylinder head in position on the cylinder block, being careful not to allow any of the valves to come in contact with any of the pistons. Do not rotate the crankshaft or camshaft separately because of possible damage which might occur to the valves.

17. Temporarily tighten the two center right and left cylinder head bolts to 14.5 ft. lbs. (20 Nm).
18. Install the camshaft sprocket together (with the timing chain) to the camshaft. Make sure that the marks you made earlier line up. If the chain will not stretch over the sprocket, the problem lies in the tensioner. See the Timing Chain Removal and Installation for timing procedure, if necessary.
19. Install the cylinder head bolts. Note that there are two sizes of bolts used; the longer bolts are installed on the driver side of the engine with a smaller bolt in the center position. The remaining small bolts are installed on the opposite side of the cylinder.
20. Tighten the cylinder head bolts in three stages on 1973–80 models: first to 29 ft. lbs. (39 Nm), second to 43 ft. lbs. (58 Nm), and lastly to 47–62 ft. lbs. (64–84 Nm). On 1970–72 models, tighten the cylinder head bolts to 36–43 ft. lbs. (49–58 Nm) in three progressive steps. Tighten the cylinder head bolts on all models in the proper sequence.
21. Install the fuel pump assembly, water pump and cylinder head cover.
22. Clean and regap the spark plugs then install plugs into the cylinder head. DO NOT OVER-TORQUE THE SPARK PLUGS!
23. Install the fan pulley and cooling fan. Connect the exhaust pipe to the exhaust manifold.
24. Install the carburetor and connect the carburetor throttle linkage, the fuel line and any other vacuum lines or electrical leads.
25. Install the alternator and its electrical connections. Install the drive belt and adjust the tension.
26. Adjust the valves. Fill the cooling system and then start the engine and run it until it reaches normal operating temperature. Retighten the cylinder head bolts to specifications. Readjust the valves. Retighten the cylinder head bolts again after 600 miles, and readjust the valves at that time.

Z20, Z22, Z24 and Z24i Engines

▶ See Figures 102 thru 107

1. Crank the engine until the No. 1 piston is at TDC of the compression stroke and disconnect the negative battery cable, drain the cooling system, and remove the air cleaner and attending hoses.

3-24 ENGINE AND ENGINE REBUILDING

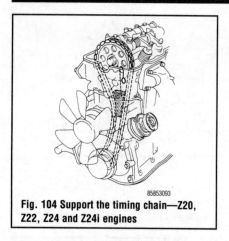

Fig. 104 Support the timing chain—Z20, Z22, Z24 and Z24i engines

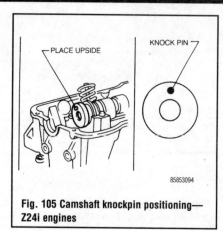

Fig. 105 Camshaft knockpin positioning—Z24i engines

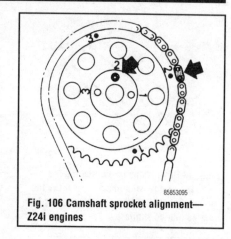

Fig. 106 Camshaft sprocket alignment—Z24i engines

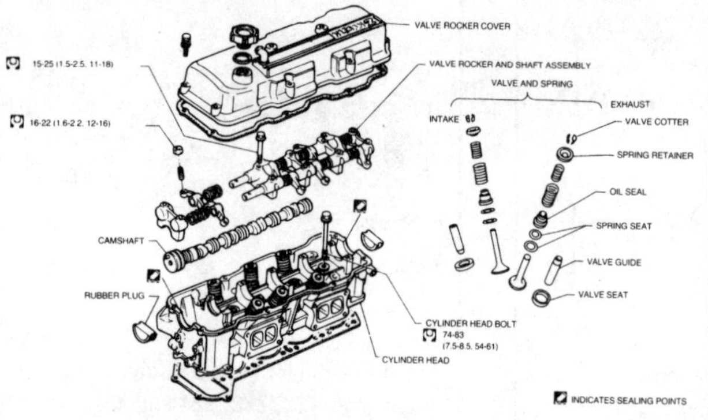

Fig. 107 Cylinder head bolt loosening sequence—Z20, Z22, Z24 and Z24i engines (L-series engines similar)

2. Remove the alternator.
3. If equipped with air conditioning, unbolt the compressor and move it aside onto the fender. Do not detach any of the compressor lines; the escaping refrigerant will freeze any surface it contacts, including your skin.
4. Disconnect the carburetor throttle linkage, the fuel line and any other vacuum lines or electrical leads, and remove the carburetor.
5. Disconnect the exhaust pipe from the exhaust manifold.
6. Remove the fan and fan pulley.
7. Disconnect the throttle linkage, the air cleaner or its intake hose assembly (fuel injection). Disconnect the fuel line (on fuel injected engines—release fuel pressure) the return fuel line and any other vacuum lines or electrical leads. Remove the carburetor (Z20, Z22 and Z24) to avoid damaging it while removing the head.

➡ A good rule of thumb when disconnecting the rather complex engine wiring of today's automobiles is to put a piece of masking tape on the wire or hose and on the connection you removed the wire or hose from, then mark both pieces of tape 1, 2, 3, etc. When replacing wiring, simply match the pieces of tape.

8. Remove the EGR tube from around the rear of the engine.
9. Remove the exhaust air induction tubes from around the front of the engine and from the exhaust manifold.
10. Unbolt the exhaust manifold from the exhaust pipe. Remove the fuel pump.
11. Remove the intake manifold supports from under the manifold. Remove the PCV valve from around the rear of the engine if necessary.
12. Remove the spark plugs to protect them from damage. Remove the cylinder head cover.

➡ The spark plug leads should be marked, however it would be wise to mark them yourself, especially the dual spark plug models.

13. Mark the relationship of the camshaft sprocket to the timing chain with paint or chalk. If this is done, it will not be necessary to locate the factory timing marks. Before removing the camshaft sprocket, it will be necessary to wedge the chain in place so that it will not fall down into the front cover. The factory procedure is to wedge the timing chain in place with the wooden wedge shown in the illustration. The problem with this procedure is that it may allow the chain tensioner to move out far enough to cock itself against the chain. If this happens, you'll find that the chain won't go back over the sprocket after you've put the sprocket back on. In this case, you'll have to remove the front cover and push the tensioner back. After you've wedged the chain, unbolt the camshaft sprocket and remove it.

14. Working from both ends in, loosen the cylinder head bolts and remove them. Remove the bolts securing the cylinder head to the front cover assembly.
15. Lift the cylinder head off the engine block. It may be necessary to tap the head lightly with a rubber mallet to loosen it.

To install:

16. Thoroughly clean the cylinder block and head surfaces, then check both for warpage.
17. Fit the new head gasket. Don't use sealant. Make sure that no open valves are in the way of raised pistons, and **never** rotate the crankshaft or camshaft separately because of possible damage which might occur to the valves.
18. Temporarily tighten the two center right and left cylinder head bolts to 14 ft. lbs. (19 Nm).
19. Install the camshaft sprocket together with the timing chain to the camshaft. Make sure the marks you made earlier line up with each other. If you get into trouble, see Timing Chain Removal and Installation for timing procedures.

    a. On the Z24i, confirm that the No. 1 cylinder is set at TDC on its compression stroke. Make sure that the front knock pin is positioned at the upper surface of the camshaft. Set the chain on the camshaft sprocket by aligning each mating mark. Then install the camshaft sprocket to the camshaft and tighten to 87–116 ft. lbs. (118–157 Nm).

➡ The camshaft sprocket should be installed by fitting the knock pin of the camshaft into its No. 2 hole. And the No. 2 timing mark must also be used.

    b. Apply sealant to the sealing point of the cylinder head and install the rubber plug.

20. Install the cylinder head bolts and torque them to 22 ft. lbs. (29 Nm), then 40 ft. lbs. (54 Nm), and then 58 ft. lbs. (78 Nm). Loosen all bolts completely and retighten 22 ft. lbs. (29 Nm), and then to 54–61 ft. lbs. (74–83 Nm); or, if you have an angle torque wrench, give all bolts a final turn of 90–95 degrees. Tighten all bolts gradually, in the order shown.
21. Clean and regap the spark plugs then install them in the cylinder head. DO NOT OVER-TORQUE THE SPARK PLUGS!
22. Install the cylinder head cover with a new gasket.
23. Install the intake manifold supports from under the manifold. Install the PCV valve if it was removed.
24. Connect the exhaust pipe to exhaust manifold. Install the fuel pump.
25. Install the exhaust air induction tubes to the front of the engine or to the exhaust manifold.
26. Install the EGR tube from around the rear of the engine.
27. Install the carburetor (Z20, Z22 and Z24). Connect the throttle linkage, the air cleaner or its intake hose assembly (Z24i). Reconnect the fuel line, the

ENGINE AND ENGINE REBUILDING   3-25

return fuel line and any other vacuum lines or electrical leads.

28. Install the power steering pump if so equipped and correctly adjust the drive belt.
29. Install the air conditioning compressor and correctly adjust the drive belt.
30. Install the alternator mounting bracket and alternator. Engage the electrical connections to the alternator and adjust the drive belt.
31. Reconnect the heater and radiator hoses.
32. Refill the cooling system. Adjust the valves.
33. Start the engine and it until it reaches normal operating temperature, check for the correct coolant level.
34. Check for leaks and roadtest vehicle for proper operation.

➥It is always wise to drain the crankcase oil after the cylinder head has been installed to avoid possible coolant contamination of the old oil.

VG30i Engines

◆ See Figures 108 thru 115

➥To remove or install the cylinder head, you'll need a special hex head wrench ST10120000 (J24239–01) or equivalent. The collector assembly and intake manifold have special bolt sequence for removal and installation. The distributor assembly is located in the left cylinder head; mark and remove it if necessary.

1. Release the fuel pressure. See the procedure in this section for timing belt removal. Set the engine to TDC and then remove the timing belt.

➥Do not rotate either the crankshaft or camshaft from this point onward, or the valves could be bent by hitting the pistons.

2. Drain the coolant from the engine. Tag and disconnect all the vacuum hoses and water hoses connected to the intake collector.
3. Remove the collector cover and the collector. Refer to the section Intake Manifold Removal And Installation for correct bolt removal sequence.
4. Remove the intake manifold and fuel tube assembly.
5. Remove the exhaust collector bracket. Remove the exhaust manifold covers. Disconnect the exhaust manifold when it connects to the exhaust pipe (three bolts).
6. Remove the camshaft pulleys and the rear timing cover securing bolts.
7. Loosen the cylinder head bolts a little at a time, in the order shown.
8. Remove the cylinder head with the exhaust manifold attached. If you need to remove the exhaust manifold, refer to the procedure in this section.

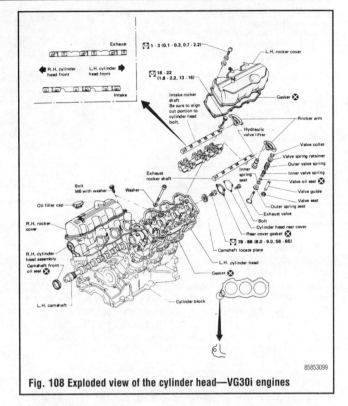

Fig. 108 Exploded view of the cylinder head—VG30i engines

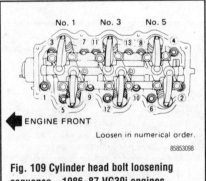

Fig. 109 Cylinder head bolt loosening sequence—1986–87 VG30i engines

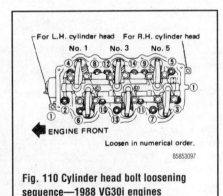

Fig. 110 Cylinder head bolt loosening sequence—1988 VG30i engines

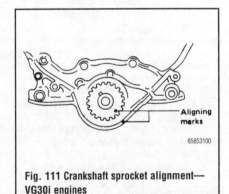

Fig. 111 Crankshaft sprocket alignment—VG30i engines

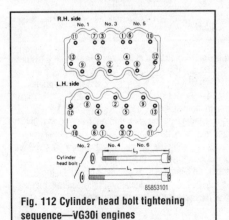

Fig. 112 Cylinder head bolt tightening sequence—VG30i engines

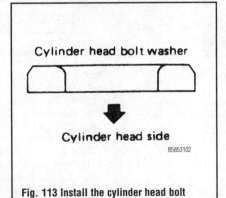

Fig. 113 Install the cylinder head bolt washer this way—VG30i engines

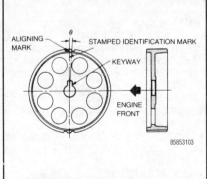

Fig. 114 Camshaft sprocket installation and positioning—VG30i engines

3-26 ENGINE AND ENGINE REBUILDING

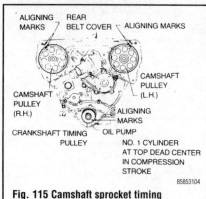

Fig. 115 Camshaft sprocket timing marks—VG30i engines

Fig. 116 Remove the carbon from the cylinder head with a wire brush and electric drill

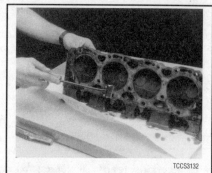

Fig. 117 Do not scratch the cylinder head mating surface when removing the old gasket material

To install:

9. Check the positions of the timing marks and camshaft sprockets to make sure they have not shifted. The mark on the crankshaft should be aligned with the one on the oil pump body and the camshaft knockpin should be at the top.
10. Install the head with a new gasket. Apply clean engine oil to the threads and seats of the bolts, then install the bolts with washers (beveled edges up) in the correct position. Note that bolts 4, 5, 12 and 13 are longer than the others.
11. Tighten the bolts in the proper sequence, in the following stages:
    a. Tighten all bolts, in order, to 22 ft. lbs. (29 Nm)
    b. Tighten all bolts, in order, to 43 ft. lbs. (59 Nm)
    c. Loosen all bolts completely.
    d. Tighten all bolts, in order, to 22 ft. lbs. (29 Nm)
    e. Tighten all bolts, in order, to 40–47 ft. lbs. (54–64 Nm). Or, if you have an angle torque wrench available, tighten them 60–65 degrees tighter rather than to the final torque.
12. Install the rear timing cover bolts. Install the camshaft pulleys. Make sure the pulley marked **R3** goes on the right and that marked **L3** goes on the left.
13. Align the timing marks if necessary and then install the timing belt and adjust the belt tension.
14. Install the front upper and lower belt covers.
15. Make sure that the cylinder head cover bolts, trays and washers are free of oil. Then, install the cylinder head covers.
16. Install the intake manifold and fuel tube.
17. Install the exhaust manifold if removed from the cylinder head.
18. Connect the exhaust manifold to the exhaust pipe connection. Install the exhaust collector bracket.
19. Install the collector and collector cover. Refer to the section for Intake Manifold Removal And Installation for the correct torque pattern.
20. Connect all the vacuum hoses and water hoses to the intake collector.
21. Refill the cooling system. Start the engine and then check the engine timing. After the engine reaches the normal operating temperature, check for the correct coolant level.
22. Roadtest the vehicle for proper operation.

CLEANING AND INSPECTION

♦ See Figures 116, 117 and 118

When the rocker assembly and valve train have been removed from the cylinder head (see Valves and Springs below), set the cylinder head on two wooden blocks on the bench, combustion chamber side up. Using a scraper or putty knife, carefully scrape away any gasket material that may have stuck to the head-to-block mating surface when the head was removed. Make sure you DO NOT gouge the mating surface with the tool.

Using a wire brush chucked into your electric drill, remove the carbon in each combustion chamber. Make sure the brush is actually removing the carbon and not merely burnishing it.

Clean all the valve guides using a valve guide brush (available at most auto parts or auto tool shops) and solvent. A fine-bristled rifle bore cleaning brush also works here.

Inspect the threads of each spark plug hole by screwing a plug into each, making sure it screws down completely. Heli-coil® any plug hole this is damaged.

✱✱ CAUTION

DO NOT hot tank the cylinder head! The head material on most engines is aluminum, which is ruined if subjected to the hot tank solution. Some of the early engines were equipped with cast iron heads, which can be hot-tanked (a service performed by most machine shops which immerses the head in a hot, caustic solution for cleaning). To be sure your engine's cylinder head is aluminum, check around its perimeter with a magnet. Your engine has an iron head if the magnet sticks.

➥Before hot-tanking any overhead cam cylinder head, check with the machine shop doing the work. Some cam bearings are easily damaged by the hot tank solution.

Finally, go over the entire head with a clean shop rag soaked in solvent to remove any grit, old gasket particles, etc. Blow out the bolt holes, coolant galleys, intake and exhaust ports, valve guides and plug holes with compressed air.

RESURFACING

♦ See Figures 119 and 120

While the head is removed, check the head-to-block mating surface for straightness. If the engine has overheated and blown a head gasket, this must be done as a matter of course. A warped mating surface must be resurfaced (milled); this is done on a milling machine and is quite similar to planing a piece of wood.

Using a precision steel straightedge and a blade-type feeler gauge, check the surface of the head across its length, width and diagonal length as shown in the illustrations. Also check the intake and exhaust manifold mating surfaces and cam cover (all) mating surfaces. If warpage exceeds 0.003 in. (0.08mm) in a 6 in. (152mm) span, or 0.005 in. (0.15mm) over the total length, the head must be milled. If warpage is highly excessive, the head must be replaced. Again, consult the machine shop operator on head milling limitations.

CYLINDER BLOCK CLEANING

While the cylinder head is removed, the top of the cylinder block and pistons should also be cleaned. Before you begin, rotate the crankshaft until one or more pistons are flush with the top of the block (on the four cylinder engines, you will either have Nos. 1 and 4 up, or Nos. 2 and 3 up). Carefully stuff clean rags into the cylinders in which the pistons are down. This will help keep grit and carbon chips out during cleaning. Using care not to gouge or scratch the block-to-head mating surface and the piston top(s), clean away any old gasket material with a wire brush and/or scraper. On the piston tops, make sure you are actually removing the carbon and not merely burnishing it.

Remove the rags from the down cylinders after you have wiped the top of the block with a solvent soaked rag. Rotate the crankshaft until the other pistons come up flush with the top of the block, and clean those pistons.

ENGINE AND ENGINE REBUILDING   3-27

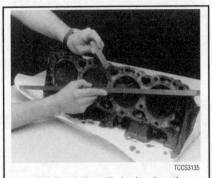
Fig. 118 Check the cylinder head mating surface straightness with a precision straightedge and a feeler gauge

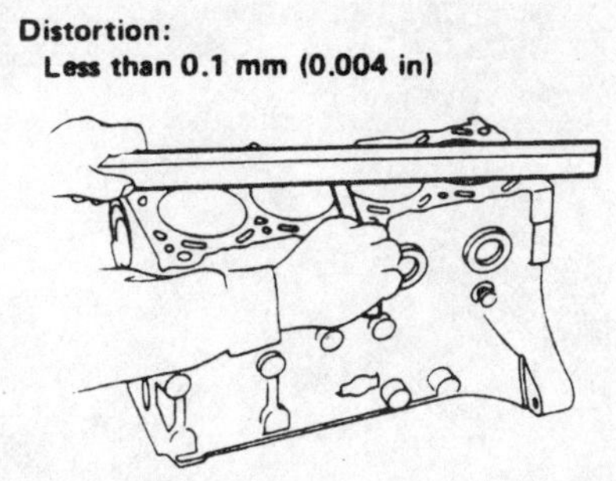

Fig. 119 Check the engine block mating surface straightness with a precision straightedge and a feeler gauge

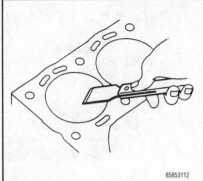
Fig. 120 Removing carbon from the piston tops-do not scratch the pistons

➡ Because you have rotated the crankshaft, you will have to re-time the engine following the procedure listed under the Timing Chain/Timing Belt removal. Make sure you wipe out each cylinder thoroughly with a solvent-soaked rag, to remove all traces of grit, before the head is reassembled to the block.

Valves and Springs

ADJUSTMENT (AFTER ENGINE SERVICE)

The valves on all engines covered here must be adjusted following any valve train disassembly. Follow the procedure listed in Section 2 for valve adjustment.

REMOVAL & INSTALLATION

◆ See Figures 121 thru 128

A valve spring compressor is needed to remove the valves and springs; these are available at most auto parts and auto tool shops. A small magnet is very helpful for removing the keepers and spring seats.

Set the head on its side on the bench. Install the spring compressor so that the fixed side of the tool is flat against the valve head in the combustion chamber, and the screw side is against the retainer. Slowly turn the screw in towards the head, compressing the spring. As the spring compresses, the keepers will be revealed; pick them off of the valve stem with the magnet as they are easily fumbled and lost. When the keepers are removed, back the screw out, then remove the retainers and springs. Remove the compressor and pull the valves

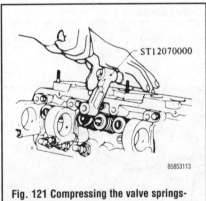
Fig. 121 Compressing the valve springs- all 4 cylinder engines

Fig. 122 Compressing the valve springs— VG30i engines

Fig. 123 Removing the valve spring

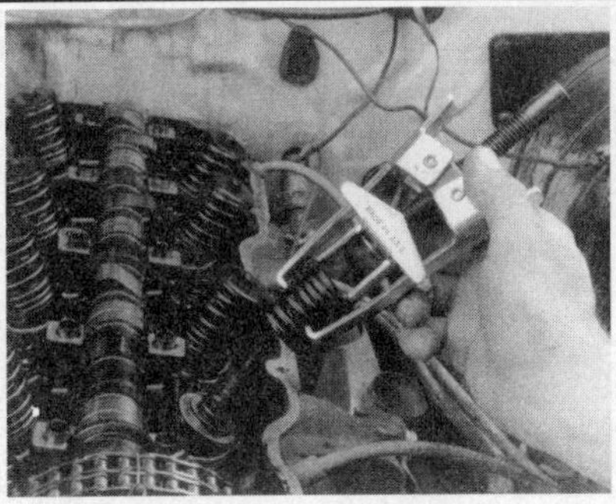

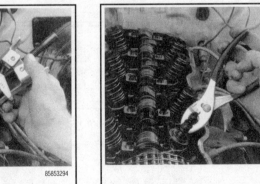
Fig. 124 Removing the valve spring

Fig. 125 Removing the oil seal

Fig. 126 View of the valve oil seal

3-28 ENGINE AND ENGINE REBUILDING

Fig. 127 Removing the valve spring seat

Fig. 128 View of the valve spring seat

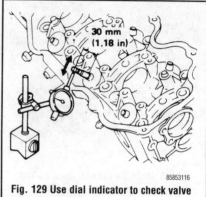

Fig. 129 Use dial indicator to check valve guide deflection

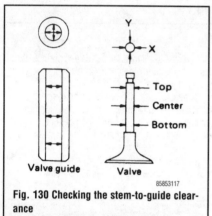

Fig. 130 Checking the stem-to-guide clearance

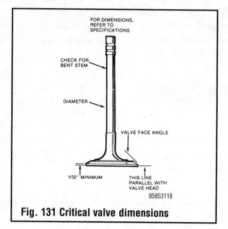

Fig. 131 Critical valve dimensions

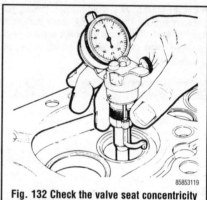

Fig. 132 Check the valve seat concentricity with a dial gauge

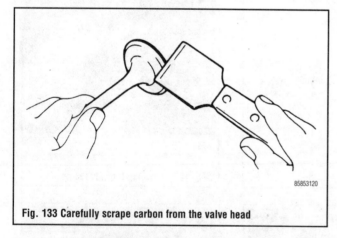

Fig. 133 Carefully scrape carbon from the valve head

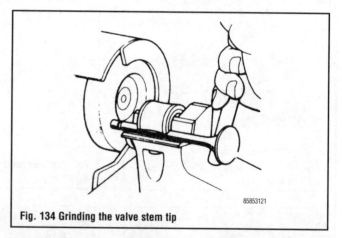

Fig. 134 Grinding the valve stem tip

out of the head from the other side. Remove the valve seals by hand and remove the spring seats with the magnet.

Since it is very important that each valve (along with it's spring, retainer, spring seat and keepers) is reassembled in its original location, you must keep these parts in order. The best way to do this to cut either eight (four cylinder) or twelve (six cylinder) holes in a piece of heavy cardboard or wood. Label each hole with the cylinder number and either **IN** or **EX**, corresponding to the location of each valve in the head. As you remove each valve, insert it into the holder. Assemble the seats, springs, keepers and retainers to the stem on the labeled side of the holder. This way each valve and its attending parts are kept together, and can be put back into the head in their proper locations.

After lapping each valve into its seat (see Valve Lapping below), oil each valve stem, and install each valve into the head in the reverse order of removal, so that all parts except the keepers are assembled on the stem. Always use new valve stem seals. Install the spring compressor tool, then compress the retainer and spring until the keeper groove on the valve stem is fully revealed. Coat the groove with a wipe of grease (to hold the keepers until the retainer is released) and install

both keepers, wide end up. Slowly back the screw of the compressor out until the spring retainer covers the keepers. Remove the tool. Lightly tap the end of each valve stem with a rubber hammer to ensure proper fit of the retainers and keepers.

INSPECTION

◆ See Figures 129 thru 134

Before the valves can be properly inspected, the stem, lower end of the stem and the entire valve face and head must be cleaned. An old valve works well for chipping carbon from the valve head, and a wire brush, gasket scraper or putty knife can be used for cleaning the valve face and the area between the face and lower stem. Do not scratch the valve face during cleaning. Clean the entire stem with a rag soaked in thinners to remove all varnish and gum.

Thorough inspection of the valves requires the use of a micrometer, and a dial indicator is needed to measure the inside diameter of the valve guides. If these instruments are not available to you, the valves and head can be taken to a

ENGINE AND ENGINE REBUILDING 3-29

reputable machine shop for inspection. Refer to the Valve Specifications chart for valve stem and stem-to-guide specifications.

If the above instruments are at your disposal, measure the diameter of each valve stem. Jot these measurements down. Using the dial indicator, measure the inside diameter of the valve guides at their bottom, top and midpoint 90° apart. Jot these measurements down also. Subtract the valve stem measurement from the valve guide inside measurement; if the clearance exceeds that listed in the specifications chart under Stem-to-Guide Clearance, replace the valve(s). Stem-to-guide clearance can also be checked at a machine shop, where a dial indicator would be used.

Check the top of each valve stem for pitting and unusual wear due to improper rocker adjustment, etc. The stem tip can be ground flat if it is worn, but no more than 0.020 in. (0.50mm) can be removed; if this limit must be exceeded to make the tip flat and square, then the valve must be replaced. If the valve stem tips are ground, make sure you fix the valve securely into a jig designed for this purpose, so the tip contacts the grinding wheel squarely at exactly 90 degrees. Most machine shops that handle automotive work are equipped for this job.

REFACING

♦ See Figures 135 and 136

Valve refacing should only be handled by a reputable machine shop, as the experience and equipment needed to do the job are beyond that of the average owner/mechanic. During the course of a normal valve job, refacing is necessary if simply lapping the valves into their seats will not correct the seat and face wear. When the valves are reground (resurfaced), the valve seats must also be recut, again requiring special equipment and experience.

Valve Springs

INSPECTION

♦ See Figures 137 and 138

Valve spring squareness, length and tension should be checked while the valve train is disassembled. Place each valve spring on a flat surface next to a steel square. Measure the length of the spring, and rotate it against the edge of the square to measure distortion. If spring length varies (by comparison) by more than 0.062 in. (1.6mm) or if distortion exceeds 0.062 in. (1.6mm), replace the spring.

Spring tension must be checked on a spring tester. Springs used on most engines should be within one pound of each other when tested at their specified installed heights.

Valve Guides

INSPECTION

♦ See Figure 139

Valve guides should be cleaned as outlined earlier, and checked when valve stem diameter and stem-to-guide clearance is checked. Generally, if the engine is using oil through the guides (assuming the valve seals are OK) and the valve stem diameter is within specification, it is the guides that are worn and need to be replaced.

Valve guides which are not excessively worn or distorted may, in some cases, be knurled rather than replaced. Knurling is a process in which metal inside the valve guide bore is displaced and raised (forming a very fine cross-hatch pattern), thereby reducing clearance. Knurling also provides for excellent oil control. The possibility of knurling rather than replacing the guides should be discussed with a machinist.

REMOVAL & INSTALLATION

♦ See Figures 140, 141, 142 and 143

All Engines Except VG30i

1. With the cylinder head removed from the engine, and the valves removed from the head, use a drift and a hammer or press. Drive the valve guides out from the combustion chamber side toward the rocker cover side. A heated cylinder head will facilitate the operation.

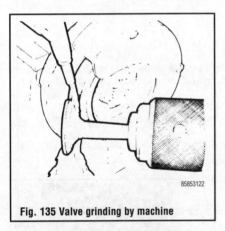

Fig. 135 Valve grinding by machine

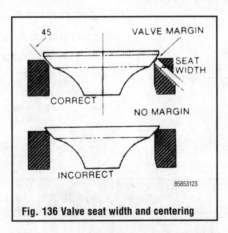

Fig. 136 Valve seat width and centering

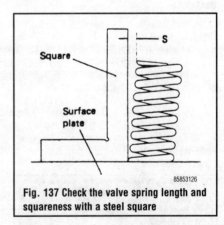

Fig. 137 Check the valve spring length and squareness with a steel square

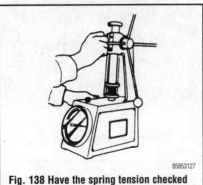

Fig. 138 Have the spring tension checked at a machine shop

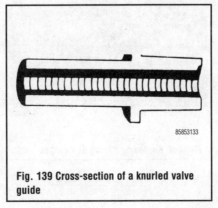

Fig. 139 Cross-section of a knurled valve guide

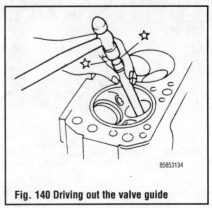

Fig. 140 Driving out the valve guide

3-30 ENGINE AND ENGINE REBUILDING

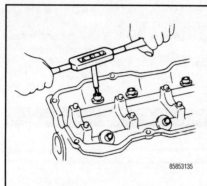

Fig. 141 Reaming the cylinder head valve guide hole

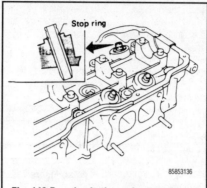

Fig. 142 Pressing in the replacement valve guide—4 cylinder engine

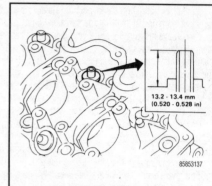

Fig. 143 Pressing in the replacement valve guide—VG30i engines

2. Ream the cylinder head side guide hole at room temperature. The guide hole should be 0.4719–0.4723 in. (11.989–11.996mm) for standard valves and 0.4797–0.4802 in. (12.184–12.197mm) for 0.0079 in. (0.2mm) oversize valves which are available for service.

3. After heating the cylinder head to 302–392°F (150–200°C) or 302–320°F (150–160°C) on the Z24i, press the new valve guide carefully into the cylinder head. The top of the valve guide should protrude out the top of the guide hole 0.4173 in. (10.5mm).

4. Ream the bore of the valve guide with the valve guide pressed into the cylinder head. The standard valve guide bore size is 0.3150–0.3157 in. (8.00–8.02mm).

5. Assemble the cylinder head and install it on the engine.

VG30i Engines

1. Remove the valve springs.
2. Heat the cylinder head to at least 320°F (160°C), then drive out the guide using an arbor press or a hammer and drift punch.

➡ Drive the valve guides toward the rocker arm cover side of the cylinder head.

3. With the valve guides removed, ream the cylinder head valve guide hole (inside diameter) to:
   a. Intake: 0.4400–0.4408 in. (11.176–11.196mm)
   b. Exhaust: 0.4793–0.4802 in. (12.174–12.197mm)
4. Heat the cylinder to at least 320°F (160°C) and press the service valve guide onto the cylinder head.
5. Ream the valve guide (inside diameter) to:
   a. Intake: 0.2756–0.2763 in. (7.000–7.018mm)
   b. Exhaust: 0.3150–0.3157 in. (8.000–8.019mm)
6. To install, use new gaskets and valve guide seals, then reverse the removal procedures.

Oil Pan

REMOVAL & INSTALLATION

♦ See Figures 144, 145 and 146

1970–86 (720-D Series)

To remove the oil pan it will be necessary to unbolt the motor mounts and jack the engine to gain clearance. Remove the stabilizer bar or any other suspension or member that may make access easier to remove the pan. Drain the oil and remove the attaching screw, then remove the oil pan and gasket. Apply a thin bead of silicone seal to the engine block at the junction of the block and front cover, then to the junction of the block and the main bearing cap. Apply a thin coat of silicone seal to the new oil pan gasket, install the gasket to the block, and install the pan. Tighten the pan bolts in a circular pattern from the center of the ends, to 4–7 ft. lbs. (5–10 Nm). Overtightening will distort the pan lip, causing leakage.

1986–88 (D21-D Series)

Z24I ENGINES

1. Remove the engine under cover and drain the engine oil.
2. Remove the bolt from the front differential carrier member on 4wd models.
3. Position a floor jack under the front differential carrier and remove the mounting bolts.
4. On 2wd models, remove the front crossmember.
5. On 4wd models, remove the transmission-to-rear engine mount bracket nuts.
6. Remove the engine mount nuts and bolts. Attach and engine hoist and raise the engine slightly.

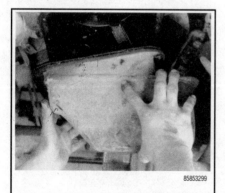

Fig. 144 Removing the oil pan

Fig. 145 Removing the oil pan gasket

Fig. 146 View of the engine with oil pan removed

ENGINE AND ENGINE REBUILDING

7. Remove the oil pan mounting bolts. Insert a seal cutter tool between the cylinder block and the oil pan, then tap it around the circumference of the pan with a hammer. Remove the oil pan.

→ Be careful not to drive the seal cutter into the oil pump or rear oil seal retainer as you will damage the aluminum mating surface.

To install:

8. Remove all traces of gasket material from the pan and block mating surfaces.
9. Apply a continuous bead of sealant 0.137–0.177 in. (3.5–4.5mm) to the oil pan mating surface. Be sure to trace the sealant bead to the inside of the bolt holes where there is no groove.
10. Install the pan and tighten all bolts in the reverse order of removal. Tighten the bolts to 4–5 ft. lbs. (4–7 Nm).
11. Wait at least 30 minutes and then refill the engine with oil. Run the engine until it reaches normal operating temperature and then check for leaks.

VG30I ENGINES

♦ See Figures 147, 148 and 149

1. Remove the engine under cover and drain the engine oil.
2. On 2wd models, remove the stabilizer bar bracket bolts.
3. On 4wd models, remove the front driveshaft and disconnect the halfshafts at the transfer case. Position a floor jack under the front differential carrier and remove the mounting bolts.
4. On 2wd models, remove the front crossmember.
5. Remove the idler arm.
6. Remove the starter motor.
7. On 4wd models, remove the transmission-to-rear engine mount bracket nut, then remove the engine mount nuts and bolts.
8. Remove the engine gussets.
9. On 4wd models, attach and engine hoist and raise the engine slightly.
10. Remove the oil pan mounting bolts in the order shown. Insert a seal cutter tool between the cylinder block and the oil pan, then tap it around the circumference of the pan with a hammer. Remove the oil pan.

→ Be careful not to drive the seal cutter into the oil pump or rear oil seal retainer as you will damage the aluminum mating surface.

To install:

11. Remove all traces of gasket material from the pan and block mating surfaces.
12. Apply sealant to the oil pump and oil seal retainer gasket.
13. Apply a continuous bead of sealant 0.137–0.177 in. (3.5–4.5mm) to the oil pan mating surface. Be sure to trace the sealant bead to the inside of the bolt holes where there is no groove.
14. Install the pan and tighten all bolts in the reverse order of removal. Tighten the bolts to 4–5 ft. lbs. (4–7 Nm).
15. Wait at least 30 minutes and then refill the engine with oil. Run the engine until it reaches normal operating temperature and then check for leaks.

Oil Pump

REMOVAL & INSTALLATION

♦ See Figures 150, 151 and 152

All Four Cylinder Engines

♦ See Figures 153, 154 and 155

The oil pump is mounted externally on the engine, eliminating the need to remove the oil pan in order to remove the oil pump.

1. Remove the distributor.
2. Drain the engine oil.
3. Remove the front stabilizer bar.
4. Remove the splash shield board.
5. Loosen the mounting bolts and remove the oil pump body with the drive spindle assembly.

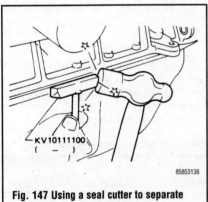

Fig. 147 Using a seal cutter to separate the oil pan from the cylinder block

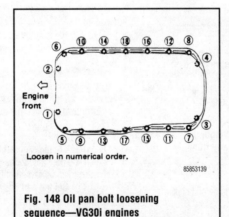

Fig. 148 Oil pan bolt loosening sequence—VG30i engines

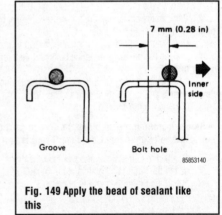

Fig. 149 Apply the bead of sealant like this

Fig. 150 Removing the oil pump-4-cylinder engines

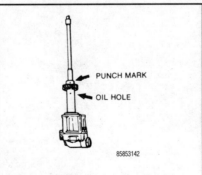

Fig. 151 Aligning the punch mark on the spindle with the hole in the oil pump-4-cylinder engines

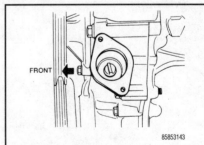

Fig. 152 The projection on the top of the oil pump, drive spindle located in the 11:25 O'clock position. The smaller crescent formed by the notch faces forward-4-cylinder engines

3-32 ENGINE AND ENGINE REBUILDING

Fig. 153 Removing the oil pump assembly

Fig. 154 Removing the oil pump mounting gasket

Fig. 155 View of the oil pump gear and drive spindle

To install:

6. Before installing the oil pump in the engine, turn the crankshaft so that the No. 1 piston is at TDC of the compression stroke.

7. Fill the pump housing with engine oil, then align the punch mark on the spindle with the hole in the oil pump.

8. With a new gasket placed over the drive spindle, install the oil pump and drive spindle assembly so that the projection on the top of the drive spindle is located in the 11:25 o'clock position (between 11 and 12 o'clock).

9. Install the distributor with the metal tip of the rotor pointing toward the No. 1 spark plug tower of the distributor cap.

10. Install the splash shield and front stabilizer bar.

11. Refill the engine with oil. Start the engine, check ignition timing and check for oil leaks.

VG30i Engines

♦ See Figure 156

1. Remove the oil pan. Remove the timing belt.
2. Remove the crankshaft timing sprocket (it may be necessary to use a puller) and the timing belt plate.
3. Remove the oil pump strainer and pick-up tube from the oil pump.
4. Loosen the oil pump retaining bolts and then remove the oil pump.

To install:

5. Use new gaskets (use silicone sealant), and a new oil seal. Tighten the 6mm bolts to 4–5 ft. lbs. (6–7 Nm) and the 8mm bolts to 9–12 ft. lbs. (12–16 Nm). Refill the engine with oil.

➡ Before installing the oil pump, be sure to pack the pump's cavity with petroleum jelly, then make sure the O-ring is properly fitted.

6. Connect the oil strainer and pick-up tube to the pump body.
7. Install the timing belt plate and the crankshaft pulley.
8. Install the timing belt and front cover. Start the engine and check for any leaks.

Timing Chain Cover

REMOVAL & INSTALLATION

♦ See Figures 157 thru 170

All Four Cylinder Engines

1. Disconnect the negative battery cable from the battery, drain the cooling system, and remove the radiator together with the upper and lower radiator hoses.

2. Loosen the alternator drive belt adjusting screw and remove the drive belt. Remove the bolts which attach the alternator bracket to the engine and position the alternator aside out of the way.

3. Remove the distributor.

4. Remove the oil pump attaching screws, then take out the pump and its drive spindle.

5. Remove the cooling fan and the fan pulley together with the drive belt.

6. Remove the water pump.

7. Remove the crankshaft pulley bolt and then remove the crankshaft pulley.

8. Remove the bolts holding the front cover to the front of the cylinder block, the four bolts which retain the front of the oil pan to the bottom of the front cover and the two bolts which are screwed down through the front of the cylinder head; into the top of the front cover.

9. Carefully pry the front cover off the front of the engine.

To install:

10. Cut the exposed front section of the oil pan gasket away from the oil pan. Do the same to the gasket at the top of the front cover. Remove the two side gaskets and clean all of the mating surfaces.

11. Cut the portions needed from a new oil pan gasket and top front cover gasket.

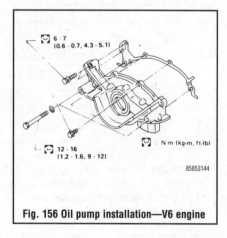

Fig. 156 Oil pump installation—V6 engine

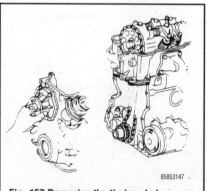

Fig. 157 Removing the timing chain cover—all 4-cylinder engines

Fig. 158 Removing the crankshaft pulley center bolt

ENGINE AND ENGINE REBUILDING   3-33

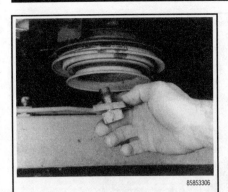
Fig. 159 View of the crankshaft pulley center bolt

Fig. 160 Removing the crankshaft pulley to hub bolts

Fig. 161 Removing the crankshaft pulley to hub spacer

Fig. 162 Matchmark the crankshaft pulley to hub

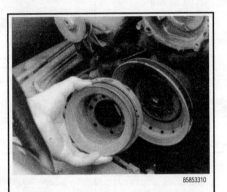
Fig. 163 Removing the crankshaft pulley

Fig. 164 Removing the crankshaft pulley hub

Fig. 165 Removing the crankshaft pulley hub plate

Fig. 166 View of the crankshaft pulley hub plate

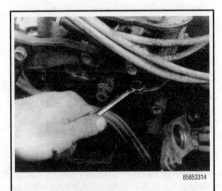
Fig. 167 Removing the timing chain cover upper mounting bolts

Fig. 168 Removing the timing chain cover center bolts

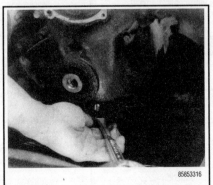
Fig. 169 Removing the timing chain cover lower mounting bolts

Fig. 170 Removing the timing chain cover—always install with new gasket

3-34 ENGINE AND ENGINE REBUILDING

12. Apply sealer to all of the gaskets and position them on the engine in their proper places.
13. Apply a light coating of oil to the crankshaft oil seal and carefully mount in the front cover to the front of the engine and install all of the mounting bolts. Tighten the 8mm bolts to 7–12 ft. lbs. (10–16 Nm) and the 6mm bolts to 3–7 ft. lbs. (4–10 Nm). Tighten the oil pan attaching bolts to 4–7 ft. lb. (6–8 Nm).
14. Before installing the oil pump, place the gasket over the shaft and make sure that the mark on the drive spindle faces (aligned with) the oil pump hole. Install the oil pump so that the projection on the top of the shaft is located in the exact position as when it was removed. Make sure the projection is at the 11:25 o'clock position (between 11 and 12 o'clock) when the piston in the No. 1 cylinder is placed at TDC on the compression stroke, if the engine was disturbed since disassembly. Tighten the oil pump attaching screws to 8–10 ft. lbs. (11–15 Nm).
15. Install the crankshaft pulley and bolt. Tighten the bolt to 87–116 ft. lbs. (118–157 Nm).
16. Install the water pump with a new gasket. Install the fan pulley and cooling fan. Install the drive belt and adjust the belt to the correct tension.
17. Install the distributor in the correct position. Reconnect the alternator bracket and alternator if it was removed. Install the drive belt and adjust the belt to the correct tension.
18. Install the radiator, reconnect the upper and lower radiator hoses, then refill the cooling system.
19. Reconnect the negative battery cable. Start the engine, check ignition timing and check for leaks.

Timing Belt Cover

REMOVAL & INSTALLATION

VG30i Engines

➥The front oil seal is a part of the oil pump assembly. To replace the oil pump seal, refer to the Oil Pump Removal and Installation procedures, in this section.

1. Remove the radiator shroud, the fan and the pulleys.
2. Drain the coolant from the radiator and remove the water pump hose.
3. Remove the power steering, A/C compressor and alternator drive belts.
4. Remove the suction pipe bracket and then remove the lower hose from the suction pipe.
5. Remove the spark plugs.
6. Set the No. 1 piston at TDC of its compression stroke and the remove the idler bracket for the compressor drive belt.
7. Remove the crankshaft pulley.
8. Loosen all bolts, then remove the upper and lower timing belt covers.

To install:

9. Install the two timing belt covers and tighten the mounting bolts to 2–4 ft. lbs. (3–5 Nm).
10. Press the crankshaft pulley onto the crankshaft and tighten the bolt to 90–98 ft. lbs. (123–132 Nm). Install the spark plugs.
11. Install the A/C compressor idler bracket.
12. Install the suction pipe bracket and connect the lower hose. Install all drive belts and adjust their tension.
13. Reconnect the water pump hose and fill the engine with coolant. Install the fan shroud and pulleys. Start the engine and check for any leaks.

Front Oil Seal

REMOVAL & INSTALLATION

♦ See Figures 171, 172, 173 and 174

Four Cylinder Engines

1. Remove the front cover.
2. Pry the old seal from the cover with a pointed piece of plastic or wood. Do not use a screwdriver in order to avoid scratching the seal surface.
3. Oil the lip of the new seal. Do not use grease. Press it into place, making sure the flat side faces forward and the lip faces the engine.
4. Install the front cover.

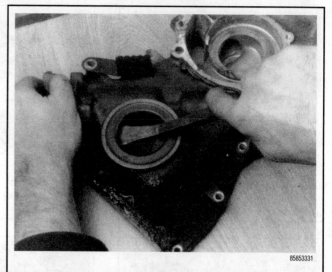

Fig. 171 Removing the front seal form the timing chain cover

Fig. 172 Installing the front seal in the timing chain cover

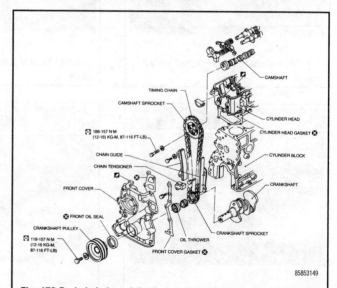

Fig. 173 Exploded view of the timing chain assembly-all 4-cylinder engines

ENGINE AND ENGINE REBUILDING 3-35

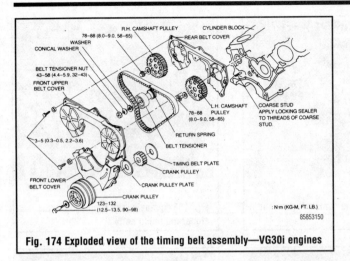

Fig. 174 Exploded view of the timing belt assembly—VG30i engines

VG30i Engines

The front oil seal is a part of the oil pump assembly. To replace the oil pump seal, please refer to the Oil Pump Removal and Installation procedures in this section.

Timing Chain and Tensioner

REMOVAL & INSTALLATION

All 4 Cylinder Engines

◆ See Figures 175 thru 192

1. Before beginning any disassembly procedures, position the No. 1 piston at TDC on the compression stroke.

2. Remove the timing chain cover. Remove the cylinder head cover.
3. With the No. 1 piston at TDC, the timing marks on the camshaft sprocket and the timing chain should be visible. Mark both of them with paint. Also mark the relationship of the camshaft sprocket to the camshaft. At this point you will see that there are three sets of timing marks and locating holes in the sprocket. They are for making adjustments to compensate for timing chain stretch. See the Timing Chain Adjustment section following for details.
4. With the timing marks on the camshaft sprocket clearly marked, locate and mark the timing marks on the crankshaft sprocket. Also mark the chain timing mark. Of course, if the chain is not to be reused, marking it is useless.
5. Unbolt the camshaft sprocket and remove the sprocket along with the chain. As you remove the chain, hold it where the chain tensioner contacts it. When the chain is removed, the tensioner is going to come apart. **Hold on to it and you won't lose any of the parts!** The crankshaft sprocket can be removed with a puller, if necessary. There is no need to remove the chain guide unless it is being replaced.

To install:

6. Install the timing chain and the camshaft sprocket together after first positioning the chain over the crankshaft sprocket. Position the sprocket so that the marks made previously line up. This is assuming that the engine has not been disturbed. The camshaft and the crankshaft keys should both be pointing upward. If a new chain and/or gear is being installed, position the sprocket so that the timing marks on the chain align with the marks on the sprocket (with both keys pointing up). The marks are on the right hand side of the sprockets as you face the engine. 1970–73 L16 and L18 engines have 42 pins between the mating marks of the chain and sprockets when the chain is installed correctly. 1974–80 L18 and L20B engines have 44 pins.

➡The factory refers to the pins as links, but in American terminology this is incorrect. Count the pins. There are two (2) pins per chain link. This is an important step! If you do not get the exact number of pins between the timing marks, valve timing will be incorrect, and the engine will either not run at all or will run very badly.

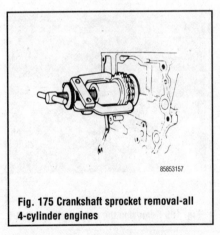

Fig. 175 Crankshaft sprocket removal—all 4-cylinder engines

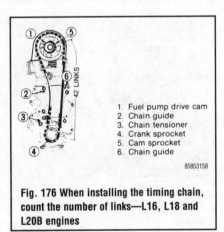

Fig. 176 When installing the timing chain, count the number of links—L16, L18 and L20B engines

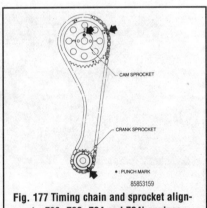

Fig. 177 Timing chain and sprocket alignment—Z20, Z22, Z24 and Z24i engines

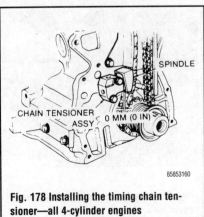

Fig. 178 Installing the timing chain tensioner—all 4-cylinder engines

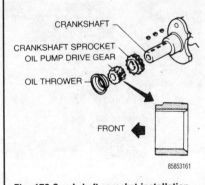

Fig. 179 Crankshaft sprocket installation—Z20, Z22, Z24 and Z24i engines

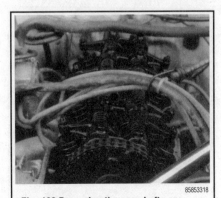

Fig. 180 Removing the camshaft gear retaining bolt

ENGINE AND ENGINE REBUILDING

Fig. 181 View of the camshaft gear retaining bolt

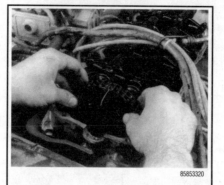
Fig. 182 Removing the camshaft gear and timing chain

Fig. 183 Removing the timing chain tensioner mounting bolts

Fig. 184 View of the timing chain tensioner assembly

Fig. 185 Removing the timing chain assembly oil thrower

Fig. 186 Removing the oil pump drive gear

Fig. 187 Marking the oil pump drive gear for correct installation

Fig. 188 Marking the timing chain if necessary

Fig. 189 Removing the crankshaft sprocket

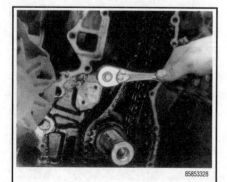
Fig. 190 Removing the timing chain guide bolt

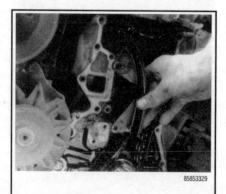
Fig. 191 Removing the timing chain guide

Fig. 192 Cleaning the timing chain case cover area

ENGINE AND ENGINE REBUILDING 3-37

➡ Z20, Z22, Z24 and Z24i engines do not use the pin counting method for finding correct valve timing. Instead, set the timing chain by aligning its mating marks with those of the crankshaft sprocket and camshaft sprocket. The camshaft sprocket should be installed by fitting the knock pin of the camshaft into its No. 2 hole. And the No. 2 timing mark must also be used.

7. Install the camshaft sprocket bolt and tighten it to 87–116 ft. lbs. (118–157 Nm).
8. Install the chain guide and tensioner. Adjust the protrusion of the chain tensioner spindle to zero clearance. Tighten the bolts to 4–7 ft. lbs. (6–10 Nm).
9. With a new seal installed in the timing chain cover and a light coat of oil applied to the seal, install the timing cover. Start the engine and check for any leaks. Check the ignition timing.

TIMING CHAIN ADJUSTMENT

L16, L18 and L20B Engines

When the timing chain stretches excessively, the valve timing will be adversely affected. There are two camshaft sprocket locating holes provided to correct the valve timing. Actually there are three sets of holes and timing marks on the camshaft sprocket; the third hole and timing mark are for 6 cylinder Datsun engines and in the case of the Datsun pick-ups, these are obviously ignored.

If the stretch of the chain roller links is excessive, adjust the camshaft sprocket location by transferring the camshaft set position of the camshaft sprocket from the factory position of the No. 1 to the No. 2 as follows:

1. Turn the crankshaft until the No. 1 piston is at TDC on its compression stroke. Examine whether the camshaft sprocket location notch is to the left of the oblong groove on the camshaft retaining plate. If the notch in the sprocket is to the left of the groove in the retaining plate, then the chain is stretched and needs to be adjusted.
2. Remove the camshaft sprocket and timing chain, then reinstall the sprocket and chain. Make sure the locating dowel on the camshaft is inserted into the No. 2 hole of the sprocket and the timing mark on the timing chain is aligned with the No. 2 marks on the sprocket. The amount of modification is 4 degrees of crankshaft rotation.
3. Recheck the valve timing as outlined in Step 1. The notch in the sprocket should be to the right of the groove in the camshaft retaining plate.
4. If and when the notch cannot be brought to the right of the groove with the sprocket installed in the No. 2 hole, the timing chain must be replaced to regain the proper valve timing.

Timing Belt

REMOVAL & INSTALLATION

▶ See Figures 193, 194, 195, 196 and 197

VG30i Engines

▶ See Figures 198 thru 205

1. Remove the upper and lower timing belt covers.
2. Turn the crankshaft so that the No. 1 cylinder is at the TDC of the compression stroke.
3. Using chalk or paint, mark the relationship of the timing belt to the camshaft and the crankshaft sprockets; also, mark the timing belt's direction of rotation.
4. Loosen the timing belt tensioner and return spring, then remove the timing belt.

To install:

✻✻ CAUTION

Before installing the timing belt, confirm that the No. 1 cylinder is set at the TDC of the compression stroke.

5. Remove both cylinder head covers and loosen all rocker arm shaft retaining bolts.

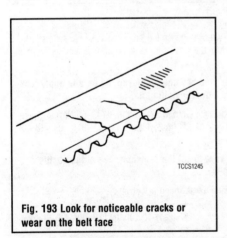
Fig. 193 Look for noticeable cracks or wear on the belt face

Fig. 194 Inspect the timing belt for cracks, fraying, glazing or damage of any kind

Fig. 195 Damage on only one side of the timing belt may indicate a faulty guide

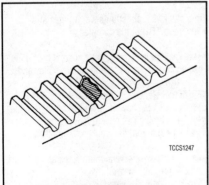
Fig. 196 Foreign materials can get in between the teeth and cause damage

Fig. 197 ALWAYS replace the timing belt at the interval specified by the manufacturer

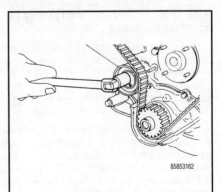
Fig. 198 Loosening the timing belt tensioner—VG30i engines

3-38 ENGINE AND ENGINE REBUILDING

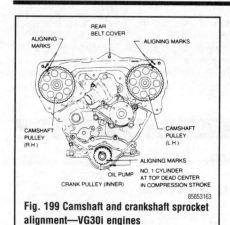

Fig. 199 Camshaft and crankshaft sprocket alignment—VG30i engines

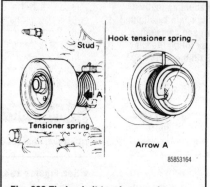

Fig. 200 Timing belt tensioner and return spring installation—VG30i engines

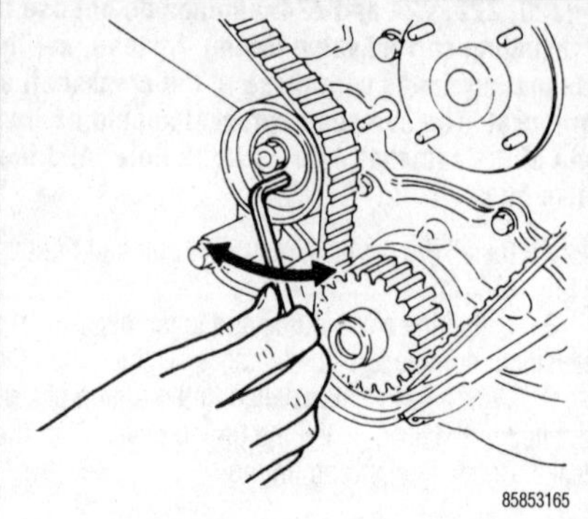

Fig. 201 Tighten the tensioner lock-nut—VG30i engines

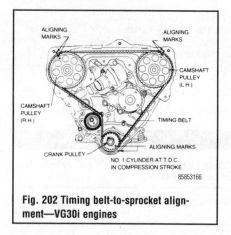

Fig. 202 Timing belt-to-sprocket alignment—VG30i engines

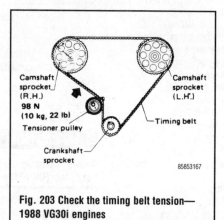

Fig. 203 Check the timing belt tension—1988 VG30i engines

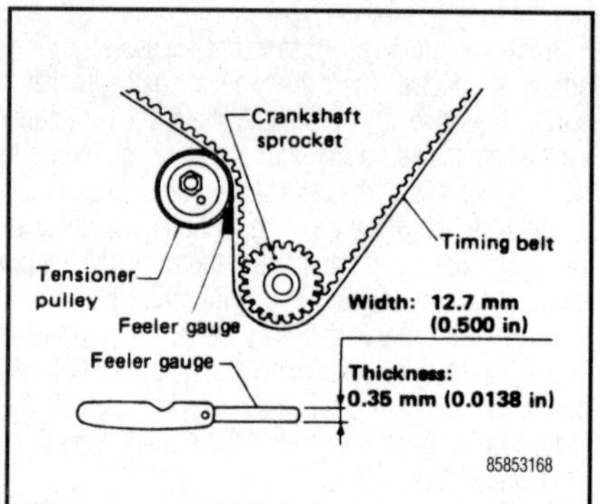

Fig. 204 Feeler gauge positioning—1988 VG30i engines

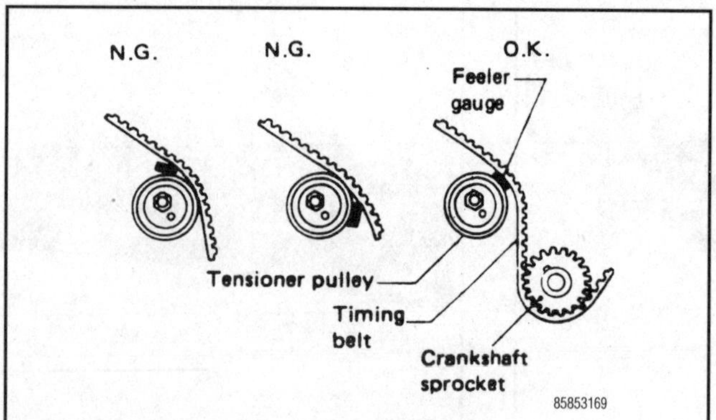

Fig. 205 Turn the crankshaft until the feeler gauge is in this position—1988 VG30i engines

➡ The rocker arm shaft bolts MUST be loosened so that the correct belt tension can be obtained.

6. Install the tensioner and the return spring. Using a hexagon wrench, turn the tensioner clockwise and temporarily tighten the lock-nut.
7. Make sure that the timing belt is clean and free from oil or water.
8. When installing the timing belt align the white lines on the belt with the punchmarks on the camshaft and crankshaft sprockets. Have the arrow on the timing belt pointing toward the front belt covers.

➡ A good way (although rather tedious!) to check for proper timing belt installation is to count the number of belt teeth between the timing marks. There are 133 teeth on the belt; there should be 40 teeth between the timing marks on the left and right side camshaft sprockets, and 43 teeth between the timing marks on the left side camshaft sprocket and the crankshaft sprocket.

9. **1986–87 Engines:**
   a. Using a hexagon wrench, loosen the tensioner lock bolt, set the tensioner and then slowly turn the tensioner clockwise and counterclockwise 2–3 times.

➡ If the coarse tensioner stud has been removed, be sure to apply locking sealer to the threads before installing it.

   b. Tighten the tensioner lock-nut to 32–43 ft. lbs. (43–58 Nm). Tighten the rocker arm shaft retaining bolts (in 2–3 stages) to 13–16 ft. lbs. (18–22 Nm).

➡ Before tightening, be sure to set the camshaft lobe at the position where the lobe is not lifted.

   c. Install the upper and lower timing belt covers.
10. **1988 Engines:**
   a. While keeping the tensioner steady, loosen the lock-nut with a hexagon wrench.
   b. Turn the tension approximately 70–80 degrees clockwise with the wrench and then tighten the lock-nut.
   c. Turn the crankshaft in a clockwise direction several times and then **slowly** set the No. 1 piston to TDC of the compression stroke.
   d. Apply 22 lbs. of pressure (push it in!) to the center span of the timing belt between the right side camshaft sprocket and the tensioner pulley and then loosen the tensioner lock-nut.
   e. Using a 0.0138 in. (0.35mm) feeler gauge (the actual width of the blade **must** be ½ in. thick!) positioned as shown in the illustration, turn the crankshaft clockwise (**slowly!**). The timing belt should move approximately 2½ teeth. Tighten the tensioner lock-nut, turn the crankshaft slightly and remove the feeler gauge.
   f. Slowly rotate the crankshaft clockwise several more times and then set the No. 1 piston to TDC of the compression stroke.
   g. Install the upper and lower timing belt covers.

ENGINE AND ENGINE REBUILDING

Camshaft Sprocket/Pulleys

REMOVAL & INSTALLATION

All 4 Cylinder Engines

1. Remove the timing chain with the camshaft sprocket.

➡ The engines are designed so that the camshaft sprocket MUST be removed at the same time that the timing chain is removed.

2. To install, use new gaskets and reverse the removal procedures. If necessary, adjust the timing chain.

VG30i Engines

1. Remove the timing belt.
2. Using an adjustable spanner wrench (to hold the camshaft pulley) and a socket wrench, remove the camshaft pulley bolt and washer.
3. Pull the camshaft pulley(s) from the camshaft(s). Be careful not to lose the woodruff key.

➡ The right and left camshaft pulleys are different parts. Install them in their correct positions. The right pulley has an R3 identification mark and the left pulley has an L3.

4. To install the camshaft pulleys, perform the following:
   a. Remove the cylinder head covers.
   b. Loosen the rocker arm shaft assembly bolts.
   c. Remove the spark plugs.
   d. Install the camshaft pulleys.
5. Install and adjust the timing belt.
6. Install the timing belt covers.

Camshaft

REMOVAL & INSTALLATION

L16, L18 and L20B Engines

♦ See Figures 206, 207, 208 and 209

➡ Removal of the cylinder head from the engine is optional. Mark and keep all parts in order for correct installation.

1. Remove the camshaft sprocket from the camshaft together with the timing chain. Refer to the Timing Chain procedures if necessary.
2. Loosen the valve rocker pivot lock-nut and remove the rocker arm by pressing down on the valve spring.
3. Remove the two retaining nuts on the camshaft retainer plate at the front of the cylinder head and carefully slide the camshaft out (towards the front of the vehicle) of the camshaft carrier.

To install:

4. Check camshaft runout, end-play, wear and journal clearance as described in this section.
5. Lightly coat the camshaft bearings with clean motor oil and carefully slide the camshaft into place in the camshaft carrier.
6. Install the camshaft retainer plate with the oblong groove in the face of the plate facing toward the front of the engine.
7. Check the valve timing as outlined under Timing Chain Removal and Installation and install the timing sprocket on the camshaft, tightening the bolt together with the fuel pump cam to 86–116 ft. lbs. (117–158 Nm).

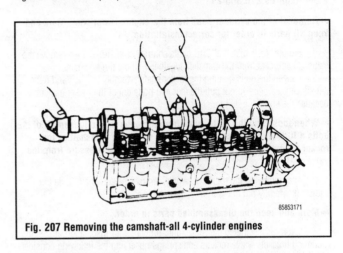

Fig. 207 Removing the camshaft-all 4-cylinder engines

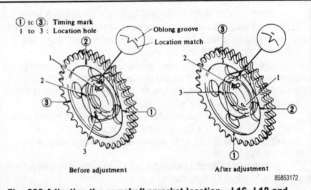

Fig. 208 Adjusting the camshaft sprocket location—L16, L18 and L20B engines

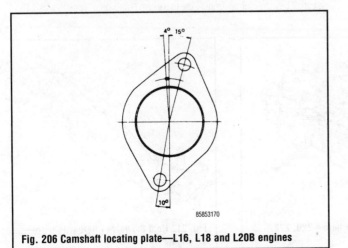

Fig. 206 Camshaft locating plate—L16, L18 and L20B engines

Fig. 209 Removing the camshaft most models similar

3-40 ENGINE AND ENGINE REBUILDING

8. Install the rocker arms by pressing down the valve springs with a screwdriver and install the valve rocker springs.
9. Install the cylinder head, if it was removed, and assemble the rest of the engine.
10. Start the engine and run it until it reaches normal operating temperature. Remove cylinder head cover, check and adjust valves if necessary. Install the cylinder head cover with a new gasket and check for oil leaks.

Z20, Z22, Z24 and Z24i Engines

◆ See Figures 210 and 211

➡ Removal of the cylinder head from the engine is optional. Mark and keep all parts in order for correct installation.

1. Set the No. 1 piston at TDC on its compression stroke, then remove the camshaft sprocket from the camshaft together with the timing chain.
2. Loosen the bolts holding the rocker shaft assembly in place and remove the six center bolts. Do not pull the four end bolts out of the rocker assembly because they hold the unit together.

➡ When loosening the bolts, work from the ends in and loosen all of the bolts a little at a time so that you do not strain the camshaft or the rocker assembly. Remember, the camshaft is under pressure from the valve springs!

3. After removing the rocker assembly, remove the camshaft. Slide the camshaft carefully out of the front of the vehicle.

➡ Mark and keep the disassembled parts in order.

4. If you disassembled the rocker unit, prepare it for installation. Install the mounting brackets, valve rockers and springs observing the following considerations:
   a. The two rocker shafts are different. Both have punch marks in the ends that face the front of the engine. The rocker shaft that goes on the side of the intake manifold has two slits in its end just below the punch mark. The exhaust side rocker shaft does not have slits.
   b. The rocker arms for the intake and exhaust valves are interchangeable between cylinders one and three and are identified by the mark **1**. Similarly, the rockers for cylinders two and four are interchangeable and are identified by the mark **2**.
   c. The rocker shaft mounting brackets are also coded for correct placement with either an **A** or a **Z** plus a number code.
5. Check camshaft runout, end-play wear and journal clearance as described in this section.
6. Apply sealant to the end camshaft saddles. Place the camshaft on the head with its knockpin pointing up.
7. Fit the rocker assembly on the head, making sure you mount it on its knock pin.
8. Tighten the bolts to 11–18 ft. lbs. (15–25 Nm), in several stages working from the middle bolts and moving outwards on both sides.

➡ Make sure that the engine is at TDC of the compression stroke for the No. 1 piston or you may damage some valves.

9. Adjust the valves.

VG30i Engines

◆ See Figures 212 and 213

➡ With the engine still mounted in the vehicle, Nissan recommends that the cylinder heads be removed from the engine, before removing the camshafts.

1. Remove the timing belt. Remove the cylinder head.
2. With cylinder head mounted on a suitable workbench, remove the rocker shafts with rocker arms. Bolts should be loosened in two or three stages.

➡ Hold the valve lifters with wire so that they will not drop from the lifter guide. Put an identification mark on the lifters to avoid mixing them up.

3. At the rear of the cylinder head, remove the cylinder head rear cover, camshaft bolt and the locating plate.
4. Remove the camshaft front oil seal and then slide the camshaft out the front of the cylinder head assembly.

To install:

5. Install camshaft, locator plate, cylinder head rear cover and front oil seal. Set the camshaft knock pin at the 12:00 o'clock position (straight up). Install cylinder head with new gasket to engine.
6. Install valve lifter guide assembly, being sure to assemble the valve lifters in their original positions. After installing them in the correct location, remove the wire holding them in lifter guide.
7. Install the rocker shafts in position with their rocker arms. Tighten the bolts in two or three stages to 13–16 ft. lbs. (18–22 Nm). Before tightening, be sure to set the camshaft lobe in a position where the lobe is not lifted or the valve closed. You can set each cylinder one at a time or follow the procedure below (the timing belt must be installed in the correct position):
   a. Set the No. 1 piston at TDC of its compression stroke and tighten the rocker shaft bolts for the No. 2, No. 4 and No. 6 cylinders.
   b. Set the No. 4 piston at TDC of its compression stroke and tighten the rocker shaft bolts for the No. 1, No. 3 and No. 5 cylinders.
   c. Tighten the rocker shaft retaining bolts to 13–16 ft. lbs. (18–22 Nm).
8. Install the rear timing belt cover and camshaft sprocket. The left and right camshaft sprockets are different parts. Install the correct sprocket in the correct position.

➡ The right and left camshaft sprockets are different parts. Install them in their correct positions. The right sprocket has an R3 identification mark and the left has an L3.

9. Install the timing belt.

CHECKING CAMSHAFT RUNOUT

◆ See Figure 214

Runout should be checked when the camshaft has been removed from the engine. An accurate dial indicator is needed for this procedure; engine specialists and most machine shops have this equipment. If you have access to a dial indicator, or can take your camshaft to someone who does, measure the camshaft bearing journal runout. The maximum (limit) runout on the L16, L18,

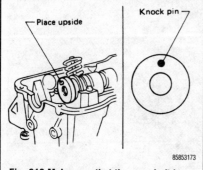

Fig. 210 Make sure that the camshaft is installed with the knockpin UP—Z20, Z22, Z24, Z24i engines

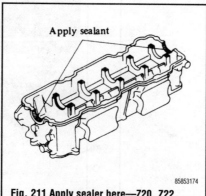

Fig. 211 Apply sealer here—Z20, Z22, Z24, Z24i engines

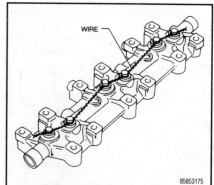

Fig. 212 Hold the valve lifters with wire—V6 engine

ENGINE AND ENGINE REBUILDING 3-41

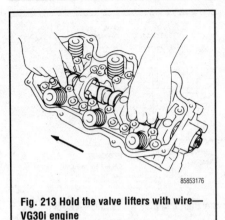

Fig. 213 Hold the valve lifters with wire—VG30i engine

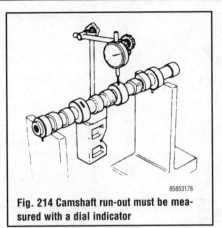

Fig. 214 Camshaft run-out must be measured with a dial indicator

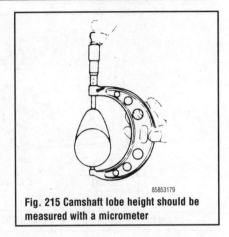

Fig. 215 Camshaft lobe height should be measured with a micrometer

L20D, Z20, Z22, Z24 and Z24i camshafts is 0.008 in. (0.2mm). The maximum (limit) runout on the VG30i camshaft is 0.0039 in. (0.1mm) If the runout exceeds the limit replace the camshaft.

CHECKING CAMSHAFT LOBE HEIGHT

♦ See Figures 215 and 216

Use a micrometer to check camshaft (lobe) height, making sure the anvil and the spindle of the micrometer are positioned directly on the heel and tip of the camshaft lobe.

CHECKING CAMSHAFT JOURNALS AND CAMSHAFT BEARING SADDLES

♦ See Figure 217

While the camshaft is still removed from the cylinder head, the camshaft bearing journals should be measured with a micrometer. Compare the measurements with those listed in the Camshaft Specifications chart in this section. If the measurements are less than the limits listed in the chart, the camshaft will require replacement, since the camshafts in all of the engines covered in this manual (except the diesels) run directly on the cylinder head surface; no actual bearings or bushings are used, so no oversize bearings or bushings are available.

Using an inside dial gauge or inside micrometer, measure the inside diameter of the camshaft saddles (the camshaft mounts that are either integrally cast as part of the cylinder head, or are a bolted on, one piece unit. The Z-series engines use a saddle-and-cap arrangement. The inside diameter of the saddles on all engines is 1.8898–1.8904 in. (48–48.01mm). On the VG30i engine, contact a Nissan dealer or local machine shop for that specification. The camshaft journal oil clearances are listed in the Camshaft Specifications chart in this section. If the saddle inside diameters exceed those listed above, the cylinder head must be replaced (again, because oversize bearings or bushings are not available).

CHECKING CAMSHAFT ENDPLAY

♦ See Figures 218, 219 and 220

After the camshaft has been installed, end-play should be checked. The camshaft sprocket should **not** be installed on the cam. Use a dial gauge to check the end-play, by moving the camshaft forward and backward in the cylinder head. Endplay specifications should be as noted in the Camshaft Specifications chart.

Pistons and Connecting Rods

REMOVAL & INSTALLATION

♦ See Figures 221, 222, 223 and 224

All Engines

➡Before removing the piston assemblies, connecting rod bearing clearance and side clearance should be checked. Refer to the Connecting Rod Inspection procedure in this section.

1. Remove the cylinder head as outlined in the appropriate procedure earlier in this section.
2. Remove the oil pan and pump.
3. Position a cylinder ridge reamer into the top of the cylinder bore. Keeping the tool square, ream the ridges from the top of the bore. Clean out the ridge material with a solvent-soaked rag, or blow it out with compressed air.
4. Remove the oil strainer if it is in the way. Unbolt the connecting rod caps, after matchmarking each cap to its connecting rod.
5. Place pieces of rubber hose over the rod bolts, to protect the cylinder walls and crank journals from scratches. Push the connecting rod and piston up and out of the cylinder from the bottom using a wooden hammer handle.

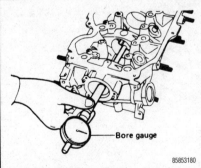

Fig. 216 Measuring the inside diameter of the camshaft saddles to determine journal clearance

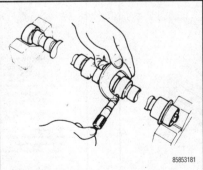

Fig. 217 Measuring outside diameter of the camshaft journals to determine journal clearance

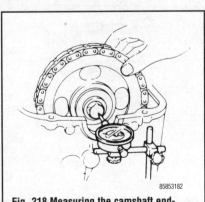

Fig. 218 Measuring the camshaft end-play—all 4-cylinder engines

3-42 ENGINE AND ENGINE REBUILDING

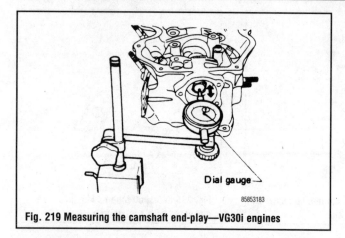

Fig. 219 Measuring the camshaft end-play—VG30i engines

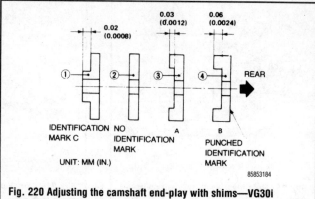

Fig. 220 Adjusting the camshaft end-play with shims—VG30i engines

→It is advisable to number the pistons, connecting rods and bearing caps in some manner so that they can be reinstalled in the same cylinder, facing the same direction, from which they were removed.

※※ CAUTION

Use care not to scratch the crank journals or the cylinder walls.

6. Mark each connecting rod with the number of the cylinder from which it was removed. Number stamps are available at most hardware or auto supply stores.

To install:

7. Apply a light coating of engine oil to the pistons, rings, and outer ends of the wrist pins.

8. Examine the piston to ensure that it has been assembled with its parts positioned correctly (see the illustrations). Be sure that the ring gaps are not pointed toward the thrust face of the piston and that they do not overlap.

9. Place pieces of rubber hose over the connecting rod bolts, to keep the threads from damaging the crank journal and cylinder bore. Install the pistons, using a ring compressor, into the cylinder bore. Be sure that the appropriate marks on the piston are facing the front of the cylinder. (see Identification And Positioning)

→It is important that the pistons, rods, bearing, etc., be returned to the same cylinder bore from which they were removed.

10. Install the connecting rod bearing caps and tighten them to the torque figures given in the Torque Specifications chart.

→Be sure that the mating marks on the connecting rods and rod bearing caps are aligned.

11. Install the oil pump. Install the oil pan.
12. Install the cylinder head.

IDENTIFICATION AND POSITIONING

◆ See Figures 225, 226, 227, 228 and 229

The pistons used in all engines are marked with a notch in the piston head. When installed in the engine, the notch markings **must** be facing towards the

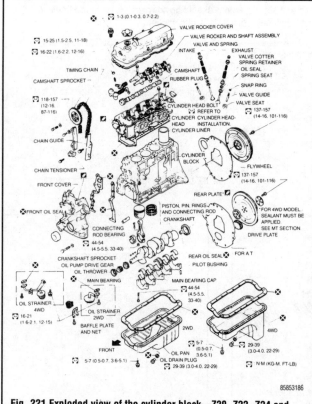

Fig. 221 Exploded view of the cylinder block—Z20, Z22, Z24 and Z24i engines (L-series engines similar)

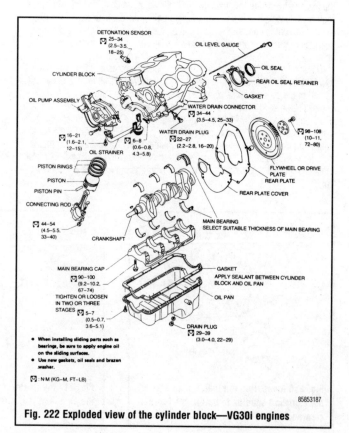

Fig. 222 Exploded view of the cylinder block—VG30i engines

ENGINE AND ENGINE REBUILDING 3-43

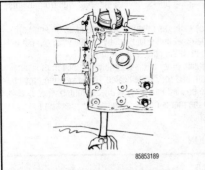

Fig. 223 Removing the piston and connecting rod assembly from the cylinder block

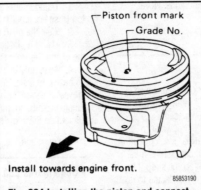

Fig. 224 Installing the piston and connecting rod

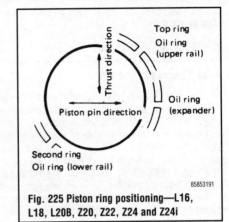

Fig. 225 Piston ring positioning—L16, L18, L20B, Z20, Z22, Z24 and Z24i

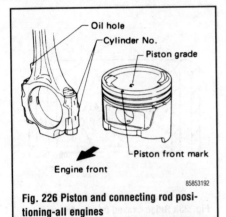

Fig. 226 Piston and connecting rod positioning-all engines

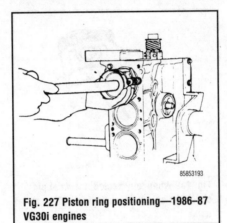

Fig. 227 Piston ring positioning—1986–87 VG30i engines

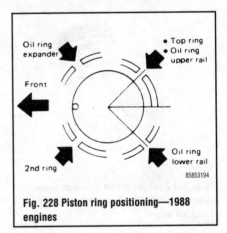

Fig. 228 Piston ring positioning—1988 engines

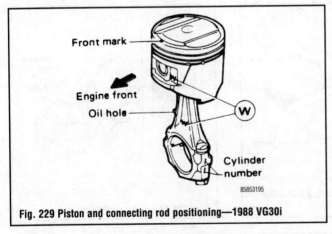

Fig. 229 Piston and connecting rod positioning—1988 VG30i

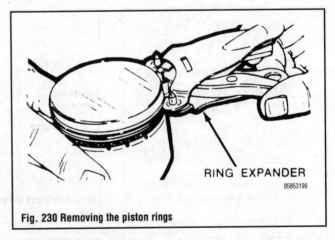

Fig. 230 Removing the piston rings

front of the engine. Additionally, late model VG30i engines have a **W** mark on the piston skirt and this must face forward.

The connecting rods should be installed in the engine with oil hole facing the right side of the engine. **Most** connecting rods also have the cylinder number stamped into the side of the rod and cap, these numbers should face the left side of the engine. Also, as with the pistons, late model VG30i engines have a **W** stamped into the connecting rod which should face the front of the engine.

➡ It is advisable to number the pistons, connecting rods and bearing caps in some manner so that they can be reinstalled in the same cylinder, facing the same direction, from which they were removed.

The piston rings must be installed with their gaps in the correct position.

PISTON RING REPLACEMENT

♦ See Figure 230

➡ The cylinder walls must be de-glazed (honed) when the piston rings are replaced. De-glazing ensures proper ring seating and oil retention.

Using a piston ring expander, remove the rings one by one. Always remove and replace the rings of each piston before going on to the next. This helps avoid mixing up the rings. When the rings have been removed from each piston, perform the end-gap check, piston inspection and piston cleaning procedures detailed later in this section. The rings are marked on one side, the mark denoting the up side for installation.

Install the rings using the ring expander, starting with the top compression ring and working down. Make sure the marks are facing up on each ring. Posi-

3-44 ENGINE AND ENGINE REBUILDING

tion the rings so that the ring and gaps are set as in the illustrations. Never align the end-gaps!

WRIST PIN REMOVAL & INSTALLATION

▶ See Figures 231 and 232

Wrist pin and/or connecting rod small-end bushing wear can be checked by rocking the piston at a right angle to the wrist pin by hand. If more than very **slight** movement is felt, the pin and/or rod busing must be replaced.

The pistons on the engines covered here must be heated in hot water to expand them before the wrist pins can be removed and installed. The four cylinder pistons must be heated to 176°F (80°C), and all six cylinder pistons must be heated to 140°F (60°C). This job can be performed at a machine shop if the idea of boiling pistons in the kitchen doesn't appeal to you. If you decide to do it, however, remember that each piston, pin and connecting rod assembly is a matched set and must be kept together until reassembly.

1. Using needlenose or snapring pliers, remove the snaprings from the piston (if so equipped).
2. Heat the piston(s) in hot water (as noted above depending on engine).
3. Using a plastic-faced hammer and driver, lightly tap the wrist pin out of the piston. Remove the piston from the connecting rod.
4. Assembly is in the opposite order of disassembly. The piston must again be heated to install the wrist pin and rod. Once heated, (while wearing protective gloves) it should be able to be pushed into place with your thumb when heated. When assembling, make sure the marks on the piston and connecting rod are aligned on the same side as shown.

CLEANING AND INSPECTION

▶ See Figures 233 thru 240

Clean the piston after removing the rings, by first scraping any carbon from the piston top. Do not scratch the piston in any way during cleaning. Use a bro-

Fig. 231 Rock the piston at a right angle to the wrist pin to check pin and small end bushing wear

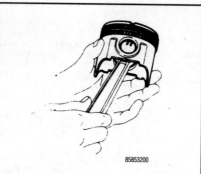

Fig. 232 When fully heated, the wrist pin should be able to be pushed into place by hand

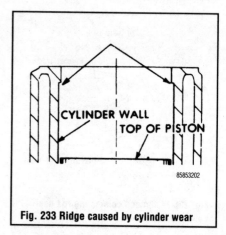

Fig. 233 Ridge caused by cylinder wear

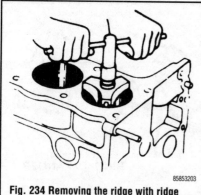

Fig. 234 Removing the ridge with ridge reamer

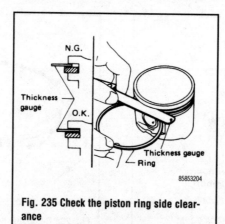

Fig. 235 Check the piston ring side clearance

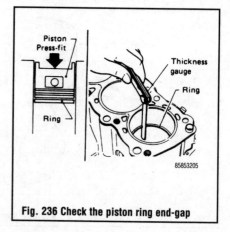

Fig. 236 Check the piston ring end-gap

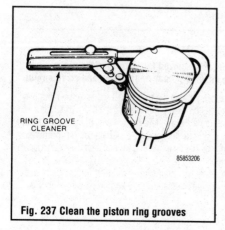

Fig. 237 Clean the piston ring grooves

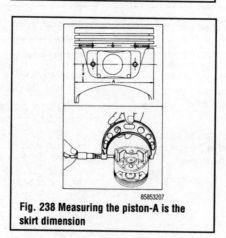

Fig. 238 Measuring the piston-A is the skirt dimension

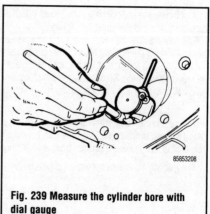

Fig. 239 Measure the cylinder bore with dial gauge

ENGINE AND ENGINE REBUILDING 3-45

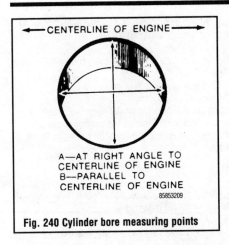

Fig. 240 Cylinder bore measuring points

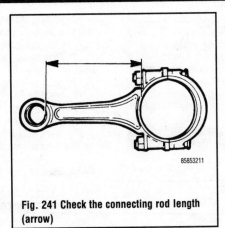

Fig. 241 Check the connecting rod length (arrow)

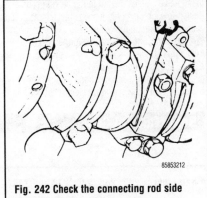

Fig. 242 Check the connecting rod side clearance with a feeler gauge

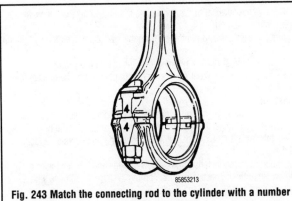

Fig. 243 Match the connecting rod to the cylinder with a number stamp

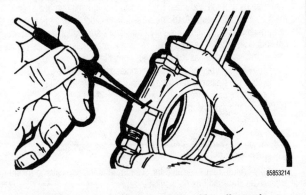

Fig. 244 Match the connecting rod and cap with scribe marks

ken piston ring or ring cleaning tool to clean out the ring grooves. Clean the entire piston with solvent and a brush (NOT a wire brush).

Once the piston is thoroughly cleaned, insert the side of a good piston ring (both No. 1 and No. 2 compression on each piston) into its respective groove. Using a feeler gauge, measure the clearance between the ring and its groove. If clearance is greater than the maximum listed under Ring Side Clearance in the Piston and Ring chart, replace the ring(s) and if necessary, the piston.

To check ring end-gap, insert a compression ring into the cylinder. Lightly oil the cylinder bore and push the ring down into the cylinder with a piston, to the bottom of its travel. Measure the ring end-gap with a feeler gauge. If the gap is not within specification, replace the ring; DO NOT file the ring ends.

CYLINDER BORE INSPECTION

Place a rag over the crankshaft journals. Wipe out each cylinder with a clean, solvent-soaked rag. Visually inspect the cylinder bores for roughness, scoring or scuffing; also check the bores by feel. Measure the cylinder bore diameter with an inside micrometer, or a telescope gauge and micrometer. Measure the bore at points parallel and perpendicular to the engine centerline at the top (below the ridge) and bottom of the bore. Subtract the bottom measurements from the top to determine cylinder taper.

Measure the piston diameter with a micrometer; since this micrometer may not be part of your tool kit as it is necessarily large, you may have to have the pistons measured at a machine shop. If you obtain a micrometer, take the measurements at right angles to the wrist pin center line, about an inch down the piston skirt from the top. Compare this measurement to the bore diameter of each cylinder. The difference is the piston clearance. If the clearance is greater than that specified in the Piston and Ring Specifications chart, have the cylinders honed or bored and replace the pistons with an oversize set. Piston clearance can also be checked by inverting a piston into an oiled cylinder, and sliding in a feeler gauge between the two.

CONNECTING ROD INSPECTION AND BEARING REPLACEMENT

♦ See Figures 241, 242, 243 and 244

Connecting rod side clearance, along with big-end bearing inspection and replacement should be performed while the rods are still installed in the engine. Determine the clearance between the connecting rod sides and the crankshaft using a feeler gauge. If clearance is below the minimum tolerance, check with a machinist about machining the rod to provide adequate clearance. If clearance is excessive, substitute an unworn rod and recheck; if clearance is still outside specifications, the crankshaft must be welded and reground, or replaced.

To check connecting rod big-end bearing clearances, remove the rod bearing caps one at a time. Using a clean, dry shop rag, thoroughly clean all oil from the crank journal and the bearing insert in the cap.

➡The Plastigage® gauging material you will be using to check clearances with is soluble in oil; therefore any oil on the journal or bearing could result in an incorrect reading.

Lay a strip of Plastigage® along the full length of the bearing insert (along the crank journal if the engine is out of the truck and inverted). Reinstall the cap and torque to specifications listed in the Torque Specifications chart.

Remove the rod cap and determine the bearing clearance by comparing the width of the now flattened Plastigage® to the scale on the Plastigage® envelope. Journal taper is determined by comparing the width of the Plastigage® strip near its ends. Rotate the crankshaft 90 degrees and retest, to determine journal eccentricity.

➡Do not rotate the crankshaft with the Plastigage® installed.

If the bearing insert and crank journal appear intact and are within tolerances, no further service is required and the bearing caps can be reinstalled (remove Plastigage® before installation). If clearances are not within tolerances, the bearing inserts in both the connecting rod and rod cap must be replaced with undersize inserts, and/or the crankshaft must be reground. To install the bearing

ENGINE AND ENGINE REBUILDING

insert halves, press them into the bearing caps and connecting rods. Make sure the tab in each insert fits into the notch in each rod and cap. Lube the face of each insert with engine oil prior to installing each rod into the engine.

The connecting rods can be further inspected when they are removed from the engine and separated from their pistons. Rod alignment (straightness and squareness) must be checked by a machinist, as the rod must be set in a special fixture. Many machine shops also perform a Magnafluxing service, which is a process that shows any tiny cracks that you may be unable to see.

Rear Main Oil Seal

REPLACEMENT

♦ See Figures 245, 246, 247, 248 and 249

All 4 Cylinder Engines

In order to replace the rear main oil seal, the rear main bearing cap must be removed. Removal of the rear main bearing cap requires the use of a special rear main bearing cap puller. Also, the oil seal is installed with a special crankshaft rear oil seal drift. Unless these or similar tools are available to you, it is recommended that the oil seal be replaced by a Nissan/Datsun service center or an independent shop that has the proper equipment.

1. Remove the engine and transmission assembly from the vehicle.
2. Remove the transmission from the engine. Remove the oil pan.
3. Remove the clutch from the flywheel.
4. Remove the flywheel from the crankshaft.
5. Remove the rear main bearing cap together with the bearing cap side seals.
6. Remove the rear main oil seal from around the crankshaft.

To install:

7. Apply lithium grease around the sealing lip of the oil seal and install the seal around the crankshaft using a suitable tool.

8. Apply sealer to the rear main bearing cap as indicated in the accompanying illustration, install the rear main bearing cap, and tighten the cap bolts to 33–40 ft. lbs. (44–54 Nm)
9. Apply sealant to the rear main bearing cap side seals and install the side seals, driving them into place with a suitable drift.
10. Install the oil pan with a new gasket.
11. Install the flywheel and clutch assembly.
12. Install the transmission to the engine, then install the engine/transmission assembly in the vehicle. Refer to the Engine Removal and Installation procedure.
13. Check all fluid levels, start the engine and check for any leaks. Roadtest the vehicle for proper operation.

VG30i Engines

1. Refer to the Engine, Removal and Installation procedures, in this section and remove the engine/transmission from the vehicle.
2. Separate the transmission from the engine.
3. Remove the clutch assembly from the flywheel (MT) or the torque converter from the drive plate (AT).
4. Remove the flywheel or the drive plate from the crankshaft, then secure the engine to a workstand.
5. If not already done, drain the oil from the crankcase, then remove the oil pan.
6. Remove the rear oil seal retainer from the rear of the engine.
7. Using a medium pry bar (or even a pair of pliers), pry the oil seal from the seal retainer.

To install:

8. Using a putty knife, clean the gasket mounting surfaces.
9. Apply oil to the sealing lip and the mounting surface of the new oil seal, then press the seal into the oil seal retainer. Install the oil seal retainer/seal around the crankshaft.
10. To complete the installation, use new gaskets and reverse the removal procedures. Refill the crankcase and the cooling system; if equipped with an automatic transmission, check the fluid.

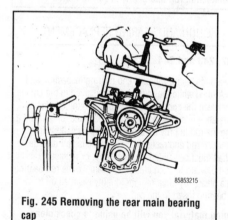

Fig. 245 Removing the rear main bearing cap

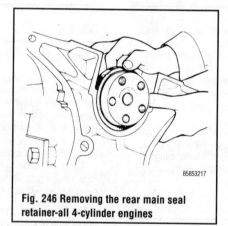

Fig. 246 Removing the rear main seal retainer-all 4-cylinder engines

Fig. 247 Installing the rear main seal

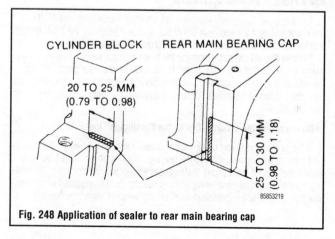

Fig. 248 Application of sealer to rear main bearing cap

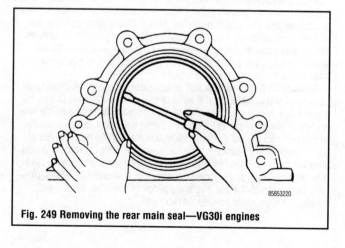

Fig. 249 Removing the rear main seal—VG30i engines

ENGINE AND ENGINE REBUILDING   3-47

Crankshaft and Main Bearing

REMOVAL & INSTALLATION

♦ See Figures 250 thru 257

➟ Before removing the crankshaft, check main bearing clearances as described later in this section.

1. Remove the piston and connecting rod assemblies following the procedure in this section.
2. Check crankshaft thrust clearance (end-play) before removing the crank from the block. Using a pry bar, pry the crankshaft the extent of its travel forward, and measure thrust clearance at the center main bearing (No. 4 bearing on V6 engines, No. 3 on 4 cylinder engines) with a feeler gauge. Pry the crankshaft the extent of its rearward travel, and measure the other side of the bearing. If clearance is greater than that specified, the thrust washers must be replaced (see main bearing installation).
3. Using a punch, mark the corresponding main bearing caps and saddles according to position: one punch on the front main cap and saddle, two on the second, three on the third, etc. This ensures correct reassembly.
4. Remove the main bearing caps after they have been marked.
5. Remove the crankshaft form the block.
6. Follow the crankshaft inspection, main bearing clearance checking and replacement procedures below before reinstalling the crankshaft.

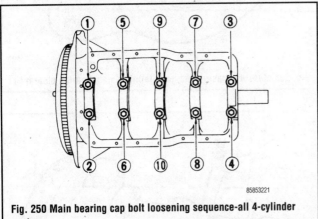
Fig. 250 Main bearing cap bolt loosening sequence-all 4-cylinder engines

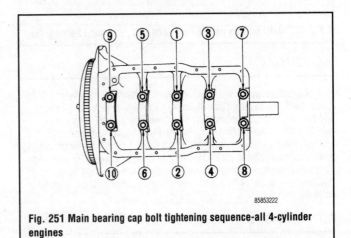
Fig. 251 Main bearing cap bolt tightening sequence-all 4-cylinder engines

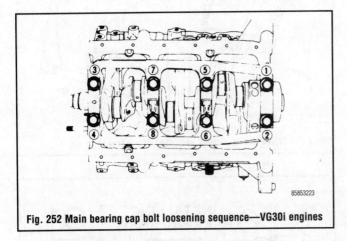
Fig. 252 Main bearing cap bolt loosening sequence—VG30i engines

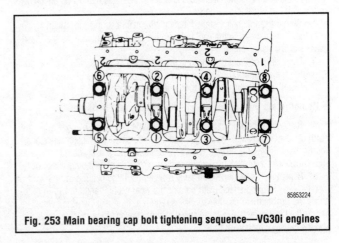
Fig. 253 Main bearing cap bolt tightening sequence—VG30i engines

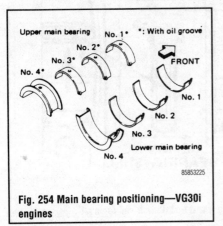
Fig. 254 Main bearing positioning—VG30i engines

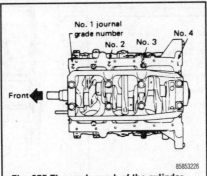
Fig. 255 The grade mark of the cylinder block main journal is stamped on the block—VG30i engines

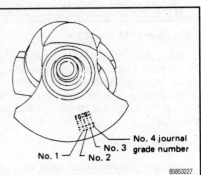
Fig. 256 The grade mark of the crankshaft main journal is stamped on the crankshaft—VG30i engines

3-48 ENGINE AND ENGINE REBUILDING

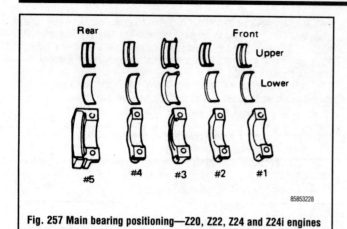

Fig. 257 Main bearing positioning—Z20, Z22, Z24 and Z24i engines

INSPECTION

Crankshaft inspection and servicing should be handled exclusively by a reputable machinist, as most of the necessary procedures require a dial indicator and fixing jig, a large micrometer, and machine tools such as a crankshaft grinder. While at the machine shop, the crankshaft should be thoroughly cleaned (especially the oil passages), Magnafluxed (to check for minute cracks) and the following checks made: main journal diameter, crank pin (connecting rod journal) diameter, taper and out-of-round, and run-out. Wear, beyond specification limits, in any of these areas means the crankshaft must be reground or replaced.

MAIN BEARING CLEARANCE CHECK

Checking main bearing clearances is done in the same manner as checking connecting rod big-end clearances.
1. With the crankshaft installed, remove the main bearing cap. Clean all oil form the bearing insert in the cap and from the crankshaft journal, as the Plastigage® material is oil-soluble.
2. Lay a strip of Plastigage® along the full width of the bearing cap (or along the width of the crank journal if the engine is out of the truck and inverted).
3. Install the bearing cap and torque to specification.

➡ Do not rotate the crankshaft with the Plastigage® installed.

4. Remove the bearing cap and determine bearing clearance by comparing the width of the now-flattened Plastigage® with the scale on the Plastigage® envelope. Journal taper is determined by comparing the width of the Plastigage® strip near its ends. Rotate the crankshaft 90 degrees and retest, to determine journal eccentricity.
5. Repeat the above for the remaining bearings. If the bearing journal and insert appear in good shape (with no unusual wear visible) and are within tolerances, no further main bearing service is required. If unusual wear is evident and/or the clearances are outside specifications, the bearings must be replaced and the cause of their wear found.

MAIN BEARING REPLACEMENT

♦ See Figures 258 thru 263

Main bearings can be replaced with the crankshaft both in the engine (with the engine still in the truck) and out of the engine (with the engine on a work stand or bench). Both procedures are covered here. The main bearings must be replaced if the crankshaft has been reground. Replacement bearings are available in various undersize increments from most auto parts jobbers or your local Nissan dealer.

Engine Out of Truck

1. Remove the crankshaft from the engine block.
2. Remove the main bearing inserts from the bearing caps and from the main bearing saddles. Remove the thrust washers from the No. 3 (4 cylinder engines) or No. 4 (V6) crank journal.

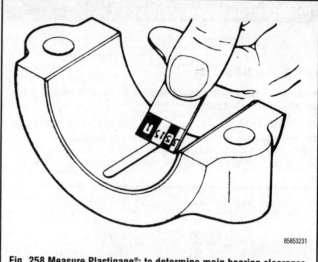

Fig. 258 Measure Plastigage®; to determine main bearing clearance

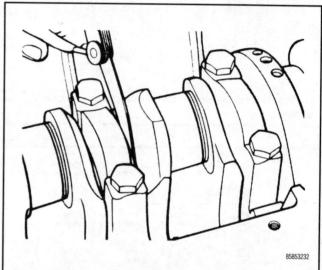

Fig. 259 Check the crankshaft end-play with a feeler gauge

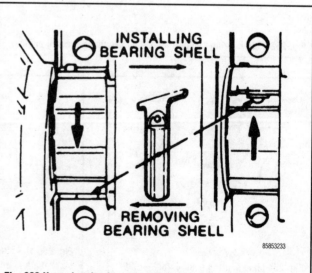

Fig. 260 Upper bearing insert installation and removal

ENGINE AND ENGINE REBUILDING 3-49

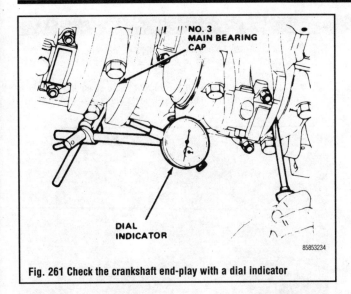

Fig. 261 Check the crankshaft end-play with a dial indicator

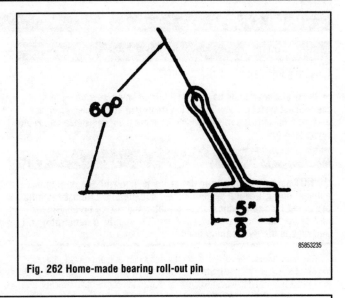

Fig. 262 Home-made bearing roll-out pin

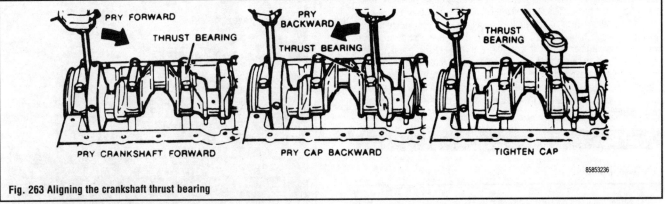

Fig. 263 Aligning the crankshaft thrust bearing

3. Thoroughly clean the saddles, bearing caps, and crankshaft.
4. Make sure the crankshaft has been fully checked and is ready for reassembly. Place the upper main bearings in the block saddles so that the oil grooves and/or oil holes are correctly aligned with their corresponding grooves or holes in the saddles.
5. Install the thrust washers on the center main bearing, with the oil grooves facing out.
6. Lubricate the faces of all bearings with clean engine oil, and place the crankshaft in the block.
7. Install the main bearing caps in numbered order with the arrows or any other orientation marks facing forward. Torque all bolts except the center cap bolts in sequence using two or three passes to achieve the specified torque. Rotate the crankshaft after each pass to ensure even tightness.
8. Align the thrust bearing by prying the crankshaft the extent of its axial travel several times with a pry bar. On last movement hold the crankshaft toward the front of the engine and torque the thrust bearing cap to specifications. Measure the crankshaft thrust clearance (end-play) as previously described in this section. If clearance is outside specifications (too sloppy), install a new set of oversize thrust washers and check clearance again.

Engine And Crankshaft Installed

1. Remove the main bearing caps and keep them in order.
2. Make a bearing roll-out pin from a cotter pin as shown.
3. Carefully roll out the old inserts from the upper side of the crankshaft journal, noting the positions of the oil grooves and/or oil holes so the new inserts can be correctly installed.
4. Roll each new insert into its saddle after lightly oiling the crankshaft-side face of each. Make sure the notches and/or oil holes are correctly positioned.
5. Replace the bearing inserts in the caps with new inserts. Oil the face of each, and install the caps in numbered order with the arrows or other orientation marks facing forward. Tighten the bolts to the specified torque in two or three passes using the sequence shown.

Flywheel and Ring Gear

REMOVAL & INSTALLATION

All Engines

→The clutch cover and the pressure plate are balanced as an assembly; if replacement of either part becomes necessary, replace both parts as an assembly. If vehicle is equipped with a automatic transmission use this procedure as a guide. See exploded view of engine block assembly for flywheel/drive plate installation and quick torque reference.

1. Remove the transmission, if the engine is installed in the truck.
2. Remove the clutch assembly, if equipped.
3. Remove the flywheel.
4. To install, use new flywheel bolts. Tighten the bolts in a criss-cross pattern to the proper torque.

3-50 ENGINE AND ENGINE REBUILDING

EXHAUST SYSTEM

Inspection

▶ See Figures 264 thru 270

➡Safety glasses should be worn at all times when working on or near the exhaust system. Older exhaust systems will almost always be covered with loose rust particles which are more than a nuisance and could injure your eye.

✳✳ CAUTION

DO NOT perform exhaust repairs or inspection with the engine or exhaust hot. Allow the system to cool completely. Exhaust systems are noted for sharp edges, flaking metal and rusted bolts. Gloves and eye protection are required. A healthy supply of penetrating oil and rags is highly recommended.

Your vehicle must be raised and supported safely at four points to inspect the exhaust system properly. Start the inspection at the exhaust manifold where the header pipe is attached and work your way to the back of the vehicle. On dual exhaust systems, remember to inspect both sides of the vehicle. Check the complete exhaust system for open seams, holes, loose connections, or other deterioration which could permit exhaust fumes to seep into the passenger compartment. Inspect all mounting brackets and hangers for deterioration, some may have rubber O-rings that can become overstretched and non-supportive (and should be replaced if worn). Many technicians use a pointed tool to poke up into the exhaust system at rust spots to see whether or not they crumble. Most models have heat shield(s) covering certain parts of the exhaust system, it is often necessary to remove these shields to visually inspect those components.

Front Pipe

REMOVAL & INSTALLATION

1. Support the vehicle securely by using jackstands or equivalent under the frame of the vehicle.
2. Remove the exhaust pipe clamps and any front exhaust pipe shield.
3. Soak the exhaust manifold front pipe mounting studs with penetrating oil. Remove attaching nuts and gasket from the manifold.

➡If these studs snap off, while removing the front pipe the manifold will have to be removed and the stud will have to be drill out and the hole tapped.

4. Remove any exhaust pipe mounting hanger or bracket.
5. Remove front pipe from the muffler/catalytic converter.

To install:

6. Install the front pipe on the manifold with seal if so equipped.
7. Connect the pipe to the muffler/catalytic converter. Assemble all parts

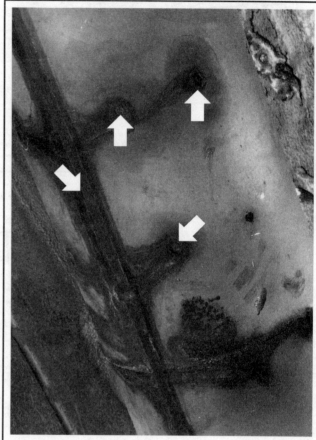

Fig. 265 Check the muffler for rotted spot welds and seams

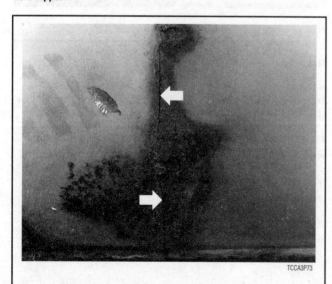

Fig. 264 Cracks in the muffler are a guaranteed leak

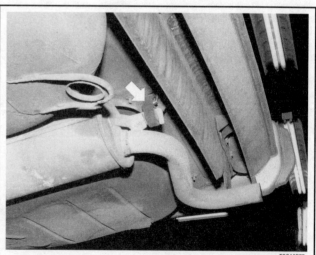

Fig. 266 Make sure the exhaust does contact the body or suspension

ENGINE AND ENGINE REBUILDING   3-51

Fig. 267 Check for overstretched or torn exhaust hangers

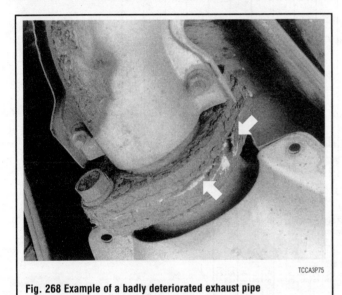

Fig. 268 Example of a badly deteriorated exhaust pipe

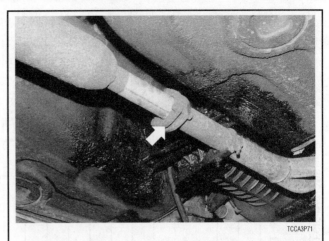

Fig. 269 Inspect flanges for gaskets that have deteriorated and need replacement

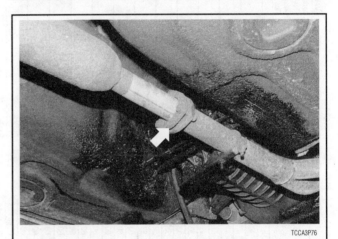

Fig. 270 Some systems, like this one, use large O-rings (donuts) in between the flanges

loosely and position the pipe to insure proper clearance from body of vehicle.
8. Tighten mounting studs, bracket bolts on exhaust clamps.
9. Install exhaust pipe shield.
10. Start engine and check for exhaust leaks.

Catalytic Converter

REMOVAL & INSTALLATION

1. Remove the converter lower shield.
2. Disconnect converter from front pipe.
3. Disconnect converter from center pipe or tail pipe assembly.
4. Remove catalytic converter.

➡Assemble all parts loosely and position the converter before tightening the exhaust clamps.

5. To install, reverse the removal procedures. Always use new clamps and exhaust seals, start the engine and check for leaks.

Tailpipe And Muffler

REMOVAL & INSTALLATION

1. Disconnect the tailpipe at the center pipe, catalytic converter or front pipe.
2. Remove all brackets and exhaust clamps.
3. Remove the tailpipe from muffler. On some models the tailpipe and muffler are one piece.
4. To install reverse the removal procedures. Always use new clamps and exhaust seals, start engine and check for leaks.

3-52 ENGINE AND ENGINE REBUILDING

VALVE SPECIFICATIONS

Year	Engine Type	Seat Angle (deg.)	Face Angle (deg.)	Spring Test Pressure (lbs.) Inner	Spring Test Pressure (lbs.) Outer	Spring Installed Height (in.) Inner	Spring Installed Height (in.) Outer	Stem-to-Guide Clearance (in.) Intake	Stem-to-Guide Clearance (in.) Exhaust	Stem Diameter (in.) Intake	Stem Diameter (in.) Exhaust
1971	L16	45	45	27 @ 1.38	64 @ 1.53	1.77	2.05	0.0006–0.0018	0.0016–0.0028	0.3136–0.3142	0.3128–0.3134
1972	L16	45	45	27 @ 1.38	64 @ 1.53	1.77	2.05	0.0006–0.0018	0.0016–0.0028	0.3136–0.3142	0.3128–0.3134
1973	L16	45	45	27 @ 1.38	64 @ 1.53	1.77	1.97	0.0008–0.0021	0.0016–0.0029	0.3136–0.3142	0.3128–0.3134
	L18	45	45	27 @ 1.38	47 @ 1.58	1.77	1.97	0.0008–0.0021	0.0016–0.0029	0.3136–0.3142	0.3128–0.3134
1974	L18	45	45	27 @ 1.38	47 @ 1.58	1.77	1.97	0.0008–0.0021	0.0016–0.0029	0.3136–0.3142	0.3128–0.3134
1975	L20B	45	45	27 @ 1.38	47 @ 1.58	1.77	1.97	0.0008–0.0021	0.0016–0.0029	0.3136–0.3142	0.3128–0.3134
1976	L20B	45	45	27 @ 1.38	47 @ 1.58	1.77	1.97	0.0008–0.0021	0.0016–0.0029	0.3136–0.3142	0.3128–0.3134
1977	L20B	45	45	27 @ 1.38	47 @ 1.58	1.77	1.97	0.0008–0.0021	0.0016–0.0029	0.3136–0.3142	0.3128–0.3134
1978	L20B	45	45.5	27 @ 1.38	47 @ 1.58	1.77	1.97	0.0008–0.0021	0.0016–0.0029	0.3136–0.3142	0.3128–0.3134
1979	L20B	45	45.5	27 @ 1.38	47 @ 1.58	1.77	1.97	0.0008–0.0021	0.0016–0.0029	0.3136–0.3142	0.3128–0.3134
1980	L20B	45	45.5	27 @ 1.38	47 @ 1.58	1.77	1.97	0.0008–0.0021	0.0016–0.0029	0.3136–0.3142	0.3128–0.3134
1981	Z22	45.5	45.5	51 @ 1.575	51 @ 1.378	1.74	1.96	0.0008–0.0021	0.0016–0.0029	0.3136–0.3142	0.3128–0.3134
	SD22	45	45	—	33 @ 1.634	—	1.93	0.0006–0.0018	0.0016–0.0028	0.3137–0.3143	0.3137–0.3143
1982	Z22	45.5	45.5	51 @ 1.575	51 @ 1.378	1.74	1.96	0.0008–0.0021	0.0016–0.0029	0.3136–0.3142	0.3128–0.3134
	SD22	45	45	—	33 @ 1.634	—	1.93	0.0006–0.0018	0.0016–0.0028	0.3137–0.3143	0.3137–0.3143
1983	Z22	45.5	45.5	51 @ 1.575	51 @ 1.378	1.74	1.96	0.0008–0.0021	0.0016–0.0029	0.3136–0.3142	0.3128–0.3134
	SD22	45	45	—	33 @ 1.634	—	1.93	0.0006–0.0018	0.0016–0.0028	0.3137–0.3143	0.3137–0.3143
1984	Z20	45.5	45.5	57 @ 0.98	115 @ 1.18	1.57	1.38	0.0008–0.0021	0.0016–0.0029	0.3136–0.3142	0.3128–0.3134
	Z24	45.5	45	57 @ 0.98	115 @ 1.18	1.57	1.38	0.0008–0.0021	0.0016–0.0029	0.3136–0.3142	0.3128–0.3134
	SD25	45	45	—	148 @ 1.224	—	1.56	0.0006–0.0018	0.0016–0.0028	0.3138–0.3144	0.3128–0.3134
1985	Z20	45.5	45.5	57 @ 0.98	115 @ 1.18	1.57	1.38	0.0008–0.0021	0.0016–0.0029	0.3136–0.3142	0.3128–0.3134
	Z24	45.5	45	57 @ 0.98	115 @ 1.18	1.57	1.38	0.0008–0.0021	0.0016–0.0029	0.3136–0.3142	0.3128–0.3134
	SD25	45	45	—	148 @ 1.224	—	1.56	0.0006–0.0018	0.0016–0.0028	0.3138–0.3144	0.3128–0.3134

GENERAL ENGINE SPECIFICATIONS

Year	Engine Type	Engine Displacement Cu. In. (cc)	Carburetor Type	Horsepower (@ rpm)	Torque @ rpm (ft. lbs.)	Bore × Stroke (in.)	Compression Ratio	Oil Pressure @ rpm (psi)
1970	L16	97.3 (1595)	2 bbl	96 @ 5600	100 @ 3600	3.27 × 2.90	8.5:1	47 @ 2000
1971	L16	97.3 (1595)	2 bbl	96 @ 5600	100 @ 3600	3.27 × 2.90	8.5:1	47 @ 2000
1972	L16	97.3 (1595)	2 bbl	96 @ 5600	100 @ 3600	3.27 × 2.90	8.5:1	47 @ 2000
1973	L16	97.3 (1595)	2 bbl	96 @ 5600	100 @ 3600	3.27 × 2.90	8.5:1	47 @ 2000
	L18	108.0 (1770)	2 bbl	100 @ 5600	100 @ 3600	3.35 × 3.07	8.5:1	47 @ 2000
1974	L18	108.0 (1770)	2 bbl	100 @ 5600	100 @ 3600	3.35 × 3.07	8.5:1	47 @ 2000
1975	L20B	119.1 (1952)	2 bbl	112 @ 5600	108 @ 3200	3.35 × 3.39	8.5:1	53 @ 2000
1976	L20B	119.1 (1952)	2 bbl	112 @ 5600	108 @ 3200	3.35 × 3.39	8.5:1	53 @ 2000
1977	L20B	119.1 (1952)	2 bbl	112 @ 5600	108 @ 3200	3.35 × 3.39	8.5:1	53 @ 2000
1978	L20B	119.1 (1952)	2 bbl	97 @ 5600	102 @ 3200	3.35 × 3.39	8.5:1	53 @ 2000
1979	L20B	119.1 (1952)	2 bbl	97 @ 5600	102 @ 3200	3.35 × 3.39	8.5:1	53 @ 2000
1980	L20B	119.1 (1952)	2 bbl	98 @ 4000	117 @ 1800	3.35 × 3.39	8.5:1	60 @ idle
1981	Z22	133.5 (2187)	2 bbl	98 @ 4000	117 @ 1800	3.43 × 3.62	8.5:1	60 @ idle
	SD22	132.0 (2164)	DFI	61 @ 4000	102 @ 1800	3.27 × 3.94	21.6:1	60 @ idle
1982	Z22	133.5 (2187)	2 bbl	98 @ 4000	117 @ 1800	3.43 × 3.62	8.5:1	60 @ idle
	SD22	132.0 (2164)	DFI	61 @ 4000	102 @ 1800	3.27 × 3.94	21.6:1	60 @ idle
1983	Z22	133.5 (2187)	2 bbl	98 @ 4000	117 @ 1800	3.43 × 3.62	8.5:1	60 @ idle
	SD22	132.0 (2164)	DFI	61 @ 4000	102 @ 1800	3.27 × 3.94	21.6:1	60 @ idle
1984	Z20	119.0 (1952)	2 bbl	97 @ 5600	102 @ 3200	3.35 × 3.39	9.4:1	60 @ idle
	Z24	146.8 (2389)	2 bbl	103 @ 4800	134 @ 2800	3.50 × 3.78	8.3:1	60 @ idle
	SD25	152.0 (2488)	DFI	70 @ 4000	115 @ 2000	3.50 × 3.94	21.4:1	60 @ idle
1985	Z20	119.0 (1952)	2 bbl	97 @ 5600	102 @ 3200	3.35 × 3.39	9.4:1	60 @ idle
	Z24	146.8 (2389)	2 bbl	103 @ 4800	134 @ 2800	3.50 × 3.78	8.3:1	60 @ idle
	SD25	152.0 (2488)	DFI	70 @ 4000	115 @ 2000	3.50 × 3.94	21.4:1	60 @ idle
1986	Z20	119.0 (1952)	2 bbl	97 @ 5600	102 @ 3200	3.35 × 3.39	9.4:1	60 @ idle
	Z24	146.8 (2389)	2 bbl	103 @ 4800	134 @ 2800	3.50 × 3.78	8.3:1	60 @ idle
	Z24i	146.8 (2389)	EFI	103 @ 4800	134 @ 2800	3.50 × 3.78	8.3:1	60 @ idle
	VG30i	181.0 (2960)	EFI	152 @ 5200	162 @ 3600	3.43 × 3.27	9.0:1	60 @ idle
1987	Z24i	146.8 (2389)	EFI	103 @ 4800	134 @ 2800	3.50 × 3.78	8.3:1	60 @ idle
	VG30i	181.0 (2960)	EFI	152 @ 5200	162 @ 3600	3.43 × 3.27	9.0:1	60 @ idle
	SD25	152.0 (2488)	DFI	70 @ 2400	115 @ 2000	3.50 × 3.94	21.4:1	60 @ idle
1988	Z24i	146.8 (2389)	EFI	106 @ 4800	137 @ 2400	3.50 × 3.78	8.3:1	60 @ idle
	VG30i	181.0 (2960)	EFI	145 @ 4800	166 @ 2800	3.43 × 3.27	9.0:1	60 @ idle

DFI—Diesel Fuel Injection
EFI—Electronic Fuel Injection

ENGINE AND ENGINE REBUILDING

VALVE SPECIFICATIONS

Year	Engine Type	Seat Angle (deg.)	Face Angle (deg.)	Spring Test Pressure (lbs.) Inner	Spring Test Pressure (lbs.) Outer	Spring Installed Height (in.) Inner	Spring Installed Height (in.) Outer	Stem-to-Guide Clearance (in.)▲ Intake	Stem-to-Guide Clearance (in.)▲ Exhaust	Stem Diameter (in.) Intake	Stem Diameter (in.) Exhaust
1986	Z20	45.5	45.5	57 @ 0.98	115 @ 1.18	1.57	1.38	0.0008–0.0021	0.0016–0.0029	0.3136–0.3142	0.3128–0.3134
	Z24	45.5	45	57 @ 0.98	115 @ 1.18	1.57	1.38	0.0008–0.0021	0.0016–0.0029	0.3136–0.3142	0.3128–0.3134
	Z24i	45.5	45.5	24 @ 1.378	51 @ 1.575	1.57	1.38	0.0008–0.0021	0.0016–0.0029	0.3136–0.3142	0.3128–0.3134
	VG30i	45.5	45.5	57 @ 0.984	118 @ 1.181	0.98	1.18	0.0008–0.0021	0.0012–0.0018	0.2742–0.2748	0.3128–0.3134
	SD25	45	45	—	148 @ 1.224	—	1.56	0.0006–0.0018	0.0016–0.0028	0.3138–0.3144	0.3128–0.3134
1987	Z24i	45.5	45.5	24 @ 1.378	51 @ 1.575	1.57	1.38	0.0008–0.0021	0.0016–0.0029	0.3136–0.3142	0.3128–0.3134
	VG30i	45.5	45.5	57 @ 0.984	118 @ 1.181	0.98	1.18	0.0006–0.0018	0.0012–0.0018	0.2742–0.2748	0.3128–0.3134
	SD25	45	45	—	148 @ 1.224	—	1.56	0.0008–0.0021	0.0016–0.0028	0.3138–0.3144	0.3128–0.3134
1988	Z24i	45.5	45.5	24 @ 1.378	51 @ 1.575	1.57	1.38	0.0008–0.0021	0.0016–0.0029	0.3136–0.3142	0.3128–0.3134
	VG30i	45.5	45.5	57 @ 0.984	118 @ 1.181	0.98	1.18	0.0008–0.0021	0.0016–0.0029	0.2742–0.2748	0.3128–0.3134

CAMSHAFT SPECIFICATIONS
(All measurements in inches)

Year	Engine	Journal Diameter 1	Journal Diameter 2	Journal Diameter 3	Journal Diameter 4	Bearing Clearance	Lobe Lift Intake	Lobe Lift Exhaust	Camshaft End Play
1970	L16	1.8877–1.8883	1.8877–1.8883	1.8877–1.8883	1.8877–1.8883	0.0015–0.0026	0.275	0.275	0.003–0.015
1971	L16	1.8877–1.8883	1.8877–1.8883	1.8877–1.8883	1.8877–1.8883	0.0015–0.0026	0.275	0.275	0.003–0.015
1972	L16	1.8877–1.8883	1.8877–1.8883	1.8877–1.8883	1.8877–1.8883	0.0015–0.0026	0.275	0.275	0.003–0.015
1973	L16	1.8877–1.8883	1.8877–1.8883	1.8877–1.8883	1.8877–1.8883	0.0015–0.0026	0.275	0.275	0.003–0.015
	L18	1.8877–1.8883	1.8877–1.8883	1.8877–1.8883	1.8877–1.8883	0.0015–0.0026	0.275	0.275	0.003–0.015
1974	L18	1.8877–1.8883	1.8877–1.8883	1.8877–1.8883	1.8877–1.8883	0.0015–0.0026	0.275	0.275	0.003–0.015
1975	L20B	1.8877–1.8883	1.8877–1.8883	1.8877–1.8883	1.8877–1.8883	0.0015–0.0026	0.275	0.275	0.003–0.015
1976	L20B	1.8877–1.8883	1.8877–1.8883	1.8877–1.8883	1.8877–1.8883	0.0015–0.0026	0.275	0.275	0.003–0.015
1977	L20B	1.8877–1.8883	1.8877–1.8883	1.8877–1.8883	1.8877–1.8883	0.0015–0.0026	0.275	0.275	0.003–0.015
1978	L20B	1.8877–1.8883	1.8877–1.8883	1.8877–1.8883	1.8877–1.8883	0.0015–0.0026	0.275	0.275	0.003–0.015
1979	L20B	1.8877–1.8883	1.8877–1.8883	1.8877–1.8883	1.8877–1.8883	0.0015–0.0026	0.275	0.275	0.003–0.015
1980	L20B	1.8877–1.8883	1.8877–1.8883	1.8877–1.8883	1.8877–1.8883	0.0015–0.0026	0.275	0.275	0.003–0.015
1981	Z22	1.2967–1.2974	1.2967–1.2974	1.2967–1.2974	1.2967–1.2974	0.0018–0.0035	0.218	0.218	0.004–0.012
	SD22	1.7887–1.7892	1.7282–1.7287	1.6228–1.6233	—	⊖	—	—	0.019–0.020
1982	Z22	1.2967–1.2974	1.2967–1.2974	1.2967–1.2974	1.2967–1.2974	⊖	0.218	0.218	0.004–0.012
	SD22	1.7887–1.7892	1.7282–1.7287	1.6228–1.6233	—	⊖	—	—	0.019–0.020
1983	Z22	1.2967–1.2974	1.2967–1.2974	1.2967–1.2974	1.2967–1.2974	⊖	0.218	0.218	0.004–0.012
	SD22	1.7887–1.7892	1.7282–1.7287	1.6228–1.6233	—	⊖	—	—	0.019–0.020
1984	Z20	1.2967–1.2974	1.2967–1.2974	1.2967–1.2974	1.2967–1.2974	⊖	0.218	0.218	0.004–0.012
	Z24	1.2967–1.2974	1.2967–1.2974	1.2967–1.2974	1.2967–1.2974	⊖	0.218	0.218	0.004–0.012
	SD25	1.7887–1.7892	1.7282–1.7287	1.6228–1.6233	—	⊖	—	—	0.003–0.011
1985	Z20	1.2967–1.2974	1.2967–1.2974	1.2967–1.2974	1.2967–1.2974	⊖	0.218	0.218	0.004–0.012
	Z24	1.2967–1.2974	1.2967–1.2974	1.2967–1.2974	1.2967–1.2974	⊖	0.218	0.218	0.004–0.012
	SD25	1.7887–1.7892	1.7282–1.7287	1.6228–1.6233	—	⊖	—	—	0.003–0.011

ENGINE AND ENGINE REBUILDING

CRANKSHAFT AND CONNECTING ROD SPECIFICATIONS
All measurements are given in inches

Year	Engine Type	Main Brg. Journal Dia.	Main Brg. Oil Clearance	Shaft End-play	Thrust on No.	Journal Diameter	Oil Clearance	Side Clearance
1970	L16	2.1631–2.1636	0.0008–0.0028	0.0020–0.0059	3	1.9670–1.9675	0.0006–0.0026	0.0079–0.0118
1971	L16	2.1631–2.1636	0.0008–0.0028	0.0020–0.0059	3	1.9670–1.9675	0.0006–0.0026	0.0079–0.0118
1972	L16	2.1631–2.1636	0.0008–0.0028	0.0020–0.0059	3	1.9670–1.9675	0.0006–0.0026	0.0079–0.0118
1973	L16	2.1631–2.1636	0.0008–0.0024	0.0020–0.0071	3	1.9670–1.9675	0.0010–0.0022	0.0079–0.0118
	L18	2.1631–2.1636	0.0008–0.0024	0.0020–0.0071	3	1.9670–1.9675	0.0010–0.0022	0.0079–0.0118
1974	L18	2.1631–2.1636	0.0008–0.0024	0.0020–0.0071	3	1.9670–1.9675	0.0010–0.0022	0.0079–0.0118
1975	L20B	2.1631–2.1636	0.0008–0.0024	0.0020–0.0071	3	1.9670–1.9675	0.0010–0.0022	0.0079–0.0118
1976	L20B	2.1631–2.1636	0.0008–0.0024	0.0020–0.0071	3	1.9670–1.9675	0.0010–0.0022	0.0079–0.0118
1977	L20B	2.1631–2.1636	0.0008–0.0024	0.0020–0.0071	3	1.9670–1.9675	0.0010–0.0022	0.0079–0.0118
1978	L20B	2.1631–2.1636	0.0008–0.0024	0.0020–0.0071	3	1.9670–1.9675	0.0010–0.0022	0.0079–0.0118
1979	L20B	2.1631–2.1636	0.0008–0.0024	0.0020–0.0071	3	1.9670–1.9675	0.0010–0.0022	0.0080–0.0120
1980	L20B	2.1631–2.1636	0.0008–0.0024	0.0020–0.0071	3	1.9670–1.9675	0.0010–0.0022	0.0080–0.0120
1981	Z22	2.1631–2.1636	0.0008–0.0024	0.0020–0.0071	3	1.9670–1.9675	0.0010–0.0022	0.0080–0.0120
	SD22	2.7916–2.7921	0.0014–0.0037	0.0024–0.0055	4	2.0832–2.0837	0.0014–0.0034	0.0039–0.0079
1982	Z22	2.1631–2.1636	0.0008–0.0024	0.0020–0.0071	3	1.9670–1.9675	0.0010–0.0022	0.0080–0.0120
	SD22	2.7916–2.7921	0.0014–0.0037	0.0024–0.0055	4	2.0832–2.0837	0.0014–0.0034	0.0039–0.0079
1983	Z22	2.1631–2.1636	0.0008–0.0024	0.0020–0.0071	3	1.9670–1.9675	0.0010–0.0022	0.0080–0.0120
	SD22	2.7916–2.7921	0.0014–0.0037	0.0024–0.0055	4	2.0832–2.0837	0.0014–0.0034	0.0039–0.0079
1984	Z20	2.1631–2.1636	0.0008–0.0024	0.0020–0.0071	3	1.9670–1.9675	0.0010–0.0022	0.0080–0.0120
	Z24	2.1631–2.1636	0.0008–0.0024	0.0020–0.0071	3	1.9670–1.9675	0.0014–0.0032	0.0080–0.0120
	SD25	2.7916–2.7921	0.0014–0.0034	0.0024–0.0055	4	2.0832–2.0837	0.0014–0.0032	0.0039–0.0079
1985	Z20	2.1631–2.1636	0.0008–0.0024	0.0020–0.0071	3	1.9670–1.9675	0.0010–0.0022	0.0080–0.0120
	Z24	2.1631–2.1636	0.0008–0.0024	0.0020–0.0071	3	1.9670–1.9675	0.0014–0.0032	0.0080–0.0120
	SD25	2.7916–2.7921	0.0014–0.0034	0.0024–0.0055	4	2.0832–2.0837	0.0014–0.0032	0.0039–0.0079

CAMSHAFT SPECIFICATIONS
(All measurements in inches)

Year	Engine	Journal Diameter 1	2	3	4	Bearing Clearance	Lobe Lift Intake	Lobe Lift Exhaust	Camshaft End Play
1986	Z20	1.2967–1.2974	1.2967–1.2974	1.2967–1.2974	1.2967–1.2974	0.0018–0.0035	0.218	0.218	0.004–0.012
	Z24	1.2967–1.2974	1.2967–1.2974	1.2967–1.2974	1.2967–1.2974	0.0018–0.0035	0.218	0.218	0.004–0.012
	Z24i	1.2961–1.2968	1.2961–1.2968	1.2961–1.2968	1.2961–1.2968	0.0024–0.0041	—	—	—
	VG30i	②	②	②	②	0.0018–0.0035	—	—	0.0012–0.0024
1987	SD25	1.7887–1.7892	1.7282–1.7287	1.6228–1.6233	—	①	—	—	0.003–0.011
	Z24i	1.2961–1.2968	1.2961–1.2968	1.2961–1.2968	1.2961–1.2968	0.0024–0.0041	—	—	—
	VG30i	②	②	②	②	0.0018–0.0035	—	—	0.0012–0.0024
1988	SD25	1.7887–1.7892	1.7282–1.7287	1.6228–1.6233	—	①	—	—	0.003–0.011
	Z24i	1.2961–1.2968	1.2961–1.2968	1.2961–1.2968	1.2961–1.2968	0.0024–0.0041	—	—	—
	VG30i	②	②	②	②	0.0018–0.0035	—	—	0.0012–0.0024

① #1, 3: 0.0009–0.0040
  #2: 0.0015–0.0045
② #1 (left side only): 1.8866–1.8874
  #2, 3 & 4: 1.8472–1.8480
  #5: 1.6701–1.6709

ENGINE AND ENGINE REBUILDING

PISTON AND RING SPECIFICATIONS
(All measurements are in inches)

Year	Engine Type	Piston Clearance 68°F	Ring Gap			Ring Side Clearance (Ring to Land)		
			Top Compression	Bottom Compression	Oil Control	Top Compression	Bottom Compression	Oil Control
1970	L16	0.0010-0.0018	0.0091-0.0150	0.0059-0.0118	0.0059-0.0118	0.0018-0.0031	0.0012-0.0025	0.0010-0.0025
1971	L16	0.0010-0.0018	0.0091-0.0150	0.0059-0.0118	0.0059-0.0118	0.0018-0.0031	0.0012-0.0025	0.0010-0.0025
1972	L16	0.0010-0.0018	0.0091-0.0150	0.0059-0.0118	0.0059-0.0118	0.0018-0.0031	0.0012-0.0025	0.0010-0.0025
1973	L16	0.0010-0.0018	0.0098-0.0157	0.0059-0.0118	0.0118-0.0354	0.0016-0.0031	0.0012-0.0028	snug
	L18	0.0010-0.0018	0.0138-0.0217	0.0118-0.0197	0.0118-0.0354	0.0018-0.0031	0.0012-0.0028	snug
1974	L18	0.0010-0.0018	0.0098-0.0157	0.0118-0.0197	0.0118-0.0354	0.0016-0.0029	0.0012-0.0028	snug
1975	L20B	0.0010-0.0018	0.0098-0.0157	0.0118-0.0197	0.0118-0.0354	0.0016-0.0029	0.0012-0.0028	snug
1976	L20B	0.0010-0.0018	0.0098-0.0157	0.0118-0.0197	0.0118-0.0354	0.0016-0.0029	0.0012-0.0028	snug
1977	L20B	0.0010-0.0018	0.0098-0.0157	0.0118-0.0197	0.0118-0.0354	0.0016-0.0029	0.0012-0.0028	snug
1978	L20B	0.0010-0.0018	0.0098-0.0157	0.0118-0.0197	0.0118-0.0354	0.0016-0.0029	0.0012-0.0028	snug
1979	L20B	0.0010-0.0018	0.0098-0.0157	0.0118-0.0197	0.0118-0.0354	0.0016-0.0029	0.0012-0.0028	snug
1980	L20B	0.0010-0.0018	0.0098-0.0157	0.0118-0.0197	0.0118-0.0354	0.0016-0.0029	0.0012-0.0028	snug
1981	Z22	0.0010-0.0018	0.0098-0.0157	0.0059-0.0118	0.0059-0.0118	0.0016-0.0029	0.0012-0.0025	0.0008-0.0024
	SD22	0.0016-0.0043	0.0118-0.0177	0.0079-0.0138	0.0118-0.0354	0.0024-0.0039	0.0016-0.0032	snug
1982	Z22	0.0010-0.0018	0.0098-0.0157	0.0059-0.0118	0.0059-0.0118	0.0016-0.0029	0.0012-0.0025	0.0008-0.0024
	SD22	0.0016-0.0043	0.0118-0.0177	0.0079-0.0138	0.0118-0.0354	0.0024-0.0039	0.0016-0.0032	snug
1983	Z22	0.0010-0.0018	0.0098-0.0157	0.0059-0.0118	0.0059-0.0118	0.0016-0.0029	0.0012-0.0025	0.0008-0.0024
	SD22	0.0016-0.0043	0.0118-0.0177	0.0079-0.0138	0.0118-0.0354	0.0024-0.0039	0.0016-0.0032	snug
1984	Z20	0.0010-0.0018	0.0098-0.0157	0.0059-0.0118	0.0059-0.0118	0.0016-0.0029	0.0012-0.0025	0.0008-0.0024
	Z24	0.0010-0.0018	0.0098-0.0157	0.0059-0.0118	0.0118-0.0354	0.0016-0.0029	0.0012-0.0025	snug
	SD25	0.0031-0.0041	0.0118-0.0177	0.0079-0.0138	0.0118-0.0354	0.0024-0.0039	0.0016-0.0032	snug
1985	Z20	0.0010-0.0018	0.0098-0.0157	0.0059-0.0118	0.0059-0.0118	0.0016-0.0029	0.0012-0.0025	0.0008-0.0024
	Z24	0.0010-0.0018	0.0098-0.0157	0.0059-0.0118	0.0118-0.0354	0.0016-0.0029	0.0012-0.0025	snug
	SD25	0.0031-0.0041	0.0118-0.0177	0.0079-0.0138	0.0118-0.0354	0.0024-0.0039	0.0016-0.0032	snug

CRANKSHAFT AND CONNECTING ROD SPECIFICATIONS
All measurements are given in inches

Year	Engine Type	Crankshaft					Connecting Rod	
		Main Brg. Journal Dia.	Main Brg. Oil Clearance	Shaft End-play	Thrust on No.	Journal Diameter	Oil Clearance	Side Clearance
1986	Z20	2.1631-2.1636	0.0008-0.0024	0.0020-0.0071	3	1.9670-1.9675	0.0010-0.0022	0.0080-0.0120
	Z24	2.1631-2.1636	0.0008-0.0024	0.0020-0.0071	3	1.9670-1.9675	0.0010-0.0022	0.0080-0.0120
	Z24i	2.3599-2.3604	①	0.0020-0.0071	3	1.9670-1.9675	0.0005-0.0021	0.0080-0.0120
	VG30i	2.4790-2.4793	0.0011-0.0022	0.0020-0.0067	4	1.9670-1.9675	0.0004-0.0020	0.0079-0.0138
	SD25	2.7916-2.7921	0.0014-0.0034	0.0024-0.0055	4	2.0832-2.0837	0.0014-0.0032	0.0039-0.0079
1987	Z24i	2.3599-2.3604	①	0.0020-0.0071	3	1.9670-1.9675	0.0005-0.0021	0.0080-0.0120
	VG30i	2.4790-2.4793	0.0011-0.0022	0.0020-0.0067	4	1.9670-1.9675	0.0004-0.0020	0.0079-0.0138
	SD25	2.7916-2.7921	0.0014-0.0034	0.0024-0.0055	4	2.0832-2.0837	0.0014-0.0032	0.0039-0.0079
1988	Z24i	2.3599-2.3604	①	0.0020-0.0071	3	1.9670-1.9675	0.0005-0.0021	0.0080-0.0120
	VG30i	2.4790-2.4793	0.0011-0.0022	0.0020-0.0067	4	1.9667-1.9675	0.0006-0.0021	0.0079-0.0138

① #1, 5: 0.0008-0.0024
#2, 3 & 4: 0.0008-0.0030

TORQUE SPECIFICATIONS
(All readings in ft. lbs.)

Year	Engine Type	Cylinder Head Bolts	Rod Bearing Bolts	Main Bearing Bolts	Crankshaft Pulley Bolt	Flywheel to Crankshaft Bolts	Manifold Intake	Manifold Exhaust
1970	L16	40③	23	36	122	72	11	11
1971	L16	40③	23	36	122	72	11	11
1972	L16	40③	23	36	122	72	11	11
1973	L16	43③	25	37	102	109	11	11
1974	L18	55③	37	37	102	109	11	11
1975	L18	55③	37	37	102	109	11	11
1976	L20B	61③	37	37	102	109	11	11
1977	L20B	61③	37	37	102	109	11	11
1978	L20B	61③	37	37	102	109	11	11
1979	L20B	61③	37	37	102	109	11	11
1980	L20B	61③	37	37	102	109	11	11
1981	Z22	58③	37	37	102	109	15	15
1981	SD22	③	40	127	239	33	13	13
1982	Z22	58③	37	37	102	109	15	15
1982	SD22	③	40	127	239	33	13	13
1983	Z22	58③	37	37	102	109	15	15
1983	SD22	③	40	127	239	33	13	13
1984	Z20	③	37	37	102	109	15	15
1984	Z24	③	37	37	102	109	15	15
1984	SD25	③	50	125	239	123	13	13
1985	Z20	③	37	37	102	109	15	15
1985	Z24	③	37	37	102	109	15	15
1985	SD25	③	50	125	239	123	13	13
1986	Z20	③	37	37	102	109	15	15
1986	Z24i	③	37	37	102	109	15	15
1986	VG30i	44	37	70	94	76	13⑤	14
1986	SD25	③	50	125	239	123	13	13
1987	Z24i	③	37	37	102	109	13	13
1987	VG30i	44	37	70	94	76	13⑤	14
1987	SD25	③	50	125	239	123	13	13
1988	Z24i	③	37	37	110	109	13	13
1988	VG30i	③	41	70	94	65	13⑤	14

① Tighten to 33 ft. lbs., then to specification
② Tighten to 23 ft. lbs., then to specification
③ Tighten to 29 ft. lbs., then 43 ft. lbs., then specification
④ Tighten to 22 ft. lbs., then 58 ft. lbs., loosen all bolts completely, then tighten to 22 ft. lbs. then 61 ft. lbs.
⑤ Small bolts: 42 ft. lbs
  Large bolts: 98 ft. lbs
⑥ Small bolts: 37 ft. lbs
  Large bolts: 91 ft. lbs
⑦ Nut: 18 ft. lbs
⑧ Tighten to 22 ft. lbs., then 43 ft. lbs., loosen all bolts completely, then tighten to 22 ft. lbs. then 61 ft. lbs.

PISTON AND RING SPECIFICATIONS
(All measurements are in inches)

Year	Engine Type	Piston Clearance 68°F	Ring Gap Top Compression	Ring Gap Bottom Compression	Ring Gap Oil Control	Ring Side Clearance Top Compression	Ring Side Clearance Bottom Compression	Ring Side Clearance Oil Control
1986	Z20	0.0010–0.0018	0.0098–0.0157	0.0059–0.0118	0.0118–0.0354	0.0016–0.0029	0.0012–0.0025	snug
1986	Z24	0.0010–0.0018	0.0098–0.0157	0.0059–0.0118	0.0118–0.0354	0.0016–0.0029	0.0012–0.0025	snug
1986	Z24i	0.0010–0.0018	0.0110–0.0150	0.0098–0.0138	0.0079–0.0236	0.0016–0.0029	0.0012–0.0025	snug
1986	VG30i	0.0010–0.0018	0.0083–0.0134	0.0071–0.0173	0.0079–0.0299	0.0016–0.0029	0.0012–0.0025	0.0006–0.0073
1986	SD25	0.0031–0.0041	0.0118–0.0177	0.0079–0.0138	0.0059–0.0118	0.0024–0.0039	0.0016–0.0032	0.0008–0.0024
1987	Z24i	0.0010–0.0018	0.0110–0.0150	0.0098–0.0138	0.0079–0.0236	0.0016–0.0029	0.0012–0.0025	snug
1987	VG30i	0.0010–0.0018	0.0083–0.0134	0.0071–0.0173	0.0079–0.0299	0.0016–0.0029	0.0012–0.0025	0.0006–0.0073
1987	SD25	0.0031–0.0041	0.0118–0.0177	0.0079–0.0138	0.0059–0.0118	0.0024–0.0039	0.0016–0.0032	0.0008–0.0024
1988	Z24i	0.0010–0.0018	0.0110–0.0150	0.0098–0.0138	0.0079–0.0236	0.0016–0.0029	0.0012–0.0025	snug
1988	VG30i	0.0010–0.0018	0.0083–0.0134	0.0071–0.0173	0.0079–0.0299	0.0016–0.0029	0.0012–0.0025	0.0006–0.0073

ENGINE AND ENGINE REBUILDING

USING A VACUUM GAUGE

White needle = steady needle Dark needle = drifting needle

The vacuum gauge is one of the most useful and easy-to-use diagnostic tools. It is inexpensive, easy to hook up, and provides valuable information about the condition of your engine.

Indication: *Normal engine in good condition*
Gauge reading: Steady, from 17–22 in.Hg.

Indication: *Sticking valve or ignition miss*
Gauge reading: Needle fluctuates from 15–20 in.Hg. at idle

Indication: *Late ignition or valve timing, low compression, stuck throttle valve, leaking carburetor or manifold gasket.*
Gauge reading: Low (15–20 in.Hg.) but steady

Indication: *Improper carburetor adjustment, or minor intake leak at carburetor or manifold*
NOTE: Bad fuel injector O-rings may also cause this reading.
Gauge reading: Drifting needle

Indication: *Weak valve springs, worn valve stem guides, or leaky cylinder head gasket (vibrating excessively at all speeds).*
NOTE: A plugged catalytic converter may also cause this reading.
Gauge reading: Needle fluctuates as engine speed increases

Indication: *Burnt valve or improper valve clearance. The needle will drop when the defective valve operates*
Gauge reading: Steady needle, but drops regularly

Indication: *Choked muffler or obstruction in system. Speed up the engine. Choked muffler will exhibit a slow drop of vacuum to zero.*
Gauge reading: Gradual drop in reading at idle

Indication: *Worn valve guides*
Gauge reading: Needle vibrates excessively at idle, but steadies as engine speed increases

TORQUE SPECIFICATIONS

Component	US	Metric
Intake manifold nut and bolt	12–14 ft. lbs.	16–20 Nm
Exhaust manifold nut and bolt (4 cyl.)	12–15 ft. lbs.	16–21 Nm
Exhaust manifold nut and bolt (6 cyl.)	13–16 ft. lbs.	18–22 Nm
Crankshaft pulley (4 cyl.)	87–116 ft. lbs.	118–157 Nm
Crankshaft pulley (6 cyl.)	90–98 ft. lbs.	123–132 Nm
Thermostat housing bolt	7–9 ft. lbs.	4–10 Nm
Cylinder head-to-front cover	3–8 ft. lbs.	1–3 Nm
Rocker cover bolts	0.7–2.2 ft. lbs.	1–3 Nm
Rocker shaft bracket bolt	11–18 ft. lbs.	15–25 Nm
Camshaft sprocket bolt	87–116 ft. lbs.	118–157 Nm
Camshaft pulley	58–65 ft. lbs.	78–88 Nm
Camshaft locating plate	58–65 ft. lbs.	78–88 Nm
Spark plug	14–22 ft. lbs.	20–29 Nm
Valve clearance adjusting lock nut	12–16 ft. lbs.	16–22 Nm
Oil strainer bolt	12–15 ft. lbs.	16–21 Nm
Oil pan bolt	5.1–5.8 ft. lbs.	7–8 Nm
Oil pan drain plug	22–29 ft. lbs.	29–39 Nm
Starter motor bolts	22–29 ft. lbs.	29–39 Nm

ENGINE AND ENGINE REBUILDING

Troubleshooting Engine Mechanical Problems

Problem	Cause	Solution
External oil leaks	• Cylinder head cover RTV sealant broken or improperly seated	• Replace sealant; inspect cylinder head cover sealant flange and cylinder head sealant surface for distortion and cracks
	• Oil filler cap leaking or missing	• Replace cap
	• Oil filter gasket broken or improperly seated	• Replace oil filter
	• Oil pan side gasket broken, improperly seated or opening in RTV sealant	• Replace gasket or repair opening in sealant; inspect oil pan gasket flange for distortion
	• Oil pan front oil seal broken or improperly seated	• Replace seal; inspect timing case cover and oil pan seal flange for distortion
	• Oil pan rear oil seal broken or improperly seated	• Replace seal; inspect oil pan rear oil seal flange; inspect rear main bearing cap for cracks, plugged oil return channels, or distortion in seal groove
	• Timing case cover oil seal broken or improperly seated	• Replace seal
	• Excess oil pressure because of restricted PCV valve	• Replace PCV valve
	• Oil pan drain plug loose or has stripped threads	• Repair as necessary and tighten
	• Rear oil gallery plug loose	• Use appropriate sealant on gallery plug and tighten
	• Rear camshaft plug loose or improperly seated	• Seat camshaft plug or replace and seal, as necessary
Excessive oil consumption	• Oil level too high	• Drain oil to specified level
	• Oil with wrong viscosity being used	• Replace with specified oil
	• PCV valve stuck closed	• Replace PCV valve
	• Valve stem oil deflectors (or seals) are damaged, missing, or incorrect type	• Replace valve stem oil deflectors
	• Valve stems or valve guides worn	• Measure stem-to-guide clearance and repair as necessary
	• Poorly fitted or missing valve cover baffles	• Replace valve cover
	• Piston rings broken or missing	• Replace broken or missing rings
	• Scuffed piston	• Replace piston
	• Incorrect piston ring gap	• Measure ring gap, repair as necessary
	• Piston rings sticking or excessively loose in grooves	• Measure ring side clearance, repair as necessary
	• Compression rings installed upside down	• Repair as necessary
	• Cylinder walls worn, scored, or glazed	• Repair as necessary

TCCS3C02

Troubleshooting Engine Mechanical Problems

Problem	Cause	Solution
Excessive oil consumption (cont.)	• Piston ring gaps not properly staggered	• Repair as necessary
	• Excessive main or connecting rod bearing clearance	• Measure bearing clearance, repair as necessary
No oil pressure	• Low oil level	• Add oil to correct level
	• Oil pressure gauge, warning lamp or sending unit inaccurate	• Replace oil pressure gauge or warning lamp
	• Oil pump malfunction	• Replace oil pump
	• Oil pressure relief valve sticking	• Remove and inspect oil pressure relief valve assembly
	• Oil passages on pressure side of pump obstructed	• Inspect oil passages for obstruction
	• Oil pickup screen or tube obstructed	• Inspect oil pickup for obstruction
	• Loose oil inlet tube	• Tighten or seal inlet tube
Low oil pressure	• Low oil level	• Add oil to correct level
	• Inaccurate gauge, warning lamp or sending unit	• Replace oil pressure gauge or warning lamp
	• Oil excessively thin because of dilution, poor quality, or improper grade	• Drain and refill crankcase with recommended oil
	• Excessive oil temperature	• Correct cause of overheating engine
	• Oil pressure relief spring weak or sticking	• Remove and inspect oil pressure relief valve assembly
	• Oil inlet tube and screen assembly has restriction or air leak	• Remove and inspect oil inlet tube and screen assembly. (Fill inlet tube with lacquer thinner to locate leaks.)
	• Excessive oil pump clearance	• Measure clearances
	• Excessive main, rod, or camshaft bearing clearance	• Measure bearing clearances, repair as necessary
High oil pressure	• Improper oil viscosity	• Drain and refill crankcase with correct viscosity oil
	• Oil pressure gauge or sending unit inaccurate	• Replace oil pressure gauge
	• Oil pressure relief valve sticking closed	• Remove and inspect oil pressure relief valve assembly
Main bearing noise	• Insufficient oil supply	• Inspect for low oil level and low oil pressure
	• Main bearing clearance excessive	• Measure main bearing clearance, repair as necessary
	• Bearing insert missing	• Replace bearing insert
	• Crankshaft end-play excessive	• Measure end-play, repair as necessary
	• Improperly tightened main bearing cap bolts	• Tighten bolts with specified torque
	• Loose flywheel or drive plate	• Tighten flywheel or drive plate attaching bolts
	• Loose or damaged vibration damper	• Repair as necessary

TCCS3C03

ENGINE AND ENGINE REBUILDING   3-59

Troubleshooting Engine Mechanical Problems

Problem	Cause	Solution
Connecting rod bearing noise	• Insufficient oil supply	• Inspect for low oil level and low oil pressure
	• Carbon build-up on piston	• Remove carbon from piston crown
	• Bearing clearance excessive or bearing missing	• Measure clearance, repair as necessary
	• Crankshaft connecting rod journal out-of-round	• Measure journal dimensions, repair or replace as necessary
	• Misaligned connecting rod or cap	• Repair as necessary
	• Connecting rod bolts tightened improperly	• Tighten bolts with specified torque
Piston noise	• Piston-to-cylinder wall clearance excessive (scuffed piston)	• Measure clearance and examine piston
	• Cylinder walls excessively tapered or out-of-round	• Measure cylinder wall dimensions, rebore cylinder
	• Piston ring broken	• Replace all rings on piston
	• Loose or seized piston pin	• Measure piston-to-pin clearance, repair as necessary
	• Connecting rods misaligned	• Measure rod alignment, straighten or replace
	• Piston ring side clearance excessively loose or tight	• Measure ring side clearance, repair as necessary
	• Carbon build-up on piston is excessive	• Remove carbon from piston
Valve actuating component noise	• Insufficient oil supply	• Check for: (a) Low oil level (b) Low oil pressure (c) Wrong hydraulic tappets (d) Restricted oil gallery (e) Excessive tappet to bore clearance
	• Rocker arms or pivots worn	• Replace worn rocker arms or pivots
	• Foreign objects or chips in hydraulic tappets	• Clean tappets
	• Excessive tappet leak-down	• Replace valve tappet
	• Tappet face worn	• Replace tappet; inspect corresponding cam lobe for wear
	• Broken or cocked valve springs	• Properly seat cocked springs; replace broken springs
	• Stem-to-guide clearance excessive	• Measure stem-to-guide clearance, repair as required
	• Valve bent	• Replace valve
	• Loose rocker arms	• Check and repair as necessary
	• Valve seat runout excessive	• Regrind valve seat/valves
	• Missing valve lock	• Install valve lock
	• Excessive engine oil	• Correct oil level

TCCS3004

Troubleshooting Engine Performance

Problem	Cause	Solution
Hard starting (engine cranks normally)	• Faulty engine control system component	• Repair or replace as necessary
	• Faulty fuel pump	• Replace fuel pump
	• Faulty fuel system component	• Repair or replace as necessary
	• Faulty ignition coil	• Test and replace as necessary
	• Improper spark plug gap	• Adjust gap
	• Incorrect ignition timing	• Adjust timing
	• Incorrect valve timing	• Check valve timing; repair as necessary
Rough idle or stalling	• Incorrect curb or fast idle speed	• Adjust curb or fast idle speed (if possible)
	• Incorrect ignition timing	• Adjust timing to specification
	• Improper feedback system operation	• Refer to Chapter 4
	• Faulty EGR valve operation	• Test EGR system and replace as necessary
	• Faulty PCV valve air flow	• Test PCV valve and replace as necessary
	• Faulty TAC vacuum motor or valve	• Repair as necessary
	• Air leak into manifold vacuum	• Inspect manifold vacuum connections and repair as necessary
	• Faulty distributor rotor or cap	• Replace rotor or cap (Distributor systems only)
	• Improperly seated valves	• Test cylinder compression, repair as necessary
	• Incorrect ignition wiring	• Inspect wiring and correct as necessary
	• Faulty ignition coil	• Test coil and replace as necessary
	• Restricted air vent or idle passages	• Clean passages
	• Restricted air cleaner	• Clean or replace air cleaner filter element
Faulty low-speed operation	• Restricted idle air vents and passages	• Clean air vents and passages
	• Restricted air cleaner	• Clean or replace air cleaner filter element
	• Faulty spark plugs	• Clean or replace spark plugs
	• Dirty, corroded, or loose ignition secondary circuit wire connections	• Clean or tighten secondary circuit wire connections
	• Improper feedback system operation	• Refer to Chapter 4
	• Faulty ignition coil high voltage wire	• Replace ignition coil high voltage wire (Distributor systems only)
	• Faulty distributor cap	• Replace cap (Distributor systems only)
Faulty acceleration	• Incorrect ignition timing	• Adjust timing
	• Faulty fuel system component	• Repair or replace as necessary
	• Faulty spark plug(s)	• Clean or replace spark plug(s)
	• Improperly seated valves	• Test cylinder compression, repair as necessary
	• Faulty ignition coil	• Test coil and replace as necessary

TCCS3005

3-60 ENGINE AND ENGINE REBUILDING

Troubleshooting Engine Performance

Problem	Cause	Solution
Faulty acceleration (cont.)	• Improper feedback system operation	• Refer to Chapter 4
Faulty high speed operation	• Incorrect ignition timing • Faulty advance mechanism • Low fuel pump volume • Wrong spark plug air gap or wrong plug • Partially restricted exhaust manifold, exhaust pipe, catalytic converter, muffler, or tailpipe • Restricted vacuum passages • Restricted air cleaner • Faulty distributor rotor or cap • Faulty ignition coil • Improperly seated valve(s) • Faulty valve spring(s) • Incorrect valve timing • Intake manifold restricted • Worn distributor shaft • Improper feedback system operation	• Adjust timing (if possible) • Check advance mechanism and repair as necessary (Distributor systems only) • Replace fuel pump • Adjust air gap or install correct plug • Eliminate restriction • Clean passages • Cleaner or replace filter element as necessary • Replace rotor or cap (Distributor systems only) • Test coil and replace as necessary • Test cylinder compression, repair as necessary • Inspect and test valve spring tension, replace as necessary • Check valve timing and repair as necessary • Remove restriction or replace manifold • Replace shaft (Distributor systems only) • Refer to Chapter 4
Misfire at all speeds	• Faulty spark plug(s) • Faulty spark plug wire(s) • Faulty distributor cap or rotor • Faulty ignition coil • Primary ignition circuit shorted or open intermittently • Improperly seated valve(s) • Faulty hydraulic tappet(s) • Improper feedback system operation • Faulty valve spring(s) • Worn camshaft lobes • Air leak into manifold • Fuel pump volume or pressure low • Blown cylinder head gasket • Intake or exhaust manifold passage(s) restricted	• Clean or relace spark plug(s) • Replace as necessary • Replace cap or rotor (Distributor systems only) • Test coil and replace as necessary • Troubleshoot primary circuit and repair as necessary • Test cylinder compression, repair as necessary • Clean or replace tappet(s) • Refer to Chapter 4 • Inspect and test valve spring tension, repair as necessary • Replace camshaft • Check manifold vacuum and repair as necessary • Replace fuel pump • Replace gasket • Pass chain through passage(s) and repair as necessary
Power not up to normal	• Incorrect ignition timing • Faulty distributor rotor	• Adjust timing • Replace rotor (Distributor systems only)

Troubleshooting Engine Performance

Problem	Cause	Solution
Power not up to normal (cont.)	• Incorrect spark plug gap • Faulty fuel pump • Faulty fuel pump • Incorrect valve timing • Faulty ignition coil • Faulty ignition wires • Improperly seated valves • Blown cylinder head gasket • Leaking piston rings • Improper feedback system operation	• Adjust gap • Replace fuel pump • Replace fuel pump • Check valve timing and repair as necessary • Test coil and replace as necessary • Test wires and replace as necessary • Test cylinder compression and repair as necessary • Replace gasket • Test compression and repair as necessary • Refer to Chapter 4
Intake backfire	• Improper ignition timing • Defective EGR component • Defective TAC vacuum motor or valve	• Adjust timing • Repair as necessary • Repair as necessary
Exhaust backfire	• Air leak into manifold vacuum • Faulty air injection diverter valve • Exhaust leak	• Check manifold vacuum and repair as necessary • Test diverter valve and replace as necessary • Locate and eliminate leak
Ping or spark knock	• Incorrect ignition timing • Distributor advance malfunction • Excessive combustion chamber deposits • Air leak into manifold vacuum • Excessively high compression • Fuel octane rating excessively low • Sharp edges in combustion chamber • EGR valve not functioning properly	• Adjust timing • Inspect advance mechanism and repair as necessary (Distributor systems only) • Remove with combustion chamber cleaner • Check manifold vacuum and repair as necessary • Test compression and repair as necessary • Try alternate fuel source • Grind smooth • Test EGR system and replace as necessary
Surging (at cruising to top speeds)	• Low fuel pump pressure or volume • Improper PCV valve air flow • Air leak into manifold vacuum • Incorrect spark advance • Restricted fuel filter • Restricted air cleaner • EGR valve not functioning properly • Improper feedback system operation	• Replace fuel pump • Test PCV valve and replace as necessary • Check manifold vacuum and repair as necessary • Test and replace as necessary • Replace fuel filter • Clean or replace air cleaner filter element • Test EGR system and replace as necessary • Refer to Chapter 4

ENGINE AND ENGINE REBUILDING 3-61

Troubleshooting the Serpentine Drive Belt

Problem	Cause	Solution
Tension sheeting fabric failure (woven fabric on outside circumference of belt has cracked or separated from body of belt)	• Grooved or backside idler pulley diameters are less than minimum recommended • Tension sheeting contacting (rubbing) stationary object • Excessive heat causing woven fabric to age • Tension sheeting splice has fractured	• Replace pulley(s) not conforming to specification • Correct rubbing condition • Replace belt • Replace belt
Noise (objectional squeal, squeak, or rumble is heard or felt while drive belt is in operation)	• Belt slippage • Bearing noise • Belt misalignment • Belt-to-pulley mismatch • Driven component inducing vibration • System resonant frequency inducing vibration	• Adjust belt • Locate and repair • Align belt/pulley(s) • Install correct belt • Locate defective driven component and repair • Vary belt tension within specifications. Replace belt.
Rib chunking (one or more ribs has separated from belt body)	• Foreign objects imbedded in pulley grooves • Installation damage • Drive loads in excess of design specifications • Insufficient internal belt adhesion	• Remove foreign objects from pulley grooves • Replace belt • Adjust belt tension • Replace belt
Rib or belt wear (belt ribs contact bottom of pulley grooves)	• Pulley(s) misaligned • Mismatch of belt and pulley groove widths • Abrasive environment • Rusted pulley(s) • Sharp or jagged pulley groove tips • Rubber deteriorated	• Align pulley(s) • Replace belt • Replace belt • Clean rust from pulley(s) • Replace pulley • Replace belt
Longitudinal belt cracking (cracks between two ribs)	• Belt has mistracked from pulley groove • Pulley groove tip has worn away rubber-to-tensile member	• Replace belt • Replace belt
Belt slips	• Belt slipping because of insufficient tension • Belt or pulley subjected to substance (belt dressing, oil, ethylene glycol) that has reduced friction • Driven component bearing failure • Belt glazed and hardened from heat and excessive slippage	• Adjust tension • Replace belt and clean pulleys • Replace faulty component bearing • Replace belt
"Groove jumping" (belt does not maintain correct position on pulley, or turns over and/or runs off pulleys)	• Insufficient belt tension • Pulley(s) not within design tolerance • Foreign object(s) in grooves	• Adjust belt tension • Replace pulley(s) • Remove foreign objects from grooves

Troubleshooting the Serpentine Drive Belt

Problem	Cause	Solution
"Groove jumping" (belt does not maintain correct position on pulley, or turns over and/or runs off pulleys)	• Excessive belt speed • Pulley misalignment • Belt-to-pulley profile mismatched • Belt cordline is distorted	• Avoid excessive engine acceleration • Align pulley(s) • Install correct belt • Replace belt
Belt broken (Note: identify and correct problem before replacement belt is installed)	• Excessive tension • Tensile members damaged during belt installation • Belt turnover • Severe pulley misalignment • Bracket, pulley, or bearing failure	• Replace belt and adjust tension to specification • Replace belt • Replace belt • Align pulley(s) • Replace defective component and belt
Cord edge failure (tensile member exposed at edges of belt or separated from belt body)	• Excessive tension • Drive pulley misalignment • Belt contacting stationary object • Pulley irregularities • Improper pulley construction • Insufficient adhesion between tensile member and rubber matrix	• Adjust belt tension • Align pulley • Correct as necessary • Replace pulley • Replace pulley • Replace belt and adjust tension to specifications
Sporadic rib cracking (multiple cracks in belt ribs at random intervals)	• Ribbed pulley(s) diameter less than minimum specification • Backside bend flat pulley(s) diameter less than minimum • Excessive heat condition causing rubber to harden • Excessive belt thickness • Belt overcured • Excessive tension	• Replace pulley(s) • Replace pulley(s) • Correct heat condition as necessary • Replace belt • Replace belt • Adjust belt tension

TCCS3C09

TCCS3C10

ENGINE AND ENGINE REBUILDING

Troubleshooting the Cooling System

Problem	Cause	Solution
High temperature gauge indication—overheating	• Coolant level low • Improper fan operation • Radiator hose(s) collapsed • Radiator airflow blocked	• Replenish coolant • Repair or replace as necessary • Replace hose(s) • Remove restriction (bug screen, fog lamps, etc.)
	• Faulty pressure cap • Ignition timing incorrect • Air trapped in cooling system • Heavy traffic driving	• Replace pressure cap • Adjust ignition timing • Purge air • Operate at fast idle in neutral intermittently to cool engine • Install proper component(s)
	• Incorrect cooling system component(s) installed • Faulty thermostat • Water pump shaft broken or impeller loose • Radiator tubes clogged • Cooling system clogged • Casting flash in cooling passages	• Replace thermostat • Replace water pump • Flush radiator • Flush system • Repair or replace as necessary. Flash may be visible by removing cooling system components or removing core plugs.
	• Brakes dragging • Excessive engine friction • Antifreeze concentration over 68%	• Repair brakes • Repair engine • Lower antifreeze concentration percentage
	• Missing air seals • Faulty gauge or sending unit • Loss of coolant flow caused by leakage or foaming • Viscous fan drive failed	• Replace air seals • Repair or replace faulty component • Repair or replace leaking component, replace coolant • Replace unit
Low temperature indication—undercooling	• Thermostat stuck open • Faulty gauge or sending unit	• Replace thermostat • Repair or replace faulty component
Coolant loss—boilover	• Overfilled cooling system	• Reduce coolant level to proper specification
	• Quick shutdown after hard (hot) run • Air in system resulting in occasional "burping" of coolant • Insufficient antifreeze allowing coolant boiling point to be too low • Antifreeze deteriorated because of age or contamination • Leaks due to loose hose clamps, loose nuts, bolts, drain plugs, faulty hoses, or defective radiator	• Allow engine to run at fast idle prior to shutdown • Purge system • Add antifreeze to raise boiling point • Replace coolant • Pressure test system to locate source of leak(s) then repair as necessary

TCCS3C11

Troubleshooting the Cooling System

Problem	Cause	Solution
Coolant loss—boilover	• Faulty head gasket • Cracked head, manifold, or block • Faulty radiator cap	• Replace head gasket • Replace as necessary • Replace cap
Coolant entry into crankcase or cylinder(s)	• Faulty head gasket • Crack in head, manifold or block	• Replace head gasket • Replace as necessary
Coolant recovery system inoperative	• Coolant level low • Leak in system • Pressure cap not tight or seal missing, or leaking • Pressure cap defective • Overflow tube clogged or leaking • Recovery bottle vent restricted	• Replenish coolant to FULL mark • Pressure test to isolate leak and repair as necessary • Repair as necessary • Replace cap • Repair as necessary • Remove restriction
Noise	• Fan contacting shroud • Loose water pump impeller • Glazed fan belt • Loose fan belt • Rough surface on drive pulley • Water pump bearing worn • Belt alignment	• Reposition shroud and inspect engine mounts (on electric fans inspect assembly • Replace pump • Apply silicone or replace belt • Adjust fan belt tension • Replace pulley • Remove belt to isolate. Replace pump. • Check pulley alignment. Repair as necessary.
No coolant flow through heater core	• Restricted return inlet in water pump • Heater hose collapsed or restricted • Restricted heater core • Restricted outlet in thermostat housing • Intake manifold bypass hole in cylinder head restricted • Faulty heater control valve • Intake manifold coolant passage restricted	• Remove restriction • Remove restriction or replace hose • Remove restriction or replace core • Remove flash or restriction • Remove restriction • Replace valve • Remove restriction or replace intake manifold

NOTE: *Immediately after shutdown, the engine enters a condition known as heat soak. This is caused by the cooling system being inoperative while engine temperature is still high. If coolant temperature rises above boiling point expansion and pressure may push some coolant out of the radiator overflow tube. If this does not occur frequently i is considered normal.*

TCCS3C12

EMISSION CONTROLS 4-2
POSITIVE CRANKCASE VENTILATION
  (PCV) SYSTEM 4-2
    OPERATION 4-2
    TESTING 4-2
    REMOVAL & INSTALLATION 4-2
EVAPORATIVE EMISSION CONTROL
  SYSTEM 4-2
    INSPECTION AND SERVICE 4-3
    REMOVAL & INSTALLATION 4-3
DUAL POINT DISTRIBUTOR 4-3
    OPERATION 4-3
    INSPECTION AND
      ADJUSTMENTS 4-3
DUAL SPARK PLUG IGNITION
  SYSTEM 4-4
    OPERATION 4-4
    ADJUSTMENT 4-5
SPARK TIMING CONTROL SYSTEM 4-5
    OPERATION 4-5
    INSPECTION AND
      ADJUSTMENTS 4-5
SPARK PLUG SWITCHING CONTROL
  SYSTEM 4-6
    OPERATION 4-6
EARLY FUEL EVAPORATION
  SYSTEM 4-6
    OPERATION 4-6
BOOST CONTROL DECELERATION
  DEVICE (BCDD) 4-6
    OPERATION 4-6
    SERVICE 4-6
INTAKE MANIFOLD VACUUM CONTROL
  SYSTEM 4-7
    OPERATION 4-7
AUTOMATIC TEMPERATURE
  CONTROLLED (ATC) AIR CLEANER 4-7
    OPERATION 4-7
    SERVICE 4-7
EXHAUST GAS RECIRCULATION (EGR)
  SYSTEM 4-8
    OPERATION 4-8
    SERVICE 4-8
    REMOVAL & INSTALLATION 4-9
AIR INJECTION SYSTEM (AIS) 4-10
    OPERATION 4-10
    SERVICE 4-11
AIR INDUCTION SYSTEM 4-11
    OPERATION 4-11
    SERVICE 4-11
FUEL SHUT-OFF SYSTEM 4-12
    OPERATION 4-12
ELECTRIC CHOKE 4-13
    OPERATION 4-13
DETONATION CONTROL SYSTEM 4-13
    OPERATION 4-13
    SERVICE 4-13
HIGH ALTITUDE COMPENSATOR
  SYSTEM 4-13
    OPERATION 4-13
MIXTURE HEATING SYSTEM 4-13
    OPERATION 4-13
CATALYTIC CONVERTER 4-13
    OPERATION 4-13
    PRECAUTIONS 4-14
    TESTING 4-14
MIXTURE RATIO FEEDBACK
  SYSTEM 4-14
    OPERATION 4-14
OXYGEN SENSOR 4-14
    OPERATION 4-14
    REMOVAL & INSTALLATION 4-15
**ELECTRONIC ENGINE
  CONTROLS 4-15**
SELF-DIAGNOSTIC SYSTEM 4-15
**VACUUM DIAGRAMS AND SYSTEM
  COMPONENTS 4-21**

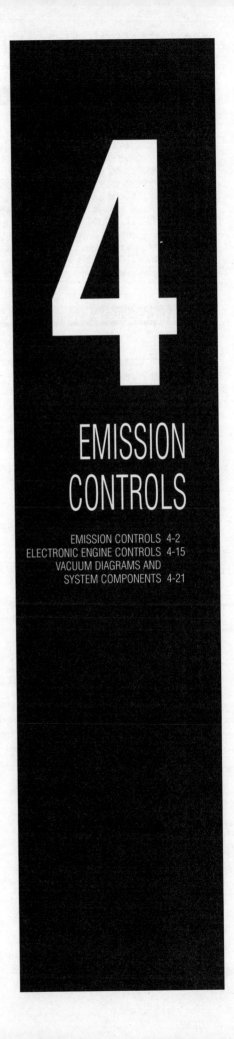

4
EMISSION CONTROLS

EMISSION CONTROLS 4-2
ELECTRONIC ENGINE CONTROLS 4-15
VACUUM DIAGRAMS AND
  SYSTEM COMPONENTS 4-21

4-2 EMISSION CONTROLS

EMISSION CONTROLS

There are three sources of automotive pollutants; crankcase fumes, exhaust gases, and gasoline evaporation. The pollutants formed from these substances fall into three categories: unburned hydrocarbons (HC), carbon monoxide (CO), and oxides of nitrogen (NOx). The equipment used to limit these pollutants is called the emission control system.

Due to varying state, federal, and provincial regulations, various specific emission control components have been devised for each. The U.S. emission equipment for vehicles covered by this manual is divided into two categories: California and 49 State (Federal). In this section, the term "California" applies only to trucks originally built to be sold in California. California emissions equipment is generally not shared with equipment installed on trucks built to be sold in the other 49 States. Models built to be sold in Canada also have specific emissions equipment, although in most years 49 State and Canadian equipment is the same.

Positive Crankcase Ventilation (PCV) System

OPERATION

The crankcase emission control equipment consists of a positive crankcase ventilation (PCV) valve, a closed filler cap and hoses to connect this equipment.

When the engine is running, a small portion of the gases which are formed in the combustion chamber during combustion leak by the piston rings and enter the crankcase. Since these gases are under pressure they tend to escape from the crankcase and enter into the atmosphere. If these gases were allowed to remain in the crankcase for any length of time, they would contaminate the engine oil and cause sludge to build up. If the gases are allowed to escape into the atmosphere, they would pollute the air, as they contain unburned hydrocarbons. The crankcase emission control equipment recycles these gases back into the engine combustion chamber where they are burned.

Crankcase gases are recycled in the following manner: while the engine is running, clean filtered air is drawn into the crankcase through the air filter and then through a hose leading to the rocker cover. As the air passes through the crankcase it picks up the combustion gases and carries them out of the crankcase, up through the PCV valve and into the intake manifold. After they enter the intake manifold they are drawn into the combustion chamber and burned.

The most critical component in the system is the PCV valve. This vacuum controlled valve regulates the amount of gases which are recycled into the combustion chamber. At low engine speeds the valve is partially closed, limiting the flow of gases into the intake manifold. As engine speed increases, the valve opens to admit greater quantities of the gases into the intake manifold. If the valve should become blocked or plugged, the gases will be prevented from escaping out of the crankcase by the normal route. Since these gases are under pressure, they will find their own way out of the crankcase. This alternate route is usually a weak oil seal or gasket in the engine. As the gas escapes by the gasket it also creates an oil leak. Besides causing oil leaks, a clogged PCV valve also allows these gases to remain in the crankcase for an extended period of time, promoting the formation of sludge in the engine.

➡ The PCV system will not function properly unless the oil filler cap is tightly sealed. Check the gasket on the cap and be certain it is not leaking. Replace the cap or gasket or both if necessary to ensure proper sealing.

TESTING

♦ See Figures 1, 2 and 3

Check the PCV system hoses and connections, to see that there are no leaks. Then replace or tighten, as necessary.

To check the valve, remove it and blow through both of its ends. When blowing from the side which goes toward the intake manifold, very little air should pass through it. When blowing from the crankcase (cylinder head cover) side, air should pass through freely.

An additional check without removing the valve may be made with the engine running, remove the ventilator hose from the PCV valve. If the valve is working, a hissing noise will be heard as air passes through the valve and a strong vacuum should be felt immediately when the valve inlet is blocked with a finger. If the valve is suspected of being plugged, it should be replaced.

If the valve fails to function as outlined replace with a new one.

➡ Do not attempt to clean or adjust the valve. Replace it with a new one.

REMOVAL & INSTALLATION

To remove the PCV valve, simply loosen the hose clamp and remove the valve from the manifold-to-crankcase hose and intake manifold; most valve pull right out, although some must be unthreaded. Install the PCV valve in the reverse order of removal.

Evaporative Emission Control System

When raw fuel evaporates, the vapors contain hydrocarbons. To prevent these fumes from escaping into the atmosphere, the fuel evaporative emission control system was developed.

There are two different evaporative emission control systems used on Datsun/Nissan trucks. The system used on 1970–1974 trucks consists of a sealed fuel tank, a vapor/liquid separator, a flow guide (check) valve, and all of the hoses connecting these components, in the above order, leading from the fuel tank to the PCV hose, which connects the crankcase to the PCV valve.

In operation, the vapor formed in the fuel tank passes through the vapor separator, into the flow guide valve and the crankcase. When the engine is not running, if the fuel vapor pressure in the vapor separator goes above 0.4 in. Hg, the flow guide valve opens and allows the vapor to enter the engine crankcase. Otherwise, the flow guide valve is closed to the vapor separator while the engine is not running. When the engine is running, and a vacuum is developed in the fuel tank or in the engine crankcase and the difference of pressure between the relief side of the valve and the fuel tank or crankcase becomes 2 in. Hg, the relief valve opens. This allows ambient air from the air cleaner into the fuel tank or the engine

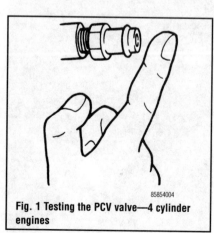

Fig. 1 Testing the PCV valve—4 cylinder engines

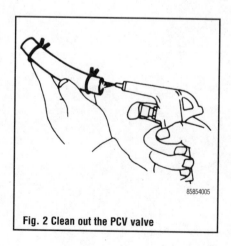

Fig. 2 Clean out the PCV valve

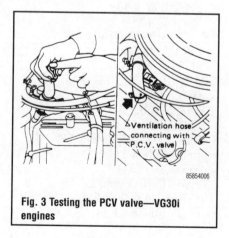

Fig. 3 Testing the PCV valve—VG30i engines

EMISSION CONTROLS 4-3

crankcase. The ambient air replaces the vapor within the fuel tank or crankcase, bringing the fuel tank or crankcase back into a neutral or positive pressure range.

The system used on 1975–88 trucks consists of a sealed fuel tank, a vapor/liquid separator, a vapor vent line, a carbon canister, a vacuum signal line and a canister purge line.

In operation, fuel vapors and/or liquid are routed to the liquid/vapor separator or check valve where liquid fuel is directed back into the fuel tank as fuel vapors flow into the charcoal filled canister. The charcoal absorbs and stores the fuel vapors when the engine is not running or is at idle. When the throttle valves in the carburetor (or air intakes for fuel injected models) are opened, vacuum from above the throttle valves is routed through a vacuum signal line to the purge control valve on the canister. The control valve opens and allows the fuel vapors to be drawn from the canister through a purge line and into the intake manifold and the combustion chambers.

INSPECTION AND SERVICE

Check the hoses for proper connections and damage. Replace as necessary. Check the vapor separator tank for fuel leaks, distortion and dents, and replace as necessary.

Flow Guide Valve—1970-74

Remove the flow guide valve and inspect it for leakage by blowing air into the ports in the valve. When air is applied from the fuel tank side, the flow guide valve is normal if air passes into the check side (crankcase side), but not leaking into the relief side (air cleaner side). When air is applied from the check side, the valve is normal if the passage of air is restricted. When air is applied from the relief side (air cleaner side), the valve is normal if air passes into the fuel tank side or into the check side.

Carbon Canister and Purge Control Valve—1975-88

To check the operation of the carbon canister purge control valve, disconnect the rubber hose between the canister control valve and the T-fitting, at the T-fitting. Apply vacuum to the hose leading to the control valve. The vacuum condition should be maintained indefinitely. If the control valve leaks, remove the top cover of the valve and check for a dislocated or cracked diaphragm. If the diaphragm is damaged, a repair kit containing a new diaphragm, retainer, and spring is available and should be installed.

The carbon canister has an air filter in the bottom of the canister. The filter element should be checked once a year or every 12,000–15,000 miles (19,200–24,000 km) miles; more frequently if the truck is operated in dusty areas, Replace the filter by pulling it out of the bottom of the canister and installing a new one.

REMOVAL & INSTALLATION

Removal and installation of the various evaporative emission control system components consists of disconnecting the hoses, loosening retaining screws, and removing the part which is to be replaced or checked. Always tag hoses before disconnecting the installation will be obvious. When replacing hoses, make sure that they are fuel and vapor resistant.

Dual Point Distributor

OPERATION

1970-73 Engines Only

The dual point distributor has two sets of breaker points which operate independently of each other and are positioned with a relative phase angle of 5° (1970), 10° (1971) or 7° (1972–73) apart. This makes one set the advanced points and the other set the retarded points.

The two sets of points, which mechanically operate continuously, are connected in parallel to the primary side of the ignition timing, depending on whether or not the retarded set of points is energized.

When both sets of points are electrically energized, the first set to open (the advanced set, 4° or 1° sooner) has no control over breaking the ignition coil primary circuit because the retarded set is still closed and maintaining a complete circuit to ground. When the retarded set of points opens, the advanced set is still open, and the primary circuit is broken causing the electromagnetic field in the coil to collapse and the ignition spark is produced.

When the retarded set of points is removed from the primary ignition circuit through the operation of a distributor relay inserted into the retarded points circuit, the advanced set of points controls the primary circuit. The retarded set of points is activated as follows:

- On 1970 and 1971 models, the retarded set of points is activated only while cruising or accelerating with the throttle partially open and the transmission in 3rd gear. Under all other conditions, the retarded set of points is removed from the ignition circuit.
- On 1972 models, the retarded set of points is activated only while cruising or accelerating with the throttle partially open, the transmission in 3rd gear, and with the ambient temperature above 50°F (10°C).
- On 1973 models, the retarded set of points is activated only while the throttle is partially open, the temperature is above 50°F (10°C), and the transmission is in any gear but 4th.

➡When the ambient temperature is below 34°F (1°C), the retarded set of points is removed from the ignition circuit no matter what switch is on.

In the case of an automatic transmission, the retarded set of points is activated at all times except under heavy acceleration and high speed cruising (wide open throttle) with the ambient temperature is above 50°F (10°C).

There are three switches which control the operation of the distributor relay on 1972–73 models and five switches on 1970–71 models. All of the switches must be **ON** in order to energize the distributor relay thus energizing the retarded set of points.

The switches and their operation are as follows:

A transmission switch located in the transmission closes an electrical circuit when the transmission is in 3rd gear (1970–72) and in any gear except 4th (1973). On 1970–71 models only, there is a transmission neutral switch which **ON** when the transmission is in all gears except Neutral.

A clutch switch mounted against the clutch pedal (1970–71) is **ON** when the clutch pedal is released (clutch engaged).

A throttle switch located on the throttle linkage at the carburetor is **ON** when the throttle valve is moved within a predetermined angle: up to 35° on 1970–71 models, 40° on 1972 models, and 45° on 1973 models.

An accelerator switch mounted to the accelerator pedal linkage (1970–72) is **ON** when the accelerator pedal is nearly completely released and **OFF** when the pedal is opened farther.

The temperature sensing switch on 1972–73 models is located near the hood release lever inside the passenger compartment. The temperature sensing switch comes **ON** between 41°F (5°F) and 55°F (13°C) when the temperature is rising and goes **OFF** at about 34°F (1°C) when the temperature falls.

The distributor vacuum advance mechanism produces a spark advance based on the amount of vacuum in the intake manifold. With a high vacuum, less air/fuel mixture enters the engine cylinders and the mixture is therefore less highly compressed. Consequently, this mixture burns more slowly and the advance mechanism gives it more time to burn. This longer burning time results in higher combustion temperatures at peak pressure and hence, more time for nitrogen (N) to react with oxygen (O_2) and form nitrogen oxides (NOx). At the same time, this advance timing results in less complete combustion due to the greater area of cylinder wall (quench area) exposed at the instant of ignition. This cooled fuel will not burn as readily and hence, results in higher unburned hydrocarbons (HC). The production of NOx and HC resulting from vacuum advance is highest during idle and moderate acceleration in lower gears.

Retardation of the ignition timing is necessary to reduce NOx and HC emissions. Various ways of retarding the ignition spark have been used in automobiles, all of which remove vacuum to the distributor vacuum advance mechanism at different times under certain conditions. Another way of accomplishing the same goal is the dual point distributor system.

INSPECTION AND ADJUSTMENTS

♦ See Figures 4, 5, 6 and 7

Phase Difference

1. Disconnect the wiring harness of the distributor from the engine harness.
2. Connect the black wire of the engine harness with the black wire of the distributor harness with a jumper wire. This connects the advanced set of points.

EMISSION CONTROLS

3. With the engine idling, adjust the ignition timing by rotating the distributor.

4. Disconnect the jumper wire from the black wire of the distributor harness and connect it to the yellow wire of the distributor harness. The retarded set of points is now activated.

5. With the engine idling, check the ignition timing. The timing should be retarded from the advanced setting as follows: 5° for 1970; 10° for 1971; and 7° for 1972–73.

6. To adjust the out-of-phase angle of the ignition timing, loosen the adjuster plate set screws on the same side as the retarded set of points.

7. Place the blade of a screwdriver in the adjusting notch of the adjuster plate and turn the plate as required to obtain the correct retarded ignition timing specification. The ignition timing is retarded when the adjuster plate is turned counterclockwise. There are graduations on the adjuster plate to make the adjustment easier; one graduation is equal to 4 degrees of crankshaft rotation.

8. Replace the distributor cap, start the engine, and check the ignition timing with the retarded set of points activated (yellow wire of the distributor wiring harness connected to the black wire of the engine wiring harness).

9. Repeat the steps above as necessary to properly set the retarded ignition timing.

Transmission Switch

Disconnect the electrical leads at the switch and connect a self-powered test light to the electrical leads. The switch should conduct electricity only when the gearshift is moved to the corresponding gear for that particular model year vehicle: 3rd gear on 1970–72 models and 4th gear on 1973 models. The neutral switch on 1970–71 models should conduct current when the transmission is shifted into **N**.

If the switch fails to perform in the above manner, replace it with a new one.

Clutch Switch

Test the clutch switch on 1970–71 models in the same manner as the transmission switch (self-powered test light). The switch should conduct current when the clutch pedal is released (clutch engaged).

Accelerator Switch

The accelerator switch is mounted on the accelerator pedal linkage (except 1973). It is checked with a self-powered test light in the same manner as outlined for the transmission switch. The switch should conduct current when the accelerator pedal is nearly completely released.

Throttle Switch

The throttle switch located on the throttle linkage at the carburetor is checked with a self-powered test light. Disconnect the electrical leads of the switch and connect the test light. The switch should not conduct current when the throttle valve is closed or opened as follows: The throttle valve opened up to 35° on 1970–71 models; 40° on 1972 models; and 45° on 1973 models. When the throttle is fully opened, the switch should conduct current.

Temperature Sensing Switch

♦ See Figure 8

The temperature sensing switch mounted in the passenger compartment (near the hood release lever) should not conduct current when the temperature is above 55°F (13°C) when connected to a self-powered test light as previously outlined for the throttle switch.

Dual Spark Plug Ignition System

OPERATION

♦ See Figure 9

Z20, Z22, Z24 and Z24i Engines

These engines have two spark plugs per cylinder. This arrangement allows the engine to burn large amounts of recirculated exhaust gases without affecting

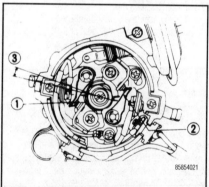

Fig. 4 (1) Advance point set (2) Retarded point set (3) Phase difference

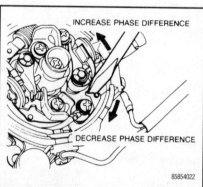

Fig. 5 Adjusting the phase angle on a dual point distributor

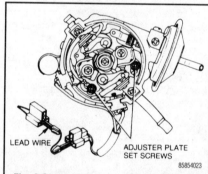

Fig. 6 Connect a jumper wire between the two wiring harnesses to activate just one set of points

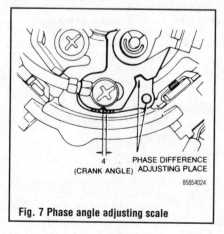

Fig. 7 Phase angle adjusting scale

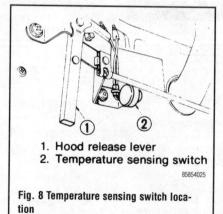

1. Hood release lever
2. Temperature sensing switch

Fig. 8 Temperature sensing switch location

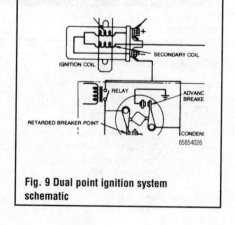

Fig. 9 Dual point ignition system schematic

EMISSION CONTROLS 4-5

performance. In fact, the system works so well it improves gas mileage under most circumstances.

Both spark plugs fire simultaneously, which substantially shortens the time required to burn the air/fuel mixture when exhaust gases (EGR) are not being recirculated. When gases are being recirculated, the dual spark plug system brings the ignition level up to that of a single plug system which is not recirculating exhaust gases.

ADJUSTMENT

The only adjustments necessary are the tune-up and maintenance procedures outlined in Sections 1 and 2.

Spark Timing Control System

OPERATION

♦ See Figure 10

There are actually two different versions of this system, the first is utilized on many 1975–80 trucks and the second can be found on 1981–86 trucks (720-D series). The 1975–80 system controls distributor vacuum advance, giving full vacuum advance when the transmission is in 4th or 5th, and partial advance in the first three gears. This provides better control of the combustion process, lowering emissions of HC and NOx.

The system components include a top gear detecting switch, installed in the transmission, and a vacuum switching valve spliced into the distributor vacuum advance hose by means of a 3-way connector. When the transmission is shifted into either of the two top gears, the transmission switch goes on, activating the vacuum switching valve which closes its air bleed, giving full advance. Shifting into any gear but 4th and 5th turns the transmission switch off, deactivating the vacuum switching valve. The valve opens a vacuum leak, providing only partial vacuum advance to the distributor.

The 1981–86 system replaces the earlier system but is very similar. The major difference is that it works solely from engine water temperature changes rather than a transmission mounted switch. The system includes a thermal vacuum valve, a vacuum delay (control) valve, and the attendant hoses. It performs the same function as the earlier system, to retard full spark advance at times when high levels of pollutants would otherwise be given off.

INSPECTION AND ADJUSTMENTS

♦ See Figures 11, 12 and 13

1975–80 Engines

1. Check all hoses and electrical wires for proper connections, leaks or corrosion, and so on.
2. Check the distributor vacuum advance unit for proper operation. This can be checked by hooking up a timing light, starting the engine, then increasing engine speed and observing whether or not the timing marks advance. If not, the advance unit must be checked for binding or leaks.
3. With the timing light installed, increase the engine speed to 2000 rpm. Have an assistant disengage the clutch, then shift between 3rd, 4th and 5th, then back down and into neutral. Spark timing should vary when the transmission is in 4th or 5th (advance should be greater). If this is not the case, check the vacuum switching valve.

VACUUM SWITCHING VALVE

1. Disconnect the valve's electrical connectors. With the timing light installed, run the engine up to about 2000 rpm and keep it there. Check the timing.
2. Connect the valve's electrical connectors directly to the battery with a pair of jumper wires. Be sure to observe correct polarity. If spark timing varies, the valve is ok. If not, replace it.

TOP GEAR TRANSMISSION SWITCH

The switch can be checked easily with an ohmmeter. Connect the ohmmeter leads to the switch leads on the transmission. Shift back and forth between either 4th or 5th and one of the other gears. If the resistance does not change, replace the switch.

1981–86 Engines

Connect a timing light and check the ignition timing while the temperature gauge is in the cold position. Write down the reading. Allow the engine to run with the timing light attached until the temperature needle reaches the center of the gauge. As the engine is warming up, check with the timing light to make sure the ignition timing retards. When the temperature needle is in the middle of the gauge, the ignition timing should advance from its previous position. If the ignition timing does not change, replace the thermal vacuum valve.

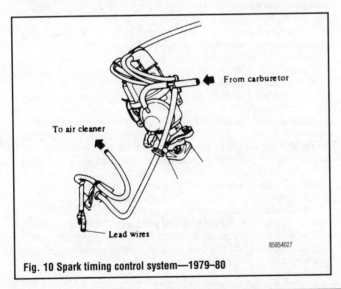

Fig. 10 Spark timing control system—1979–80

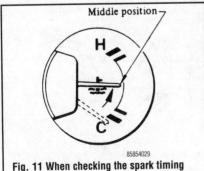

Fig. 11 When checking the spark timing control system, the ignition timing should advance when the temperature gauge reaches the middle—1981–86

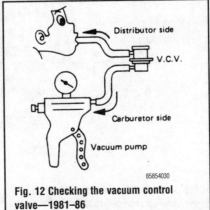

Fig. 12 Checking the vacuum control valve—1981–86

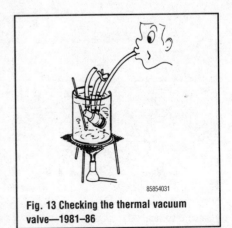

Fig. 13 Checking the thermal vacuum valve—1981–86

4-6 EMISSION CONTROLS

Spark Plug Switching Control System

OPERATION

♦ See Figure 14

This system, used only on the 1984–86 Canadian trucks (Z24), is designed to change the ignition system from 2-plug ignition to 1-plug ignition during heavy load driving conditions in order to reduce engine noise. The system also functions to advance ignition timing by the proper amount during 1-plug ignition.

The main component of the system is an ignition control unit installed in the distributor. The unit has a switching function which allows it to change from 2-plug to 1-plug operation by means of a vacuum switch in the intake manifold.

Early Fuel Evaporation System

OPERATION

♦ See Figure 15

The early fuel evaporation system is used on certain 1973–77 L-series engines. The system's purpose is to heat the air/fuel mixture when the engine is below normal operating temperature. The L-series engines use a system much similar to the old style exhaust manifold heat riser. The only adjustment necessary is to occasionally lubricate the counterweight. Other than that, the system should be trouble-free.

Most later carbureted engines use coolant water heat instead of exhaust gas heat to prewarm the fuel mixture. This system should be trouble-free.

Boost Control Deceleration Device (BCDD)

OPERATION

The BCDD reduces hydrocarbon emissions during coasting conditions. High manifold vacuum during coasting prevents the complete combustion of the air/fuel mixture because of the reduced amount of air. This condition will result in large HC emissions. Enriching the air/fuel mixture for a short time (during the high vacuum condition) will reduce the emission of HC in conjunction with the AIR system.

However, enriching the air/fuel mixture with only the mixture adjusting screw will cause poor engine idle, or invite an increase in the carbon monoxide (CO) content of the exhaust gases.

The BCDD consists of an independently operated auxiliary fuel system. This system functions when the engine is coasting to enrich the air/fuel mixture which minimizes the hydrocarbon content of the exhaust gases through more efficient combustion. This is accomplished without adversely affecting engine idle and the carbon monoxide content of the exhaust gases.

When intake manifold vacuum exceeds a predetermined value, a vacuum actuated diaphragm opens an air passage allowing additional air to enter the intake manifold. When the additional air passage is opened, vacuum is brought to bear on another diaphragm which opens a fuel passage allowing additional fuel to enter the intake manifold.

When the engine changes from a coasting condition to that of idling, the transmission speed sensor closes an electrical circuit, energizing the vacuum control solenoid valve. When energized, the vacuum control solenoid valve vents the intake manifold vacuum to the atmosphere, thus causing the two diaphragms to return to their normal positions, closing off the additional air and fuel mixture. The transmission switch is not used on 1978–79 models.

SERVICE

♦ See Figures 16 and 17

Normally, the BCDD never needs adjustment. However, if the need should arise because of suspected malfunction of the system, proceed as follows:
1. Connect a tachometer to the engine.
2. Connect a quick-response vacuum gauge to the intake manifold.
3. Disconnect the BCDD solenoid valve electrical leads.
4. Start and warm up the engine until it reaches normal operating temperature.
5. Adjust the idle speed to the proper specification.
6. Raise the engine speed to 3000–3500 rpm under no-load (transmission in **N** or **P**), then allow the throttle to close quickly. Take notice as to whether or not the engine rpm returns to idle speed and if it does, how long the fall in rpm is interrupted before it reaches idle speed.

At the moment the throttle is snapped closed at high engine rpm, the vacuum in the intake manifold reaches 27.7 in. Hg on pre—1975 vehicles and 23.6 in. Hg on 1975 and later models, and then gradually falls to about 16.5 in. Hg at idle speed. The process of the fall of intake manifold vacuum and engine rpm will take one of the following three forms:

- When the operating pressure of the BCDD is too high, the system remains inoperative, and the vacuum in the intake manifold decreases without interruption just like that of an engine without a BCDD.
- When the operating pressure is lower than that of the case given, but still higher than the properly set pressure, the fall of vacuum in the intake manifold is interrupted and kept constant at a certain level (operating pressure) for about 1 second and then gradually falls down to the normal vacuum at idle speed.
- When the set operating pressure of the BCDD is lower than the intake manifold vacuum when the throttle is suddenly released, the engine speed will not lower to idle speed.

To adjust the set operating pressure of the BCDD, remove the adjusting screw cover from the BCDD mechanism mounted on the side of the carburetor.

The adjusting screw is a Left-hand threaded screw. Turning the screw ⅛ of a turn in either direction will change the operation pressure about 0.79 in. Hg. Turning the screw counterclockwise will increase the amount of vacuum needed to operate the mechanism and turning the screw clockwise will decrease the amount of vacuum needed to operate the mechanism.

The operating pressure for the BCDD on a vehicle with a manual transmission is 18.91–20.49 in. Hg and for a vehicle with an automatic transmission 18.11–19.69 in. Hg through 1974. The decrease in intake manifold vacuum should be interrupted at these levels for about 1 second when the BCDD is operating correctly. The figures for later years are:

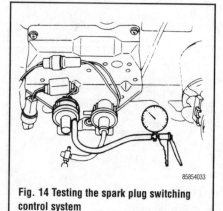

Fig. 14 Testing the spark plug switching control system

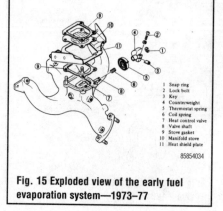

1 Snap ring
2 Lock bolt
3 Key
4 Counterweight
5 Thermostat spring
6 Coil spring
7 Heat control valve
8 Valve shaft
9 Stove gasket
10 Manifold stove
11 Heat shield plate

Fig. 15 Exploded view of the early fuel evaporation system—1973–77

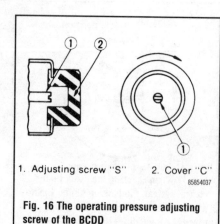

1. Adjusting screw "S"   2. Cover "C"

Fig. 16 The operating pressure adjusting screw of the BCDD

EMISSION CONTROLS 4-7

- 1975–76: 20.7 to –21.1—manual transmission; 19.9 to 20.3—automatic transmission
- 1977: 20.1 to 21.7—manual transmission; 19.3 to 20.9—automatic transmission
- 1978: 21.26 to 22.84—all models
- 1979 and later: 20.90 to 22.44—all models.

Don't forget to install the adjusting screw cover when the system is adjusted.

Intake Manifold Vacuum Control System

OPERATION

♦ See Figure 18

This system, used in 1979–84, is designed to reduce the engine's oil consumption when the intake manifold vacuum increases to an extremely high level during deceleration. The system consists of two units. A boost control unit as the vacuum sensor, and a by-pass air control unit as an actuator. The boost control unit senses the manifold vacuum. When the level of the manifold vacuum increases above the pre-determined value, the boost control valve opens and transmits the manifold vacuum to the by-pass air control unit. The manifold vacuum then pulls the diaphragm in and opens the by-pass air control valve, thereby causing the air to be bypassed to the intake manifold. After completion of the air by-pass, the manifold vacuum is lowered. This results in the closing of the boost control valve and then the closing of the air control valve. This system operates in a tightly controlled circuit so that the manifold vacuum can be kept very close to the pre-determined value during deceleration.

Aside from a routine check of the hoses and their connections, no service or adjustments should ever be necessary on this system. If at some time you feel that an adjustment is required, it is suggested that you take the truck to a Nissan/Datsun dealer or an authorized service representative.

Automatic Temperature Controlled (ATC) Air Cleaner

OPERATION

♦ See Figures 19, 20, 21 and 22

The rate of fuel atomization varies with the temperature of the air with which the fuel is being mixed. The air/fuel ratio cannot be held constant for efficient fuel combustion with a wide range of air temperatures. Cold air being drawn into the engine causes a denser and richer air/fuel mixture, inefficient fuel atomization, and thus, more hydrocarbons in the exhaust gas. Hot air being drawn into the engine causes a leaner air/fuel mixture, for efficient atomization and combustion which decreases in the exhaust gases.

The automatic temperature controlled air cleaner is designed so that the temperature of the ambient air being drawn into the engine is automatically controlled, to hold the temperature of the air and ,consequently, the fuel/air ratio at a constant rate for efficient fuel combustion.

A temperature sensing vacuum switch controls vacuum applied to a vacuum motor operating a valve in the intake snorkel of the air cleaner. When the engine is cold or the air being drawn into the engine is cold, the vacuum motor opens the valve, allowing air heated by the exhaust manifold to be drawn into the engine. As the engine warms up, the temperature sensing unit shuts off the vacuum applied to the motor which allows the valve to close, shutting off the heated air and allowing cooler, outside (underhood) air to be drawn into the engine.

SERVICE

♦ See Figures 23, 24, 25 and 26

When the air around the temperature sensor of the unit mounted inside the air cleaner housing reaches 100°F (38°C), the sensor should block the flow of vacuum to the air control valve vacuum motor. When the temperature around the

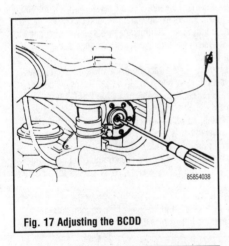

Fig. 17 Adjusting the BCDD

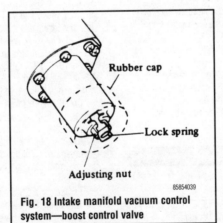

Fig. 18 Intake manifold vacuum control system—boost control valve

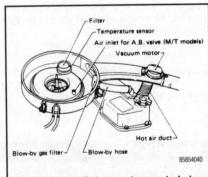

Fig. 19 Automatic temperature control air cleaner—1985–86 Z20 and Z24 engines (USA)

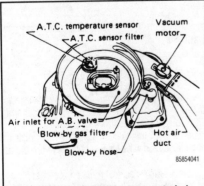

Fig. 20 Automatic temperature control air cleaner—1986–88 Z24i engines

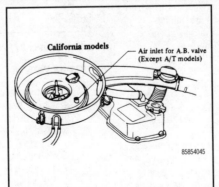

Fig. 21 Automatic temperature control air cleaner—1984

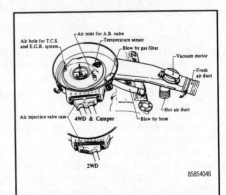

Fig. 22 Automatic temperature control air cleaner—1985–86 Z24 engines (Canada)

4-8 EMISSION CONTROLS

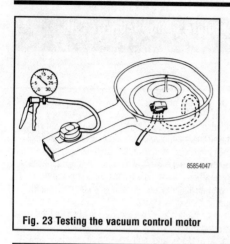

Fig. 23 Testing the vacuum control motor

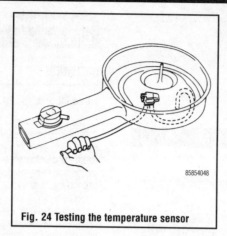

Fig. 24 Testing the temperature sensor

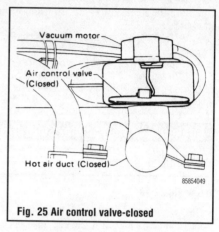

Fig. 25 Air control valve-closed

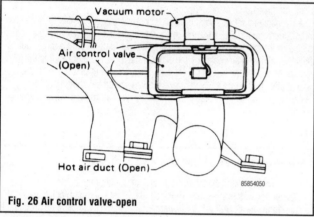

Fig. 26 Air control valve-open

temperature sensor is below 100°F (38°C), the sensor should allow vacuum to pass onto the air valve vacuum motor, thus blocking off the air cleaner snorkel to underhood (unheated) air.

When the temperature around the sensor is about 118°F (48°C), the air control valve should be completely open to underhood air.

When the engine is operating under a heavy load (wide open throttle acceleration), the air control valve fully opens to underhood air in order to obtain full power no matter what the temperature is around the temperature sensor.

If the air cleaner fails to operate correctly, check for loose or broken vacuum hoses. If the hoses are not the cause, replace the vacuum motor in the air cleaner.

Exhaust Gas Recirculation (EGR) System

OPERATION

Exhaust gas recirculation is used to reduce combustion temperatures in the engine, thereby reducing the oxides of nitrogen (NOx) emissions.

An EGR valve is mounted on the center of the intake manifold. The recycled exhaust gas is drawn into the bottom of the intake manifold riser portion through the exhaust manifold heat stove and EGR valve. A vacuum diaphragm is connected to a timed signal port at the carburetor flange.

As the throttle valve is opened, vacuum is applied to the EGR valve vacuum diaphragm. When the vacuum reaches about 2 in. Hg, the diaphragm moves against spring pressure and is in a fully up position at 8 in. Hg of vacuum. As the diaphragm moves up, it opens the exhaust gas metering valve which allows exhaust gas to be pulled into the engine intake manifold. The system does not operate when the engine is idling because the exhaust gas recirculation would cause a rough idle.

On 1974–75 models, an electrically operated solenoid is located in the vacuum line between the EGR valve and the carburetor. The operation of the solenoid is controlled by a temperature sensing switch mounted in the coolant outlet housing. When the temperature of the coolant is below normal operating temperature, the solenoid is electrically activated and blocks the vacuum line leading to the EGR valve, thus preventing exhaust gas recirculation. When the temperature of the engine coolant reaches operating temperature, the solenoid is deactivated and the vacuum is allowed to act upon the EGR valve diaphragm; exhaust gas recirculation takes place.

On 1975–86 models, a thermal vacuum valve inserted in the engine thermostat housing controls the application of vacuum to the EGR valve. When the engine coolant reaches a predetermined temperature, the thermal vacuum valve opens and allows vacuum to be routed to the EGR valve. Below the pre-determined temperature, the thermal vacuum valve closes and blocks vacuum to the EGR valve.

For 1978–80 and all 1986–86 models a Back Pressure Transducer (BPT) valve is installed between the EGR valve and the thermal vacuum valve. The BPT valve has a diaphragm raised or lowered by exhaust back pressure. The diaphragm opens or closes an air bleed, which is connected into the EGR vacuum line. High pressure results in higher levers of EGR, because the diaphragm is raised, closing off the air bleed, which allows more vacuum to reach and open the EGR valve. Thus, the amount of recirculated exhaust gas varies with exhaust pressure.

All 1981–84 models use a Venturi Vacuum Transducer valve (VVT) instead of the BPT valve. The VVT valve monitors exhaust pressure and carburetor vacuum in order to activate the diaphragm which controls the throttle vacuum applied to the EGR control valve. This system expands the operating range of the EGR flow rate as compared to the BPT unit.

All 1978–79 California models have a vacuum delay valve installed in the line between the thermal vacuum valve and the EGR valve. This valve delays rapid drops in vacuum in the EGR line, thus effecting a longer EGR time.

On all 1975 trucks (except Canadian models) and all 1976–77 49 States trucks, the EGR system is equipped with a warning system which monitors the distance the pick–up has traveled and activates a warning light when the EGR system must be checked and possibly serviced. The EGR warning light, mounted on top of the dash, comes on when a predetermined number of miles has been traveled and every time the starter is engaged as a check for a burned out bulb.

To reset the EGR counter, which is mounted on the right fender apron under the hood, remove the grommet installed in the side of the counter and insert the tip of a small screwdriver into the hole. Press down on the knob inside the hole. reinstall the grommet.

SERVICE

♦ See Figures 27, 28, 29 and 30

1974–75 Vehicles

1. Check the operation of the EGR system as follows:

    a. Visually inspect the entire EGR control system. Clean the mechanism so its free of oil and dirt. Replace any rubber hoses found to be cracked or broken.

    b. Make sure that the EGR solenoid valve is properly wired.

    c. Increase the engine speed from idling to 3000–3500 rpm. The plate of the EGR control valve diaphragm and the valve shaft should move upward as the engine speed is increased.

    d. Disconnect the EGR solenoid valve electrical leads and connect them directly to the vehicle's 12V electrical supply (the battery). Race the engine again with the EGR solenoid valve connected to a 12V power source . The EGR control valve should remain stationary.

EMISSION CONTROLS 4-9

e. With the engine running at idle, push up the EGR control valve diaphragm by pressing it up with your finger. When this is done, the engine idle should become rough and uneven.

2. Inspect the two components of the EGR system as necessary in the following manner:

a. Remove the EGR control valve from the intake manifold.

b. Apply 4.7–5.1 in. Hg of vacuum to the EGR control valve by sucking on a tube attached to the outlet on top of the valve. The valve should move to the full up position. The valve should remain open for more than 30 seconds after the application of vacuum is discontinued and the vacuum hose is blocked.

c. Inspect the EGR valve for any signs of warpage or damage.

d. Clean the EGR valve seat with a brush and compressed air to prevent clogging.

e. Connect the EGR solenoid valve to a 12V DC power source and notice if the valve clicks when intermittently electrified. If the valve clicks, it is considered to be working properly.

f. Check the EGR temperature sensing switch by removing it from the engine and placing it in a container of water together with a thermometer. Connect a self-powered test light to the 2 electrical leads of the switch.

g. Heat the container of water.

h. The switch should conduct current when the water temperature is below 77°F (25°C) and stop conducting current when the water reaches a temperature somewhere between 88–106°F (31–41°C). Replace the switch if it behaves otherwise.

1975–88 Vehicles

1. Remove the EGR valve and apply enough vacuum to the diaphragm to open the valve.

2. The valve should remain open for over 30 seconds after the vacuum is removed.

3. Check the valve for damage, such as warpage, cracks, and excessive wear around the valve and seat.

4. Clean the seat with a brush and compressed air and remove any deposits from around the valve and port (seat).

5. To check the operation of the thermal vacuum valve, remove the valve from the engine and apply vacuum to the ports of the valve. The valve should not allow vacuum to pass.

6. Place the Thermal Vacuum valve in a container of water with a thermometer and heat the water. When the temperature of the water reaches 134–145°F (57–63°C), carefully remove the valve and apply vacuum to the ports; the valve should allow vacuum to pass through it.

7. To test the BPT valve, disconnect the two vacuum hoses from the valve. Plug one of the ports. While applying pressure to the bottom of the valve, apply vacuum to the unplugged port and check for leakage. If any exists, replace the valve.

8. To test the check valve installed in some models, remove the valve and blow into the side which connects to the EGR valve. Air should flow. When air is applied to the other side, air flow resistance should be greater. If not, replace the valve.

9. To check the VVT valve, disconnect the top and bottom center hoses and apply vacuum to the top hose. Check for leaks. If a leak is present, replace the valve.

REMOVAL & INSTALLATION

▶ See Figures 31 thru 36

1. Remove the nuts which attach the EGR tube and/or the Back Pressure (BP) tube to the EGR valve (if so equipped).

2. Unscrew the mounting bolts and remove the heat shield plate from the EGR control valve (if so equipped).

3. Tag and disconnect the EGR vacuum hose(s).

4. Unscrew the mounting bolts and remove the EGR control valve.

To install:

5. Install the EGR valve assembly with mounting bolts to intake manifold location.

6. Connect all vacuum hoses and install the heat shield if so equipped.

7. Connect EGR tube or Back Pressure (BP) tube to the EGR valve if so equipped.

➡ Always be sure that the new valve is identical to the old one.

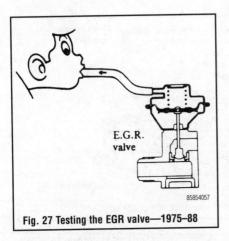
Fig. 27 Testing the EGR valve—1975–88

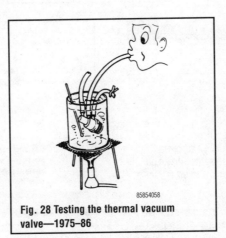
Fig. 28 Testing the thermal vacuum valve—1975–86

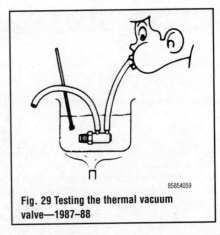
Fig. 29 Testing the thermal vacuum valve—1987–88

Fig. 30 Cleaning the EGR valve

Fig. 31 EGR valve—1980

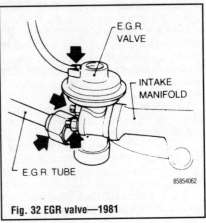
Fig. 32 EGR valve—1981

4-10 EMISSION CONTROLS

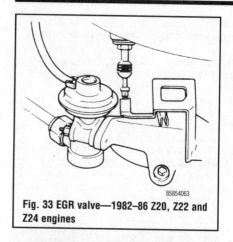

Fig. 33 EGR valve—1982–86 Z20, Z22 and Z24 engines

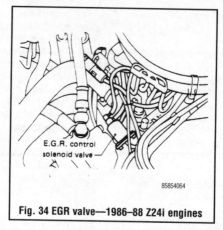

Fig. 34 EGR valve—1986–88 Z24i engines

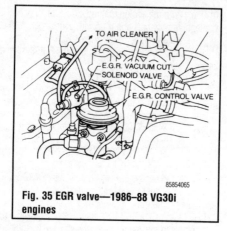

Fig. 35 EGR valve—1986–88 VG30i engines

Fig. 36 Removing the EGR valve

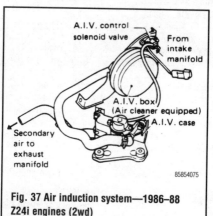

Fig. 37 Air induction system—1986–88 Z24i engines (2wd)

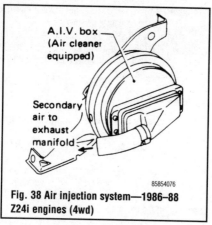

Fig. 38 Air injection system—1986–88 Z24i engines (4wd)

Air Injection System (AIS)

OPERATION

♦ See Figures 37, 38 and 39

In gasoline engines, it is difficult to burn the air/fuel mixture completely through normal combustion in the combustion chambers. Under certain operating conditions, unburned fuel is exhausted into the atmosphere.

The air injection reactor system is designed so that ambient air, pressurized by an air pump, is injected through the injection nozzles into the exhaust ports near each exhaust valve. The exhaust gases are at high temperatures and ignite when brought into contact with the oxygen of the ambient air. Thus, the unburned fuel is burned in the exhaust ports and manifold.

A check valve is installed in the air pump discharge line to prevent the airflow from reversing due to a broken drive belt, relief valve spring failure, or backfire in the exhaust manifold. Reversed airflow could damage the air pump.

The air pump relief valve bleeds off excess air from the pump at high speeds. The valve is mounted on the carburetor air cleaner.

Trucks with a catalytic converter have protection devices to prevent converter overheating due to large quantities of injected air. All 1976–77 models use an emergency air relief valve and an air control valve. The emergency valve has a diaphragm operated by engine vacuum. When intake manifold vacuum reaches a predetermined level, the valve opens, diverting air from the pump into the atmosphere. When vacuum drops, the valve closes allowing normal AIS operation.

The air control valve is also controlled by engine vacuum. High vacuum and high pressure from the air pump open the control valve, venting air from the pump into the air cleaner.

All 1978–79 models have a combined air control valve instead of the relief valve, emergency valve, and air control valve. The combined air control valve regulates the amount of injected air according to intake manifold and air pump discharge pressure, to prevent the converter from overheating.

An anti-backfire valve is installed in an air delivery hose. The purpose of the valve is to prevent backfiring in the exhaust manifold during deceleration. When

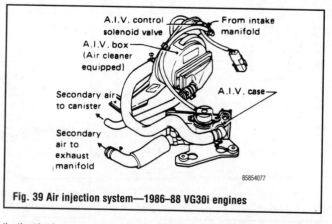

Fig. 39 Air injection system—1986–88 VG30i engines

the throttle closes suddenly, an overly rich air/fuel mixture exists in the intake manifold due to the lack of air getting past the throttle valves. This rich mixture will not completely burn in the combustion chamber. If the unburned gases were to come in contact with the oxygen pumped into the exhaust ports by the air pump, they would ignite and causing a backfire and damage.

The anti-backfire valve is connected to the intake manifold by a vacuum line and when the vacuum rises, the valve opens a port in the intake manifold, allowing extra filtered air from the air chambers, leaning out the overly rich mixture.

All 1979 cab and chassis models have a transistorized programmed control unit, a vacuum switching valve, and an air control switch which govern air flow through the AIS. The air control switch, located between the intake manifold and the control unit, turns off when manifold vacuum is high, and turns on when vacuum is low. This provides a signal to the control unit, which determines when to turn the vacuum switching valve on or off accordingly. The vacuum switching valve controls the upper chamber of the combined air control (CAC) valve diaphragm, opening or closing the CAC valve according to signals received from the control unit. Thus, the amount of air injected into the AIS is monitored and adjusted as conditions warrant.

EMISSION CONTROLS 4-11

SERVICE

Air Pump

If the air pump makes an abnormal noise and cannot be corrected without removing the pump from the vehicle, check the following:

1. Turn the pulley ¾ of a turn in the clockwise direction and ¼ of a turn in the counterclockwise direction. If the pulley is binding and if rotation is not smooth, a defective bearing is indicated.
2. Check the inner wall of the pump body, vanes, and rotor for wear. If the rotor has abnormal wear, replace the air pump.
3. Check the needle roller bearing for wear and damage. If the bearings are defective, the air pump should be replaced.
4. Check and replace the rear side seal if abnormal wear or damage is noticed.
5. Check and replace the carbon shoes holding the vanes if they are found to be worn or damaged.
6. Deposits of carbon particles on the inner wall of the pump body and vanes are normal, but should be removed with compressed air before reassembling the air pump.

Check Valve

Remove the check valve from the air pump discharge line. Test it for leakage by blowing air into the valve from the air pump side and from the air manifold side. Air should only pass through the valve from the air pump side if the valve is functioning normally. A small amount of air leakage from the manifold side can be overlooked. Replace the check valve if it is found to be defective.

Anti-Backfire Valve

To check the valve, disconnect the hose from the air cleaner and place a finger on the end. Run the engine up to about 3000 rpm, then quickly release the throttle. If the valve is performing correctly, suction should be felt at the end of the hose. If no suction is felt, replace the anti-backfire valve.

Air Pump Relief Valve

1. Disconnect the hoses leading to the check valve (on the air injection manifold) and the air control valve from the air hose connector. Plug the connector.
2. Start the engine and increase the engine speed to about 3000 rpm. Place you finger on the outlet of the relief valve (inside the air cleaner housing) and check for air discharge. If you do not feel any air coming out, the relief valve is faulty, and must be replaced.

Air Injection Nozzles

Check around the air manifold for air leakage with the engine running at 2000 rpm. If air is leaking form the eye joint bolt, retighten or replace the gasket. Check the air nozzles for restrictions by blowing air into the nozzles.

Hoses

Check and replace hoses if they are found to be weakened or cracked. Check all hose connections and clips. Be sure that the hoses are not in contact with other parts of the engine.

Emergency Air Relief Valve

1. Warm up the engine.
2. Check all hoses for leaks, kinks, improper connections, etc.
3. Run the engine up to 2000 rpm under no load. No air should be discharged from the valve.
4. Disconnect the vacuum hose from the valve. This is the hose which runs to the intake manifold. Run the engine up to 2000 rpm. Air should be discharged from the valve. If not, replace it.

Combined Air Control Valve

1. Check all hoses for leaks, kinks, and improper connections.
2. Thoroughly warm up the engine.
3. With the engine idling, check for air discharge from the relief opening in the air cleaner case.
4. Disconnect and plug the vacuum hose from the valve. Air should be discharged from the valve with the engine idling. If the disconnected vacuum hose is not plugged. The engine will stumble.
5. Connect a hand operated vacuum pump to the vacuum fitting on the valve and apply 7.8–9.8 in. Hg of vacuum. Run the engine speed up to 3000 rpm. No air should be discharged from the valve.
6. Disconnect and plug the air hose at the check valve, with the conditions as in the preceding step. This should cause the valve to discharge air. If not, or if any of the conditions in this procedure are not met, replace the valve.

Air Induction System

OPERATION

♦ See Figures 40 thru 49

The air induction system is designed to send secondary air to the exhaust manifold, utilizing a vacuum caused by exhaust pulsation in the exhaust manifold.

The pressure in the exhaust manifold usually pulsates in response to the opening and closing of the exhaust valve. It decreases below atmospheric pressure periodically.

If a secondary air intake pipe is opened to the atmosphere under vacuum conditions, secondary air can be drawn into the exhaust manifold in proportion to the vacuum.

Therefore, the air induction system reduces CO and HC emissions in exhaust gases. The system consists of two air induction valves, a filter, hoses and E.A.I. tube(s).

AIR INDUCTION VALVE CASE

The air induction valve case consists of 2 reed valves, a rubber seal and a filter. The valve case is attached to the air cleaner. There are 2 types of air induction valve cases. Type A is equipped with 2 hose connectors and is installed on California models, while Type B is equipped with 1 connector and is installed on non-California models.

AIR INDUCTION VALVE

Two reed valve type check valves are installed in the air cleaner. When the exhaust pressure is below atmospheric pressure (negative pressure), secondary air is sent to the exhaust manifold.

When the exhaust pressure is above atmospheric pressure, the reed valves prevent secondary air from being sent back to the air cleaner.

AIR INDUCTION VALVE FILTER

The air induction valve filter is installed at the dust side of the air cleaner. It purifies secondary air to be sent to the exhaust manifold.

AIR INDUCTION PIPE

The secondary air fed from the air induction valve goes through the Exhaust Air Injection (EAI) pipe to the exhaust manifold.

At this point, the mixture in the intake manifold becomes too rich to ignite and burn in the combustion chamber and burns easily in the exhaust system with injected air in the exhaust manifold.

The Anti-backfire (AB) valve provides air to the intake manifold to make the air/fuel mixture leaner and prevents backfire.

The correct function of this valve reduces hydrocarbon emission during deceleration.

SERVICE

Air Induction Valve and Filter

Remove the valve and filter on the air cleaner. The air induction valve and valve filter can then be taken out easily. Installation is in the reverse sequence of removal.

AB Valve

1. Remove air cleaner.
2. Remove air hoses and vacuum tube. Then the AB valve can be taken out.

4-12 EMISSION CONTROLS

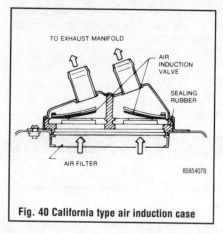
Fig. 40 California type air induction case

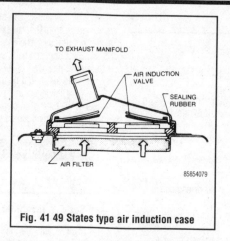
Fig. 41 49 States type air induction case

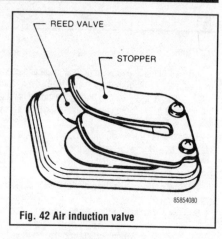
Fig. 42 Air induction valve

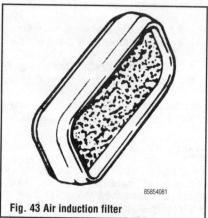
Fig. 43 Air induction filter

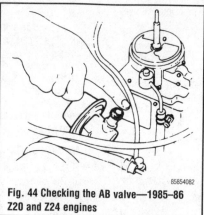
Fig. 44 Checking the AB valve—1985–86 Z20 and Z24 engines

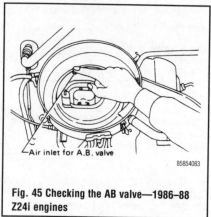
Fig. 45 Checking the AB valve—1986–88 Z24i engines

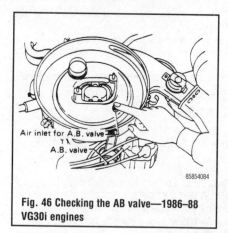
Fig. 46 Checking the AB valve—1986–88 VG30i engines

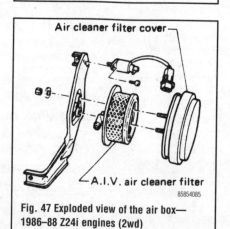
Fig. 47 Exploded view of the air box—1986–88 Z24i engines (2wd)

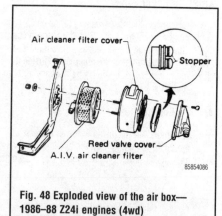
Fig. 48 Exploded view of the air box—1986–88 Z24i engines (4wd)

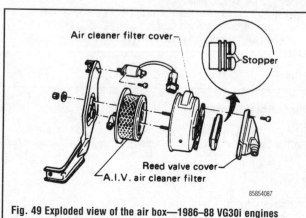
Fig. 49 Exploded view of the air box—1986–88 VG30i engines

Fuel Shut-Off System

OPERATION

This system is designed to reduce HC emissions and also to improve fuel economy during deceleration.

The system is operated by an anti-dieseling solenoid valve in the carburetor which is controlled by a vacuum switch. When the intake manifold vacuum increases to an extremely high level (which it does during deceleration), the fuel flow of the slow system is shut off by the anti-dieseling solenoid valve. When the intake manifold vacuum drops to a low level again, the fuel flow to the slow system is resupplied.

The fuel shut-off system is further controlled by the clutch switch and gear position switches such as the neutral switch (manual transmission) and the inhibitor switch (automatic transmission) to ensure that fuel cannot be shut off even if the manifold vacuum is high enough to trigger the normal fuel shut-off operation.

EMISSION CONTROLS 4-13

Electric Choke

OPERATION

The purpose of the electric choke is to shorten the time that the choke is in operation after the engine is started, thus shortening the time of high HC output.

An electric heater warms the bimetal spring which controls the opening and closing of the choke valve. The heater begins to warm-up heat as the engine starts.

Detonation Control System

OPERATION

♦ See Figures 50, 51 and 52

This system is used on 1984–86 models and its purpose is to sense engine detonation or knock. When detonation occurs in the cylinders, the sensor will detect the vibrations and send a signal to the detonation control unit which will in turn make minor adjustments to the ignition timing to keep engine performance at its optimum.

SERVICE

1. Connect a timing light as per the manufacturer's instructions.
2. With engine speed at approximately 2200 rpm, disconnect the electrical lead at the detonation sensor and check that the timing drops by approximately 10 degrees.
3. If the timing does not drop, check the distributor or the detonation control unit.
4. Locate the control unit behind the right side kick panel and connect a volt meter between ground and terminal **4**—make sure the engine is at 2200 rpm. Voltage should be 0.4–0.7V, if not, check the distributor and harness.
5. With the engine still idling at 2200 rpm and one voltmeter lead still grounded, insert the other lead into terminal **3**. Voltage should be 3.7–3.8V, if not, replace the control unit.
6. If both the distributor and control unit test properly, replace the sensor.

High Altitude Compensator System

OPERATION

When the truck is operated at particularly high altitudes, where the air is thinner, the mixture ratio and intake manifold boost vary greatly; exhaust emissions also increase considerably. In order to decrease these emissions, an altitude compensation system is employed to correct the air/fuel ratio to that of sea level.

When the atmospheric pressure decreases (as altitude increases) to a certain value, an altitude switch is turned on, applying voltage to an altitude solenoid valve. When the solenoid valve turns on, additional air is let into the carburetor, allowing a leaner air/fuel ratio.

Mixture Heating System

OPERATION

♦ See Figure 53

This system is found in 1983 California trucks with 4wd and certain Canada trucks. It is employed to warm the air/fuel mixture after initial start-up. Operation occurs by means of a water temperature switch and a relay, that controls a heater/insulator plate positioned between the manifold and carburetor. It aids engine start-up ability and improves initial emissions discharge.

Catalytic Converter

OPERATION

♦ See Figure 54

The catalytic converter is a muffler like container built into the exhaust system to aid in the reduction of exhaust emissions. The catalyst element consists of individual pellets or a honeycomb monolithic substrate coated with a noble metal such as platinum, palladium, rhodium or a combination. When the exhaust gases come into contact with the catalyst, a chemical reaction occurs which will reduce the pollutants into harmless substances like water and carbon dioxide.

There are essentially two types of catalytic converters. An oxidizing type is used on many models. It requires the addition of oxygen to spur the catalyst into reducing the engine's HC and CO emissions into H_2O and CO_2. Because of this need for oxygen, the Air Injection System is used with all these models.

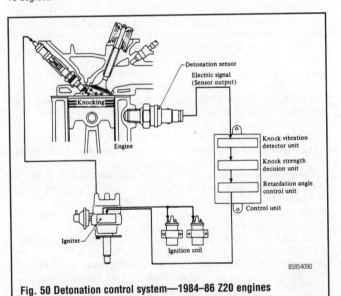

Fig. 50 Detonation control system—1984–86 Z20 engines

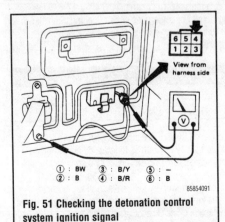

Fig. 51 Checking the detonation control system ignition signal

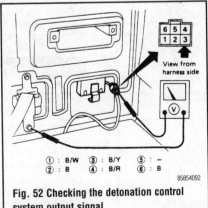

Fig. 52 Checking the detonation control system output signal

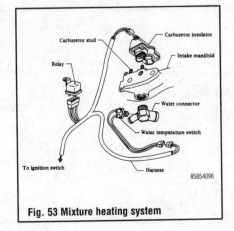

Fig. 53 Mixture heating system

4-14 EMISSION CONTROLS

The oxidizing catalytic converter, while effectively reducing HC and CO emissions, does little, if anything in the way of reducing NOx emissions. Thus, the three way catalytic converter was developed to address this problem.

The three way converter, unlike the oxidizing type, is capable of reducing HC, CO and NOx emissions; all at the same time. In theory, it seems impossible to reduce all three pollutants in one system since the reduction of HC and CO requires the addition of oxygen, while the reduction of NOx calls for the removal of oxygen. In actuality, the three way system really can reduce all three pollutants, but only if the amount of oxygen in the exhaust system is precisely controlled. Due to this precise oxygen control requirement, the three way converter system is used only in trucks equipped with an oxygen sensor system.

The 1976–78 models utilize a floor temperature warning system, consisting of a temperature sensor installed onto the floor of the truck above the converter, a relay, located under the passenger seat, and a light, installed on the instrument panel. The lamp illuminates when floor temperatures become abnormally high, due to converter or engine malfunction. The light also comes on when the ignition switch is turned to **START** to check its operation. The 1979 and later models do not have the warning system.

Trucks with the catalytic converter also have a combined air control valve in 1978–1979, which control the amount of secondary air injected into the exhaust manifold. It is regulated by engine vacuum and air pump pressure, and works to keep the converter temperatures within proper limits. The combined air control valve replaces the air pump relief valve, found in the system of trucks not equipped with a catalytic converter. The 1976–77 models have an emergency air relief valve for catalyst protection. See the AIS section for a description.

All models with the three way converter have an oxygen sensor warning light on the dashboard, which illuminates at the first 30,000 mile interval, signaling the need for oxygen sensor replacement. The oxygen sensor is part of the Mixture Ratio Feedback System. The Feedback System uses the three way converter as one of its major components.

No regular maintenance is required for the catalytic converter system, except for periodic replacement of the Air Induction System filter (if so equipped). The Air Induction System is described earlier in this section. Filter replacement procedures are in Section 1. The Air Induction System is used to supply the catalytic converter with fresh air. Oxygen present in the air is used in the oxidation process.

PRECAUTIONS

1. Use only unleaded fuel.
2. Avoid prolonged idling. The engine should not run longer than 20 min. at curb idle and no longer than 10 min. at fast idle.
3. Do not disconnect any of the spark plug leads while the engine is running.
4. Make engine compression checks as quickly as possible.

TESTING

Testing the catalytic converter operation in the field is a difficult problem. The most reliable test is a 12 hour and 40 min. soak test (CVS) which must be done in a laboratory.

In most cases an infrared HC/CO tester is not sensitive enough to measure the higher tailpipe emissions from a failing converter. Thus, a bad converter may allow enough emissions to escape so that the truck is no longer in compliance with Federal or state stands, but will still not cause the needle on a tester to move off zero.

The chemical reactions which occur inside a catalytic converter generate a great deal of heat. Most converter problems can be traced to fuel or ignition system problems which cause unusually high emissions. As a result of the increased intensity of the chemical reactions, the converter literally burns itself up.

As long as you avoid severe overheating and the use of leaded fuels it is reasonably safe to assume that the converter is working properly. If you are in doubt, take the truck to a diagnostic center that has a tester.

➡ **If the catalytic converter becomes blocked the engine will not run. The converter has 5 year or 50,000 mile warranty; contact your local Datsun/Nissan dealer for more information.**

Mixture Ratio Feedback System

OPERATION

The need for better fuel economy coupled to increasingly strict emission control regulations dictates a more exact control of the engine air/fuel mixture. Datsun/Nissan has developed a mixture ratio feedback system in response to these needs.

The principle of the system is to control the air/fuel mixture exactly, so that more complete combustion can occur in the engine. In doing so a more thorough oxidation and reduction of the exhaust gases can occur in the catalytic converter. The object is to maintain a stoichiometric air/fuel mixture, which is chemically correct for complete combustion. The stoichiometric ratio is 14.7:1 (air to fuel). At that point, the converter's efficiency is greatest in oxidizing and reducing HC, CO, and NOx into CO_2, H_2O, O_2, and N_2.

Components used in the system include an oxygen sensor (installed in the exhaust manifold upstream of the converter), a three way oxidation reduction catalytic converter, an electronic control unit, and the fuel injection system itself.

The oxygen sensor reads the oxygen content of the exhaust gases. It generates an electric signal which is sent to the control unit. The control unit then decides how to adjust the mixture to keep it at the correct air/fuel ratio. For example, if the mixture is too lean, the control unit increases the fuel metering to the injectors. The monitoring process is a continual one, so that fine mixture adjustments are going on at all times.

The system has two modes of operation: open loop and closed loop. Open loop operation takes place when the engine is still cold. In this mode, the control unit ignores signals from the oxygen sensor and provides a fixed signal to the fuel injection unit. Closed loop operation takes place when the engine and catalytic converter have warmed to normal operating temperature. In closed loop operation, the control unit uses the oxygen sensor signals to adjust the mixture. The burned mixture's oxygen content is read by the oxygen sensor, which continues to signal the control unit, and so on. Thus, the closed loop mode is an interdependent system of information feedback.

Mixture is, of course, not readily adjustable in this system. All system adjustments require the use of a CO meter. Thus, they should be entrusted to a qualified dealer with access to the equipment and special training in the system's repair. The only regularly scheduled maintenance is replacement of the oxygen sensor at 30,000 mile intervals. This procedure is covered in the following section.

It should be noted that proper operation of the system is entirely dependent on the oxygen sensor. Thus, if the sensor is not replaced at the correct interval, or if the sensor fails during normal operation, the engine fuel mixture will be incorrect, resulting in poor fuel economy, starting problems, or stumbling and stalling of the engine when warm.

Oxygen Sensor

OPERATION

The three-way catalytic converter, which is capable of reducing HC, CO and NOx into CO_2, H_2O, O_2 and N_2 can only function as long as the air/fuel mixture is kept within a critically precise range. The oxygen sensor system is what keeps the oxygen range in control.

Basically, the oxygen sensor system works like this: As soon as the engine warms up, the computer begins to work. The oxygen sensor, located in the exhaust manifold, senses the oxygen content of the exhaust gases which varies according to

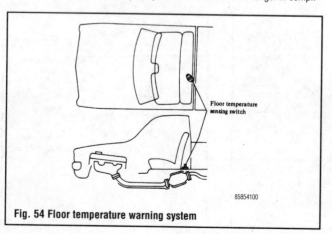

Fig. 54 Floor temperature warning system

EMISSION CONTROLS 4-15

the air/fuel mixture. The O₂ sensor produces a small voltage that varies depending on the amount of oxygen in the exhaust at the time. This voltage is picked up by the ECU. The computer works together with the fuel distributor and together they will vary the amount of fuel which is delivered to the engine at any given time.

If the amount of oxygen in the exhaust system is low, which indicates a rich mixture, the sensor voltage will be high. The higher the voltage signal sent to the computer, the more it will reduce the amount of fuel supplied to the engine. The amount of fuel is reduced until the amount of oxygen in the exhaust system increases, indicating a lean mixture. When the mixture is lean, the sensor will send a low voltage signal to the computer. The computer will then increase the quantity of fuel until the sensor voltage increases again. Then the cycle will start all over.

REMOVAL & INSTALLATION

The oxygen sensor is installed in the exhaust manifold and is removed in the same manner as a spark plug. Exercise care when handling the sensor do not drop or handle the sensor roughly. Care should be used not to get compound on the sensor itself.

1. Disconnect the negative battery cable.
2. Unplug the wiring connector leading from the O₂ sensor.

➡ **Be careful not to bend the waterproof hose as the oxygen sensor will not function properly if the air passage is blocked.**

3. Unscrew the sensor from the exhaust manifold.

To install:

4. Coat the threads of the replacement sensor with a nickel base anti-seize compound. Do not use other types of compounds, since they may electrically insulate the sensor. Do not get compound on sensor housing. Install the sensor into the manifold. Installation torque for the sensor is about 18–25 ft. lbs. (24–34 Nm). Connect the electrical lead. Be careful handling the electrical lead. It is easily damaged.
5. Reconnect the battery cable.

ELECTRONIC ENGINE CONTROLS

Self-Diagnostic System

The self-diagnostic system is useful to diagnose malfunctions in major sensors and actuators of the ECCS system. The ECU constantly monitors the function of these sensor and actuator circuits, regardless of ignition key position. If a malfunction occurs, information is stored in the ECU and can be retrieved from the memory by turning on the diagnostic mode selector, located on the side of the ECU. When activated the malfunction is indicated by flashing a red and green LED light emitting diode, also located on the ECU. Since all the self-diagnostic results are stored in the ECU memory, even intermittent malfunctions can be diagnosed.

A malfunctioning parts group is indicated by the number of both the red and green LEDs flashing. First, the red flashes, then the green flashes follow. The red LED refers to the number of the tens digit while the green one refers to the number of the units digit. For example, when the red LED flashes three times and then the green on flashes twice, this means the number 32. In this way, all problems are classified by the code numbers.

Perform self-diagnosis with engine sufficiently warmed up. After a malfunctioning component has been corrected, be sure to erase memory. To erase code memory:

1. Turn ignition switch **ON**.
2. Turn diagnosis mode selector ON.
3. Wait for 2 seconds.
4. Turn diagnosis mode selector OFF.
5. Wait 2 seconds. Memory erasure has been completed.

➡ **The stored memory would be lost if battery terminal is disconnected**

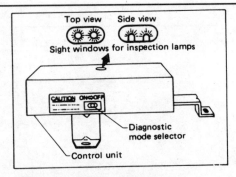

DISPLAY CODE TABLE

Code No.	Self-diagnostic items
11	Crank angle sensor
12	Air flow meter
13	Water temperature sensor
21	Ignition signal
23	Idle switch
24	Neutral & Clutch/Inhibitor switch
32	Start signal
42	Throttle sensor
43	Injector
44	All self-diagnostic items: O.K.

Fig. 55 ECU code table—Z24i engine through 1986

4-16 EMISSION CONTROLS

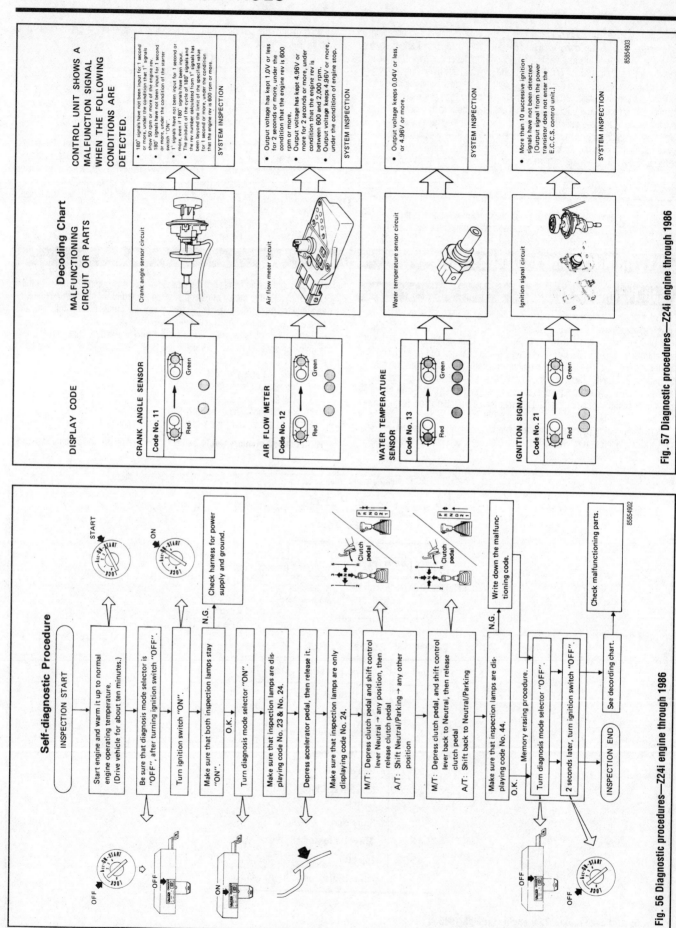

Fig. 57 Diagnostic procedures—Z24i engine through 1986

Fig. 56 Diagnostic procedures—Z24i engine through 1986

EMISSION CONTROLS 4-17

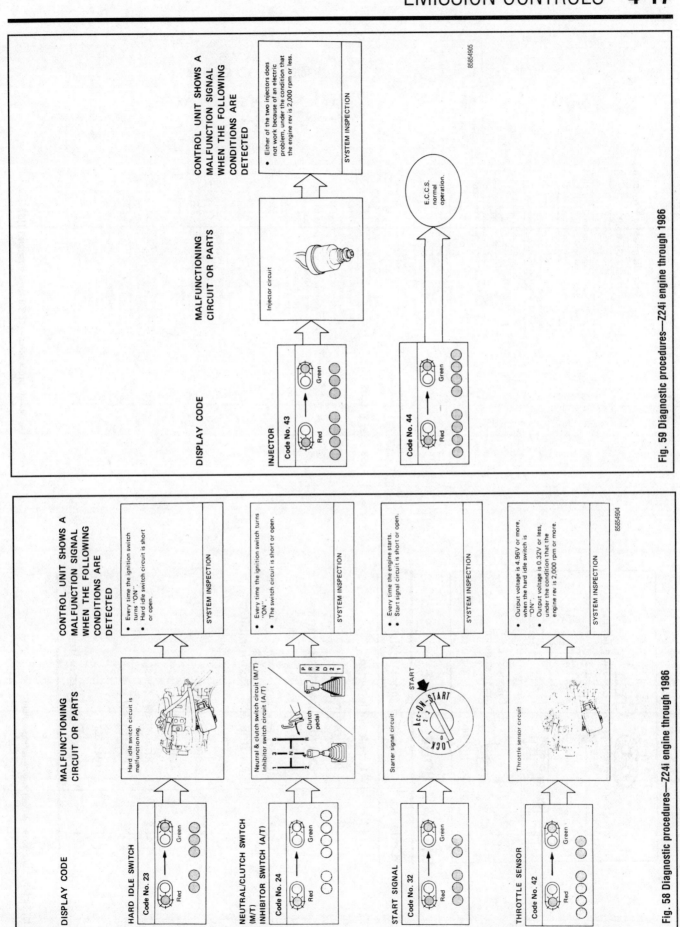

Fig. 58 Diagnostic procedures—Z24i engine through 1986

Fig. 59 Diagnostic procedures—Z24i engine through 1986

4-18 EMISSION CONTROLS

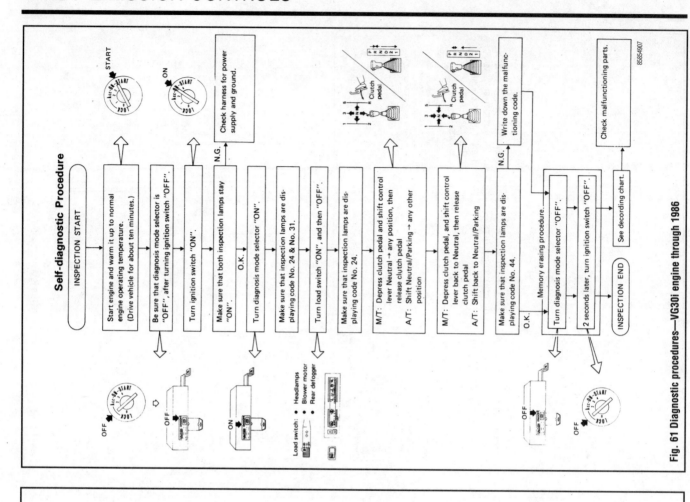

Fig. 61 Diagnostic procedures—VG30i engine through 1986

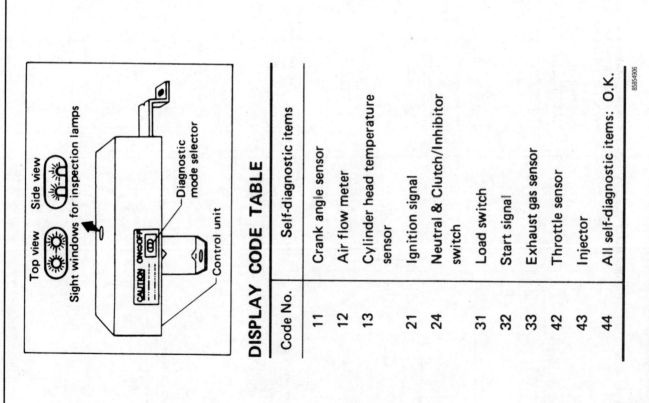

Fig. 60 ECU code table—VG30i engine through 1986

DISPLAY CODE TABLE

Code No.	Self-diagnostic items
11	Crank angle sensor
12	Air flow meter
13	Cylinder head temperature sensor
21	Ignition signal
24	Neutral & Clutch/Inhibitor switch
31	Load switch
32	Start signal
33	Exhaust gas sensor
42	Throttle sensor
43	Injector
44	All self-diagnostic items: O.K.

EMISSION CONTROLS 4-19

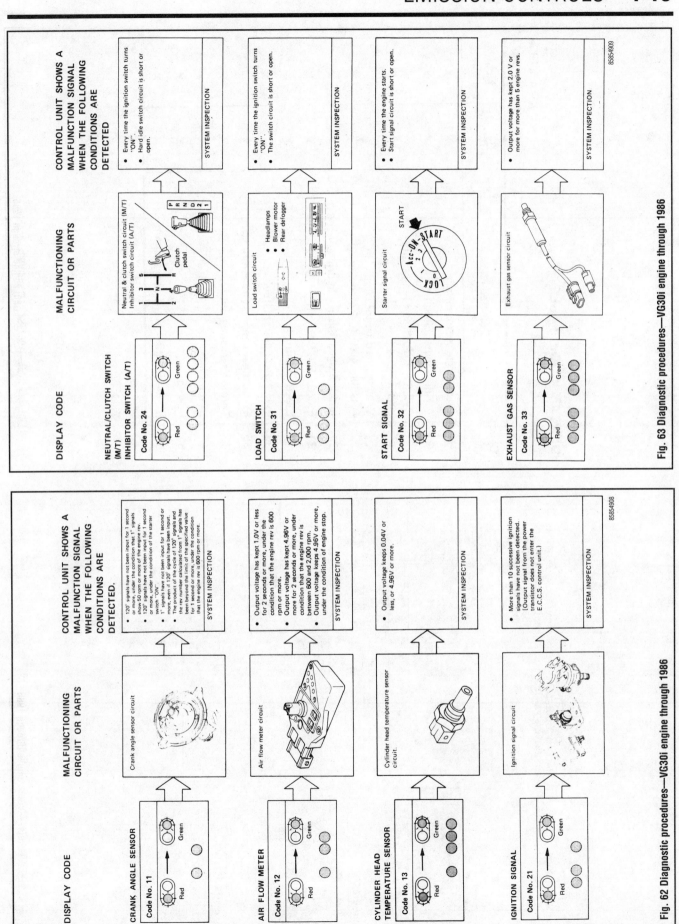

Fig. 63 Diagnostic procedures—VG30i engine through 1986

Fig. 62 Diagnostic procedures—VG30i engine through 1986

4-20 EMISSION CONTROLS

DISPLAY CODE TABLE

X: Available
–: Not available

Code No.	Detected items	California	Non-California
11	Crank angle sensor circuit	X	X
12	Air flow meter circuit	X	X
13	Cylinder head/Water temperature sensor circuit	X	X
14	Vehicle speed sensor circuit (VG30i: 4WD A/T model only)	X	X
21	Ignition signal missing in primary coil	X	X
31	E.C.U. (E.C.C.S. control unit)	X	X
32	E.G.R. circuit	X	–
33	Exhaust gas sensor circuit	X	X
35	Exhaust gas temperature sensor circuit	X	–
43	Throttle sensor circuit	X	X
45	Injector leak	X	–
51	Injector	X	X
55	No malfunction in the above circuit	X	X

Fig. 65 ECU code table—1987–88 Z24i and VG30i engines

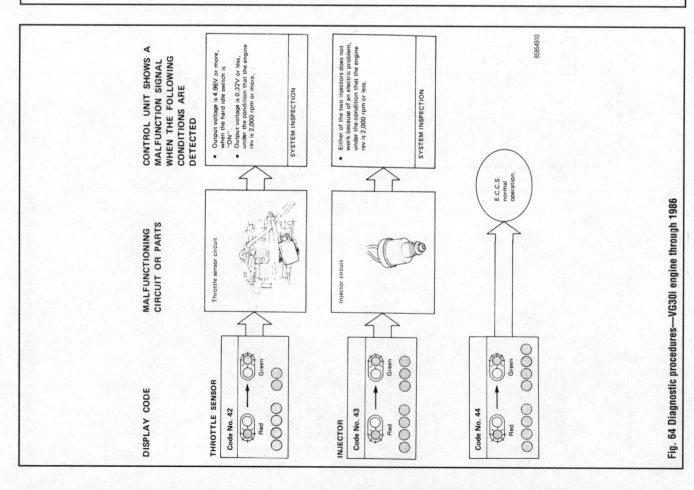

Fig. 64 Diagnostic procedures—VG30i engine through 1986

EMISSION CONTROLS 4-21

VACUUM DIAGRAMS AND SYSTEM COMPONENTS

Following are vacuum diagrams for most of the engine and emissions package combinations covered by this manual. Because vacuum circuits will vary based on various engine and vehicle options, always refer first to the vehicle emission control information label, if present. Should the label be missing, or should vehicle be equipped with a different engine from the vehicle's original equipment, refer to the diagrams below for the same or similar configuration.

If you wish to obtain a replacement emissions label, most manufacturers make the labels available for purchase. The labels can usually be ordered from a local dealer.

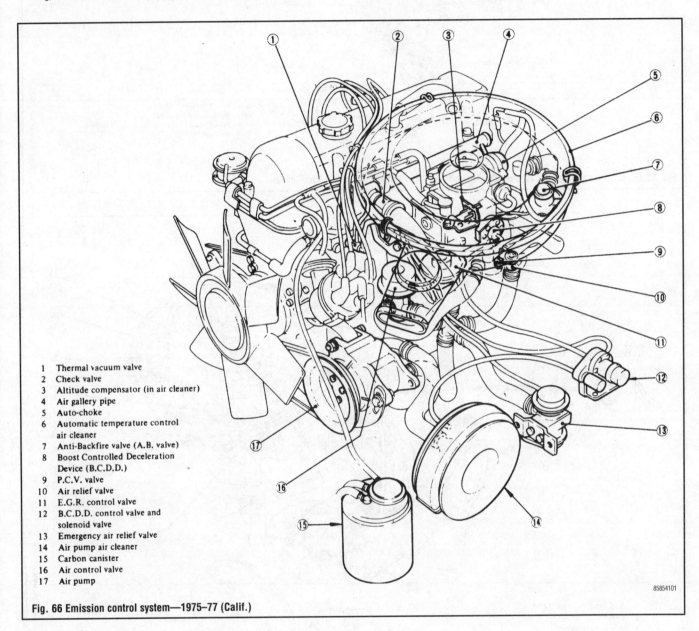

1. Thermal vacuum valve
2. Check valve
3. Altitude compensator (in air cleaner)
4. Air gallery pipe
5. Auto-choke
6. Automatic temperature control air cleaner
7. Anti-Backfire valve (A.B. valve)
8. Boost Controlled Deceleration Device (B.C.D.D.)
9. P.C.V. valve
10. Air relief valve
11. E.G.R. control valve
12. B.C.D.D. control valve and solenoid valve
13. Emergency air relief valve
14. Air pump air cleaner
15. Carbon canister
16. Air control valve
17. Air pump

Fig. 66 Emission control system—1975-77 (Calif.)

4-22 EMISSION CONTROLS

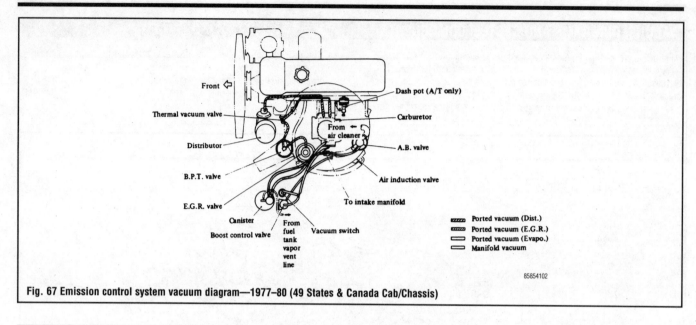

Fig. 67 Emission control system vacuum diagram—1977-80 (49 States & Canada Cab/Chassis)

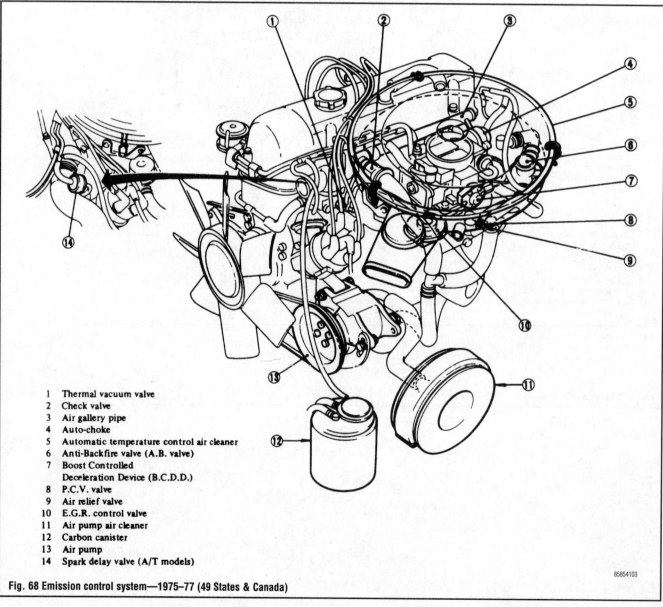

1. Thermal vacuum valve
2. Check valve
3. Air gallery pipe
4. Auto-choke
5. Automatic temperature control air cleaner
6. Anti-Backfire valve (A.B. valve)
7. Boost Controlled Deceleration Device (B.C.D.D.)
8. P.C.V. valve
9. Air relief valve
10. E.G.R. control valve
11. Air pump air cleaner
12. Carbon canister
13. Air pump
14. Spark delay valve (A/T models)

Fig. 68 Emission control system—1975-77 (49 States & Canada)

EMISSION CONTROLS 4-23

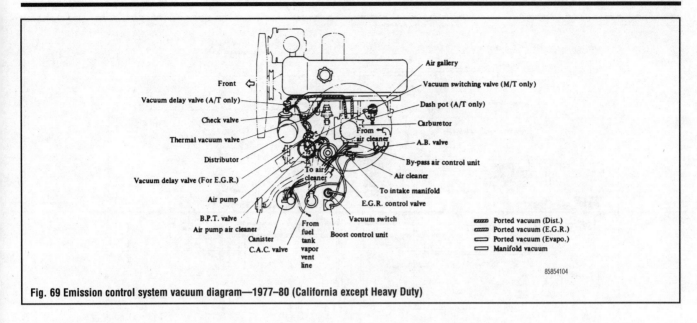

Fig. 69 Emission control system vacuum diagram—1977–80 (California except Heavy Duty)

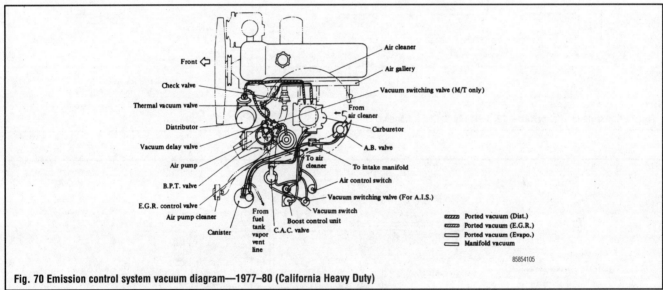

Fig. 70 Emission control system vacuum diagram—1977–80 (California Heavy Duty)

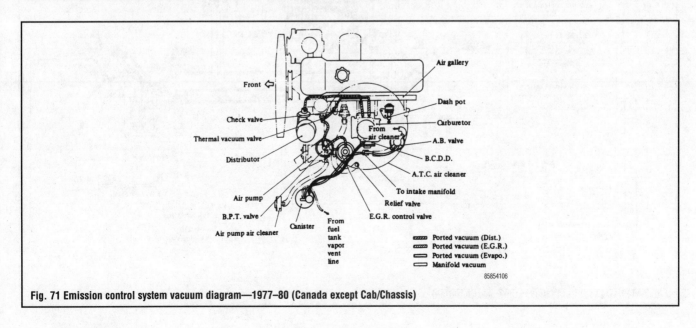

Fig. 71 Emission control system vacuum diagram—1977–80 (Canada except Cab/Chassis)

4-24 EMISSION CONTROLS

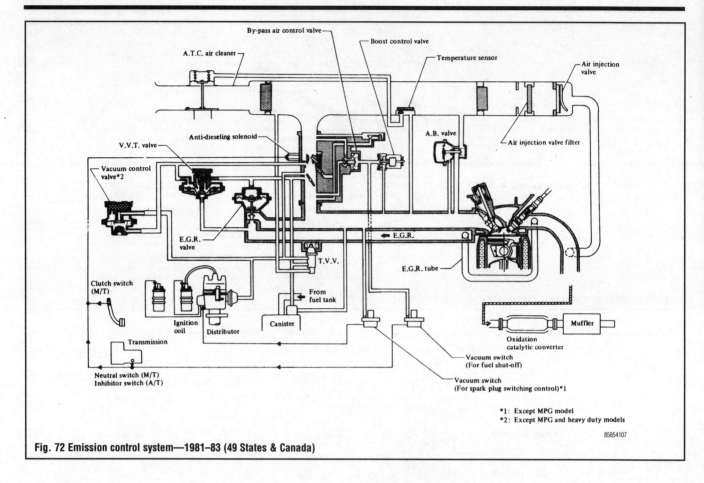

Fig. 72 Emission control system—1981–83 (49 States & Canada)

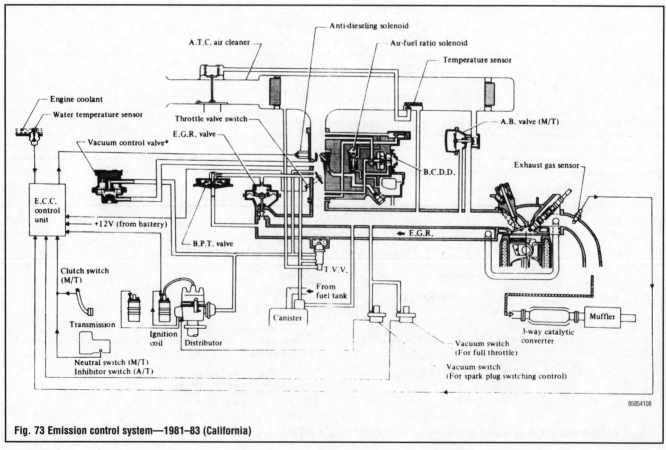

Fig. 73 Emission control system—1981–83 (California)

EMISSION CONTROLS 4-25

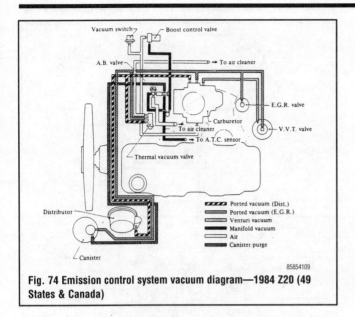

Fig. 74 Emission control system vacuum diagram—1984 Z20 (49 States & Canada)

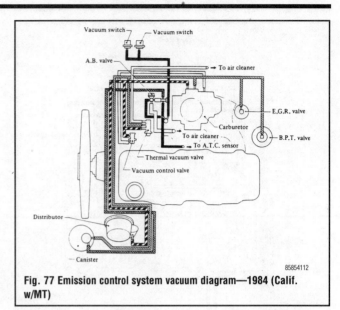

Fig. 77 Emission control system vacuum diagram—1984 (Calif. w/MT)

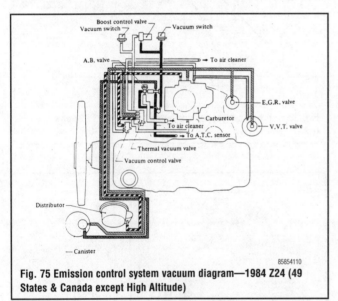

Fig. 75 Emission control system vacuum diagram—1984 Z24 (49 States & Canada except High Altitude)

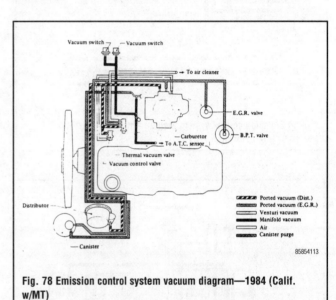

Fig. 78 Emission control system vacuum diagram—1984 (Calif. w/MT)

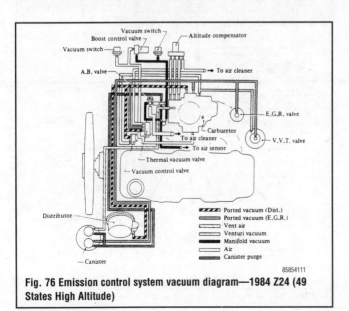

Fig. 76 Emission control system vacuum diagram—1984 Z24 (49 States High Altitude)

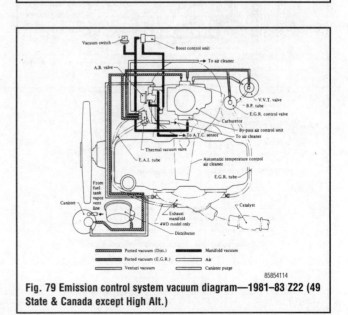

Fig. 79 Emission control system vacuum diagram—1981-83 Z22 (49 State & Canada except High Alt.)

4-26 EMISSION CONTROLS

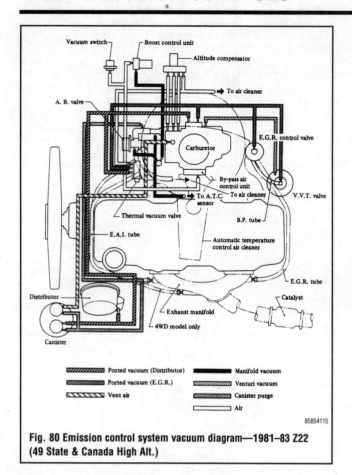

Fig. 80 Emission control system vacuum diagram—1981-83 Z22 (49 State & Canada High Alt.)

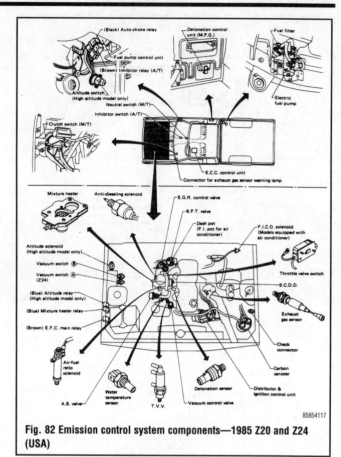

Fig. 82 Emission control system components—1985 Z20 and Z24 (USA)

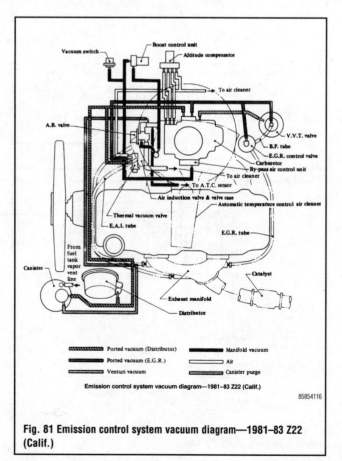

Fig. 81 Emission control system vacuum diagram—1981-83 Z22 (Calif.)

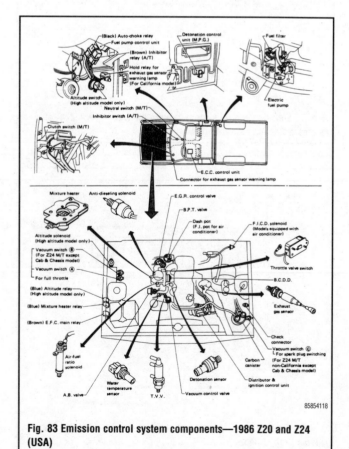

Fig. 83 Emission control system components—1986 Z20 and Z24 (USA)

EMISSION CONTROLS 4-27

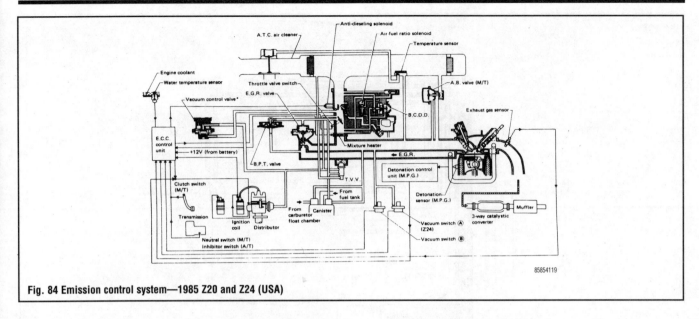

Fig. 84 Emission control system—1985 Z20 and Z24 (USA)

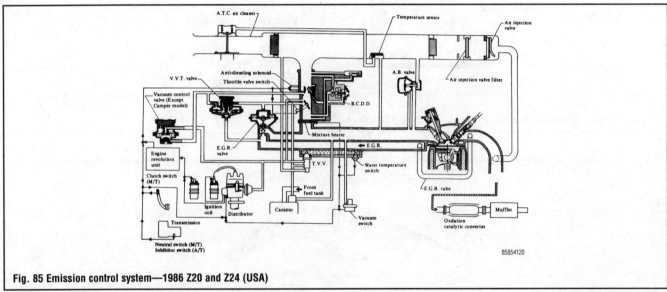

Fig. 85 Emission control system—1986 Z20 and Z24 (USA)

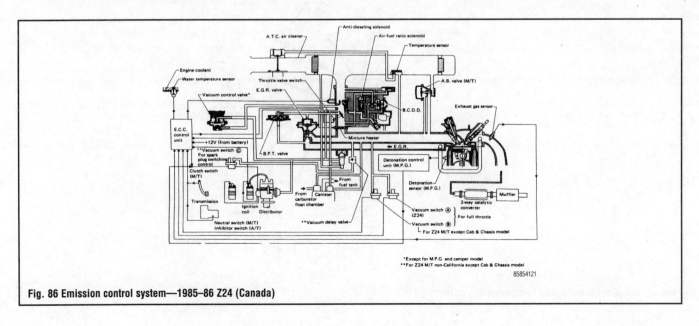

Fig. 86 Emission control system—1985-86 Z24 (Canada)

4-28 EMISSION CONTROLS

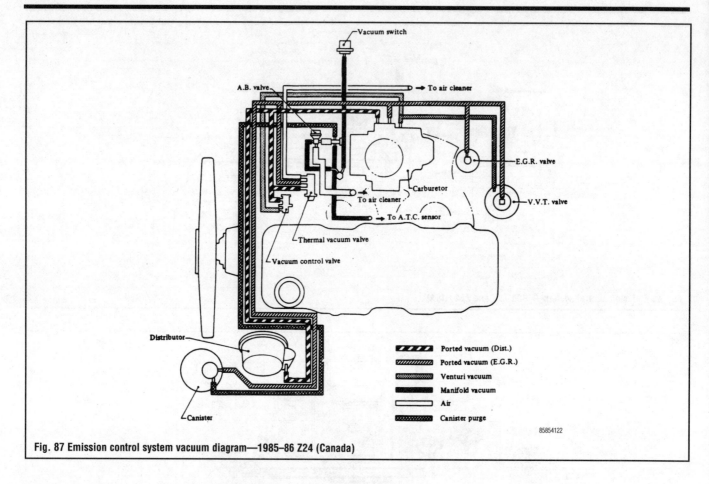

Fig. 87 Emission control system vacuum diagram—1985–86 Z24 (Canada)

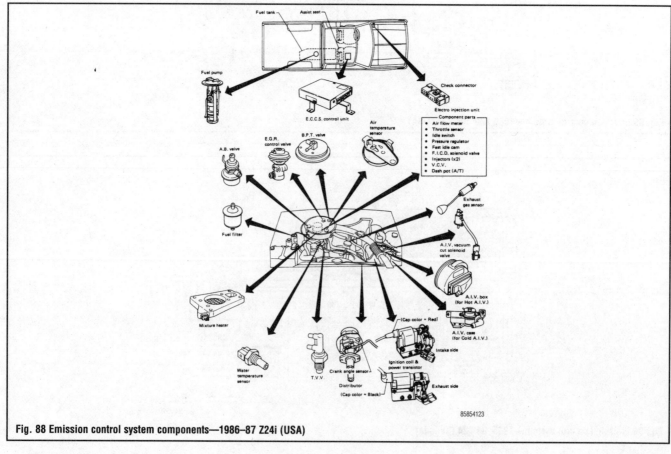

Fig. 88 Emission control system components—1986–87 Z24i (USA)

EMISSION CONTROLS 4-29

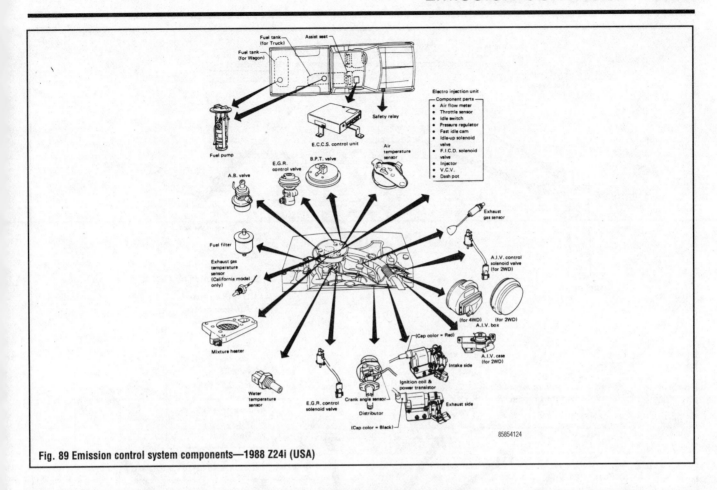

Fig. 89 Emission control system components—1988 Z24i (USA)

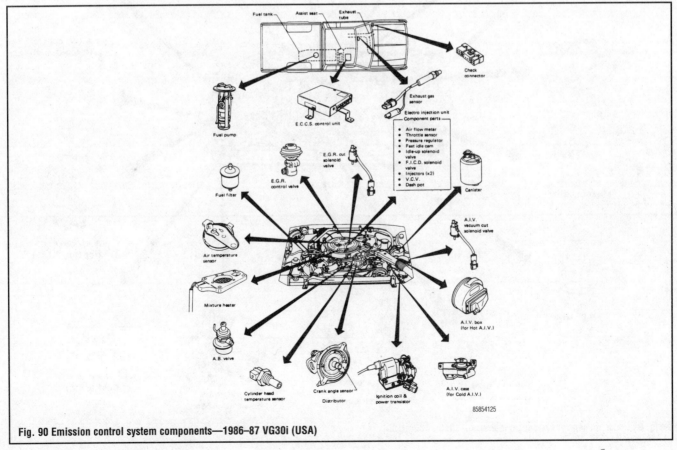

Fig. 90 Emission control system components—1986-87 VG30i (USA)

4-30 EMISSION CONTROLS

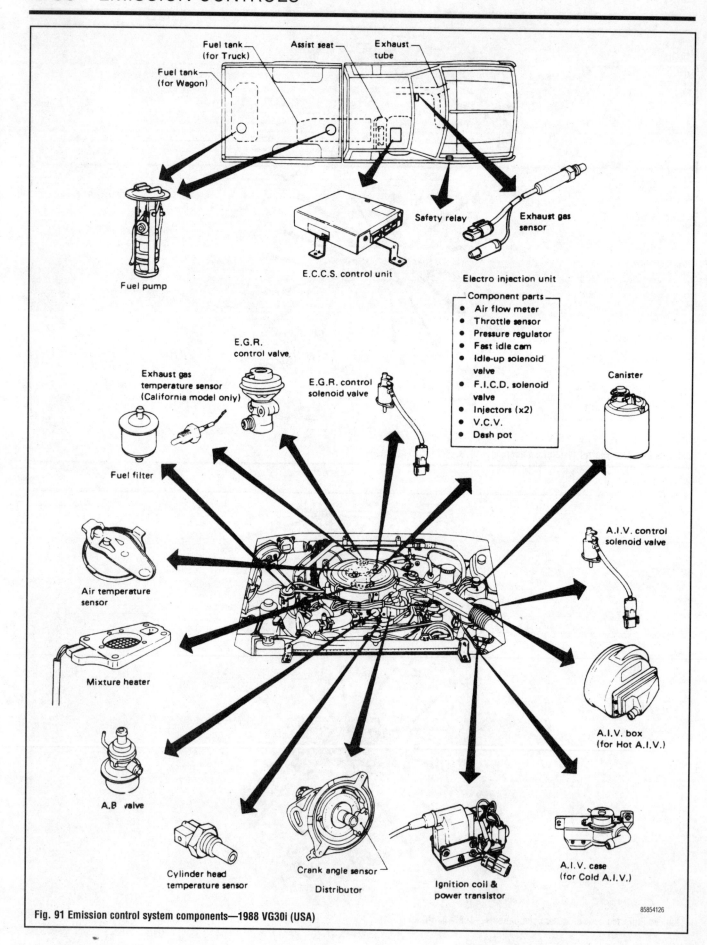

Fig. 91 Emission control system components—1988 VG30i (USA)

CARBURETED FUEL SYSTEM 5-2
UNDERSTANDING THE FUEL
  SYSTEM 5-2
MECHANICAL FUEL PUMP 5-2
    OPERATION 5-2
    REMOVAL & INSTALLATION 5-2
    TESTING 5-2
ELECTRIC FUEL PUMP 5-2
    OPERATION 5-2
    REMOVAL & INSTALLATION 5-3
    TESTING 5-3
CARBURETOR 5-4
    REMOVAL & INSTALLATION 5-5
    ADJUSTMENTS 5-6
    OVERHAUL 5-9
FUEL INJECTION SYSTEM 5-10
TROUBLESHOOTING 5-10
FUEL SYSTEM PRESSURE 5-10
    RELEASE PROCEDURE 5-10
ELECTRIC FUEL PUMP 5-10
    DESCRIPTION 5-10
    REMOVAL & INSTALLATION 5-10
    TESTING 5-11
THROTTLE BODY/CHAMBER 5-11
    REMOVAL & INSTALLATION 5-11
FUEL INJECTORS 5-12
    REMOVAL & INSTALLATION 5-12
    ADJUSTMENTS 5-13
FUEL TANK 5-14
FUEL TANK LOCATION 5-14
    REMOVAL & INSTALLATION 5-14
    GAUGE UNIT 5-14

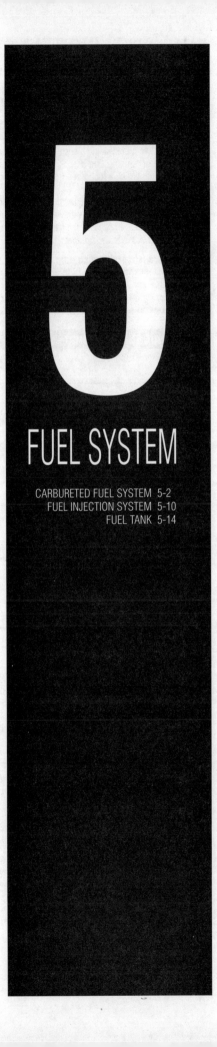

5
FUEL SYSTEM

CARBURETED FUEL SYSTEM 5-2
FUEL INJECTION SYSTEM 5-10
FUEL TANK 5-14

5-2 FUEL SYSTEM

CARBURETED FUEL SYSTEM

Understanding the Fuel System

An automotive fuel system consists of everything between the fuel tank and the carburetor or fuel injection unit. This includes the tank itself, all the lines, one or more fuel filters, a fuel pump (mechanical or electric), and the carburetor or fuel injection unit.

With the exception of the carburetor or fuel injection unit, the fuel system is quite simple in operation. Fuel is drawn from the tank through the fuel line by the fuel pump, which forces it to the fuel filter, and from there to the carburetor where it is distributed to the cylinders.

➡ When there is a problem starting or driving a vehicle, two of the most important checks involve the ignition and the fuel systems. You must have fuel and spark for the vehicle to operate properly. If the ignition system checks out there is spark, then you must determine if the fuel system is operating properly.

Mechanical Fuel Pump

OPERATION

♦ See Figure 1

Except 1977–83 Without A/C and 1979–83— Cab/Chassis

The fuel pump is a mechanically operated, diaphragm type driven by the fuel pump eccentric cam on the front of the camshaft.

Design of the fuel pump permits disassembly, cleaning, and repair or replacement of defective parts.

If the fuel pump is suspected of being faulty, tests for both pressure and volume should be performed. Never replace the pump without performing these simple tests first. Always check all hoses for leaks or clogs before testing the pump.

REMOVAL & INSTALLATION

※ CAUTION

Never smoke when working around gasoline! Avoid all sources of sparks or ignition. Gasoline vapors are EXTREMELY volatile!

1. Disconnect the negative battery cable. Disconnect the two fuel lines from the fuel pump. Be sure to keep the line leading from the fuel tank up high to prevent the excessive loss of fuel.
2. Remove the two fuel pump mounting nuts and remove the fuel pump assembly from the side of the engine.

To install:

3. Install the fuel pump using a NEW gasket and sealer on the mating surface.
4. Reconnect the two fuel lines.

TESTING

1. Disconnect the line between the carburetor and the fuel pump, at the carburetor.
2. Connect a fuel pump pressure gauge into the line.
3. Start the engine. The pressure should be between 3.0 and 3.9 psi (2.8–3.8 psi—early models). There is usually enough gas in the float bowl to perform this test.
4. If the pressure is OK, perform a capacity test. Remove the gauge from the line. Use a graduated container to catch the gas from the fuel line. Fill the carburetor float bowl with gas. Run the engine for one minute at about 1000 rpm. The pump should deliver 1000cc in one minute or less.

Electric Fuel Pump

OPERATION

♦ See Figures 2, 3 and 4

1977–83 with A/C, 1979–83 Cab/Chassis and 1984–86 All Models

An electric fuel pump is used on these models. The pump is mounted on a bracket located on the right frame rail next to the fuel tank. There is a filter

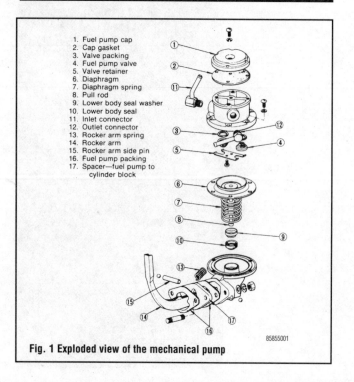

Fig. 1 Exploded view of the mechanical pump

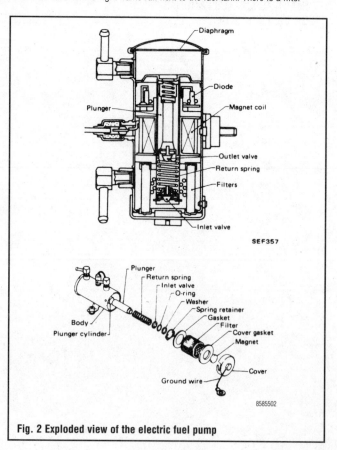

Fig. 2 Exploded view of the electric fuel pump

FUEL SYSTEM

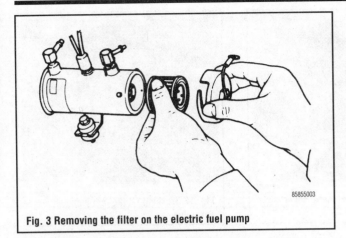

Fig. 3 Removing the filter on the electric fuel pump

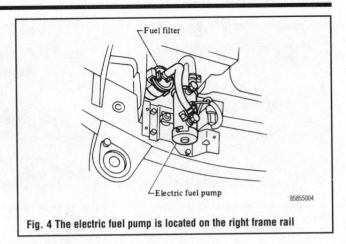

Fig. 4 The electric fuel pump is located on the right frame rail

mounted in the body of the pump, which does not normally require service. The pump can be disassembled, if necessary, but all electronic parts within the body (one transistor, two diodes, and three resistors) must be replaced.

REMOVAL & INSTALLATION

▶ See Figures 5, 6, 7, 8 and 9

1. Disconnect the negative battery cable.
2. Remove the fuel pump protector.
3. Remove the inlet and outlet hoses, catching the fuel that escapes in a metal container.
4. Disconnect the wiring harness at the connector.
5. Remove the two bolts securing the pump to the bracket and remove the pump.

To install:

6. Unscrew the pump end cover and slide out the pump filter. Check that the filter is not clogged and then replace it.
7. Install the pump in the bracket and tighten the mounting screws.
8. Connect the wiring harness and the fuel lines.
9. Install the pump protector and reconnect the battery cable. Run the engine and check for leaks.

TESTING

▶ See Figures 10 thru 18

1. Disconnect the hose from the pump outlet at the pump.
2. Connect a length of hose to the outlet. The hose should have an inside diameter of 6mm (0.24 in.). The diameter of the hose is important for accurate measurements.

Fig. 5 View of the electric fuel pump assembly

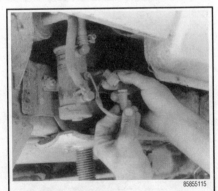

Fig. 6 Removing the electric fuel pump electrical connection

Fig. 7 View of the gas line clamp — note the fuel inlet hose pinched

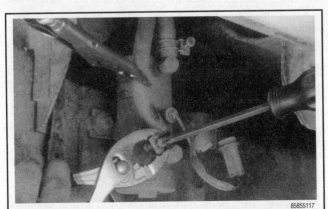

Fig. 8 Removing the gas hose clamp from the electric fuel pump

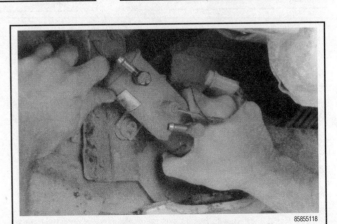

Fig. 9 Removing the electric fuel pump from the frame rail

5-4 FUEL SYSTEM

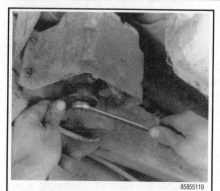
Fig. 10 View of the fuel pump protector installed

Fig. 11 Cleaning the fuel pump cover assembly

Fig. 12 Brushing off the fuel pump cover assembly

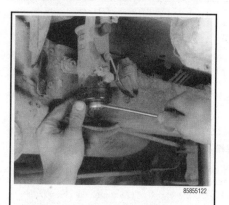
Fig. 13 Removing the fuel pump cover

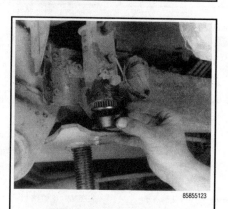
Fig. 14 Removing the fuel pump filter

Fig. 15 View of the fuel pump filter and cover

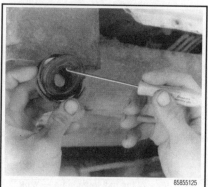
Fig. 16 Removing the fuel pump cover gasket

Fig. 17 View of the fuel pump cover gasket and magnets

Fig. 18 Removing the fuel pump cover magnet

3. Raise the end of the hose above the level of the pump. Turn the ignition switch on and catch the gasoline in a graduated container. Pump output should be 1400cc in one minute or less.

4. Fuel pump pressure should be 4.6 psi through 1978, 3.1–3.8 psi for 1979–83 and 2.7–3.4 psi for 1984–86 models.

Carburetor

The carburetor is the most complex part of the entire fuel system. Carburetors vary greatly in construction, but they all operate basically the same way; their job is to supply the correct mixture of fuel and air to the engine in response to varying conditions.

Despite their complexity in operation, carburetors function because of a simple physical principle (the venturi principle). Air is drawn into the engine by the pumping action of the pistons. As the air enters the top of the carburetor, it passes through a venturi, which is nothing more than a restriction in the throttle bore. The air speeds up as it passes through the venturi, causing a slight drop in pressure. This pressure drop pulls fuel from the float bowl through a nozzle into the throttle bore, where it mixes with the air and forms a fine mist, which is distributed to the cylinders through the intake manifold.

There are six different systems (air/fuel circuits) in a carburetor that make it work; the Float system, Main Metering system, Idle and Low-Speed system, Accelerator Pump system, Power system, and the Choke system. The way these systems are arranged in the carburetor determines the carburetor's size and shape.

It's hard to believe that the 2-bbl carburetor used on 4 cylinder engines have all the same basic systems as the enormous 4-bbl carburetors used on V8 engines. Of course, the 4-bbl have more throttle bores ("barrels") and a lot of other hardware you won't find on the little 2-bbl. But basically, all carburetors are similar, and if you understand a simple 2-bbl, you can use that knowledge to understand a 4-bbl. If you'll study the explanations of the various systems on this stage, you'll discover that carburetors aren't as tricky as you thought they were. In fact, they're fairly simple, considering the job they have to do.

It's important to remember that carburetors seldom give trouble during normal operation. Other than changing the fuel and air filters and making sure the

FUEL SYSTEM 5-5

idle speed and mixture are OK at every tune-up, there's not much maintenance you can perform on the average carburetor.

The carburetors used on Nissan and Datsun pickups are conventional 2-bbl, downdraft types. The main circuits are: primary, for normal operational requirements; secondary, to supply high speed fuel needs; float, to supply fuel to the primary and secondary circuits; accelerator, to supply fuel for quick and safe acceleration; choke, for reliable starting in cold weather; and power valve, for fuel economy. Although slight differences in appearance may be noted, these carburetors are basically alike. Of course, different jets and settings are demanded by the different engines to which they are fitted.

REMOVAL & INSTALLATION

▸ See Figures 19 thru 29

1. Disconnect the negative battery cable.
2. Loosen the radiator drain plug and drain the coolant into a suitable container.

✲✲✲ CAUTION

When draining the coolant, keep in mind that cats and dogs are attracted by the ethylene glycol antifreeze, and are quite likely to drink any that is left in an uncovered container or in puddles on the ground. This will prove fatal in sufficient quantity. Always drain the coolant into a sealable container. Coolant should be reused unless it is contaminated or several years old.

3. Unscrew the mounting screws and remove the air filter housing. Disconnect all hoses and lines leading from the air cleaner.
4. Tag and disconnect all fuel, vacuum, coolant and electrical lines or hoses leading from the carburetor.
5. Disconnect the accelerator linkage from the carburetor. On trucks equipped with an automatic transmission, disconnect the throttle cable linkage running from the transmission.

Fig. 19 View of the carburetor installed on the engine

Fig. 20 Brushing the gas line lock lever

Fig. 21 Removing the gas line lock lever

Fig. 22 Removing the fuel filter set screw

Fig. 23 View of the fuel filter set screw

Fig. 24 Removing the carburetor hold down bolts

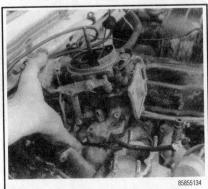
Fig. 25 Removing the carburetor from the engine

Fig. 26 Removing the carburetor gasket — if gasket is cracked it must be replaced

Fig. 27 View of the intake manifold carburetor ports

5-6 FUEL SYSTEM

Fig. 28 View of the carburetor mounting gasket — some gaskets have to be installed in the correct position

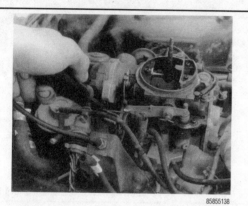

Fig. 29 Adjust the idle speed after carburetor installation

6. Remove the four carburetor mounting bolts and lift off the carburetor and its gasket.

To install:

➡ Cover the manifold opening with a clean rag to prevent anything from falling into the engine.

7. Install the carburetor, tighten the mounting bolts EVENLY IN STEPS and reconnect all linkage.
8. Start the engine and check for any leaks. Check the float level. Road test the vehicle for proper operation.

ADJUSTMENTS

Automatic Choke

1970–80

♦ See Figure 30

1. With the engine cold, make sure the choke is fully closed (press the gas pedal all the way to the floor and release, or pull the choke knob out on early models with that system).
2. Check the choke linkage for binding. The choke plate should be easily opened and closed with your finger. If the choke sticks or binds, it can usually be freed with a liberal application of a carburetor cleaner make for the purpose. A couple of quick shots from a spray can of this stuff normally does the trick. If not, the carburetor will have to be disassembled for repairs.
3. The choke is correctly adjusted when the index mark on the choke housing (notch) aligns with the center mark on the carburetor body. If the setting is incorrect, loosen the three screws clamping the choke body in place and rotate the choke cover left or right until the marks align. Tighten the screws carefully to avoid cracking the housing.

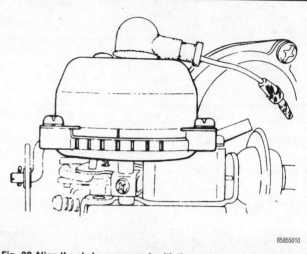

Fig. 30 Align the choke cover mark with the center notch on the carburetor

1981–86

♦ See Figures 31, 32, 33 and 34

These carburetors utilize an electric choke which cannot be adjusted. If the choke is not functioning properly, perform the following tests and replace the defective parts.

Choke Heater Circuit

✳✳✳ CAUTION

Use only those test leads illustrated.

1. With the ignition off, check for continuity between leads **A** and **B** in the illustration.
2. If continuity is found, the heater is good. If continuity is not found, check for shorts or open wires.
3. With the engine at idle, check for voltage across **A** & **B**. A reading of 12 volts should be indicated. If not, check for a short or open circuit.

Choke Relay

4. Remove the relay, located on the right side of the firewall.
5. Check for continuity between **4** and **5**; and between **1** and **2**. Continuity should exist each time.
6. Check for continuity between **1** and **3**. There should be none.

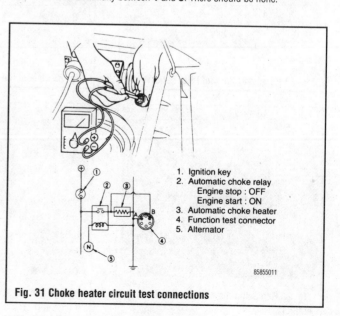

1. Ignition key
2. Automatic choke relay
   Engine stop : OFF
   Engine start : ON
3. Automatic choke heater
4. Function test connector
5. Alternator

Fig. 31 Choke heater circuit test connections

FUEL SYSTEM

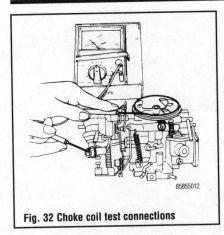

Fig. 32 Choke coil test connections

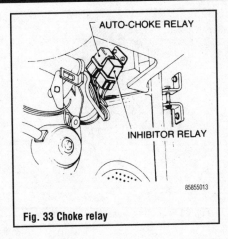

Fig. 33 Choke relay

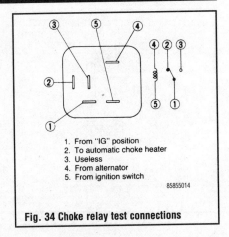

1. From "IG" position
2. To automatic choke heater
3. Useless
4. From alternator
5. From ignition switch

Fig. 34 Choke relay test connections

7. Apply 12 volts across **4** and **5**. Continuity should now exist between **1** and **3**, but not between **1** and **2**.
8. If all these conditions are not met, replace the relay.

Throttle Linkage

On all models, make sure the throttle is wide open when the accelerator pedal is floored. Some models have an adjustable accelerator pedal stop to prevent strain on the linkage.

Secondary Throttle Linkage

♦ See Figure 35

All Datsun/Nissan carburetors discussed in this manual are two stage type carburetors. On this type of carburetor, the engine runs on the primary barrel most of the time, with the secondary barrel being used for acceleration purposes. When the throttle valve on the primary side opens to an angle of approximately 50 degrees (from its fully closed position), the secondary throttle valve is pulled open by the connecting linkage. The fifty degree angle of throttle valve opening works out to a clearance measurement of somewhere between 0.26–0.32 in. between the throttle valve and the carburetor body. The easiest way to measure this is to use a drill bit. Drill bits from size H to size P (standard letter size drill bits) should fit. If an adjustment is necessary, bend the connecting link between the two linkage assemblies.

Float Level

♦ See Figure 36

The fuel level is normal if it is within the lines on the window glass of the float chamber when the vehicle is resting on level ground and the engine is off.

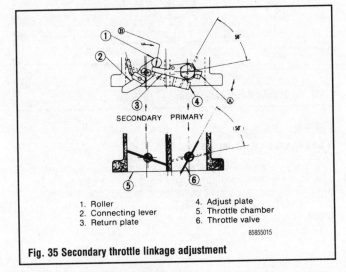

Fig. 35 Secondary throttle linkage adjustment

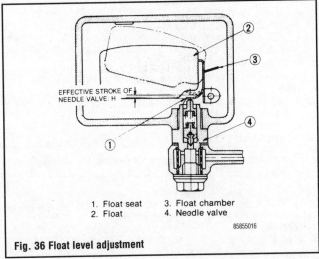

1. Float seat
2. Float
3. Float chamber
4. Needle valve

Fig. 36 Float level adjustment

If the fuel level is outside the lines, remove the float housing cover. Have an absorbent cloth under the cover to catch the fuel from the fuel bowl. Adjust the float level by bending the needle seat on the float.

The needle valve should have an effective stroke of about 0.0591 in. (1.5mm). When necessary, the needle valve stroke can be adjusted by bending the float stopper.

➡ Be careful not to bend the needle valve rod when installing the float and baffle plate, if removed.

Fast Idle Speed

♦ See Figures 37, 38 and 39

1. With the carburetor removed from the vehicle, place the upper side of the fast idle screw on the 2nd step (1st step for 1977–82 engines) of the fast idle cam and measure the clearance between the throttle valve and the wall of the throttle valve chamber at the center of the throttle valve. Check it against the following specifications:

1970–74:
- 0.035–0.039 in. (0.9–1.0mm)—M/T
- 0.044–0.048 in. (1.12–1.22mm)—A/T

1975–76:
- 0.040–0.048 in. (1.01–1.21mm)—M/T
- 0.048–0.052 in. (1.23–1.33mm)—A/T

1977–79:
- 0.052–0.058 in. (1.33–1.47mm)—M/T
- 0.062–0.068 in. (1.58–1.72mm)—A/T

1980:
- 0.032–0.037 in. (0.81–0.95mm)—M/T
- 0.040–0.046 in. (1.02–1.16mm)—A/T

5-8 FUEL SYSTEM

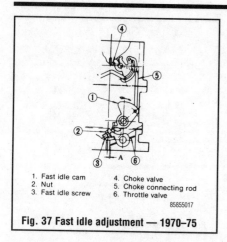

Fig. 37 Fast idle adjustment — 1970–75

1. Fast idle cam
2. Nut
3. Fast idle screw
4. Choke valve
5. Choke connecting rod
6. Throttle valve

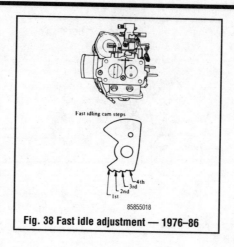

Fig. 38 Fast idle adjustment — 1976–86

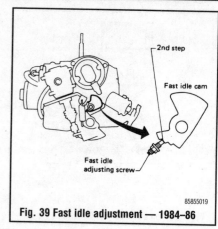

Fig. 39 Fast idle adjustment — 1984–86

1981:
- 0.032–0.037 in. (0.81–0.95mm)—M/T
- 0.039–0.044 in. (0.98–1.12mm)—A/T (49 State)
- 0.039–0.043 in. (1.00–1.10mm)—A/T (Calif.)

1982–83:
- 0.032–0.037 in. (0.81–0.95mm)—M/T
- 0.038–0.044 in. (0.97–1.11mm)—A/T

1984–86:
- 0.030–0.035 in. (0.76–0.90mm)—M/T (Z20)
- 0.028–0.034 in. (0.71–0.85mm)—M/T (Z24)
- 0.034–0.040 in. (0.87–1.01mm)—A/T

M/T means manual transmission. A/T means automatic transmission.

➡ The first step of the fast idle adjustment procedure is not absolutely necessary.

2. Install the carburetor on the engine.
3. Start the engine and measure the fast idle rpm with the engine at operating temperature. The cam should be at the 2nd step.

1970–76:
- 1900–2100 rpm—M/T
- 2300–2500 rpm—A/T

1977–80:
- 1900–2800 rpm—M/T
- 2200–3200 rpm—A/T

1981–83:
- 1900–2800 rpm—M/T
- 2200–3200 rpm—A/T

1984–86:
- 2600–3000 rpm—M/T (Z20)
- 2600–3000 rpm—M/T (Z24)
- 2200–2600 rpm—A/T

4. To adjust the fast idle speed, turn the fast idle adjusting screw counterclockwise to increase the fast idle speed and clockwise to decrease the fast idle speed.

Choke Unloader

♦ See Figure 40

1. Close the choke valve completely.
2. Hold the choke valve closed by stretching a rubber band between the choke piston lever and a stationary part of the carburetor.
3. Open the throttle lever fully.
4. With the throttle lever fully open, adjust the clearance between the choke valve and the carburetor body to the figure indicated:
- 1973–74: 0.1730 in. (4.4mm)
- 1975–77: 0.0960 in. (2.45mm)
- 1978–86: 0.0965 in. (2.45mm)

➡ Make sure that the throttle valve opens completely when the carburetor is mounted on the engine.

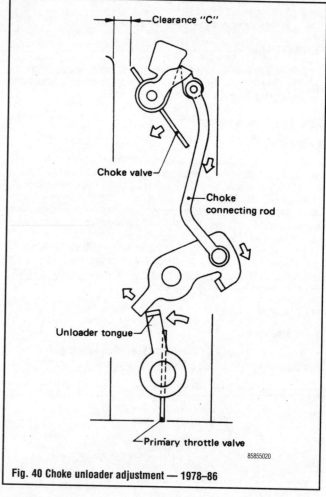

Fig. 40 Choke unloader adjustment — 1978–86

Dashpot

♦ See Figures 41, 42 and 43

The purpose of this device is to prevent the throttle from suddenly snapping shut. The dashpot has a plunger which extends when the throttle is closed suddenly. The plunger contacts a tab on the throttle lever and holds the throttle open slightly for a second, then closes the throttle slowly over the period of another second or so.

FUEL SYSTEM 5-9

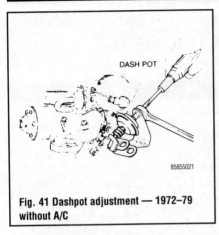

Fig. 41 Dashpot adjustment — 1972–79 without A/C

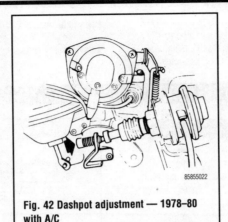

Fig. 42 Dashpot adjustment — 1978–80 with A/C

Fig. 43 Dashpot adjustment — 1981–86

1. Adjust the idle speed and mixture before making adjustments to the dashpot. Warm the engine to operating temperature, and connect a tachometer to the engine.
2. Move the throttle lever by hand, and note the engine speed when the dashpot plunger just touches the throttle lever.
3. The engine speed should be as indicated.
- 1970–72: 1800–2000 rpm
- 1973: 1600–1800 rpm
- 1974–80: 1900–2100 rpm, M/T; 1650–1850 rpm, A/T
- 1981–83: 1400–1600 rpm
- 1984: 1400–1600 rpm, A/T; 1700–1900 rpm, M/T (Calif.)
- 1985: 1300–1700 rpm
- 1986: 1600–2000 rpm, M/T; 1300–1700 rpm, A/T
4. If not, loosen the locknut and turn the adjusting screw until the engine speed is in the proper range. Tighten the locknut. On 1978–79 models with air conditioning, a different dashpot is used. Adjustment is made by turning the screw on the throttle lever which contacts the plunger.
5. Open the throttle and allow it to close by itself. The dashpot should smoothly reduce the idling speed from 2000 to 1000 rpm in about three seconds.

OVERHAUL

Efficient carburetion depends greatly on careful cleaning and inspection during overhaul, since dirt, gum, water, or varnish in or on the carburetor parts are often responsible for poor performance.

Overhaul your carburetor in a clean, dust-free area. Carefully disassemble the carburetor, referring often to the exploded views. Keep all similar and look-alike parts segregated during disassembly and cleaning to avoid accidental interchange during assembly. Make a note of all jet sizes.

When the carburetor is disassembled, wash all parts (except diaphragms, electric choke units, pump plunger, and any other plastic, leather, fiber, or rubber parts) in clean carburetor solvent. Do not leave parts in the solvent any longer than is necessary to sufficiently loosen the deposits. Excessive cleaning may remove the special finish from the float bowl and choke valve bodies, leaving these parts unfit for service. Rinse all parts in clean solvent and blow them dry with compressed air to allow them to air dry. Wipe clean all cork, plastic, leather, and fiber parts with a clean, lint-free cloth.

➥Carburetor solvent is available in various-sized solvent cans, which are designed with a removable small parts basket in the top. The carburetor choke chamber and body, and all small parts can be soaked in this can until clean. These solvent cans are available at most auto parts stores, and are quite handy for soaking other small engine parts.

Blow out all passages and jets with compressed air and be sure that there are not restrictions or blockages. Never use wire or similar tools to clean jets, fuel passages, or air bleeds. Clean all jets and valves separately to avoid accidental interchange.

Check all parts for wear or damage. If wear or damage is found, replace the defective parts. Especially check the following:
1. Check the float needle and seat for wear. If wear is found, replace the complete assembly.
2. Check the float hinge pin for wear and the float(s) for dents or distortion. Replace the float if fuel has leaked into it.
3. Check the throttle and choke shaft bores for wear or an out-of-round condition. Damage or wear to the throttle arm, shaft, or shaft bore will often require replacement of the throttle body. These parts require a close tolerance of fit; wear may allow air leakage, which could affect starting and idling.

➥Throttle shafts and bushings are not included in overhaul kits. They can be purchased separately.

4. Inspect the idle mixture adjusting needles for burrs or grooves. Any such condition requires replacement of the needle, since you will not be able to obtain a satisfactory idle.
5. Test the accelerator pump check valves. They should pass air one way but not the other. Test for proper seating by blowing and sucking on the valve. Replace the valve if necessary. If the valve is satisfactory, wash the valve again to remove breath moisture.
6. Check the bowl cover for warped surfaces with a straight edge.
7. Closely inspect the valves and seats for wear and damage, replacing as necessary.
8. After the carburetor is assembled, check the choke valve for freedom of operation.

Carburetor overhaul kits are recommended for each overhaul. These kits contain all gaskets and new parts to replace those that deteriorate most rapidly. Failure to replace all parts supplied with the kit (especially gaskets) can result in poor performance and a leaky carburetor later.

Most carburetor manufacturers supply overhaul kits in at least one of three basic types: minor repair; major repair; and gasket kits. Basically, they contain the following, and are available at most auto parts jobbers and Nissan dealers:

- **Minor Repair Kits:**
- All gaskets
- Float needle valve
- Volume control screw
- All diaphragms
- Spring for the pump diaphragm
- **Major Repair Kits:**
- All jets and gaskets
- All diaphragms
- Float needle valve
- Volume control screw
- Pump ball valve
- Main jet carrier
- Float
- **Gasket Kits:**

5-10 FUEL SYSTEM

- All gaskets

After cleaning and checking all components, reassemble the carburetor, using new parts and referring to the exploded view. When reassembling, make sure that all screws and jets are tight in their seats, but do not overtighten as the tips will be distorted. Tighten all screws gradually in rotation. Do not tighten needle valves into their seats; uneven jetting will result. Always use new gaskets. Be sure to adjust the float level when reassembling.

FUEL INJECTION SYSTEM

Troubleshooting

Engine troubles are not usually caused by the EFI system. When troubleshooting, always check first the condition of all other related systems.

Many times the most frequent cause of problems is a bad contact in a wiring connector, so always make sure that the connections are secure. When inspecting the connector, pay particular attention to the following

1. Check to see that the terminals are not bent.
2. Check to see that the connector is pushed in all the way and locked.
3. Check that there is no change in signal when the connector is tapped or wiggled.

Actual troubleshooting of the EFI system and the EFI computer is a complex process which requires the use of a few expensive and hard to find tools. Other than checking the operation of the main components individually, we suggest that you leave any further troubleshooting to an authorized service facility.

➡The worst enemy of any fuel injection system is water or moisture. The best (i.e., cheapest and simplest) insurance for your truck's injection system is to change the fuel filter as frequently as the maintenance schedule recommends. When you follow the filter change interval strictly, many possible expensive injection system problems are eliminated.

✱✱ CAUTION

Before disconnecting the fuel lines or any of the fuel system components, it is important to release the fuel system pressure. Please refer to the Fuel System Pressure Release procedure, which follows.

Fuel System Pressure

RELEASE PROCEDURE

♦ See Figures 44 and 45

✱✱ CAUTION

Never smoke when working around gasoline! Avoid all sources of sparks or ignition. Gasoline vapors are EXTREMELY volatile! Any time the fuel system is being worked on always keep a dry chemical (Class B) fire extinguisher near the work area.

1. Remove the fuel pump fuse from the fuse block, fuel pump relay or disconnect the harness connector at the tank while engine is running.
2. It should run and then stall when the fuel in the lines is exhausted. When the engine stops, crank the starter a few times for about 5 seconds to make sure all pressure in the fuel lines is released.
3. Install the fuel pump fuse, relay or harness connector after repair is made.
4. On some late models the "Check Engine Light" will stay on after test has been completed. The memory code in the control unit must be erased. To erase the code disconnect the battery cable for 10 seconds then reconnect.

Electric Fuel Pump

DESCRIPTION

See Figure 46

The fuel pump with a damper is located in the fuel tank. The vane rollers are directly coupled to the motor which is cooled by fuel. a relief valve in the pump is designed to open at 44–64 psi, should a malfunction arise.

REMOVAL & INSTALLATION

1. Before disconnecting the fuel lines or any of the fuel system components, refer to Fuel Pressure Release procedures and release the fuel pressure.

✱✱ WARNING

Reducing the fuel pressure to zero is a very important step for correct removal of the electric fuel pump. See Fuel Pressure Release procedures in this section

2. Disconnect the negative battery cable. Disconnect the fuel gauge electrical connector and remove the fuel tank inspection cover.

➡If the truck has no fuel tank inspection cover the fuel tank must be lowered or removed to gain access to the in-tank fuel pump.

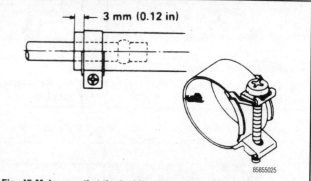

Fig. 45 Make sure that the fuel line hose clamps are installed properly

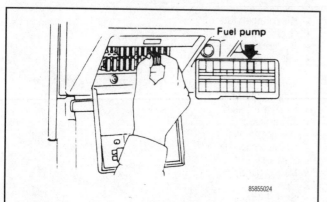

Fig. 44 Remove the fuel pump fuse when releasing the fuel pressure

FUEL SYSTEM   5-11

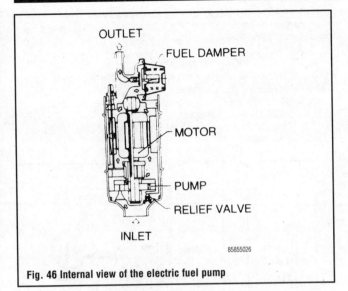

Fig. 46 Internal view of the electric fuel pump

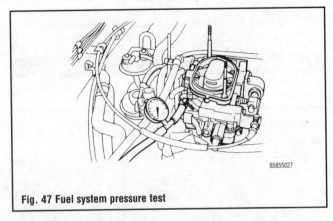

Fig. 47 Fuel system pressure test

3. Disconnect the fuel outlet and the return hoses. Remove the fuel tank if necessary.
4. Remove the ring retaining bolts and the O-ring, then lift the fuel pump assembly from the fuel tank. Plug the opening with a clean rag to prevent dirt from entering the system.

To install:

➡ When removing or installing the fuel pump assembly, be careful not to damage or deform it. Always install a new O-ring.

5. Install the fuel pump assembly in the fuel tank with a NEW O-ring. Install the ring retaining bolts. Install the fuel tank if removed.
6. Reconnect the fuel lines and the electrical connection.
7. Connect battery cable, start engine and check for fuel leaks.

➡ On some late models the "Check Engine Light" will stay on after installation is completed. The memory code in the control unit must be erased. To erase the code disconnect the battery cable for 10 seconds then reconnect after installation of fuel pump.

TESTING

♦ See Figure 47

1. Release the fuel pressure. Connect a fuel pressure gauge between the fuel filter outlet and fuel feed pipe.
2. Start the engine and check that the pressure is approximately 37 psi.

➡ Make sure that the fuel filter is not blocked before replacing any fuel system components.

3. If pressure is not as specified, replace the pressure regulator and repeat the test. If the pressure is still incorrect, check for clogged or deformed fuel lines, then replace the fuel pump.

Throttle Body/Chamber

REMOVAL & INSTALLATION

♦ See Figures 48, 49 and 50

❋❋ CAUTION

Never smoke when working around gasoline! Avoid all sources of sparks or ignition. Gasoline vapors are EXTREMELY volatile!

1. Disconnect the negative battery cable and remove the intake duct from the throttle chamber.
2. Disconnect the vacuum hoses and the electrical harness connector from the throttle chamber. Disconnect the accelerator cable from the throttle chamber.
3. Remove the mounting bolts and the throttle chamber from the intake manifold.

To install:

4. Use a NEW gasket and reverse the removal procedures. Torque the throttle chamber bolts EVENLY to 9–13 ft. lbs. (12–18 Nm). Adjust the throttle cable if necessary.

Check the throttle for smooth operation and make sure the by-pass port is free of obstacles and is clean. Check to make sure the idle speed adjusting screw moves smoothly.

Do not touch the EGR vacuum port screw or, on some later models, the throttle valve stopper screw, as they are factory adjusted.

Because of the sensitivity of the air flow meter, there cannot be any air leaks in the fuel system. Even the smallest leak could unbalance the system and affect the performance of the vehicle.

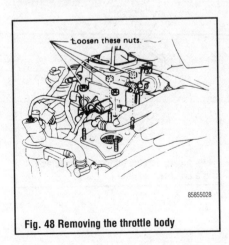

Fig. 48 Removing the throttle body

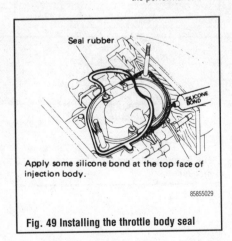

Fig. 49 Installing the throttle body seal

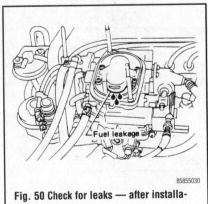

Fig. 50 Check for leaks — after installation

5-12 FUEL SYSTEM

During every check pay attention to hose connections, dipstick and oil filler cap for evidence of air leaks. Should you encounter any, take steps to correct the problem.

Fuel Injectors

REMOVAL & INSTALLATION

♦ See Figures 51 thru 59

1. Remove the throttle body assembly as outlined earlier.
2. Remove the rubber seal and the injector harness grommet from the top of the injection body.
3. Remove the injector cover.
4. Use a hollow bar with an inside diameter of not less than 5.5mm (0.217 in.) and with the throttle valve kept fully open, tap the bottom of the fuel injector with the hollow bar and plastic hammer.
5. Disconnect the harness of the injector from the harness connector.
   a. Remove the terminal retainer.
   b. Using a small screwdriver, tilt the lock tongue, and at the same time push out the terminal.

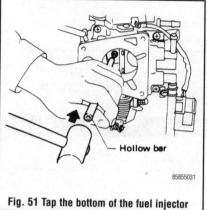
Fig. 51 Tap the bottom of the fuel injector

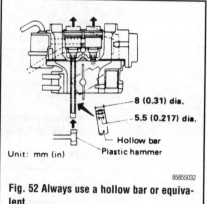
Fig. 52 Always use a hollow bar or equivalent

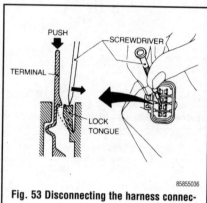
Fig. 53 Disconnecting the harness connector

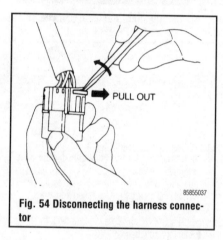
Fig. 54 Disconnecting the harness connector

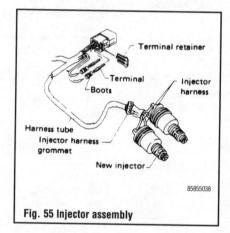
Fig. 55 Injector assembly

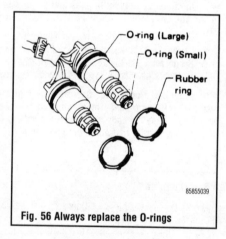
Fig. 56 Always replace the O-rings

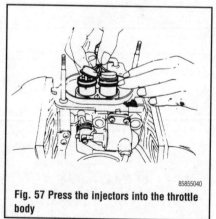
Fig. 57 Press the injectors into the throttle body

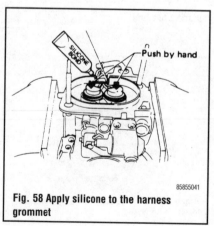
Fig. 58 Apply silicone to the harness grommet

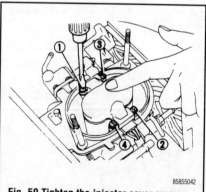
Fig. 59 Tighten the injector cover screws in a criss-cross pattern

FUEL SYSTEM

To install:

6. Put the harness of the new injector into a new injector harness grommet and the harness tube.

➡ **Every time a harness grommet is removed it should be replaced with a new one. When assembling the connector, pay attention to the harness color and position, otherwise injector damage could occur.**

7. Replace all injector O-rings with new ones coated with some silicone oil and put the injector assembly into the injection body.

8. Push the injectors into the injector body by hand, until the O-rings are fully seated. Invert the injection body and insure that the injector tips are properly seated.

9. Apply some silicone bond to the injector harness grommet.

➡ **Air tight sealing is essential to ensure stable and proper idling condition.**

10. Use locking sealer on the screw threads and reinstall the injector cover. Tighten the screws in a criss-cross pattern to ensure proper seating of the injector and cover.

11. Apply some silicone bond to the bottom of the rubber seal and attach the seal to the top face of the injection body.

➡ **Do not reinstall the air cleaner until the silicone bond has hardened.**

12. Install the injection unit to the intake manifold and tighten the bolts EVENLY to 9–13 ft. lbs. 12–18 Nm).

ADJUSTMENTS

Fast Idle Speed

♦ See Figure 60

1. Start the engine and run it until it reaches normal operating temperature.
2. Make sure that the aligning mark stamped on the fast idle cam meets the center of the roller installed on the cam follow lever. If not, correct the location of the fast idle cam by turning the adjusting screw (**S1**).

➡ **If it is not adjustable, replace the thermo element.**

3. Measure the clearance **G** between the roller and the fast idle cam. The clearance should be 0.020–0.118 in. (0.508–2.99mm) for the VG30i engine and 0.028–0.118 in. (0.71–2.99mm) for the Z24i engine.

4. If not correct, adjust clearance **G** by turning the adjusting screw (**S2**). Make sure the engine is warmed up sufficiently and adjust to 0.031–0.047 in. (0.787–1.194mm) for the VG30i and 0.047–0.063 in. (1.194–1.600mm) for the Z24i.

FICD Solenoid

♦ See Figure 61

1. With the engine at normal operating temperature, check the idle speed. (Refer to the Tune-Up Specification Chart).
2. Turn the air conditioner switch **ON**. When the A/C is on, the idle speed should be 850–950 rpm with the transmission in **N**.
3. If out of specification, adjust the idle speed by turning the adjusting screw.

Dashpot

♦ See Figure 62

1. Run the engine to normal operating temperature.
2. Turn the throttle valve by hand, and read the engine speed when the dashpot just touches the adjusting screw.
3. The dashpot touch speed is; 1300–1500 rpm for the VG30i and 1600–2000 rpm for the Z24i.
4. Adjust by turning the adjusting screw.

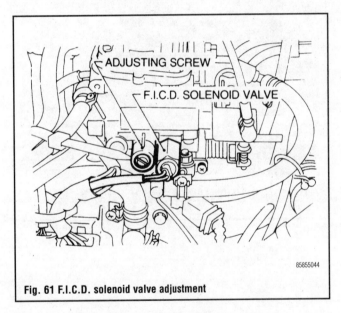

Fig. 61 F.I.C.D. solenoid valve adjustment

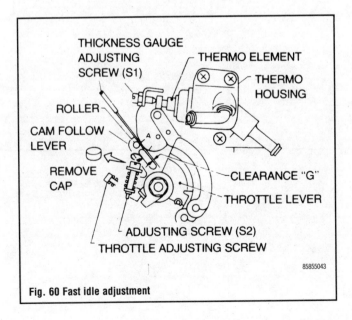

Fig. 60 Fast idle adjustment

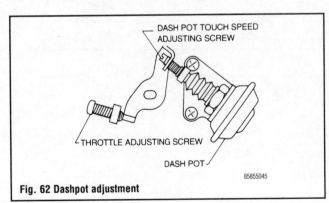

Fig. 62 Dashpot adjustment

FUEL TANK

Fuel Tank Location

The fuel tank is located under the floor of the bed on the right side, directly behind the cab. DISPOSE OF ANY GASOLINE IN THE PROPER MANNER, IF NECESSARY.

REMOVAL & INSTALLATION

▶ See Figures 63 and 64

1. Disconnect the negative cable from the battery.
2. Remove the drain plug at the bottom of the tank and drain the fuel into a suitable container.
3. Disconnect the filler tube from the filler hose.
4. Disconnect the ventilation hoses, the fuel return hose and fuel outlet hose from the tank. Disconnect the gauge unit wires at the electrical connector.

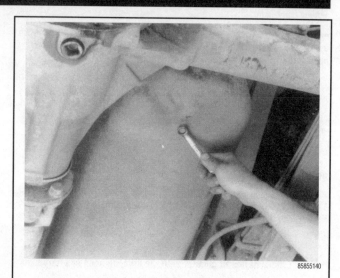

Fig. 64 Draining the gas tank — before removal of gas tank

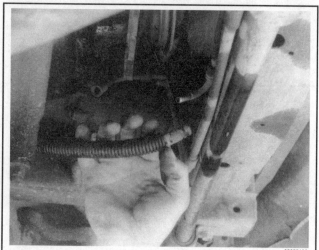

Fig. 63 Removing the fuel line — always replace the fuel line clamps

5. Remove the mounting bolts and remove the fuel tank.

To install:

6. Installation is the reverse of the removal procedure. When installing, tighten the clamps EVENLY and securely, but do not crimp any of the lines. Install the clips holding the fuel tube to the underbody securely. Do not attach the filler hose to the tube until the tank is in place. Failure to do this will cause leaks around the connection.

GAUGE UNIT

The fuel tank must be removed for access to the gauge unit. The unit is installed into the tank with a bayonet type of mount. Turn it counterclockwise with a screwdriver to remove. Use a new O-ring when installing, aligning the tab in the unit with the notch in the tank.

UNDERSTANDING AND
TROUBLESHOOTING ELECTRICAL
SYSTEMS 6-2
BASIC ELECTRICAL THEORY 6-2
    HOW DOES ELECTRICITY WORK: THE
      WATER ANALOGY 6-2
    OHM'S LAW 6-2
ELECTRICAL COMPONENTS 6-2
    POWER SOURCE 6-2
    GROUND 6-3
    PROTECTIVE DEVICES 6-3
    SWITCHES & RELAYS 6-3
    LOAD 6-4
    WIRING & HARNESSES 6-4
    CONNECTORS 6-4
TEST EQUIPMENT 6-5
    JUMPER WIRES 6-5
    TEST LIGHTS 6-5
    MULTIMETERS 6-5
TROUBLESHOOTING ELECTRICAL
  SYSTEMS 6-6
TESTING 6-6
    OPEN CIRCUITS 6-6
    SHORT CIRCUITS 6-6
    VOLTAGE 6-6
    VOLTAGE DROP 6-7
    RESISTANCE 6-7
WIRE AND CONNECTOR REPAIR 6-7
**HEATING AND AIR
  CONDITIONING 6-8**
HEATER ASSEMBLY 6-8
    REMOVAL & INSTALLATION 6-8
HEATER CORE 6-8
    REMOVAL & INSTALLATION 6-8
BLOWER MOTOR 6-9
    REMOVAL & INSTALLATION 6-9
AIR CONDITIONING COMPONENTS 6-10
    REMOVAL & INSTALLATION 6-10
CONTROL HEAD 6-10
    REMOVAL & INSTALLATION 6-10
    ADJUSTMENT 6-11
RADIO 6-12
ADJUSTMENTS 6-12
    REMOVAL & INSTALLATION 6-12
WINDSHIELD WIPERS 6-12
BLADE AND ARM 6-12
    REMOVAL & INSTALLATION 6-12
WINDSHIELD WIPER MOTOR 6-13
    REMOVAL & INSTALLATION 6-13
WIPER LINKAGE 6-13
    REMOVAL & INSTALLATION 6-13
REAR WIPER 6-14
    REMOVAL & INSTALLATION 6-14
INSTRUMENT AND SWITCHES 6-15
INSTRUMENT CLUSTER 6-15
    REMOVAL & INSTALLATION 6-15
WINDSHIELD WIPER SWITCH 6-15
    REMOVAL & INSTALLATION 6-15
HEADLIGHT SWITCH 6-16
    REMOVAL & INSTALLATION 6-16
TURN SIGNAL/COMBINATION
  SWITCH 6-16
    REMOVAL & INSTALLATION 6-16
IGNITION SWITCH 6-16
    REMOVAL & INSTALLATION 6-16
BACK–UP LIGHT SWITCH 6-16
    REMOVAL & INSTALLATION 6-16
SPEEDOMETER CABLE 6-16
    REPLACEMENT 6-16
LIGHTING 6-17
HEADLIGHTS 6-17
    REMOVAL & INSTALLATION 6-17
SIGNAL AND MARKER LIGHTS 6-17
    REMOVAL & INSTALLATION 6-17
TRAILER WIRING 6-19
CIRCUIT PROTECTION 6-19
FUSES AND FLASHERS 6-19
    FUSES 6-19
    FLASHERS AND RELAYS 6-19
FUSIBLE LINK 6-26
    FUSE LINK 6-26
CIRCUIT BREAKERS 6-27
WIRING DIAGRAMS 6-28

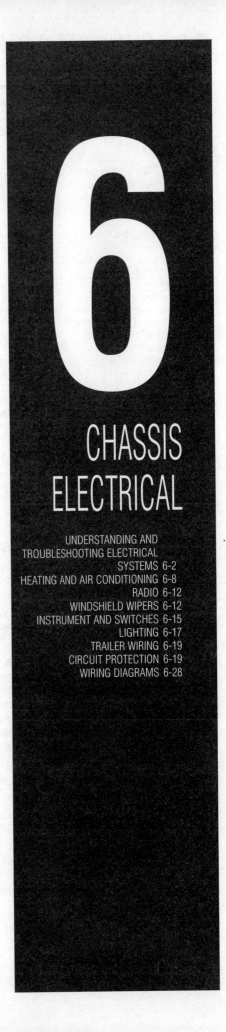

6

CHASSIS ELECTRICAL

UNDERSTANDING AND
TROUBLESHOOTING ELECTRICAL
SYSTEMS 6-2
HEATING AND AIR CONDITIONING 6-8
RADIO 6-12
WINDSHIELD WIPERS 6-12
INSTRUMENT AND SWITCHES 6-15
LIGHTING 6-17
TRAILER WIRING 6-19
CIRCUIT PROTECTION 6-19
WIRING DIAGRAMS 6-28

CHASSIS ELECTRICAL

UNDERSTANDING AND TROUBLESHOOTING ELECTRICAL SYSTEMS

Basic Electrical Theory

♦ See Figure 1

For any 12 volt, negative ground, electrical system to operate, the electricity must travel in a complete circuit. This simply means that current (power) from the positive (+) terminal of the battery must eventually return to the negative (-) terminal of the battery. Along the way, this current will travel through wires, fuses, switches and components. If, for any reason, the flow of current through the circuit is interrupted, the component fed by that circuit will cease to function properly.

Perhaps the easiest way to visualize a circuit is to think of connecting a light bulb (with two wires attached to it) to the battery—one wire attached to the negative (-) terminal of the battery and the other wire to the positive (+) terminal. With the two wires touching the battery terminals, the circuit would be complete and the light bulb would illuminate. Electricity would follow a path from the battery to the bulb and back to the battery. It's easy to see that with longer wires on our light bulb, it could be mounted anywhere. Further, one wire could be fitted with a switch so that the light could be turned on and off.

The normal automotive circuit differs from this simple example in two ways. First, instead of having a return wire from the bulb to the battery, the current travels through the frame of the vehicle. Since the negative (-) battery cable is attached to the frame (made of electrically conductive metal), the frame of the vehicle can serve as a ground wire to complete the circuit. Secondly, most automotive circuits contain multiple components which receive power from a single circuit. This lessens the amount of wire needed to power components on the vehicle.

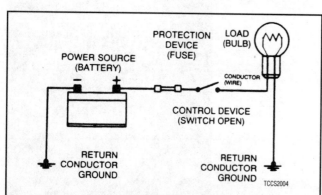

Fig. 1 This example illustrates a simple circuit. When the switch is closed, power from the positive (+) battery terminal flows through the fuse and the switch, and then to the light bulb. The light illuminates and the circuit is completed through the ground wire back to the negative (-) battery terminal. In reality, the two ground points shown in the illustration are attached to the metal frame of the vehicle, which completes the circuit back to the battery

HOW DOES ELECTRICITY WORK: THE WATER ANALOGY

Electricity is the flow of electrons—the subatomic particles that constitute the outer shell of an atom. Electrons spin in an orbit around the center core of an atom. The center core is comprised of protons (positive charge) and neutrons (neutral charge). Electrons have a negative charge and balance out the positive charge of the protons. When an outside force causes the number of electrons to unbalance the charge of the protons, the electrons will split off the atom and look for another atom to balance out. If this imbalance is kept up, electrons will continue to move and an electrical flow will exist.

Many people have been taught electrical theory using an analogy with water. In a comparison with water flowing through a pipe, the electrons would be the water and the wire is the pipe.

The flow of electricity can be measured much like the flow of water through a pipe. The unit of measurement used is amperes, frequently abbreviated as amps (a). You can compare amperage to the volume of water flowing through a pipe.

When connected to a circuit, an ammeter will measure the actual amount of current flowing through the circuit. When relatively few electrons flow through a circuit, the amperage is low. When many electrons flow, the amperage is high.

Water pressure is measured in units such as pounds per square inch (psi); The electrical pressure is measured in units called volts (v). When a voltmeter is connected to a circuit, it is measuring the electrical pressure.

The actual flow of electricity depends not only on voltage and amperage, but also on the resistance of the circuit. The higher the resistance, the higher the force necessary to push the current through the circuit. The standard unit for measuring resistance is an ohm. Resistance in a circuit varies depending on the amount and type of components used in the circuit. The main factors which determine resistance are:

- **Material**—some materials have more resistance than others. Those with high resistance are said to be insulators. Rubber materials (or rubber-like plastics) are some of the most common insulators used in vehicles as they have a very high resistance to electricity. Very low resistance materials are said to be conductors. Copper wire is among the best conductors. Silver is actually a superior conductor to copper and is used in some relay contacts, but its high cost prohibits its use as common wiring. Most automotive wiring is made of copper.
- **Size**—the larger the wire size being used, the less resistance the wire will have. This is why components which use large amounts of electricity usually have large wires supplying current to them.
- **Length**—for a given thickness of wire, the longer the wire, the greater the resistance. The shorter the wire, the less the resistance. When determining the proper wire for a circuit, both size and length must be considered to design a circuit that can handle the current needs of the component.
- **Temperature**—with many materials, the higher the temperature, the greater the resistance (positive temperature coefficient). Some materials exhibit the opposite trait of lower resistance with higher temperatures (negative temperature coefficient). These principles are used in many of the sensors on the engine.

OHM'S LAW

There is a direct relationship between current, voltage and resistance. The relationship between current, voltage and resistance can be summed up by a statement known as Ohm's law.

Voltage (E) is equal to amperage (I) times resistance (R): $E = I \times R$
Other forms of the formula are $R = E/I$ and $I = E/R$

In each of these formulas, E is the voltage in volts, I is the current in amps and R is the resistance in ohms. The basic point to remember is that as the resistance of a circuit goes up, the amount of current that flows in the circuit will go down, if voltage remains the same.

The amount of work that the electricity can perform is expressed as power. The unit of power is the watt (w). The relationship between power, voltage and current is expressed as:

Power (w) is equal to amperage (I) times voltage (E): $W = I \times E$

This is only true for direct current (DC) circuits; The alternating current formula is a tad different, but since the electrical circuits in most vehicles are DC type, we need not get into AC circuit theory.

Electrical Components

POWER SOURCE

Power is supplied to the vehicle by two devices: The battery and the alternator. The battery supplies electrical power during starting or during periods when the current demand of the vehicle's electrical system exceeds the output capacity of the alternator. The alternator supplies electrical current when the engine is running. Just not does the alternator supply the current needs of the vehicle, but it recharges the battery.

The Battery

In most modern vehicles, the battery is a lead/acid electrochemical device consisting of six 2 volt subsections (cells) connected in series, so that the unit is capable of producing approximately 12 volts of electrical pressure. Each sub-

CHASSIS ELECTRICAL 6-3

section consists of a series of positive and negative plates held a short distance apart in a solution of sulfuric acid and water.

The two types of plates are of dissimilar metals. This sets up a chemical reaction, and it is this reaction which produces current flow from the battery when its positive and negative terminals are connected to an electrical load. The power removed from the battery is replaced by the alternator, restoring the battery to its original chemical state.

The Alternator

On some vehicles there isn't an alternator, but a generator. The difference is that an alternator supplies alternating current which is then changed to direct current for use on the vehicle, while a generator produces direct current. Alternators tend to be more efficient and that is why they are used.

Alternators and generators are devices that consist of coils of wires wound together making big electromagnets. One group of coils spins within another set and the interaction of the magnetic fields causes a current to flow. This current is then drawn off the coils and fed into the vehicles electrical system.

GROUND

Two types of grounds are used in automotive electric circuits. Direct ground components are grounded to the frame through their mounting points. All other components use some sort of ground wire which is attached to the frame or chassis of the vehicle. The electrical current runs through the chassis of the vehicle and returns to the battery through the ground (-) cable; if you look, you'll see that the battery ground cable connects between the battery and the frame or chassis of the vehicle.

➡It should be noted that a good percentage of electrical problems can be traced to bad grounds.

PROTECTIVE DEVICES

♦ See Figure 2

It is possible for large surges of current to pass through the electrical system of your vehicle. If this surge of current were to reach the load in the circuit, the surge could burn it out or severely damage it. It can also overload the wiring, causing the harness to get hot and melt the insulation. To prevent this, fuses, circuit breakers and/or fusible links are connected into the supply wires of the electrical system. These items are nothing more than a built-in weak spot in the system. When an abnormal amount of current flows through the system, these protective devices work as follows to protect the circuit:

- Fuse—when an excessive electrical current passes through a fuse, the fuse "blows" (the conductor melts) and opens the circuit, preventing the passage of current.

- Circuit Breaker—a circuit breaker is basically a self-repairing fuse. It will open the circuit in the same fashion as a fuse, but when the surge subsides, the circuit breaker can be reset and does not need replacement.
- Fusible Link—a fusible link (fuse link or main link) is a short length of special, high temperature insulated wire that acts as a fuse. When an excessive electrical current passes through a fusible link, the thin gauge wire inside the link melts, creating an intentional open to protect the circuit. To repair the circuit, the link must be replaced. Some newer type fusible links are housed in plug-in modules, which are simply replaced like a fuse, while older type fusible links must be cut and spliced if they melt. Since this link is very early in the electrical path, it's the first place to look if nothing on the vehicle works, yet the battery seems to be charged and is properly connected.

✳✳ CAUTION

Always replace fuses, circuit breakers and fusible links with identically rated components. Under no circumstances should a component of higher or lower amperage rating be substituted.

SWITCHES & RELAYS

♦ See Figures 3 and 4

Switches are used in electrical circuits to control the passage of current. The most common use is to open and close circuits between the battery and the various electric devices in the system. Switches are rated according to the amount of amperage they can handle. If a sufficient amperage rated switch is not used in a circuit, the switch could overload and cause damage.

Some electrical components which require a large amount of current to operate use a special switch called a relay. Since these circuits carry a large amount of current, the thickness of the wire in the circuit is also greater. If this large wire were connected from the load to the control switch, the switch would have to carry the high amperage load and the fairing or dash would be twice as large to accommodate the increased size of the wiring harness. To prevent these problems, a relay is used.

Relays are composed of a coil and a set of contacts. When the coil has a current passed though it, a magnetic field is formed and this field causes the contacts to move together, completing the circuit. Most relays are normally open, preventing current from passing through the circuit, but they can take any electrical form depending on the job they are intended to do. Relays can be considered "remote control switches." They allow a smaller current to operate devices that require higher amperages. When a small current operates the coil, a larger current is allowed to pass by the contacts. Some common circuits which may use relays are the horn, headlights, starter, electric fuel pump and other high draw ciruits.

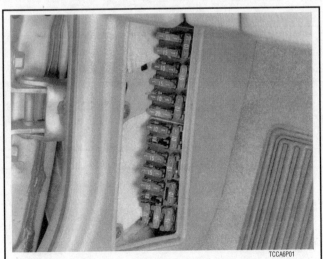

Fig. 2 Most vehicles use one or more fuse panels. This one is located on the driver's side kick panel

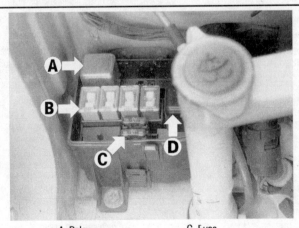

A. Relay
B. Fusible link
C. Fuse
D. Flasher

Fig. 3 The underhood fuse and relay panel usually contains fuses, relays, flashers and fusible links

6-4 CHASSIS ELECTRICAL

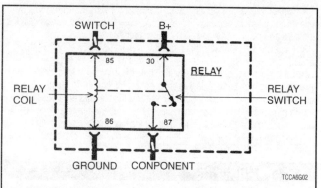

Fig. 4 Relays are composed of a coil and a switch. These two components are linked together so that when one operates, the other operates at the same time. The large wires in the circuit are connected from the battery to one side of the relay switch (B+) and from the opposite side of the relay switch to the load (component). Smaller wires are connected from the relay coil to the control switch for the circuit and from the opposite side of the relay coil to ground

LOAD

Every electrical circuit must include a "load" (something to use the electricity coming from the source). Without this load, the battery would attempt to deliver its entire power supply from one pole to another. This is called a "short circuit." All this electricity would take a short cut to ground and cause a great amount of damage to other components in the circuit by developing a tremendous amount of heat. This condition could develop sufficient heat to melt the insulation on all the surrounding wires and reduce a multiple wire cable to a lump of plastic and copper.

WIRING & HARNESSES

The average vehicle contains meters and meters of wiring, with hundreds of individual connections. To protect the many wires from damage and to keep them from becoming a confusing tangle, they are organized into bundles, enclosed in plastic or taped together and called wiring harnesses. Different harnesses serve different parts of the vehicle. Individual wires are color coded to help trace them through a harness where sections are hidden from view.

Automotive wiring or circuit conductors can be either single strand wire, multi-strand wire or printed circuitry. Single strand wire has a solid metal core and is usually used inside such components as alternators, motors, relays and other devices. Multi-strand wire has a core made of many small strands of wire twisted together into a single conductor. Most of the wiring in an automotive electrical system is made up of multi-strand wire, either as a single conductor or grouped together in a harness. All wiring is color coded on the insulator, either as a solid color or as a colored wire with an identification stripe. A printed circuit is a thin film of copper or other conductor that is printed on an insulator backing. Occasionally, a printed circuit is sandwiched between two sheets of plastic for more protection and flexibility. A complete printed circuit, consisting of conductors, insulating material and connectors for lamps or other components is called a printed circuit board. Printed circuitry is used in place of individual wires or harnesses in places where space is limited, such as behind instrument panels.

Since automotive electrical systems are very sensitive to changes in resistance, the selection of properly sized wires is critical when systems are repaired. A loose or corroded connection or a replacement wire that is too small for the circuit will add extra resistance and an additional voltage drop to the circuit.

The wire gauge number is an expression of the cross-section area of the conductor. Vehicles from countries that use the metric system will typically describe the wire size as its cross-sectional area in square millimeters. In this method, the larger the wire, the greater the number. Another common system for expressing wire size is the American Wire Gauge (AWG) system. As gauge number increases, area decreases and the wire becomes smaller. An 18 gauge wire is smaller than a 4 gauge wire. A wire with a higher gauge number will carry less current than a wire with a lower gauge number. Gauge wire size refers to the size of the strands of the conductor, not the size of the complete wire with insulator. It is possible, therefore, to have two wires of the same gauge with different diameters because one may have thicker insulation than the other.

It is essential to understand how a circuit works before trying to figure out why it doesn't. An electrical schematic shows the electrical current paths when a circuit is operating properly. Schematics break the entire electrical system down into individual circuits. In a schematic, usually no attempt is made to represent wiring and components as they physically appear on the vehicle; switches and other components are shown as simply as possible. Face views of harness connectors show the cavity or terminal locations in all multi-pin connectors to help locate test points.

CONNECTORS

▶ See Figures 5 and 6

Three types of connectors are commonly used in automotive applications—weatherproof, molded and hard shell.

• Weatherproof—these connectors are most commonly used where the connector is exposed to the elements. Terminals are protected against moisture and dirt by sealing rings which provide a weathertight seal. All repairs require the use of a special terminal and the tool required to service it. Unlike standard blade type terminals, these weatherproof terminals cannot be straightened once they are bent. Make certain that the connectors are properly seated and all of the sealing rings are in place when connecting leads.

• Molded—these connectors require complete replacement of the connector if found to be defective. This means splicing a new connector assembly into the harness. All splices should be soldered to insure proper contact. Use care when probing the connections or replacing terminals in them, as it is possible to create a short circuit between opposite terminals. If this happens to the wrong terminal pair, it is possible to damage certain components. Always use jumper

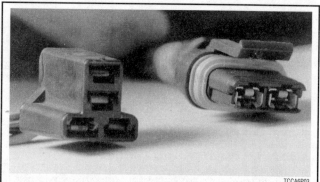

Fig. 5 Hard shell (left) and weatherproof (right) connectors have replaceable terminals

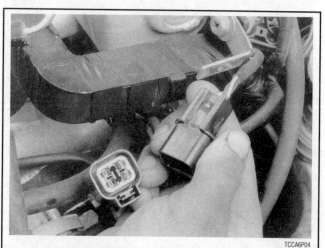

Fig. 6 Weatherproof connectors are most commonly used in the engine compartment or where the connector is exposed to the elements

CHASSIS ELECTRICAL 6-5

wires between connectors for circuit checking and NEVER probe through weatherproof seals.

- Hard Shell—unlike molded connectors, the terminal contacts in hard-shell connectors can be replaced. Replacement usually involves the use of a special terminal removal tool that depresses the locking tangs (barbs) on the connector terminal and allows the connector to be removed from the rear of the shell. The connector shell should be replaced if it shows any evidence of burning, melting, cracks, or breaks. Replace individual terminals that are burnt, corroded, distorted or loose.

Test Equipment

Pinpointing the exact cause of trouble in an electrical circuit is most times accomplished by the use of special test equipment. The following describes different types of commonly used test equipment and briefly explains how to use them in diagnosis. In addition to the information covered below, the tool manufacturer's instructions booklet (provided with the tester) should be read and clearly understood before attempting any test procedures.

JUMPER WIRES

> **※※ CAUTION**
>
> **Never use jumper wires made from a thinner gauge wire than the circuit being tested. If the jumper wire is of too small a gauge, it may overheat and possibly melt. Never use jumpers to bypass high resistance loads in a circuit. Bypassing resistances, in effect, creates a short circuit. This may, in turn, cause damage and fire. Jumper wires should only be used to bypass lengths of wire or to simulate switches.**

Jumper wires are simple, yet extremely valuable, pieces of test equipment. They are basically test wires which are used to bypass sections of a circuit. Although jumper wires can be purchased, they are usually fabricated from lengths of standard automotive wire and whatever type of connector (alligator clip, spade connector or pin connector) that is required for the particular application being tested. In cramped, hard-to-reach areas, it is advisable to have insulated boots over the jumper wire terminals in order to prevent accidental grounding. It is also advisable to include a standard automotive fuse in any jumper wire. This is commonly referred to as a "fused jumper". By inserting an in-line fuse holder between a set of test leads, a fused jumper wire can be used for bypassing open circuits. Use a 5 amp fuse to provide protection against voltage spikes.

Jumper wires are used primarily to locate open electrical circuits, on either the ground (-) side of the circuit or on the power (+) side. If an electrical component fails to operate, connect the jumper wire between the component and a good ground. If the component operates only with the jumper installed, the ground circuit is open. If the ground circuit is good, but the component does not operate, the circuit between the power feed and component may be open. By moving the jumper wire successively back from the component toward the power source, you can isolate the area of the circuit where the open is located. When the component stops functioning, or the power is cut off, the open is in the segment of wire between the jumper and the point previously tested.

You can sometimes connect the jumper wire directly from the battery to the "hot" terminal of the component, but first make sure the component uses 12 volts in operation. Some electrical components, such as fuel injectors or sensors, are designed to operate on about 4 to 5 volts, and running 12 volts directly to these components will cause damage.

TEST LIGHTS

▶ See Figure 7

The test light is used to check circuits and components while electrical current is flowing through them. It is used for voltage and ground tests. To use a 12 volt test light, connect the ground clip to a good ground and probe wherever necessary with the pick. The test light will illuminate when voltage is detected. This does not necessarily mean that 12 volts (or any particular amount of voltage) is present; it only means that some voltage is present. It is advisable before using the test light to touch its ground clip and probe across the battery posts or terminals to make sure the light is operating properly.

> **※※ WARNING**
>
> **Do not use a test light to probe electronic ignition, spark plug or coil wires. Never use a pick-type test light to probe wiring on computer controlled systems unless specifically instructed to do so. Any wire insulation that is pierced by the test light probe should be taped and sealed with silicone after testing.**

Like the jumper wire, the 12 volt test light is used to isolate opens in circuits. But, whereas the jumper wire is used to bypass the open to operate the load, the 12 volt test light is used to locate the presence of voltage in a circuit. If the test light illuminates, there is power up to that point in the circuit; if the test light does not illuminate, there is an open circuit (no power). Move the test light in successive steps back toward the power source until the light in the handle illuminates. The open is between the probe and a point which was previously probed.

The self-powered test light is similar in design to the 12 volt test light, but contains a 1.5 volt penlight battery in the handle. It is most often used in place of a multimeter to check for open or short circuits when power is isolated from the circuit (continuity test).

The battery in a self-powered test light does not provide much current. A weak battery may not provide enough power to illuminate the test light even when a complete circuit is made (especially if there is high resistance in the circuit). Always make sure that the test battery is strong. To check the battery, briefly touch the ground clip to the probe; if the light glows brightly, the battery is strong enough for testing.

➡ **A self-powered test light should not be used on any computer controlled system or component. The small amount of electricity transmitted by the test light is enough to damage many electronic automotive components.**

MULTIMETERS

Multimeters are an extremely useful tool for troubleshooting electrical problems. They can be purchased in either analog or digital form and have a price range to suit any budget. A multimeter is a voltmeter, ammeter and ohmmeter (along with other features) combined into one instrument. It is often used when testing solid state circuits because of its high input impedance (usually 10 megaohms or more). A brief description of the multimeter main test functions follows:

- Voltmeter—the voltmeter is used to measure voltage at any point in a circuit, or to measure the voltage drop across any part of a circuit. Voltmeters usually have various scales and a selector switch to allow the reading of different voltage ranges. The voltmeter has a positive and a negative lead. To avoid damage to the meter, always connect the negative lead to the negative (-) side of the circuit (to ground or nearest the ground side of the circuit) and connect the positive lead to the positive (+) side of the circuit (to the power source or the nearest power source). Note that the negative voltmeter lead will always be black and that the positive voltmeter will always be some color other than black (usually red).

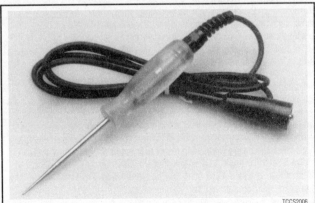

Fig. 7 A 12 volt test light is used to detect the presence of voltage in a circuit

- Ohmmeter—the ohmmeter is designed to read resistance (measured in ohms) in a circuit or component. Most ohmmeters will have a selector switch which permits the measurement of different ranges of resistance (usually the selector switch allows the multiplication of the meter reading by 10, 100, 1,000 and 10,000). Some ohmmeters are "auto-ranging" which means the meter itself will determine which scale to use. Since the meters are powered by an internal battery, the ohmmeter can be used like a self-powered test light. When the ohmmeter is connected, current from the ohmmeter flows through the circuit or component being tested. Since the ohmmeter's internal resistance and voltage are known values, the amount of current flow through the meter depends on the resistance of the circuit or component being tested. The ohmmeter can also be used to perform a continuity test for suspected open circuits. In using the meter for making continuity checks, do not be concerned with the actual resistance readings. Zero resistance, or any ohm reading, indicates continuity in the circuit. Infinite resistance indicates an opening in the circuit. A high resistance reading where there should be none indicates a problem in the circuit. Checks for short circuits are made in the same manner as checks for open circuits, except that the circuit must be isolated from both power and normal ground. Infinite resistance indicates no continuity, while zero resistance indicates a dead short.

✶✶ WARNING

Never use an ohmmeter to check the resistance of a component or wire while there is voltage applied to the circuit.

- Ammeter—an ammeter measures the amount of current flowing through a circuit in units called amperes or amps. At normal operating voltage, most circuits have a characteristic amount of amperes, called "current draw" which can be measured using an ammeter. By referring to a specified current draw rating, then measuring the amperes and comparing the two values, one can determine what is happening within the circuit to aid in diagnosis. An open circuit, for example, will not allow any current to flow, so the ammeter reading will be zero. A damaged component or circuit will have an increased current draw, so the reading will be high. The ammeter is always connected in series with the circuit being tested. All of the current that normally flows through the circuit must also flow through the ammeter; if there is any other path for the current to follow, the ammeter reading will not be accurate. The ammeter itself has very little resistance to current flow and, therefore, will not affect the circuit, but it will measure current draw only when the circuit is closed and electricity is flowing. Excessive current draw can blow fuses and drain the battery, while a reduced current draw can cause motors to run slowly, lights to dim and other components to not operate properly.

Troubleshooting Electrical Systems

When diagnosing a specific problem, organized troubleshooting is a must. The complexity of a modern automotive vehicle demands that you approach any problem in a logical, organized manner. There are certain troubleshooting techniques, however, which are standard:

- Establish when the problem occurs. Does the problem appear only under certain conditions? Were there any noises, odors or other unusual symptoms? Isolate the problem area. To do this, make some simple tests and observations, then eliminate the systems that are working properly. Check for obvious problems, such as broken wires and loose or dirty connections. Always check the obvious before assuming something complicated is the cause.
- Test for problems systematically to determine the cause once the problem area is isolated. Are all the components functioning properly? Is there power going to electrical switches and motors. Performing careful, systematic checks will often turn up most causes on the first inspection, without wasting time checking components that have little or no relationship to the problem.
- Test all repairs after the work is done to make sure that the problem is fixed. Some causes can be traced to more than one component, so a careful verification of repair work is important in order to pick up additional malfunctions that may cause a problem to reappear or a different problem to arise. A blown fuse, for example, is a simple problem that may require more than another fuse to repair. If you don't look for a problem that caused a fuse to blow, a shorted wire (for example) may go undetected.

Experience has shown that most problems tend to be the result of a fairly simple and obvious cause, such as loose or corroded connectors, bad grounds or damaged wire insulation which causes a short. This makes careful visual inspection of components during testing essential to quick and accurate troubleshooting.

Testing

OPEN CIRCUITS

♦ See Figure 8

This test already assumes the existence of an open in the circuit and it is used to help locate the open portion.

1. Isolate the circuit from power and ground.
2. Connect the self-powered test light or ohmmeter ground clip to the ground side of the circuit and probe sections of the circuit sequentially.
3. If the light is out or there is infinite resistance, the open is between the probe and the circuit ground.
4. If the light is on or the meter shows continuity, the open is between the probe and the end of the circuit toward the power source.

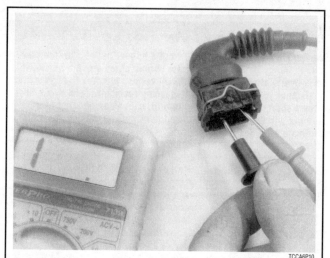

Fig. 8 The infinite reading on this multimeter indicates that the circuit is open

SHORT CIRCUITS

➡ **Never use a self-powered test light to perform checks for opens or shorts when power is applied to the circuit under test. The test light can be damaged by outside power.**

1. Isolate the circuit from power and ground.
2. Connect the self-powered test light or ohmmeter ground clip to a good ground and probe any easy-to-reach point in the circuit.
3. If the light comes on or there is continuity, there is a short somewhere in the circuit.
4. To isolate the short, probe a test point at either end of the isolated circuit (the light should be on or the meter should indicate continuity).
5. Leave the test light probe engaged and sequentially open connectors or switches, remove parts, etc. until the light goes out or continuity is broken.
6. When the light goes out, the short is between the last two circuit components which were opened.

VOLTAGE

This test determines voltage available from the battery and should be the first step in any electrical troubleshooting procedure after visual inspection. Many electrical problems, especially on computer controlled systems, can be caused by a low state of charge in the battery. Excessive corrosion at the battery cable terminals can cause poor contact that will prevent proper charging and full battery current flow.

CHASSIS ELECTRICAL 6-7

1. Set the voltmeter selector switch to the 20V position.
2. Connect the multimeter negative lead to the battery's negative (-) post or terminal and the positive lead to the battery's positive (+) post or terminal.
3. Turn the ignition switch **ON** to provide a load.
4. A well charged battery should register over 12 volts. If the meter reads below 11.5 volts, the battery power may be insufficient to operate the electrical system properly.

VOLTAGE DROP

♦ See Figure 9

When current flows through a load, the voltage beyond the load drops. This voltage drop is due to the resistance created by the load and also by small resistances created by corrosion at the connectors and damaged insulation on the wires. The maximum allowable voltage drop under load is critical, especially if there is more than one load in the circuit, since all voltage drops are cumulative.

1. Set the voltmeter selector switch to the 20 volt position.
2. Connect the multimeter negative lead to a good ground.
3. Operate the circuit and check the voltage prior to the first component (load).
4. There should be little or no voltage drop in the circuit prior to the first component. If a voltage drop exists, the wire or connectors in the circuit are suspect.
5. While operating the first component in the circuit, probe the ground side of the component with the positive meter lead and observe the voltage readings. A small voltage drop should be noticed. This voltage drop is caused by the resistance of the component.
6. Repeat the test for each component (load) down the circuit.
7. If a large voltage drop is noticed, the preceding component, wire or connector is suspect.

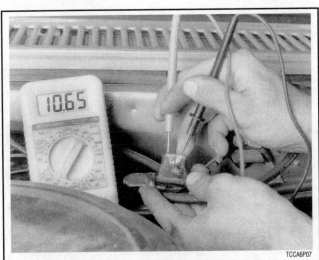

Fig. 9 This voltage drop test revealed high resistance (low voltage) in the circuit

RESISTANCE

♦ See Figures 10 and 11

*** WARNING

Never use an ohmmeter with power applied to the circuit. The ohmmeter is designed to operate on its own power supply. The normal 12 volt electrical system voltage could damage the meter!

1. Isolate the circuit from the vehicle's power source.
2. Ensure that the ignition key is **OFF** when disconnecting any components or the battery.
3. Where necessary, also isolate at least one side of the circuit to be checked, in order to avoid reading parallel resistances. Parallel circuit resistances will always give a lower reading than the actual resistance of either of the branches.

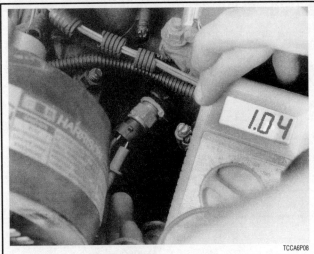

Fig. 10 Checking the resistance of a coolant temperature sensor with an ohmmeter. Reading is 1.04 kilohms

4. Connect the meter leads to both sides of the circuit (wire or component) and read the actual measured ohms on the meter scale. Make sure the selector switch is set to the proper ohm scale for the circuit being tested, to avoid misreading the ohmmeter test value.

Wire and Connector Repair

Almost anyone can replace damaged wires, as long as the proper tools and parts are available. Wire and terminals are available to fit almost any need. Even the specialized weatherproof, molded and hard shell connectors are now available from aftermarket suppliers.

Be sure the ends of all the wires are fitted with the proper terminal hardware and connectors. Wrapping a wire around a stud is never a permanent solution and will only cause trouble later. Replace wires one at a time to avoid confusion. Always route wires exactly the same as the factory.

➥**If connector repair is necessary, only attempt it if you have the proper tools. Weatherproof and hard shell connectors require special tools to release the pins inside the connector. Attempting to repair these connectors with conventional hand tools will damage them.**

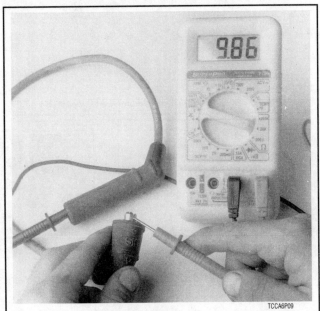

Fig. 11 Spark plug wires can be checked for excessive resistance using an ohmmeter

CHASSIS ELECTRICAL

HEATING AND AIR CONDITIONING

Please refer to Section 1 for all discharging, evacuating and charging procedures for the air conditioning system.

Heater Assembly

REMOVAL & INSTALLATION

♦ See Figures 12 thru 21

1970–79

1. Disconnect the negative battery cable.
2. Drain the engine coolant.

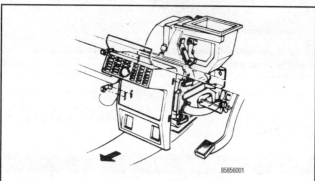

Fig. 12 Removing the heater assembly front cover on 1970–79 models

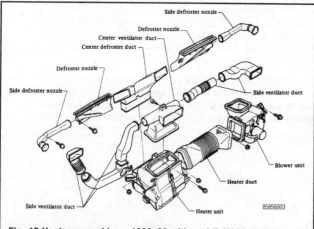

Fig. 13 Heater assembly — 1980–86 without A/C (720D series)

3. Remove the defroster hoses.
4. Remove the three cable retaining clips and disconnect the control cables from the valves and water cock.
5. Disconnect the two fan motor leads from each connector.
6. Disconnect the two resistor lead wires from each connector.
7. Disconnect the water hoses from the heater core and water cock.
8. Remove the three heater housing mounting bolts and remove the heater assembly from the vehicle.

To install:

9. Install the heater assembly and tighten the mounting screws.
10. Connect the heater hoses at the core. Connect the two resistor wires and the fan motor leads.
11. Connect the control cables to the valves and water cock.
12. Fill the engine with coolant, connect the battery cable and start the engine. Check for any leaks.

1980–88 All Series

1. Disconnect the negative battery cable.
2. Drain the cooling system.
3. On models with air conditioning, disconnect the heater hose from the engine.
4. On models without air conditioning, remove the heater duct and disconnect the heater hose at the heater.
5. Remove the console box and instrument panel assembly.
6. Disconnect the air intake control cable from the blower motor.
7. On models equipped with A/C, remove the blower. Remove the evaporator unit nuts and bolts, but do not remove the evaporator unit.
8. Remove the heater assembly.

To install:

9. Installation the heater assembly and tighten the mounting screws.
10. Install the blower on A/C models and connect the air intake control cable.
11. Install the instrument panel and the console box.
12. Install the heater duct.
13. Connect the heater hoses and fill the engine with coolant. Adjust the control cable for proper operation. Start the engine and check for any leaks.

Heater Core

REMOVAL & INSTALLATION

♦ See Figures 22, 23, 24 and 25

1970–79

1. Drain the engine coolant.
2. Remove the defroster hoses.
3. Disconnect the water hoses from the inlet and outlet pipes of the heater core.

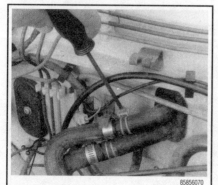

Fig. 14 Removing the heater hoses from the heater assembly

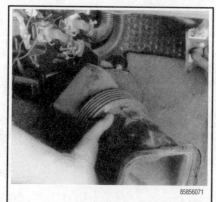

Fig. 15 Removing the side ventilator duct

Fig. 16 Removing the heater cock cover

CHASSIS ELECTRICAL 6-9

Fig. 17 Removing the heater cock retaining screw

Fig. 18 Removing the necessary brackets

Fig. 19 Removing the underdash panel

Fig. 20 Removing the heater control cable clip

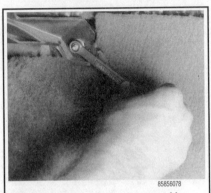
Fig. 21 Removing the heater assembly holddown bolts

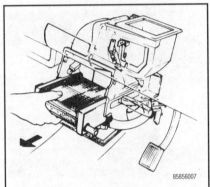
Fig. 22 Removing the heater core — 1970–79

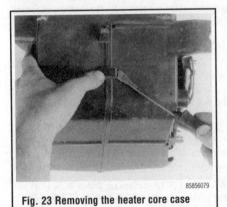
Fig. 23 Removing the heater core case clips

Fig. 24 Removing the heater core from the case

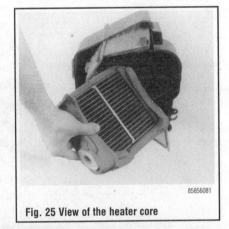
Fig. 25 View of the heater core

4. Remove the four clips and front cover.
5. Remove the heater core from the heater housing.

To install:

6. Install the heater core in the housing and press in the clips.
7. Connect the heater hoses and the defroster ducts.
8. Fill the engine with coolant, start the engine and check for any leaks.

1980–88 All Series

1. Remove the heater assembly.
2. Remove the screws and clips and separate the heater case halves.

To install:

3. Slide out the heater core.
4. Install the heater core in the heater case and close the two halves. Install the clips.
5. Install the heater assembly.

Blower Motor

REMOVAL & INSTALLATION

♦ See Figures 26 thru 32

1970–79

1. Disconnect the negative battery cable. Remove the heater assembly from the vehicle.
2. Remove the nine spring clips and disassemble the heater housing.
3. Remove the fan from the electric motor.

To install:

4. Remove the fan motor retaining screws and remove the motor.
5. Install the blower motor into the heater assembly and then install the heater assembly.

6-10 CHASSIS ELECTRICAL

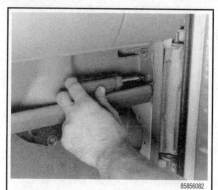
Fig. 26 Removing the underdash panel screws

Fig. 27 Removing the underdash panel

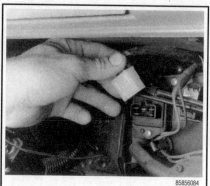
Fig. 28 Removing the necessary electrical connections

Fig. 29 Removing the inline electrical connection, if necessary

Fig. 30 Removing the blower motor hose

Fig. 31 Removing the blower motor retaining screws

Fig. 32 Removing the blower motor assembly

1980–88 720D, D21D Series

1. Disconnect the negative battery cable.
2. Remove the package tray.
3. Remove the heater duct on models without air conditioning.
4. Remove the resistor connector and disconnect the control cable.
5. Remove the blower.

To install:

6. Install the blower motor and connect the control cable and resistor.
7. Install the heater ducts and the package tray.
8. Connect the battery cable. Adjust the control cable for proper operation.

Air Conditioning Components

REMOVAL & INSTALLATION

Repair or service of air conditioning components is not covered by this manual, because of the risk of personal injury or death, and because of the legal ramifications of servicing these components without the proper EPA certification and experience. Cost, personal injury or death, environmental damage, and legal considerations (such as the fact that it is a federal crime to vent refrigerant into the atmosphere), dictate that the A/C components on your vehicle should be serviced only by a Motor Vehicle Air Conditioning (MVAC) trained, and EPA certified automotive technician.

➡If your vehicle's A/C system uses R-12 refrigerant and is in need of recharging, the A/C system can be converted over to R-134a refrigerant (less environmentally harmful and expensive). Refer to Section 1 for additional information on R-12 to R-134a conversions, and for additional considerations dealing with your vehicle's A/C system.

Control Head

REMOVAL & INSTALLATION

1970–88 All Series

1. Disconnect the negative battery cable.
2. Remove the package tray.
3. Tag and disconnect all control cables at the heater assembly and blower motor.
4. Remove the control knob(s) and slide the panel out through the front of the instrument panel.
5. Installation is the reverse of the removal procedure. Check operation of system.

CHASSIS ELECTRICAL   6-11

ADJUSTMENT

1970–86 720D Series

♦ See Figures 33, 34 and 35

AIR INTAKE DOOR

1. Set the air intake lever in the **RECIRC** position.
2. Clamp the cable while at the same time pushing the sheathing and the door lever in the direction as shown.

AIR MIX DOOR/WATER COCK

1. Set the temperature control lever in the **COLD** position.
2. Pull the control cable sheathing in the direction shown in the illustration until the clearance between the ends of the rod and water cock lever is approximately 0.08 in. (2mm).
3. Clamp the cable in position.

1986–88 D21D Series

♦ See Figures 36 thru 41

VENTILATOR DOOR CONTROL ROD

1. Move the side link as shown in the illustration.
2. Hold the upper and lower doors as shown and then connect the rods to their respective doors.

DEFROSTER DOOR CONTROL ROD

1. Move the side link as shown in the illustration.
2. Connect the rod to the side link to the rod while pushing the door lever as shown.

AIR CONTROL CABLE

Push the cable sheathing and side link in the direction illustrated and tighten the clamp.

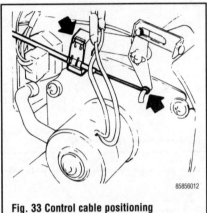
Fig. 33 Control cable positioning

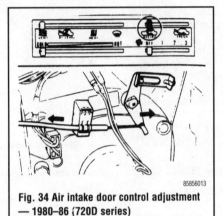
Fig. 34 Air intake door control adjustment — 1980–86 (720D series)

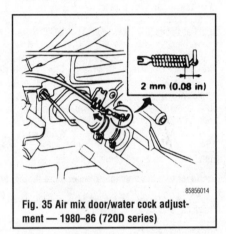
Fig. 35 Air mix door/water cock adjustment — 1980–86 (720D series)

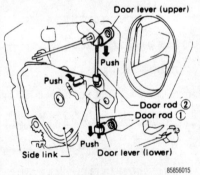
Fig. 36 Ventilation door control rod adjustment — 1986–88 (D21D series)

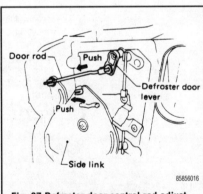
Fig. 37 Defroster door control rod adjustment — 1986–88 (D21D series)

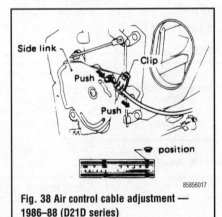
Fig. 38 Air control cable adjustment — 1986–88 (D21D series)

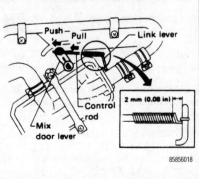
Fig. 39 Water cock control rod adjustment — 1986–88 (D21D series)

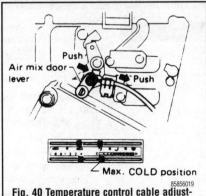
Fig. 40 Temperature control cable adjustment — 1986–88 (D21D series)

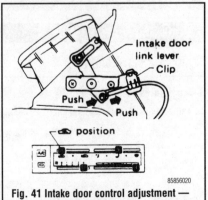
Fig. 41 Intake door control adjustment — 1986–88 (D21D series)

6-12 CHASSIS ELECTRICAL

WATER COCK CONTROL ROD

➡ When adjusting the control rod, disconnect the temperature control cable at the air mix door lever and then adjust air mix door control cable and then the control rod. Reconnect the temperature control cable and then readjust it.

1. Push the air mix door lever in the direction shown in the illustration.
2. Pull the control rod in the direction shown until there is an 0.08 in. (2mm) clearance between the ends of the rod and link lever. Connect the rod to the door lever.

TEMPERATURE CONTROL CABLE

Push the cable sheathing and the air mix door lever in the direction shown and then tighten the clamp.

INTAKE DOOR CABLE

Push the cable sheathing and the intake door lever in the direction shown and then tighten the clamp.

RADIO

ADJUSTMENTS

Observe the following cautions when working on the radio:
1. Always observe the proper polarity of the connections (positive to positive and negative to negative).
2. Never operate the radio without a speaker, to prevent damage to the output transistors. If a new speaker is installed, make sure it has the correct impedance (ohms) for the radio.

If a new antenna or antenna cable is used, or if poor AM reception is noted, the antenna trimmer can be adjusted. Turn the radio to a weak station around 1400 kHz. Adjust the trimmer screw until best reception and maximum volume are obtained. The trimmer screw for the factory installed radio is located on the bottom in the left rear corner on 1970–71 models, in the lower left corner of the rear of the radio case 1972–78, above the left knob on the front of the radio in 1979, above the right station pre-set button on 1980–86 720D series models, and on 1986–88 D21D series models, either above the left station pre-set button or in the lower left corner of the facia.

➡ Never turn the antenna trimmer more than ½ turn on 1980–88 models.

For best FM reception, raise the antenna to 31 in. For best AM reception, raise the antenna to its full height.

REMOVAL & INSTALLATION

♦ See Figure 42

1970–79

1. Disconnect the negative battery cable. Carefully pull the knobs off the radio control shafts.
2. Remove the radio retaining nuts and washer from the radio control shafts.
3. Remove the bezel plate from the front of the radio.
4. Disconnect the antenna cable and the power and speaker wires from under the instrument panel.
5. Remove the radio from the instrument panel.

To install:

6. Install the radio in the instrument panel.
7. Connect the speaker and power leads, plug the antenna in and then position the bezel.

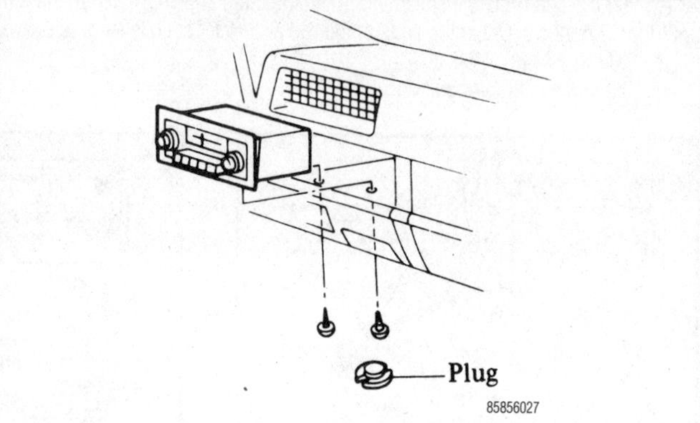

Fig. 42 Removing the radio — 1980–86 (720D series)

8. Slide the washers over the control shafts and then tighten the retaining nuts.
9. Press the knobs back onto the control shafts.

1980–88 All Series

1. Disconnect the negative battery cable.
2. Remove the ash tray and heater/air conditioner control panel.
3. Disconnect the wiring plug at the back of the radio.
4. Remove the plug covering the mounting screws, remove the screws and pull the radio from the dash.
5. Disconnect the wiring harness and the antenna.

To install:

6. Reconnect the wiring harness into the rear of the radio and then slide the radio into the instrument panel.
7. Install and tighten the radio mounting screws and then press the plug into position.
8. Reach through the control head opening and connect the antenna and any electrical leads.
9. Install the control head and connect the battery cable. Adjust the heater control head if necessary.

WINDSHIELD WIPERS

Blade and Arm

REMOVAL & INSTALLATION

♦ See Figures 43, 44, 45 and 46

➡ Wiper blade element replacement is covered in Section 1.

1. To remove the wiper blades, lift up on the spring release tab on the wiper blade–to–wiper arm connector.
2. Pull the blade assembly off the wiper arm.
3. There are two types of replacements:
   a. Replace the entire wiper blade as an assembly. Simply snap the replacement into place on the arm.
   b. Press the old wiper blade insert down, away from the blade assembly, to free it from the retaining clips on the blade ends. Slide the insert out of the blade. Slide the new insert into the blade assembly and bend the insert upward slightly to engage the retaining clips.
4. To replace a wiper arm, unscrew the acorn nut which secures it to the pivot and carefully pull the arm upward and off the pivot.

➡ Some models may be equipped with a cover over the acorn nut. To expose the nut, lift the wiper arm and the cover at the same time; this will afford access to the nut.

5. The wiper arms should be installed so that the blades are 0.98 in. (25mm) above, and parallel to, the windshield molding. If the motor has been run, be sure the motor and linkage is in its parked position before installing the wiper arms. To do this, turn the ignition switch **ON**, and cycle the motor three or four times. Shut off the motor with the wiper switch (not the ignition switch), and allow the motor to return to the park position.

CHASSIS ELECTRICAL 6-13

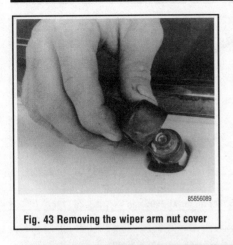
Fig. 43 Removing the wiper arm nut cover

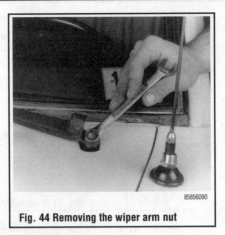
Fig. 44 Removing the wiper arm nut

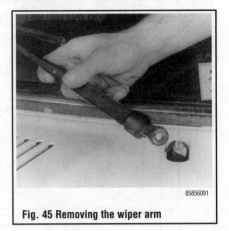
Fig. 45 Removing the wiper arm

Fig. 46 Removing the windshield washer hose

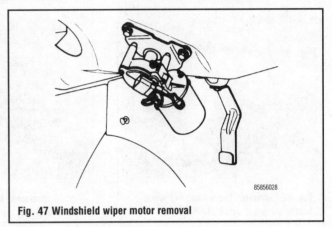
Fig. 47 Windshield wiper motor removal

Windshield Wiper Motor

REMOVAL & INSTALLATION

♦ See Figures 47 thru 56

1. Remove the wiper blades and arms as an assembly from the pivots. The arms are retained to the pivots by nuts. Remove the nuts and pull the arms straight off.
2. Remove the cowl top grille. It is retained by four screws at its front edge. Remove the screws and pull the grille forward to disengage the tabs at the rear.
3. Remove the stop ring which connects the wiper motor arm to the connecting rod.
4. Disconnect the wiper motor harness at the connector on the wiper motor body from under the instrument panel.
5. Remove the three retaining screws and pull the wiper motor outward and remove the motor from the vehicle.

To install:

6. Install the wiper motor and connect the harness.
7. Connect the linkage to the motor arm and then install the cowling.
8. The wiper arms should be installed so that the blades are 0.98 in. (25mm) above, and parallel to, the windshield molding. If the motor has been run, be sure the motor and linkage is in its parked position before installing the wiper arms. To do this, turn the ignition switch **ON**, and cycle the motor three or four times. Shut off the motor with the wiper switch (not the ignition switch), and allow the motor to return to the park position.

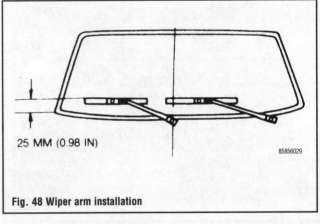
Fig. 48 Wiper arm installation

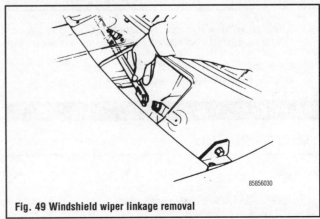
Fig. 49 Windshield wiper linkage removal

Wiper Linkage

REMOVAL & INSTALLATION

1. Remove the wiper blade and arm from the pivot. See the preceding section.
2. Remove the cowl top grille.

CHASSIS ELECTRICAL

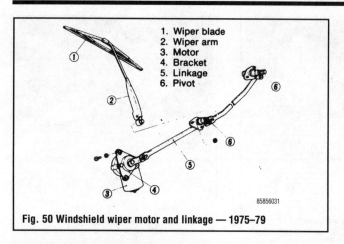

Fig. 50 Windshield wiper motor and linkage — 1975–79

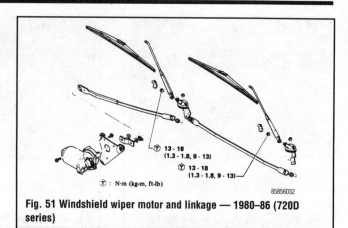

Fig. 51 Windshield wiper motor and linkage — 1980–86 (720D series)

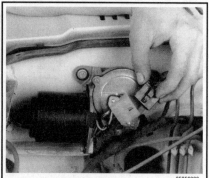

Fig. 52 Removing the windshield wiper motor electrical connection

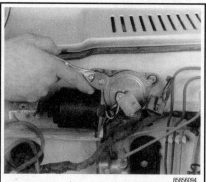

Fig. 53 Removing the windshield wiper motor retaining bolts

Fig. 54 Removing the windshield wiper motor with linkage still attached

Fig. 55 Removing the windshield wiper motor linkage nut

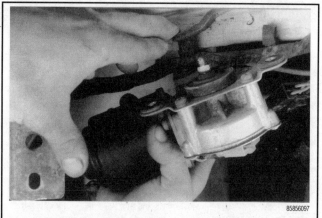

Fig. 56 View of the windshield wiper motor and linkage

3. Remove the two flange nuts retaining the wiper linkage pivot to the cowl top.
4. Remove the stop ring which retains the connecting rod to the wiper motor arm.
5. Remove the wiper motor linkage assembly from the truck.
6. Install the linkage in the reverse order of removal.

Rear Wiper

REMOVAL & INSTALLATION

Pathfinder

1. Disconnect the negative battery cable.
2. Pop up the acorn nut cover, remove the nut and pull off the rear wiper.

3. Remove the pivot nut.
4. Inside, pop out the 4 clips and remove the wiper motor cover.
5. Disconnect the electrical lead and the washer hose, remove the mounting bolts and lift out the wiper motor.

To install:

6. Position the wiper motor and install the mounting bolts.
7. Connect the lead and the washer hose.
8. Position the wiper motor cover over the opening and press in the retaining clips.
9. Install the pivot nut.
10. Install the wiper arm and tighten the acorn nut. Connect the battery cable.

CHASSIS ELECTRICAL 6-15

INSTRUMENT AND SWITCHES

Instrument Cluster

REMOVAL & INSTALLATION

♦ See Figures 57 thru 63

1970–79

1. Disconnect the negative battery cable.
2. Working through the openings of the instrument cluster cover, remove the screws retaining the cluster cover to the instrument panel and remove the cover.
3. From underneath the instrument panel, remove the screw retaining the cluster assembly to the lower instrument panel.
4. Withdraw the cluster lid slightly. Press the windshield wiper control knob in, turn it counterclockwise and pull it off the switch. Remove the headlight/parking light switch knob in the same manner.
5. From behind the instrument cluster, disconnect the speedometer cable at the speedometer head and the multiple connector from the printed circuit.
6. On vehicles with a clock, disconnect the wires at each connection on the instrument panel printed circuit.
7. Remove the screws retaining the cluster assembly to the cluster lid.
8. Remove the instrument cluster assembly from under the instrument panel.

To install:

9. Install the instrument cluster into the instrument panel and tighten the cluster–to–lid screws.
10. Connect the clock, speedometer cable and multi–connector.
11. Install the headlight and windshield wiper control knobs.
12. Tighten the cluster–to–panel retaining screws and then reconnect the battery cable.

1980–88

1. Disconnect the negative battery cable.
2. Remove the cluster lid.
3. Remove the cluster assembly.
4. Remove the gauges from the cluster, individually.

To install:

5. Install the gauges into the cluster and then position the cluster in the instrument panel.
6. Install the cluster lid and connect the battery cable.

Windshield Wiper Switch

REMOVAL & INSTALLATION

1970–79

1. Disconnect the negative battery cable.
2. Press the wiper control knob in and turn it counterclockwise. Remove the switch.
3. Install the wiper control knob and connect the battery cable.

1980–88

1. Disconnect the negative battery cable.
2. Pry out the horn pad and remove the steering wheel.
3. Remove the terminals from the connector.
4. Slide the switch assembly off the steering column.

To install:

5. Install the switch on the steering column and connect the electrical leads.
6. Press the steering wheel (refer to the necessary service procedures in this manual) onto the column and install the horn pad.

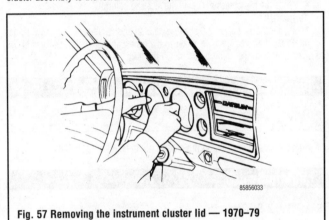

Fig. 57 Removing the instrument cluster lid — 1970–79

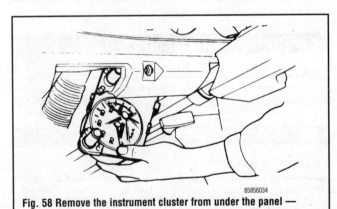

Fig. 58 Remove the instrument cluster from under the panel — 1970–1979

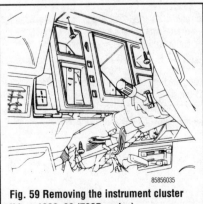

Fig. 59 Removing the instrument cluster lid — 1980–86 (720D series)

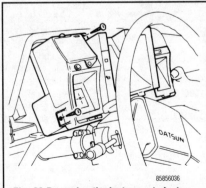

Fig. 60 Removing the instrument cluster — 1980–86 (720D series)

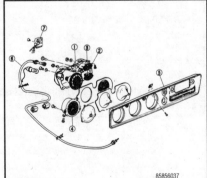

Fig. 61 Exploded view of the instrument cluster — 1970–79

6-16 CHASSIS ELECTRICAL

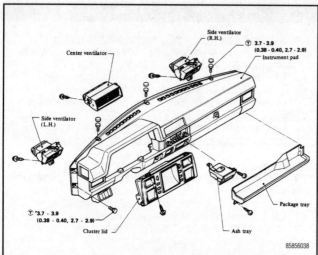

Fig. 62 Exploded view of the instrument panel — 1980–86 (720D series)

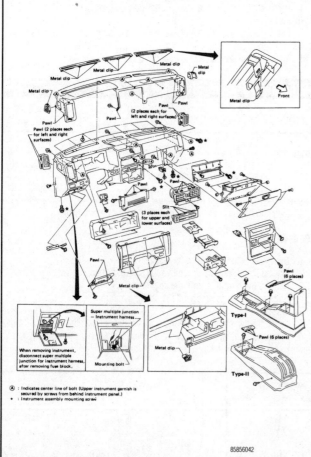

Fig. 63 Exploded view of the instrument cluster — 1986–88 (D21D series)

Headlight Switch

REMOVAL & INSTALLATION

1970–79

1. Disconnect the negative battery cable.
2. Press the headlight control knob in and turn it counterclockwise. Remove the switch.
3. Install the headlight control knob and connect the battery cable.

1980–88

1. Disconnect the negative battery cable.
2. Pry out the horn pad and remove the steering wheel.
3. Remove the terminals from the connector.
4. Slide the switch assembly off the steering column.

To install:

5. Install the switch on the steering column and connect the electrical leads.
6. Press the steering wheel (refer to the necessary service procedures in this manual) onto the column and install the horn pad.

Turn Signal/Combination Switch

REMOVAL & INSTALLATION

All removal and installation procedures are detailed in Section 8.

Ignition Switch

REMOVAL & INSTALLATION

All removal and installation procedures are detailed in Section 8.

Back–Up Light Switch

REMOVAL & INSTALLATION

All removal and installation procedures are detailed in Section 7.

Speedometer Cable

REPLACEMENT

1. Reach up under the instrument panel and disconnect the cable housing from the back of the speedometer. It is attached by a knurled knob which simply unscrews. On many later models, the speedometer cable is connected to the speedometer by means of a press–fit. When you remove the combination meter (cluster), they simply come unplugged.
2. Pull the cable from the cable housing. If the cable is broken, the other half of the cable will have to be removed from the transmission end. Unscrew the retaining knob and remove the cable from the transmission extension housing.
3. Lubricate the cable with graphite powder (sold as speedometer cable lubricant, curiously enough) and feed the cable into the housing. It is best to start at the speedometer end and feed the cable down towards the transmission. It is also usually necessary to unscrew the transmission connection and install the cable end to the gear, then reconnect the housing to the transmission. Slip the cable end into the speedometer, and reconnect the cable housing.

CHASSIS ELECTRICAL 6-17

LIGHTING

Headlights

REMOVAL & INSTALLATION

♦ See Figures 64 thru 70

1. Remove the radiator grille retaining screws and remove the radiator grille (ONLY IF NECESSARY).
2. Loosen and remove, if necessary, the retaining ring screws. Do not disturb the aiming adjusting screws.
3. Remove the retaining ring. On round headlamp systems, rotate the ring clockwise to remove it.
4. Remove the headlight from the mounting ring and disconnect the electrical connector from behind the light.

To install:
5. Change the headlight and connect the wiring connector to the new light.
6. Place the headlight in position so that the three locating tabs behind the light fit in the three holes on the mounting ring.
7. Install the headlight retaining ring and tighten the retaining screws.
8. Install the radiator grille.

Signal And Marker Lights

REMOVAL & INSTALLATION

Front Turn Signal And Parking Lights

♦ See Figures 71 thru 76

1. Remove turn signal/parking light lens with retaining screws.
2. Slightly depress the bulb and turn it counterclockwise to release it.

To install:
3. Carefully push bulb down and turn bulb clockwise at the same time.
4. Install the turn signal/parking light lens with retaining screws.

Side Marker Lights

♦ See Figures 77, 78, 79, 80 and 81

1. Remove side marker light lens with retaining screws.
2. Turn the bulb socket counterclockwise to release it from lens.
3. Pull bulb straight out.

To install:
4. Carefully push bulb straight in.
5. Turn the bulb socket clockwise to install it in lens.
6. Install the side marker light lens with retaining screws.

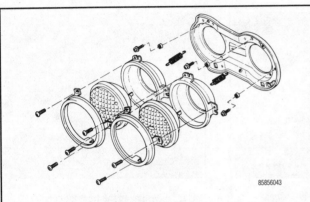

Fig. 64 Headlamp assembly — 1970–79

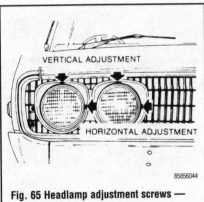

Fig. 65 Headlamp adjustment screws — 1970–79

Fig. 66 Removing the headlight assembly bezel

Fig. 67 View of the headlight assembly bezel lower retaining clip

Fig. 68 Removing the headlamp retaining ring screw

Fig. 69 Removing the headlamp

Fig. 70 Removing the headlamp electrical connection

6-18 CHASSIS ELECTRICAL

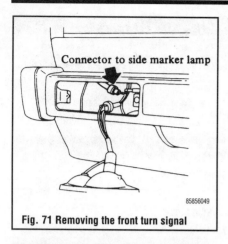
Fig. 71 Removing the front turn signal

Fig. 72 Removing the front turn signal lens screw

Fig. 73 Removing the front turn signal lens

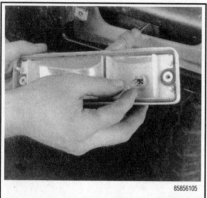
Fig. 74 Removing the side marker bulb

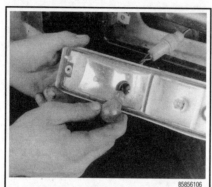
Fig. 75 Removing the front turn signal bulb

Fig. 76 Removing the front turn signal assembly electrical connection

Fig. 77 Removing the front side marker lamp lens screw

Fig. 78 Removing the front side marker lamp lens

Fig. 79 Removing the front side marker lamp from lens

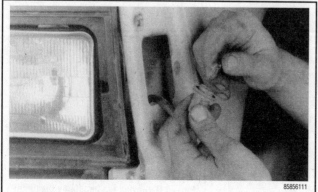
Fig. 80 Removing the front side marker lamp from socket

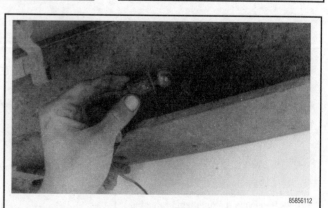
Fig. 81 Removing the rear license plate light

CHASSIS ELECTRICAL   6-19

Rear Turn Signal, Brake And Parking Lights

1. Remove rear trim panel if necessary to gain access to the bulb socket.
2. Slightly depress the bulb and turn it counterclockwise to release it.
3. To install the bulb, carefully push down and turn the bulb clockwise at the same time.
4. Install the trim panel if necessary.

TRAILER WIRING

Wiring the truck for towing is fairly easy. There are a number of good wiring kits available and these should be used, rather than trying to design your own. All trailers will need brake lights and turn signals as well as tail lights and side marker lights. Most states require extra marker lights for overly wide trailers. Also, most states have recently required backup lights for trailers, and most trailer manufacturers have been building trailers with backup lights for several years.

Additionally, some Class I, most Class II and just about all Class III trailers will have electric brakes.

Add to this number an accessories wire, to operate trailer internal equipment or to charge the trailer's battery, and you can have as many as seven wires in the harness.

Determine the equipment on your trailer and buy the wiring kit necessary. The kit will contain all the wires needed, plus a plug adapter set which included the female plug, mounted on the bumper or hitch, and the male plug, wired into, or plugged into the trailer harness.

When installing the kit, follow the manufacturer's instructions. The color coding of the wires is standard throughout the industry.

One point to note, some domestic vehicles, and most imported vehicles, have separate turn signals. On most domestic vehicles, the brake lights and rear turn signals operate with the same bulb. For those vehicles with separate turn signals, you can purchase an isolation unit so that the brake lights won't blink whenever the turn signals are operated, or, you can go to your local electronics supply house and buy four diodes to wire in series with the brake and turn signal bulbs. Diodes will isolate the brake and turn signals. The choice is yours. The isolation units are simple and quick to install, but far more expensive than the diodes. The diodes, however, require more work to install properly, since they require the cutting of each bulb's wire and soldering in place of the diode.

One final point, the best kits are those with a spring loaded cover on the vehicle mounted socket. This cover prevents dirt and moisture from corroding the terminals. Never let the vehicle socket hang loosely. Always mount it securely to the bumper or hitch.

CIRCUIT PROTECTION

Fuses And Flashers

FUSES

♦ See Figures 82, 83, 84 and 85

Fuses protect all the major electrical systems in the truck. In case of an electrical overload, the fuse melts, breaking the circuit and stopping the flow of electricity.

If a fuse blows, the cause should be investigated and corrected before the installation of a new fuse. This, however, is easier to say than to do. Because each fuse protects a limited number of components, your job is narrowed down somewhat. Begin your investigation by looking for obvious fraying, loose connections, breaks in insulation, etc. Use the techniques outlined at the beginning of this section. Electrical problems are almost always a real headache to solve, but patience and persistence, coupled with logic, usually provide a solution.

The amperage of each fuse and the circuit it protects are marked on the cover of the fuse box, which is located under the instrument panel next to the steering column on but 1970–71 trucks where the fuse box is in the engine compartment on the firewall.

➡ NEVER USE A FUSE OF HIGHER AMPERAGE THAN RECOMMENDED

FLASHERS AND RELAYS

♦ See Figures 86 thru 98

The turn signal and four-way hazard flashers are located under the instrument panel on opposite sides of the steering column. The turn signal flasher is the larger of the two. Replacement is made by unplugging the old flasher and plugging in the new one. Later model pickups may combine the two flashers into one.

Relays are used for the horn, headlights, wiper, heater, choke heater, catalyst floor sensor, air conditioner compressor, and transmission switches, although obviously not all relay are used on all models. All relays used are grouped together, and mounted on the right fender in the engine compartment.

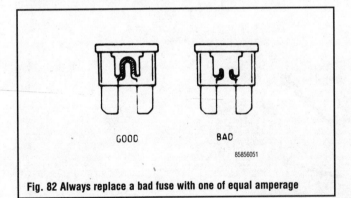

Fig. 82 Always replace a bad fuse with one of equal amperage

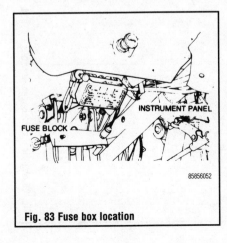

Fig. 83 Fuse box location

Fig. 84 View of the fuse box

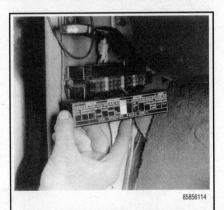

Fig. 85 Removing the fuse box cover

6-20 CHASSIS ELECTRICAL

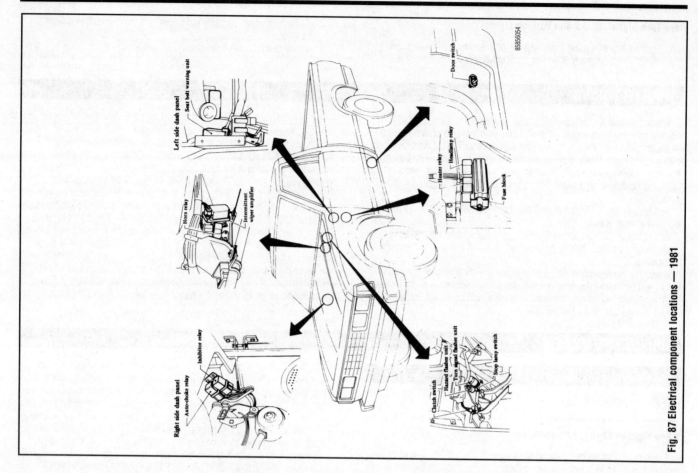

Fig. 87 Electrical component locations — 1981

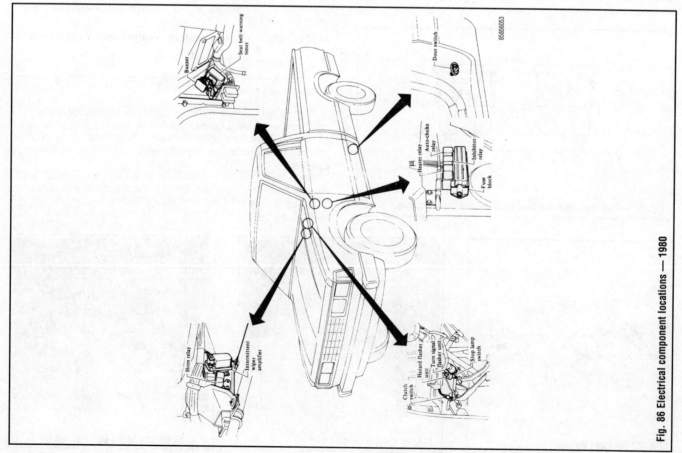

Fig. 86 Electrical component locations — 1980

CHASSIS ELECTRICAL 6-21

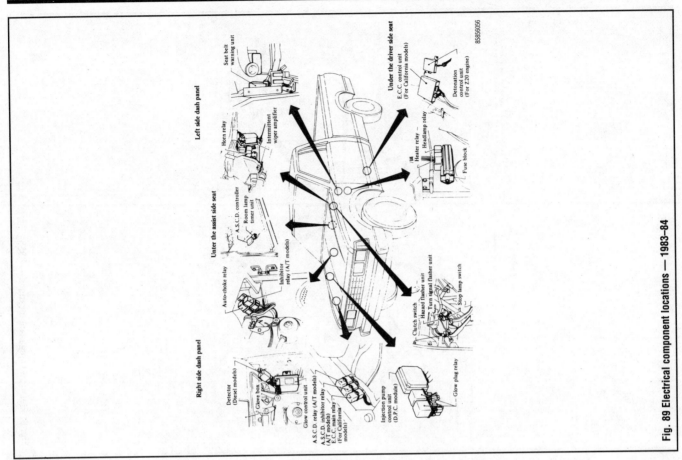

Fig. 89 Electrical component locations — 1983-84

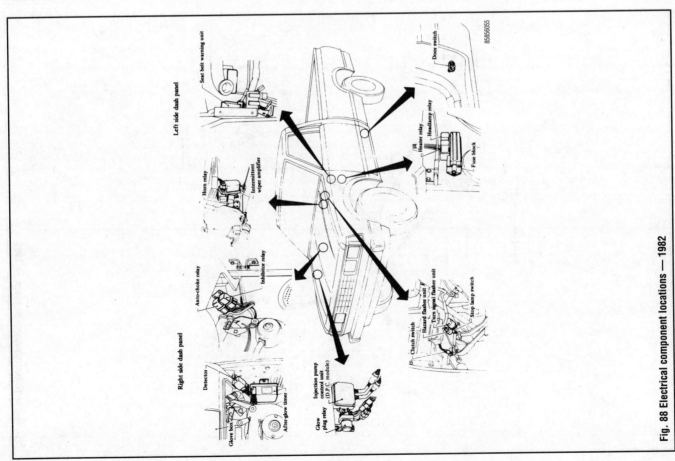

Fig. 88 Electrical component locations — 1982

6-22 CHASSIS ELECTRICAL

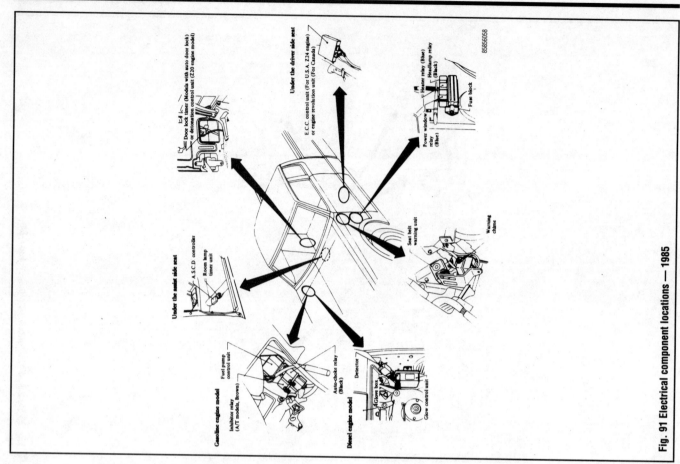

Fig. 91 Electrical component locations — 1985

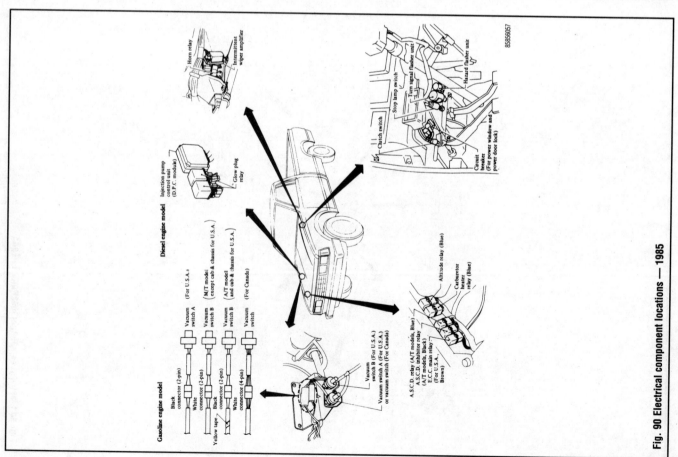

Fig. 90 Electrical component locations — 1985

CHASSIS ELECTRICAL 6-23

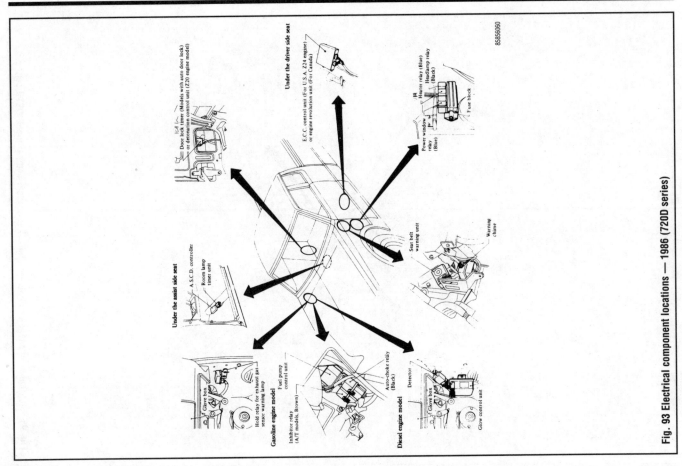

Fig. 93 Electrical component locations — 1986 (720D series)

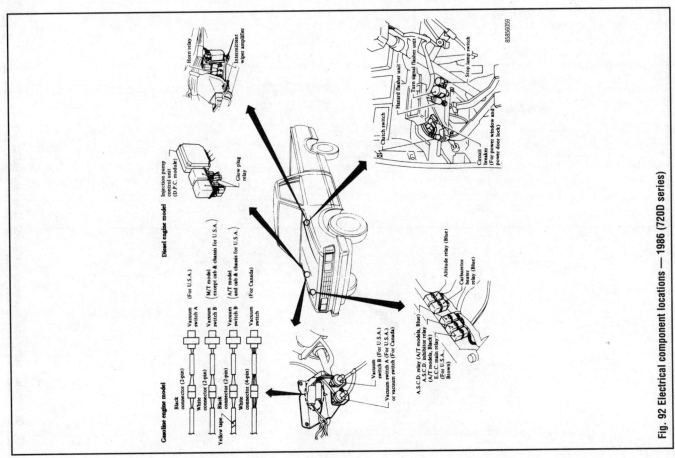

Fig. 92 Electrical component locations — 1986 (720D series)

6-24 CHASSIS ELECTRICAL

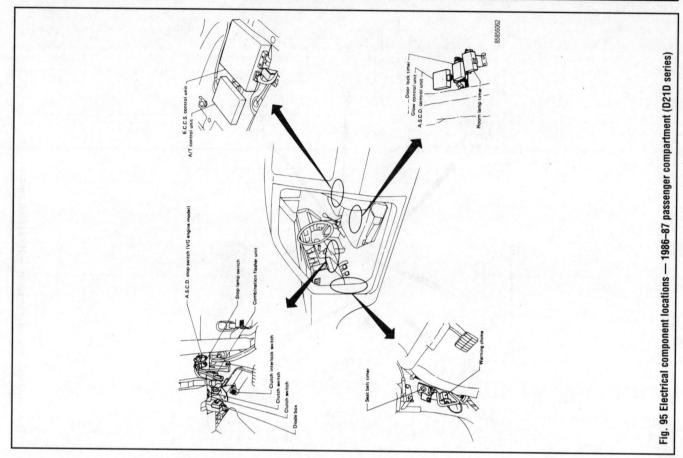

Fig. 95 Electrical component locations — 1986-87 passenger compartment (D21D series)

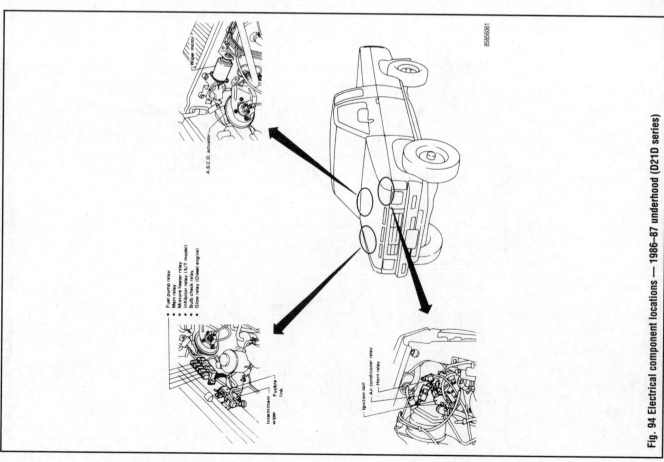

Fig. 94 Electrical component locations — 1986-87 underhood (D21D series)

CHASSIS ELECTRICAL 6-25

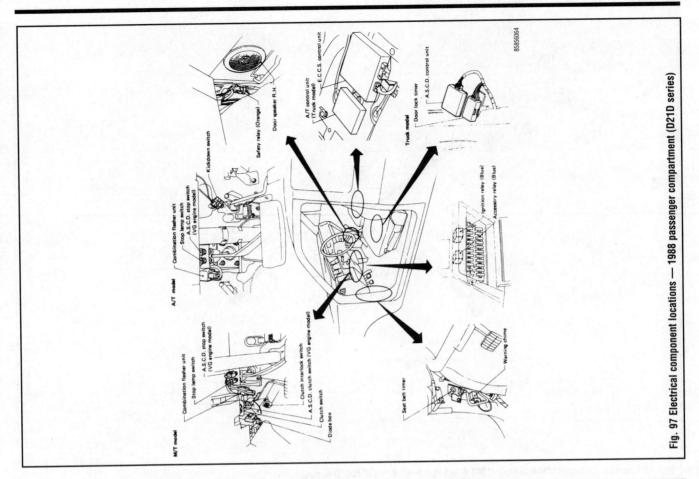

Fig. 97 Electrical component locations — 1988 passenger compartment (D21D series)

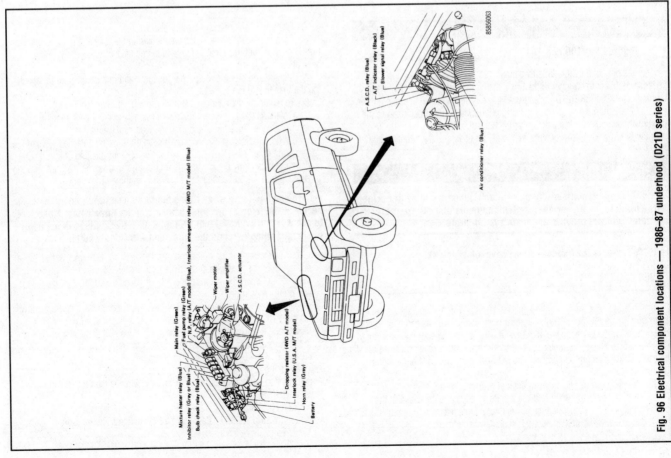

Fig. 96 Electrical component locations — 1986–87 underhood (D21D series)

6-26 CHASSIS ELECTRICAL

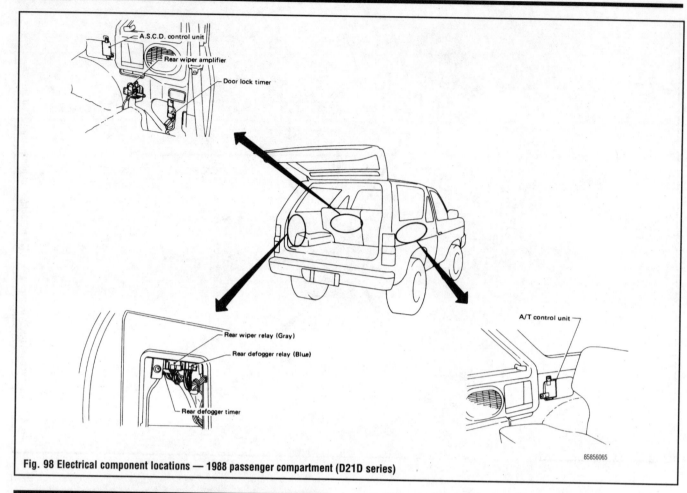

Fig. 98 Electrical component locations — 1988 passenger compartment (D21D series)

Fusible Link

► See Figures 99, 100 and 101

There is only one fusible link used on all 1972–86 pickups (620 and 720D series) and that is the thinner of the two wires connected to the positive battery terminal. On 1986–88 D21D series trucks there is also a brown one used in the headlight circuit, brown one used in the ignition switch, green one used in the power windows, brown one used in the EFI control unit and a brown one used with the EFI injector. Replacements are simply plugged into the connectors in this wire.

※※ CAUTION

Use only replacements of the same electrical capacity as the original, available from your dealer. Replacements of a different electrical value will not provide adequate system protection.

➥1970–71 trucks (521 series) do not have a fusible link.

FUSE LINK

The fuse link is a short length of special, Hypalon (high temperature) insulated wire, integral with the engine compartment wiring harness and should not be confused with standard wire. It is several wire gauges smaller than the circuit which protects. Under no circumstances should a fuse link replacement repair be made using a length of standard wire out from bulk stock or from another wiring harness.

To repair any blown fuse link use the following procedure:
1. Determine which circuit is damaged, its location and the cause of the open fuse link. If the damaged fuse link is one of three fed by a common No. 10 or 12 gauge feed wire, determine the specific effected circuit.
2. Disconnect the negative battery cable.
3. Cut the damaged fuse link from the wiring harness and discard it. If the fuse link is one of three circuits fed by a single feed wire, cut it out of the harness at each splice end and discard it.
4. Identify and procure the proper fuse link and butt connectors for attaching the fuse link to the harness.
5. To repair any fuse link in a 3–link ground with one feed:
   a. After cutting the open link out of the harness, cut each of the remaining undamaged fuse links closed to the feed wire weld.
   b. Strip approximately ½ in. of insulation from the detached ends of the two good fuse links. Then insert two wire ends into one end of a butt connector and carefully push one strip end of the replacement fuse link into the same end of the butt connector and crimp all three firmly together.

➥**Care must be taken when fitting the three fuse links into the butt connector as the internal diameter is a snug fit for three wires. Make sure to use a proper crimping tool. Pliers, side cutters, etc., will not apply the proper crimp to retain the wires and withstand a pull test.**

   c. After crimping the butt connector to the three fuse links, cut the weld portion from the feed wire and strip approximately ½ inch of insulation from the end cut. Insert the stripped end into the open end of the butt connector and crimp very firmly.
   d. To attach the remaining end of the replacement fuse link, strip approximately ½ in. of insulation from the wire end of the circuit from which the blown fuse link was removed, and firmly crimp a butt connector or equivalent to the stripped wire. Then, insert the end of the replacement link into the other end of the butt connector and crimp firmly.
   e. Using resin core solder with a consistency of 60 percent tin and 40 percent lead, solder the connectors and the wires at the repairs and insulate with electrical tape.
6. To replace any fuse link on a single circuit in a harness, cut out the damaged portion, strip approximately ½ in. of insulation from the two wire ends and

CHASSIS ELECTRICAL 6-27

attach the appropriate replacement fuse link to the stripped wire ends with two proper size butt connectors. Solder the connectors and wires and insulate with tape.

7. To repair any fuse link which has an eyelet terminal on one end of such as the charging circuit, cut off the open fuse link behind the weld, strip approximately ½ in. of insulation from the cut end and attach the appropriate new eyelet fuse link to the cut stripped wire with an appropriate size butt connector. Solder the connectors and wires at the repair and insulate with tape.

8. Connect the negative battery cable to the battery and test the system for proper operation.

➡ Do not mistake a resistor wire for a fuse link. The resistor wire is generally longer and has print stating, resistor—don't cut or splice. When attaching a single No. 16, 17, 18, or 20 gauge fuse link to a heavy gauge wire, always double the stripped wire end of the fuse link before inserting and crimping it into the butt connector for positive wire retention.

Circuit Breakers

Circuit breakers are also located in the fuse block. A circuit breaker is an electrical switch which breaks the circuit during an electrical overload. The circuit breaker will remain open until the short or overload condition in the circuit is corrected.

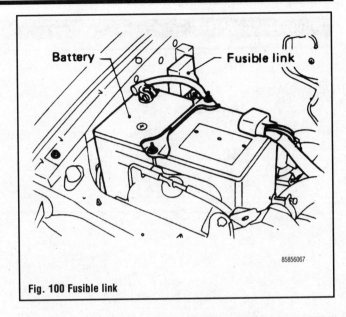
Fig. 100 Fusible link

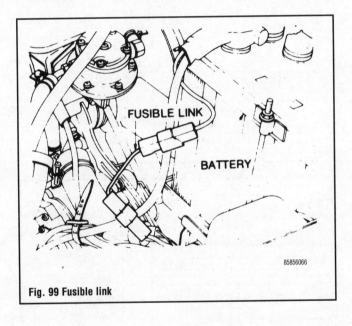
Fig. 99 Fusible link

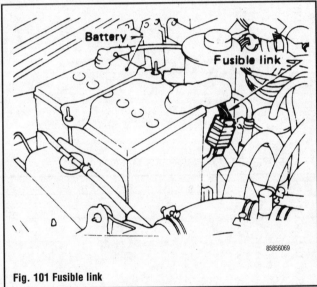
Fig. 101 Fusible link

6-28 CHASSIS ELECTRICAL

WIRING DIAGRAMS

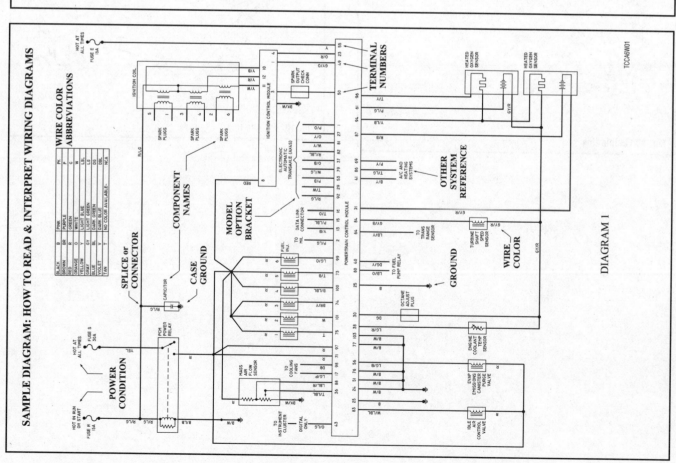

CHASSIS ELECTRICAL 6-29

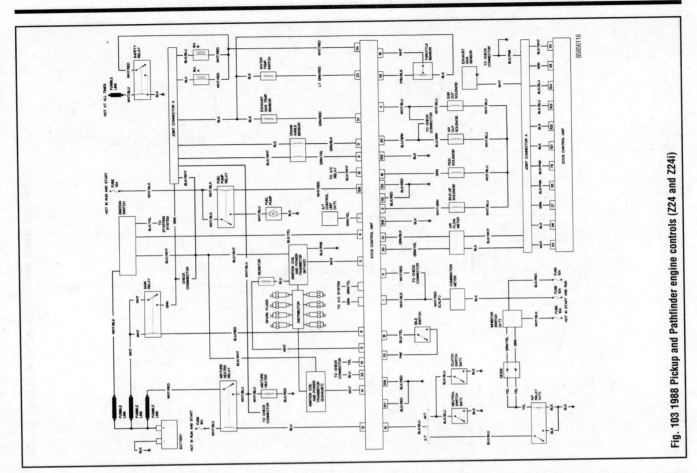

Fig. 103 1988 Pickup and Pathfinder engine controls (Z24 and Z24i)

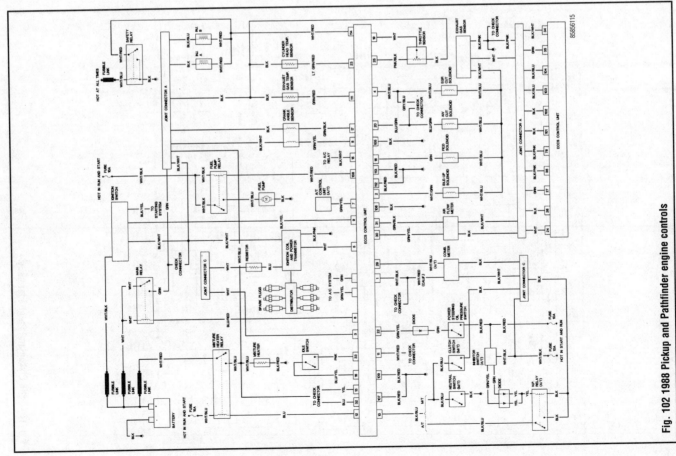

Fig. 102 1988 Pickup and Pathfinder engine controls

6-30 CHASSIS ELECTRICAL

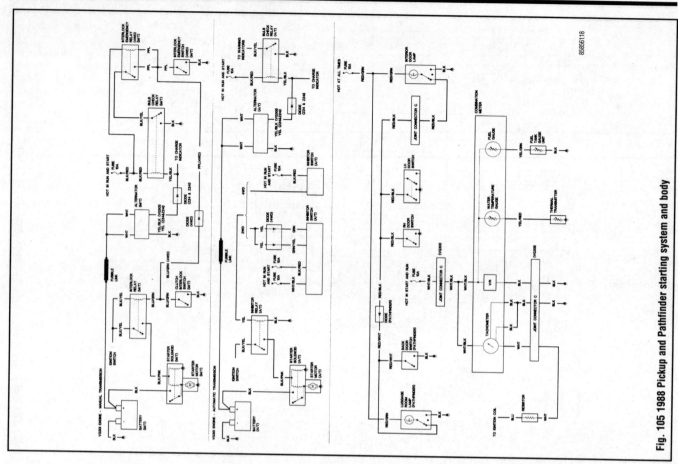

Fig. 105 1988 Pickup and Pathfinder starting system and body

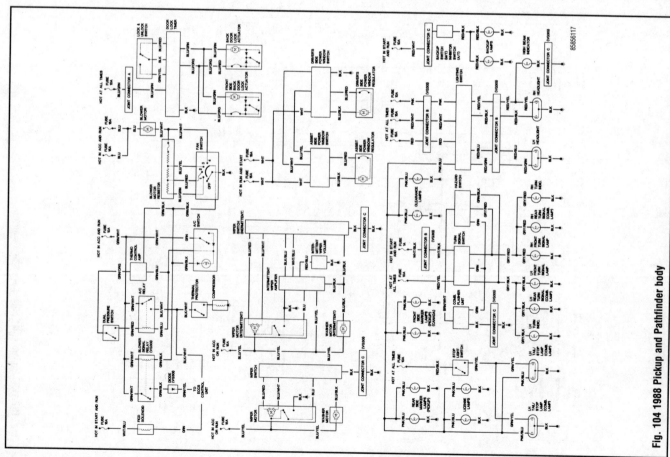

Fig. 104 1988 Pickup and Pathfinder body

CHASSIS ELECTRICAL 6-31

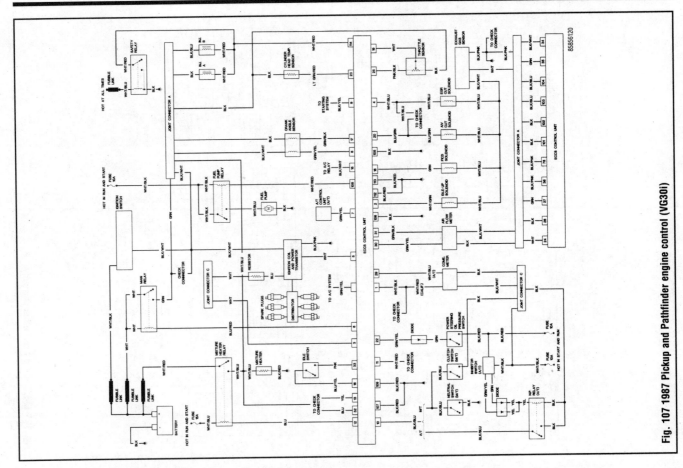

Fig. 107 1987 Pickup and Pathfinder engine control (VG30i)

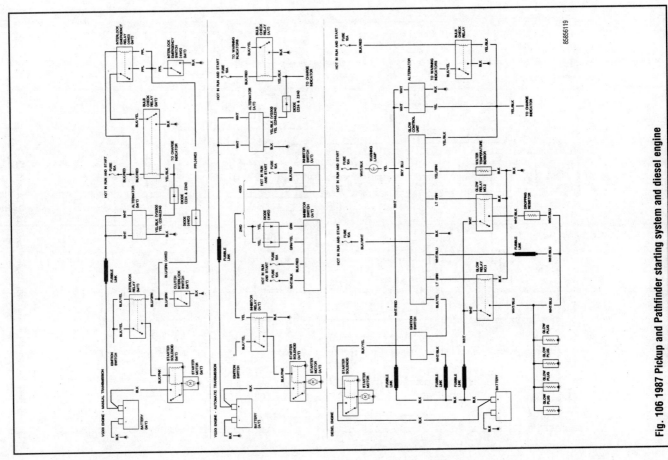

Fig. 106 1987 Pickup and Pathfinder starting system and diesel engine

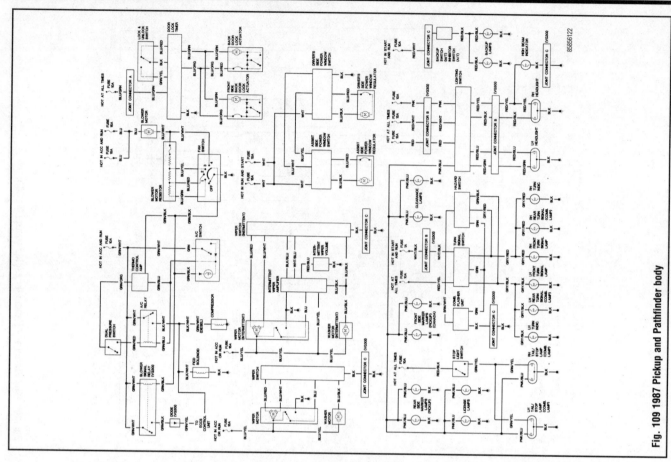

Fig. 109 1987 Pickup and Pathfinder body

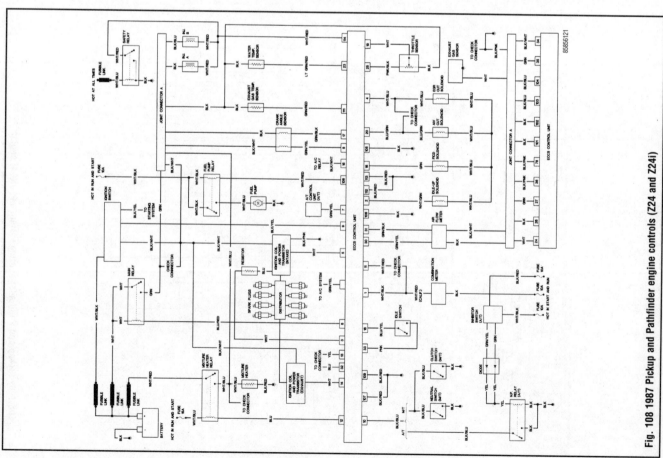

Fig. 108 1987 Pickup and Pathfinder engine controls (Z24 and Z24i)

CHASSIS ELECTRICAL 6-33

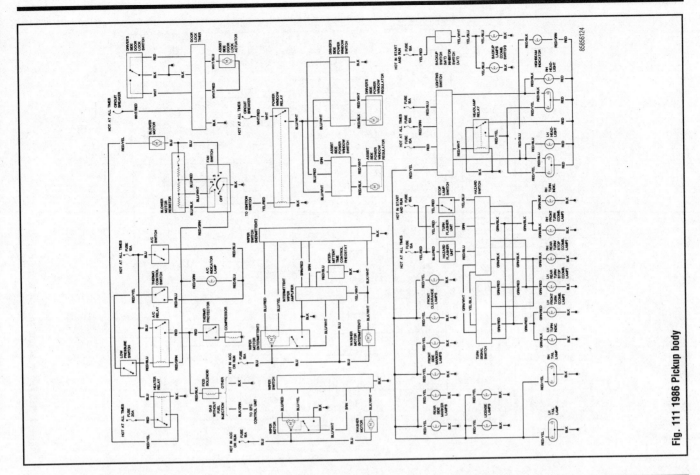

Fig. 111 1986 Pickup body

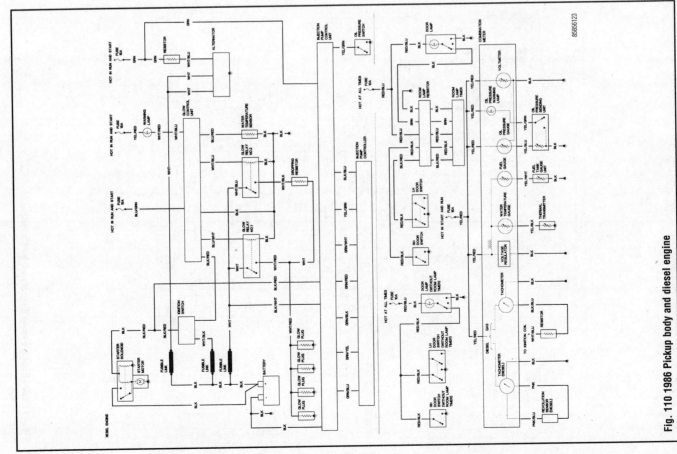

Fig. 110 1986 Pickup body and diesel engine

6-34 CHASSIS ELECTRICAL

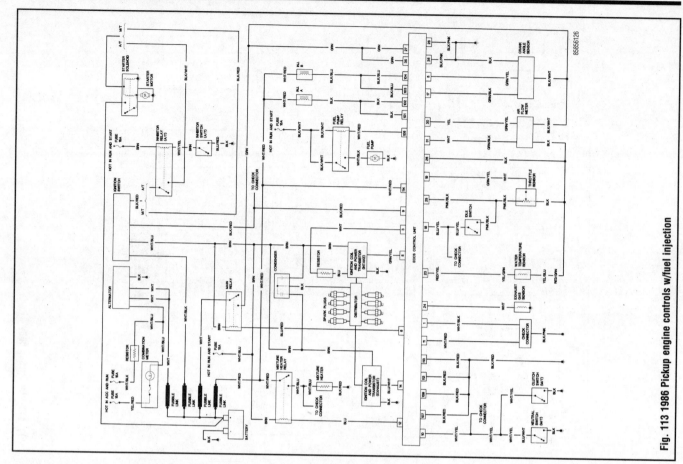

Fig. 113 1986 Pickup engine controls w/fuel injection

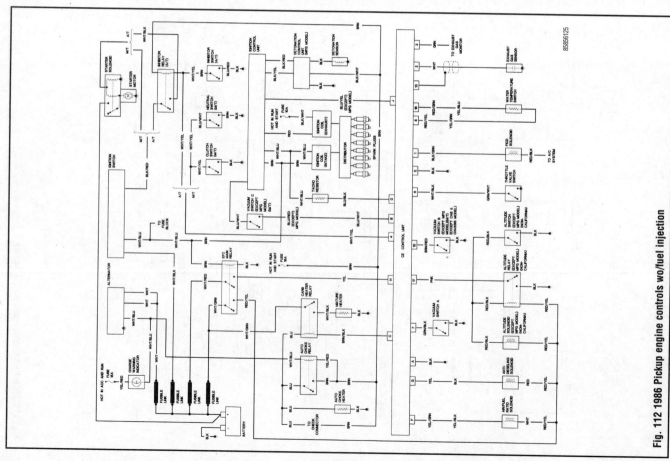

Fig. 112 1986 Pickup engine controls wo/fuel injection

CHASSIS ELECTRICAL 6-35

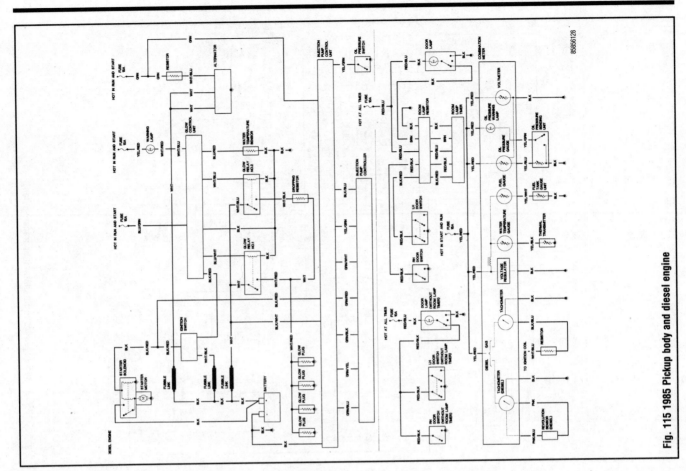

Fig. 115 1985 Pickup body and diesel engine

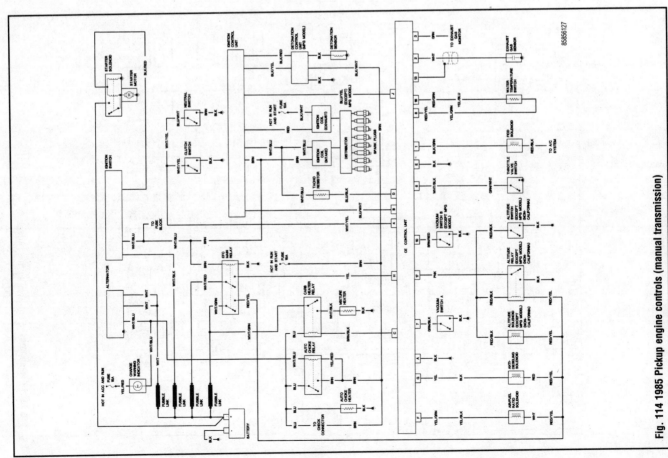

Fig. 114 1985 Pickup engine controls (manual transmission)

6-36 CHASSIS ELECTRICAL

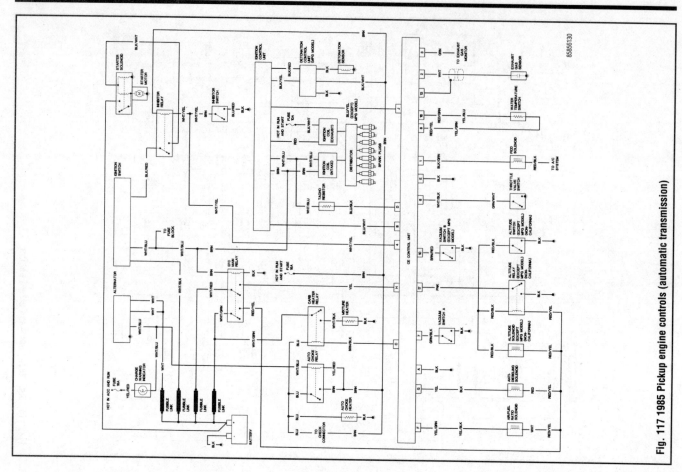

Fig. 117 1985 Pickup engine controls (automatic transmission)

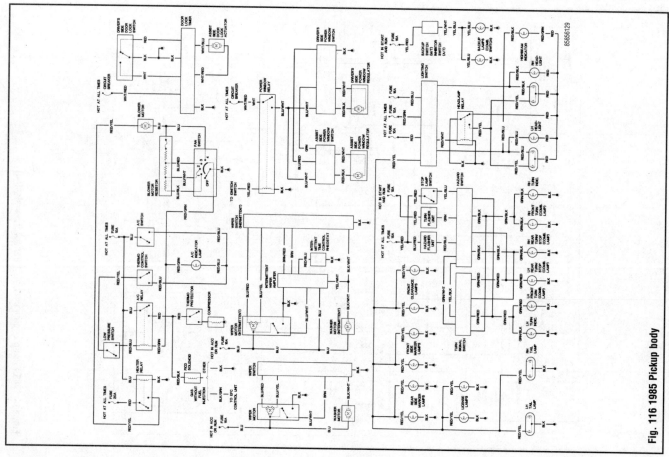

Fig. 116 1985 Pickup body

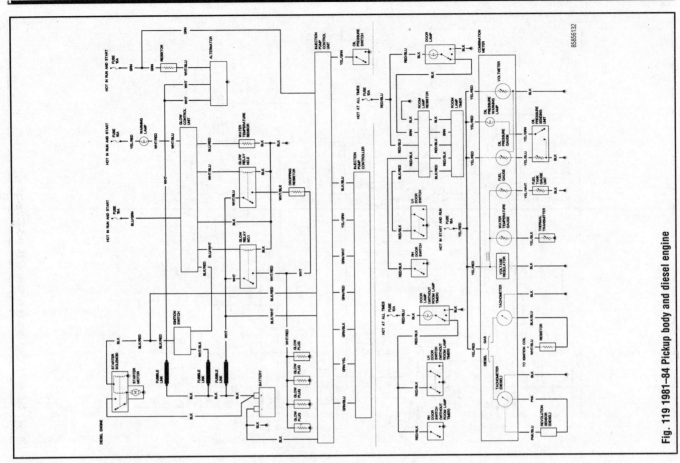

Fig. 119 1981–84 Pickup body and diesel engine

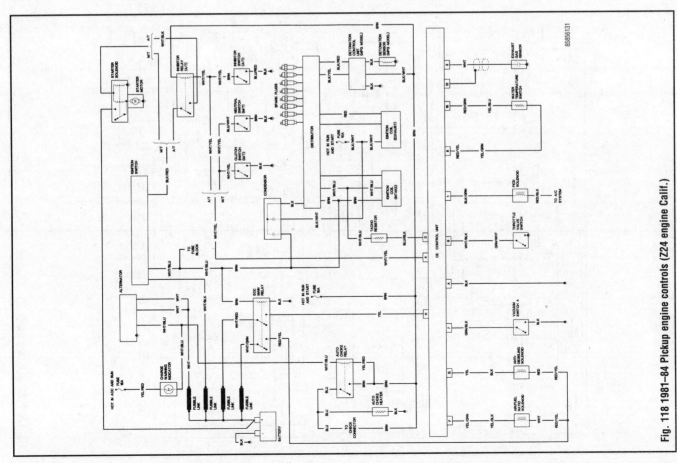

Fig. 118 1981–84 Pickup engine controls (Z24 engine Calif.)

6-38 CHASSIS ELECTRICAL

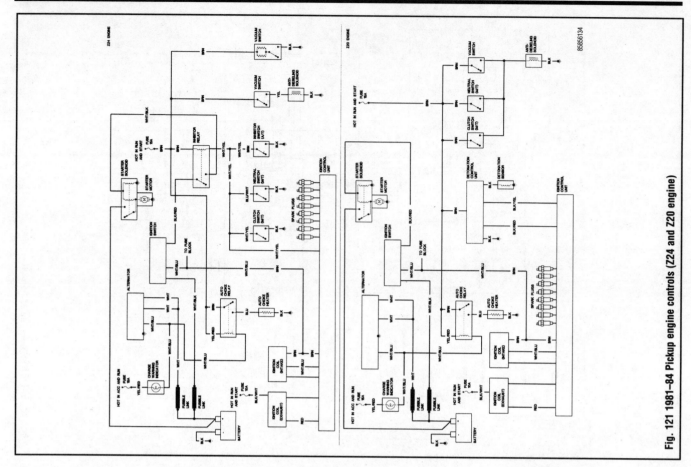

Fig. 121 1981-84 Pickup engine controls (Z24 and Z20 engine)

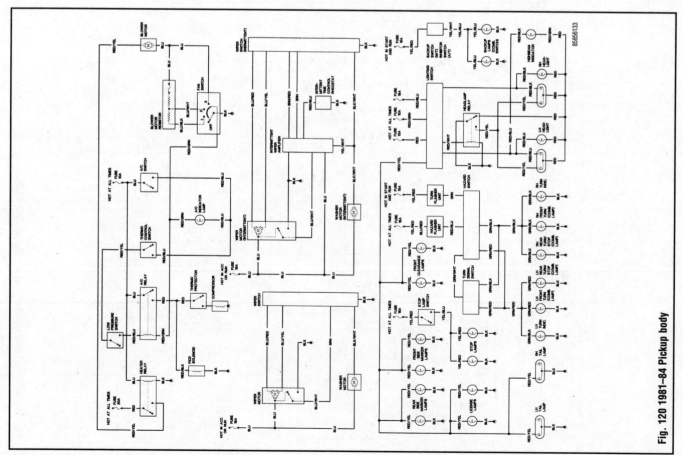

Fig. 120 1981-84 Pickup body

CHASSIS ELECTRICAL 6-39

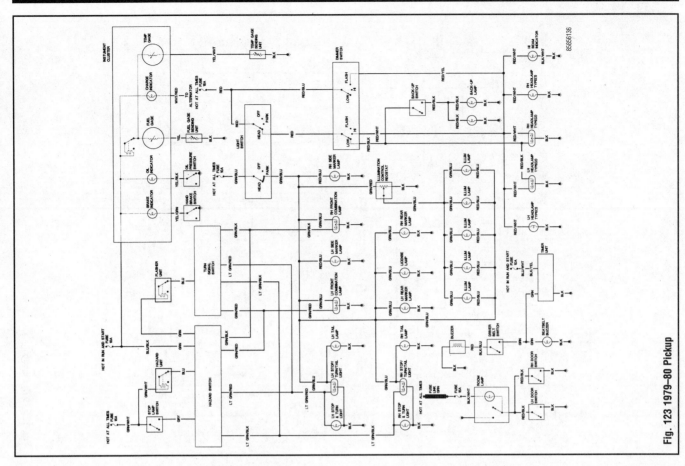

Fig. 123 1979-80 Pickup

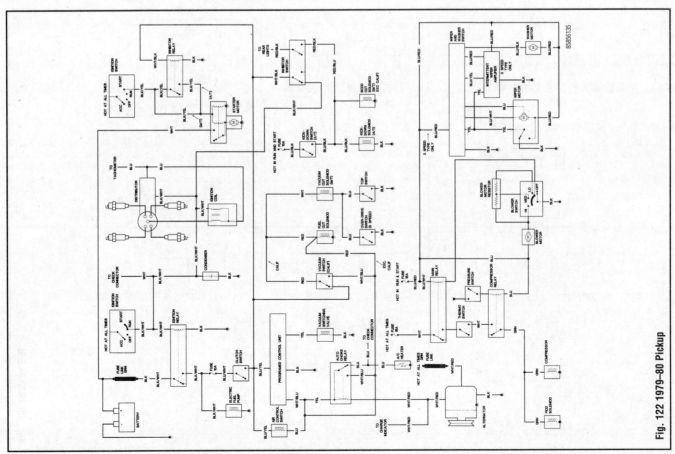

Fig. 122 1979-80 Pickup

6-40 CHASSIS ELECTRICAL

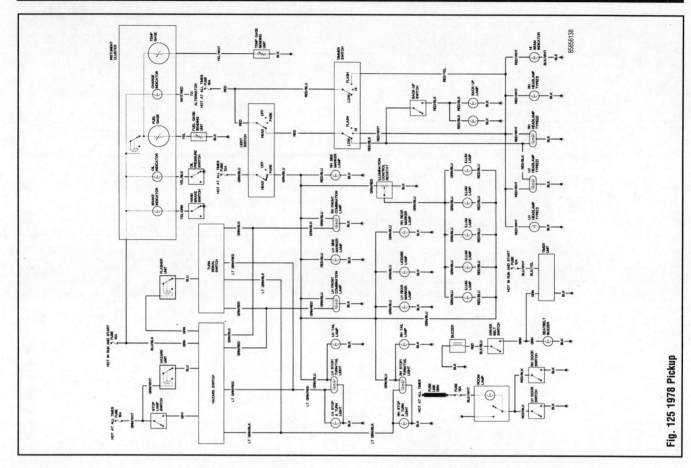

Fig. 125 1978 Pickup

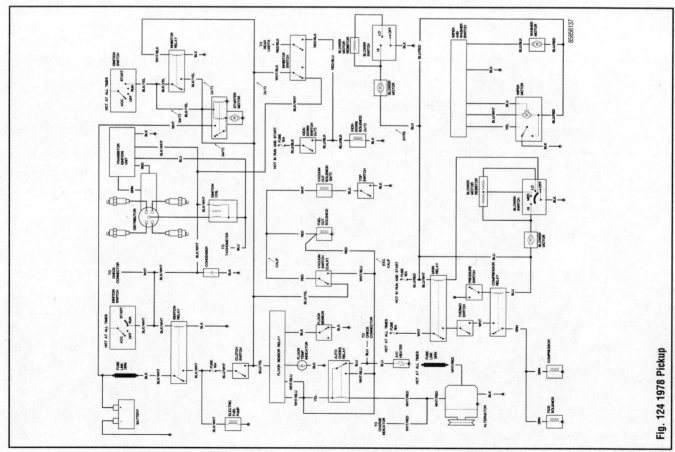

Fig. 124 1978 Pickup

CHASSIS ELECTRICAL 6-41

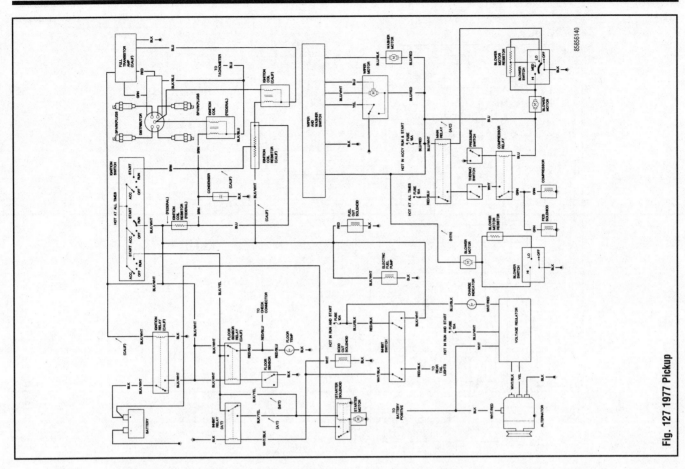

Fig. 127 1977 Pickup

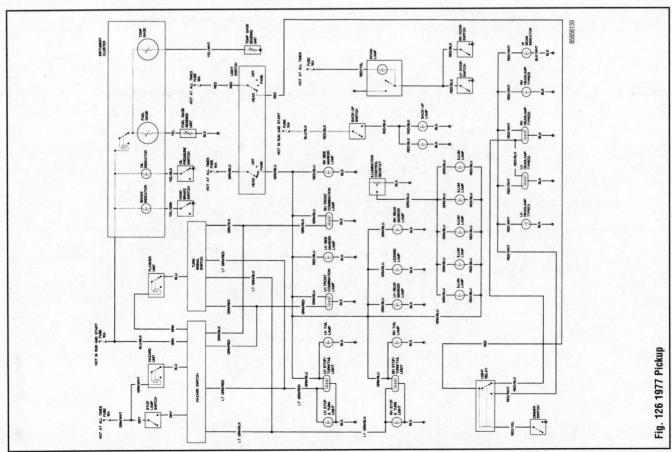

Fig. 126 1977 Pickup

6-42 CHASSIS ELECTRICAL

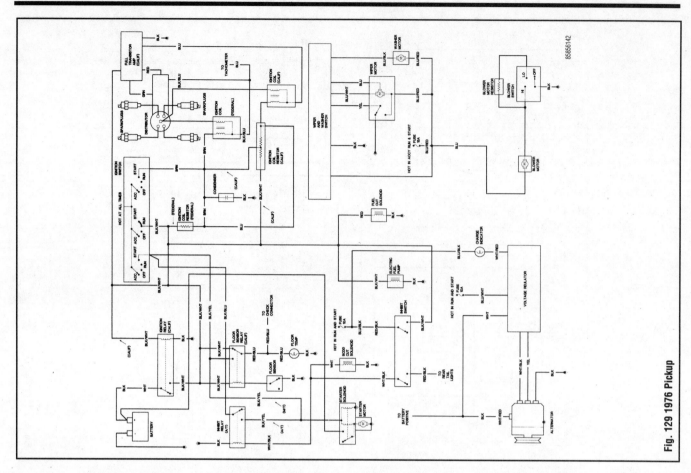

Fig. 129 1976 Pickup

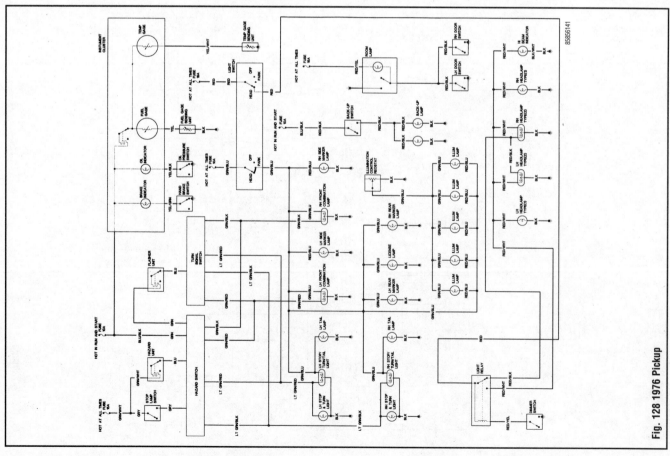

Fig. 128 1976 Pickup

CHASSIS ELECTRICAL 6-43

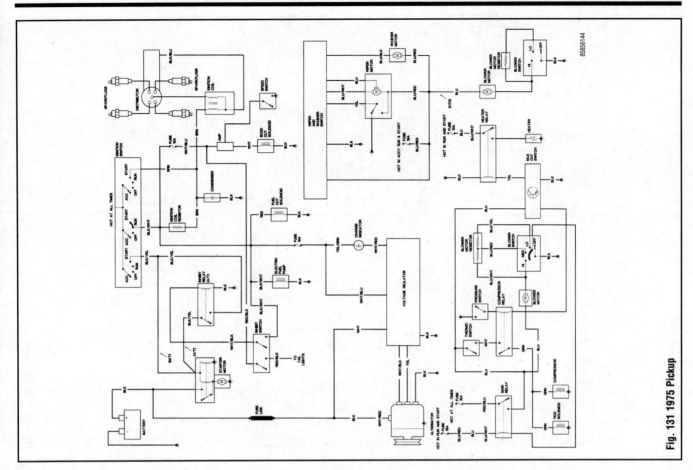

Fig. 131 1975 Pickup

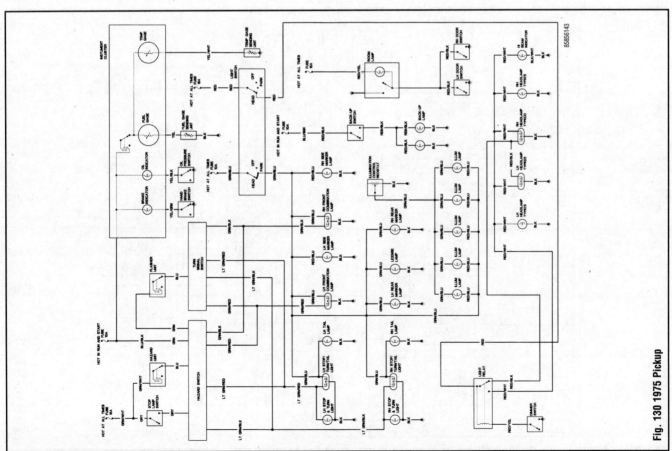

Fig. 130 1975 Pickup

6-44 CHASSIS ELECTRICAL

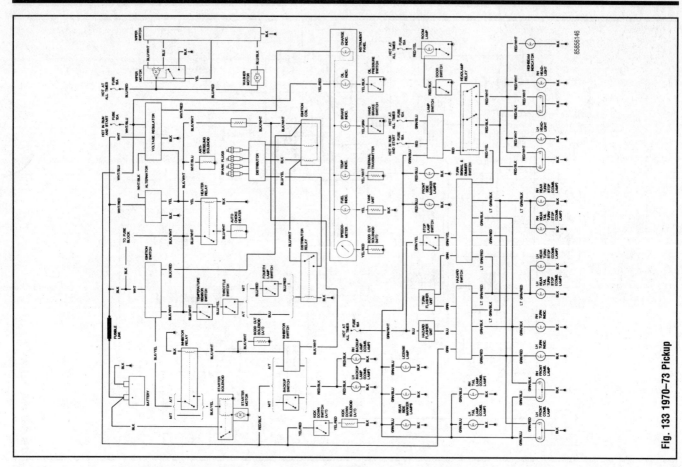

Fig. 133 1970-73 Pickup

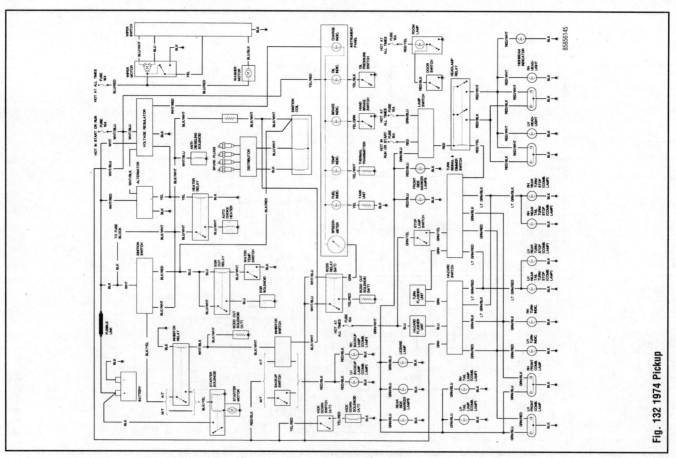

Fig. 132 1974 Pickup

MANUAL TRANSMISSION 7-2
UNDERSTANDING THE MANUAL
 TRANSMISSION 7-2
IDENTIFICATION 7-2
ADJUSTMENTS 7-2
BACK-UP LIGHT SWITCH 7-2
 REMOVAL & INSTALLATION 7-2
TRANSMISSION 7-2
 REMOVAL & INSTALLATION 7-2
CLUTCH 7-5
UNDERSTANDING THE CLUTCH 7-5
ADJUSTMENTS 7-5
 PEDAL HEIGHT 7-5
 PEDAL FREE-PLAY 7-6
 CLUTCH INTERLOCK 7-6
DRIVEN DISC AND PRESSURE
 PLATE 7-6
 REMOVAL & INSTALLATION 7-6
CLUTCH MASTER CYLINDER 7-8
 REMOVAL & INSTALLATION 7-8
 OVERHAUL 7-8
CLUTCH RELEASE CYLINDER 7-8
 REMOVAL & INSTALLATION 7-8
 OVERHAUL 7-8
CLUTCH DAMPER 7-9
 REMOVAL & INSTALLATION 7-9
 OVERHAUL 7-9
 BLEEDING THE CLUTCH HYDRAULIC
 SYSTEM 7-9
AUTOMATIC TRANSMISSION 7-10
UNDERSTANDING THE AUTOMATIC
 TRANSMISSION 7-10
IDENTIFICATION 7-10
FLUID PAN 7-10
ADJUSTMENTS 7-10
 BRAKE BAND 7-10
 SHIFT LINKAGE 7-10
 KICKDOWN SWITCH AND DOWN-
 SHIFT SOLENOID 7-11
NEUTRAL SAFETY/INHIBITOR
 SWITCH 7-11
 1973–86 (620 AND 720-D
 SERIES) 7-11
 1986–88 (D21-D SERIES) 7-12
TRANSMISSION 7-12
 REMOVAL & INSTALLATION 7-12
TRANSFER CASE 7-12
TRANSFER CASE 7-12
 REMOVAL & INSTALLATION 7-12
DRIVELINE 7-13
FRONT DRIVESHAFT AND
 U-JOINTS 7-13
 REMOVAL & INSTALLATION 7-13
 U-JOINT OVERHAUL 7-14
REAR DRIVESHAFT AND U-JOINTS 7-14
 REMOVAL & INSTALLATION 7-14
 U-JOINT OVERHAUL 7-16
CENTER BEARING 7-17
 REMOVAL & INSTALLATION 7-17

REAR DRIVE AXLE 7-18
AXLE SHAFT, BEARING AND SEAL 7-18
 REMOVAL & INSTALLATION 7-18
FINAL DRIVE 7-19
 REMOVAL & INSTALLATION 7-19
PINION SEAL 7-20
 REMOVAL & INSTALLATION 7-20
AXLE HOUSING 7-20
 REMOVAL & INSTALLATION 7-20
FRONT DRIVE AXLE 7-21
FREE RUNNING HUB 7-21
 REMOVAL & INSTALLATION 7-21
AXLE SHAFT 7-24
 REMOVAL & INSTALLATION 7-24
PINION SEAL 7-26
 REMOVAL & INSTALLATION 7-26

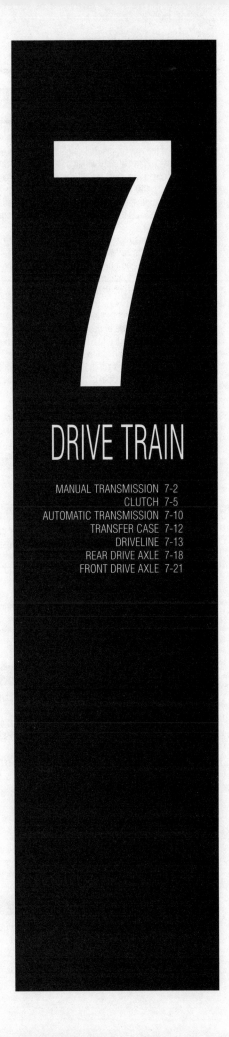

7

DRIVE TRAIN

MANUAL TRANSMISSION 7-2
CLUTCH 7-5
AUTOMATIC TRANSMISSION 7-10
TRANSFER CASE 7-12
DRIVELINE 7-13
REAR DRIVE AXLE 7-18
FRONT DRIVE AXLE 7-21

7-2 DRIVE TRAIN

MANUAL TRANSMISSION

Understanding the Manual Transmission

Because of the way an internal combustion engine breathes, it can produce torque (or twisting force) only within a narrow speed range. Most overhead valve pushrod engines must turn at about 2500 rpm to produce their peak torque. Often by 4500 rpm, they are producing so little torque that continued increases in engine speed produce no power increases.

The torque peak on overhead camshaft engines is, generally, much higher, but much narrower.

The manual transmission and clutch are employed to vary the relationship between engine RPM and the speed of the wheels so that adequate power can be produced under all circumstances. The clutch allows engine torque to be applied to the transmission input shaft gradually, due to mechanical slippage. The vehicle can, consequently, be started smoothly from a full stop.

The transmission changes the ratio between the rotating speeds of the engine and the wheels by the use of gears. 4-speed or 5-speed transmissions are most common. The lower gears allow full engine power to be applied to the rear wheels during acceleration at low speeds.

The clutch driveplate is a thin disc, the center of which is splined to the transmission input shaft. Both sides of the disc are covered with a layer of material which is similar to brake lining and which is capable of allowing slippage without roughness or excessive noise.

The clutch cover is bolted to the engine flywheel and incorporates a diaphragm spring which provides the pressure to engage the clutch. The cover also houses the pressure plate. When the clutch pedal is released, the driven disc is sandwiched between the pressure plate and the smooth surface of the flywheel, thus forcing the disc to turn at the same speed as the engine crankshaft.

The transmission contains a mainshaft which passes all the way through the transmission, from the clutch to the driveshaft. This shaft is separated at one point, so that front and rear portions can turn at different speeds.

Power is transmitted by a countershaft in the lower gears and reverse. The gears of the countershaft mesh with gears on the mainshaft, allowing power to be carried from one to the other. Countershaft gears are often integral with that shaft, while several of the mainshaft gears can either rotate independently of the shaft or be locked to it. Shifting from one gear to the next causes one of the gears to be freed from rotating with the shaft and locks another to it. Gears are locked and unlocked by internal dog clutches which slide between the center of the gear and the shaft. The forward gears usually employ synchronizers; friction members which smoothly bring gear and shaft to the same speed before the toothed dog clutches are engaged.

Identification

All models covered in this book have the manual transmission serial number stamped on the front upper face of the transmission case.

1970–74 models use an F4W63 4-speed transmission.
1975–83 models use an F4W71B 4-speed transmission. or an optional FS5W71B 5-speed transmission.
1984–86 models (720–D series) also use the FS5W71B5 5-speed transmission
1986–87 models (D21–D series) with the Z24i engine use an FS5W71C 5-speed transmission, while 1988 models use an F4W71C 4-speed transmission or the FS5W71C 5-speed transmission.
1986–88 models with the VG30i engines use an FS5R30A 5-speed transmission.

The F4W63 is a bottom cover unit, with an extension housing for the shift rail, while all other models have a one piece case, an adapter plate which supports the mainshaft and countershaft, and an extension housing.

Adjustments

Most models utilize a floor-mounted shifter and an internally-mounted shift linkage.

No external adjustments are either necessary or possible.

Back-Up Light Switch

REMOVAL & INSTALLATION

▶ See Figure 1

All Models

1. Raise vehicle and support it safely with floor stands.
2. Disconnect the electrical connections from the switch.
3. Unscrew the switch and remove it from the transmission housing. When removing, be sure to position a drain pan under the transmission to catch any leaking fluid.
4. Install the switch (with new gasket if so equipped) and connect the electrical lead. Lower the truck and check the fluid level.

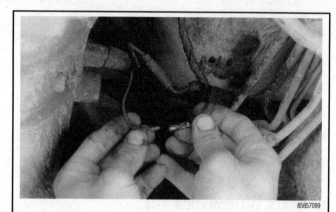

Fig. 1 Removing the electrical connection on back-up light switch

Transmission

REMOVAL & INSTALLATION

1970–86 (521, 620 and 720–D Series)

▶ See Figures 2 thru 12

F4W63, F4W71B AND FS5W71B

1. Disconnect the negative battery cable.
2. On 1975–86 models only, remove the shift lever from inside the cab. It is retained to the shaft rail by a C–clip, accessible under the boot. Remove the C-clip and retaining pin, then remove the lever.
3. Raise the vehicle and support it with jackstands.
4. On 1970–74 models, unscrew the nut securing the bottom of the shifter to the transmission shifting mechanism.
5. Disconnect the exhaust pipe from the exhaust manifold. On trucks with a catalytic converter, also remove the exhaust pipe bracket next to the speedometer cable by unscrewing the two mounting bolts.
6. Remove the clutch slave cylinder from the transmission case.
7. Disconnect the speedometer cable from the transmission extension housing, then disengage the back-up light and transmission switch wires at the switch(es).
8. Remove the bracket holding the center bearing of the driveshaft on the third crossmember of the frame.
9. Remove the driveshaft(s).

➡On 4wd models, this requires removal of the transfer case, which should be performed at this time.

Drive Train 7-3

10. Support the engine with a floor jack located under the oil pan. Place a block of wood between the jack and the oil pan to prevent damage to the oil pan. Support the transmission with a jack.

11. Remove the rear engine mount securing bolts and the crossmember mounting bolts. The 1970–71 models (521 series) do not have a removable crossmember; only the rear engine/transmission extension housing mount is removable from the crossmember.

12. Remove the starter motor.

13. Remove the bolts securing the transmission to the engine, pull the transmission toward the rear until the transmission mainshaft is free of the back of the engine.

14. On 1970–71 models, place the rear of the transmission on the crossmember and then pull the transmission down toward the front of the truck and out from under the vehicle.

15. On 1972–86 models, separate the transmission from the engine, then lower the transmission out from under the truck.

To install:

16. Before installing the transmission, clean the mating surfaces of the engine and transmission thoroughly.

17. Lightly coat the input shaft splines with grease.

18. Reverse the removal procedures. Tighten the engine-to-transmission bolts to 17–20 ft. lbs. (23–27 Nm) for 1970–73 vehicles, 29–36 ft. lbs. (39–49

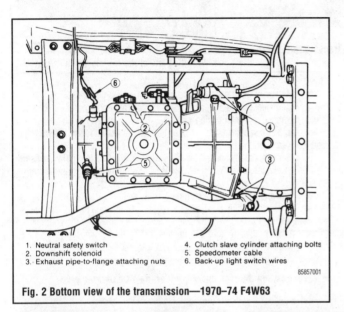

1. Neutral safety switch
2. Downshift solenoid
3. Exhaust pipe-to-flange attaching nuts
4. Clutch slave cylinder attaching bolts
5. Speedometer cable
6. Back-up light switch wires

Fig. 2 Bottom view of the transmission—1970–74 F4W63

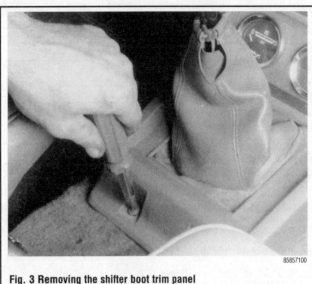

Fig. 3 Removing the shifter boot trim panel

Fig. 4 Removing the shifter E-clip

Fig. 5 Removing the shifter lever assembly

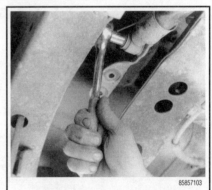

Fig. 6 Removing the transmission damper bolt

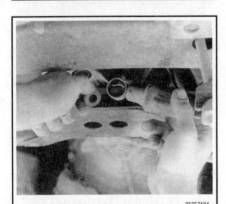

Fig. 7 Removing the damper bushing

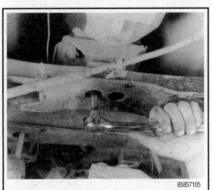

Fig. 8 Removing the transmission crossmember mount bolts

Fig. 9 Removing the transmission to frame mounting bolts

7-4 DRIVE TRAIN

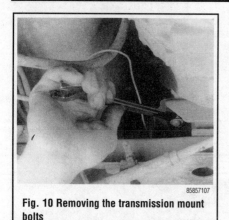

Fig. 10 Removing the transmission mount bolts

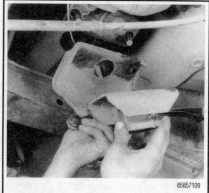

Fig. 11 Removing the transmission crossmember

Fig. 12 View of the transmission mount

Nm) for 1974–76 vehicles or to 32–43 ft. lbs. (43–58 Nm) for 1977–86 vehicles.

➡ On the 5-speed transmission, the two bottom bolts are tightened to 7–9 ft. lbs. (9–12 Nm).

19. Tighten the crossmember-to-chassis bolts to 20–27 ft. lbs. (27–37 Nm) and the clutch slave cylinder mounting bolts to 18–22 ft. lbs. (24–30 Nm). Be sure to align the marks made earlier on the U-joint and differential flange when installing the driveshaft, to maintain driveline balance.

1986–88 (D21-D Series)

F4W71C, FS5W71C AND FS5R30A

◆ See Figures 13, 14, 15, 16 and 17

1. Disconnect the negative battery cable.
2. Disconnect the accelerator linkage if necessary.
3. Raise the front of the truck and support it with jack stands.
4. Disconnect the exhaust pipe from the manifold and bracket if necessary to gain clearance for transmission removal.
5. Tag and disconnect any switches that are connected to the transmission case (back-up, neutral, top gear or overdrive).
6. Disconnect the speedometer cable where it attaches to the transmission.
7. Remove the driveshaft(s). Don't forget to plug the opening in the rear extension so that oil won't flow out.
8. Remove the clutch slave cylinder.
9. Remove the rubber boot and console box (if so equipped). Place the shift lever in neutral, remove the E-ring (later models only) and then remove the shifter. On 4wd models remove the transfer case shift lever also.
10. Support the engine by placing a jack under the oil pan with a wooden block used between the jack and the pan.

➡ Never position the jack directly under the oil pan drain plug.

11. Support the transmission with a transmission jack.

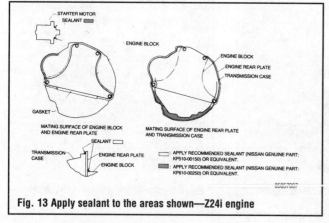

Fig. 13 Apply sealant to the areas shown—Z24i engine

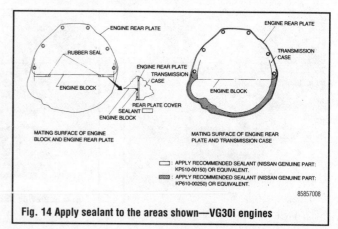

Fig. 14 Apply sealant to the areas shown—VG30i engines

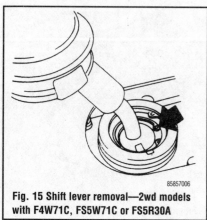

Fig. 15 Shift lever removal—2wd models with F4W71C, FS5W71C or FS5R30A

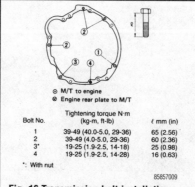

Fig. 16 Transmission bolt installation—Z24i engines

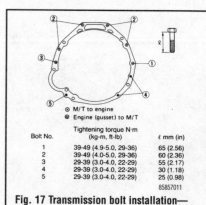

Fig. 17 Transmission bolt installation—VG30i engines

DRIVE TRAIN   7-5

12. Loosen the rear engine mount securing nuts temporarily and then remove the crossmember. On 4wd models, remove the torsion bar springs.
13. Lower the rear of the engine slightly to allow additional clearance.
14. Remove the starter electrical connections and the starter motor.
15. Remove the transmission-to-engine mounting bolts, lower the transmission and remove it toward the rear.

To install:

16. Install the transmission in the correct position. Tighten all the transmission-to-engine mounting bolts.
    a. On Z24i engines, tighten the 4 longest bolts (1—65mm and 3—60mm) to 29–36 ft. lbs. (39–49 Nm); tighten the 2 shortest bolts (1—25mm with nut and 1—16mm) to 14–18 ft. lbs. (19–25 Nm).
    b. On VG30i engines, tighten the 5 longest bolts (1—65mm and 4—60mm) to 29–36 ft. lbs. (39–49 Nm); tighten the 4 shortest bolts (1—55mm, 2—30mm and 1-16mm) to 22–29 ft. lbs. (29–39 Nm).

17. Install the starter motor and electrical connections.
18. Install the crossmember assembly and tighten all retaining nuts to crossmember and rear engine mounts. Install the torsion bars on 4wd models.
19. Install the shifter. Install the rubber boot and console box if so equipped.
20. Install the clutch slave cylinder.
21. Install the driveshaft(s) and connect the speedometer cable.
22. Connect any switches that are connected to the transmission case (back-up, neutral, top gear or overdrive).
23. Connect the exhaust pipe to the manifold and bracket if necessary.
24. Connect the accelerator linkage.
25. Connect the negative battery cable. Bleed the clutch hydraulic system if necessary. Road test the vehicle for proper shift pattern operation.

CLUTCH

✱✱ CAUTION

The clutch driven disc contains asbestos, which has been determined to be a cancer causing agent. Never clean clutch surfaces with compressed air. Avoid inhaling any dust from any clutch surface. When cleaning clutch surfaces, use a commercially available brake cleaning fluid.

Understanding the Clutch

The purpose of the clutch is to disconnect and connect engine power at the transmission. A vehicle at rest requires a lot of engine torque to get all that weight moving. An internal combustion engine does not develop a high starting torque (unlike steam engines) so it must be allowed to operate without any load until it builds up enough torque to move the vehicle. To a point, torque increases with engine rpm. The clutch allows the engine to build up torque by physically disconnecting the engine from the transmission, relieving the engine of any load or resistance.

The transfer of engine power to the transmission (the load) must be smooth and gradual; if it weren't, drive line components would wear out or break quickly. This gradual power transfer is made possible by gradually releasing the clutch pedal. The clutch disc and pressure plate are the connecting link between the engine and transmission. When the clutch pedal is released, the disc and plate contact each other (the clutch is engaged) physically joining the engine and transmission. When the pedal is pushed in, the disc and plate separate (the clutch is disengaged) disconnecting the engine from the transmission.

Most clutch assemblies consists of the flywheel, the clutch disc, the clutch pressure plate, the throw out bearing and fork, the actuating linkage and the pedal. The flywheel and clutch pressure plate (driving members) are connected to the engine crankshaft and rotate with it. The clutch disc is located between the flywheel and pressure plate, and is splined to the transmission shaft. A driving member is one that is attached to the engine and transfers engine power to a driven member (clutch disc) on the transmission shaft. A driving member (pressure plate) rotates (drives) a driven member (clutch disc) on contact and, in so doing, turns the transmission shaft.

There is a circular diaphragm spring within the pressure plate cover (transmission side). In a relaxed state (when the clutch pedal is fully released) this spring is convex; that is, it is dished outward toward the transmission. Pushing in the clutch pedal actuates the attached linkage. Connected to the other end of this is the throw out fork, which hold the throw out bearing. When the clutch pedal is depressed, the clutch linkage pushes the fork and bearing forward to contact the diaphragm spring of the pressure plate. The outer edges of the spring are secured to the pressure plate and are pivoted on rings so that when the center of the spring is compressed by the throw out bearing, the outer edges bow outward and, by so doing, pull the pressure plate in the same direction – away from the clutch disc. This action separates the disc from the plate, disengaging the clutch and allowing the transmission to be shifted into another gear. A coil type clutch return spring attached to the clutch pedal arm permits full release of the pedal. Releasing the pedal pulls the throw out bearing away from the diaphragm spring resulting in a reversal of spring position. As bearing pressure is gradually released from the spring center, the outer edges of the spring bow outward, pushing the pressure plate into closer contact with the clutch disc. As the disc and plate move closer together, friction between the two increases and slippage is reduced until, when full spring pressure is applied (by fully releasing the pedal) the speed of the disc and plate are the same. This stops all slipping, creating a direct connection between the plate and disc which results in the transfer of power from the engine to the transmission. The clutch disc is now rotating with the pressure plate at engine speed and, because it is splined to the transmission shaft, the shaft now turns at the same engine speed.

The clutch is operating properly if:

1. It will stall the engine when released with the vehicle held stationary.
2. The shift lever can be moved freely between 1st and reverse gears when the vehicle is stationary and the clutch disengaged.

Adjustments

PEDAL HEIGHT

♦ See Figures 18, 19 and 20

The pedal height measurement is gauged from the angle section of the floorboard to the center of the clutch pedal pad.

Adjust the pedal height by loosening the locknut on the pedal stopper, clutch switch or ASCD switch and turning the adjusting bolt to provide the following specified heights:

- 1970–73: 5.90 in. (150mm)
- 1974–77: 6.02 in. (153mm)
- 1978–80: 6.41 in. (163mm)
- 1981–82 Z22: 6.73 in. (171mm)
- 1983 Z22 6.61 in. (168mm)
- 1984–86 Z20 and Z24: 7.24 in. (184mm)
- 1986–88 Z24i: 9.29–9.68 in. (236–246mm)
- 1986–88 VG30i: 8.93–9.33 in. (227–237mm)

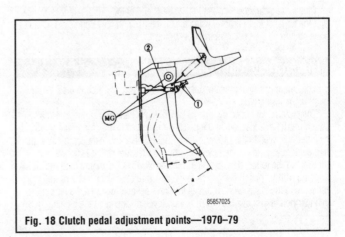

Fig. 18 Clutch pedal adjustment points—1970–79

7-6 DRIVE TRAIN

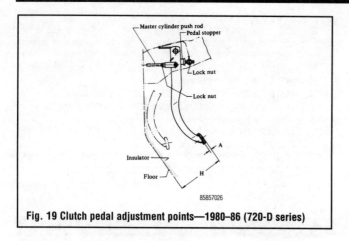

Fig. 19 Clutch pedal adjustment points—1980–86 (720-D series)

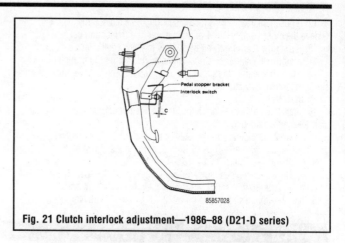

Fig. 21 Clutch interlock adjustment—1986–88 (D21-D series)

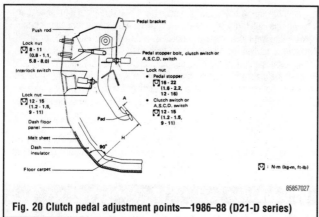

Fig. 20 Clutch pedal adjustment points—1986–88 (D21-D series)

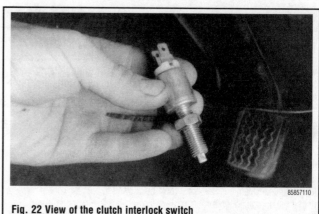

Fig. 22 View of the clutch interlock switch

PEDAL FREE-PLAY

The free-play measurement is the total travel of the clutch pedal from the fully released position to where resistance is felt as the pedal is pushed downward.

Adjust the pedal free-play by loosening the pushrod locknut and turning the clevis. free-play is as follows:
- 1970–77: 0.078 in. (2mm)
- 1978–84: 0.012 in. (3mm)
- 1985–88: 0.039–0.059 in. (1–1.5mm)

CLUTCH INTERLOCK

1986–88 (D21-D Series)

♦ See Figures 21 and 22

Check the clearance between the threaded end of the clutch interlock switch and the pedal stopper bracket when the clutch pedal is fully depressed. Clearance should be 0.011–0.039 in. (0.3–1.0mm).

Driven Disc And Pressure Plate

The clutch is a hydraulically operated single plate, dry friction disc, diaphragm spring type.

The clutch is operated by a pedal which is mechanically connected to a clutch master cylinder. When the pedal is depressed, the piston in the master cylinder is moved in the master cylinder bore. This movement compresses the hydraulic fluid in the master cylinder causing pressure which is transferred through a tube to the slave cylinder. The slave cylinder is mounted to the clutch housing with its piston connected to the clutch release lever. The hydraulic pressure in the slave cylinder forces the slave cylinder piston to travel out the cylinder bore and move the clutch release lever, disengaging the clutch.

REMOVAL & INSTALLATION

♦ See Figures 23 thru 34

✲✲✲ CAUTION

The clutch driven disc contains asbestos, which has been determined to be a cancer causing agent. Never clean clutch surfaces with compressed air. Avoid inhaling any dust from any clutch surface. When cleaning clutch surfaces, use a commercially available brake cleaning fluid.

1. Raise the vehicle and support it with floor stands.
2. Remove the transmission. On 1970–71 models with the non-removable crossmember, you can move the transmission back and rest it on the crossmember while working on the clutch, if you prefer. You won't have much working area, but it will save you the trouble of getting the transmission out from under the truck.
3. Mark the clutch assembly-to-flywheel relationship with paint or a center punch so that the clutch assembly can be reassembled in the same position from which it is removed. Insert a clutch aligning tool (dummy shaft) into the hub. This tool is available from your local Nissan dealer or an auto parts store. It is important to support the weight of the clutch while the retaining bolts are being removed.
4. Loosen the clutch cover-to-flywheel attaching bolts, one turn at a time in an alternating sequence, until the spring tension is relieved to avoid distorting or bending the clutch cover. Remove the clutch assembly.

To install:

5. Inspect the flywheel for scoring, roughness, or signs of overheating. Light scoring may be cleaned up with emery cloth, but any deep grooves or scoring warrant replacement or refacing (if possible) of the flywheel. If the clutch facings or flywheel are oily, inspect the transmission front cover oil seal, the pilot bushing, and engine rear seals, etc. for leakage, and correct before replacing the

DRIVE TRAIN 7-7

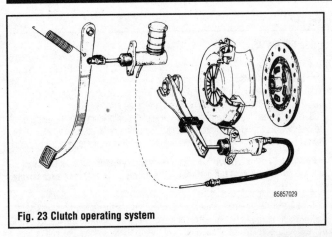
Fig. 23 Clutch operating system

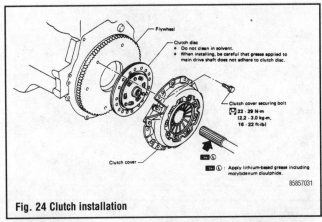
Fig. 24 Clutch installation

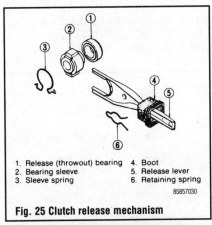
Fig. 25 Clutch release mechanism

1. Release (throwout) bearing
2. Bearing sleeve
3. Sleeve spring
4. Boot
5. Release lever
6. Retaining spring

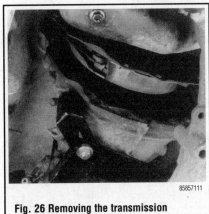
Fig. 26 Removing the transmission

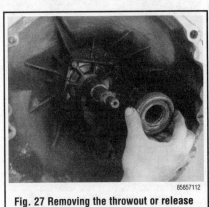
Fig. 27 Removing the throwout or release bearing

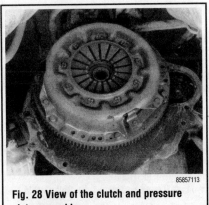
Fig. 28 View of the clutch and pressure plate assembly

Fig. 29 Removing the pressure plate bolts evenly in stages

Fig. 30 Removing the clutch disc from the pressure plate

Fig. 31 View of the flywheel and pilot bearing

Fig. 32 Removing the flywheel bolts-note position of tool to hold flywheel in place

Fig. 33 Marking the flywheel before removal

7-8 DRIVE TRAIN

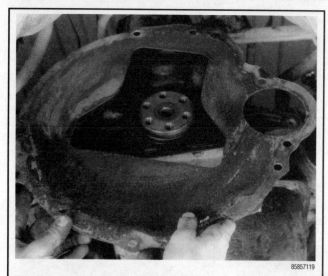

Fig. 34 Removing the transmission end plate

clutch. If the pilot bushing in the crankshaft is worn, replace it. Install it using a soft hammer. The factory supplied part does not have to be oiled, but check the procedure if you are using an aftermarket part. Inspect the clutch cover for wear or scoring, and replace as necessary. The pressure plate and spring cannot be disassembled; you must replace the clutch cover as an assembly.

6. Inspect the clutch release bearing. If it is rough or noisy, it should be replaced. The bearing can be removed from the sleeve with a puller; this requires a press to install the new bearing. After installation, coat the groove in the sleeve, the contact surfaces of the release lever, pivot pin and sleeve, and the release bearing contact surfaces on the transmission front cover with a light coat of grease. Be careful not to use too much grease, which will run at high temperatures and get onto the clutch facings. Reinstall the release bearing on the lever.

7. Apply a thin coat of grease to the pressure plate wire ring, diaphragm spring, clutch cover grooves and the drive bosses on the pressure plate.

8. Apply a thin coat of Lubriplate® to the splines in the driven plate. Slide the clutch disc onto the splines, and move it back and forth several times. Remove the disc and wipe off the excess lubricant. Be very careful not to get any grease on the clutch facings.

9. Assemble the clutch cover and the clutch plate on the clutch alignment arbor.

10. Align the marks made on the clutch cover and the flywheel (if the old cover is being used) and install the clutch cover-to-flywheel attaching bolts. Three dowels are used to locate the clutch cover on the flywheel properly. Tighten the bolts in an alternating sequence one turn at a time to 12–15 ft. lbs. (17–22 Nm) on 1970–79 models and 16–22 ft. lbs. (22–29 Nm) on 1980–88 models. Remove the aligning arbor.

11. Install the transmission.

Clutch Master Cylinder

REMOVAL & INSTALLATION

1. Disconnect the master cylinder pushrod from the clutch pedal.
2. Remove the hydraulic line from the master cylinder being careful not to damage the compression fitting.
3. Remove the two bolts holding the master cylinder to the engine compartment.

❈❈ CAUTION

Brake fluid dissolves paint. Do not allow it to drip onto the body when removing the master cylinder.

To install:

4. Install the master cylinder. Partially tighten the hydraulic line and then tighten the cylinder mounting bolts.
5. Connect the pushrod to the clutch pedal.
6. Adjust the clutch pedal and bleed the system.

OVERHAUL

▸ See Figure 35

1. Disassemble the master cylinder by unscrewing the clutch pedal clevis from the pushrod. Also remove the locknut.
2. Pull off the rubber boot to expose an internal snapring. Remove the snapring and withdraw the piston and compression spring.
3. Take a clean rag and wipe out the inside of the cylinder. Inspect the inside of the cylinder for scoring and deposits. Use crocus cloth or a small hone to refinish the inside of the cylinder. If light honing will not remove score marks replace the cylinder.

➡Be careful not to remove too much from the cylinder walls as the cups will not be able to seal the cylinder if the diameter is enlarged excessively.

4. Wash all metal parts in solvent.
5. Further disassembly should be avoided unless the reservoir is leaking. If the reservoir needs to be replaced, remove the cap and remove the master cylinder reservoir bolt located at the bottom of the reservoir. Tighten the bolt upon reassembly.
6. With new parts from the rebuilding kit assemble the master cylinder. Coat the cylinder wall with brake fluid so that the edges of the new cups will not be damaged. Coat the piston with lithium soap based glycol grease.

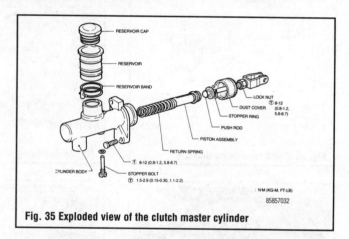

Fig. 35 Exploded view of the clutch master cylinder

Clutch Release Cylinder

REMOVAL & INSTALLATION

▸ See Figures 36, 37 and 38

1. Raise the front of the truck and support it on jackstands.
2. Remove the tension spring on the clutch fork.
3. Remove the hydraulic line from the release cylinder. Be careful not to damage the fitting.
4. Turn the release cylinder pushrod in sufficiently to gain clearance from the fork.
5. Remove the mounting bolts and withdraw the cylinder.

To install:

6. Install the hydraulic line from the master cylinder.
7. Position the cylinder on the clutch housing and install the clamp and retaining screws. Tighten the attaching bolts to 18–25 ft. lbs. (25–35 Nm) on 1970–79 models and 22–30 ft. lbs. (30–40 Nm) on 1980–88 models.
8. Adjust the fork tip clearance to 0.079 in. (2mm) on 1970–71 models

➡The system must be bled after the cylinder is reinstalled.

OVERHAUL

▸ See Figure 39

1. Remove the pushrod, rubber boot, piston and cups from the cylinder.
2. Clean the inside of the cylinder with a rag and inspect for scoring. If there is no serious damage, hone the cylinder just enough to remove deposits.

DRIVE TRAIN   7-9

Fig. 36 Removing the clutch release cylinder bolts

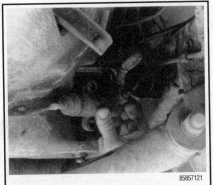
Fig. 37 Removing the clutch release cylinder assembly

Fig. 38 Bleeding the clutch release cylinder

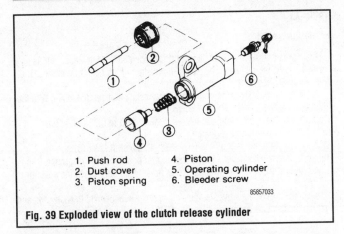
Fig. 39 Exploded view of the clutch release cylinder

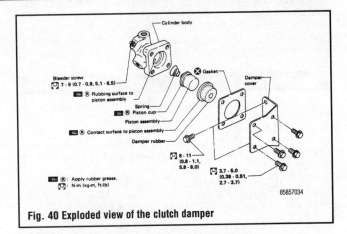
Fig. 40 Exploded view of the clutch damper

Replace the cylinder if light honing does not remove the score marks. Wash all the parts in brake fluid before assembly.

3. Coat the new rubber parts in brake fluid and reassemble. Coat the piston with lithium soap based glycol grease.

Clutch Damper

REMOVAL & INSTALLATION

1986–88 Only (D21-D Series)

1. Loosen the union nuts and disconnect the two hydraulic lines at the damper.
2. Remove the mounting bolts and then remove the clutch damper from the firewall.

To install:

3. Install the damper and tighten the bolts to 6–8 ft. lbs. (8–11 Nm).
4. Reconnect the hydraulic lines being careful not to damage the union nuts.
5. Bleed the system.

OVERHAUL

♦ See Figure 40

1. Remove the damper cover and gasket from the cylinder body.
2. Remove the rubber damper, piston and cups and spring from the cylinder.
3. Clean the inside of the cylinder with a rag and inspect for scoring. If there is no serious damage, hone the cylinder just enough to remove deposits. Replace the cylinder if light honing does not remove the score marks. Wash all the parts in brake fluid before assembly.
4. Coat the new rubber parts in brake fluid and reassemble. Coat the piston with lithium soap based glycol grease.
5. Install a new gasket and tighten the damper cover to 3–4 ft. lbs. (3–5 Nm).

BLEEDING THE CLUTCH HYDRAULIC SYSTEM

♦ See Figure 41

→This procedure may be utilized when either the clutch master or release cylinder has been removed or if any of the hydraulic lines have been disturbed.

❉❉ CAUTION

Do not spill brake fluid on the body of the vehicle as it will destroy the paint.

1. Fill the master cylinder reservoir with brake fluid.

→On 1986–88 models that incorporate a clutch damper in the hydraulic system, perform Steps 1–10 for the clutch damper and then move on to the release cylinder.

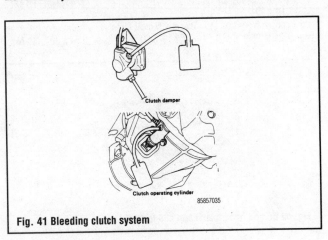
Fig. 41 Bleeding clutch system

7-10 DRIVE TRAIN

2. Remove the cap and loosen the bleeder screw on the clutch release cylinder. Cover the hole with your finger.
3. Have an assistant pump the clutch pedal several times. Take your finger off the hole while the pedal is being depressed so that the air in the system can be released. Put your finger back on the hole and release the pedal.
4. After fluid pressure can be felt (with your finger) tighten the bleeder screw.
5. Put a short length of hose over the bleeder screw and place the other end into a jar half full of clean brake fluid.
6. Depress the clutch pedal and loosen the bleeder screw. Allow the fluid to flow into the jar.
7. Tighten the plug and then release the clutch pedal.
8. Repeat Steps 6–7 until no air bubbles are visible in the bleeder tube.
9. When there are no more air bubbles in the system, tighten the plug fully with the pedal depressed. Replace the plastic cap.
10. Fill the master cylinder to the correct level with brake fluid.
11. Check the system for leaks.

AUTOMATIC TRANSMISSION

Understanding the Automatic Transmission

The automatic transmission allows engine torque and power to be transmitted to the rear wheels within a narrow range of engine operating speeds. It will allow the engine to turn fast enough to produce plenty of power and torque at very low speeds, while keeping it at a sensible rpm at high vehicle speeds (and it does this job without driver assistance). The transmission uses a light fluid as the medium for the transmission of power. This fluid also works in the operation of various hydraulic control circuits and as a lubricant. Because the transmission fluid performs all of these functions, trouble within the unit can easily travel from one part to another.

Identification

The optional automatic transmission is a JATCO (Japan Automatic Transmission Co., Ltd.) Model L3N71B It is used on all models except the D21-D series truck. The D21-D series trucks introduced in 1986 use a model L4N71B with the Z24i engine, a model E4N71B with the VG30i engine in 1986–87, and in 1988, a model E4N71B for 2wd models with the VG30i engine and a model RE4R01A for 4wd models.

All of these transmissions are fully automatic units, with a three element torque converter and tow planetary gear sets. The transmission shifts gears in response to signals of both engine speed and manifold vacuum.

While it is unlikely that you will ever disassemble the transmission yourself, there are a few adjustments you can perform which will prolong the transmission's life if performed accurately. The most important thing is to change the fluid regularly, which is covered in Section One.

Fluid Pan

Refer to Section 1 for fluid pan removal procedures.

Adjustments

BRAKE BAND

L3N71B Only

♦ See Figure 42

1. Remove the fluid pan.
2. Loosen the locknut on the piston stem. Tighten the piston stem to 9–11 ft. lbs. (12–15 Nm).
3. Loosen the piston stem **exactly** two (2) turns. Hold the stem and tighten the locknut to 20 ft. lbs. (27 Nm) for 1973–79 vehicles or to 14 ft. lbs. (19 Nm) for 1980–86 vehicles. If the stem turns when the locknut is tightened, loosen the locknut and repeat the adjustment.
4. Replace the fluid pan and refill the transmission.

SHIFT LINKAGE

1970–79

♦ See Figure 43

Adjustment of the shift linkage is a critical operation. If the adjustment is made sloppily, the result will be partial application of the band or clutches, and will eventually burn up the transmission.

1. If the control knob is removed prior to installation set dimension **A** in the illustration to 0.43–0.47 in. (11–12mm).
2. Install the control knob, adjusting dimension **B** to 0.004–0.043 in. (0.1–1.1mm) by turning the pushing rod (2).
3. Loosen the adjusting nuts (H). Set both the shift lever (3) and the transmission selector lever (4) into the neutral positions. Set clearance **C** to 0.040 in. (1mm) by turning the adjusting nuts which connect to the selector rod (6).

After making the adjustments, check for proper engagement in each gear, and that the mechanism operates without binding. Readjust as necessary.

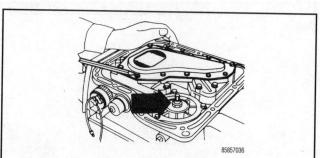

Fig. 42 Brake band piston stem and locknut (arrow)

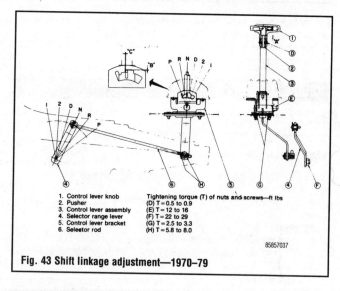

Fig. 43 Shift linkage adjustment—1970–79

1980–86 (720-D Series)

♦ See Figure 44

Adjustment is made at the locknuts at the base of the shifter, which control the length of the shift control rod.

1. Place the shift lever in **D**.
2. Loosen the locknuts and move the shift lever until it is firmly in the **D** range, the pointer is aligned, and the transmission is in **D** range.
3. Tighten the locknuts.
4. Check the adjustment. Start the truck and apply the parking brake. Shift through all the ranges, starting in **P**. As the lever is moved from **P** to **1**, you should be able to feel the detents in each range. If proper adjustment is not possible, the grommets are probably worn and should be replaced.

DRIVE TRAIN 7-11

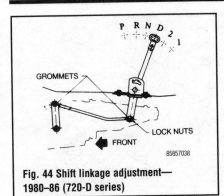

Fig. 44 Shift linkage adjustment—1980–86 (720-D series)

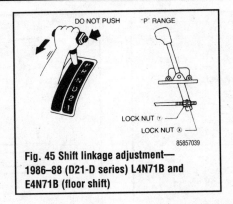

Fig. 45 Shift linkage adjustment—1986–88 (D21-D series) L4N71B and E4N71B (floor shift)

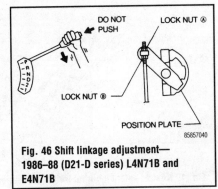

Fig. 46 Shift linkage adjustment—1986–88 (D21-D series) L4N71B and E4N71B

1986–88 (D21-D Series)

L4N71B AND E4N71B—FLOOR SHIFT MODELS

♦ See Figure 45

Move the gear selector lever slowly through the ranges from **P** to **1**. You should be able to feel the detents in each range. If the detents can't be felt, or if the indicator point is out of alignment, the linkage needs adjustment.

1. Position the selector lever in **P**.
2. Loosen the locknuts.
3. Tighten the locknut **X** until it touches the trunnion, pulling the selector lever toward the **R** side without pushing the button.
4. Back off the locknut **X** ¼–½ turn (1986–87) or 1 turn (1988) and tighten the lock nut **Y** to 6–8 ft. lbs. (8–11 Nm) on 1986–87 models; 8–11 ft. lbs. (11–15 Nm) on 1988 models.
5. Move the selector lever from the **P** range to the **1** range. Make sure the selector lever moves smoothly.

L4N71B AND E4N71B—COLUMN SHIFT MODELS

♦ See Figure 46

Move the gear selector lever slowly through the ranges from **P** to **1**. You should be able to feel the detents in each range. If the detents can't be felt, or if the indicator point is out of alignment, the linkage needs adjustment.

1. Position the selector lever in **P**.
2. Loosen the locknuts.
3. Tighten the locknut **A** until it touches the trunnion, pulling the selector lever toward the **R** side without pushing the button.
4. Back off the locknut **A** 2 turns and tighten the locknut **B** to 6–8 ft. lbs. (8–11 Nm) on 1986–87 models; 8–11 ft. lbs. (11–15 Nm) on 1988 models.
5. Move the selector lever from the **P** range to the **1** range. Make sure the selector lever moves smoothly.

RE4R01A—FLOOR SHIFT MODELS

♦ See Figure 47

Move the gear selector lever slowly through the ranges from **P** to **1**. You should be able to feel the detents in each range. If the detents can't be felt, or if the indicator point is out of alignment, the linkage needs adjustment.

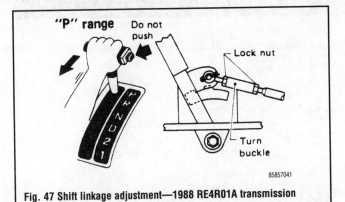

Fig. 47 Shift linkage adjustment—1988 RE4R01A transmission

1. Position the selector lever in **P**.
2. Loosen the locknuts.
3. Tighten the turnbuckle until it aligns with the inner cable, pulling the selector lever toward the **R** side without pushing the button.
4. Back off the turnbuckle 1 turn and tighten the locknuts to 3.3–4.3 ft. lbs. (4.4–5.9 Nm).
5. Move the selector lever from the **P** range to the **1** range. Make sure the selector lever moves smoothly.

KICKDOWN SWITCH AND DOWNSHIFT SOLENOID

L3N71B Models Only

♦ See Figure 48

1. Turn the key to the **ON** position (without starting the engine), and depress the accelerator all the way. The solenoid in the transmission should make an audible click.
2. If the solenoid does not work, inspect the wiring, and test it electrically to determine whether the problem is in the wiring, the kickdown switch, or the solenoid.
3. If the solenoid requires replacement, drain a little over 2 pts (1 liter) of fluid from the transmission before removing it.

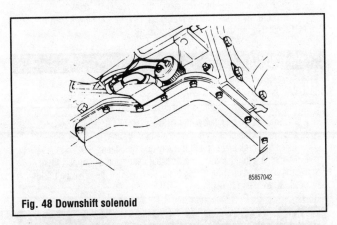

Fig. 48 Downshift solenoid

Neutral Safety/Inhibitor Switch

1973–86 (620 and 720-D SERIES)

♦ See Figure 49

The switch unit is bolted to the left side of the transmission case, behind the transmission shift lever. The switch prevents the engine from being started in any transmission position except **P** or **N**. It also controls the back-up lights.

1. Apply the brakes and check to see that the starter works only in the **P** and **N** transmission ranges. If the starter works with the transmission in gear, adjust the switch as described below.

7-12 DRIVE TRAIN

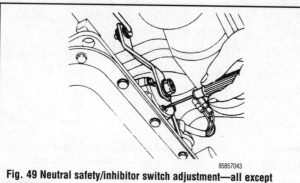

Fig. 49 Neutral safety/inhibitor switch adjustment—all except RE4R01A

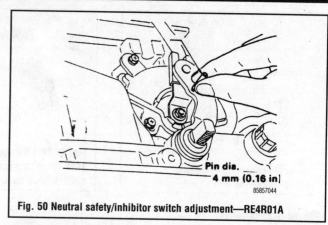

Fig. 50 Neutral safety/inhibitor switch adjustment—RE4R01A

2. Remove the transmission shift lever retaining nut and the lever.
3. Remove the switch.

To install:

4. Remove the machine screw in the case under the switch.
5. Align the switch to the case by inserting a 0.059 in. (1.5mm) pin, through the hole in the switch into the screw hole. Mark the switch location.
6. Remove the pin, replace the machine screw, install the switch as marked, then replace the transmission shift lever and retaining nut.
7. Make sure while holding the brakes on, that the engine will start only in **P** or **N**. Check that the back-up lights go on only in **R**.

1986–88 (D21-D SERIES)

▶ See Figure 50

The switch unit is bolted to the transmission case, behind the transmission shift lever. The switch prevents the engine from being started in any transmission position except **P** or **N**. It also controls the back-up lights.

1. Place the transmission selector lever in the **N**.
2. Remove the screw from the switch.
3. Loosen the attaching bolts. Using a 0.16 in. (4.0mm) aligning pin to gauge the adjustment, move the switch until the pin falls into the hole in the rotor.
4. Tighten the attaching bolts equally.
5. Make sure while holding the brakes on, that the engine will start only in **P** or **N**. Check that the back-up lights go on only in **R**.

Transmission

REMOVAL & INSTALLATION

1. Disconnect the negative battery cable.
2. Disconnect the shaft from the accelerator linkage.
3. Raise the truck and support it safely on floor stands.
4. Matchmark the U-joint and differential flange and disconnect them. Remove the center bearing mounting bolts, then remove the driveshaft. Plug the transmission extension housing.

TRANSFER CASE

Transfer Case

REMOVAL & INSTALLATION

1981–86 Model T100L (720-D Series)

▶ See Figure 51

1. Disconnect the negative battery cable.
2. Raise the vehicle and support it with jackstands.
3. Remove the transfer case shield.
4. Remove the primary driveshaft securing nuts.
5. Remove the front and rear driveshafts.

5. Disconnect the exhaust pipe from the manifold and discard the gasket. Use a new gasket upon assembly. On trucks with a catalytic converter, disconnect the exhaust pipe bracket.
6. Disconnect the shift linkage at the transmission.
7. Disconnect the neutral safety (inhibitor) switch wires. Disconnect the vacuum hose from the diaphragm, and the wire from the downshift solenoid. Disconnect the speedometer cable from the extension housing.
8. Remove the fluid filler tube.
9. Disconnect the fluid cooler lines at the transmission. Use a flare nut wrench if one is available.
10. Support the engine with a jack under the oil pan, placing a wooden block between the pan and the jack as a buffer. Also support the transmission with a jack.
11. Remove the torque converter cover. Matchmark the converter and the drive plate for reassembly; they were balanced as a unit at the factory. Remove the bolts attaching the converter to the drive plate (flywheel). You will have to rotate the engine to do this, using a wrench on the crankshaft pulley bolt.
12. Remove the bolts for the rear engine mount and the crossmember. Remove the crossmember.
13. Remove the starter.
14. Remove the transmission-to-engine bolts. Lower the transmission back and down, out from under the truck.

To install:

15. Before installing the transmission, check the drive plate runout with a dial indicator. Turn the crankshaft one full turn. Maximum allowable runout is 0.012 in. (0.3mm). Replace the drive plate if runout exceeds 0.5mm; otherwise, reface it.
16. After connecting the torque converter to the transmission, lay a straight-edge across the face of the transmission and measure the distance from the top of the mounting bolt to the straight-edge. It should be at least 1.38 in. (35mm) on all transmissions except the RE4R01A, where it should be at least 1.02 in. (26mm).
17. When installing the torque converter, be sure to line up the notch in the converter with the projection on the oil pump. Align the marks made during removal and bolt the converter to the drive plate, tightening the bolts to 29–36 ft. lbs. (39–49 Nm). Then rotate the engine a few turns to make sure the transmission rotates freely without binding. The engine-to-transmission bolt torque is 29–36 ft. lbs. (39–49 Nm). Adjust the shift linkage and neutral safety switches and check the transmission fluid level.

6. Disconnect the 4wd switch wire.
7. Disconnect the speedometer cable.
8. Remove the exhaust pipe.
9. Support the transfer case with a jack.
10. Temporarily loosen the transfer case insulator bolts.
11. Remove the shift lever rubber boot from the floor.
12. Unbolt and remove the transfer case and primary driveshaft from the vehicle. Remove the insulators from the transfer case.

To install:

13. Install the insulators on the transfer case and then install the case itself. Tighten all bolts to 20–26 ft. lbs. (27–35 Nm).
14. Install the shift lever boot.
15. Connect the exhaust pipe to the manifold.
16. Connect the speedometer cable and the 4wd switch.

Drive Train 7-13

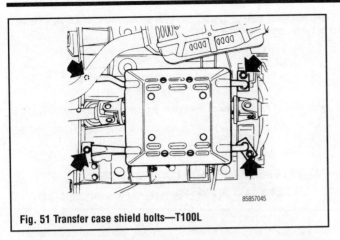

Fig. 51 Transfer case shield bolts—T100L

17. Install the front and rear driveshafts, then tighten the primary driveshaft nuts.
18. Install the case shield. Refill the transfer case with fluid, lower the truck and connect the battery cable. Road test the truck and check for any leaks of improper operation.

1986–88 Model TX100 (D21-D Series)

1. Disconnect the negative battery cable.
2. Raise the front of the vehicle and support it with jackstands.

3. Drain the fluid from the transmission and transfer cases.
4. Remove the front and rear driveshafts. Be sure to plug the oil seal openings after removal.

➡ Be very careful not to damage the transfer case spline, yoke or oil seal while removing the driveshafts.

5. Remove the torsion bar spring.
6. Remove the second crossmember.
7. Disconnect the transfer control lever at the outer shift lever ball joint and position it out of the way.
8. Position a floor jack underneath the transfer case, then remove the case-to-transmission mounting bolts. Separate the transfer case from the transmission and slowly lower it out and away from the transmission.

To install:
9. Carefully position the transfer case so that it mates with the transmission and tighten the mounting bolts to 23–30 ft. lbs. (31–41 Nm). On models with manual transmissions, be sure to coat the case mating surface with sealant.
10. Connect the transfer control lever to the outer shift lever and tighten the nut to 18–22 ft. lbs. (25–30 Nm).
11. Install the second crossmember and tighten the bolts to 43–58 ft. lbs. (59–78 Nm). Install the torsion bar spring.
12. Unplug the oil seals and install the two driveshafts.
13. Refill the transmission and transfer case with fluid, lower the vehicle and connect the battery cable. Road test the truck and check for any leaks or improper operation.

DRIVELINE

Front Driveshaft And U-Joints

REMOVAL & INSTALLATION

◆ See Figures 52, 53, 54 and 55

1981–86 720-D Series

PRIMARY DRIVESHAFT

1. Matchmark the flanges and separate the primary driveshaft from the transfer case.
2. Remove the transfer case.
3. Pull the primary shaft from the transmission and plug the opening.

To install:
4. Slide the front end of the driveshaft into the transmission and support the driveshaft with wire.
5. Install the transfer case.
6. Position the rear end of the driveshaft at the transfer case so the marks made previously align and then tighten the flange bolts to 58–65 ft. lbs. (78–88 Nm).

FRONT DRIVESHAFT

1. Matchmark the flanges and unbolt the front driveshaft at the front differential.
2. Matchmark the flanges and unbolt the front driveshaft at the transfer case.

To install:
3. Align the matchmarks at the transfer case and install the driveshaft. Tighten the flange bolts to 25–33 ft. lbs. (34–44 Nm).
4. Align the matchmarks at the front differential and install the driveshaft. Tighten the flange bolts to 25–33 ft. lbs. (34–44 Nm).

1986–88 D21-D Series

1. Matchmark the flanges and unbolt the front driveshaft at the front differential.
2. Matchmark the flanges and unbolt the front driveshaft at the transfer case.

To install:
3. Align the matchmarks at the transfer case and install the driveshaft. Tighten the flange bolts to 29–33 ft. lbs. (39–44 Nm).
4. Align the matchmarks at the front differential and install the driveshaft. Tighten the flange bolts to 29–33 ft. lbs. (39–44 Nm).

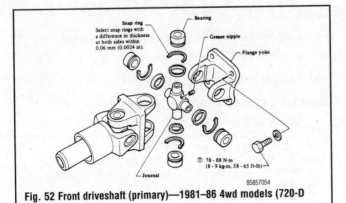

Fig. 52 Front driveshaft (primary)—1981–86 4wd models (720-D series)

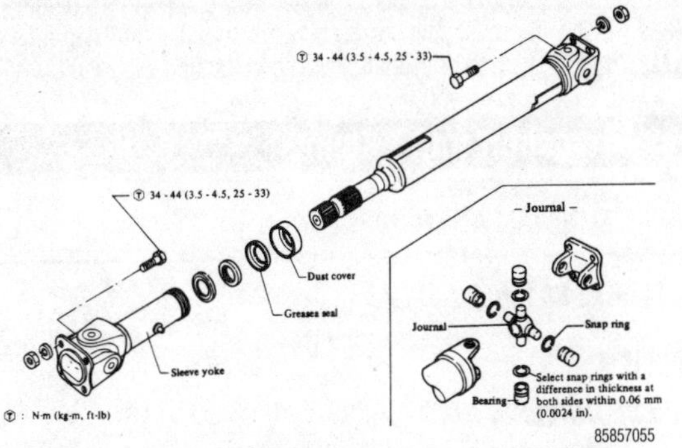

Fig. 53 Front driveshaft (front)—1981–86 4wd models (720-D series)

7-14 DRIVE TRAIN

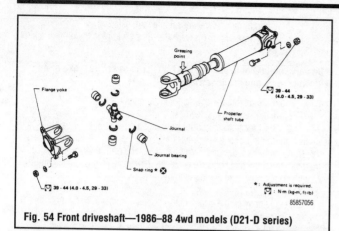

Fig. 54 Front driveshaft—1986–88 4wd models (D21-D series)

Fig. 55 Removing the front driveshaft—most models similar

U-JOINT OVERHAUL

1. Matchmark the yoke and the driveshaft.
2. Remove the snaprings from the bearings.
3. Position the yoke on vise jaws. Using a bearing remover and a hammer, gently tap the remover until the bearing is driven out of the yoke about 1 in. (25mm).
4. Place the tool in the vise and drive the yoke away from the tool until the bearing is removed.
5. Repeat Steps 3 and 4 for the other bearings.
6. Check for worn or damaged parts. Inspect the bearing journal surfaces for wear.

To assemble:

7. Install the bearing cups, seals, and O-rings in the spider.
8. Grease the spider and the bearings.
9. Position the spider in the yoke.
10. Start the bearings in the yoke and then press them into place, using a vise.
11. If the axial play of the spider is greater than 0.0007 in. (0.02mm), select snaprings which will provide the correct play. Be sure that the snaprings are the same size on both sides or driveshaft noise and vibration will result.

Rear Driveshaft and U-Joints

REMOVAL & INSTALLATION

▶ See Figures 56 thru 62

2wd Models

ONE-PIECE DRIVESHAFT

1. Jack up the rear of the truck and support the rear axle housing with jackstands.
2. Paint a mating mark on the two halves of the rear universal joint flange.
3. Remove the bolts which hold the rear flange together.
4. Remove the splined end of the driveshaft from the transmission.

➡If you don't want to lose a lot of gear or transmission oil, plug the end of the transmission with a rag.

5. Remove the driveshaft from under the truck.

To install:

6. Apply multipurpose grease to the splined end of the shaft.
7. Insert the driveshaft sleeve into the transmission.

➡Be careful not to damage the extension housing grease seal.

8. Align the mating marks on the rear flange and replace the bolts. Tighten to 58–65 ft. lbs. (78–88 Nm).
9. Remove the jackstands and lower the vehicle.

TWO-PIECE DRIVESHAFT WITH CENTER BEARING

1. Raise the rear of the truck and support the rear axle housing on jackstands.
2. Before you begin to disassemble the driveshaft components, you must first paint accurate alignment marks on the mating flanges. Do this on the rear universal joint flange, the center flange, and on the transmission flange.
3. Remove the bolts attaching the rear universal joint flange to the drive pinion flange.
4. Drop the rear section of the shaft slightly and pull the unit out of the center bearing sleeve yoke.
5. Remove the center bearing support from the crossmember.
6. Separate the transmission output flange and remove the front half of the driveshaft together with the center bearing assembly.

To install:

7. Connect the output flange of the transmission to the flange on the front half of the shaft.
8. Install the center bearing support to the crossmember, but do not fully tighten the bolts.
9. Install the rear section of the shaft making sure that all mating marks are aligned.
10. Tighten all flange bolts to 17–24 ft. lbs. (24–32 Nm) on 1974–86 models. On 1986–88 models (D21-D series), tighten the bolts to 29–33 ft. lbs. (39–44 Nm)—Z24i engines; or 58–65 ft. lbs. (78–88 Nm)—VG30i engines.
11. Tighten the center bearing support bolts to 12–16 ft. lbs. (16–22 Nm).

4wd Models

ONE-PIECE DRIVESHAFT

1. Raise the rear of the truck and support the rear axle housing with jackstands.
2. Paint a mating mark on the two halves of the rear universal joint flange.
3. Remove the bolts which hold the rear flange together.
4. Remove the splined end of the driveshaft from the transmission. If you don't want to lose a lot of gear oil, plug the end of the transmission with a rag.

➡The rear driveshaft on 1981–86 models is connected to the transfer case by means of a flange, simply unbolt it.

5. Remove the driveshaft from under the truck.

To install:

6. Apply multipurpose grease to the splined end of the shaft.
7. Insert the driveshaft sleeve into the transmission (1986–88 D21-D) or mount the flange and tighten the bolts to 58–65 ft. lbs. (78–88 Nm) on 1981–86 720-D models.

➡Be careful not to damage the extension housing grease seal.

8. Align the mating marks on the rear flange and replace the bolts. Tighten to 58–65 ft. lbs. (78–88 Nm).
9. Remove the jackstands and lower the vehicle.

TWO-PIECE DRIVESHAFT WITH CENTER BEARING

1. Raise the rear of the truck and support the rear axle housing on jackstands.
2. Before you begin to disassemble the driveshaft components, you must first paint accurate alignment marks on the mating flanges. Do this on the rear universal joint flange, the center flange, and on the transmission flange.
3. Remove the bolts attaching the rear universal joint flange to the drive pinion flange.
4. Drop the rear section of the shaft slightly and pull the unit out of the center bearing sleeve yoke.
5. Remove the center bearing support from the crossmember.

DRIVE TRAIN 7-15

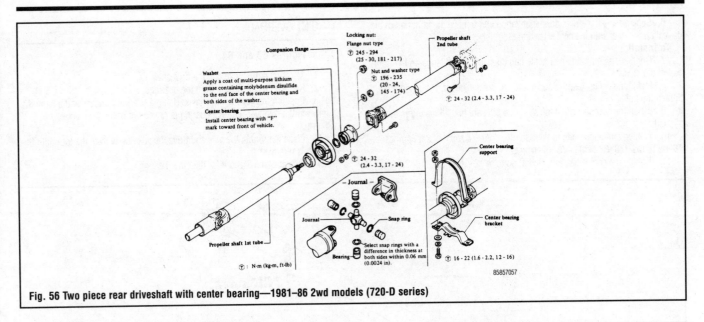

Fig. 56 Two piece rear driveshaft with center bearing—1981–86 2wd models (720-D series)

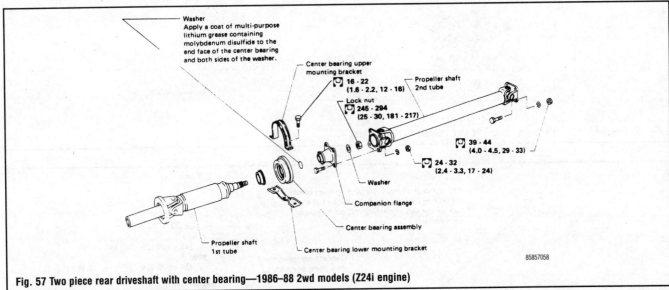

Fig. 57 Two piece rear driveshaft with center bearing—1986–88 2wd models (Z24i engine)

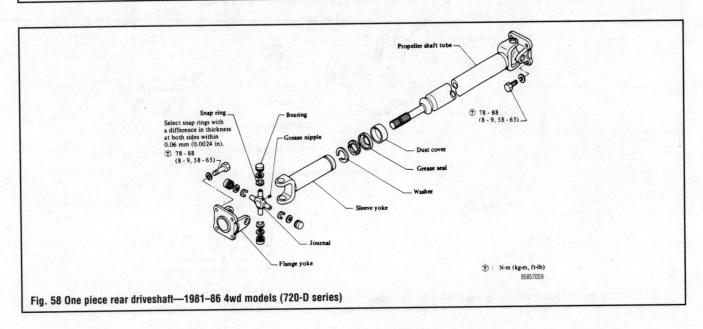

Fig. 58 One piece rear driveshaft—1981–86 4wd models (720-D series)

7-16 DRIVE TRAIN

6. Separate the transmission output flange and remove the front half of the driveshaft together with the center bearing assembly.

To install:

7. Connect the output flange of the transmission to the flange on the front half of the shaft.

8. Install the center bearing support to the crossmember, but do not fully tighten the bolts.

9. Install the rear section of the shaft making sure that all mating marks are aligned.

10. Tighten all flange bolts to 29–33 ft. lbs. (39–44 Nm)—Z24i engines; or 58–65 ft. lbs. (78–88 Nm)—VG30i engines.

11. Tighten the center bearing support bolts to 12–16 ft. lbs. (16–22 Nm).

U-JOINT OVERHAUL

▶ See Figures 63 and 64

1. Matchmark the yoke and the driveshaft.
2. Remove the snaprings from the bearings.
3. Position the yoke on vise jaws. Using a bearing remover and a hammer, gently tap the remover until the bearing is driven out of the yoke about 1 in. (25mm).
4. Place the tool in the vise and drive the yoke away from the tool until the bearing is removed.
5. Repeat Steps 3 and 4 for the other bearings.

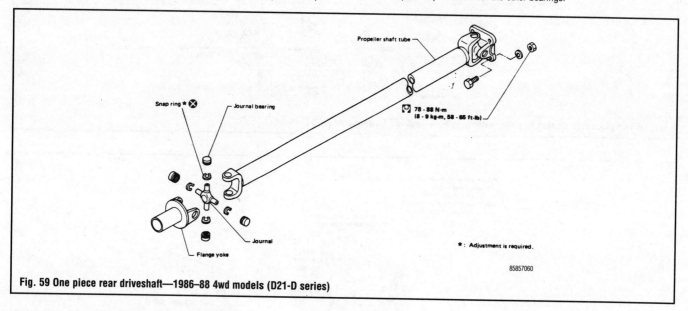

Fig. 59 One piece rear driveshaft—1986–88 4wd models (D21-D series)

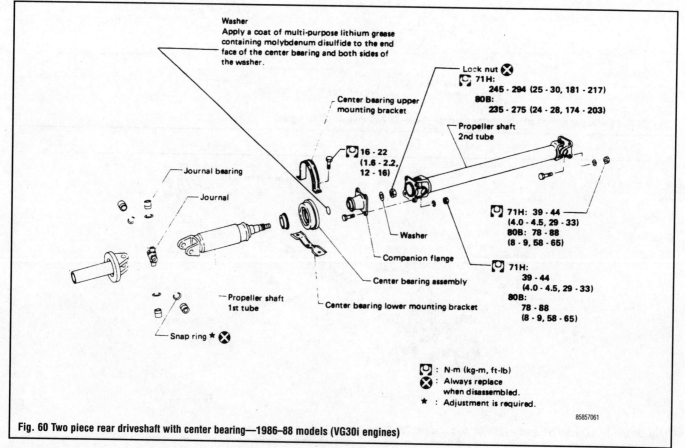

Fig. 60 Two piece rear driveshaft with center bearing—1986–88 models (VG30i engines)

DRIVE TRAIN 7-17

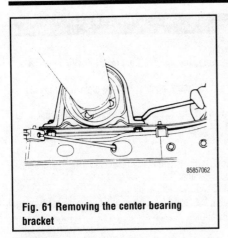

Fig. 61 Removing the center bearing bracket

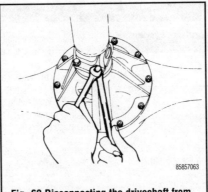

Fig. 62 Disconnecting the driveshaft from the differential flange

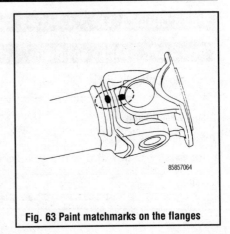

Fig. 63 Paint matchmarks on the flanges

6. Check for worn or damaged parts. Inspect the bearing journal surfaces for wear.

To assemble:

7. Install the bearing cups, seals, and O-rings in the spider.
8. Grease the spider and the bearings.
9. Position the spider in the yoke.
10. Start the bearings in the yoke and then press them into place, using a vise.
11. Repeat for the other bearings.
12. If the axial play of the spider is greater than 0.0007 in. (0.02mm), select snaprings which will provide the correct play. Be sure that the snaprings are the same size on both sides or driveshaft noise and vibration will result.

Center Bearing

REMOVAL & INSTALLATION

▶ See Figures 65, 66 and 67

➡ The following procedure requires the use of special lock nut removal tool, a puller to remove the companion flange, and a press to remove the center bearing. The center bearing is a sealed unit which must be replaced as an assembly if defective.

1. Remove the driveshaft.
2. Matchmark the flange yoke and the companion flange which connect the front half of the driveshaft to the rear. Also matchmark the companion flange and the front driveshaft. Remove the bolts and separate the shafts.
3. You must devise a way to hold the driveshaft while unbolting the companion flange from the front driveshaft. Do not place the front driveshaft tube in a vise, because the chances are it will get crushed. The best way is to grip the flange somehow while loosening the nut. It is going to require some strength to remove. There are special lock nut removal tools available. Use Tool No. ST315300 for models through 1986 (except D21-D series). On D21-D series

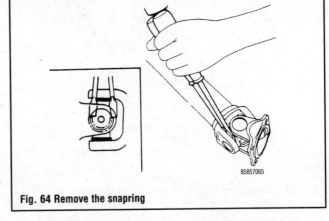

Fig. 64 Remove the snapring

trucks with 2wd use Tool No. ST38060002, on 4wd models use tool No. KV38104700.

4. Remove the companion flange off the front driveshaft with a puller and press the center bearing from its mount.

To install:

5. The new bearing is already lubricated. Install it into the mount, making sure that the seals and so on are facing the same way as then removed.
6. Slide the companion flange onto the front driveshaft, aligning the marks made during removal. Install the washer and locknut. Tighten the nut to 145–175 ft. lbs. (197–238 Nm) on all 1970–80 models. On 1981–86 trucks (720-D), tighten to 181–217 ft. lbs. (245–294 Nm). On 1986–88 models with the Z24i engine, tighten to 181–217 ft. lbs. (245–294 Nm). On models with the VG30i engines, tighten to 174–203 ft. lbs. (235–275 Nm). Check that the bearing rotates freely around the driveshaft.
7. Connect the companion flange to the flange yoke, aligning the marks made during disassembly.
8. Install the driveshaft, aligning the marks made during removal.

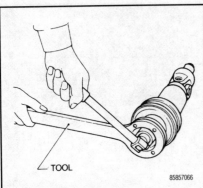

Fig. 65 Removing the center bearing locknut with the special tool

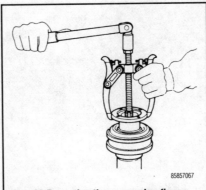

Fig. 66 Removing the companion flange with a puller

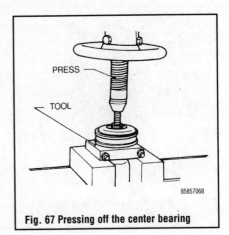

Fig. 67 Pressing off the center bearing

7-18 DRIVE TRAIN

REAR DRIVE AXLE

Axle Shaft, Bearing and Seal

REMOVAL & INSTALLATION

Single Rear Wheels

♦ See Figures 68 thru 75

1. Raise the rear of the vehicle and support it. Remove the rear wheel and tire.
2. Disconnect the rear parking brake cable by removing the adjusting nut and clamps.
3. Disconnect the brake tube at the rear brake backing plate. Plug the end of the brake tube to prevent loss of brake fluid.
4. Remove the brake drum.
5. Remove the nuts securing the wheel bearing retainer to the brake backing plate.
6. Pull out the axle shaft assembly together with the brake backing plate using a slide hammer.
7. Remove the oil seal in the axle housing if necessary. It can be pried out with a screwdriver. Oil the lips of the new seal and install it carefully to avoid damage to the lip.

To install:

8. To replace the bearing, unbend and discard the lockwasher. Remove the locknut with a soft drift and a hammer.
9. Press the old bearing and cage off the shaft.
10. Remove the oil seal in the cage. Use a brass drift to remove the bearing cup after the seal has been removed.

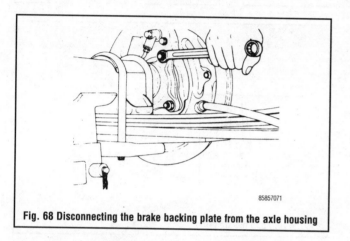

Fig. 68 Disconnecting the brake backing plate from the axle housing

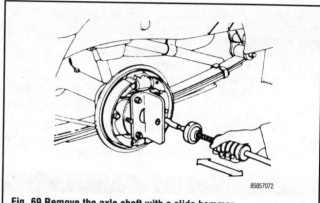

Fig. 69 Remove the axle shaft with a slide hammer

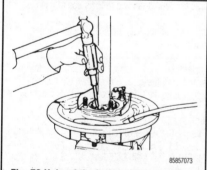

Fig. 70 Unbend the lockwasher to remove the bearing locknut-use a new one for installation

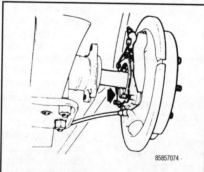

Fig. 71 Axle shaft end-play is adjusted by the addition or subtraction of shims behind the brake backing plate

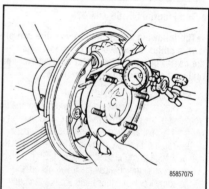

Fig. 72 Measure the axial end-play with a dial indicator

Fig. 73 Removing the nuts securing the axleshaft to the axle housing

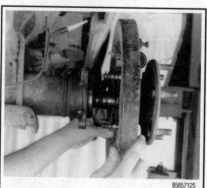

Fig. 74 Removing the backing plate from the axle housing

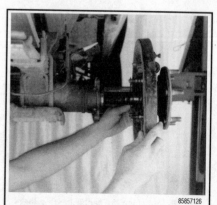

Fig. 75 Removing the axleshaft assembly

DRIVE TRAIN 7-19

11. Install the new cup with a brass drift. Install a new oil seal over the bearing cup. Lubricate the area between the seal lips with grease after installation.
12. Place the bearing cage and spacer on the axle shaft, then fit the bearing, tapping it into place with a soft drift and light hammer blows.
13. Place the flat bearing lockwasher over the bearing, then the new nut lockwasher. Install the locknut, tightening to 108 ft. lbs. (147 Nm). Continue to tighten after that until the grooves line up with the lockwasher tabs. The nut can be tightened up to 145 ft. lbs. (196 Nm). Bend the lockwasher tabs into place.
14. Lubricate the bearing and recess in the axle housing with wheel bearing grease. Coat the axle splines with gear oil. Coat the seal surface of the shaft with grease.
15. Install the axle shaft and then check the axle end-play. It should be 0.012–0.035 in. (0.3–0.9mm) on 1970–74 models; 0.0008–0.0059 in. (0.02–0.15mm) on 1975–88 models. The end-play is adjusted by adding or removing shims behind the brake backing plate. Tighten the backing plate attaching nuts to 27–35 ft. lbs. (37–47 Nm) on 1970–73 models, or 39–46 ft. lbs. (53–63 Nm) on 1974–88 models.

Dual Rear Wheels

▶ See Figures 76 and 77

1. Raise the rear of the vehicle and support it. Remove the rear wheel and tire.
2. Disconnect the rear parking brake cable by removing the adjusting nut and clamps.
3. Disconnect the brake tube at the rear brake backing plate. Plug the end of the brake tube to prevent loss of brake fluid.
4. Remove the brake drum.
5. Remove the nuts securing the wheel bearing retainer to the brake backing plate.
6. Pull out the axle shaft assembly together with the brake backing plate using a slide hammer.
7. Remove the attaching screws and detach the lockwasher from the rear wheel bearing nut.
8. Remove the rear wheel bearing nut.
9. Remove the bearing and seal, then drive out the races with a brass drift.

To install:
10. Coat the axles shaft splines with 90W gear oil and coat the seal lip with chassis lube.
11. Install new bearing races with an installing drift and pack the hub with chassis lube.
12. Pack each bearing and the O-ring with chassis lube.
13. Install the bearings and axle shaft. Be careful not to damage the seal with the shaft. Always use new seals. Make sure that the axle shaft end-play is 0.003 in. (0.08mm). Observe the following torques:
   - Wheel bearing locknut: 123–145 ft. lbs (167–196 Nm).
   - Backing plate nut: 62–80 ft. lbs. (84–108 Nm).
   - Wheel lugs: 159–188 ft. lbs. (216–255 Nm).

Final Drive

REMOVAL & INSTALLATION

▶ See Figures 78 thru 83

All Except C200 Models

1. Raise the rear of the truck and support it with safety stands.
2. Disconnect the driveshaft at the final drive unit.
3. Drain all fluid from the final drive and then remove the axle shafts.
4. Loosen the final drive-to-axle housing mounting bolts and remove the final drive.

To install:
5. Install the final drive and tighten the mounting bolts to 12–18 ft. lbs. (17–25 Nm). Be sure that the gasket on H233B models is installed in the correct position.
6. Install the axle shafts and connect the driveshaft.
7. Lower the vehicle and fill the final drive with gear oil.

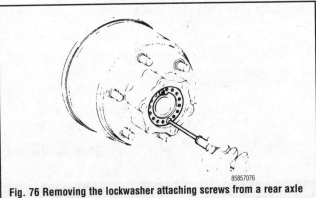
Fig. 76 Removing the lockwasher attaching screws from a rear axle assembly with dual rear wheels

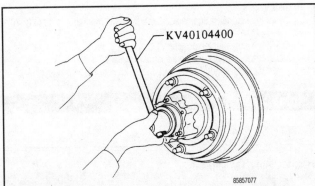
Fig. 77 Removing the bearing locknut from a rear axle assembly with dual rear wheels

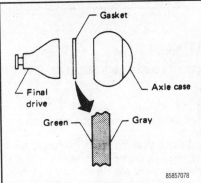
Fig. 78 Gasket installation on the H233B final drive assembly

Fig. 79 Removing brake line from the rear axle cover

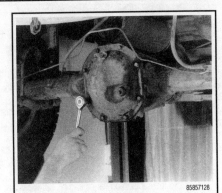
Fig. 80 Removing rear axle cover retaining bolts

DRIVE TRAIN

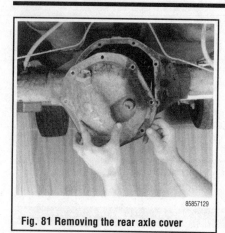

Fig. 81 Removing the rear axle cover

Fig. 82 View of the rear axle assembly-rear axle cover removed

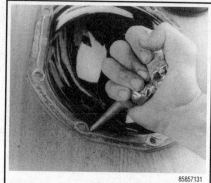

Fig. 83 Applying sealer to the rear axle cover

1984–86 (720-D Series) C200 Models

1. Raise the rear of the truck and support it with safety stands.
2. Disconnect the driveshaft at the final drive unit.
3. Drain all fluid from the final drive and then remove the axle shafts.
4. Remove the rear cover and gasket.

To install:

5. Install the rear cover and gasket and tighten the mounting bolts to 8–10 ft. lbs. (11–14 Nm).
6. Install the axle shafts and connect the driveshaft.
7. Lower the vehicle and fill the final drive with gear oil.

1986–88 (D21-D Series) C200 Models

1. Raise the rear of the truck and support it with safety stands.
2. Disconnect the driveshaft at the final drive unit.
3. Drain all fluid from the final drive, then remove the axle shafts.
4. Remove the axle housing assembly.
5. Remove the rear cover and gasket.

To install:

6. Install the rear cover and gasket and tighten the mounting bolts to 8–10 ft. lbs. (11–14 Nm).
7. Install the axle housing assembly.
8. Install the axle shafts and connect the driveshaft.
9. Lower the vehicle and fill the final drive with gear oil.

Pinion Seal

REMOVAL & INSTALLATION

H190-ML and H190A Models

1. Raise the rear of the vehicle and support it with safety stands.
2. Remove the final drive unit from the axle housing assembly.
3. Matchmark the side bearing caps to the case and then remove them.
4. Pry out the differential case assembly.
5. Remove the pinion nut.
6. Remove the companion flange with a suitable puller.
7. Knock out the drive pinion with a rubber mallet and then remove the collapsible spacer and washer from the pinion.
8. Pry the oil seal from the final drive unit and remove the pinion bearing inner race.

To install:

9. Coat the cavity between the seal lips with grease and then drive the seal into final drive so it is flush with the end of the housing.
10. Position a **new** washer and collapsible spacer on the drive pinion and then coat the rear bearing with gear oil. Insert the assembly into the gear carrier.
11. Install the companion flange and hold it firmly while tapping the drive pinion in with a rubber mallet.
12. Hold the companion flange and tighten the pinion nut until there is no axial play. Tighten the nut gradually until the pre-load is 9.5–13.9 inch lbs. (1.1–1.6 Nm). After tightening, rotate the pinion several times to set the bearing roller.

13. Install the differential case assembly and the side bearing rollers into the final drive housing and then install the side bearing cap.
14. Install the final drive. Lower the vehicle and fill with gear oil.

C200 Models

1. Raise the rear of the vehicle and support it with safety stands.
2. Remove the rear cover from the final drive unit.
3. Matchmark the side bearing caps to the case and then remove them.
4. Pry out the differential case assembly.
5. Remove the pinion nut.
6. Remove the companion flange with a suitable puller.
7. Knock out the drive pinion with a rubber mallet, then remove the collapsible spacer and washer from the pinion.
8. Pry the oil seal from the final drive unit and remove the pinion bearing inner race.

To install:

9. Coat the cavity between the seal lips with grease and then drive the seal into final drive so it is flush with the end of the housing.
10. Position a **new** washer and collapsible spacer on the drive pinion and then coat the rear bearing with gear oil. Insert the assembly into the gear carrier.
11. Install the companion flange and hold it firmly while tapping the drive pinion in with a rubber mallet.
12. Hold the companion flange and tighten the pinion nut until there is no axial play. Tighten the nut gradually until the pre-load is 9.5–14.8 inch lbs. (1.1–1.7 Nm). After tightening, rotate the pinion several times to set the bearing roller.
13. Install the differential case assembly and the side bearing rollers into the final drive housing and then install the side bearing caps. Tighten to 65–72 ft. lbs. (88–98 Nm).
14. Install the rear cover with a **new** gasket. Lower the vehicle and fill with gear oil.

Axle Housing

REMOVAL & INSTALLATION

▶ See Figures 84 and 85

Pick-Ups with Leaf Spring Suspension

1. Raise the rear of the vehicle and support it with safety stands. Remove the rear wheels.
2. Remove the driveshaft.
3. Disconnect the parking brake cable and the brake line.
4. Position a floor jack under the center of the axle housing and raise it just enough to support the assembly.
5. Disconnect the lower end of each shock absorber at the spring carrier.
6. Remove the spring carrier U-bolts and let the springs drop down slightly.
7. On 2wd models, carefully maneuver the axle housing out through the springs. This will probably require two floor jacks or another set of safety stands. On 4wd models, the axle housing is below the leaf springs; simply lower the housing and remove it.

DRIVE TRAIN 7-21

To install:

8. Reinstall the axle housing and support it in position. Slide the spring carrier U-bolts over the axle tube (or leaf springs on 4wd models) and tighten the nuts to 65–72 ft. lbs. (88–98 Nm).
9. Reconnect the shock absorbers and tighten the mounting bolts to 12–16 ft. lbs. (16–22 Nm) on 1970–86 2wd models; or, 22–30 ft. lbs. (30–40 Nm) on 1981–86 4wd models and all 1986–88 models.
10. Connect the parking brake cable and the brake lines.
11. Connect the driveshaft, install the wheels and lower the vehicle.

Pathfinders with 5-Link Suspension

1. Raise the rear of the vehicle and support it with safety stands. Remove the rear wheels.
2. Remove the driveshaft.
3. Disconnect the parking brake cable and the brake line.
4. Position a floor jack under the center of the axle housing and raise it just enough to support the assembly.
5. Remove the stabilizer-to-body mounting bolts.
6. Disconnect the upper and lower links at the body.
7. Disconnect the panhard rod at the body.
8. Remove the upper shock absorber mounting nuts.
9. Lower the entire axle housing assembly (suspension and all) out and away from the vehicle.

To install:

10. Position the axle housing assembly under the body of the truck and raise it until the upper ends of the shock absorbers can be connected. Tighten the bolts to 22–30 ft. lbs. (30–40 Nm).
11. Connect the panhard rod and tighten the bolts to 80–108 ft. lbs. (108–147 Nm).
12. Reconnect the upper and lower links and then tighten the bolts to 80–108 ft. lbs. (108–147 Nm).
13. Connect the stabilizer bar to the body and tighten the bolts to 30–35 ft. lbs. (41–47 Nm).
14. Connect the parking brake cable and the brake lines.
15. Install the driveshaft. Install the wheels and then lower the vehicle.

FRONT DRIVE AXLE

Free Running Hub

REMOVAL & INSTALLATION

♦ See Figures 93 thru 107

1981–83

♦ See Figures 86 and 87

1. Raise the front of the vehicle and support the front axle on stands.
2. Set the hub in the **Lock** position.

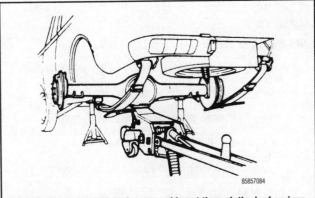
Fig. 84 Slide the axle housing assembly out through the leaf springs

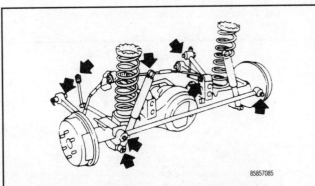
Fig. 85 The axle housing assembly on the Pathfinder is removed with the suspension intact

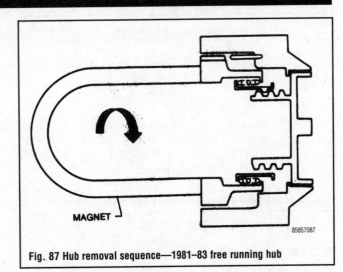
Fig. 87 Hub removal sequence—1981–83 free running hub

3. Remove the driven clutch by turning it clockwise.

➡A pin is located inside the hub case to lock the driven clutch. Pull and turn the clutch while attracting the pin with a magnet.

4. Remove the lockpin.

To install:

5. Set the hub at the **Free** position.
6. Screw the driven clutch into place by turning it counterclockwise until it bottoms.
7. Turn it clockwise until it aligns with the bolt hole.
8. Install the lockpin.

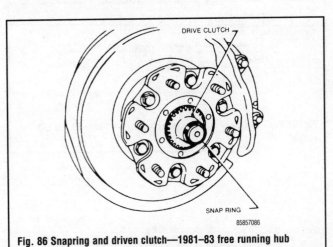
Fig. 86 Snapring and driven clutch—1981–83 free running hub

7-22 DRIVE TRAIN

1984–86 (720-D Series)

MANUAL LOCK

▶ See Figures 88 and 89

1. Raise the front of the vehicle and support the front axle on stands.
2. Remove the wheels.
3. Remove the locking hub cover using a Torx® wrench.
4. Pull out the free running hub.
5. Remove the snapring and pull out the drive clutch.
6. Remove the snapring and lock washer and then remove the wheel bearing locknut using tool KV40104300, or its equivalent.

To install:

7. Install the wheel bearing locknut. Install a new lock washer and snapring.
8. Press on the driven clutch and install a new snapring.
9. Press on the free running hub.
10. Install the hub cover and tighten the screws to 18–25 ft. lbs. (25–34 Nm).
11. Install the wheels, remove the stands and lower the vehicle.

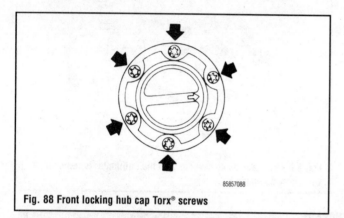

Fig. 88 Front locking hub cap Torx® screws

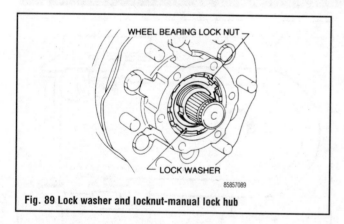

Fig. 89 Lock washer and locknut-manual lock hub

AUTO LOCK

▶ See Figure 90

1. Raise the front of the vehicle and support the front axle on jackstands.
2. Remove the wheels.
3. Remove the locking hub cover using a Torx® wrench.
4. Remove the automatic free running hub with the O-ring spring and brake A.
5. Remove the washers then remove the snapring.
6. Remove the large snapring, lock washer and wheel bearing lock nut, using tool No. KV401043, or its equivalent.

To install:

7. Install the wheel bearing locknut. Install a new lock washer and large snapring.
8. Install the snapring and then the washers.
9. Install the free running hub along with the brake and O-ring spring.
10. Install the hub cover.
11. Install the wheels, remove the stands and lower the vehicle.

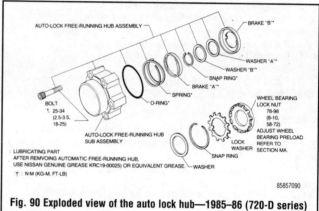

Fig. 90 Exploded view of the auto lock hub—1985–86 (720-D series)

1986–88 (D21-D Series)

MANUAL LOCK

▶ See Figure 91

1. Raise the front of the vehicle and support the front axle on stands.
2. Remove the wheels.
3. Set the knob of the manual lock to the **FREE** position.
4. Remove the locking hub cover using a Torx® wrench, while the brake pedal is depressed.
5. Remove the snapring and pull out the drive clutch.

To install:

6. Install the drive clutch and snapring. Make sure the hub is in the **FREE** position.
7. Install the hub cover and tighten the bolts to 18–25 ft. lbs. (25–34 Nm).
8. Install the wheels, remove the stands and lower the vehicle.

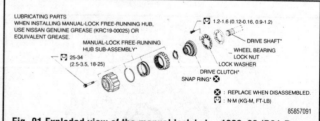

Fig. 91 Exploded view of the manual lock hub—1986–88 (D21-D series)

DRIVE TRAIN 7-23

AUTO LOCK
♦ See Figure 92

1. Raise the front of the vehicle and support the front axle on jackstands.
2. Remove the wheels.
3. Set the knob of the auto lock to the **FREE** position.
4. Remove the locking hub cover using a Torx® wrench, while the brake pedal is depressed.
5. Remove the snapring.
6. Remove washer **B**, washer **A** and brake **B**.

To install:

7. Make sure the hub is in the **FREE** position and then install washer **B**, washer **A** and brake **B**.
8. Install the snapring.

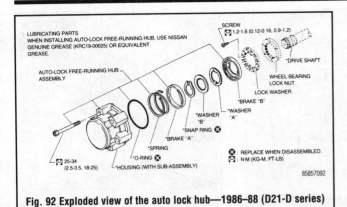
Fig. 92 Exploded view of the auto lock hub—1986–88 (D21-D series)

Fig. 93 Removing the hub retaining bolts

Fig. 94 Removing the housing cover

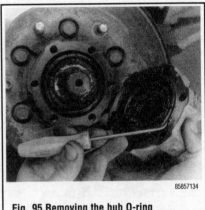
Fig. 95 Removing the hub O-ring

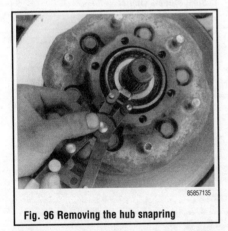
Fig. 96 Removing the hub snapring

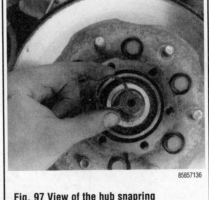
Fig. 97 View of the hub snapring

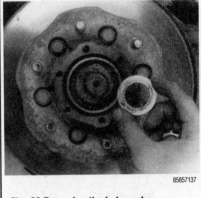
Fig. 98 Removing the hub washer

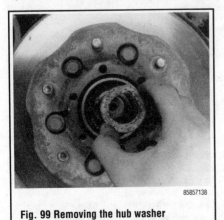
Fig. 99 Removing the hub washer

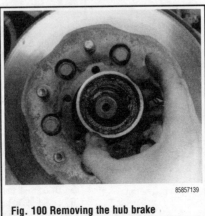
Fig. 100 Removing the hub brake

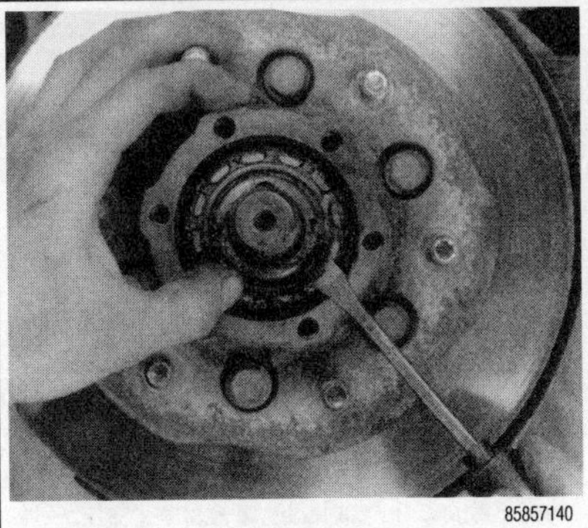

Fig. 101 Removing the hub bearing snapring

7-24 DRIVE TRAIN

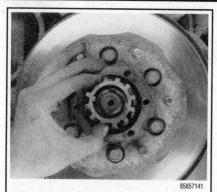
Fig. 102 Removing the hub bearing lock washer

Fig. 103 Removing the hub bearing locknut

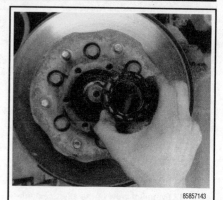
Fig. 104 View of the hub bearing locknut

Fig. 105 Removing wheel bearing

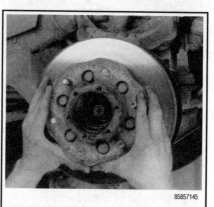
Fig. 106 Removing the front hub assembly

Fig. 107 View of locking hub assembly-most models similar

9. Install the hub cover and tighten the bolts to 18–25 ft. lbs. (25–34 Nm).
10. Install the wheels, remove the stands and then lower the vehicle.

Axle Shaft

REMOVAL & INSTALLATION

▶ See Figures 112, 113, 114, 115 and 116

1981–83

▶ See Figure 108

1. Remove the free running hub.
2. Remove the snapring and remove the driven clutch.
3. Remove the front rebound bumper.
4. Disconnect the stabilizer bar at the lower link.
5. Remove the bolts attaching the axle shaft to the carrier. DO NOT REMOVE THE RUBBER BOOTS!
6. Lower the inner end of the axle shaft and then pull the shaft out of the wheel assembly.

To install:

7. Install the outer end of the axle shaft into the wheel and then connect it to the differential. Observe the following points:
   a. Apply multi-purpose wheel bearing grease to the copper portion of the wheel bearing support.
   b. Adjust the axle shaft axial end-play by installing the proper thickness of snaprings on the end of the shaft.
   c. Tighten the axle shaft flange bolts to 20–27 ft. lbs. (27–37 Nm); the free running hub bolts to 18–25 ft. lbs. (25–34 Nm); the stabilizer bar-to-lower link bolts to 12–16 ft. lbs. (16–22 Nm) and the wheel nuts to 87–108 ft. lbs. (118–147 Nm).

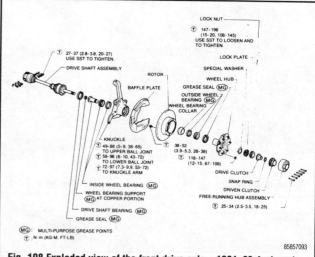
Fig. 108 Exploded view of the front drive axle—1981–83 4wd models

1984–86 (720-D Series)

▶ See Figure 109

1. Remove the locking hub.
2. Remove the snapring and drive clutch.
3. Disconnect the lower ball joint.
4. Disconnect the lower end of the shock absorber.
5. Disconnect the axle shaft from the differential.
6. Lower the inner end of the axle shaft and then pull the axle shaft from the wheel housing. It helps to turn the steering wheel to the right when pulling the right shaft and left when pulling the left shaft.

Drive Train 7-25

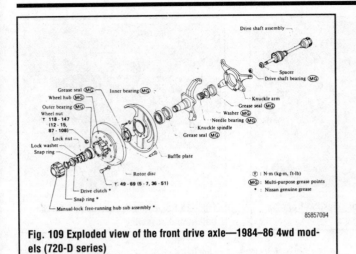

Fig. 109 Exploded view of the front drive axle—1984–86 4wd models (720-D series)

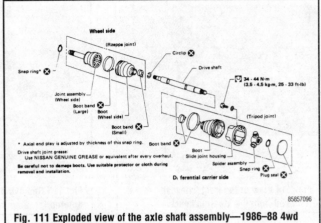

Fig. 111 Exploded view of the axle shaft assembly—1986–88 4wd models (D21-D series)

To install:

7. Install the axle shaft into the wheel housing and then connect it to the differential. Please note the following:
   a. Apply chassis lube to all bearing surfaces.
   b. Before installing the shaft make sure that the spacer is in place.
   c. Adjust the axle shaft end-play by using various thicknesses of snaprings. The end-play should be 0.004–0.012 in. (0.1–0.3mm).
   d. Observe the following torques:
- axle shaft-to-differential: 20–27 ft. lbs. (27–37 Nm).
- locking hub: 18–25 ft. lbs. (25–34 Nm).
- ball joint-to-lower link: 87–123 ft. lbs. (118–165 Nm).

1986–88 (D21-D Series)

▶ See Figures 110 and 111

1. Remove the bolts attaching the axle shaft to the differential while the brake pedal is being depressed.

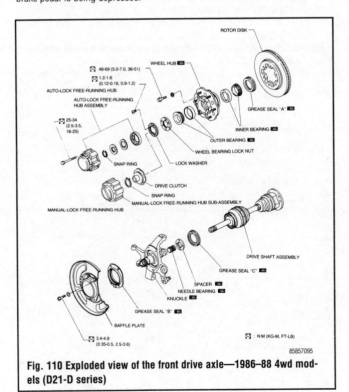

Fig. 110 Exploded view of the front drive axle—1986–88 4wd models (D21-D series)

Fig. 112 View of the front axleshaft installed

Fig. 113 Removing the axleshaft from the steering knuckle

DRIVE TRAIN

Fig. 114 View of the front axleshaft removed from the steering knuckle

Fig. 115 Removing the axleshaft from the differential retaining nuts

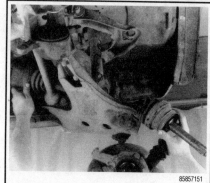

Fig. 116 Removing the axleshaft from the differential assembly

2. Remove the free running hub assembly with the brake pedal depressed.
3. Remove the brake caliper assembly without disconnecting the hydraulic brake line. Support or hang the brake caliper with a wire to avoid breaking the hose.
4. Remove the tie rod ball joint.
5. Support the lower link with a jack and remove the nuts attaching the lower ball joint on the lower link.
6. Remove the upper ball joint attaching bolts.
7. Remove the shock absorber lower attaching bolt.
8. Cover the axle shaft boot with a suitable protector, and then remove the axle shaft with the knuckle still attached.
9. Separate the axle shaft from the knuckle by lightly tapping it with a rubber mallet.

To install:
10. Install the axle shaft into the knuckle and then install the assembly.
11. When installing the bearing spacer onto the axle shaft, make sure that the bearing spacer is facing in the proper direction. Temporarily install a new snapring on the axle shaft at the same thickness as it was before removal and then measure the axial end-play of the axle shaft with a dial gauge. The axial end-play should be 0.004–0.012 in. (0.1–0.3mm). Select another snapring if not within specifications.
12. Connect the shock absorber and tighten the bolt to 43–58 ft. lbs. (59–78 Nm).
13. Connect the upper ball joint and tighten the bolts to 12–15 ft. lbs. (16–21 Nm).
14. Connect the lower ball joint to the lower link and tighten the nuts to 35–45 ft. lbs. (47–61 Nm).
15. Install the tie rod ball joint and the brake caliper.
16. Install the hub and then connect the axle shaft to the differential and tighten the bolts to 25–33 ft. lbs. (34–44 Nm).
17. Install the wheels, remove the stands and lower the vehicle.

Pinion Seal

REMOVAL & INSTALLATION

1. Drain the gear oil from the differential.
2. Raise the front of the vehicle and support it with safety stands.
3. Disconnect the front driveshaft at the differential.
4. Using a flange wrench and a 27mm socket, remove the drive pinion nut.
5. Remove the companion flange and then pry out the oil seal.

To install:
6. Coat the cavity between the lips of the oil seal with grease and then install the seal with an oil seal installation tool.
7. Press the companion flange in and install the drive pinion nut. Tighten the nut to 167–196 ft. lbs. (123–145 Nm).
8. Install the driveshaft, remove the stands and lower the vehicle. Refill the differential with gear oil.

FRONT SUSPENSION 8-2
TORSION BARS 8-2
   REMOVAL & INSTALLATION 8-2
SHOCK ABSORBER 8-5
   TESTING 8-5
   REMOVAL & INSTALLATION 8-5
TENSION ROD AND STABILIZER BAR 8-5
   REMOVAL & INSTALLATION 8-5
COMPRESSION ROD AND STABILIZER BAR 8-7
   REMOVAL & INSTALLATION 8-7
KINGPINS 8-7
   INSPECTION 8-7
   REMOVAL & INSTALLATION 8-8
UPPER BALL JOINT 8-9
   INSPECTION 8-9
   REMOVAL & INSTALLATION 8-9
LOWER BALL JOINT 8-10
   INSPECTION 8-10
   REMOVAL & INSTALLATION 8-10
CONTROL ARMS 8-11
   REMOVAL & INSTALLATION 8-11
UPPER CONTROL ARM 8-11
   REMOVAL & INSTALLATION 8-11
LOWER CONTROL ARM 8-12
   REMOVAL & INSTALLATION 8-12
STEERING KNUCKLE AND SPINDLE 8-13
   REMOVAL & INSTALLATION 8-13
FRONT AXLE HUB AND WHEEL BEARING 8-16
   REMOVAL & INSTALLATION 8-16
FRONT END ALIGNMENT 8-16
   CASTER 8-16
   CAMBER 8-16
   TOE 8-16
   STEERING ANGLE ADJUSTMENT 8-16
REAR SUSPENSION 8-16
COIL SPRINGS 8-16
   REMOVAL & INSTALLATION 8-16
LEAF SPRINGS 8-17
   REMOVAL & INSTALLATION 8-17
SHOCK ABSORBERS 8-17
   INSPECTION AND TESTING 8-17
   REMOVAL & INSTALLATION 8-17
CONTROL ARMS 8-18
   REMOVAL & INSTALLATION 8-18
PANHARD ROD 8-18
   REMOVAL & INSTALLATION 8-18
STABILIZER BAR 8-18
   REMOVAL & INSTALLATION 8-18
STEERING 8-20
STEERING WHEEL 8-20
   REMOVAL & INSTALLATION 8-20
TURN SIGNAL AND DIMMER SWITCH 8-20
   REMOVAL & INSTALLATION 8-20
COMBINATION SWITCH 8-20
   REMOVAL & INSTALLATION 8-20
IGNITION SWITCH 8-21
   REMOVAL & INSTALLATION 8-21
IGNITION LOCK/SWITCH 8-21
   REMOVAL & INSTALLATION 8-21
STEERING LINKAGE 8-21
   REMOVAL & INSTALLATION 8-21
MANUAL STEERING GEAR 8-23
   ADJUSTMENTS 8-23
   REMOVAL & INSTALLATION 8-24
POWER STEERING GEAR 8-24
   ADJUSTMENT 8-24
   REMOVAL & INSTALLATION 8-24
POWER STEERING PUMP 8-25
   REMOVAL AND INSTALLATION 8-25
   BLEEDING 8-25
SPECIFICATIONS CHARTS
   WHEEL ALIGNMENT 8-26
   TORQUE SPECIFICATIONS 8-26

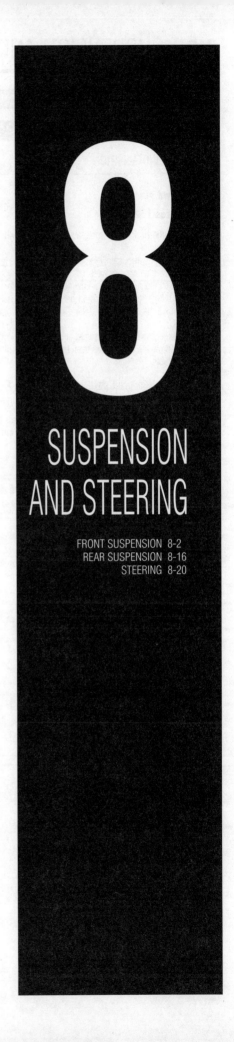

8

SUSPENSION AND STEERING

FRONT SUSPENSION 8-2
REAR SUSPENSION 8-16
STEERING 8-20

SUSPENSION AND STEERING

FRONT SUSPENSION

Torsion Bars

REMOVAL & INSTALLATION

1970–83 2wd Models

♦ See Figures 1, 2, 3 and 4

1. Raise the front of the vehicle and support it with jackstands. Remove the wheel.
2. On trucks with a catalytic converter, the converter must be removed if the left torsion bar is being removed.
3. Loosen the ride height adjusting nuts at the anchor (rear) end of the torsion bar, allowing the anchor arm to hang down.
4. Remove the dust cover at the rear end of the torsion bar and remove the snapring.
5. Pull the anchor arm rearward and off the torsion bar.
6. Withdraw the torsion bar from the lower control arm and remove it from under the vehicle.

To install:

7. Before installing the torsion bar, apply a light coat of grease to the splines. Install the torsion bar to the lower control arm.

➡The torsion bars are marked on the end with an L(left) or an R(right). The torsion bars must be installed on the same side from which they are removed.

8. Install the anchor arm on the rear end of the torsion bar. On 1970–71 models, with the lower arm against the rebound bumper, dimension **A** must be 2.697 in. (68.5mm). On 1972–83 models, dimension **A** must be:

- 1972–76: 0.20–0.60 in. (5–15mm)—standard bed models; 0.59–0.98 in. (15–25mm)—long bed models.
- 1977: 0.59–0.98 in. (15–25mm)—all models.
- 1978–83: 0.28–0.67 in. (7–17mm)—all models.

➡There are two different methods used for measuring this distance. Be sure you are using the correct illustration for your truck.

9. Install a **new** retaining snapring and dust boot to the anchor arm end of the torsion bar.

➡Always use a **new** snapring. Never reinstall the old one.

10. On 1970–71 models, tighten the adjusting nut until dimension **A** is reached: 3.86 in. (98mm) for standard bed models or 3.62 in. (92mm) for long bed models. On all other models, tighten the adjusting nut until the link protrudes above the support bracket; 2.36–2.76 in. (60–70mm) (dimension **B**). Again, make sure you are looking at the correct illustration for your truck.
11. Install the wheel and lower the vehicle.
12. Adjust the vehicle ride height with the truck at curb weight (full tank of gas and no passengers). Tighten the locknut to 23–30 ft. lbs.

1981–83 4wd Models

♦ See Figures 5 thru 11

1. Raise and support the front end on jackstands.
2. Remove the torsion bar spring anchor bolt.
3. Pull the anchor arm out rearward.
4. Pull the torsion bar spring rearward.
5. Remove the torsion bar.

To install:

6. Install the torsion bar to the lower control arm. Tighten the outer bolt to 20–27 ft. lbs. (26–36 Nm) and the inner bolt to 26–33 ft. lbs. (35–45 Nm).
7. Coat the serrated end of the torsion bar with grease and install it into the torque arm.
8. Install the anchor arm to the serrated end of the torsion bar spring and install the anchor arm adjusting bolt. Turn the bolt until the bottom of the nut is about 0.28–0.67 in. (7–17mm) (Dimension **A**) from the end of the bolt.
9. Install the dust cover.

Fig. 1 Anchor arm adjusting nut — most models similar

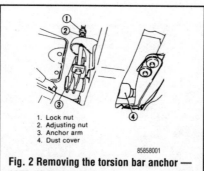

Fig. 2 Removing the torsion bar anchor — 1970–79 2wd models

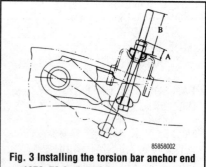

Fig. 3 Installing the torsion bar anchor end — 1972–79 2wd models

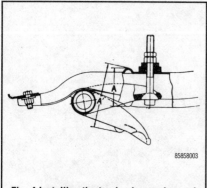

Fig. 4 Installing the torsion bar anchor end — 1970–71 2wd models

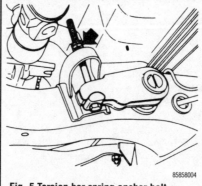

Fig. 5 Torsion bar spring anchor bolt — 1981–83 4wd models

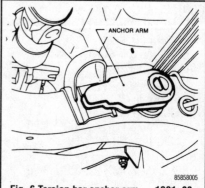

Fig. 6 Torsion bar anchor arm — 1981–83 4wd models

SUSPENSION AND STEERING 8-3

10. Adjust the anchor arm position until the distance between the end of the dust cover and the bottom of the nut (Dimension **B**) is about 2.36–2.76 in. (60–70mm).
11. Lower the vehicle.
12. Turn the anchor bolt adjusting nut until the center link spindle is 5.28–5.47 in. (134–139mm) above the tension rod attaching bolts. This is dimension **H**.

1984–86 2wd Models (720D Series)

▶ See Figures 12 thru 17

1. Block the rear wheels and raise and support the front end with jackstands under the frame rails.
2. Remove the torsion bar spring anchor bolt.
3. Remove the dust cover and remove the snapring from the anchor arm.
4. Pull the anchor arm off toward the rear.
5. Pull the torsion bar out toward the rear.
6. Remove the torsion bar spring torque arm.

To install:

7. Check the torsion bars for wear, cracks or other damage. Replace them if they are suspect.
8. Install the torque arm on the lower link (control arm). Tighten the outer side to 20–27 ft. lbs. (26–36 Nm); the inner side to 26–33 ft. lbs. (35–45 Nm).
9. Install the snapring and dust cover on the torsion bar.
10. Coat the splines on the torsion bar with chassis lube and install it in the torque arm. The torsion bars are marked **L** and **R** and are **not** interchangeable.
11. Place the lower link in position so that clearance between it and the rebound bumper is
12. On 1984 models, install the anchor arm so that dimension **G** in the illustration is:
   - Z20 and Z24 engines: left side—4.33–4.72 in. (110–120mm); right side—5.12–5.51 in. (130–140mm).

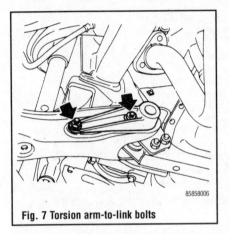

Fig. 7 Torsion arm-to-link bolts

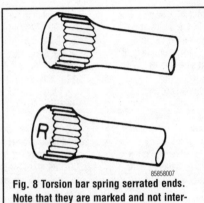

Fig. 8 Torsion bar spring serrated ends. Note that they are marked and not interchangeable

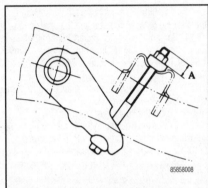

Fig. 9 Anchor arm adjusting bolt measurement — 1981–83

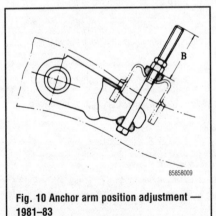

Fig. 10 Anchor arm position adjustment — 1981–83

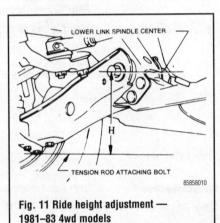

Fig. 11 Ride height adjustment — 1981–83 4wd models

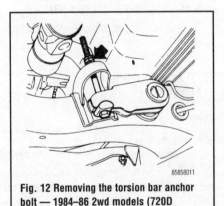

Fig. 12 Removing the torsion bar anchor bolt — 1984–86 2wd models (720D series)

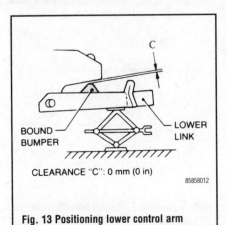

Fig. 13 Positioning lower control arm

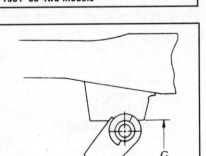

Fig. 14 Anchor arm installation — 1984 2wd models

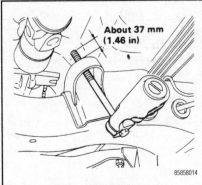

Fig. 15 Anchor arm installation — 1985–86 2wd models (720D series)

8-4 SUSPENSION AND STEERING

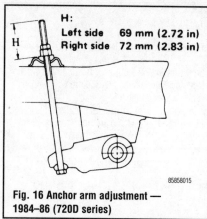

Fig. 16 Anchor arm adjustment — 1984–86 (720D series)

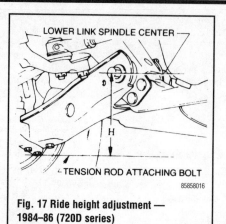

Fig. 17 Ride height adjustment — 1984–86 (720D series)

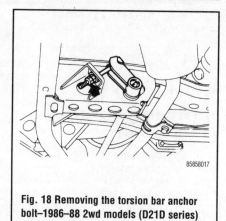

Fig. 18 Removing the torsion bar anchor bolt–1986–88 2wd models (D21D series)

13. On 1985–86 models, install the anchor arm bolt through the seat so that the distance between the seat and the upper end of the bolt is 1.46 in. (37mm).

14. Temporarily tighten the anchor arm bolt so that dimension **H** in the illustration is: 2.72 in. (69mm) on the left side and 2.83 in. (72mm) on the right side for 1984 models. Or 2.36–2.76 in. (60–70mm) for both sides on 1985–86 models.

15. Install the snapring on the anchor arm, turning it to make sure that it is completely in the groove.

16. Install the dust cover.

17. Lower the truck so that it is resting on its wheels. Turn the anchor bolt adjusting nut so that dimension **H** in the illustration is: 4.65–4.80 in. (118–122mm) on regular cab models and 4.45–4.61 in. (113–117mm) on the King Cab models in 1984. On all 1985–86 models, **H** should be 5.04–5.20 in. (128–132mm). Torque the adjusting nut to 22–30 ft. lbs. (30–40 Nm).

➡ Dimension H can be calculated by subtracting dimension B from dimension A.

1984–86 4wd Models (720D Series)

1. Raise and support the front end with jackstands under the frame rails.
2. Remove the torsion bar anchor bolt.
3. Pull the anchor arm out toward the rear.
4. Pull the torsion bar out toward the rear.
5. Remove the torque arm.

To install:

6. Check the torsion bar for signs of wear and/or damage and replace as necessary.
7. Install the torque arm to the lower link (control arm) and tighten the bolts to 66–87 ft. lbs. (89–118 Nm).
8. Coat the spines on the inner end of the torsion bar with chassis lube and install it into the torque arm.

➡ The torsion bars are marked L and R. They are not interchangeable.

9. Using a floor jack, position the lower link so that there is 0 clearance between it and the rebound bumper.

10. Install the anchor arm so that dimension **G** is:
   - 1984 Z20 and Z24 engines: left side—4.33–4.72 in. (110–120mm); right side—5.12–5.51 in. (130–140mm).
   - 1985–86 models: left side—3.74 in. (95mm); right side—4.33 in. (110mm).

11. Temporarily tighten the anchor arm bolt so that dimension **H** is:
   - 1984 models: left side—2.72 in. (69mm); right side—2.83 in. (72mm).
   - 1985–86 models: left side—3.50 in. (89mm); right side—3.86 in. (98mm).

12. Lower the truck so that it is resting on its wheels. Adjust the anchor bolt so that dimension **H**:
   - 1984 models: 1.54–1.69 in. (39–43mm) for King Cab models and 1.73–1.89 in. (44–48mm) for regular cab models.
   - 1985–86 models: 2.09–2.24 in. (53–57mm).

➡ Dimension H can be calculated by subtracting dimension B from dimension A.

1986–88 2wd Models (D21D Series)

◆ See Figures 18 thru 24

1. Block the rear wheels and raise and support the front end with jackstands under the frame rails.
2. Remove the torsion bar spring adjusting nut.
3. Remove the dust cover and remove the snapring from the anchor arm.
4. Pull the anchor arm off toward the rear and then remove the torsion bar spring.
5. Remove the torque arm.

To install:

6. Check the torsion bars for wear, cracks or other damage. Replace them if they are suspect.
7. Install the torque arm on the lower link (control arm) and tighten the bolts to 37–50 ft. lbs. (50–68 Nm).
8. Install the snapring and dust cover on the torsion bar.

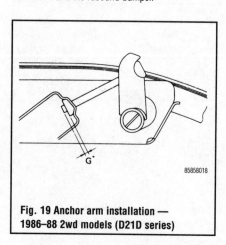

Fig. 19 Anchor arm installation — 1986–88 2wd models (D21D series)

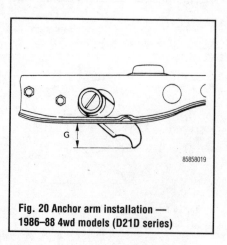

Fig. 20 Anchor arm installation — 1986–88 4wd models (D21D series)

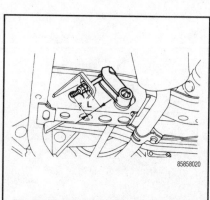

Fig. 21 Tighten the anchor arm adjusting nut — 1986–88 2wd models (D21D series)

SUSPENSION AND STEERING

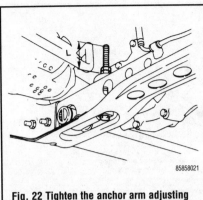

Fig. 22 Tighten the anchor arm adjusting nut — 1986–88 4wd models (D21D series)

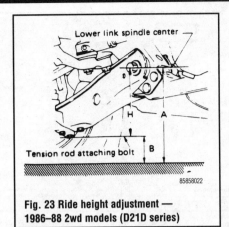

Fig. 23 Ride height adjustment — 1986–88 2wd models (D21D series)

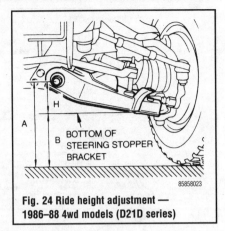

Fig. 24 Ride height adjustment — 1986–88 4wd models (D21D series)

9. Coat the splines on the inner end of the torsion bar with chassis lube and install it into the torque arm. The torsion bars are marked **L** and **R** and are **not** interchangeable.

10. Position a floor jack under the lower link and raise it so that clearance between the link and the rebound bumper is 0.

11. Install the anchor arm so that dimension **G** in the illustration is 0.24–0.71 in. (6–18mm).

12. Install the snapring to the anchor arm and dust cover. Make sure that the snapring is properly installed in the groove of the anchor arm.

13. Tighten the anchor arm adjusting nut until dimension **L** is 1.38 in. (35mm) for Heavy Duty, Cab/Chassis and STD models; or 1.93 in. (49mm) for all other models.

14. Lower the truck so that it is resting on its wheels and bounce it several times to set the suspension. Turn the anchor bolt adjusting nut so that dimension **H** in the illustration is 4.37–4.53 in. (111–115mm) on 1986–87 models; or 4.25–4.65 in. (108–118mm) on 1988 models.

1986–88 4wd Models (D21D Series)

1. Block the rear wheels and raise and support the front end with jackstands under the frame rails.
2. Remove the torsion bar spring adjusting nut.
3. Pull back the dust boot and remove the anchor arm snapring.
4. Remove the torque arm attaching nuts, then withdraw the torsion bar spring forward with the torque arm still attached.

To install:

5. Check the torsion bar for wear, cracks or other damage. Replace them if they are suspect.
6. Coat the splines on the torsion bar with chassis lube and install it in the anchor arm. The torsion bars are marked **L** and **R** and are **not** interchangeable.
7. Position a floor jack under the lower link (control arm) and raise it so that the clearance between the link and the rebound bumper is 1.97–2.36 in. (50–60mm).
8. Install the snapring on the anchor arm and pull the dust boot over it.
9. Tighten the anchor arm adjusting nut until dimension **L** is 3.03 in. (77mm).
10. Lower the truck so that it is resting on its wheels and bounce it several times to set the suspension. Turn the anchor bolt adjusting nut so that dimension **H** is 1.73–1.89 in. (44–48mm) on 1986–87 models; or 1.61–2.01 in. (41–51mm) on 1988 models.

Shock Absorber

TESTING

The function of the shock absorber is to dampen harsh spring movement and provide a means of controlling the motion of the wheels so that the bumps encountered by the wheels are not totally transmitted to the body of the truck and, therefore, to you and your passengers. As the wheel moves up and down, the shock absorber shortens and lengthens, thereby imposing a restraint on excessive movement by its hydraulic action.

A good way to see if your shock absorbers are working properly is to push on one corner of the truck until it is moving up and down for almost the full suspension travel, then release it and watch its recovery. If the truck bounces slightly about one more time and then comes to a rest, you can be fairly certain that the shock is OK. If the truck continues to bounce excessively, the shocks will probably require replacement.

REMOVAL & INSTALLATION

▶ See Figures 25 thru 30

1. Raise the front of the vehicle and support it with safety stands. Remove the wheel.
2. Hold the upper stem of the shock absorber and remove the nuts, washer, and rubber bushing.
3. Remove the bolt from the lower end of the shock absorber and remove the shock absorber from the vehicle.

To install:

4. Install the shock absorber. Replace all of the rubber bushings with new ones if a new shock absorber is being installed. Install the lower retaining bolt from the front of the truck. Tighten the upper attaching nut to 12–16 ft. lbs. (16–22 Nm) and the lower nut to 23–30 ft. lbs. (30–40 Nm) on 1970–83 models; 43–58 ft. lbs. (59–68 Nm) on 1984–87 2wd models and 1984–88 4wd models; or 36–47 ft. lbs. (49–64 Nm) on 1988 2wd models.

Tension Rod and Stabilizer Bar

REMOVAL & INSTALLATION

2wd Models Only

1. With the truck resting on its wheels, remove the underpan.
2. If the tension rod installation is correct, the white painted marks on the stabilizer bar, at the bushings, should be visible.
3. The tension bar and stabilizer bar can be unbolted and removed with the vehicle supported on jackstands.

To install:

4. Position the component and tighten the nuts and bolts. Tighten the stabilizer bar through-bolt and the bar bushing clamp bolts to 12–16 ft. lbs. (16–22 Nm). Tighten the tension rod-to-lower link bolts to 36–47 ft. lbs. (49–64 Nm); and the tension rod-to-frame anchor nut to 87–116 ft. lbs. (118–157 Nm). Replace the bushings whenever the parts are changed. Replace any bushing that appears dry, cracked or compressed.
5. Check the stabilizer bar with the truck on its wheels to see if both white painted marks on the stabilizer bar are visible at the bushings.

8-6 SUSPENSION AND STEERING

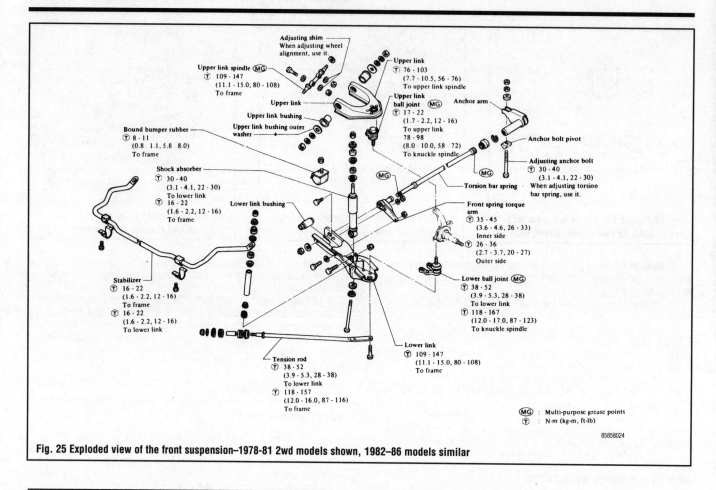

Fig. 25 Exploded view of the front suspension—1978-81 2wd models shown, 1982-86 models similar

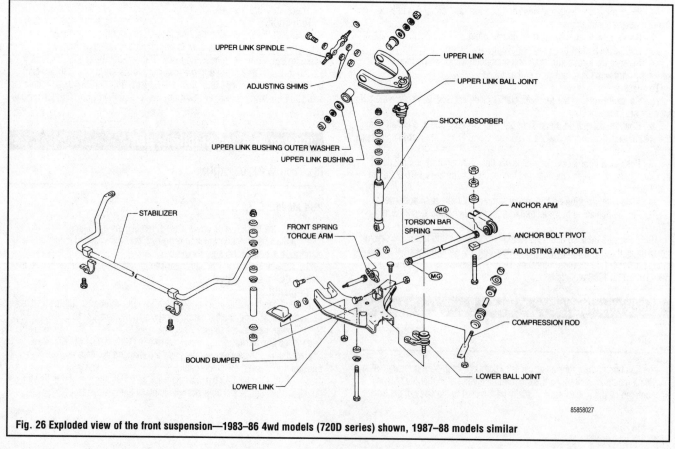

Fig. 26 Exploded view of the front suspension—1983-86 4wd models (720D series) shown, 1987-88 models similar

SUSPENSION AND STEERING   8-7

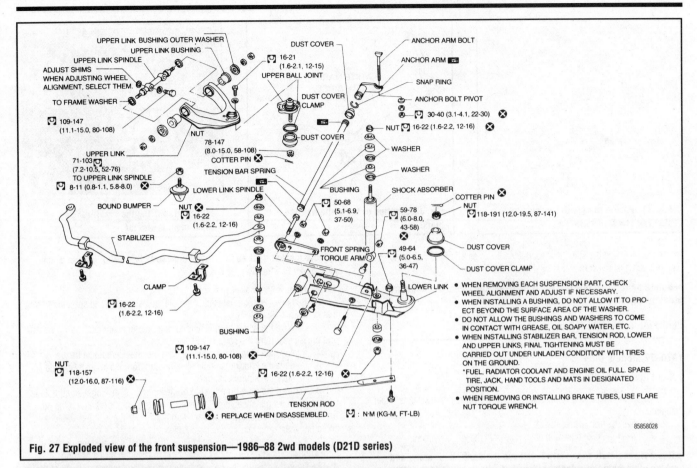

Fig. 27 Exploded view of the front suspension—1986-88 2wd models (D21D series)

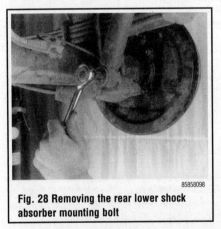

Fig. 28 Removing the rear lower shock absorber mounting bolt

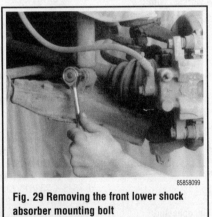

Fig. 29 Removing the front lower shock absorber mounting bolt

Fig. 30 Removing the front upper shock absorber mounting nut

Compression Rod and Stabilizer Bar

REMOVAL & INSTALLATION

▶ See Figures 31, 32 and 33

4wd Models Only

1. With the truck resting on its wheels, remove the underpan.
2. If the compression rod installation is correct, the white painted marks on the stabilizer bar, at the bushings, should be visible.
3. The compression rod and stabilizer bar can be unbolted and removed with the vehicle supported on jackstands.

To install:

4. Position the component and tighten the nuts and bolts. Tighten the stabilizer bar through-bolt and the bar bushing clamp bolts to 12–16 ft. lbs. (16–22 Nm). Tighten the compression rod-to-lower link bolts to 36–47 ft. lbs. (49–64 Nm); and the compression rod-to-frame anchor nut to 87–116 ft. lbs. (118–157 Nm). Replace the bushings whenever the parts are changed. Replace any bushing that appears dry, cracked or compressed.

5. Check the stabilizer bar with the truck on its wheels to see if both white painted marks on the stabilizer bar are visible at the bushings.

Kingpins

➡ Kingpins are used on 1970–77 trucks only.

INSPECTION

1. Raise the vehicle so that the tire on the side to be checked is off the ground. Adjust wheel bearing preload to the proper specification.
2. Grasp the top and bottom of the tire and try to move the top and bottom of the tire alternately in and out. If there is noticeable play between the steering

8-8 SUSPENSION AND STEERING

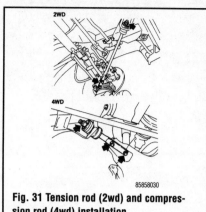

Fig. 31 Tension rod (2wd) and compression rod (4wd) installation

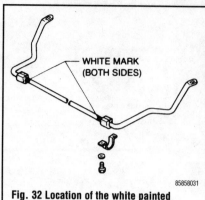

Fig. 32 Location of the white painted marks

Fig. 33 Removing the stabilizer bar — most models similar

knuckle/spindle and the spindle support, then it can be assumed that the kingpins or bushings are worn and should be replaced.

➡Before performing this test make sure that the wheel bearings are properly adjusted.

REMOVAL & INSTALLATION

1970–77 Models Only

▶ See Figures 34, 35, 36 and 37

1. Raise the front of the vehicle and support it by placing jackstands under the frame.
2. Remove the front wheel.
3. Remove the brake hose and connector from the wheel cylinder.

➡It is not absolutely necessary to remove the drum, hub, brake and backing plate from the spindle, although it will make working with the spindle a great deal easier. If you choose to leave the parts in place, skip down to Step 8.

4. Remove the brake drum.
5. Remove the hub dust cap, cotter pin, adjusting cap and spindle nut from the spindle.
6. Remove the wheel hub, inner and outer wheel bearings, bearing washer and grease seal from the spindle.
7. Remove the brake backing plate from the knuckle/spindle flange.
8. Remove the knuckle/spindle steering arm from the knuckle/spindle.
9. Remove the kingpin locknut.
10. Remove the plug from the top of the kingpin by drilling a small hole in the plug, screwing a sheet metal screw into the hole, and pulling out the plug.
11. Drive out the kingpin together with the lower plug with a suitable drift and a hammer.
12. Tap the steering knuckle/spindle lightly with a hammer and detach it from knuckle/spindle support. Be careful not to drop the thrust bearing.
13. Drive the steering knuckle/spindle bushing and grease seal out of the kingpin bore with a kingpin bushing driver. Do not try to use a drift, because it will probably score the inner wall of the knuckle spindle.

To install:

14. After cleaning the pin bores thoroughly, install the new bushing carefully by using a bushing driver. Position the bushings in the spindle so that they are flush with the counterbores for the plugs. The bushings in the factory rebuilding kit have a grease gallery which should align with the grease nipple hole in the spindle (see the illustration).
15. Remove the grease nipples and drill grease holes through the bushings, placing the drill through the threaded grease nipple hole. The grease hole should be 1/8 in. (3mm) or less. Remove all metal filings and burrs after drilling the grease holes. This step is not necessary if you have used the factory bushings and installed them as outlined in Step 14.
16. Ream the inside of the kingpin bushings, if necessary, to 0.7878–0.7888 in. (20.01–20.03mm). The fit should be such that the kingpin, when greased, can be turned or pushed in or out with thumb pressure. Use the lower bore as a guide for reaming the upper bore, and vice versa, to keep the bores aligned.

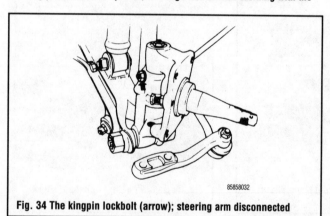

Fig. 34 The kingpin lockbolt (arrow); steering arm disconnected

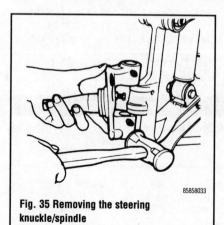

Fig. 35 Removing the steering knuckle/spindle

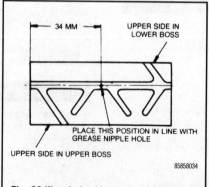

Fig. 36 Kingpin bushing to be aligned with the grease nipple hole in the spindle

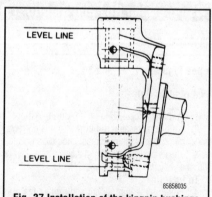

Fig. 37 Installation of the kingpin bushings flush with the plug counterbores

SUSPENSION AND STEERING

17. Press fit the grease seal on the upper bushing. Take care not to damage the grease seal lip.
18. Install the steering knuckle/spindle to the steering knuckle/spindle support as follows:
19. Insert the O-ring in the lower end of the knuckle/spindle support. Install the thrust bearing and shim together with the steering knuckle/spindle to the knuckle/spindle support.

Select the spindle shims which will obtain 0.004 in. (0.1mm) or less clearance between the steering knuckle/spindle and the support. To measure this clearance with a feeler gauge, raise up the bottom of the spindle slightly.

➡ **The thrust bearing is installed so that the covered side faces upward. you will probably be able to use the same shims that were originally installed.**

20. Drive the new kingpin into the kingpin bores, securing the steering knuckle/spindle to the support.
21. Align the locking bolt hole of the knuckle/spindle support with the notch in the kingpin and install the lockbolt.
22. Install the upper and lower kingpin plugs.
23. Install the steering knuckle/spindle arm to the steering knuckle/spindle together with a new lockplate. Tighten the steering knuckle arm attaching bolts to 75–88 ft. lbs. Bend the tabs of the lockplate to engage the flats on the bolt head.
24. Install the brake backing plate, hub and wheel bearings, brake drum and wheel. Bleed the brake hydraulic system and grease the newly installed bushings until the grease is visible around the upper and lower grease seals.

Upper Ball Joint

➡ **Ball joints are used on all 1978–88 Nissans, replacing the kingpins used in 1970–77.**

INSPECTION

The ball joint should be replaced when play becomes excessive. Nissan does not publish specifications on just what constitutes excessive play, relying instead on a method of determining the force (in inch lbs.) required to keep the ball joint turning. This method is not very helpful to the backyard mechanic since it involves removing the ball joint, which is what we are trying to avoid in the first place. An effective way to determine ball joint play is to raise the truck until the wheel is just a couple of inches off the ground and the ball joint is unloaded, which means that you can't jack directly under the ball joint. Place a long bar under the tire and move the wheel and tire assembly up and down. Keep one hand on top of the tire while doing this. If there is over ¼ in. (6mm) of play at the top of the tire, the ball joint is probably bad. This assuming that the wheel bearings are in good shape and properly adjusted. As a double check, have someone watch the ball joint while you move the tire up and down with the bar. If considerable play is seen, besides feeling play at the top of the wheel, the ball joints need to be replaced.

REMOVAL & INSTALLATION

1978–83

1. Raise and support the truck on stands placed on the frame rails.
2. Remove the wheels.
3. Loosen the torsion bar anchor lock and adjusting nuts to relieve spring tension.
4. Remove and discard the cotter pin from the ball joint stud and remove the nut. Separate the stud from the knuckle spindle with a ball joint removal tool.
5. Loosen the bolts retaining the ball joint to the control arm, and remove the joint.

To install:

6. Install the new ball joint into the control arm, tightening the bolts to 12–16 ft. lbs. (16–22 Nm). Install the ball joint stud into the knuckle spindle and install the nut. Tighten the nut to 60 ft. lbs., then continue to tighten until the holes align (limit: 72 ft. lbs.). Install a new cotter pin. Install the wheel, lower the truck, and adjust the ride height. Have the alignment checked.

1984–88 Models

▶ See Figures 38, 39, 40 and 41

1. Raise and support the front end with jackstands under the frame rails.
2. Remove the front wheels.
3. Support the lower control arm with a floor jack and remove the upper ball joint-to-knuckle nut.
4. Using a ball joint separator, such as tool ST29020001, remove the ball joint from the knuckle.
5. Unbolt the ball joint from the upper arm.

To install:

6. Install the ball joint in the upper control arm and tighten the bolts to 12–15 ft. lbs. (16–21 Nm). Press the ball stud into the steering knuckle and

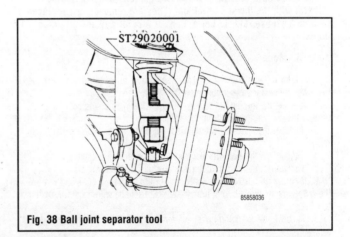

Fig. 38 Ball joint separator tool

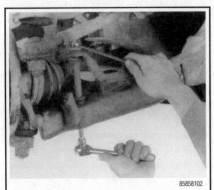

Fig. 39 Removing the stabilizer link on the front suspension

Fig. 40 Installing the upper ball joint to A-frame

Fig. 41 Installing the upper ball joint nuts — note position of pry bar

8-10 SUSPENSION AND STEERING

tighten the nut to 58–72 ft. lbs. (78–98 Nm) on all 1984–86 2wd models (720D series) or 58–108 ft. lbs. (78–147 Nm) on all 1984–86 4wd models (720D series) and all 1986–88 models (D21D series).

7. Have the front end alignment checked.

Lower Ball Joint

➡ Ball joints are used on all 1978–88 Nissans, replacing the kingpins used in 1970–77.

INSPECTION

The ball joint should be replaced when play becomes excessive. Nissan does not publish specifications on just what constitutes excessive play, relying instead on a method of determining the force (in inch lbs.) required to keep the ball joint turning. This method is not very helpful to the backyard mechanic since it involves removing the ball joint, which is what we are trying to avoid in the first place. An effective way to determine ball joint play is to raise the truck until the wheel is just a couple of inches off the ground and the ball joint is unloaded, which means that you can't jack directly under the ball joint. Place a long bar under the tire and move the wheel and tire assembly up and down. Keep one hand on top of the tire while doing this. If there is over ¼ in. (6mm) of play at the bottom of the tire, the ball joint is probably bad. This assuming that the wheel bearings are in good shape and properly adjusted. As a double check, have someone watch the ball joint while you move the tire up and down with the bar. If considerable play is seen, besides feeling play at the top of the wheel, the ball joints need to be replaced.

REMOVAL & INSTALLATION

◆ See Figures 42, 43, 44 and 45

➡ The lower ball joint on 1986–88 2wd models (D21D series) is integral with the lower control arm. They are removed and replaced as a unit; please refer to Lower Control Arm for any and all procedures.

1978–83 Models

1. Perform Steps 1–2 of the Upper Ball Joint removal procedure. Remove the lower shock absorber mounting bolt.
2. Loosen the torsion bar spring anchor lock and adjusting nuts, and remove the anchor arm bolt from the anchor arm.
3. Remove the snapring, then move the anchor arm and torsion bar fully rearward.
4. Disconnect the stabilizer bar from the lower arm, if equipped.
5. Disconnect the tension/compression rod from the lower arm.
6. Remove and discard the cotter pin from the ball joint stud, and remove the nut. Separate the ball joint from the knuckle spindle with a ball joint removal tool.
7. Remove the attaching bolts, and remove the ball joint from the lower arm.

To install:

8. Install the new ball joint in the arm and tighten the bolts to 28–38 ft. lbs. (38–52 Nm). Install the ball joint stud into the knuckle spindle and tighten the nut to 87–123 ft. lbs. (118–167 Nm). Continue to tighten until the holes align, then install the new cotter pin (limit: 141 ft. lbs.). The torsion bar ride height must be adjusted after assembly.

1984–86 2wd Models and 1984–88 4wd Models

➡ The lower ball joint on 1986–88 2wd models (D21D series) is integral with the lower control arm. They are removed and replaced as a unit; please refer to Lower Control Arm for any and all procedures.

1. Raise and support the front of the vehicle on jackstands under the frame rails.
2. Remove the front wheels.
3. Remove the torsion bar as previously described.
4. Unbolt the shock absorber from the lower arm.
5. Remove the ball joint nut.
6. Using a ball joint separator such as tool ST29020001, separate the ball joint from the knuckle.
7. Unbolt the ball joint from the lower arm.

To install:

8. Install the ball joint to the lower arm and tighten the nuts to 28–38 ft. lbs. (38–52 Nm) on all 1984–86 models (720D series); or 35–45 ft. lbs. (47–61 Nm) on all 1986–88 4wd models (D21D series).
9. Press the ball stud into the knuckle and tighten the nut to 87–123 ft. lbs. (118–167 Nm) on all 1984–86 models (720D series); or 87–141 ft. lbs. (118–191 Nm) on all 1986–88 4wd models (D21D series).

Fig. 42 Removing the cotter pin on the lower ball joint

Fig. 43 Separating the lower ball joint with puller type tool

Fig. 44 Removing the lower ball joint

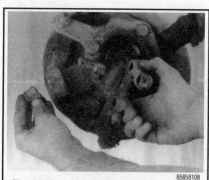

Fig. 45 View of the lower ball joint and nut — always replace the nut and cotter pin upon installation

SUSPENSION AND STEERING 8-11

Control Arms

REMOVAL & INSTALLATION

1970–77 Models

1. Raise the truck on a hoist or jack up the front end and support it with jackstands placed under the frame.
2. Remove the wheel and brake drum.
3. Remove the hub.
4. Remove the brake backing plate from the steering knuckle/spindle support.
5. Remove the steering knuckle/spindle arm, torsion bar, stabilizer bar, shock absorber and strut rod, in this order.
6. Remove the upper fulcrum bolt securing the knuckle/spindle support to the upper control arm assembly and detach the two.
7. Remove the upper control arm bushings from the knuckle/spindle support.
8. Remove the screw bushings from both ends of the lower control arm fulcrum pin.
9. Loosen the nut at the lower end of the knuckle/spindle support from the inside and pull out the cotter pin retaining the fulcrum.
10. Drive the fulcrum pin out of the lower control arm and remove the knuckle/spindle support and steering knuckle/spindle from the lower control arm.
11. Remove the bolts retaining the upper control arm pivot shaft and remove the upper control arm pivot shaft with the camber adjusting shims from the body bracket.
12. Remove the nut retaining the lower control arm pivot shaft and remove the lower control arm pivot shaft. Remove the lower control arm, with the torque arm, from the mounting bracket.
13. The lower control arm bushing is removed with a drift and hammer.

To install:

14. Install the upper and lower control arms. Tighten the lower control arm attaching nut to 54–58 ft. lbs. Tighten the upper control arm and camber adjusting shim bolts to 51–65 ft. lbs.
15. Coat the threads of the fulcrum pin with grease and line up the notch of the fulcrum pin with the knuckle/spindle support for the insertion of the cotter pin. Install the fulcrum pin to the knuckle/spindle support with a soft hammer, attaching the support to the upper control arm. Install the cotter pin and tighten the locknut to 5.8–8.0 ft. lbs.
16. Coat the inner threaded portion of the screw bushing with grease. Position the support at the center of the lower control arm and install the screw bushings. Check the dimensions of the installed screw bushing against those in the illustration, then tighten the bushing to 145–216 ft. lbs.
17. Replace the grease filler plug with a grease fitting and pump grease in until it comes out around the dust cover. Reinstall the filler plug.
18. Install the upper control arm bushing to the knuckle/spindle support and then connect the knuckle/spindle support to the upper control arm. Insert the connecting bolt from the rear and tighten the nut to 28–38 ft. lbs.
19. Install the strut rod, shock absorber, stabilizer rod, torsion bar and steering knuckle arm.
20. Install the brake backing plate to the steering knuckle/spindle and tighten the attaching bolts to 30–36 ft. lbs.
21. Install the brake drum and wheel and adjust the wheel bearing preload.

Upper Control Arm

REMOVAL & INSTALLATION

1978–83 Models

▶ See Figures 46 and 47

1. Perform Steps 1–4 of the Upper Ball Joint removal procedure.
2. Remove the bolts retaining the upper arm pivot shaft and remove the shaft, arm and camber adjusting shims from the body. Note the location of the shims so that they may be installed in their original positions during assembly.

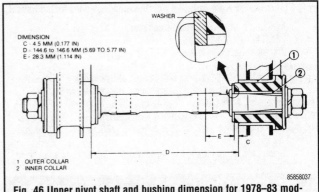

Fig. 46 Upper pivot shaft and bushing dimension for 1978–83 models

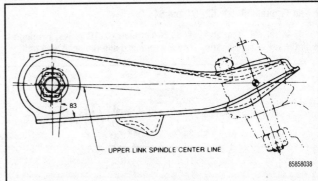

Fig. 47 1978–83 upper arm pivot shaft installation before tightening shaft nuts

3. To remove the upper arm shaft and bushings from the arm, remove the nuts and washers from the shaft. Use a press, first on one end of the shaft and then the other, to press out the bushings. Remove the shaft.

To install:

4. Coat the bushing with soapy water and press it into the upper arm. Install the washers onto the shaft and install the shaft into the arm. Be sure the chamfered side of the washer is against the shaft flange. Measure the distance between the outer collar on the bushing and the washer on the shaft (dimension **C** in the illustration); it should exceed 0.177 in. (4.5mm).
5. Press the other bushing into the arm, and check dimension **C**. Also check the distance between the outer collars of both bushings (dimension **D**) and the distance between the end of the bushing and the centerline of the shaft mounting bolt bore (dimension **E**). **D** should be 5.69–5.77 in. (144.6–146.6mm); **E** should be 1.114 in. (28.3mm).
6. Rotate the pivot shaft in the arm until the angle is as specified in the illustration. Install the nuts and washers on the shaft. Tighten the bushings to 56–76 ft. lbs.
7. Install the upper arm and shaft assembly to the body, replacing the camber shims in their original locations. Tighten the bolts to 80–108 ft. lbs.
8. Follow Step 6 of the upper ball joint removal procedure.

1984–88 Models

▶ See Figures 48 and 49

1. Separate the upper ball joint from the knuckle as previously described.
2. Disconnect the shock absorber at the upper end.
3. Unbolt the control arm spindle. Lift out the control arm.

To install:

4. The bushings may now be pressed out form both sides of the control arm.
5. Apply a soapy solution to new bushings and press them into position in one end of the arm, so that the flange on the bushing firmly contacts the end surface of the upper link collar.
6. Install the spindle and press in the remaining bushings.

8-12 SUSPENSION AND STEERING

➡ The inner washers are installed with the rounded edges facing inward.

7. Temporarily tighten the spindle end nuts.
8. Install the upper ball joint.
9. Bolt the control arm to the frame. Tighten the bolts to 80–108 ft. lbs. (109–147 Nm).
10. Tighten the spindle end nut with camber adjusting shims. Torque the nuts to 52–76 ft. lbs. (71–83 Nm). Check the dimensions **A** and **B** in the illustration. Dimension **A** should be 5.34–5.42 in. (135.6–137.6mm) for 1984–86 models (720D series); or 4.33 (110mm) for 1986–88 models (D21D series). Dimension **B** should be 1.114 in. (28.3mm) for the 720D series; or 1.26 in. (32mm) for the D21D series.
11. Install the ball joint to the knuckle and check the front end align-ment.

Lower Control Arm

REMOVAL & INSTALLATION

◆ See Figures 50, 51, 52, 53 and 54

➡ The lower ball joint on 1986–88 2wd models (D21D series) is integral with the lower control arm. They are removed and replaced as a unit.

1978–83 Models

1. Perform Steps 1–6 of the Lower Ball Joint removal procedure.
2. Remove the lower arm pivot shaft bolt and washer. Tap the pivot shaft out of the bushing. Push down on the torsion bar and remove the lower arm.

To install:

3. Use a bushing driver to tap the lower arm bushing from the frame.
4. Drive the new bushing into the frame.
5. Install the arm and pivot shaft, tightening the nut to 80–108 ft. lbs.
6. Follow Step 8 of the lower ball joint removal procedure.

1984–86 Models (720D Series)

1. Disconnect the lower ball joint from the knuckle as previously described.
2. Remove the torsion bar as previously described.
3. Unbolt the shock absorber from the lower arm.
4. Unbolt the stabilizer bar and tension/compression rod from the arm.
5. Remove the torque arm from the control arm.
6. Unbolt the control arm from the frame.
7. Unbolt the ball joint.
8. Using a driver, remove the lower arm spindle bushings from the frame.

To install:

9. Obtain new bushings.
10. Install the ball joint on the lower arm.
11. Using a driver, install the new bushings, coated with a soapy solution, in the frame.
12. Install the torque arm on the torsion bar.
13. Position the control arm on the frame and then install the torque arm onto the control arm. Tighten the inner bolt to 26–33 ft. lbs. (35–45 Nm) and the outer side to 20–27 ft. lbs. (26–36 Nm).
14. Install the ball joint on the knuckle.
15. Connect the shock absorber.
16. Install the tension/compression rod and stabilizer bar.
17. Lower the truck so that it is resting normally on its wheels.
18. Check wheel alignment.

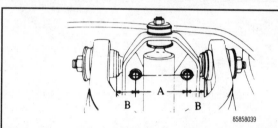

Fig. 48 Upper control arm measuring points — 1984–86 (720D series)

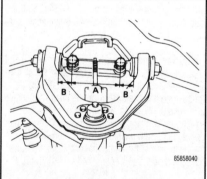

Fig. 49 Upper control arm measuring points — 1986–88 (D21D series)

Fig. 50 Removing the lower pivot shaft bushing nut

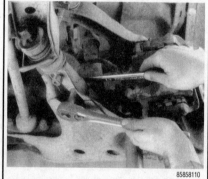

Fig. 51 Removing the lower pivot shaft retaining nuts

Fig. 52 Removing the lower pivot shaft

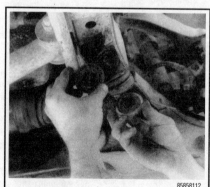

Fig. 53 Removing the lower pivot shaft bushing washers

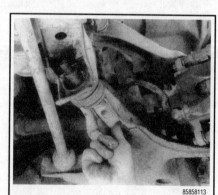

Fig. 54 Installing the lower pivot shaft in the lower arm

SUSPENSION AND STEERING

1986–88 Models (D21D Series)

➡ **The lower ball joint on 1986–88 2wd models (D21D series) is integral with the lower control arm. They are removed and replaced as a unit.**

1. Make matching marks on the anchor arm crossmember when loosening the adjusting nut until there is no tension on the torsion bar and remove the torsion bar.
2. Separate the lower ball joint from the knuckle spindle on 2wd models. On 4wd models, separate it from the control arm.
3. Remove the front lower control arm attaching nut.
4. If necessary, remove the bushing of the lower control arm spindle from the frame using a suitable tool.

To install:

5. Coat the control arm bushing with soapy water and then install the arm to the frame. Tighten the bolt to 80–108 ft. lbs. (109–147 Nm).
6. Connect the ball joint to the knuckle on 2wd models or to the control arm on 4wd models.
7. Install the torsion bar and lower the vehicle.
8. Check the front end alignment.

Steering Knuckle and Spindle

REMOVAL & INSTALLATION

♦ **See Figures 55 thru 74**

1970–79 2wd Models

1. Raise the front of the vehicle and support it safely with jackstands.
2. Remove the front wheels.
3. Disconnect the brake hose from the steering knuckle at the bracket.
4. Remove the brake caliper.
5. Remove the wheel hub cap, and then remove the cotter pin, adjusting cap and spindle nut from the knuckle spindle.
6. Remove the wheel hub and rotor assembly.
7. Remove the hub from the rotor assembly.
8. Remove the outer bearing cone with fingers and remove the inner bearing cone by prying out the grease seal. Discard the grease seal.
9. If it is necessary to replace the bearing outer race, drive it out from the hub with a brass drift and mallet. Evenly tap the bearing outer race through the hole inside the hub.
10. Remove the baffle plate.
11. Separate the knuckle from the spindle arm.
12. Loosen the torsion bar spring anchor nut. and adjusting nut to cancel the torsion of the torsion bar spring.
13. Remove the upper and lower ball joint securing nuts and then remove the ball joints from the knuckle spindle using ball joint removal Tool ST29020001.

To install:

14. Install the knuckle spindle to the upper and lower ball joints. Tighten the upper ball stud nut to 58–72 ft. lbs. and the lower ball stud nut to 124–141 ft. lbs.
15. Tighten the anchor arm adjusting bolt and lock nut to the dimensions show in the illustration.
16. Install the baffle plate.
17. Install and grease the inner and outer bearings and seal if removed. Refer to Section One.
18. Install the knuckle arm and caliper and tighten all retaining bolts to 53–72 ft. lbs.

1980–88 2wd Models

1. Raise the front of the vehicle and support it safely with jackstands.
2. Remove the front wheels.
3. Disconnect the brake hose from the knuckle at the bracket.
4. Remove the brake caliper.
5. Remove the wheel hub cap, and then remove the cotter pin, adjusting cap and spindle nut from the knuckle spindle.
6. Remove the wheel hub and rotor assembly.
7. Remove the hub from the rotor assembly.
8. Remove the outer bearing cone with fingers and remove the inner bearing cone by prying out the grease seal. Discard the grease seal.
9. If it is necessary to replace the bearing outer race, drive it out from the hub with a brass drift and mallet. Evenly tap the bearing outer race through the hole inside the hub.
10. Remove the baffle plate.
11. Loosen but do not remove the upper and lower ball joint tightening nut.
12. Separate the upper and lower ball joint from the knuckle spindle.

➡ **During Step 12, never remove the ball joint nut which was loosened in Step 11.**

13. Jack up the lower control arm (link), then remove the ball joint tightening nut.
14. Separate the knuckle spindle from the upper and lower control arms (links).
15. Installation is the reverse of removal with the following exceptions:
    a. While jacking up the lower link, install the knuckle spindle to the upper and lower ball joints.
    b. When installing the knuckle arm, torque the retaining bolts to 53–72 ft. lbs.
    c. Install the front hub wheel bearings as outlined in Section One.
    d. When attaching the disc rotor to the hub, torque the bolts to 36–51 ft. lbs.

1981–83 4wd Models

1. Block the rear wheels, raise and support the front of the vehicle on jackstands.
2. Remove the wheels.
3. Remove the brake caliper and suspend it out of the way. Do not disconnect the brake hose.
4. Remove the axle shaft.
5. Remove the bolt securing the knuckle arm to the knuckle.
6. Loosen, but do not remove the upper and lower ball joint tightening nuts.
7. Separate the ball joints from the knuckle with a ball joint removing tool.

❋❋ CAUTION

NEVER REMOVE THE BALL JOINT NUT IN THE ABOVE STEP!

8. Jack up the lower link and remove the ball joint tightening nut.
9. Remove the knuckle.
10. Unbend the lockwasher with a small prybar and remove the front hub locknut.
11. Remove the lockwasher and special washer.
12. Push the wheel bearing support out of the hub.
13. Separate the knuckle from the hub with a puller.
14. Remove the bearing collar.
15. Remove the inside bearing and seal. Drive the race out with a brass driver.
16. Separate the hub from the rotor.
17. Knock the hub on a wood block to move the outer bearing away from the hub surface, then pull it the rest of the way with a bearing puller. Remove the grease seal.
18. Remove the axle shaft bearing from the bearing support with a brass driver.
19. Clean and thoroughly repack the bearings.
20. When assembling, note the following points:
    a. Install the bearing outer race into each side of the knuckle with a brass driver.
    b. Install the outer grease seal and bearing with a brass driver.
    c. Pack the seal lip with wheel bearing grease. Be sure that the seal faces the right direction.
    d. The wheel bearing collar thickness determines end play. Determine what thickness to use as follows:
- Install the collar which was removed.
- Install the inside bearing with a brass driver.
- Install the special washer and lockwasher.
- Tighten the locknut to 108–145 ft. lbs.
- Turn the hub several times in both directions to seat the bearings.
- Using a spring scale as shown, check the preload to see that it falls between 2.2 and 9.5 ft. lbs.
- If not, adjust by replacing the collar with one of a different thickness, as shown by the number stamped on the collar. The larger the number, the thickness the collar.

8-14 SUSPENSION AND STEERING

- When preload has been correctly set, secure the nut by bending the lockwasher tip.

21. Installation is the reverse of the removal procedure. Observe the following torques:
- Upper ball joint-to-knuckle: 36–65 ft. lbs.
- Lower ball joint-to-knuckle: 43–72 ft. lbs.
- Knuckle arm-to-knuckle: 53–72 ft. lbs.
- Caliper-to-knuckle: 53–72 ft. lbs.
- Axle shaft-to-carrier: 20–27 ft. lbs.
- Free running hub: 18–25 ft. lbs.
- Stabilizer bar: 12–16 ft. lbs.
- Wheel nut: 87–108 ft. lbs.

1984–86 4wd Models (720D Series)

1. Raise and support the front end with jackstands under the frame rails.
2. Remove the front wheels.
3. Remove the calipers and suspend them out of the way.
4. Remove the locking hub assembly.
5. Remove the tie rod using tool HT2520000, or equivalent.
6. Unbolt the knuckle arm from the knuckle.
7. Support the lower control arm with a floor jack and remove the upper and lower ball joint-to-knuckle nuts.
8. Separate the ball joints from the knuckle.
9. Remove the snapring and lock washer from the hub.
10. Remove the hub locknut using tool KV40104300 or equivalent.
11. Separate the hub and rotor from the knuckle.
12. Installation is the reverse of the removal procedure.

1986–88 4wd Models (D21D Series)

1. Remove the Auto-lock or Manual-lock free running hub assembly as detailed in Section 7.
2. Separate the axle shaft from the knuckle spindle by slightly tapping the axle shaft end.
3. Loosen, but do not remove the upper and lower ball joint-to-spindle nuts.
4. Separate the knuckle spindle from the upper and lower ball joint studs with Tool HT72520000

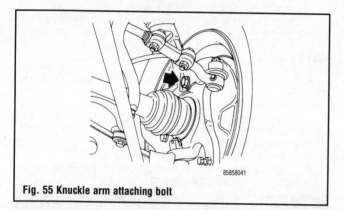
Fig. 55 Knuckle arm attaching bolt

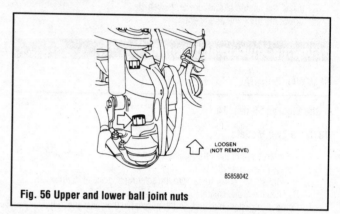
Fig. 56 Upper and lower ball joint nuts

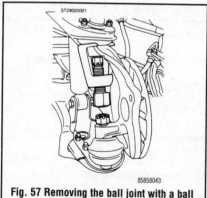
Fig. 57 Removing the ball joint with a ball joint removal type tool

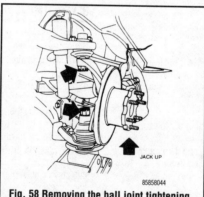
Fig. 58 Removing the ball joint tightening nuts

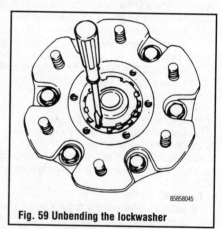
Fig. 59 Unbending the lockwasher

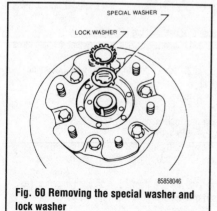
Fig. 60 Removing the special washer and lock washer

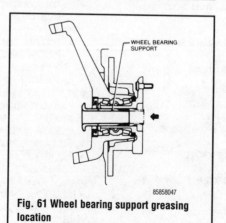
Fig. 61 Wheel bearing support greasing location

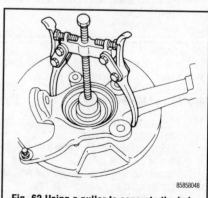
Fig. 62 Using a puller to separate the hub from the knuckle

SUSPENSION AND STEERING 8-15

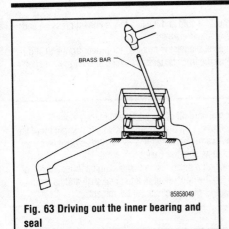

Fig. 63 Driving out the inner bearing and seal

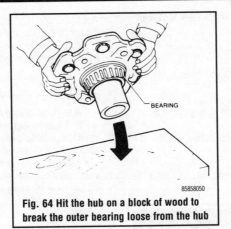

Fig. 64 Hit the hub on a block of wood to break the outer bearing loose from the hub

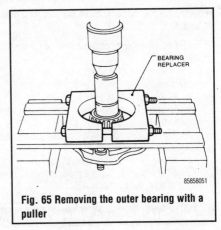

Fig. 65 Removing the outer bearing with a puller

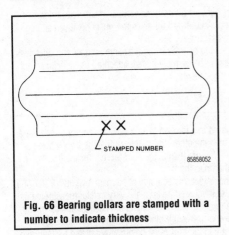

Fig. 66 Bearing collars are stamped with a number to indicate thickness

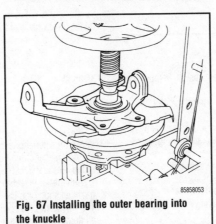

Fig. 67 Installing the outer bearing into the knuckle

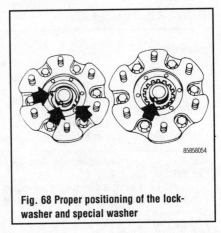

Fig. 68 Proper positioning of the lock-washer and special washer

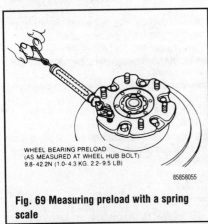

Fig. 69 Measuring preload with a spring scale

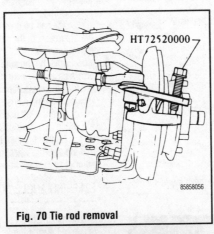

Fig. 70 Tie rod removal

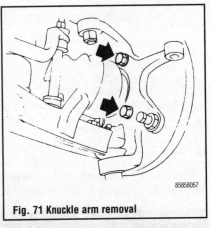

Fig. 71 Knuckle arm removal

Fig. 72 View of the steering knuckle assembly on 4wd model — most models similar

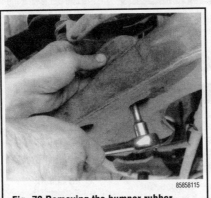

Fig. 73 Removing the bumper rubber assembly nut

Fig. 74 Removing the bumper rubber assembly

8-16 SUSPENSION AND STEERING

➡ **During Step 4, never remove the ball joint nuts which were loosened in Step 3.**

5. Support the lower control arm with a floor jack and remove the ball joint tightening nuts.
6. Remove the knuckle spindle from the upper and lower control arms.
7. When installing, follow these notes:
    a. When installing the needle bearing into the knuckle spindle, apply multi-purpose grease and make sure that the needle bearing is facing in the proper direction.
    b. With the lower control arm jacked up, install the knuckle spindle to the upper and lower ball joints.
    c. Adjust the wheel bearing preload.
    d. When installing the axle shaft, never reuse the snapring, and check axial end play. Refer to Section 7.

Front Axle Hub and Wheel Bearing

REMOVAL & INSTALLATION

2wd Models

1. Raise the front of the truck and support it with safety stands. Remove the wheels.
2. Remove the brake caliper and suspend it with wire, out of the way. Remove the caliper torque plate if equipped.
3. Remove the axle end cap and then remove the cotter pin, nut lock and nut.
4. Pull the hub/disc assembly off the spindle with the outer bearing. Don't let the bearing fall out.
5. Pry the inner oil seal out and remove the inner bearing from the hub.

To install:

6. Clean the bearings and outer races and inspect them for wear or cracks.
7. Using a brass drift and a hammer, drive out the bearing outer race. Press a new one into position.
8. Pack the bearings with grease until it oozes out the other side. Coat the inside of the hub and cap with grease.
9. Position the inner bearing into the hub, coat the oil seal with grease and press it into the hub.
10. Press the hub assembly onto the spindle and install the outer bearing and thrust washer.
11. Install the hub nut. Turn the hub a few times to seat the bearings and then loosen the nut until there is 0.5–1.0mm axial play. Using a spring tension gauge, check that the preload is 1.3–4.0 lbs.
12. Install the locknut, new cotter pin and hub grease cap.
13. Install the brake torque plate. Install the brake caliper.
14. Install the wheels and lower the truck.

4wd Models

Hub and bearing removal and installation procedures for these models are detailed in the Front Drive Axle section of Section 7.

Front End Alignment

Alignment should only be performed after it has been verified that all parts of the steering and suspension systems are in good operating condition. The truck must be empty. The tires must be cold and inflated to the correct pressure and the test surface must be level and horizontal.

Because special, elaborate equipment is required for proper front end alignment, it is recommended that the truck be taken to a reputable alignment shop.

CASTER

Caster is the forward or rearward tilt of the upper end of the kingpin (1970–77), or the upper ball joint (1978–88), which results in a slight tilt of the steering axis forward or backward. Rearward tilt is referred to as positive caster, while forward tilt is referred to as negative caster.

Caster is adjusted by creating a difference in the total number (thickness) of shims, front and rear, between the upper control arm pivot shaft and its mounting bracket. Adjustment requires the use of special equipment.

CAMBER

Camber is the inward or outward tilt from the vertical, measured in degrees, of the front wheels at the top. An outward tilt gives the wheel positive camber. Proper camber is critical to assure even tire wear.

Camber is adjusted by adding or subtracting the same number and thickness of shims at the front and rear upper arm pivot shaft attaching bolts. Adjustment requires the use of special equipment.

TOE

Toe is the amount measured in a fraction of an inch, that the front wheels are closer together at one end than the other. Toe-in means that the front wheels are closer together at the front of the tire than at the rear; toe-out means that the rear of the tires are closer together than the front.

Although it is recommended that this adjustment be made by your dealer or a qualified shop, you can make it yourself if you make very careful measurement. The wheels must be dead straight ahead. The truck must have a full tank of gas, all fluids must be at their proper levels, all other suspension and steering adjustments must be correct and the tires must be properly inflated to their cold specification.

1. Toe can be determined by measuring the distance between the centers of the tire treads, at the front of the tire and the rear. If the tread pattern of your truck's tires makes this impossible, you can measure between the edges of the wheel rims, but be sure to move the truck and measure in a few places to avoid errors caused by bent rims or wheel runout.
2. If the measurement is not within specifications loosen the retaining clamp lock nuts on the adjustable tie rods.
3. Turn the left and right tie rods EQUAL amounts until the measurements are within specifications.
4. Tighten the lock bolts and then recheck the measurements. Check to see that the steering wheel is still in the proper position. If not, remove it and reposition it as detailed later in this section.

STEERING ANGLE ADJUSTMENT

The maximum steering angle is adjusted by stopper bolts located on the inside of the steering knuckle/spindle. Loosen the locknut on the stopper bolt, turn the stopper bolt, turn the stopper bolt in or out as required to obtain the proper maximum steering angle and retighten the locknut.

REAR SUSPENSION

Coil Springs

REMOVAL & INSTALLATION

✳✳ CAUTION

The leaf springs are under a considerable amount of tension. Be very careful when removing or installing them; they can exert enough force to cause serious injuries.

1988 Pathfinder

▶ See Figure 75

1. Raise the rear of the truck and remove the rear axle as detailed in Section 7 under Rear Axle—5-Link.
2. Remove the coil springs and their spring seats. Be careful to keep all components in their proper order.

To install:

3. Install the spring seats on the rear axle in the proper directions and then raise the axle housing until the springs can be inserted.
4. Install the rear axle housing as detailed in Section 7.

SUSPENSION AND STEERING   8-17

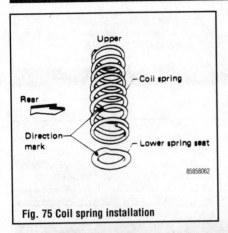

Fig. 75 Coil spring installation

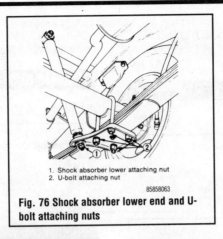

1. Shock absorber lower attaching nut
2. U-bolt attaching nut

Fig. 76 Shock absorber lower end and U-bolt attaching nuts

Fig. 77 Removing the leaf spring shackle assembly

Leaf Springs

REMOVAL & INSTALLATION

♦ See Figures 76 and 77

✲✲✲ CAUTION

The leaf springs are under a considerable amount of tension. Be very careful when removing or installing them; they can exert enough force to cause serious injuries.

1970–88 Pickups and 1986–87 Pathfinder

1. Raise the rear of the truck and support it with jackstands placed under the frame.
2. Disconnect the shock absorbers at their lower end. Disconnect the parking brake cables from the springs.
3. Remove the nuts securing the U-bolts around the axle housing.
4. Place a jack under the rear axle housing and raise the housing just enough to remove the weight from the springs.
5. Remove the nuts from the spring shackles, drive out the shackle pins and remove the spring from the vehicle.

To install:

6. Install the spring in the reverse order of removal. The weight of the truck must be on the rear wheels before tightening the front pin, shackle, and shock absorber attaching nuts. Bounce the truck several times to set the suspension and then tighten the front pin and shackle nuts to :
   • 83–94 ft. lbs. on 1970–77 models
   • 37–50 ft. lbs. (50–68 Nm) on 1978–86 models (720D series) and for the spring shackle nuts only on 1986–88 2wd models (D21D series)
   • 58–72 ft. lbs. (78–98 Nm) on 1986–88 models (D21D series) except the shackle nuts on 2wd models
7. Tighten the U-bolt nuts to 65–72 ft. lbs. (88–98 Nm).
8. Tighten the shock absorber lower end nut to:
   • 12–16 ft. lbs. (16–22 Nm) on all 1970–86 2wd models (720D series)
   • 22–30 ft. lbs. (30–40 Nm) on all 1981–86 4wd models (720D series) and all 1986–88 models (D21D series)

Shock Absorbers

INSPECTION AND TESTING

Inspect and test the rear shock absorbers in the same manner as outlined for the front shock absorbers.

REMOVAL & INSTALLATION

♦ See Figures 78 thru 83

1. Raise the rear of the vehicle.
2. Support the rear axle housing with jackstands.
3. Unfasten the upper shock absorber retaining nuts and/or bolts from the upper frame member.
4. Depending upon the type of rear spring used, either disconnect the lower end of the shock absorber from the spring seat, or the rear axle housing, by removing its cotter pins, nuts and/or bolts.
5. Remove the shock absorber. Inspect the shock for wear, leaks, or other signs of damage.

To install:

6. Install the shock absorber and tighten the upper bolts to 22–30 ft. lbs. (30–40 Nm).

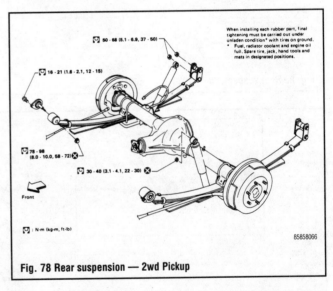

Fig. 78 Rear suspension — 2wd Pickup

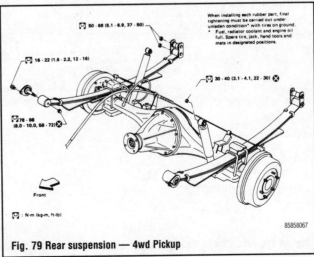

Fig. 79 Rear suspension — 4wd Pickup

8-18 SUSPENSION AND STEERING

7. Tighten the shock absorber lower bolt to:
- 12–16 ft. lbs. (16–22 Nm) on all 1970–86 2wd models (720D series)
- 22–30 ft. lbs. (30–40 Nm) on all 1981–86 4wd models (720D series) and all 1986–88 models (D21D series)

Control Arms

REMOVAL & INSTALLATION

1988 Pathfinder

Control arm removal and installation is fairly simple; raise the vehicle and support the rear axle housing and then unbolt the control arms. Always install the bolts in the same direction that they were removed. All bolts should be tightened to 80–108 ft. lbs. (108–147 Nm) with the vehicle on the ground. Bounce the truck several times to set the suspension.

Panhard Rod

REMOVAL & INSTALLATION

1988 Pathfinder

Panhard rod removal and installation is fairly simple; raise the vehicle and support the rear axle housing and then unbolt the rod. Tighten the right side bolt to 80–108 ft. lbs. (108–147 Nm) and the left side bolt to 36–51 ft. lbs. (49–69 Nm) with the vehicle on the ground. Bounce the truck several times to set the suspension.

Stabilizer Bar

REMOVAL & INSTALLATION

1988 Pathfinder

1. Raise the truck and support it with safety stands.
2. Disconnect the stabilizer bar connecting rod at the body. Remove the retainer and cushion from the link.
3. Disconnect the stabilizer bar bracket and cushion from the axle housing.
4. Remove the stabilizer bar.

To install:

5. Position the stabilizer bar at the axle housing and install the bracket and cushion. Tighten the mounting bolts to 19–24 ft. lbs. (25–32 Nm).
6. Install the connecting rod to the body with the retainers and cushion. Tighten the mounting bolts to 19–24 ft. lbs. (25–32 Nm).
7. Lower the truck.

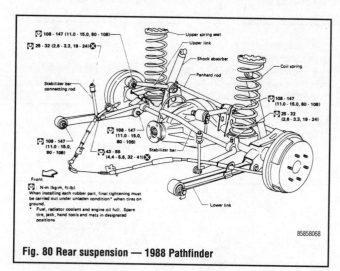

Fig. 80 Rear suspension — 1988 Pathfinder

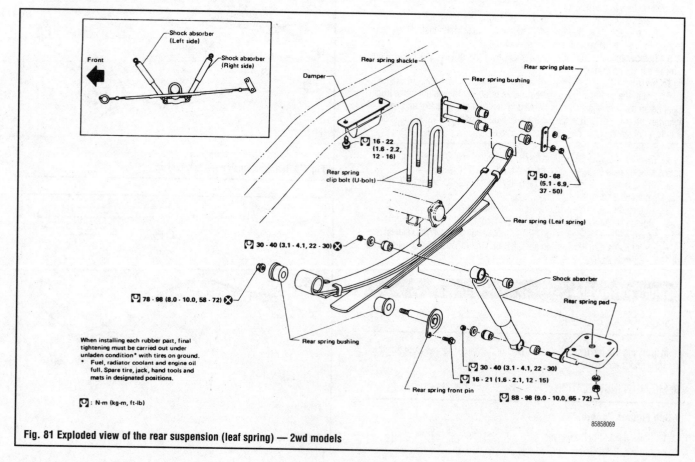

Fig. 81 Exploded view of the rear suspension (leaf spring) — 2wd models

SUSPENSION AND STEERING 8-19

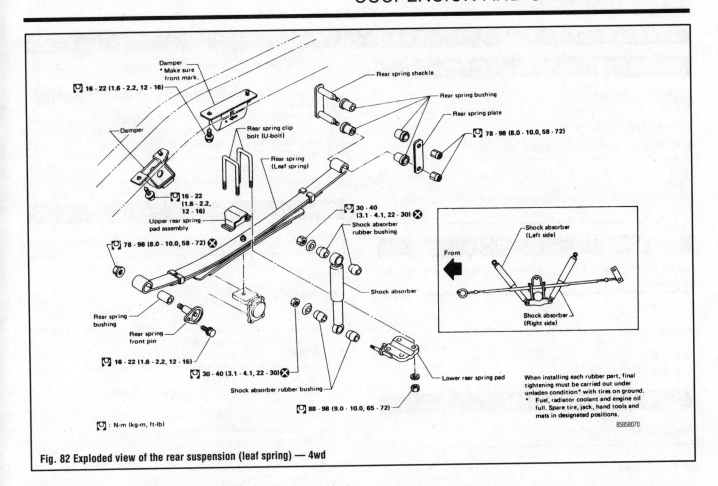

Fig. 82 Exploded view of the rear suspension (leaf spring) — 4wd

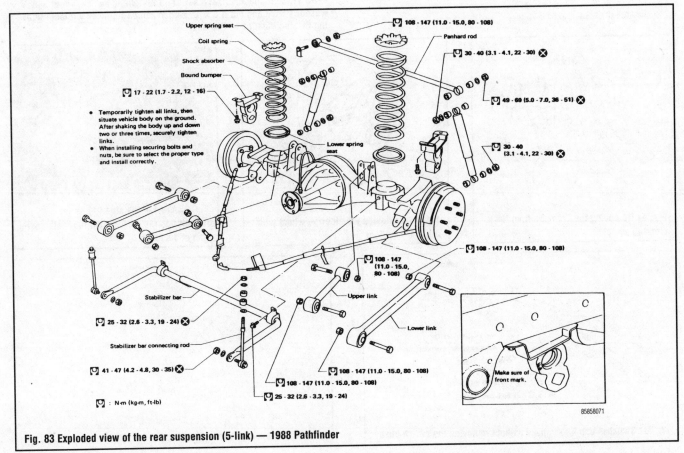

Fig. 83 Exploded view of the rear suspension (5-link) — 1988 Pathfinder

8-20 SUSPENSION AND STEERING

STEERING

Steering Wheel

REMOVAL & INSTALLATION

▶ See Figures 84, 85 and 86

1. Position the wheels in the straight ahead position.
2. Disconnect the negative battery cable.
3. Remove the horn pad by unscrewing the two screws from the rear side of the steering wheel crossbar.
4. Punchmark the top of the steering column shaft and the steering wheel flange.
5. Remove the attaching nut and remove the steering wheel with a puller.

CAUTION

Do not strike the shaft with a hammer, which may cause the column to collapse.

To install:

6. Install the steering wheel so that the punchmarks are aligned. Tighten the steering wheel attaching nut to 51–54 ft. lbs. for 1970–79 models; 29–36 ft. lbs. (39–49 Nm) on 1980–86 models (720D series); and 22–29 ft. lbs. (29–39 Nm) on 1986–88 models (D21D series).
7. Install the horn pad.

Turn Signal and Dimmer Switch

REMOVAL & INSTALLATION

1970–79 Models

1. Disconnect the negative battery cable.
2. Remove the steering wheel.
3. Disconnect the wiring harness from the clip which retains it to the lower instrument panel.
4. Disconnect the multi-connector and lead wire from the instrument panel wiring harness.
5. Remove the steering column shell covers (upper and lower).
6. Loosen the 2 screws attaching the switch assembly to the steering column jacket and remove the switch assembly.

To install:

7. Install the turn signal and dimmer switch and connect the electrical leads.
8. Install the steering column covers and the steering wheel.

Combination Switch

REMOVAL & INSTALLATION

1980–88

▶ See Figures 87 and 88

1. Disconnect the negative battery cable.
2. Unscrew the two retaining bolts and remove the steering column garnish.
3. Remove the upper and lower steering column covers.
4. Remove the steering wheel as detailed previously.
5. Trace the switch wiring harness to the multi-connector. Push in the lock levers and pull apart the connector.
6. Unscrew the mounting screws and remove the switch.

To install:

7. Install the switch and tighten the mounting screws. Be sure to align the protrusion on the switch body with the hole in the steering column.
8. Connect the switch multi-connector.
9. Install the steering wheel and column covers. Connect the negative battery cable.

➥On 1986–88 models (D21D series), the lighting switch, wiper and washer switch and the A.S.C.D. switch can be replaced without removing the combination switch base.

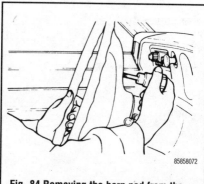
Fig. 84 Removing the horn pad from the steering wheel

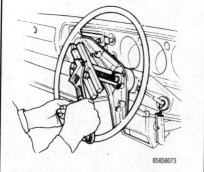
Fig. 85 Removing the steering wheel with a puller type tool

Fig. 86 View of the steering wheel installed in the correct position, note position of 3 spokes

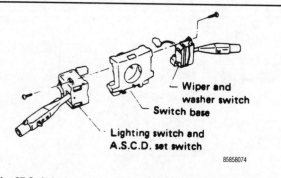
Fig. 87 Switches can be removed without removing the switch base

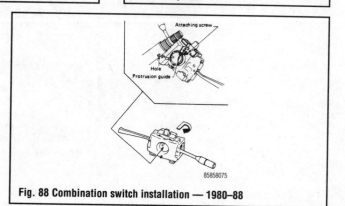
Fig. 88 Combination switch installation — 1980–88

SUSPENSION AND STEERING 8-21

Ignition Switch

REMOVAL & INSTALLATION

1970–79

1. Disconnect the negative cable from the battery.
2. Unscrew and remove the escutcheon from the front of the ignition switch.
3. Remove the ignition switch and wiring harness with spacer from the steering shell cover.
4. Disconnect the wiring connector from the back of the ignition switch.

To install:

5. Install the ignition switch and connect the electrical lead.
6. Screw the escutcheon onto the switch and connect the battery cable.

Ignition Lock/Switch

REMOVAL & INSTALLATION

♦ See Figures 89 and 90

1980–88

1. Disconnect the battery ground cable.
2. Remove the steering wheel and the column covers.
3. Drill out the shear bolts holding the lock assembly in place and remove the conventional bolts.
4. Disconnect the wiring from the switch and remove the assembly.
5. Unscrew the retaining bolts in the lock cylinder and separate the switch from the lock.

To install:

6. Connect the switch to the lock cylinder and tighten the retaining screws.
7. Make sure that the hole in the column and the mating part of the lock cylinder are aligned. Install new shear bolts and break off their heads.
8. Connect the electrical lead to the switch and then install the column covers.
9. Install the steering wheel and connect the battery cable.

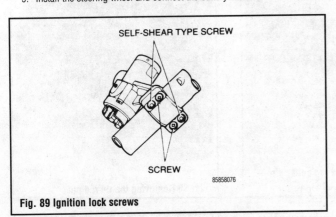

Fig. 89 Ignition lock screws

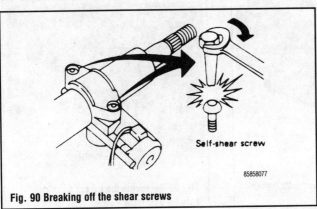

Fig. 90 Breaking off the shear screws

Steering Linkage

REMOVAL & INSTALLATION

♦ See Figures 91 and 92

1970–79 Models

1. Raise the front of the truck and support it with jackstands placed under the frame.
2. Remove the cotter pins and nuts securing the side rod ball studs to the steering knuckle/spindle arms.
3. Use a puller to disconnect the side rod ball studs from the steering knuckle arms. If a puller is not available, strike the side of the steering knuckle arm boss with a hammer, backing it up with a heavy hammer on the opposite side, and at the same time having an assistant pull the ball stud out of the steering knuckle arm.

➥ **Do not strike the ball stud head, the ball socket on the side rod, or the side rod with the hammer.**

4. Remove the nut securing the steering gear arm on the sector shaft and remove the gear arm with a puller. If a puller is not available, and the steering

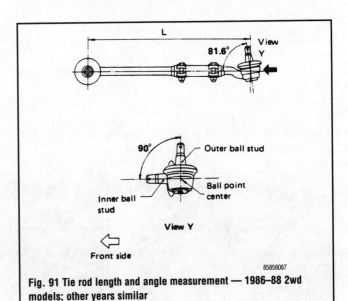

Fig. 91 Tie rod length and angle measurement — 1986–88 2wd models; other years similar

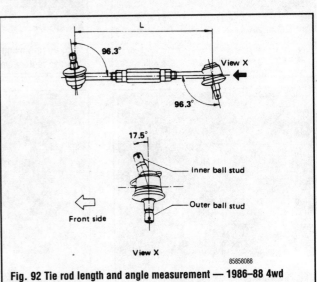

Fig. 92 Tie rod length and angle measurement — 1986–88 4wd models; other years similar

8-22 SUSPENSION AND STEERING

gear arm need not be removed, disconnect the side arm and tie rod ball studs from the steering gear arm in the same manner as outlined in Step 3.

5. Remove the idler arm assembly from the frame by unscrewing the two attaching nuts.

To install:

6. Install the steering linkage in the reverse order of removal. Tighten the ball stud nuts to 40–55 ft. lbs., idler arm assembly attaching nuts to 23–27 ft. lbs., and the tie rod adjustment locknuts to 58–72 ft. lbs. Adjust the toe-in and steering angle.

1980–88 Models

◆ See Figures 93 thru 107

➡ Before working on any of the following steering linkage components, disconnect the battery cable, raise the front of the truck and support it with safety stands.

PITMAN ARM

1. Remove the strut bar.
2. Loosen the Pitman arm nut.
3. Using a tie rod end puller or the like, disconnect the Pitman arm from the sector shaft.
4. Using a tie rod end puller or the like, disconnect the Pitman arm from the cross rod.

To install:

5. Align the marks on the Pitman arm and sector shaft and connect them. Tighten the nut to 94–108 ft. lbs. (127–147 Nm) on models with manual steering; or 101–130 ft. lbs. (137–177 Nm) on models with power steering.
6. Connect the arm to the cross rod and tighten the nut. Install a new cotter pin.
7. Install the strut bar.

TIE ROD

1. Using a tie rod end puller, disconnect the tie rod from the cross rod.
2. Using a tie rod end puller, disconnect the tie rod from the knuckle arm.
3. Remove the tie rod and remove the tie rod ends.

To install:

4. Screw the tie rod ends onto the tie rod. The tie rod length should be:
- 1980–86 2wd (720D series): 13.07 in. (332mm).
- 1986–88 2wd (D21D series): 13.54 in. (344mm).
- 1981–83 4wd: 10.83 in. (275mm).
- 1984–86 4wd (720D series): 11.54 in. (293mm).
- 1986–88 4wd (D21D series): 11.06 in. (281mm).

The remaining length of threads on both ends should always be equal. On 1986–88 models (D21D series), the tie rod ends should always be screwed on at least 1.38 in. (35mm).

5. Turn the tie rod ends so they cross at about 90° (17.5° on 1986–88 4wd models). Tighten the clamp nuts to 8–12 ft. lbs. (11–17 Nm) on 1980–86 2wd models (720D series); or 10–14 ft. lbs (14–20 Nm) on 1986–88 2wd models (D21D series). Tighten the locknuts to 58–72 ft. lbs. (78–98 Nm) on all 4wd models.

6. Connect the tie rod to the knuckle arm and cross rod and tighten the mounting nuts to 40–72 ft. lbs. (54–98 Nm).

CROSS ROD

1. Disconnect the tie rod ends from the cross rod.
2. Using a tie rod end puller, disconnect the Pitman arm from the cross rod.
3. Using a tie rod end puller, disconnect the idler arm from the cross rod.
4. Remove the rod and inspect it for cracks or other damage.

To install:

5. Connect the cross rod to the idler arm and tighten the nut 40–72 ft. lbs. (54–98 Nm).
6. Connect the cross rod to the Pitman arm and tighten the nut to 40–72 ft. lbs. (54–98 Nm).
7. Connect the tie rod ends to the cross rod and tighten the nuts to 40–72 ft. lbs. (54–98 Nm).

STEERING DAMPER

1. Disconnect the steering damper at the cross rod.
2. Disconnect the damper at the frame and remove the damper with all washers and cushions.

Fig. 93 Loosening the tie rod lock nut

Fig. 94 Removing the tie rod cotter pin — always replace upon installation

Fig. 95 Removing the tie rod nut

Fig. 96 View of the tie rod assembly after being greased

Fig. 97 Separating the tie rod with puller type tool

Fig. 98 Removing the tie rod from the spindle assembly

SUSPENSION AND STEERING 8-23

Fig. 99 Removing the tie rod end-count the threads to remove, install the same amount

Fig. 100 Removing the idle arm cotter pin, replace upon installation

Fig. 101 Removing the idle arm nut

Fig. 102 Removing the idle arm assembly with a puller type tool

Fig. 103 Removing the idle arm from the frame bracket

Fig. 104 View of the idler arm and washer assembly

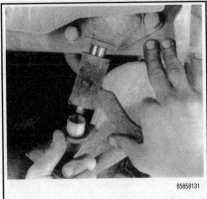

Fig. 105 Installing the idler arm assembly

Fig. 106 View of the steering damper assembly

Fig. 107 Removing the steering damper

To install:

3. Install the damper to the frame bracket and tighten the nut to 7–8 ft. lbs. (9–12 Nm) on 1981–86 models (720D series), or 13–17 ft. lbs. (18–24 Nm) on 1986–88 models (D21D series).

4. Connect the other end of the steering damper to the cross rod and tighten the nut to 14–19 ft. lbs. (19–25 Nm) on 1981–86 models (720D series), or 27–36 ft. lbs. (37–49 Nm) on 1986–88 models (D21D series).

IDLER ARM BRACKET

1. Disconnect the cross rod from the idler arm.
2. Remove the mounting bolts and remove the idler arm bracket with the arm attached.

To install:

3. Position the bracket and arm on the frame and tighten the bolts to 36–51 ft. lbs. (49–69 Nm) on 1981–86 models (720D series), or 58–72 ft. lbs. (78–98 Nm) on 1986&–88 models (D21D series).

4. Connect the idler arm to the cross rod and tighten the nut to 40–72 ft. lbs. (54–98 Nm). Install a new cotter pin.

Manual Steering Gear

ADJUSTMENTS

Adjustments to the manual steering gear are not necessary during normal service. Adjustments are performed only as part of overhaul.

Worm Bearing Preload

♦ See Figures 108 and 109

1. Mount the gear in a vise.
2. Using an inch lbs. torque wrench and spanner KV48101400, or its equiv-

8-24 SUSPENSION AND STEERING

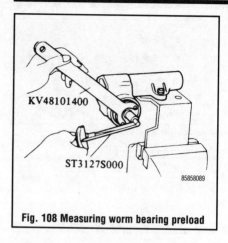
Fig. 108 Measuring worm bearing preload

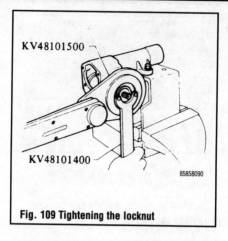
Fig. 109 Tightening the locknut

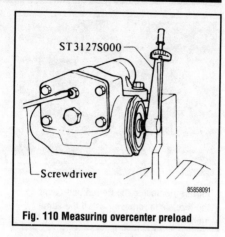
Fig. 110 Measuring overcenter preload

alent, rotate the worm shaft a few turns in each direction to settle the bearing and measure the existing preload.

3. If preload is not 1.7–5.2 inch lbs., loosen the locknut and turn the adjusting plug with the spanner, in a clockwise rotation ONLY. Never adjust preload by turning the adjusting plug counterclockwise! If preload cannot be obtained in this manner, rebuild the gear.

4. Apply liquid sealer on the shaft threads and tighten the locknut to 181–231 ft. lbs. (245–314 Nm).

Overcenter Preload

♦ See Figure 110

1. Mount the gear in a vise.
2. With an inch lb. torque wrench on the sector shaft, rotate the sector shaft lock-to-lock, counting the total number of turns. Divide the total by two and position the shaft at this midpoint.
3. Rotate the shaft one turn to either side of center using the torque wrench and noting the preload.
4. Adjust the preload by loosening the adjusting screw locknut and turning the adjusting screw in a clockwise rotation ONLY. Preload should be 5.2–8.7 inch lbs.
5. If adjustment will not correct preload, the unit must be rebuilt.

REMOVAL & INSTALLATION

♦ See Figure 111

1. Raise and support the truck on jackstands.
2. Unbolt the wormshaft pinch bolt at the rubber coupling.

3. Matchmark the Pitman arm and sector shaft, and with the wheels in a straight ahead position, remove the Pitman arm with a puller.
4. Unbolt and remove the gear from the frame.

To install:

5. Install the gear and tighten the bolts to 62–71 ft. lbs. (84–96 Nm).
6. Press the Pitman arm onto the sector shaft so that the marks are aligned and then tighten the nut to 94–108 ft. lbs. (127–147 Nm).
7. Slide the worm shaft into the coupling pinch bolt and tighten the bolt to 29–36 ft. lbs. (39–49 Nm) except on 1986–88 models (D21D series) where it should be 17–22 ft. lbs. (24–29 Nm).

Power Steering Gear

ADJUSTMENT

Turning Torque

♦ See Figures 112, 113 and 114

1. Mount the gear on a holding fixture in a vise.
2. Turn the stub shaft (the shaft that connects with the steering column) several turns in either direction.
3. Mount an inch lb. torque wrench on the stub shaft and turn it lock-to-lock, counting the total number of turns. Divide that number by 2 and position the torque wrench and shaft at the mid-point.
4. Measure the amount of force needed to turn the shaft past the midpoint in both directions. The force should be 3.5 inch lbs.
5. To correct the adjustment, loosen the locknut on the adjusting screw and turn the screw to give the correct torque. Tighten the locknut to 21–25 ft. lbs. (28–34 Nm) on all except 1986–88 models (D21D series) where it should be 25–29 ft. lbs. (34–39 Nm).

REMOVAL & INSTALLATION

♦ See Figure 115

1. Matchmark and remove the Pitman arm from the sector shaft, using a puller such as special tool 290200001.
2. Matchmark and disconnect the steering stub shaft from the gear at the coupling.
3. Disconnect the fluid lines from the gear and cap the lines and openings in the gear.
4. Unbolt and remove the gear assembly from the frame.
5. Installation is the reverse of the removal procedure. When installing, observe the following torques:
   - Gear housing-to-frame: 62–71 ft. lbs. (84–96 Nm)
   - Steering stub shaft-to-coupling: 29–36 ft. lbs. (39–49 Nm)—except 1986–88 models (D21D series); 17–22 ft. lbs. (24–29 Nm)—1986–88 models (D21D series).
   - Pitman arm-to-sector shaft: 101–130 ft. lbs. (137–177 Nm)

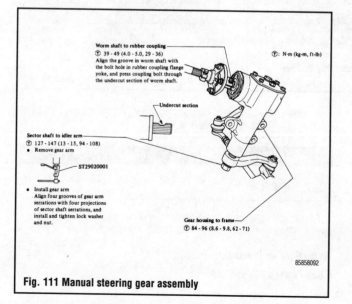
Fig. 111 Manual steering gear assembly

SUSPENSION AND STEERING 8-25

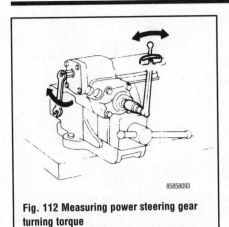

Fig. 112 Measuring power steering gear turning torque

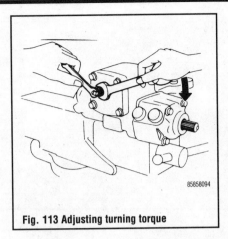

Fig. 113 Adjusting turning torque

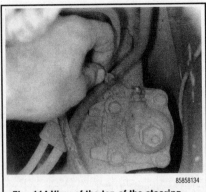

Fig. 114 View of the top of the steering gear or steering box, most models similar

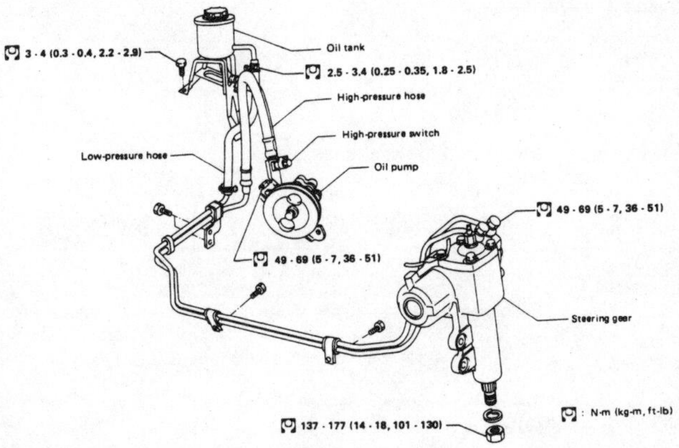

![Fig. 115 Power steering gear assembly]

Fig. 115 Power steering gear assembly

Power Steering Pump

REMOVAL AND INSTALLATION

1. Remove the fan shroud.
2. Unfasten the nut from the center of the pump pulley.

➡ Use the drive belt as a brake to keep the pulley from rotating.

3. Remove the drive belt.
4. Remove the pulley and the bracket from the pump shaft.
5. Detach the intake and outlet hoses from the pump reservoir.

➡ Tie the hose ends up high so the fluid cannot flow out of them. Drain or plug the pump to prevent fluid leakage.

6. Remove the bolt from the rear mounting brace.
7. Remove the bracket bolts and then remove the pump.

To install:

8. Install the pump and tighten the pump pulley mounting bolt to 23–31 ft. lbs. (31–42 Nm).
9. Adjust the pump drive belt tension. The belt should deflect 8–10mm under thumb pressure applied midway between the air pump and power steering pump.
10. Fill the reservoir with Dexron®II automatic transmission fluid. Bleed the air from the system.

BLEEDING

1. Raise the front of the truck and support it securely with jackstands.
2. Fill the pump reservoir with Dexron®II automatic transmission fluid.
3. Rotate the steering wheel from lock-to-lock several times. Add fluid as necessary.

➡ Never hold the steering wheel in the lock position for more than 15 seconds.

4. Repeat Step 3 until the fluid level in the reservoir remains the same.
5. Start the engine. With the engine idling, turn the steering wheel from lock-to-lock several times.
6. Lower the front of the truck and repeat Step 5.
7. Center the wheel at the midpoint of its travel. Stop the engine.
8. The fluid level should not have risen more than 5mm If it does, repeat Step 6.
9. Check for fluid leakage.

8-26 SUSPENSION AND STEERING

TORQUE SPECIFICATIONS

Component	US	Metric
Wheel hub nut	87–108 ft. lbs.	118–147 Nm
Knuckle arm-to-tie-rod	40–72 ft. lbs.	54–98 Nm
Knuckle arm-to-spindle	53–72 ft. lbs.	72–97 Nm
Caliper-to-knuckle spindle	53–72 ft. lbs.	72–97 Nm
Upper ball joint-to-upper link	12–15 ft. lbs.	16–21 Nm
Lower ball joint-to-knuckle spindle (2WD)	87–141 ft. lbs.	118–191 Nm
Lower ball joint-to-lower link (4WD)	35–45 ft. lbs.	47–61 Nm
Front shock absorber upper end-to-frame	12–16 ft. lbs.	16–22 Nm
Front shock absorber lower end-to-lower link	43–58 ft. lbs.	59–78 Nm
Free running hub-to-wheel hub	18–25 ft. lbs.	25–34 Nm
Rear shock absorber upper end nut	22–30 ft. lbs.	30–40 Nm
Rear shock absorber lower end nut	22–30 ft. lbs.	30–40 Nm
Leaf spring U-bolt	65–72 ft. lbs.	88–98 Nm

WHEEL ALIGNMENT

Year	Model	Caster (deg.) Range	Caster (deg.) Preferred	Camber (deg.) Range	Camber (deg.) Preferred	(in.)	Steering Angle (deg.) Inner	Steering Angle (deg.) Outer
1970	Pick-Up	1¹/₁₆P–2¹/₂P	2P	¼P–2¼P	1¼P	0.125	36	31
1971	Pick-Up	1¹/₁₆P–2¹/₂P	2P	¼P–2¼P	1¼P	0.125	36	31
1972	Pick-Up	1¹/₁₆P–2¹/₂P	2P	¼P–2¼P	1¼P	0.125	36	31
1973	Pick-Up	1¹/₁₆P–2¹/₂P	2P	¼P–2¼P	1¼P	0.125	36	31
1974	Pick-Up	1¹/₁₆P–2¹/₂P	2P	¼P–2¼P	1¼P	0.125	36	31
1975	Pick-Up	1¹/₁₆P–2¹/₂P	2P	¼P–2¼P	1¼P	0.125	36	31
1976	Pick-Up	1¹/₁₆P–2¹/₂P	2P	¼P–2¼P	1¼P	0.125	36	31
1977	Pick-Up	1¹/₁₆P–2¹/₂P	2P	¼P–2¼P	1¼P	0.125	36	31
1978	Pick-Up	½P–2½P	1½P	¼P–1¼P	¾P	0.125	35	30.5
1979	Pick-Up	½P–2½P	1½P	¼P–1¼P	¾P	0.250	35	30.5
1980	Pick-Up	¹³/₁₆P–1¹³/₁₆P	1⁵/₁₆P	0–1P	½P	0.250	35	31
1981	Pick-Up (2wd)	¹³/₁₆P–1¹³/₁₆P	1⁵/₁₆P	0–1P	½P	0.250	35	31
1981	Pick-Up (4wd)	¹³/₁₆P–2¹³/₁₆P	1¹¹/₁₆P	0–1P	½P	0.250	31	28
1982	Pick-Up (2wd)	¹³/₁₆P–1¹³/₁₆P	1⁵/₁₆P	0–1P	½P	0.250	35	31
1982	Pick-Up (4wd)	¹³/₁₆P–2¹³/₁₆P	1¹¹/₁₆P	0–1P	½P	0.250	31	28
1983	Pick-Up (2wd)	¹³/₁₆P–1¹³/₁₆P	1⁵/₁₆P	0–1P	½P	0.250	35	31
1983	Pick-Up (4wd)	¹⁵/₁₆P–2¹³/₁₆P	1¹¹/₁₆P	0–1P	½P	0.250	31	28
1984	Pick-Up (2wd)	¹⁵/₁₆P–1¹³/₁₆P	1⁵/₁₆P	0–1P	½P	⊖	35	31
1984	Pick-Up (4wd)	¹⁵/₁₆P–1¹⁵/₁₆P	1⁷/₁₆P	1P–1³/₁₆P	1/16P	0.125	32	31
1985	Pick-Up (2wd)	¹⁵/₁₆P–1¹³/₁₆P	1⁵/₁₆P	0–1P	½P	⊖	35	31
1985	Pick-Up (4wd)	¹⁵/₁₆P–1¹⁵/₁₆P	1⁷/₁₆P	1P–1³/₁₆P	1/16P	0.125	32	31
1986①	Pick-Up (2wd)	¹⁵/₁₆P–1¹³/₁₆P	1⁵/₁₆P	0–1P	½P	0.125	32	31
1986②	Pick-Up (4wd)	¹/₈P–1⁷/₈P	½P	1P–1³/₁₆P	1/16P	ⓒ	37	34
1987	Pick-Up (2wd)	¹/₈N–⁷/₈P	1⁵/₁₆P	³/₁₆P–1³/₁₆P	11/16P	ⓒ	34④	32
1987	Pick-Up (4wd)	¹/₈N–⁷/₈P	½P	¹/₁₆N–1⁵/₁₆P	5/16P	ⓒ	37	34
1988	Pick-Up (2wd)	¹/₈N–⁷/₈P	1⁵/₁₆P	¹/₁₆N–1⁵/₁₆P	11/16P	ⓒ	34④	32
1988	Pick-Up (4wd)	¹³/₁₆P–1¹³/₁₆P	1⁵/₁₆P	³/₁₆P–1³/₁₆P	11/16P	ⓒ	34④	32

N—Negative
P—Positive
① Radial: 0.125
② Bias: 0.250
③ 720-D series
④ D21-D series
⑤ Radial: 0.08–0.16
⑥ Bias: 0.16–0.24
⑦ Radial: 0.12–0.20
⑧ Bias: 0.16–0.24
⑨ 31X10.5R15 tires: inner—28, outer—26

BRAKE OPERATING SYSTEM 9-2
BASIC OPERATING PRINCIPLES 9-2
    DISC BRAKES 9-2
    DRUM BRAKES 9-2
BRAKE SYSTEM 9-3
ADJUSTMENTS 9-3
    DISC BRAKES 9-3
    DRUM BRAKES 9-3
    BRAKE PEDAL 9-4
BRAKE LIGHT SWITCH 9-5
    REMOVAL & INSTALLATION 9-5
MASTER CYLINDER 9-5
    REMOVAL & INSTALLATION 9-5
    OVERHAUL 9-5
POWER BRAKE BOOSTER 9-8
    REMOVAL & INSTALLATION 9-8
LOAD SENSING PROPORTIONING VALVE 9-8
    REMOVAL & INSTALLATION 9-8
    ADJUSTMENT 9-8
BRAKE HOSES AND LINES 9-9
    HYDRAULIC BRAKE LINE CHECK 9-9
BLEEDING 9-9
FRONT DRUM BRAKES 9-10
BRAKE DRUM 9-10
    REMOVAL & INSTALLATION 9-10
    INSPECTION 9-10
BRAKE SHOES 9-10
    INSPECTION 9-10
    REMOVAL & INSTALLATION 9-10
WHEEL CYLINDERS 9-11
    REMOVAL & INSTALLATION 9-11
    OVERHAUL 9-11
FRONT DISC BRAKES 9-12
BRAKE PADS 9-12
    INSPECTION 9-12
    REMOVAL & INSTALLATION 9-12
CALIPER 9-13
    REMOVAL & INSTALLATION 9-13
    OVERHAUL 9-14
BRAKE DISC 9-15
    REMOVAL & INSTALLATION 9-15
    INSPECTION 9-16
    WHEEL BEARING PRELOAD ADJUSTMENT 9-16
REAR DRUM BRAKES 9-16
BRAKE DRUMS 9-16
    INSPECTION 9-16
    REMOVAL & INSTALLATION 9-16
BRAKE SHOES 9-17
    REMOVAL & INSTALLATION 9-17
WHEEL CYLINDERS 9-19
    REMOVAL & INSTALLATION 9-19
    OVERHAUL 9-20
REAR DISC BRAKES 9-21
BRAKE PADS 9-21
    INSPECTION 9-21
    REMOVAL & INSTALLATION 9-21
CALIPER 9-21
    REMOVAL & INSTALLATION 9-21
    OVERHAUL 9-22
BRAKE DISC 9-22
    REMOVAL & INSTALLATION 9-22
    INSPECTION 9-22
PARKING BRAKE 9-22
CABLES 9-22
    ADJUSTMENT 9-22
    REMOVAL & INSTALLATION 9-23
PARKING BRAKE SHOES 9-23
    ADJUSTMENT 9-23
SPECIFICATIONS CHART
    BRAKE SPECIFICATIONS 9-24

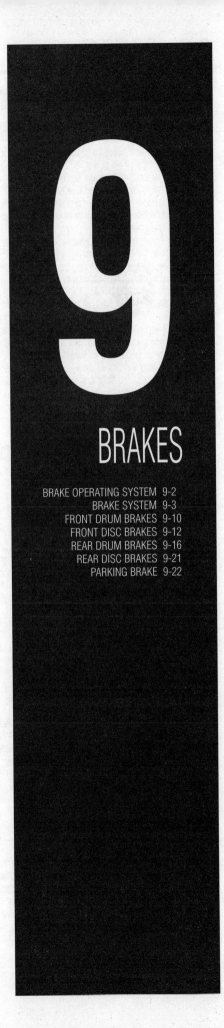

9
BRAKES

BRAKE OPERATING SYSTEM 9-2
BRAKE SYSTEM 9-3
FRONT DRUM BRAKES 9-10
FRONT DISC BRAKES 9-12
REAR DRUM BRAKES 9-16
REAR DISC BRAKES 9-21
PARKING BRAKE 9-22

BRAKE OPERATING SYSTEM

Basic Operating Principles

Hydraulic systems are used to actuate the brakes of all modern automobiles. The system transports the power required to force the frictional surfaces of the braking system together from the pedal to the individual brake units at each wheel. A hydraulic system is used for two reasons.

First, fluid under pressure can be carried to all parts of an automobile by small pipes and flexible hoses without taking up a significant amount of room or posing routing problems.

Second, a great mechanical advantage can be given to the brake pedal end of the system, and the foot pressure required to actuate the brakes can be reduced by making the surface area of the master cylinder pistons smaller than that of any of the pistons in the wheel cylinders or calipers.

The master cylinder consists of a fluid reservoir along with a double cylinder and piston assembly. Double type master cylinders are designed to separate the front and rear braking systems hydraulically in case of a leak. The master cylinder coverts mechanical motion from the pedal into hydraulic pressure within the lines. This pressure is translated back into mechanical motion at the wheels by either the wheel cylinder (drum brakes) or the caliper (disc brakes).

Steel lines carry the brake fluid to a point on the vehicle's frame near each of the vehicle's wheels. The fluid is then carried to the calipers and wheel cylinders by flexible tubes in order to allow for suspension and steering movements.

In drum brake systems, each wheel cylinder contains two pistons, one at either end, which push outward in opposite directions and force the brake shoe into contact with the drum.

In disc brake systems, the cylinders are part of the calipers. At least one cylinder in each caliper is used to force the brake pads against the disc.

All pistons employ some type of seal, usually made of rubber, to minimize fluid leakage. A rubber dust boot seals the outer end of the cylinder against dust and dirt. The boot fits around the outer end of the piston on disc brake calipers, and around the brake actuating rod on wheel cylinders.

The hydraulic system operates as follows: When at rest, the entire system, from the piston(s) in the master cylinder to those in the wheel cylinders or calipers, is full of brake fluid. Upon application of the brake pedal, fluid trapped in front of the master cylinder piston(s) is forced through the lines to the wheel cylinders. Here, it forces the pistons outward, in the case of drum brakes, and inward toward the disc, in the case of disc brakes. The motion of the pistons is opposed by return springs mounted outside the cylinders in drum brakes, and by spring seals, in disc brakes.

Upon release of the brake pedal, a spring located inside the master cylinder immediately returns the master cylinder pistons to the normal position. The pistons contain check valves and the master cylinder has compensating ports drilled in it. These are uncovered as the pistons reach their normal position. The piston check valves allow fluid to flow toward the wheel cylinders or calipers as the pistons withdraw. Then, as the return springs force the brake pads or shoes into the released position, the excess fluid reservoir through the compensating ports. It is during the time the pedal is in the released position that any fluid that has leaked out of the system will be replaced through the compensating ports.

Dual circuit master cylinders employ two pistons, located one behind the other, in the same cylinder. The primary piston is actuated directly by mechanical linkage from the brake pedal through the power booster. The secondary piston is actuated by fluid trapped between the two pistons. If a leak develops in front of the secondary piston, it moves forward until it bottoms against the front of the master cylinder, and the fluid trapped between the pistons will operate the rear brakes. If the rear brakes develop a leak, the primary piston will move forward until direct contact with the secondary piston takes place, and it will force the secondary piston to actuate the front brakes. In either case, the brake pedal moves farther when the brakes are applied, and less braking power is available.

All dual circuit systems use a switch to warn the driver when only half of the brake system is operational. This switch is usually located in a valve body which is mounted on the firewall or the frame below the master cylinder. A hydraulic piston receives pressure from both circuits, each circuit's pressure being applied to one end of the piston. When the pressures are in balance, the piston remains stationary. When one circuit has a leak, however, the greater pressure in that circuit during application of the brakes will push the piston to one side, closing the switch and activating the brake warning light.

In disc brake systems, this valve body also contains a metering valve and, in some cases, a proportioning valve. The metering valve keeps pressure from traveling to the disc brakes on the front wheels until the brake shoes on the rear wheels have contacted the drums, ensuring that the front brakes will never be used alone. The proportioning valve controls the pressure to the rear brakes to lessen the chance of rear wheel lock-up during very hard braking.

Warning lights may be tested by depressing the brake pedal and holding it while opening one of the wheel cylinder bleeder screws. If this does not cause the light to go on, substitute a new lamp, make continuity checks, and, finally, replace the switch as necessary.

The hydraulic system may be checked for leaks by applying pressure to the pedal gradually and steadily. If the pedal sinks very slowly to the floor, the system has a leak. This is not to be confused with a springy or spongy feel due to the compression of air within the lines. If the system leaks, there will be a gradual change in the position of the pedal with a constant pressure. Check for leaks along all lines and at wheel cylinders. If no external leaks are apparent, the problem is inside the master cylinder.

DISC BRAKES

Instead of the traditional expanding brakes that press outward against a circular drum, disc brake systems utilize a disc (rotor) with brake pads positioned on either side of it. An easily-seen analogy is the hand brake arrangement on a bicycle. The pads squeeze onto the rim of the bike wheel, slowing its motion. Automobile disc brakes use the identical principle but apply the braking effort to a separate disc instead of the wheel.

The disc (rotor) is a casting, usually equipped with cooling fins between the two braking surfaces. This enables air to circulate between the braking surfaces making them less sensitive to heat buildup and more resistant to fade. Dirt and water do not drastically affect braking action since contaminants are thrown off by the centrifugal action of the rotor or scraped off the by the pads. Also, the equal clamping action of the two brake pads tends to ensure uniform, straight line stops. Disc brakes are inherently self-adjusting. There are three general types of disc brake:

1. A fixed caliper.
2. A floating caliper.
3. A sliding caliper.

The fixed caliper design uses two pistons mounted on either side of the rotor (in each side of the caliper). The caliper is mounted rigidly and does not move.

The sliding and floating designs are quite similar. In fact, these two types are often lumped together. In both designs, the pad on the inside of the rotor is moved into contact with the rotor by hydraulic force. The caliper, which is not held in a fixed position, moves slightly, bringing the outside pad into contact with the rotor. There are various methods of attaching floating calipers. Some pivot at the bottom or top, and some slide on mounting bolts. In any event, the end result is the same.

DRUM BRAKES

Drum brakes employ two brake shoes mounted on a stationary backing plate. These shoes are positioned inside a circular drum which rotates with the wheel assembly. The shoes are held in place by springs. This allows them to slide toward the drums (when they are applied) while keeping the linings and drums in alignment. The shoes are actuated by a wheel cylinder which is mounted at the top of the backing plate. When the brakes are applied, hydraulic pressure forces the wheel cylinder's actuating links outward. Since these links bear directly against the top of the brake shoes, the tops of the shoes are then forced against the inner side of the drum. This action forces the bottoms of the two shoes to contact the brake drum by rotating the entire assembly slightly (known as servo action). When pressure within the wheel cylinder is relaxed, return springs pull the shoes back away from the drum.

Most modern drum brakes are designed to self-adjust themselves during application when the vehicle is moving in reverse. This motion causes both shoes to rotate very slightly with the drum, rocking an adjusting lever, thereby causing rotation of the adjusting screw. Some drum brake systems are designed to self-adjust during application whenever the brakes are applied. This on-board adjustment system reduces the need for maintenance adjustments and keeps both the brake function and pedal feel satisfactory.

BRAKES

BRAKE SYSTEM

⚠ WARNING

Clean, high quality brake fluid is essential to the safe and proper operation of the brake system. You should always buy the highest quality brake fluid that is available. If the brake fluid becomes contaminated, drain and flush the system, then refill the master cylinder with new fluid. Never reuse any brake fluid. Any brake fluid that is removed from the system should be discarded.

⚠ CAUTION

Brake shoes contain asbestos, which has been determined to be a cancer causing agent. Never clean the brake surfaces with compressed air! Avoid inhaling any dust from any brake surface! When cleaning brake surfaces, use a commercially available brake cleaning fluid.

Adjustments

DISC BRAKES

All disc brakes are inherently self-adjusting. No periodic adjustment is either necessary or possible.

On models with rear disc brakes, the parking brake is actuated by means of conventional drum brake shoes. For adjustment of these shoes, please refer to Parking Brake at the end of this section.

DRUM BRAKES

▶ See Figures 1 and 2

Front

1970–77

1. Jack up the wheel to be adjusted until it completely clears the ground.
2. Make sure that the parking brake is completely released if the rear brakes are being adjusted.
3. Remove the rubber boot from the rear of the brake backing plate.
4. Lightly tap the adjuster housing forward with a hammer and screwdriver.
5. Turn the adjuster wheel downward with a screwdriver to spread the brake shoes. Stop turning the adjuster wheel when the brake drum is locked and the wheel cannot be turned by hand.
6. Turn the adjuster wheel upward, backing off the shoes from the brake drum 12 notches, to obtain the correct clearance between the brake shoes and drum. Turn the wheel to make sure that the brake drum turn without dragging.
7. Install the rubber boot.

Rear

1970–88

▶ See Figures 3, 4 and 5

➡1984–88 Nissan trucks utilize self-adjusting brakes. The following procedure is necessary only after the brake shoes have been changed.

1. Raise and support the rear of the vehicle until the wheel to be adjusted completely clears the ground.
2. Make sure that the parking brake is completely released.
3. Remove the rubber boot from the rear of the brake backing plate.
4. Lightly tap the adjuster housing forward with a hammer and screwdriver.
5. Turn the adjuster wheel downward with a screwdriver to spread the brake shoes. Stop turning the adjuster wheel when the brake drum is locked and the wheel cannot be turned by hand.
6. Turn the adjuster wheel upward, backing off the shoes from the brake drum 12 notches, to obtain the correct clearance between the brake shoes and drum. Turn the wheel to make sure that the brake drum will turn without dragging.
7. Install the rubber boot.
8. Adjust the other wheel in the same manner.
9. Lower the vehicle.

Fig. 1 Adjusting the front drum brake

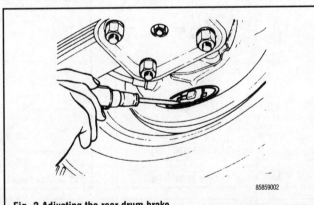

Fig. 2 Adjusting the rear drum brake

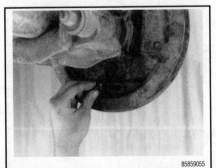

Fig. 3 Removing the rear brake adjuster rubber plug

Fig. 4 View of the brake adjuster rubber plug

Fig. 5 Adjusting the rear brakes, note tool used for this procedure

9-4 BRAKES

BRAKE PEDAL

Pedal Height

♦ See Figures 6, 7 and 8

1970–71

These models have non-adjustable master cylinder pushrods. The freeplay must be adjusted by the use of shims between the master cylinder and the firewall.

1. Loosen the pedal stopper so that it does not contact the pedal arm.
2. With the master cylinder pushrod completely extended, the pedal should be 5.45 in. (139mm) from the tow board (rugs removed). The distance can be adjusted with shims. Use the same thickness of shim for both the upper and lower master cylinder mounting bolts.

1972–88

1. Measure the distance between the center (upper surface) of the pedal pad and the floor pad.
2. If out of specifications, loosen the brake light switch.
3. Turn the pedal pushrod (input rod) until the pedal height is within specifications.
   - 1972–75: 5.5 in. (140mm).
   - 1976–77: 5.8 in. (147mm).
   - 1978–79: 6.06 in. (154mm).
   - 1980–83: 6.7 in. (170mm).
   - 1984–86 (720D series): 7.125 in. (181mm).
   - 1986–88 (D21-D series): AT—8.35–8.74 in. (212–222mm); MT—8.23–8.62 in. (209–219mm).
4. Move the brake light switch until clearance between the plunger and the pedal is:
   - 1972–75: 0.04–0.12 in. (1–3mm).
   - 1976–77: 0.024–0.047 in. (0.6–1.2mm).
   - 1978–83: 0.04–0.20 in. (1–5mm).
   - 1984–88: 0.012–0.039 in. (0.3–1.0mm).Tighten the switch.
5. Check the brake pedal free-play.

Free-Play

♦ See Figure 9

1970–71

Depress the brake pedal until resistance is felt. Adjust the pedal height with the stopper, so that the front of the pedal pad is 5.33 in. (135mm) from the toe board.

1972–88

1. With the engine turned off, depress the brake pedal several times until there is no vacuum left in the brake booster.
2. Push the pedal down until resistance is first felt. Measure this distance; it should be 0.04–0.12 in. (1–3mm).
3. Adjust the free-play by turning the pedal pushrod.
4. Start the engine and recheck the free-play.
5. Recheck the pedal height.

Reserve Distance

♦ See Figure 10

Depress the brake pedal to the bottom of the pedal travel and measure the distance from the center (upper surface) of the pedal pad to the floor mat. If the distance is out of specifications, recheck the other pedal adjustments and the master cylinder. Pedal depressed height should be:
- 1970–77: 1.69–1.93 in. (43–49mm).
- 1978: at least 2.95 in. (75mm).
- 1979: at least 2.56 in. (65mm).
- 1980–83: at least 3.23 in. (82mm).
- 1984–86 (720D series): at least 3.35 in. (85mm).
- 1986–88 (D21-D series): at least 4.72 in. (120mm).

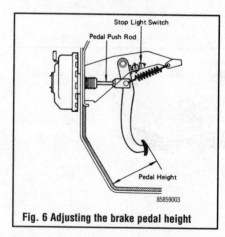

Fig. 6 Adjusting the brake pedal height

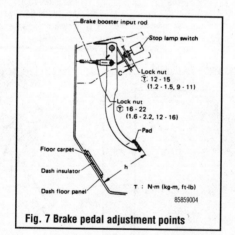

Fig. 7 Brake pedal adjustment points

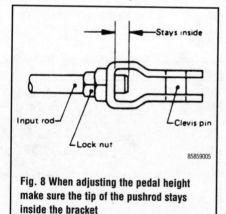

Fig. 8 When adjusting the pedal height make sure the tip of the pushrod stays inside the bracket

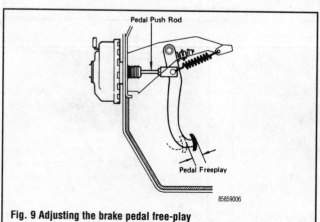

Fig. 9 Adjusting the brake pedal free-play

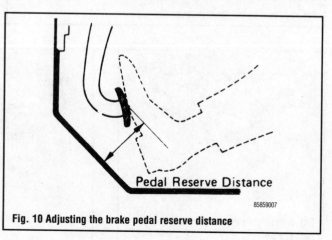

Fig. 10 Adjusting the brake pedal reserve distance

BRAKES 9-5

Brake Light Switch

REMOVAL & INSTALLATION

1. Disconnect the electrical harness at the switch.
2. Remove the mounting bolt and slide the switch up and down. Remove the switch from the brake pedal.
3. Installation is the reverse of the removal procedure.

➡ It is not necessary to remove the pushrod from the stud.

Master Cylinder

REMOVAL & INSTALLATION

♦ See Figures 11, 12, 13 and 14

✽✽✽ CAUTION

Be careful not to spill brake fluid on the painted surfaces of the vehicle; it will damage the paint.

1. Unfasten the hydraulic lines from the master cylinder. On early models, disconnect the lines running to the master cylinder reservoir.
2. Disconnect the hydraulic fluid pressure differential switch wiring connectors. On models with fluid level sensors, disconnect the fluid level sensor wiring connectors, as well.
3. Loosen the master cylinder reservoir mounting bolts.
4. Then do one of the following:
    a. On models with manual brakes, remove the master cylinder securing bolts and the clevis pin from the brake pedal. Remove the master cylinder;
    b. On models with power brakes, unfasten the nuts and remove the master cylinder assembly from the power brake unit.

To install:
5. Install the master cylinder and note the following:
    a. Certain models may have an **UP** mark on the cylinder boot, make sure this is in the correct position.
    b. Before tightening the master cylinder mounting nuts or bolts, screw the hydraulic line into the cylinder body a few turns.

✽✽✽ WARNING

Clean, high quality brake fluid is essential to the safe and proper operation of the brake system. You should always buy the highest quality brake fluid that is available. If the brake fluid becomes contaminated, drain and flush the system, then refill the master cylinder with new fluid. Never reuse any brake fluid. Any brake fluid that is removed from the system should be discarded.

    c. After installation is completed, bleed the master cylinder and the brake system.
    d. Check and adjust the brake pedal.

OVERHAUL

♦ See Figures 15 thru 33

1. Place the cylinder securely in a vise. Remove the reservoir caps and floats. Unscrew the bolts which secure the reservoir(s) to the main body.
2. Remove the pressure differential warning switch assembly. Then, working from the rear of the cylinder, remove the boot, snapring, stop washer, piston No. 1, spacer, cylinder cup, spring retainer, and spring, in that order.
3. Remove the end plug and gasket from the front of the cylinder (if equipped), and then remove the front piston stop bolt from underneath. Pull out the spring, retainer, piston No. 2, spacer, and the cylinder cup.
4. Remove the two outlet fittings, washers, check valves and springs.
5. Remove the piston cups from their seats only if they are to be replaced. After washing all parts in clean brake fluid, dry them with compressed air (if

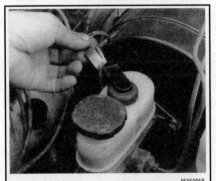
Fig. 11 Removing the electrical connection from the master cylinder

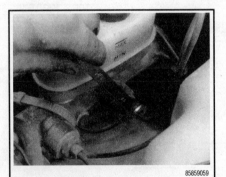
Fig. 12 Removing the brake lines from the master cylinder, note tool used for this procedure

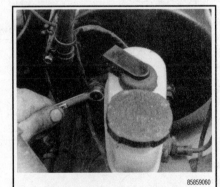
Fig. 13 Removing the master cylinder mounting bolts

available). Drying parts with a shop rag can deposit lint and dirt particles inside the assembled master cylinder. Inspect the cylinder bore for wear, scuff marks, or nicks. Cylinders may be honed slightly, but the limits is 0.15mm. In view of the importance of the master cylinder, it is recommended that it is replaced rather than overhauled if worn or damaged.
6. Absolute cleanliness is essential. Coat all parts with clean brake fluid prior to assembly.

✽✽✽ WARNING

Clean, high quality brake fluid is essential to the safe and proper operation of the brake system. You should always buy the highest quality brake fluid that is available. If the brake fluid becomes contaminated, drain and flush the system, then refill the master cylinder with new fluid. Never reuse any brake fluid. Any brake fluid that is removed from the system should be discarded.

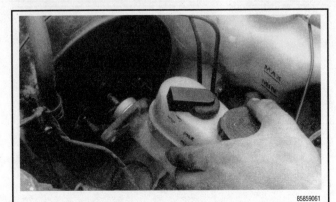
Fig. 14 Removing the master cylinder assembly

9-6 BRAKES

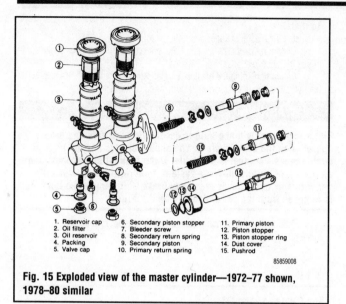

Fig. 15 Exploded view of the master cylinder—1972–77 shown, 1978–80 similar

1. Reservoir cap
2. Oil filter
3. Oil reservoir
4. Packing
5. Valve cap
6. Secondary piston stopper
7. Bleeder screw
8. Secondary return spring
9. Secondary piston
10. Primary return spring
11. Primary piston
12. Piston stopper
13. Piston stopper ring
14. Dust cover
15. Pushrod

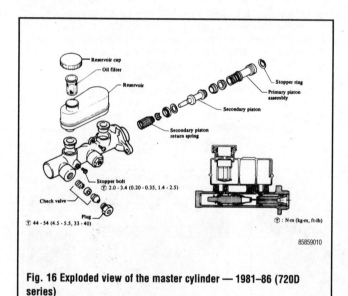

Fig. 16 Exploded view of the master cylinder — 1981–86 (720D series)

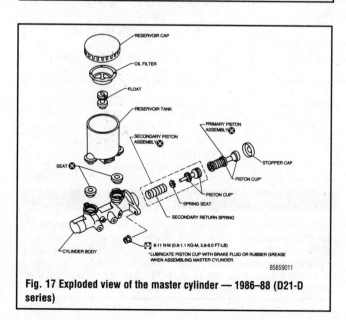

Fig. 17 Exploded view of the master cylinder — 1986–88 (D21-D series)

Fig. 18 Cleaning the master cylinder assembly

Fig. 19 Removing the reservoir hold-down screw

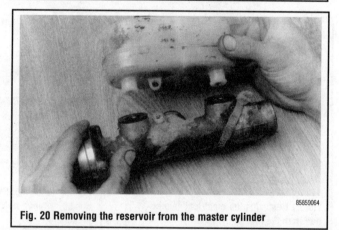

Fig. 20 Removing the reservoir from the master cylinder

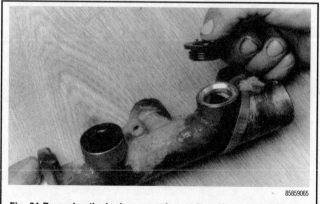

Fig. 21 Removing the brake reservoir seat from the master cylinder

BRAKES 9-7

Fig. 22 Removing the stopper ring from the master cylinder

Fig. 23 Removing the primary piston assembly from the master cylinder

Fig. 24 Removing the stopper bolt

Fig. 25 View of the stopper bolt removed from the master cylinder

Fig. 26 Removing the secondary piston assembly from the master cylinder

Fig. 27 View of the master cylinder disassembled

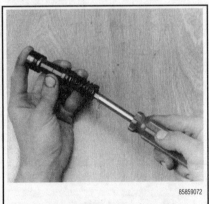
Fig. 28 Removing the piston assembly

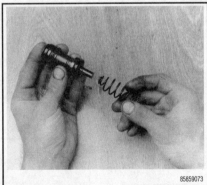
Fig. 29 Removing the return spring seat from the piston

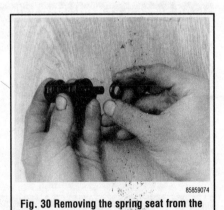
Fig. 30 Removing the spring seat from the piston

Fig. 31 View of the piston assembly

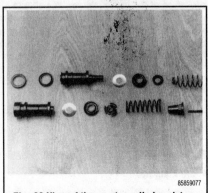
Fig. 33 View of the master cylinder piston assemblies

Fig. 32 Removing the piston cup

9-8 BRAKES

7. Bleed the hydraulic system after the master cylinder is installed.

Power Brake Booster

➡ Vacuum boosters can be found only on models equipped with power brakes.

REMOVAL & INSTALLATION

1. Remove the master cylinder as previously detailed.
2. Locate the clevis rod where it attaches to the brake pedal. Pull out the clip and then remove the clevis pin.
3. Disconnect the vacuum hose from the booster.
4. Loosen the four nuts and then pull out the vacuum booster, the bracket and the gasket.

➡ Some 4wd models may have two extra brackets that must be removed when removing the brake booster.

To install:

5. Install the booster and tighten the mounting bolts to 6–8 ft. lbs. (0.8–1.1 Nm).
6. Connect the clevis rod to the brake pedal.

⚠ WARNING

Clean, high quality brake fluid is essential to the safe and proper operation of the brake system. You should always buy the highest quality brake fluid that is available. If the brake fluid becomes contaminated, drain and flush the system, then refill the master cylinder with new fluid. Never reuse any brake fluid. Any brake fluid that is removed from the system should be discarded.

7. Install the master cylinder. Check the brake pedal adjustment and bleed the brakes.

Load Sensing Proportioning Valve

The purpose of this valve is to control the fluid pressure applied to the brakes to prevent rear wheel lockup during weight transfer at high speed stops.

REMOVAL & INSTALLATION

♦ See Figures 34, 35 and 36

1. Disconnect the brake lines going to the valve.
2. Remove the mounting bolts, if used, and remove the valve.

➡ This valve can not be rebuilt. It must be replaced.

To install:

3. Installation is the reverse of removal.

⚠ WARNING

Clean, high quality brake fluid is essential to the safe and proper operation of the brake system. You should always buy the highest quality brake fluid that is available. If the brake fluid becomes contaminated, drain and flush the system, then refill the master cylinder with new fluid. Never reuse any brake fluid. Any brake fluid that is removed from the system should be discarded.

4. Bleed the brake system.

ADJUSTMENT

1986–88 (D21-D Series)

HEAVY DUTY MODELS WITH VG30I ENGINE

♦ See Figure 37

1. Position approximately 220 lbs. of weight over the rear axle.
2. Install pressure gauges at the front and rear brakes.

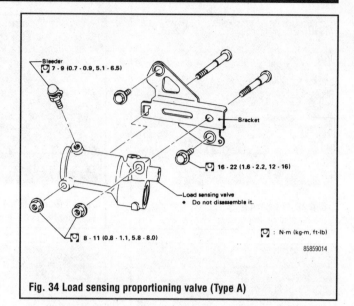

Fig. 34 Load sensing proportioning valve (Type A)

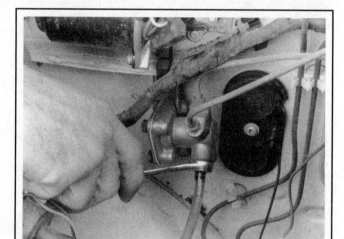

Fig. 35 Removing brake line from load sensing proportioning valve

Fig. 36 Bleeding at proportioning valve

Brakes 9-9

3. Depress the brake pedal until the front brake pressure is approximately 711 lbs. Check that the rear brake pressure is 327–469 lbs.
4. Depress the brake pedal until the front brake pressure is approximately 1422 lbs. Check that the rear brake pressure is 455–654 lbs.
5. If the rear brake pressure is not within specifications, move the spring bracket to the left if the pressure is high or to the right if the pressure is low. Repeat this process until the rear brake pressure is correct.

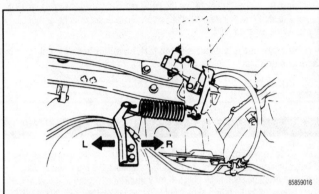

Fig. 37 Adjusting the proportioning valve (Type B) — 1986–88 HD with VG30i engines

Brake Hoses and Lines

HYDRAULIC BRAKE LINE CHECK

The hydraulic brake lines and brake linings are to be inspected at the recommended intervals in the maintenance schedule. Follow the steel tubing from the master cylinder to the flexible hose fitting at each wheel. If a section of the tubing is found to be damaged, replace the entire section with tubing of the same type (steel, not copper), size, shape, and length. When installing a new section of brake tubing, flush clean brake fluid or denatured alcohol through to remove any dirt or foreign material from the line. Be sure to flare both ends to provide sound, leak-proof connections. When bending the tubing to fit the underbody contours, be careful not to kink or crack the line. Torque all hydraulic connections to 10–15 lbs.

Check the flexible brake hoses that connect the steel tubing to each wheel cylinder. Replace the hose if it shows any signs of softening, cracking, or other damage. When installing a new front brake hose, position the hose to avoid contact with other chassis parts. Place a new copper gasket over the hose fitting and thread the hose assembly into the front wheel cylinder. A new rear brake hose must be positioned clear of the exhaust pipe or shock absorber. Thread the hose into the rear brake tube connector. When installing either a new front or rear brake hose, engage the opposite end of the hose to the bracket on the frame. Install the horseshoe type retaining clip and connect the tube to the hose with the tube fitting nut.

※※ WARNING

Clean, high quality brake fluid is essential to the safe and proper operation of the brake system. You should always buy the highest quality brake fluid that is available. If the brake fluid becomes contaminated, drain and flush the system, then refill the master cylinder with new fluid. Never reuse any brake fluid. Any brake fluid that is removed from the system should be discarded.

Always bleed the system after hose or line replacement. Before bleeding, make sure that the master cylinder is topped up with high temperature, extra heavy duty fluid of at least SAE 70R3 quality.

Bleeding

▶ See Figures 38 and 39

The purpose of bleeding the brakes is to expel air trapped in the hydraulic system. The system must be bled whenever the pedal feels spongy, indicating that compressible air has entered the system. It must also be bled whenever the system has been opened or repaired. You will need a helper for this job.

※※ CAUTION

Never reuse brake fluid which has been bled from the brake system.

※※ WARNING

Clean, high quality brake fluid is essential to the safe and proper operation of the brake system. You should always buy the highest quality brake fluid that is available. If the brake fluid becomes contaminated, drain and flush the system, then refill the master cylinder with new fluid. Never reuse any brake fluid. Any brake fluid that is removed from the system should be discarded.

1. The sequence for bleeding is as follows:
- 1970–71: Right rear, left rear, right front, left front;
- 1972–75: Master cylinder front, master cylinder rear, then the 1970–71 sequence;
- 1976–79: Master cylinder front, master cylinder rear, NLSV front, right front, left front, left rear, right rear, NLSV rear, NLSV center.

Fig. 38 Bleeding the front disc brakes

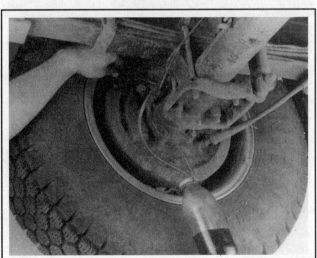

Fig. 39 Bleeding the rear drum brakes

9-10 BRAKES

- 1980–86 (720D series): NLSV, rear wheels, front wheels.
- 1986–88 (D21-D series) equipped with LSV: LSV air bleeder, left rear wheel cylinder, right rear wheel cylinder, left front caliper, right front caliper.
- 1986–88 (D21-D series) not equipped with LSV: left rear wheel cylinder, right rear wheel cylinder, left front caliper, right front caliper.

It is not necessary to run the engine on 1972–79 models with a vacuum booster.

2. Clean all the bleeder screws. You may want to give each one a shot of a penetrating lubricant to loosen it up; seizure is a common problem with bleeder screw, which then break off, sometimes requiring replacement of the part to which they are attached.

3. Fill the master cylinder with DOT 3 brake fluid.

→Brake fluid picks up moisture from the air. Don't leave the master cylinder or the fluid container uncovered any longer than necessary. Be careful! Brake fluid eats paint. Check the level of the fluid often when bleeding, and refill the reservoirs as necessary. Don't let them run dry, or you will have to repeat the process.

4. Attach a length of clear vinyl tubing to the bleeder screw on the wheel cylinder (or master cylinder). Insert the other end of the tube into a clear, clean jar half filled with brake fluid.

5. Have you helper slowly depress the brake pedal. As this is done, open the bleeder screw 1/3–1/2 of a turn, and allow the fluid to run through the tube. Then close the bleeder screw before the pedal reaches the end of its travel. Have you assistant slowly release the pedal. Repeat this process until no air bubbles appear in the expelled fluid.

→If the brake pedal is depressed too fast, small air bubbles will form in the brake fluid.

6. Repeat the procedure on the other three brakes, checking the level of fluid in the cylinder reservoirs often.

FRONT DRUM BRAKES

※※ CAUTION

Brake shoes contain asbestos, which has been determined to be a cancer causing agent. Never clean the brake surfaces with compressed air! Avoid inhaling any dust from any brake surface! When cleaning brake surfaces, use a commercially available brake cleaning fluid.

Brake Drum

REMOVAL & INSTALLATION

1. Remove the hub cap and loosen the lug nuts.
2. Raise the front of the vehicle and support it on jackstands.
3. Remove the lug nuts, tire and wheel.
4. Remove the axle hub grease cap.
5. Remove the cotter pin, and then loosen the hub nut. When the nut is close to the end of the spindle, pull the drum and hub assembly toward you. If it does not slide off the brake shoes, loosen the brake shoe adjuster star wheels. Remove the spindle nut, brake drum and hub, the washer, and the wheel bearings.

→Be careful not to get foreign matter in the wheel bearings. The heavy coating of grease will hold many particles. These will damage the bearings.

6. Inspect the brake drum as outlined below.

※※ CAUTION

Do not depress the brake pedal with the brake drum removed.

7. Installation is the reverse of the removal procedure. Always use a NEW cotter pin upon installation. For instructions on preloading the front wheel bearings, see the appropriate section.

INSPECTION

1. Clean the drum with a rag and a little paint thinner.

※※ CAUTION

Do not blow the brake dust out of the drum with compressed air or lung power. Brake linings contain asbestos, a known cancer causing agent.

2. Inspect the drum for cracks, grooves, scoring and out-of-roundness.
3. Light scoring may be removed with fine emery paper, Heavy scores or grooves will have to be removed by having the drum turned on a lathe. This can be done at many automotive machine shops and some service stations.
4. Before cutting the drum it must be measured to determine whether or not the inside dimension of the drum is within limitations after removing the score marks.

5. Check the drum for concentricity. An inside micrometer is necessary for an exact measurement, so unless this tool is available, the drum should be taken to a machine shop to be checked. Any drum which is out of round will result in an inaccurate brake adjustment and other problems, and must be refinished or replaced.

→Make all measurements at right angles to each other and at the open and closed edges of the drum machined surface.

Brake Shoes

INSPECTION

After removing the brake drum, inspect the brake shoes. If the lining is worn down so that the thickness is less than 0.0394 in. (1mm), the brake shoes must be replaced.

→This figure may disagree with your state inspection laws.

If the brake lining is soaked with brake fluid, it must be replaced. Also the brake drum should be sanded with crocus cloth to remove all traces of brake fluid and the wheel cylinders rebuilt. Clean all grit off the brake drum before installing it.

If the brake lining is chipped, cracked, or otherwise damaged, it must be replace with new lining.

→Always replace the brake linings (shoes) in sets of two on both ends of the axle. Never replace just one shoe or both shoes on just one side.

Check the condition of the shoes, retracting springs and hold-down springs for signs of overheating. If the shoes or springs have a slight blue color, this indicates overheating and replacement of the springs and shoes is recommended. The wheel cylinders should be rebuilt as a precaution against future problems.

REMOVAL & INSTALLATION

♦ See Figures 40 and 41

1. Raise and support the vehicle until the wheel which is to be serviced is off the ground. Remove the wheel and brake drum.
2. Remove the hub dust cap.
3. Straighten the cotter pin and remove it from the spindle.
4. Unscrew the spindle nut and remove the adjusting cap, spindle nut, and spindle washer.
5. Wiggle the hub assembly until the outer bearing comes unseated and can be removed from the hub. Remove the outer bearing.
6. Pull the hub assembly off the spindle.
7. Unhook the upper, lower, and after shoe return springs, and remove them from the brake assembly.
8. Remove the brake shoes from the wheel cylinder at the top and the adjuster assembly at the bottom.

To install:

9. Clean the brake backing plate and adjuster assembly so they are free of

Brakes 9-11

all dust and dirt. To remove the adjuster assembly for cleaning, remove the rubber boot at the back of the adjuster assembly and slide the adjuster shim, lockplate and retaining spring off the rear of the adjuster assembly.

10. Check the wheel cylinders by carefully pulling the lower edges of the wheel cylinder boots away from the cylinders. If there is leakage, the inside of the cylinder will be wet with fluid. If leakage exists, a wheel cylinder overhaul is in order. Do not delay, because brake failure could result.

➡ **A trace of fluid will be present, which acts as a lubricant for the wheel cylinder pistons.**

11. Apply brake grease to the adjuster assembly housing bore, adjuster wheel, and adjuster screw. Assemble the adjuster assembly with the adjuster screw turned all the way in. Apply brake grease to the sliding surfaces of the adjuster assembly, brake backing plate, and the retaining spring. Install the adjuster assembly to the backing plate in the reverse order of removal.

12. Before installing the brake shoes, apply brake grease to the notches into which the brake shoes fit on the wheel cylinder and adjuster mechanism, and brake shoe-to-backing plate contact surfaces.

13. Install the brake shoes.

14. Install the hub, brake drum, and wheel in the reverse order of removal and adjust the wheel bearings and the brake shoes. Bleed the brakes. Lower the vehicle and road test it.

Wheel Cylinders

REMOVAL & INSTALLATION

1. Raise the front of the truck and support it with safety stands.
2. Remove the wheel, brake drum, hub assembly, and brake shoes.
3. Disconnect the brake hose from the wheel cylinder.
4. Unscrew the wheel cylinder securing nut and remove the wheel cylinder from the brake backing plate.

※※ WARNING

Clean, high quality brake fluid is essential to the safe and proper operation of the brake system. You should always buy the highest quality brake fluid that is available. If the brake fluid becomes contaminated, drain and flush the system, then refill the master cylinder with new fluid. Never reuse any brake fluid. Any brake fluid that is removed from the system should be discarded.

5. Install the wheel cylinder, assemble the remaining components, and bleed the brake hydraulic system.

OVERHAUL

▸ See Figure 42

Refer to the Rear Drum Brakes section for overhaul procedures.

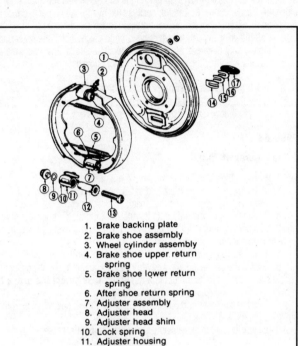

1. Brake backing plate
2. Brake shoe assembly
3. Wheel cylinder assembly
4. Brake shoe upper return spring
5. Brake shoe lower return spring
6. After shoe return spring
7. Adjuster assembly
8. Adjuster head
9. Adjuster head shim
10. Lock spring
11. Adjuster housing
12. Adjuster wheel
13. Adjuster screw
14. Retaining spring
15. Lockplate
16. Adjuster shim
17. Rubber boot

Fig. 40 Exploded view of the front drum brake assembly — 1970–77

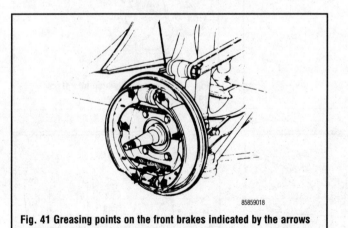

Fig. 41 Greasing points on the front brakes indicated by the arrows

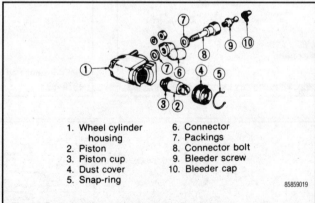

1. Wheel cylinder housing
2. Piston
3. Piston cup
4. Dust cover
5. Snap-ring
6. Connector
7. Packings
8. Connector bolt
9. Bleeder screw
10. Bleeder cap

Fig. 42 Exploded view of the front wheel cylinder

9-12 BRAKES

FRONT DISC BRAKES

> ✱✱ **CAUTION**
>
> Brake shoes contain asbestos, which has been determined to be a cancer causing agent. Never clean the brake surfaces with compressed air! Avoid inhaling any dust from any brake surface! When cleaning brake surfaces, use a commercially available brake cleaning fluid.

Brake Pads

INSPECTION

The pads should be removed so that the thickness of the remaining friction material can be measured. If the pads are less than 2mm (0.08 in.) thick, they must be replaced. This measurement may disagree with your state inspection laws.

➡ Always replace all pads on both wheels at the same time. The factory kit includes four pads, slips, pins, and springs; all parts should be used.

REMOVAL & INSTALLATION

1978–83

▶ See Figures 43, 44 and 45

1. Raise and support the front of the truck. Remove the wheels.
2. Remove the retaining clip from the outboard pad.
3. Remove the pad pins retaining the anti-squeal springs.
4. Remove the pads.

➡ When replacing the pads, always check the surface of the rotors for scoring or wear. The rotors should be removed for resurfacing if badly worn.

To install:

5. Open the bleeder screw slightly and push the outer piston into the cylinder until the dust seal groove aligns with the end of the seal retaining ring, then close the bleeder screw. Be careful, because the piston can be pushed too far, requiring disassembly of the caliper to repair. Install the inner pad.
6. Pull the yoke to push the inner piston into place. Install the outer pad.
7. Lightly coat the areas where the pins touch the pads, and where the pads touch the caliper (at the top) with grease. Do not allow the grease to get on the pad friction surfaces.
8. Install the anti-squeal springs and pad pins. Install the clip.
9. Apply the brakes a few times to seat the pads. Check the master cylinder level; add fluid if necessary. Bleed the brakes if necessary.

1984–88

▶ See Figures 46 thru 51

1. Remove the hub cap and loosen the lug nuts.
2. Raise the front of the truck and safely support it with jackstands.
3. Remove the lug nuts and the wheel.
4. Attach a clear vinyl tube onto the bleeder plug on the brake cylinder, and insert the other end into a jar half filled with brake fluid. Bleed off a small amount of brake fluid.
5. Remove the caliper slide pin bolt on the sub-pin (lower) side.
6. Swivel the caliper up and away from the torque plate. Tie the caliper to a suspension member so its out of the way. **Do not disconnect the brake line.**
7. Lift the 2 brake pads out of the torque plate.
8. Remove the inner and outer shims. Remove the 2 pad retainers if they are not still attached to the pads.
9. Check the pad thickness and replace the pads, if necessary.

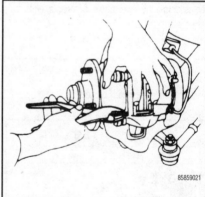

Fig. 43 Removing the pad pins — 1978–83

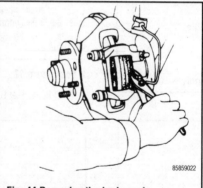

Fig. 44 Removing the brake pads — 1978–83

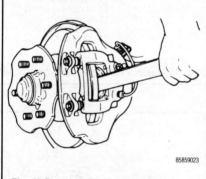

Fig. 45 Pressing the piston into place — 1978–83

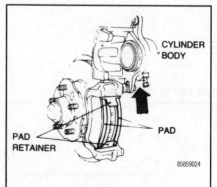

Fig. 46 To remove the pads, swivel the caliper upward — single piston caliper

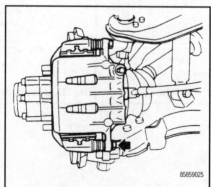

Fig. 47 Remove the guide pin bolt — twin piston calipers

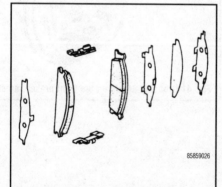

Fig. 48 Swivel the caliper upward to remove the pads — twin piston calipers

BRAKES 9-13

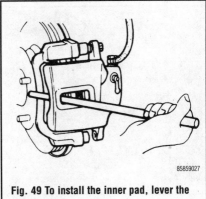
Fig. 49 To install the inner pad, lever the cylinder body outward

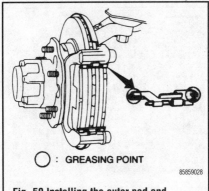
Fig. 50 Installing the outer pad and retainer

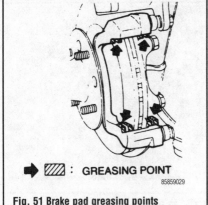
Fig. 51 Brake pad greasing points

➥This minimum thickness measurement may disagree with your state inspection laws.

To install:
10. Install the inner and outer shims into the torque plate.
11. Install a pad retainer to the bottom of each pad.
12. Install the pads into the torque plate.

✴✴ CAUTION

When installing new brake pads, make sure your hands are clean. Do not allow any grease or oil to touch the contact face of the pads.

13. Use a C-clamp or hammer handle and press the caliper piston back into the housing.

➥**Never press the piston into the caliper when the pads are out on both sides of the truck.**

14. Untie the caliper and swivel it back into position over the torque plate so that the dust boot is not pinched. Install the slide pin and tighten it to 16–23 ft. lbs. (22–31 Nm) on 1984–86 models (720D series); or 53–72 ft. lbs. (72–97 Nm) on 1986–88 models (D21-D series).
15. Check the condition of the cylinder side bushing boot. Pull on it to relieve any air from the cylinder side pin mounting area. Check that the hole plug on the main pin side is there. Push on the center of the plug to relieve any air from the inner portion of the main pin.
16. Install the wheel and lower the truck. Bleed the brakes and road test the vehicle.

Caliper

REMOVAL & INSTALLATION

♦ **See Figures 52 thru 58**

1. Remove the hub cap and loosen the lug nuts.
2. Raise the front of the truck and safely support it with jackstands.
3. Remove the lug nuts and the wheel.
4. Attach a clear vinyl tube onto the bleeder plug on the brake cylinder, and insert the other end into a jar half filled with brake fluid. Bleed off a small amount of brake fluid.
5. Disconnect and plug the brake line.
6. Remove the caliper slide pin bolts and lift out the caliper.

To install:
7. Press the caliper piston(s) back into the housing until they are flush and then install the caliper. Tighten the mounting bolts to 16–23 ft. lbs. (22–31 Nm) on 1984–86 models (720D series); and 53–72 ft. lbs. (72–97 Nm) on 1978–83 models and all 1986–88 models (D21-D series).

✴✴ WARNING

Clean, high quality brake fluid is essential to the safe and proper operation of the brake system. You should always buy the highest quality brake fluid that is available. If the brake fluid becomes contaminated, drain and flush the system, then refill the master cylinder with new fluid. Never reuse any brake fluid. Any brake fluid that is removed from the system should be discarded.

Fig. 52 Compressing the piston with a C-clamp

Fig. 53 Removing the caliper lower mounting bolt or pin

Fig. 54 Removing the brake pad

9-14 BRAKES

Fig. 55 Removing the retainer

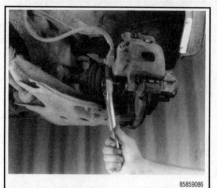
Fig. 56 Using the correct tool to remove the caliper bolts

Fig. 57 Removing the caliper assembly

Fig. 58 Hanging the caliper — never let caliper assembly hang without support

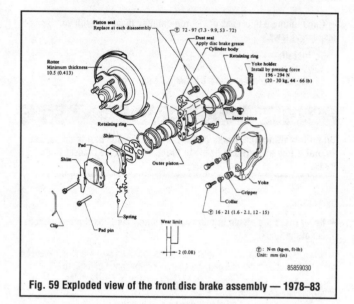
Fig. 59 Exploded view of the front disc brake assembly — 1978–83

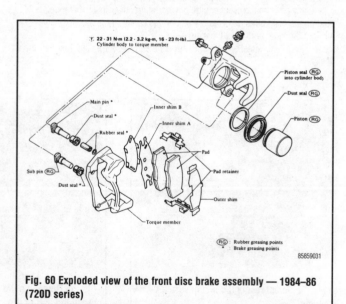
Fig. 60 Exploded view of the front disc brake assembly — 1984–86 (720D series)

OVERHAUL

▶ See Figures 59 thru 70

1. Raise and support the truck on jackstands.
2. Remove the caliper.
3. Remove the pads.
4. Remove the gripper or caliper pin attaching nuts and separate the yoke/torque member from the caliper body.
5. Remove the yoke/torque member holder from the piston and remove the retaining rings and dust seals from the ends of both pistons.
6. Apply air pressure gradually into the fluid chamber of the caliper, to force the piston(s) from the cylinders.
7. Remove the piston seals.
8. Inspect the parts for wear or damage. Check the inside surface of the cylinder for scoring or wear, and replace the caliper as necessary. Minor damage can be cleaned up with crocus cloth, buy deep pitting or scoring warrants replacement of the caliper. The piston should be examined for wear, but do not polish it with crocus cloth; it has a plated surface which will be damaged by sanding. Replace the piston as necessary.
9. To assembly, coat the seals and pistons with clean brake fluid. Install the seals into the cylinder bore.
10. On dual piston calipers, perform the follwoing:
    a. Slide the **A** piston into the cylinder, followed by the **B** piston, so that its yoke groove coincides with the yoke groove of the cylinder.
    b. Install the dust seal and secure tightly with the retaining ring.
    c. Install the yoke holder onto the **A** piston and install the gripper to the yoke. If you lightly coat the gripper pins with soapy water, they will be easier to install.
    d. Support the end of the **B** piston, and press the yoke into the yoke holder. This will require a good deal of force. Be careful to insert the yoke straight into the holder, to avoid cracking the yoke holder.
11. On single piston calipers, replace the piston seal and dust boot. If the support pins are damaged at all, replace them.
12. Assembly is the reverse of disassembly. Coat all metal parts with clean brake fluid prior to assembly.
13. Install the pads, anti-squeal springs, and pad pins and retain with the clip. Apply a thin coating of silicone brake lubricant to the support pins and bushings.
14. Tighten the gripper or caliper pin attaching nuts to 12–15 ft. lbs. (16–21 Nm), and install the caliper on the spindle.

BRAKES 9-15

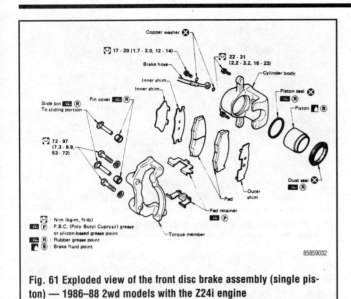

Fig. 61 Exploded view of the front disc brake assembly (single piston) — 1986–88 2wd models with the Z24i engine

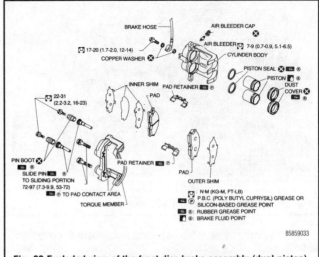

Fig. 62 Exploded view of the front disc brake assembly (dual piston) — 1986–88 2wd models with VG30i engine and all 4wd models

Brake Disc

REMOVAL & INSTALLATION

1. Remove the brake pads and the caliper, as detailed in the appropriate section.
2. Check the disc run-out, as detailed following, at this point. Make a note of the results for use during installation.
3. Remove the grease cap from the hub. Remove the cotter pin and the castellated nut.
4. Remove the wheel hub with the brake disc attached.
5. Perform the disc inspection procedure, as outlined in the following section.

To install:

6. Coat the hub oil seal lip with multipurpose grease and install the disc/hub assembly.
7. Adjust the wheel bearing preload, as detailed following.
8. Measure the disc run-out. Check it against the specifications in the "Brake Specifications" chart and against the figures noted during removal.

➡ If the wheel bearing nut is improperly tightened, disc run-out will be affected.

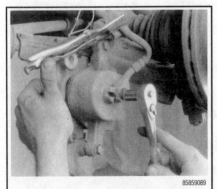

Fig. 63 Removing the brake caliper inlet line with socket and ratchet wrench

Fig. 64 Removing the brake caliper inlet line with box wrench

Fig. 65 View of the brake caliper inlet line — note copper washer

Fig. 66 Removing the brake caliper assembly

Fig. 67 Removing the brake caliper piston

Fig. 68 Removing the brake caliper dust seal

9-16 BRAKES

Fig. 69 Removing the brake caliper O-ring

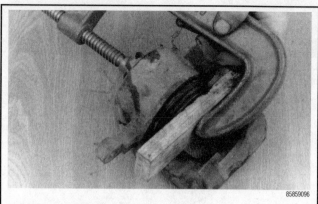

Fig. 70 Installing caliper piston with C-clamp

9. Install the remainder of the components as outlined in the appropriate sections.
10. Bleed the brake system.
11. Road test the truck. Check the wheel bearing preload.

INSPECTION

▶ See Figure 71

Examine the disc. If it is worn, warped or scored, it must be machined or replaced. Check the thickness of the disc against the specifications given in the "Brake Specifications" chart. If it is below specifications, replace it. Use a micrometer to measure the thickness.

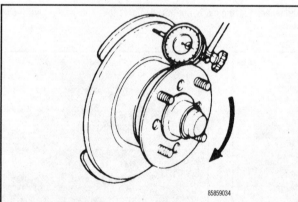

Fig. 71 Measure the disc runout with a dial indicator

The disc run-out should be measured before the disc is removed and again, after the disc is installed. Use a dial indicator mounted on a stand to determine run-out. If run-out exceeds 0.0059 in. (0.15mm) on 1978–83 models or 0.0028 in. (0.07mm) on 1984–88 models, replace the disc.

➡Be sure that the wheel bearing nut is properly tightened. If it is not, an inaccurate run-out reading may be obtained. If different run-out readings are obtained with the same disc, between removal and installation, this is probably the cause.

WHEEL BEARING PRELOAD ADJUSTMENT

➡For wheel bearing removal, installation and adjustment refer to Sections 1 or 7

1. With the front hub/disc assembly installed, tighten the castellated nut to the torque.
2. Rotate the disc back and forth, two or three times, to allow the bearing to seat properly.
3. Loosen the castellated nut until it is only finger tight.
4. Tighten the nut firmly, using a box wrench. Make sure the disc rotates smoothly.
5. Measure the bearing preload with a spring scale attached to a wheel mounting stud.
6. Install the NEW cotter pin.

➡If the hole does not align with the nut (or cap) holes, tighten the nut slightly until it does.

7. Finish installing the dust cap, brake components and wheel.

REAR DRUM BRAKES

Brake Drums

✻✻ CAUTION

Brake shoes contain asbestos, which has been determined to be a cancer causing agent. Never clean the brake surfaces with compressed air! Avoid inhaling any dust from any brake surface! When cleaning brake surfaces, use a commercially available brake cleaning fluid.

INSPECTION

1. Clean the drum with a rag and a little paint thinner.

✻✻ CAUTION

Do not blow the brake dust out of the drum with compressed air or lung power. Brake linings contain asbestos, a known cancer causing agent.

2. Inspect the drum for cracks, grooves, scoring and out-of-roundness.
3. Light scoring may be removed with fine emery paper. Heavy scores or grooves will have to be removed by having the drum turned on a lathe. This can be done at many automotive machine shops and some service stations.
4. Before cutting the drum it must be measured to determine whether or not the inside dimension of the drum is within limitations after removing the score marks.
5. Check the drum for concentricity. An inside micrometer is necessary for an exact measurement, so unless this tool is available, the drum should be taken to a machine shop to be checked.

➡Make all measurements at right angles to each other and at the open and closed edges of the drum machined surface.

REMOVAL & INSTALLATION

1. Remove the hub cap and loosen the lug nuts.
2. Raise the rear of the vehicle and support it on jackstands.
3. Remove the lug nuts, tire and wheel.

Brakes 9-17

4. Loosen the brake adjustment, if necessary. Remove the brake drum. Inspect the brake drum.

> **CAUTION**
> Do not depress the brake pedal with the brake drum removed.

5. Installation is the reverse of the removal procedure. Adjust the brakes, if necessary.

Brake Shoes

REMOVAL & INSTALLATION

◆ See Figures 72 thru 92

1. Raise and support the vehicle until the wheel to be serviced is off the ground and remove the wheel and brake drum.
2. With a pair of pliers, remove the brake shoe hold-down anti-rattle spring retainers. Depress the retainer while rotating it 90 degrees to align the slot in the retainer with the flanged end of the pin. Remove the retainers, springs, spring seats, and pins.
3. Open the brake shoes outward against the return springs and remove the parking brake extension link.
4. Disconnect the brake shoe return springs.
5. Remove the brake shoes from the backing plate. The secondary (after) brake shoe must be disconnected from the parking brake toggle lever after withdrawing the toggle lever clevis pin.
6. Remove the rubber boot from behind the brake backing plate and slide the adjuster shim, lockplate, and adjuster springs off the back of the adjuster assembly. Remove the adjuster assembly from the backing plate.

To install:

7. Clean the backing plate and adjuster assembly so they are free of all dust and dirt.
8. Check the wheel cylinders.
9. Apply brake grease to the adjuster assembly housing bore, adjuster wheel, and adjuster screw. Assemble the adjuster assemble with the adjuster screw turned all the way in. Apply brake grease to the sliding surfaces of the adjuster assembly, brake backing plate, and the retaining spring. Install the adjuster assembly to the backing plate.

➡ On 1986–88 models (D21-D series) with 4wd, after installing the crank lever on the back plate, make sure there is no play between the crank lever and the back plate when pulling the crank lever. If play exists, adjust bolt "A" and locknut "A".

10. Assemble the secondary (after) brake shoe to the parking brake toggle lever and adjust the clearance between the toggle lever and the brake shoe. On

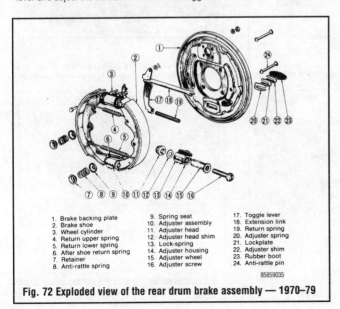

Fig. 72 Exploded view of the rear drum brake assembly — 1970–79

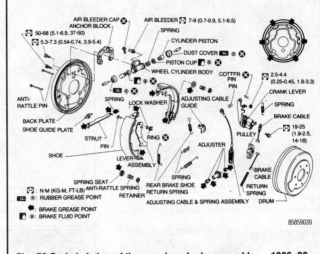

Fig. 73 Exploded view of the rear drum brake assembly — 1986–88 4wd models (D21-D series)

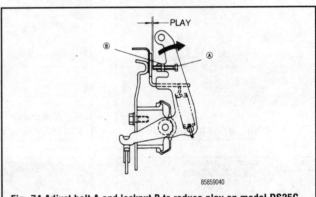

Fig. 74 Adjust bolt A and locknut B to reduce play on model DS25C brake system

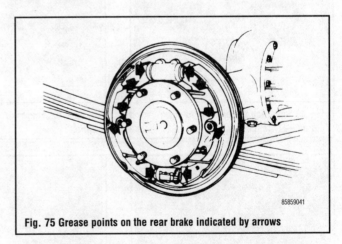

Fig. 75 Grease points on the rear brake indicated by arrows

1970–79 models, use the proper thickness toggle pin washer to adjust the clearance which should be 0.012 in. (0.3mm). Toggle pin washers are available in the following thicknesses: 0.079 in. (2mm), 0.091 in. (2.3mm), 0.102 in. (2.6mm), 0.114 in. (2.9mm) and 0.126 in. (3.2mm).

11. Before assembling the brake shoes to the backing plate apply brake grease to the following areas: the brake shoe grooves in the parking brake extension link, the inside surfaces of the anti-rattle (retaining) spring seats, and the contact surfaces between the brake backing plate and the brake shoes.
12. Assemble the brake shoes to the backing plate. Measure the inner diam-

9-18 BRAKES

Fig. 76 Removing the rear drum

Fig. 77 View of the rear drum brakes

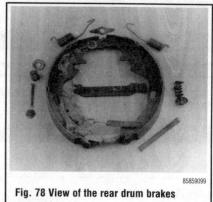
Fig. 78 View of the rear drum brakes removed

Fig. 79 Applying grease to backing plate

Fig. 80 Removing the rear brake shoes from the parking brake

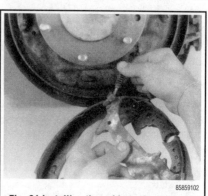
Fig. 81 Installing the cable to the brake shoe

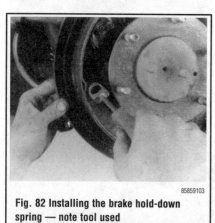
Fig. 82 Installing the brake hold-down spring — note tool used

Fig. 83 Installing the hold-down pin through backing plate for hold-down spring

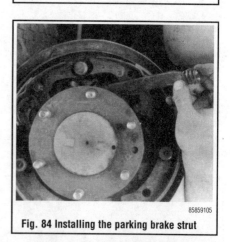
Fig. 84 Installing the parking brake strut

Fig. 85 Installing the brake self-adjuster lever

Fig. 86 Installing the return spring

Fig. 87 Installing the self-adjuster cable to lever

BRAKES 9-19

Fig. 88 Installing the self-adjuster cable to guide

Fig. 89 Installing the self-adjuster cable to backing plate

Fig. 90 Installing the shoe guide plate

Fig. 91 Installing the brake return spring — note position of tool

Fig. 92 Removing the brake return spring — note position of tool

eter of the brake drum and then measure the outer diameter of the shoes (at the center). The shoe outer diameter should be 0.0098–0.0157 in. (0.25–0.40mm) less than the drum inner diameter; if not, adjust it by rotating the star wheel adjuster.

13. Install the brake drum and the wheel.
14. Adjust the brakes. Bleed the brakes.

➡ On 1980–88 models, adjust the shoe-to-drum clearance by operating the parking brake lever several times. On earlier models refer to the adjustment procedure for drum brakes outlined earlier.

Wheel Cylinders

REMOVAL & INSTALLATION

▸ See Figures 93 thru 98

1. Raise the rear of the truck and support it with safety stands.
2. Remove the wheel, brake drum, hub assembly, and brake shoes.
3. Disconnect the brake hose from the wheel cylinder.
4. Unscrew the wheel cylinder securing nut and remove the wheel cylinder from the brake backing plate.

Fig. 93 Removing the brake line from the wheel cylinder

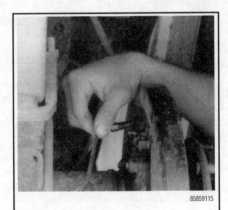

Fig. 94 View of the brake line

Fig. 95 Removing the wheel cylinder retaining bolts

9-20 BRAKES

Fig. 96 Removing the wheel cylinder air bleeder valve

Fig. 97 Removing the wheel cylinder from the backing plate

Fig. 98 Removing the wheel cylinder to brake shoe links

※※ WARNING

Clean, high quality brake fluid is essential to the safe and proper operation of the brake system. You should always buy the highest quality brake fluid that is available. If the brake fluid becomes contaminated, drain and flush the system, then refill the master cylinder with new fluid. Never reuse any brake fluid. Any brake fluid that is removed from the system should be discarded.

5. Install the wheel cylinder, assemble the remaining components, and bleed the brake hydraulic system.

OVERHAUL

♦ See Figures 99, 100, 101 and 102

➡ This is one of those jobs where it is usually easier just to replace the part rather than rebuild it. If you decide to rebuild the wheel cylinders, be sure you get the correct parts for your truck. Datsun obtains parts from two manufacturers: Nabco and Tokiko. Parts are not interchangeable. The name of the manufacturer is on the part.

1. Remove the wheel cylinder from the backing plate.
2. Remove the snapring from the piston bore.

Fig. 99 Removing the wheel cylinder dust cover

Fig. 100 Removing the wheel cylinder piston

Fig. 101 Installing the seal on wheel cylinder piston

Fig. 102 Exploded view of the wheel cylinder assembly

3. Remove the dust boot and take out the piston. Discard the piston cup. The dust boot can be reused, if necessary, but it is better to replace it.
4. Wash all of the components in clean brake fluid.
5. Inspect the piston and piston bore. Replace any components which are severely corroded, scored, or worn. The piston and piston bore can be polished lightly with crocus cloth. Move the crocus cloth around the piston bore; not in and out of the piston bore.
6. Wash the wheel cylinder and piston thoroughly in clean brake fluid, allowing them to remain lubricated for assembly.
7. Coat all of the new components to be installed in the wheel cylinder with clean brake fluid prior to assembly.
8. Assemble the wheel cylinder and install it to the backing plate. Assemble the remaining components and bleed the brake hydraulic system.

Brakes 9-21

REAR DISC BRAKES

✳✳ CAUTION

Brake shoes contain asbestos, which has been determined to be a cancer causing agent. Never clean the brake surfaces with compressed air! Avoid inhaling any dust from any brake surface! When cleaning brake surfaces, use a commercially available brake cleaning fluid.

Brake Pads

INSPECTION

The pads should be removed so that the thickness of the remaining friction material can be measured. If the pads are less than 2mm (0.08 in.) thick, they must be replaced. This measurement may disagree with your state inspection laws.

➙ Always replace all pads on both wheels at the same time. The factory kit includes four pads, slips, pins, and springs; all parts should be used.

REMOVAL & INSTALLATION

♦ See Figures 103, 104 and 105

1988

1. Remove the hub cap and loosen the lug nuts.
2. Raise the rear of the truck and safely support it with jackstands.
3. Remove the lug nuts and the wheel.
4. Attach a clear vinyl tube onto the bleeder plug on the brake cylinder, and insert the other end into a jar half filled with brake fluid. Bleed off a small amount of brake fluid.
5. Remove the caliper guide pin on the lower side.
6. Swivel the caliper up and away from the torque plate. Tie the caliper to a suspension member so its out of the way. **Do not disconnect the brake line.**
7. Lift the 2 brake pads out of the torque plate.
8. Remove the inner and outer shims and cover. Remove the pad retainer if it is not still attached to the pad.
9. Check the pad thickness and replace the pads, if necessary.

➙ This minimum thickness measurement may disagree with your state inspection laws.

To install:

10. Install the inner and outer shims into the torque plate.
11. Install the pad retainer.
12. Install the pads into the torque plate.

✳✳ CAUTION

When installing new brake pads, make sure your hands are clean. Do not allow any grease or oil to touch the contact face of the pads or the brakes will not stop the truck properly.

13. Use a C-clamp or hammer handle and press the caliper piston back into the housing.

➙ Never press the piston into the caliper when the pads are out on both sides of the truck.

14. Untie the caliper and swivel it back into position over the torque plate so that the dust boot is not pinched. Install the guide pin and tighten it to 23–30 ft. lbs. (31–41 Nm).
15. Check the condition of the cylinder side bushing boot. Pull on it to relieve any air from the cylinder side pin mounting area. Check that the hole plug on the main pin side is there. Push on the center of the plug to relieve any air from the inner portion of the main pin.
16. Install the wheel and lower the truck. Bleed the brakes and road test the vehicle.

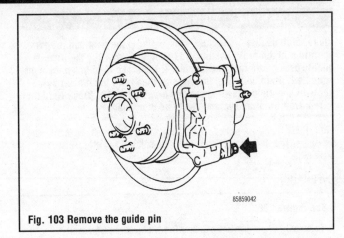

Fig. 103 Remove the guide pin

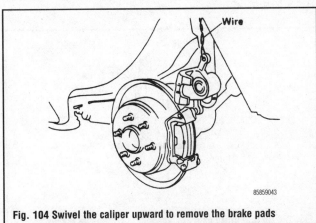

Fig. 104 Swivel the caliper upward to remove the brake pads

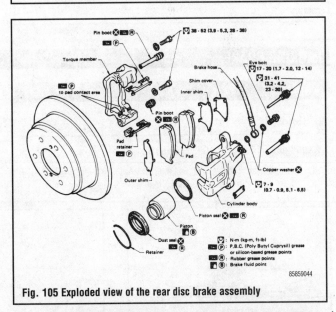

Fig. 105 Exploded view of the rear disc brake assembly

Caliper

REMOVAL & INSTALLATION

1. Remove the hub cap and loosen the lug nuts.
2. Raise the rear of the truck and safely support it with jackstands.
3. Remove the lug nuts and the wheel.

9-22 BRAKES

4. Disconnect and plug the brake line.
5. Remove the caliper slide pin bolts and lift out the caliper.

※※ WARNING

Clean, high quality brake fluid is essential to the safe and proper operation of the brake system. You should always buy the highest quality brake fluid that is available. If the brake fluid becomes contaminated, drain and flush the system, then refill the master cylinder with new fluid. Never reuse any brake fluid. Any brake fluid that is removed from the system should be discarded.

6. Press the caliper piston into the housing until it is flush and then install the caliper. Tighten the mounting bolts 23–30 ft. lbs. (31–41 Nm). Bleed the brake system.

OVERHAUL

▶ See Figure 106

Refer to the Front Disc Brake Caliper Overhaul procedure for overhauling the rear disc brake caliper.

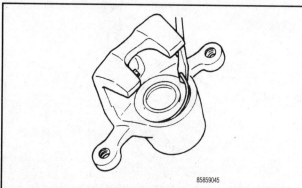

Fig. 106 On rear brake calipers, you must first remove the piston retainer

Brake Disc

REMOVAL & INSTALLATION

1. Remove the brake pads and the caliper, as detailed in the appropriate section.
2. Check the disc run-out, as detailed following, at this point. Make a note of the results for use during installation.
3. Loosen the parking brake shoes by rotating the star wheel upward.
4. Remove the two mounting bolts and then remove the brake disc assembly.
5. Perform the disc inspection procedure, as outlined in the following section.

To install:

6. Install the disc/hub assembly and tighten the mounting bolts.
7. Measure the disc run-out. Check it against the specifications in the "Brake Specifications" chart and against the figures noted during removal.

➡ If the wheel bearing nut is improperly tightened, disc run-out will be affected.

8. Install the remainder of the components as outlined in the appropriate sections.
9. Bleed the brake system.
10. Road test the truck. Check the wheel bearing preload.

INSPECTION

Examine the disc. If it is worn, warped or scored, it must be replaced. Check the thickness of the disc against the specifications given in the "Brake Specifications" chart. If it is below specifications, replace it. Use a micrometer to measure the thickness.

The disc run-out should be measured before the disc is removed and again, after the disc is installed. Use a dial indicator mounted on a stand to determine run-out.

➡ Be sure that the wheel bearing nut is properly tightened. If it is not, an inaccurate run-out reading may be obtained. If different run-out readings are obtained with the same disc, between removal and installation, this is probably the cause.

PARKING BRAKE

Cables

ADJUSTMENT

▶ See Figures 107, 108, 109, 110 and 111

1. Raise the rear of the vehicle until the rear wheels clear the ground.
2. Adjust the rear brakes as outlined under Brake System Adjustment.
3. Loosen the locknut at the parking cable lever assembly mounted on the driveshaft center bearing crossmember.
4. Turn the adjusting nut until the parking brake control lever operating stroke is 6–10 notches on 1970–83 models; 13–16 notches 1984–86 models (720D series); 10–12 notches (center lever and 2wd with stick lever) and 9–11 notches (4wd with stick lever) on 1986–87 models (D21-D series); 1988 models are the same except for Pathfinders with a center lever where is should be 7–9 notches. Notches are measured from the rest position (in or down) to the full-on position (out or up).

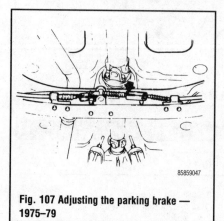

Fig. 107 Adjusting the parking brake — 1975–79

Fig. 108 Adjusting the parking brake — 1980–86 (720D series)

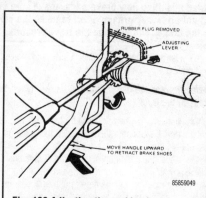

Fig. 109 Adjusting the parking brake — 1986–88 (D21-D series)

BRAKES 9-23

5. Release the parking brake and make sure that the rear wheels turn freely with no drag.
6. On 1986–88 models (D21-D series), the brake warning light should come on after 1 notch (pickups with center lever) or 2 notches (pickups with stick lever and Pathfinders with center lever). If not, adjust the switch.
7. Lower the vehicle.

REMOVAL & INSTALLATION

♦ See Figures 112 and 113

1. Fully release the parking brake control lever.
2. Loosen the adjusting nut at the cable lever mounted to the frame crossmember.
3. Disconnect the cable from the control lever.
4. Remove the rear brake drums, and disconnect the parking brake cables from the parking brake toggle levers of the rear service brake assemblies.
5. Remove the lockplate, spring and clip, and pull the parking brake cable out toward the cable lever.
6. Remove the cotter pin at the cable lever and disconnect the cable.
7. Install the cables in the reverse order of removal. Apply a light coat of grease to the cables to make sure that they slide properly. Adjust the parking brakes.

Parking Brake Shoes

ADJUSTMENT

Rear Disc Brakes Only

♦ See Figures 114 and 115

➡ Refer to the necessary illustration and drum brake service procedures as a guide for removal and installation of parking brake shoes.

1. Raise the rear of the truck and support it with safety stands.
2. Remove the adjuster hole plug at the rear of the brake backing plate.
3. Make sure that the parking brake is fully released and rotate the star wheel adjuster downward with a brake adjusting tool until the shoes are touching the brake drum.
4. Back off the star wheel 7–8 latches.
5. Install the hole plug and rotate the wheel a few times to ensure that the shoes are not dragging on the drums.

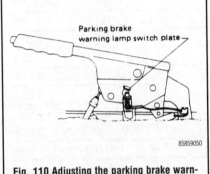

Fig. 110 Adjusting the parking brake warning lamp switch — 1986–88 (D21-D series)

Fig. 111 Adjusting the parking brake — most models similar

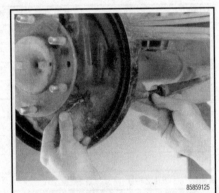

Fig. 112 Installing the parking brake cable into the backing plate

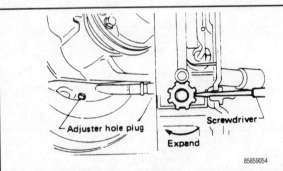

Fig. 113 Adjusting the parking brake shoes — models with rear disc brakes

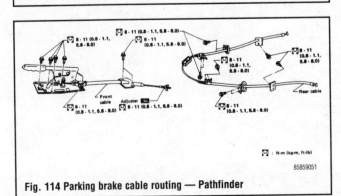

Fig. 114 Parking brake cable routing — Pathfinder

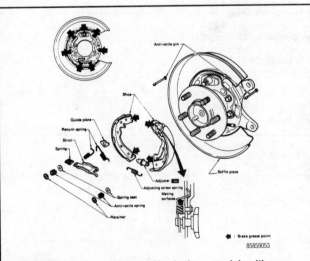

Fig. 115 Exploded view of the parking brake — models with rear disc brakes

BRAKE SPECIFICATIONS
(All measurements given are (in.) unless noted)

Year	Model	Master Cylinder Bore	Brake Disc Minimum Thickness	Brake Disc Maximum Runout	Brake Drum Diameter	Brake Drum Max. Machine O/S	Brake Drum Max. Wear Limit	Minimum Lining Thickness Front	Minimum Lining Thickness Rear
1970	521	0.750	—	—	10.00	10.09	10.06	0.039	0.059
1971	521	0.750	—	—	10.00	10.09	10.06	0.039	0.059
1972	521	0.750	—	—	10.00	10.09	10.06	0.039	0.059
1973	620	0.750	—	—	10.00	10.09	10.06	0.039	0.059
1974	620	0.750	—	—	10.00	10.09	10.06	0.039	0.059
1975	620	0.750	—	—	10.00	10.09	10.06	0.039	0.059
1976	620	0.750	—	—	10.00	10.09	10.06	0.039	0.059
1977	620	0.750	—	—	10.00	10.09	10.06	0.039	0.059
1978	620	0.813	0.413	0.0059	10.00	10.09	10.06	0.079	0.059
1979	720-D	0.813	0.413	0.0059	10.00	10.09	10.06	0.079	0.059
1980	720-D	0.875	0.413	0.0059	10.00	10.09	10.06	0.079	0.059
1981	720-D	0.875	0.413	0.0059	10.00	10.09	10.06	0.079	0.059
1982	720-D	0.875	0.413	0.0059	10.00	10.09	10.06	0.079	0.059
1983	720-D	0.875	0.413	0.0059	10.00	10.09	10.06	0.079	0.059
1984	720-D	0.938	0.787	0.0028	①	②	③	0.079	0.059
1985	720-D	0.938	0.787	0.0028	①	②	③	0.079	0.059
1986	720-D	0.938	0.787	0.0028	①	②	③	0.079	0.059
	D21-D	0.938	④	0.0028	⑤	③	⑥	0.079	0.059
1987	D21-D	0.938	④	0.0028	⑤	③	⑥	0.079	0.059
1988	D21-D	0.938	④	0.0028	⑤	③	⑥	0.079	0.059 ⑦

① Single rear wheels: 10.00
　Dual rear wheels: 8.66
② Single rear wheels: 10.06
　Dual rear wheels: 8.72
③ Single rear wheels: 10.09
　Dual rear wheels: 8.75
④ CL28VA: 0.787
　CL28VD: 0.945
　AD14VB (Rear): 0.630
⑤ 2wd exc. HD & C/C: 10.24
　2wd C/C: 8.66
　2wd HD: 10.00
　4dw: 10.00 or 7.48
⑥ 2wd exc. HD & C/C: 10.30
　2wd C/C: 8.72
　2wd HD: 10.06
　4wd: 10.06 or 7.52
⑦ Rear disc: 0.079

EXTERIOR 10-2
FRONT DOOR 10-2
    ADJUSTMENT 10-2
DOOR LOCKS 10-2
    REMOVAL & INSTALLATION 10-2
HOOD 10-2
    REMOVAL & INSTALLATION 10-2
    ADJUSTMENT 10-3
TAILGATE 10-3
    REMOVAL & INSTALLATION 10-3
    ALIGNMENT 10-3
FRONT OR REAR BUMPER 10-3
    REMOVAL & INSTALLATION 10-3
MIRRORS 10-4
    REMOVAL & INSTALLATION 10-4
ANTENNA 10-4
    REMOVAL & INSTALLATION 10-4
WINDSHIELD AND FIXED GLASS 10-4
    REMOVAL & INSTALLATION 10-4
    WINDSHIELD CHIP REPAIR 10-4
INTERIOR 10-5
DOOR TRIM PANELS 10-5
    REMOVAL & INSTALLATION 10-5
DOOR GLASS AND REGULATOR 10-5
    REMOVAL & INSTALLATION 10-5
    ADJUSTMENT 10-6
HEADLINER 10-6
    REMOVAL & INSTALLATION 10-6
FRONT AND REAR SEAT BELTS 10-6
    REMOVAL & INSTALLATION 10-6
FRONT BENCH AND FRONT
  SPLIT-BENCH SEATS 10-6
    REMOVAL & INSTALLATION 10-6
FRONT BUCKET SEATS 10-6
    REMOVAL & INSTALLATION 10-6
REAR BENCH SEAT 10-6
    REMOVAL & INSTALLATION 10-6

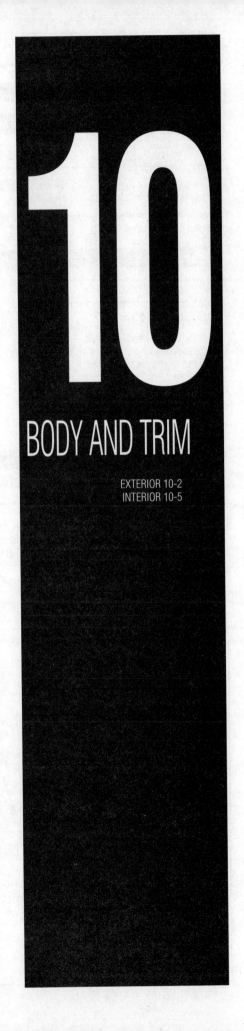

10

BODY AND TRIM

EXTERIOR 10-2
INTERIOR 10-5

10-2 BODY AND TRIM

EXTERIOR

Front Door

ADJUSTMENT

To adjust the door alignment, loosen the door hinge and door lock striker bolts and move the door to the desired position.

➡ Make sure the weather-strip contacts the body opening evenly to prevent the entry of water.

Door Locks

REMOVAL & INSTALLATION

♦ See Figures 1, 2 and 3

1. Remove the door inside trim.
2. Disengage the rod holder from the inside handle unlock rod.
3. Remove the door inside handle.
4. Remove the door lock cylinder.
5. Disengage the rod holder from the door lock rod.
6. Remove the door lock assembly.
7. Remove the front door outside handle.
8. Installation is the reverse of removal.

Hood

REMOVAL & INSTALLATION

♦ See Figures 4, 5, 6 and 7

1. Place protective covers over the front fender and cowl top grille.
2. Open the hood and mark the hinge locations on the hood for reinstalling.
3. Remove the hood hinge to hood retaining bolts and carefully lift the hood from the vehicle.
4. Installation is the reverse of the removal procedure. Adjust the hood for proper alignment.

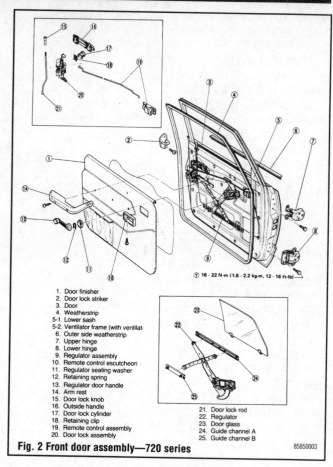

1. Door finisher
2. Door lock striker
3. Door
4. Weatherstrip
5-1. Lower sash
5-2. Ventilator frame (with ventilator)
6. Outer side weatherstrip
7. Upper hinge
8. Lower hinge
9. Regulator assembly
10. Remote control escutcheon
11. Regulator seating washer
12. Retaining spring
13. Regulator door handle
14. Arm rest
15. Door lock knob
16. Outside handle
17. Door lock cylinder
18. Retaining clip
19. Remote control assembly
20. Door lock assembly
21. Door lock rod
22. Regulator
23. Door glass
24. Guide channel A
25. Guide channel B

Fig. 2 Front door assembly—720 series

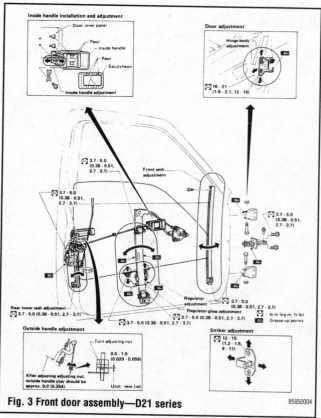

Fig. 3 Front door assembly—D21 series

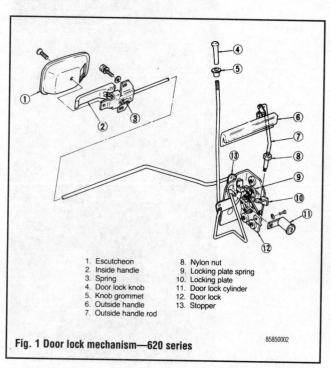

1. Escutcheon
2. Inside handle
3. Spring
4. Door lock knob
5. Knob grommet
6. Outside handle
7. Outside handle rod
8. Nylon nut
9. Locking plate spring
10. Locking plate
11. Door lock cylinder
12. Door lock
13. Stopper

Fig. 1 Door lock mechanism—620 series

BODY AND TRIM 10-3

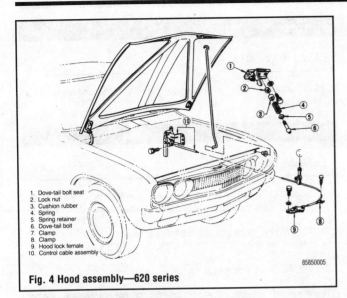

Fig. 4 Hood assembly—620 series

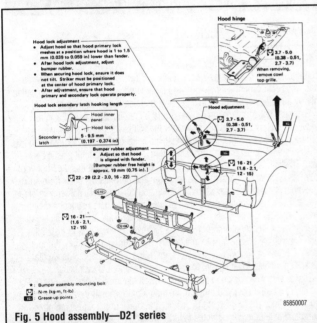

Fig. 5 Hood assembly—D21 series

ADJUSTMENT

1. Loosen the bolts attaching the hood hinge.
2. Adjust the hood back and forth and side to side until it is in the proper position.
3. Loosen the bolts attaching the hood lock and adjust the hood lock back and forth and side to side until it is in the proper position and opens and closes smoothly.
4. Loosen the lock nut on the dovetail bolt and turn the dovetail bolt in or out as necessary to obtain the correct height.
5. Tighten the lock nut firmly while holding the dovetail bolt with a screwdriver to secure the adjustment. Torque the locknut to 14–19 ft. lbs.

➥ Make sure that the safety catch hooks the hood properly when the hood latch has been disengaged.

Tailgate

REMOVAL & INSTALLATION

♦ See Figures 8, 9 and 10

1. Open the rear gate.
2. On earlier models, remove the gate chain.
3. Remove the gate hinge attaching bolts and remove the rear gate.
4. Installation is the reverse of the removal procedure. Adjust the rear gate for proper alignment.

ALIGNMENT

The rear gate may be adjusted by loosening the hinge attaching bolts and moving the gate as required. The height may be adjusted by adding or removing shims at the rear gate hinge.

Front or Rear Bumper

REMOVAL & INSTALLATION

1. Support the bumper.
2. Remove the nuts and bolts attaching the bumper to the frame.
3. Installation is the reverse of removal.

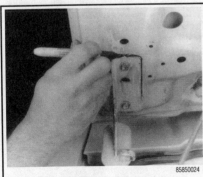

Fig. 6 Marking the hood hinges before removal of the hood

Fig. 7 Removing the hood hinge retaining bolts mark the hood hinge before removal

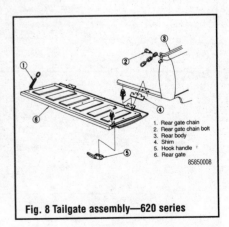

Fig. 8 Tailgate assembly—620 series

10-4 BODY AND TRIM

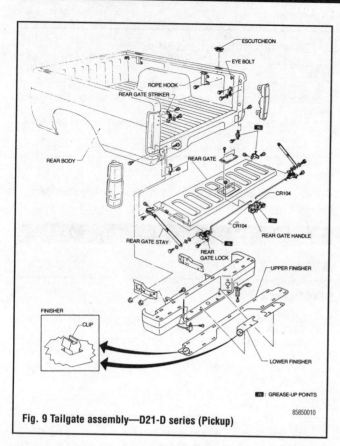

Fig. 9 Tailgate assembly—D21-D series (Pickup)

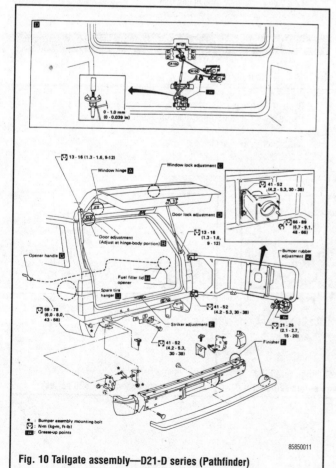

Fig. 10 Tailgate assembly—D21-D series (Pathfinder)

Mirrors

REMOVAL & INSTALLATION

All mirrors are removed by removing the mounting screws and lifting off the mirror and gasket.

Antenna

REMOVAL & INSTALLATION

1. Disconnect the antenna cable at the radio by pulling it straight out of the set.
2. Working under the instrument panel, disengage the cable from its retainers.
3. Outside, unsnap the cap from the antenna base.
4. Remove the screw(s) and lift off the antenna, pulling the cable with it, carefully.
5. Installation is the reverse of removal.

Windshield and Fixed Glass

REMOVAL & INSTALLATION

If your windshield, or other fixed window, is cracked or chipped, you may decide to replace it with a new one yourself. However, there are two main reasons why replacement windshields and other window glass should be installed only by a professional automotive glass technician: safety and cost.

The most important reason a professional should install automotive glass is for safety. The glass in the vehicle, especially the windshield, is designed with safety in mind in case of a collision. The windshield is specially manufactured from two panes of specially-tempered glass with a thin layer of transparent plastic between them. This construction allows the glass to "give" in the event that a part of your body hits the windshield during the collision, and prevents the glass from shattering, which could cause lacerations, blinding and other harm to passengers of the vehicle. The other fixed windows are designed to be tempered so that if they break during a collision, they shatter in such a way that there are no large pointed glass pieces. The professional automotive glass technician knows how to install the glass in a vehicle so that it will function optimally during a collision. Without the proper experience, knowledge and tools, installing a piece of automotive glass yourself could lead to additional harm if an accident should ever occur.

Cost is also a factor when deciding to install automotive glass yourself. Performing this could cost you much more than a professional may charge for the same job. Since the windshield is designed to break under stress, an often life saving characteristic, windshields tend to break VERY easily when an inexperienced person attempts to install one. Do-it-yourselfers buying two, three or even four windshields from a salvage yard because they have broken them during installation are common stories. Also, since the automotive glass is designed to prevent the outside elements from entering your vehicle, improper installation can lead to water and air leaks. Annoying whining noises at highway speeds from air leaks or inside body panel rusting from water leaks can add to your stress level and subtract from your wallet. After buying two or three windshields, installing them and ending up with a leak that produces a noise while driving and water damage during rainstorms, the cost of having a professional do it correctly the first time may be much more alluring. We here at Chilton, therefore, advise that you have a professional automotive glass technician service any broken glass on your vehicle.

WINDSHIELD CHIP REPAIR

▶ See Figures 11 and 12

➡ Check with your state and local authorities on the laws for state safety inspection. Some states or municipalities may not allow chip repair as a viable option for correcting stone damage to your windshield.

Although severely cracked or damaged windshields must be replaced, there is something that you can do to prolong or even prevent the need for replacement of a chipped windshield. There are many companies which offer wind-

BODY AND TRIM 10-5

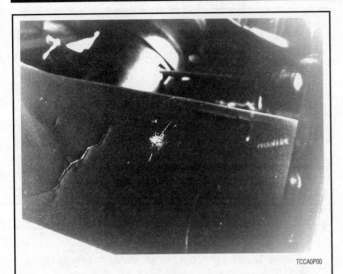

Fig. 11 Small chips on your windshield can be fixed with an aftermarket repair kit, such as the one from Loctite®

shield chip repair products, such as Loctite's® Bullseye™ windshield repair kit. These kits usually consist of a syringe, pedestal and a sealing adhesive. The syringe is mounted on the pedestal and is used to create a vacuum which pulls the plastic layer against the glass. This helps make the chip transparent. The adhesive is then injected which seals the chip and helps to prevent further stress cracks from developing

➡ Always follow the specific manufacturer's instructions.

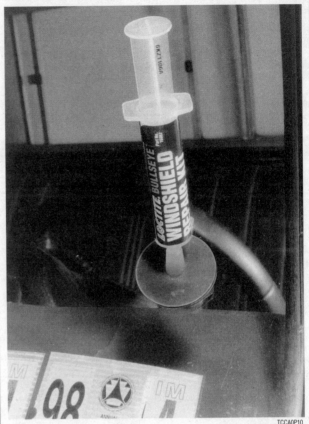

Fig. 12 Most kits use a self-stick applicator and syringe to inject the adhesive into the chip or crack

INTERIOR

Door Trim Panels

REMOVAL & INSTALLATION

1. Fully lower the door glass.
2. Remove the arm rest, door lock knob and inside door handle escutcheon.
3. Remove the regulator handle.
4. Gently pry the door panel away from the door.
5. Installation is the reverse of removal. Install the regulator handle (correct position) with the door glass closed.

Door Glass And Regulator

REMOVAL & INSTALLATION

♦ See Figures 13 and 14

1. Remove the door trim panel.
2. Remove the front door lower sash or the front door ventilator frame, if so equipped.
3. Remove the door glass to regulator attaching bolts and remove the door glass by lifting upwards.
4. Remove the regulator attaching bolts from the bottom of the regulator.
5. Remove the regulator through the large access hole in the door inside panel.
6. Installation is the reverse of removal. Grease the regulator sliding surfaces and adjust the door glass and regulator.

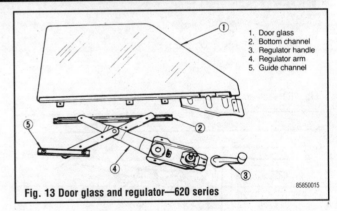

1. Door glass
2. Bottom channel
3. Regulator handle
4. Regulator arm
5. Guide channel

Fig. 13 Door glass and regulator—620 series

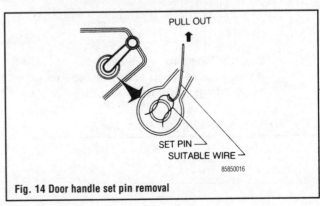

Fig. 14 Door handle set pin removal

10-6 BODY AND TRIM

ADJUSTMENT

1. In-and-out and fore-and-aft adjustments can be made by moving the front or rear sash and guide channel as required.

The ease with which the window assembly raises and lowers depends on the adjustment of the rear lower sash. The rear lower sash should be parallel with the front lower sash.

2. Fore and aft adjustment is determined by position of the guide channel and front lower sash. Moving the front lower sash backward reduces play in the window assembly.

Headliner

REMOVAL & INSTALLATION

♦ See Figures 15, 16, 17 and 18

All Except D21 Series and Pathfinder

➡ The headliner assembly is of the suspension type, which is held in place by listing wires. Use this service procedure as guide for this type of repair.

1. Remove the dome lamp, assist grips inside rear view mirror and sun visors, if so equipped.
2. Remove the rear finisher and rear side finisher.
3. Remove the windshield glass, if necessary weather-strip and windshield pillar cloth.
4. Remove the back window glass and weather-strip, if necessary.
5. Disengage the listing wires from the roof rail and remove the headlining from back to front.
6. Installation is the reverse of removal. Install the headlining from the front to the rear. Be careful not to deform the listing wires.

D21 Series and Pathfinder

For removal and installation of the headliner on these models please refer to the illustration.

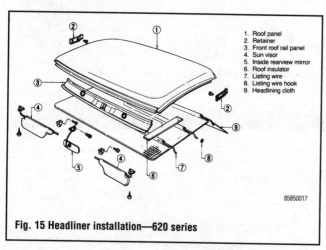

Fig. 15 Headliner installation—620 series

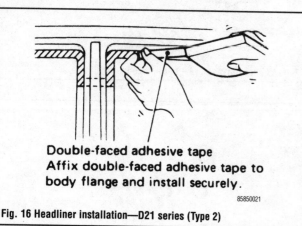

Fig. 16 Headliner installation—D21 series (Type 2)

Fig. 17 Headliner installation—D21 series (Type 2)

Front and Rear Seat Belts

REMOVAL & INSTALLATION

1. Remove the seat assembly or necessary trim panel.
2. Remove the seat belt mounting bolts. Remove the seat belt assembly—do not repair assembly always replace.
3. Installation is the reverse of the removal procedure.

Front Bench And Front Split-Bench Seats

REMOVAL & INSTALLATION

1. Remove the seat track-to-floor pan bolts and lift out the seat.
2. Apply sealer to the hole areas and install the seat. Tighten the bolts.

Front Bucket Seats

REMOVAL & INSTALLATION

1. Remove the seat track-to-floor pan bolts and lift out the seat.
2. Repeat Step 1 for the other seat.
3. Apply sealer to the hole areas and install the seat. Tighten the bolts.

Rear Bench Seat

REMOVAL & INSTALLATION

Pathfinder Only

1. Release the seat back locks on each side of the seat.
2. Remove the seat track-to-floor pan bolts and lift out the seat.
3. Apply sealer to the hole areas and install the seat. Tighten the bolts.

BODY AND TRIM 10-7

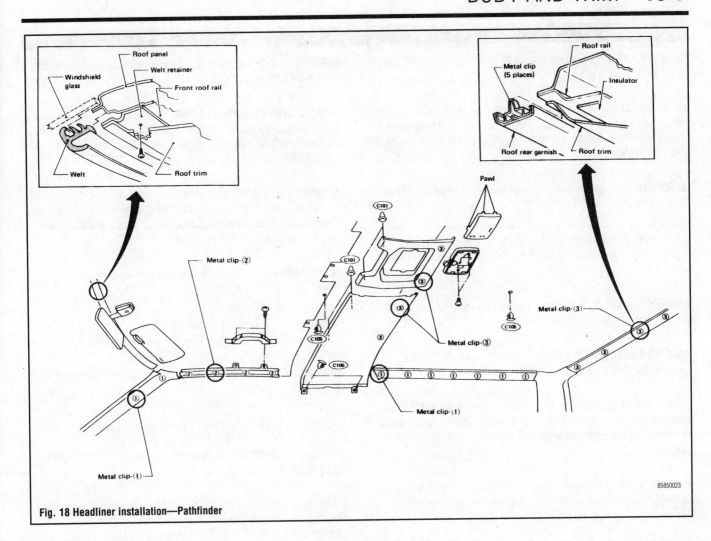

Fig. 18 Headliner installation—Pathfinder

Glossary

AIR/FUEL RATIO: The ratio of air-to-gasoline by weight in the fuel mixture drawn into the engine.

AIR INJECTION: One method of reducing harmful exhaust emissions by injecting air into each of the exhaust ports of an engine. The fresh air entering the hot exhaust manifold causes any remaining fuel to be burned before it can exit the tailpipe.

ALTERNATOR: A device used for converting mechanical energy into electrical energy.

AMMETER: An instrument, calibrated in amperes, used to measure the flow of an electrical current in a circuit. Ammeters are always connected in series with the circuit being tested.

AMPERE: The rate of flow of electrical current present when one volt of electrical pressure is applied against one ohm of electrical resistance.

ANALOG COMPUTER: Any microprocessor that uses similar (analogous) electrical signals to make its calculations.

ARMATURE: A laminated, soft iron core wrapped by a wire that converts electrical energy to mechanical energy as in a motor or relay. When rotated in a magnetic field, it changes mechanical energy into electrical energy as in a generator.

ATMOSPHERIC PRESSURE: The pressure on the Earth's surface caused by the weight of the air in the atmosphere. At sea level, this pressure is 14.7 psi at 32°F (101 kPa at 0°C).

ATOMIZATION: The breaking down of a liquid into a fine mist that can be suspended in air.

AXIAL PLAY: Movement parallel to a shaft or bearing bore.

BACKFIRE: The sudden combustion of gases in the intake or exhaust system that results in a loud explosion.

BACKLASH: The clearance or play between two parts, such as meshed gears.

BACKPRESSURE: Restrictions in the exhaust system that slow the exit of exhaust gases from the combustion chamber.

BAKELITE: A heat resistant, plastic insulator material commonly used in printed circuit boards and transistorized components.

BALL BEARING: A bearing made up of hardened inner and outer races between which hardened steel balls roll.

BALLAST RESISTOR: A resistor in the primary ignition circuit that lowers voltage after the engine is started to reduce wear on ignition components.

BEARING: A friction reducing, supportive device usually located between a stationary part and a moving part.

BIMETAL TEMPERATURE SENSOR: Any sensor or switch made of two dissimilar types of metal that bend when heated or cooled due to the different expansion rates of the alloys. These types of sensors usually function as an on/off switch.

BLOWBY: Combustion gases, composed of water vapor and unburned fuel, that leak past the piston rings into the crankcase during normal engine operation. These gases are removed by the PCV system to prevent the buildup of harmful acids in the crankcase.

BRAKE PAD: A brake shoe and lining assembly used with disc brakes.

BRAKE SHOE: The backing for the brake lining. The term is, however, usually applied to the assembly of the brake backing and lining.

BUSHING: A liner, usually removable, for a bearing; an anti-friction liner used in place of a bearing.

CALIPER: A hydraulically activated device in a disc brake system, which is mounted straddling the brake rotor (disc). The caliper contains at least one piston and two brake pads. Hydraulic pressure on the piston(s) forces the pads against the rotor.

CAMSHAFT: A shaft in the engine on which are the lobes (cams) which operate the valves. The camshaft is driven by the crankshaft, via a belt, chain or gears, at one half the crankshaft speed.

CAPACITOR: A device which stores an electrical charge.

CARBON MONOXIDE (CO): A colorless, odorless gas given off as a normal byproduct of combustion. It is poisonous and extremely dangerous in confined areas, building up slowly to toxic levels without warning if adequate ventilation is not available.

CARBURETOR: A device, usually mounted on the intake manifold of an engine, which mixes the air and fuel in the proper proportion to allow even combustion.

CATALYTIC CONVERTER: A device installed in the exhaust system, like a muffler, that converts harmful byproducts of combustion into carbon dioxide and water vapor by means of a heat-producing chemical reaction.

CENTRIFUGAL ADVANCE: A mechanical method of advancing the spark timing by using flyweights in the distributor that react to centrifugal force generated by the distributor shaft rotation.

CHECK VALVE: Any one-way valve installed to permit the flow of air, fuel or vacuum in one direction only.

GLOSSARY 10-9

CHOKE: A device, usually a moveable valve, placed in the intake path of a carburetor to restrict the flow of air.

CIRCUIT: Any unbroken path through which an electrical current can flow. Also used to describe fuel flow in some instances.

CIRCUIT BREAKER: A switch which protects an electrical circuit from overload by opening the circuit when the current flow exceeds a predetermined level. Some circuit breakers must be reset manually, while most reset automatically.

COIL (IGNITION): A transformer in the ignition circuit which steps up the voltage provided to the spark plugs.

COMBINATION MANIFOLD: An assembly which includes both the intake and exhaust manifolds in one casting.

COMBINATION VALVE: A device used in some fuel systems that routes fuel vapors to a charcoal storage canister instead of venting them into the atmosphere. The valve relieves fuel tank pressure and allows fresh air into the tank as the fuel level drops to prevent a vapor lock situation.

COMPRESSION RATIO: The comparison of the total volume of the cylinder and combustion chamber with the piston at BDC and the piston at TDC.

CONDENSER: 1. An electrical device which acts to store an electrical charge, preventing voltage surges. 2. A radiator-like device in the air conditioning system in which refrigerant gas condenses into a liquid, giving off heat.

CONDUCTOR: Any material through which an electrical current can be transmitted easily.

CONTINUITY: Continuous or complete circuit. Can be checked with an ohmmeter.

COUNTERSHAFT: An intermediate shaft which is rotated by a mainshaft and transmits, in turn, that rotation to a working part.

CRANKCASE: The lower part of an engine in which the crankshaft and related parts operate.

CRANKSHAFT: The main driving shaft of an engine which receives reciprocating motion from the pistons and converts it to rotary motion.

CYLINDER: In an engine, the round hole in the engine block in which the piston(s) ride.

CYLINDER BLOCK: The main structural member of an engine in which is found the cylinders, crankshaft and other principal parts.

CYLINDER HEAD: The detachable portion of the engine, usually fastened to the top of the cylinder block and containing all or most of the combustion chambers. On overhead valve engines, it contains the valves and their operating parts. On overhead cam engines, it contains the camshaft as well.

DEAD CENTER: The extreme top or bottom of the piston stroke.

DETONATION: An unwanted explosion of the air/fuel mixture in the combustion chamber caused by excess heat and compression, advanced timing, or an overly lean mixture. Also referred to as "ping".

DIAPHRAGM: A thin, flexible wall separating two cavities, such as in a vacuum advance unit.

DIESELING: A condition in which hot spots in the combustion chamber cause the engine to run on after the key is turned off.

DIFFERENTIAL: A geared assembly which allows the transmission of motion between drive axles, giving one axle the ability to turn faster than the other.

DIODE: An electrical device that will allow current to flow in one direction only.

DISC BRAKE: A hydraulic braking assembly consisting of a brake disc, or rotor, mounted on an axle, and a caliper assembly containing, usually two brake pads which are activated by hydraulic pressure. The pads are forced against the sides of the disc, creating friction which slows the vehicle.

DISTRIBUTOR: A mechanically driven device on an engine which is responsible for electrically firing the spark plug at a predetermined point of the piston stroke.

DOWEL PIN: A pin, inserted in mating holes in two different parts allowing those parts to maintain a fixed relationship.

DRUM BRAKE: A braking system which consists of two brake shoes and one or two wheel cylinders, mounted on a fixed backing plate, and a brake drum, mounted on an axle, which revolves around the assembly.

DWELL: The rate, measured in degrees of shaft rotation, at which an electrical circuit cycles on and off.

ELECTRONIC CONTROL UNIT (ECU): Ignition module, module, amplifier or igniter. See Module for definition.

ELECTRONIC IGNITION: A system in which the timing and firing of the spark plugs is controlled by an electronic control unit, usually called a module. These systems have no points or condenser.

END-PLAY: The measured amount of axial movement in a shaft.

ENGINE: A device that converts heat into mechanical energy.

EXHAUST MANIFOLD: A set of cast passages or pipes which conduct exhaust gases from the engine.

FEELER GAUGE: A blade, usually metal, or precisely predetermined thickness, used to measure the clearance between two parts.

Glossary

FIRING ORDER: The order in which combustion occurs in the cylinders of an engine. Also the order in which spark is distributed to the plugs by the distributor.

FLOODING: The presence of too much fuel in the intake manifold and combustion chamber which prevents the air/fuel mixture from firing, thereby causing a no-start situation.

FLYWHEEL: A disc shaped part bolted to the rear end of the crankshaft. Around the outer perimeter is affixed the ring gear. The starter drive engages the ring gear, turning the flywheel, which rotates the crankshaft, imparting the initial starting motion to the engine.

FOOT POUND (ft. lbs. or sometimes, ft.lb.): The amount of energy or work needed to raise an item weighing one pound, a distance of one foot.

FUSE: A protective device in a circuit which prevents circuit overload by breaking the circuit when a specific amperage is present. The device is constructed around a strip or wire of a lower amperage rating than the circuit it is designed to protect. When an amperage higher than that stamped on the fuse is present in the circuit, the strip or wire melts, opening the circuit.

GEAR RATIO: The ratio between the number of teeth on meshing gears.

GENERATOR: A device which converts mechanical energy into electrical energy.

HEAT RANGE: The measure of a spark plug's ability to dissipate heat from its firing end. The higher the heat range, the hotter the plug fires.

HUB: The center part of a wheel or gear.

HYDROCARBON (HC): Any chemical compound made up of hydrogen and carbon. A major pollutant formed by the engine as a byproduct of combustion.

HYDROMETER: An instrument used to measure the specific gravity of a solution.

INCH POUND (inch lbs.; sometimes in.lb. or in. lbs.): One twelfth of a foot pound.

INDUCTION: A means of transferring electrical energy in the form of a magnetic field. Principle used in the ignition coil to increase voltage.

INJECTOR: A device which receives metered fuel under relatively low pressure and is activated to inject the fuel into the engine under relatively high pressure at a predetermined time.

INPUT SHAFT: The shaft to which torque is applied, usually carrying the driving gear or gears.

INTAKE MANIFOLD: A casting of passages or pipes used to conduct air or a fuel/air mixture to the cylinders.

JOURNAL: The bearing surface within which a shaft operates.

KEY: A small block usually fitted in a notch between a shaft and a hub to prevent slippage of the two parts.

MANIFOLD: A casting of passages or set of pipes which connect the cylinders to an inlet or outlet source.

MANIFOLD VACUUM: Low pressure in an engine intake manifold formed just below the throttle plates. Manifold vacuum is highest at idle and drops under acceleration.

MASTER CYLINDER: The primary fluid pressurizing device in a hydraulic system. In automotive use, it is found in brake and hydraulic clutch systems and is pedal activated, either directly or, in a power brake system, through the power booster.

MODULE: Electronic control unit, amplifier or igniter of solid state or integrated design which controls the current flow in the ignition primary circuit based on input from the pick-up coil. When the module opens the primary circuit, high secondary voltage is induced in the coil.

NEEDLE BEARING: A bearing which consists of a number (usually a large number) of long, thin rollers.

OHM: (Ω) The unit used to measure the resistance of conductor-to-electrical flow. One ohm is the amount of resistance that limits current flow to one ampere in a circuit with one volt of pressure.

OHMMETER: An instrument used for measuring the resistance, in ohms, in an electrical circuit.

OUTPUT SHAFT: The shaft which transmits torque from a device, such as a transmission.

OVERDRIVE: A gear assembly which produces more shaft revolutions than that transmitted to it.

OVERHEAD CAMSHAFT (OHC): An engine configuration in which the camshaft is mounted on top of the cylinder head and operates the valve either directly or by means of rocker arms.

OVERHEAD VALVE (OHV): An engine configuration in which all of the valves are located in the cylinder head and the camshaft is located in the cylinder block. The camshaft operates the valves via lifters and pushrods.

OXIDES OF NITROGEN (NOx): Chemical compounds of nitrogen produced as a byproduct of combustion. They combine with hydrocarbons to produce smog.

GLOSSARY

OXYGEN SENSOR: Use with the feedback system to sense the presence of oxygen in the exhaust gas and signal the computer which can reference the voltage signal to an air/fuel ratio.

PINION: The smaller of two meshing gears.

PISTON RING: An open-ended ring with fits into a groove on the outer diameter of the piston. Its chief function is to form a seal between the piston and cylinder wall. Most automotive pistons have three rings: two for compression sealing; one for oil sealing.

PRELOAD: A predetermined load placed on a bearing during assembly or by adjustment.

PRIMARY CIRCUIT: the low voltage side of the ignition system which consists of the ignition switch, ballast resistor or resistance wire, bypass, coil, electronic control unit and pick-up coil as well as the connecting wires and harnesses.

PRESS FIT: The mating of two parts under pressure, due to the inner diameter of one being smaller than the outer diameter of the other, or vice versa; an interference fit.

RACE: The surface on the inner or outer ring of a bearing on which the balls, needles or rollers move.

REGULATOR: A device which maintains the amperage and/or voltage levels of a circuit at predetermined values.

RELAY: A switch which automatically opens and/or closes a circuit.

RESISTANCE: The opposition to the flow of current through a circuit or electrical device, and is measured in ohms. Resistance is equal to the voltage divided by the amperage.

RESISTOR: A device, usually made of wire, which offers a preset amount of resistance in an electrical circuit.

RING GEAR: The name given to a ring-shaped gear attached to a differential case, or affixed to a flywheel or as part of a planetary gear set.

ROLLER BEARING: A bearing made up of hardened inner and outer races between which hardened steel rollers move.

ROTOR: 1. The disc-shaped part of a disc brake assembly, upon which the brake pads bear; also called, brake disc. 2. The device mounted atop the distributor shaft, which passes current to the distributor cap tower contacts.

SECONDARY CIRCUIT: The high voltage side of the ignition system, usually above 20,000 volts. The secondary includes the ignition coil, coil wire, distributor cap and rotor, spark plug wires and spark plugs.

SENDING UNIT: A mechanical, electrical, hydraulic or electro-magnetic device which transmits information to a gauge.

SENSOR: Any device designed to measure engine operating conditions or ambient pressures and temperatures. Usually electronic in nature and designed to send a voltage signal to an on-board computer, some sensors may operate as a simple on/off switch or they may provide a variable voltage signal (like a potentiometer) as conditions or measured parameters change.

SHIM: Spacers of precise, predetermined thickness used between parts to establish a proper working relationship.

SLAVE CYLINDER: In automotive use, a device in the hydraulic clutch system which is activated by hydraulic force, disengaging the clutch.

SOLENOID: A coil used to produce a magnetic field, the effect of which is to produce work.

SPARK PLUG: A device screwed into the combustion chamber of a spark ignition engine. The basic construction is a conductive core inside of a ceramic insulator, mounted in an outer conductive base. An electrical charge from the spark plug wire travels along the conductive core and jumps a preset air gap to a grounding point or points at the end of the conductive base. The resultant spark ignites the fuel/air mixture in the combustion chamber.

SPLINES: Ridges machined or cast onto the outer diameter of a shaft or inner diameter of a bore to enable parts to mate without rotation.

TACHOMETER: A device used to measure the rotary speed of an engine, shaft, gear, etc., usually in rotations per minute.

THERMOSTAT: A valve, located in the cooling system of an engine, which is closed when cold and opens gradually in response to engine heating, controlling the temperature of the coolant and rate of coolant flow.

TOP DEAD CENTER (TDC): The point at which the piston reaches the top of its travel on the compression stroke.

TORQUE: The twisting force applied to an object.

TORQUE CONVERTER: A turbine used to transmit power from a driving member to a driven member via hydraulic action, providing changes in drive ratio and torque. In automotive use, it links the driveplate at the rear of the engine to the automatic transmission.

TRANSDUCER: A device used to change a force into an electrical signal.

TRANSISTOR: A semi-conductor component which can be actuated by a small voltage to perform an electrical switching function.

TUNE-UP: A regular maintenance function, usually associated with the replacement and adjustment of parts and components in the electrical and fuel systems of a vehicle for the purpose of attaining optimum performance.

GLOSSARY

TURBOCHARGER: An exhaust driven pump which compresses intake air and forces it into the combustion chambers at higher than atmospheric pressures. The increased air pressure allows more fuel to be burned and results in increased horsepower being produced.

VACUUM ADVANCE: A device which advances the ignition timing in response to increased engine vacuum.

VACUUM GAUGE: An instrument used to measure the presence of vacuum in a chamber.

VALVE: A device which control the pressure, direction of flow or rate of flow of a liquid or gas.

VALVE CLEARANCE: The measured gap between the end of the valve stem and the rocker arm, cam lobe or follower that activates the valve.

VISCOSITY: The rating of a liquid's internal resistance to flow.

VOLTMETER: An instrument used for measuring electrical force in units called volts. Voltmeters are always connected parallel with the circuit being tested.

WHEEL CYLINDER: Found in the automotive drum brake assembly, it is a device, actuated by hydraulic pressure, which, through internal pistons, pushes the brake shoes outward against the drums.

MASTER INDEX

ADJUSTMENTS (AUTOMATIC TRANSMISSION) 7-10
    BRAKE BAND 7-10
    KICKDOWN SWITCH AND DOWNSHIFT SOLENOID 7-11
    SHIFT LINKAGE 7-10
ADJUSTMENTS (BRAKE SYSTEM) 9-3
    BRAKE PEDAL 9-4
    DISC BRAKES 9-3
    DRUM BRAKES 9-3
ADJUSTMENTS (CLUTCH) 7-5
    CLUTCH INTERLOCK 7-6
    PEDAL FREE-PLAY 7-6
    PEDAL HEIGHT 7-5
ADJUSTMENTS (MANUAL TRANSMISSION) 7-2
ADJUSTMENTS (RADIO) 6-12
    REMOVAL & INSTALLATION 6-12
ADJUSTMENTS (VALVE LASH) 2-14
    1981-82 Z22 ENGINES 2-14
    L16, L18 AND L20B ENGINES 2-14
    VG30I ENGINES 2-16
    Z20, Z22 (EXCEPT 1981-82), Z24 & Z24I ENGINES 2-15
AIR CLEANER 1-10
    REMOVAL & INSTALLATION 1-10
AIR CONDITIONING COMPONENTS 6-10
    REMOVAL & INSTALLATION 6-10
AIR CONDITIONING COMPRESSOR 3-19
    REMOVAL & INSTALLATION 3-19
AIR CONDITIONING CONDENSER 3-20
    REMOVAL & INSTALLATION 3-20
AIR CONDITIONING SYSTEM 1-19
    ISOLATING THE COMPRESSOR 1-20
    PREVENTIVE MAINTENANCE 1-19
    SYSTEM INSPECTION 1-20
    SYSTEM SERVICE & REPAIR 1-19
AIR INDUCTION SYSTEM 4-11
    OPERATION 4-11
    SERVICE 4-11
AIR INJECTION/INDUCTION VALVE FILTER 1-13
    REMOVAL & INSTALLATION 1-13
AIR INJECTION SYSTEM (AIS) 4-10
    OPERATION 4-10
    SERVICE 4-11
ALTERNATOR 3-5
    ALTERNATOR PRECAUTIONS 3-5
    REMOVAL & INSTALLATION 3-5
ALTERNATOR AND REGULATOR SPECIFICATIONS 3-7
ANTENNA 10-4
    REMOVAL & INSTALLATION 10-4
AUTOMATIC TEMPERATURE CONTROLLED (ATC) AIR
  CLEANER 4-7
    OPERATION 4-7
    SERVICE 4-7
AUTOMATIC TRANSMISSION 7-10
AUTOMATIC TRANSMISSION (FLUIDS AND
  LUBRICANTS) 1-27
    DRAIN AND REFILL 1-28
    FLUID LEVEL CHECK 1-27
    FLUID RECOMMENDATIONS 1-27
AVOIDING THE MOST COMMON MISTAKES (HOW TO USE
  THIS BOOK) 1-2
AVOIDING TROUBLE (HOW TO USE THIS BOOK) 1-2
AXLE HOUSING 7-20
    REMOVAL & INSTALLATION 7-20
AXLE SHAFT 7-24
    REMOVAL & INSTALLATION 7-24
AXLE SHAFT, BEARING AND SEAL 7-18
    REMOVAL & INSTALLATION 7-18
BACK-UP LIGHT SWITCH (INSTRUMENT AND SWITCHES) 6-16
    REMOVAL & INSTALLATION 6-16
BACK-UP LIGHT SWITCH (MANUAL TRANSMISSION) 7-2
    REMOVAL & INSTALLATION 7-2
BASIC CHARGING SYSTEM PROBLEMS 2-20

10-14 MASTER INDEX

BASIC ELECTRICAL THEORY 6-2
    HOW DOES ELECTRICITY WORK: THE WATER
        ANALOGY 6-2
    OHM'S LAW 6-2
BASIC OPERATING PRINCIPLES (BRAKES) 9-2
    DISC BRAKES 9-2
    DRUM BRAKES 9-2
BASIC STARTING SYSTEM PROBLEMS 2-19
BATTERY (ENGINE ELECTRICAL) 3-9
    REMOVAL & INSTALLATION 3-9
BATTERY (FLUIDS AND LUBRICANTS) 1-33
BATTERY (ROUTINE MAINTENANCE AND TUNE-UP) 1-14
    BATTERY FLUID 1-14
    CABLES 1-15
    CHARGING 1-15
    GENERAL MAINTENANCE 1-14
    PRECAUTIONS 1-14
    REPLACEMENT 1-16
BATTERY AND STARTER SPECIFICATIONS 3-7
BLADE AND ARM 6-12
    REMOVAL & INSTALLATION 6-12
BLEEDING (BRAKES) 9-9
BLOWER MOTOR 6-9
    REMOVAL & INSTALLATION 6-9
BOLTS, NUTS AND OTHER THREADED RETAINERS 1-5
BOOST CONTROL DECELERATION DEVICE (BCDD) 4-6
    OPERATION 4-6
    SERVICE 4-6
BRAKE DISC (FRONT DISC BRAKES) 9-15
    INSPECTION 9-16
    REMOVAL & INSTALLATION 9-15
    WHEEL BEARING PRELOAD ADJUSTMENT 9-16
BRAKE DISC (REAR DISC BRAKES) 9-22
    INSPECTION 9-22
    REMOVAL & INSTALLATION 9-22
BRAKE DRUM (FRONT DRUM BRAKES) 9-10
    INSPECTION 9-10
    REMOVAL & INSTALLATION 9-10
BRAKE DRUMS (REAR DRUM BRAKES) 9-16
    INSPECTION 9-16
    REMOVAL & INSTALLATION 9-16
BRAKE HOSES AND LINES 9-9
    HYDRAULIC BRAKE LINE CHECK 9-9
BRAKE LIGHT SWITCH 9-5
    REMOVAL & INSTALLATION 9-5
BRAKE OPERATING SYSTEM 9-2
BRAKE PADS (FRONT DISC BRAKES) 9-12
    INSPECTION 9-12
    REMOVAL & INSTALLATION 9-12
BRAKE PADS (REAR DISC BRAKES) 9-21
    INSPECTION 9-21
    REMOVAL & INSTALLATION 9-21
BRAKE SHOES (FRONT DRUM BRAKES) 9-10
    INSPECTION 9-10
    REMOVAL & INSTALLATION 9-10
BRAKE SHOES (REAR DRUM BRAKES) 9-17
    REMOVAL & INSTALLATION 9-17
BRAKE SPECIFICATIONS 9-24
BRAKE SYSTEM 9-3
CABLES 9-22
    ADJUSTMENT 9-22
    REMOVAL & INSTALLATION 9-23
CALIPER (FRONT DISC BRAKES) 9-13
    OVERHAUL 9-14
    REMOVAL & INSTALLATION 9-13
CALIPER (REAR DISC BRAKES) 9-21
    OVERHAUL 9-22
    REMOVAL & INSTALLATION 9-21

CAMSHAFT 3-39
    CHECKING CAMSHAFT ENDPLAY 3-41
    CHECKING CAMSHAFT JOURNALS AND CAMSHAFT BEARING
        SADDLES 3-41
    CHECKING CAMSHAFT LOBE HEIGHT 3-41
    CHECKING CAMSHAFT RUNOUT 3-40
    REMOVAL & INSTALLATION 3-39
CAMSHAFT SPECIFICATIONS 3-53
CAMSHAFT SPROCKET/PULLEYS 3-39
    REMOVAL & INSTALLATION 3-39
CAPACITIES 1-40
CARBURETED ENGINES (ELECTRONIC IGNITION) 2-7
CARBURETED FUEL SYSTEM 5-2
CARBURETOR (CARBURETED FUEL SYSTEM) 5-4
    ADJUSTMENTS 5-6
    OVERHAUL 5-9
    REMOVAL & INSTALLATION 5-5
CARBURETOR (IDLE SPEED AND MIXTURE ADJUSTMENTS) 2-16
    ADJUSTMENT PROCEDURES 2-16
CATALYTIC CONVERTER (EMISSION CONTROLS) 4-13
    OPERATION 4-13
    PRECAUTIONS 4-14
    TESTING 4-14
CATALYTIC CONVERTER (EXHAUST SYSTEM) 3-51
    REMOVAL & INSTALLATION 3-51
CENTER BEARING 7-17
    REMOVAL & INSTALLATION 7-17
CHASSIS GREASING 1-33
    AUTOMATIC TRANSMISSION LINKAGE 1-34
    MANUAL TRANSMISSION AND CLUTCH LINKAGE 1-34
    PARKING BRAKE LINKAGE 1-34
CHECKING AND ADJUSTMENT (IGNITION TIMING) 2-13
    1970-86 CARBURETED ENGINES 2-13
    1986-88 FUEL INJECTED ENGINES 2-13
CHECKING ENGINE COMPRESSION 3-10
CIRCUIT BREAKERS 6-27
CIRCUIT PROTECTION 6-19
CLUTCH 7-5
CLUTCH DAMPER 7-9
    BLEEDING THE CLUTCH HYDRAULIC SYSTEM 7-9
    OVERHAUL 7-9
    REMOVAL & INSTALLATION 7-9
CLUTCH MASTER CYLINDER 7-8
    OVERHAUL 7-8
    REMOVAL & INSTALLATION 7-8
CLUTCH RELEASE CYLINDER 7-8
    OVERHAUL 7-8
    REMOVAL & INSTALLATION 7-8
COIL SPRINGS 8-16
    REMOVAL & INSTALLATION 8-16
COMBINATION SWITCH 8-20
    REMOVAL & INSTALLATION 8-20
COMPRESSION ROD AND STABILIZER BAR 8-7
    REMOVAL & INSTALLATION 8-7
CONTROL ARMS (FRONT SUSPENSION) 8-11
    REMOVAL & INSTALLATION 8-11
CONTROL ARMS (REAR SUSPENSION) 8-18
    REMOVAL & INSTALLATION 8-18
CONTROL HEAD 6-10
    ADJUSTMENT 6-11
    REMOVAL & INSTALLATION 6-10
COOLING 1-36
    ENGINE 1-36
COOLING SYSTEM 1-30
    CHECKING SYSTEM PROTECTION 1-31
    DRAIN AND REFILL 1-31
    FLUID LEVEL CHECK 1-30
    FLUID RECOMMENDATIONS 1-30

MASTER INDEX 10-15

SYSTEM INSPECTION 1-31
CRANKSHAFT AND CONNECTING RODS SPECIFICATIONS 3-54
CRANKSHAFT AND MAIN BEARING 3-47
    INSPECTION 3-47
    MAIN BEARING CLEARANCE CHECK 3-48
    MAIN BEARING REPLACEMENT 3-48
    REMOVAL & INSTALLATION 3-47
CYLINDER HEAD 3-22
    CLEANING AND INSPECTION 3-26
    CYLINDER BLOCK CLEANING 3-26
    REMOVAL & INSTALLATION 3-22
    RESURFACING 3-26
CYLINDER HEAD COVER 3-13
    REMOVAL & INSTALLATION 3-13
DETONATION CONTROL SYSTEM 4-13
    OPERATION 4-13
    SERVICE 4-13
DISTRIBUTOR 3-3
    INSTALLATION 3-3
    REMOVAL 3-3
DISTRIBUTOR SERVICE 2-8
    CARBURETED ENGINES 2-8
    FUEL INJECTED ENGINES 2-10
    PICK-UP COIL AND RELUCTOR REPLACEMENT 2-9
    RELUCTOR AND IC IGNITION UNIT 2-10
DO'S 1-4
DON'TS 1-5
DOOR GLASS AND REGULATOR 10-5
    ADJUSTMENT 10-6
    REMOVAL & INSTALLATION 10-5
DOOR LOCKS 10-2
    REMOVAL & INSTALLATION 10-2
DOOR TRIM PANELS 10-5
    REMOVAL & INSTALLATION 10-5
DRIVE AXLES (DIFFERENTIALS) 1-29
    DRAIN AND REFILL 1-30
    FLUID LEVEL CHECK 1-29
    FLUID RECOMMENDATIONS 1-29
DRIVE BELTS 1-16
    ADJUSTMENT 1-16
    INSPECTION 1-16
DRIVELINE 7-13
DRIVEN DISC AND PRESSURE PLATE 7-6
    REMOVAL & INSTALLATION 7-6
DUAL POINT DISTRIBUTOR 4-3
    INSPECTION AND ADJUSTMENTS 4-3
    OPERATION 4-3
DUAL SPARK PLUG IGNITION SYSTEM 4-4
    ADJUSTMENT 4-5
    OPERATION 4-4
EARLY FUEL EVAPORATION SYSTEM 4-6
    OPERATION 4-6
ELECTRIC CHOKE 4-13
    OPERATION 4-13
ELECTRIC FUEL PUMP (CARBURETED FUEL SYSTEM) 5-2
    OPERATION 5-2
    REMOVAL & INSTALLATION 5-3
    TESTING 5-3
ELECTRIC FUEL PUMP (FUEL INJECTION SYSTEM) 5-10
    DESCRIPTION 5-10
    REMOVAL & INSTALLATION 5-10
    TESTING 5-11
ELECTRICAL COMPONENTS 6-2
    CONNECTORS 6-4
    GROUND 6-3
    LOAD 6-4
    POWER SOURCE 6-2

    PROTECTIVE DEVICES 6-3
    SWITCHES & RELAYS 6-3
    WIRING & HARNESSES 6-4
ELECTRONIC ENGINE CONTROLS 4-15
ELECTRONIC FUEL INJECTION (EFI) 2-17
    IDLE SPEED ADJUSTMENT PROCEDURE 2-17
ELECTRONIC IGNITION 2-7
EMISSION CONTROLS 4-2
ENGINE (ENGINE MECHANICAL) 3-10
    REMOVAL & INSTALLATION 3-10
ENGINE (FLUIDS AND LUBRICANTS) 1-24
    OIL AND FILTER CHANGE 1-24
    OIL LEVEL CHECK 1-24
ENGINE ELECTRICAL 3-2
ENGINE IDENTIFICATION 1-9
ENGINE MECHANICAL 3-9
ENGINE MECHANICAL PROBLEMS 3-59
ENGINE OVERHAUL TIPS 3-9
    INSPECTION TECHNIQUES 3-9
    OVERHAUL TIPS 3-9
    REPAIRING DAMAGED THREADS 3-9
    TOOLS 3-9
ENGINE PERFORMANCE 3-60
ENGINE SERIAL NUMBER 1-8
    L16, L18 AND L20B ENGINES 1-9
    VG30I ENGINES 1-9
    Z20, Z22, Z24 AND Z24I ENGINES 1-9
EVAPORATIVE CANISTER 1-13
    SERVICING 1-13
EVAPORATIVE EMISSION CONTROL SYSTEM 4-2
    INSPECTION AND SERVICE 4-3
    REMOVAL & INSTALLATION 4-3
EXHAUST GAS RECIRCULATION (EGR) SYSTEM 4-8
    OPERATION 4-8
    REMOVAL & INSTALLATION 4-9
    SERVICE 4-8
EXHAUST MANIFOLD 3-18
    REMOVAL & INSTALLATION 3-18
EXHAUST SYSTEM 3-50
EXTERIOR 10-2
FASTENERS, MEASUREMENTS AND CONVERSIONS 1-5
FINAL DRIVE 7-19
    REMOVAL & INSTALLATION 7-19
FIRING ORDERS 2-5
FLUID PAN 7-10
FLUIDS AND LUBRICANTS 1-23
FLYWHEEL AND RING GEAR 3-49
    REMOVAL & INSTALLATION 3-49
FREE RUNNING HUB 7-21
    REMOVAL & INSTALLATION 7-21
FRONT AND REAR SEAT BELTS 10-6
    REMOVAL & INSTALLATION 10-6
FRONT AXLE HUB AND WHEEL BEARING 8-16
    REMOVAL & INSTALLATION 8-16
FRONT BENCH AND FRONT SPLIT-BENCH SEATS 10-6
    REMOVAL & INSTALLATION 10-6
FRONT BUCKET SEATS 10-6
    REMOVAL & INSTALLATION 10-6
FRONT DISC BRAKES 9-12
FRONT DOOR 10-2
    ADJUSTMENT 10-2
FRONT DRIVE AXLE 7-21
FRONT DRIVESHAFT AND U-JOINTS 7-13
    REMOVAL & INSTALLATION 7-13
    U-JOINT OVERHAUL 7-14
FRONT DRUM BRAKES 9-10
FRONT END ALIGNMENT 8-16
    CAMBER 8-16

MASTER INDEX

CASTER 8-16
    STEERING ANGLE ADJUSTMENT 8-16
    TOE 8-16
FRONT OIL SEAL 3-34
    REMOVAL & INSTALLATION 3-34
FRONT OR REAR BUMPER 10-3
    REMOVAL & INSTALLATION 10-3
FRONT PIPE 3-50
    REMOVAL & INSTALLATION 3-50
FRONT SUSPENSION 8-2
FUEL FILTER 1-11
    REMOVAL & INSTALLATION 1-11
FUEL INJECTED ENGINES 2-8
FUEL INJECTION SYSTEM 5-10
FUEL INJECTORS 5-12
    ADJUSTMENTS 5-13
    REMOVAL & INSTALLATION 5-12
FUEL SHUT-OFF SYSTEM 4-12
    OPERATION 4-12
FUEL SYSTEM PRESSURE 5-10
    RELEASE PROCEDURE 5-10
FUEL TANK 5-14
FUEL TANK LOCATION 5-14
    GAUGE UNIT 5-14
    REMOVAL & INSTALLATION 5-14
FUSES AND FLASHERS 6-19
    FLASHERS AND RELAYS 6-19
    FUSES 6-19
FUSIBLE LINK 6-26
    FUSE LINK 6-26
GASOLINE ENGINE TUNE-UP SPECIFICATIONS 2-18
GENERAL ENGINE SPECIFICATIONS 3-52
GENERAL RECOMMENDATIONS 1-36
HEADLIGHT SWITCH 6-16
    REMOVAL & INSTALLATION 6-16
HEADLIGHTS 6-17
    REMOVAL & INSTALLATION 6-17
HEADLINER 10-6
    REMOVAL & INSTALLATION 10-6
HEAT RISER 1-14
    SERVICING 1-14
HEATER ASSEMBLY 6-8
    REMOVAL & INSTALLATION 6-8
HEATER CORE 6-8
    REMOVAL & INSTALLATION 6-8
HEATING AND AIR CONDITIONING 6-8
HIGH ALTITUDE COMPENSATOR SYSTEM 4-13
    OPERATION 4-13
HITCH (TONGUE) WEIGHT 1-36
HOOD 10-2
    ADJUSTMENT 10-3
    REMOVAL & INSTALLATION 10-2
HOSES 1-18
    REPLACEMENT 1-18
HOW TO USE THIS BOOK 1-2
IDENTIFICATION (AUTOMATIC TRANSMISSION) 7-10
IDENTIFICATION (MANUAL TRANSMISSION) 7-2
IDLE SPEED AND MIXTURE ADJUSTMENTS 2-16
IGNITION COIL 3-2
    REMOVAL & INSTALLATION 3-2
    TESTING 3-2
IGNITION LOCK/SWITCH 8-21
    REMOVAL & INSTALLATION 8-21
IGNITION SWITCH (INSTRUMENT AND SWITCHES) 6-16
    REMOVAL & INSTALLATION 6-16
IGNITION SWITCH (STEERING) 8-21
    REMOVAL & INSTALLATION 8-21

IGNITION TIMING 2-11
INSPECTION (EXHAUST SYSTEM) 3-50
INSTRUMENT AND SWITCHES 6-15
INSTRUMENT CLUSTER 6-15
    REMOVAL & INSTALLATION 6-15
INTAKE MANIFOLD 3-16
    REMOVAL & INSTALLATION 3-16
INTAKE MANIFOLD VACUUM CONTROL SYSTEM 4-7
    OPERATION 4-7
INTERIOR 10-5
JACKING 1-37
JACKING PRECAUTIONS 1-38
JUMP STARTING A DEAD BATTERY 1-37
JUMP STARTING PRECAUTIONS 1-37
JUMP STARTING PROCEDURE 1-37
KINGPINS 8-7
    INSPECTION 8-7
    REMOVAL & INSTALLATION 8-8
LEAF SPRINGS 8-17
    REMOVAL & INSTALLATION 8-17
LIGHTING 6-17
LOAD SENSING PROPORTIONING VALVE 9-8
    ADJUSTMENT 9-8
    REMOVAL & INSTALLATION 9-8
LOWER BALL JOINT 8-10
    INSPECTION 8-10
    REMOVAL & INSTALLATION 8-10
LOWER CONTROL ARM 8-12
    REMOVAL & INSTALLATION 8-12
MAINTENANCE INTERVALS 1-39
MAINTENANCE OR REPAIR? 1-2
MANUAL STEERING GEAR 8-23
    ADJUSTMENTS 8-23
    REMOVAL & INSTALLATION 8-24
MANUAL TRANSMISSION 7-2
MANUAL TRANSMISSION (FLUIDS AND LUBRICANTS) 1-26
    CHECKING WATER ENTRY 1-27
    DRAIN AND REFILL 1-26
    FLUID LEVEL CHECK 1-26
    FLUID RECOMMENDATIONS 1-26
MASTER CYLINDER (BRAKE SYSTEM) 9-5
    OVERHAUL 9-5
    REMOVAL & INSTALLATION 9-5
MASTER CYLINDERS (FLUIDS AND LUBRICANTS) 1-31
    FLUID LEVEL CHECK 1-32
    FLUID RECOMMENDATIONS 1-32
MECHANICAL FUEL PUMP 5-2
    OPERATION 5-2
    REMOVAL & INSTALLATION 5-2
    TESTING 5-2
MIRRORS 10-4
    REMOVAL & INSTALLATION 10-4
MIXTURE HEATING SYSTEM 4-13
    OPERATION 4-13
MIXTURE RATIO FEEDBACK SYSTEM 4-14
    OPERATION 4-14
NEUTRAL SAFETY/INHIBITOR SWITCH 7-11
    1973-86 (620 AND 720-D SERIES) 7-11
    1986-88 (D21-D SERIES) 7-12
OIL AND FUEL RECOMMENDATIONS 1-23
    FUEL 1-24
    OIL 1-23
    OPERATION IN FOREIGN COUNTRIES 1-24
OIL PAN 3-30
    REMOVAL & INSTALLATION 3-30
OIL PUMP 3-31
    REMOVAL & INSTALLATION 3-31

MASTER INDEX 10-17

OXYGEN SENSOR 4-14
    OPERATION 4-14
    REMOVAL & INSTALLATION 4-15
PANHARD ROD 8-18
    REMOVAL & INSTALLATION 8-18
PARKING BRAKE 9-22
PARKING BRAKE SHOES 9-23
    ADJUSTMENT 9-23
PCV VALVE 1-12
    REMOVAL, TESTING & INSTALLATION 1-13
PINION SEAL (FRONT DRIVE AXLE) 7-26
    REMOVAL & INSTALLATION 7-26
PINION SEAL (REAR DRIVE AXLE) 7-20
    REMOVAL & INSTALLATION 7-20
PISTON AND RING SPECIFICATIONS 3-55
PISTONS AND CONNECTING RODS 3-41
    CLEANING AND INSPECTION 3-44
    CONNECTING ROD INSPECTION AND BEARING
      REPLACEMENT 3-45
    CYLINDER BORE INSPECTION 3-45
    IDENTIFICATION AND POSITIONING 3-42
    PISTON RING REPLACEMENT 3-43
    REMOVAL & INSTALLATION 3-41
    WRIST PIN REMOVAL & INSTALLATION 3-44
POINT TYPE IGNITION 2-5
    ADJUSTMENT OF THE BREAKER POINTS 2-6
    INSPECTION AND CLEANING 2-5
    REMOVAL & INSTALLATION 2-6
POSITIVE CRANKCASE VENTILATION (PCV) SYSTEM 4-2
    OPERATION 4-2
    REMOVAL & INSTALLATION 4-2
    TESTING 4-2
POWER BRAKE BOOSTER 9-8
    REMOVAL & INSTALLATION 9-8
POWER STEERING GEAR 8-24
    ADJUSTMENT 8-24
    REMOVAL & INSTALLATION 8-24
POWER STEERING PUMP (FLUIDS AND LUBRICANTS) 1-32
    FLUID LEVEL CHECK 1-33
    FLUID RECOMMENDATIONS 1-32
POWER STEERING PUMP (STEERING) 8-25
    BLEEDING 8-25
    REMOVAL AND INSTALLATION 8-25
RADIATOR 3-20
    REMOVAL & INSTALLATION 3-20
RADIO 6-12
REAR BENCH SEAT 10-6
    REMOVAL & INSTALLATION 10-6
REAR DISC BRAKES 9-21
REAR DRIVE AXLE 7-18
REAR DRIVESHAFT AND U-JOINTS 7-14
    REMOVAL & INSTALLATION 7-14
    U-JOINT OVERHAUL 7-16
REAR DRUM BRAKES 9-16
REAR MAIN OIL SEAL 3-46
    REPLACEMENT 3-46
REAR SUSPENSION 8-16
REAR WIPER 6-14
    REMOVAL & INSTALLATION 6-14
REGULATOR 3-5
    ADJUSTMENT 3-6
    REMOVAL & INSTALLATION 3-5
ROCKER ARM/SHAFT ASSEMBLY 3-13
    INSPECTION 3-15
    REMOVAL & INSTALLATION 3-13
ROCKER ARMS AND ROCKER PIVOTS 3-13
    REMOVAL & INSTALLATION 3-13
ROUTINE MAINTENANCE AND TUNE-UP 1-10

SELF-DIAGNOSTIC SYSTEM 4-15
SERIAL NUMBER IDENTIFICATION 1-7
SERVICING YOUR VEHICLE SAFELY 1-4
SHOCK ABSORBER (FRONT SUSPENSION) 8-5
    REMOVAL & INSTALLATION 8-5
    TESTING 8-5
SHOCK ABSORBERS (REAR SUSPENSION) 8-17
    INSPECTION AND TESTING 8-17
    REMOVAL & INSTALLATION 8-17
SIGNAL AND MARKER LIGHTS 6-17
    REMOVAL & INSTALLATION 6-17
SPARK PLUG SWITCHING CONTROL SYSTEM 4-6
    OPERATION 4-6
SPARK PLUG WIRES 2-4
    CHECKING AND REPLACEMENT 2-4
SPARK PLUGS 2-2
    INSPECTION & GAPPING 2-3
    INSTALLATION 2-4
    REMOVAL 2-3
SPARK TIMING CONTROL SYSTEM 4-5
    INSPECTION AND ADJUSTMENTS 4-5
    OPERATION 4-5
SPECIAL TOOLS 1-4
SPECIFICATION CHARTS
    ALTERNATOR AND REGULATOR SPECIFICATIONS 3-7
    BATTERY AND STARTER SPECIFICATIONS 3-7
    BRAKE SPECIFICATIONS 9-24
    CAMSHAFT SPECIFICATIONS 3-53
    CAPACITIES 1-40
    CRANKSHAFT AND CONNECTING RODS
      SPECIFICATIONS 3-54
    ENGINE IDENTIFICATION 1-9
    GASOLINE ENGINE TUNE-UP SPECIFICATIONS 2-18
    GENERAL ENGINE SPECIFICATIONS 3-52
    PISTON AND RING SPECIFICATIONS 3-55
    TORQUE SPECIFICATIONS 3-56
    TORQUE SPECIFICATIONS 8-26
    VALVE SPECIFICATIONS 3-52
    WHEEL ALIGNMENT 8-26
SPEEDOMETER CABLE 6-16
    REPLACEMENT 6-16
STABILIZER BAR 8-18
    REMOVAL & INSTALLATION 8-18
STANDARD AND METRIC MEASUREMENTS 1-7
STARTER 3-8
    OVERHAUL 3-8
    REMOVAL & INSTALLATION 3-8
STEERING 8-20
STEERING GEAR 1-33
    FLUID LEVEL CHECK 1-33
    FLUID RECOMMENDATIONS 1-33
STEERING KNUCKLE AND SPINDLE 8-13
    REMOVAL & INSTALLATION 8-13
STEERING LINKAGE 8-21
    REMOVAL & INSTALLATION 8-21
STEERING WHEEL 8-20
    REMOVAL & INSTALLATION 8-20
TAILGATE 10-3
    ALIGNMENT 10-3
    REMOVAL & INSTALLATION 10-3
TAILPIPE AND MUFFLER 3-51
    REMOVAL & INSTALLATION 3-51
TENSION ROD AND STABILIZER BAR 8-5
    REMOVAL & INSTALLATION 8-5
TEST EQUIPMENT 6-5
    JUMPER WIRES 6-5
    MULTIMETERS 6-5
    TEST LIGHTS 6-5

10-18 MASTER INDEX

TESTING 6-6
    OPEN CIRCUITS 6-6
    RESISTANCE 6-7
    SHORT CIRCUITS 6-6
    VOLTAGE 6-6
    VOLTAGE DROP 6-7
THERMOSTAT 3-15
    REMOVAL & INSTALLATION 3-15
THROTTLE BODY/CHAMBER 5-11
    REMOVAL & INSTALLATION 5-11
TIMING BELT 3-37
    REMOVAL & INSTALLATION 3-37
TIMING BELT COVER 3-34
    REMOVAL & INSTALLATION 3-34
TIMING CHAIN AND TENSIONER 3-35
    REMOVAL & INSTALLATION 3-35
    TIMING CHAIN ADJUSTMENT 3-37
TIMING CHAIN COVER 3-32
    REMOVAL & INSTALLATION 3-32
TIRES AND WHEELS 1-21
    INFLATION & INSPECTION 1-22
    TIRE DESIGN 1-21
    TIRE ROTATION 1-21
    TIRE STORAGE 1-21
TOOLS AND EQUIPMENT 1-2
TORQUE 1-6
    TORQUE ANGLE METERS 1-7
    TORQUE WRENCHES 1-6
TORQUE SPECIFICATIONS (ENGINE AND ENGINE REBUILDING) 3-56
TORQUE SPECIFICATIONS (SUSPENSION AND STEERING) 8-26
TORSION BARS 8-2
    REMOVAL & INSTALLATION 8-2
TRAILER TOWING 1-36
TRAILER WEIGHT 1-36
TRAILER WIRING 6-19
TRANSFER CASE 7-12
TRANSFER CASE (FLUIDS AND LUBRICANTS) 1-28
    DRAIN AND REFILL 1-28
    FLUID LEVEL CHECK 1-28
    FLUID RECOMMENDATIONS 1-28
TRANSFER CASE (TRANSFER CASE) 7-12
    REMOVAL & INSTALLATION 7-12
TRANSMISSION (AUTOMATIC TRANSMISSION) 7-12
    REMOVAL & INSTALLATION 7-12
TRANSMISSION (MANUAL TRANSMISSION) 7-2
    REMOVAL & INSTALLATION 7-2
TRANSMISSION (SERIAL NUMBER IDENTIFICATION) 1-9
TRANSMISSION (TRAILER TOWING) 1-36
TROUBLESHOOTING (ELECTRONIC IGNITION) 2-10
    CARBURETED ENGINES 2-10
TROUBLESHOOTING (FUEL INJECTION SYSTEM) 5-10
TROUBLESHOOTING CHARTS
  BASIC CHARGING SYSTEM PROBLEMS 2-20
  BASIC STARTING SYSTEM PROBLEMS 2-19
  ENGINE MECHANICAL PROBLEMS 3-59
  ENGINE PERFORMANCE 3-60
  TROUBLESHOOTING ELECTRICAL SYSTEMS 6-6

TUNE-UP PROCEDURES 2-2
TURN SIGNAL AND DIMMER SWITCH 8-20
    REMOVAL & INSTALLATION 8-20
TURN SIGNAL/COMBINATION SWITCH 6-16
    REMOVAL & INSTALLATION 6-16
UNDERSTANDING AND TROUBLESHOOTING ELECTRICAL SYSTEMS 6-2
UNDERSTANDING THE AUTOMATIC TRANSMISSION 7-10
UNDERSTANDING THE CLUTCH 7-5
UNDERSTANDING THE FUEL SYSTEM 5-2
UNDERSTANDING THE MANUAL TRANSMISSION 7-2
UPPER BALL JOINT 8-9
    INSPECTION 8-9
    REMOVAL & INSTALLATION 8-9
UPPER CONTROL ARM 8-11
    REMOVAL & INSTALLATION 8-11
VACUUM DIAGRAMS AND SYSTEM COMPONENTS 4-21
VALVE GUIDES 3-29
    INSPECTION 3-29
    REMOVAL & INSTALLATION 3-29
VALVE LASH 2-13
VALVE SPECIFICATIONS 3-52
VALVE SPRINGS 3-29
    INSPECTION 3-29
VALVES AND SPRINGS 3-27
    ADJUSTMENT (AFTER ENGINE SERVICE) 3-27
    INSPECTION 3-28
    REFACING 3-29
    REMOVAL & INSTALLATION 3-27
VEHICLE IDENTIFICATION NUMBER 1-7
WATER PUMP 3-21
    REMOVAL & INSTALLATION 3-21
WHEEL ALIGNMENT 8-26
WHEEL BEARINGS 1-34
    ADJUSTMENT AND LUBRICATION 1-34
WHEEL CYLINDERS (FRONT DRUM BRAKES) 9-11
    OVERHAUL 9-11
    REMOVAL & INSTALLATION 9-11
WHEEL CYLINDERS (REAR DRUM BRAKES) 9-19
    OVERHAUL 9-20
    REMOVAL & INSTALLATION 9-19
WHERE TO BEGIN 1-2
WINDSHIELD AND FIXED GLASS 10-4
    REMOVAL & INSTALLATION 10-4
    WINDSHIELD CHIP REPAIR 10-4
WINDSHIELD WIPER MOTOR 6-13
    REMOVAL & INSTALLATION 6-13
WINDSHIELD WIPER SWITCH 6-15
    REMOVAL & INSTALLATION 6-15
WINDSHIELD WIPERS 6-12
WINDSHIELD WIPERS (ROUTINE MAINTENANCE AND TUNE-UP) 1-20
    ELEMENT (REFILL) CARE & REPLACEMENT 1-20
WIPER LINKAGE 6-13
    REMOVAL & INSTALLATION 6-13
WIRE AND CONNECTOR REPAIR 6-7
WIRING DIAGRAMS 6-28

Don't Miss These Other Important Titles From NP/CHILTON'S.

TOTAL CAR CARE MANUALS
The ULTIMATE in automotive repair manuals

Features:
- Based on actual teardowns
- Each manual covers all makes and models (unless otherwise indicated)
- Expanded photography from vehicle teardowns
- Actual vacuum and wiring diagrams—not general representations
- Comprehensive coverage
- Maintenance interval schedules
- Electronic engine and emission controls

ACURA
Coupes and Sedans 1986-93
PART NO. 8426/10300

AMC
Coupes/Sedans/Wagons 1975-88
PART NO. 14300

BMW
Coupes and Sedans 1970-88
PART NO. 8789/18300
318/325/M3/525/535/M5 1989-93
PART NO. 8427/18400

CHRYSLER
Aspen/Volare 1976-80
PART NO. 20100
Caravan/Voyager/Town & Country 1984-95
PART NO. 8155/20300
Caravan/Voyager/Town & Country 1996-99
PART NO. 20302
Cirrus/Stratus/Sebring/Avenger 1995-98
PART NO. 20320
Colt/Challenger/Conquest/Vista 1971-89
PART NO. 20340
Colt/Vista 1990-93
PART NO. 8418/20342
Concorde/Intrepid/New Yorker/LHS/Vision 1993-97
PART NO. 8817/20360
Front Wheel Drive Cars-4 Cyl 1981-95
PART NO. 8673/20382
Front Wheel Drive Cars-6 Cyl 1988-95
PART NO. 8672/20384
Full-Size Trucks 1967-88
PART NO. 8662/20400
Full-Size Trucks 1989-96
PART NO. 8166/20402
Full-Size Vans 1967-88
PART NO. 20420
Full-Size Vans 1989-98
PART NO. 8169/20422
Neon 1995-99
PART NO. 20600
Omni/Horizon/Rampage 1978-89
PART NO. 8787/20700
Ram 50/D50/Arrow 1979-93
PART NO. 20800

FORD
Aerostar 1986-96
PART NO. 8057/26100
Aspire 1994-97
PART NO. 26120
Contour/Mystique/Cougar 1995-99
PART NO. 26170
Crown Victoria/Grand Marquis 1989-94
PART NO. 8417/26180
Escort/Lynx 1981-90
PART NO. 8270/26240
Escort/Tracer 1991-99
PART NO. 26242
Fairmont/Zephyr 1978-83
PART NO. 26320
Ford/Mercury Full-Size Cars 1968-88
PART NO. 8665/26360
Full-Size Vans 1961-88
PART NO. 26400
Full-Size Vans 1989-96
PART NO. 8157/26402
Ford/Mercury Mid-Size Cars 1971-85
PART NO. 8667/26580
Mustang/Cougar 1964-73
PART NO. 26600
Mustang/Capri 1979-88
PART NO. 8580/26604
Mustang 1989-93
PART NO. 8253/26606
Mustang 1994-98
PART NO. 26608
Pick-Ups and Bronco 1976-86
PART NO. 8576/26662
Pick-Ups and Bronco 1987-96
PART NO. 8136/26664
Pick-Ups/Expedition/Navigator 1997-00
PART NO. 26666
Probe 1989-92
PART NO. 8266/26680
Probe 1993-97
PART NO. 8411/46802
Ranger/Bronco II 1983-90
PART NO. 8159/26686
Ranger/Explorer/Mountaineer 1991-97
PART NO. 26688
Taurus/Sable 1986-95
PART NO. 8251/26700
Taurus/Sable 1996-99
PART NO. 26702
Tempo/Topaz 1984-94
PART NO. 8271/26720
Thunderbird/Cougar 1983-96
PART NO. 8268/26760
Windstar 1995-98
PART NO. 26840

GENERAL MOTORS
Astro/Safari 1985-96
PART NO. 8056/28100
Blazer/Jimmy 1969-82
PART NO. 28140
Blazer/Jimmy/Typhoon/Bravada 1983-93
PART NO. 8139/28160
Blazer/Jimmy/Bravada 1994-99
PART NO. 8845/28862
Bonneville/Eighty Eight/LeSabre 1986-99
PART NO. 8423/28200
Buick/Oldsmobile/Pontiac Full-Size 1975-90
PART NO. 8584/28240
Cadillac 1967-89
PART NO. 8587/28260
Camaro 1967-81
PART NO. 28280
Camaro 1982-92
PART NO. 8260/28282
Camaro/Firebird 1993-98
PART NO. 28284
Caprice 1990-93
PART NO. 8421/28300
Cavalier/Sunbird/Skyhawk/Firenza 1982-94
PART NO. 8269/28320
Cavalier/Sunfire 1995-00
PART NO. 28322
Celebrity/Century/Ciera/6000 1982-96
PART NO. 8252/28360
Chevette/1000 1976-88
PART NO. 28400
Chevy Full-Size Cars 1968-78
PART NO. 28420
Chevy Full-Size Cars 1979-89
PART NO. 8531/28422
Chevy Mid-Size Cars 1964-88
PART NO. 8594/28440
Citation/Omega/Phoenix/Skylark/XII 1980-85
PART NO. 28460
Corsica/Beretta 1988-96
PART NO. 8254/28480
Corvette 1963-82
PART NO. 28500
Corvette 1984-96
PART NO. 28502
Cutlass RWD 1970-87
PART NO. 8668/28520
DeVille/Fleetwood/Eldorado/Seville 1990-93
PART NO. 8420/28540
Electra/Park Avenue/Ninety-Eight 1990-93
PART NO. 8430/28560
Fiero 1984-88
PART NO. 28580
Firebird 1967-81
PART NO. 28600
Firebird 1982-92
PART NO. 8534/28602
Full-Size Trucks 1970-79
PART NO. 28620
Full-Size Trucks 1980-87
PART NO. 8577/28622
Full-Size Trucks 1988-98
PART NO. 8055/28624
Full-Size Vans 1967-86
PART NO. 28640
Full-Size Vans 1987-97
PART NO. 8040/28642
Grand Am/Achieva 1985-98
PART NO. 8257/28660
Lumina/Silhouette/Trans Sport/Venture 1990-99
PART NO. 8134/28680
Lumina/Monte Carlo/Grand Prix/Cutlass Supreme/Regal 1988-96
PART NO. 8258/28682
Metro/Sprint 1985-99
PART NO. 8424/28700
Nova/Chevy II 1962-79
PART NO. 28720
Pontiac Mid-Size 1974-83
PART NO. 28740
Chevrolet Nova/GEO Prizm 1985-93
PART NO. 8422/28760
Regal/Century 1975-87
PART NO. 28780
Chevrolet Spectrum/GEO Storm 1985-93
PART NO. 8425/28800
S10/S15/Sonoma Pick-Ups 1982-93
PART NO. 8141/28860
S10/Sonoma/Blazer/Jimmy/Bravada Hombre 1994-99
PART NO. 8845/28862

HONDA
Accord/Civic/Prelude 1973-83
PART NO. 8591/30100
Accord/Prelude 1984-95
PART NO. 8255/30150
Civic, CRX and del SOL 1984-95
PART NO. 8256/30200

HYUNDAI
Coupes/Sedans 1986-93
PART NO. 8412/32100
Coupes/Sedans 1994-98
PART NO. 32102

ISUZU
Amigo/Pick-Ups/Rodeo/Trooper 1981-96
PART NO. 8686/36100
Cars and Trucks 1981-91
PART NO. 8069/36150

JEEP
CJ 1945-70
PART NO. 40200
CJ/Scrambler 1971-86
PART NO. 8536/40202
Wagoneer/Commando/Cherokee 1957-83
PART NO. 40600
Wagoneer/Comanche/Cherokee 1984-98
PART NO. 8143/40602
Wrangler/YJ 1987-95
PART NO. 8535/40650

MAZDA
Trucks 1972-86
PART NO. 46600
Trucks 1987-93
PART NO. 8264/46602
Trucks 1994-98
PART NO. 46604
323/626/929/GLC/MX-6/RX-7 1978-89
PART NO. 8581/46800
323/Protege/MX-3/MX-6/626 Millenia/Ford Probe 1990-98
PART NO. 8411/46802

MERCEDES
Coupes/Sedans/Wagons 1974-84
PART NO. 48300

MITSUBISHI
Cars and Trucks 1983-89
PART NO. 7947/50200
Eclipse 1990-98
PART NO. 8415/50400
Pick-Ups and Montero 1983-95
PART NO. 8666/50500

NISSAN
Datsun 210/1200 1973-81
PART NO. 52300
Datsun 200SX/510/610/710/810/Maxima 1973-84
PART NO. 52302
Nissan Maxima 1985-92
PART NO. 8261/52450
Maxima 1993-98
PART NO. 52452
Pick-Ups and Pathfinder 1970-88
PART NO. 8585/52500
Pick-Ups and Pathfinder 1989-95
PART NO. 8145/52502

Total Car Care, continued

Sentra/Pulsar/NX 1982-96
PART NO. 8263/52700
Stanza/200SX/240SX 1982-92
PART NO. 8262/52750
240SX/Altima 1993-98
PART NO. 52752
Datsun/Nissan Z and ZX 1970-88
PART NO. 8846/52800

RENAULT
Coupes/Sedans/Wagons 1975-85
PART NO. 58300

SATURN
Coupes/Sedans/Wagons 1991-98
PART NO. 8419/62300

SUBARU
Coupes/Sedan/Wagons 1970-84
PART NO. 8790/64300
Coupes/Sedans/Wagons 1985-96
PART NO. 8259/64302

SUZUKI
Samurai/Sidekick/Tracker 1986-98
PART NO. 66500

TOYOTA
Camry 1983-96
PART NO. 8265/68200
Celica/Supra 1971-85
PART NO. 68250
Celica 1986-93
PART NO. 8413/68252

Celica 1994-98
PART NO. 68254
Corolla 1970-87
PART NO. 8586/68300
Corolla 1988-97
PART NO. 8414/68302
Cressida/Corona/Crown/MkII 1970-82
PART NO. 68350
Cressida/Van 1983-90
PART NO. 68352
Pick-ups/Land Cruiser/4Runner 1970-88
PART NO. 8578/68600
Pick-ups/Land Cruiser/4Runner 1989-98
PART NO. 8163/68602
Previa 1991-97
PART NO. 68640

Tercel 1984-94
PART NO. 8595/68700

VOLKSWAGEN
Air-Cooled 1949-69
PART NO. 70200
Air-Cooled 1970-81
PART NO. 70202
Front Wheel Drive 1974-89
PART NO. 8663/70400
Golf/Jetta/Cabriolet 1990-93
PART NO. 8429/70402

VOLVO
Coupes/Sedans/Wagons 1970-89
PART NO. 8786/72300
Coupes/Sedans/Wagons 1990-98
PART NO. 8428/72302

SELOC MARINE MANUALS

OUTBOARDS
Chrysler Outboards, All Engines 1962-84
PART NO. 018-7(1000)
Force Outboards, All Engines 1984-96
PART NO. 024-1(1100)
Honda Outboards, All Engines 1988-98
PART NO. 1200
Johnson/Evinrude Outboards, 1.5-40HP, 2-Stroke 1956-70
PART NO. 007-1(1300)
Johnson/Evinrude Outboards, 1.25-60HP, 2-Stroke 1971-89
PART NO. 008-X(1302)
Johnson/Evinrude Outboards, 1-50 HP, 2-Stroke 1990-95
PART NO. 026-8(1304)
Johnson/Evinrude Outboards, 50-125 HP, 2-Stroke 1958-72
PART NO. 009-8(1306)
Johnson/Evinrude Outboards, 60-235 HP, 2-Stroke 1973-91
PART NO. 010-1(1308)
Johnson/Evinrude Outboards, 80-300 HP, 2-Stroke 1992-96
PART NO. 040-3(1310)
Mariner Outboards, 2-60 HP, 2-Stroke 1977-89
PART NO. 015-2(1400)

Mariner Outboards, 45-220 HP, 2 Stroke 1977-89
PART NO. 016-0(1402)
Mercury Outboards, 2-40 HP, 2-Stroke 1965-91
PART NO. 012-8(1404)
Mercury Outboards, 40-115 HP, 2-Stroke 1965-92
PART NO. 013-6(1406)
Mercury Outboards, 90-300 HP, 2-Stroke 1965-91
PART NO. 014-4(1408)
Mercury/Mariner Outboards, 2.5-25 HP, 2-Stroke 1990-94
PART NO. 035-7(1410)
Mercury/Mariner Outboards, 40-125 HP, 2-Stroke 1990-94
PART NO. 036-5(1412)
Mercury/Mariner Outboards, 135-275 HP, 2-Stroke 1990-94
PART NO. 037-3(1414)
Mercury/Mariner Outboards, All Engines 1995-99
PART NO. 1416
Suzuki Outboards, All Engines 1985-99
PART NO. 1600

Yamaha Outboards, 2-25 HP, 2-Stroke and 9.9 HP, 4-Stroke 1984-91
PART NO. 021-7(1700)
Yamaha Outboards, 30-90 HP, 2-Stroke 1984-91
PART NO. 022-5(1702)
Yamaha Outboards, 115-225 HP, 2-Stroke 1984-91
PART NO. 023-3(1704)
Yamaha Outboards, All Engines 1992-98
PART NO. 1706

STERN DRIVES
Marine Jet Drive 1961-96
PART NO. 029-2(3000)
Mercruiser Stern Drive Type 1, Alpha, Bravo I, II, 1964-92
PART NO. 005-5(3200)
Mercruiser Stern Drive Alpha 1 Generation II 1992-96
PART NO. 039-X(3202)
Mercruiser Stern Drive Bravo I, II, III 1992-96
PART NO. 046-2(3204)
OMC Stern Drive 1964-86
PART NO. 004-7(3400)
OMC Cobra Stern Drive 1985-95
PART NO. 025-X(3402)

Volvo/Penta Stern Drives 1968-91
PART NO. 011-X(3600)
Volvo/Penta Stern Drives 1992-93
PART NO. 038-1(3602)
Volvo/Penta Stern Drives 1992-95
PART NO. 041-1(3604)

INBOARDS
Yanmar Inboard Diesels 1988-91
PART NO. 7400

PERSONAL WATERCRAFT
Kawasaki 1973-91
PART NO. 032-2(9200)
Kawasaki 1992-97
PART NO. 042-X(9202)
Polaris 1992-97
PART NO. 045-4(9400)
Sea Doo/Bombardier 1988-91
PART NO. 033-0(9000)
Sea Doo/Bombardier 1992-97
PART NO. 043-8(9002)
Yamaha 1987-91
PART NO. 034-9(9600)
Yamaha 1992-97
PART NO. 044-6(9602)

"...and even more from CHILTON"

General Interest / Recreational Books

ATV Handbook
PART NO. 9123
Auto Detailing
PART NO. 8394
Auto Body Repair
PART NO. 7898
Briggs & Stratton Vertical Crankshaft Engine
PART NO. 61-1-2
Briggs & Stratton Horizontal Crankshaft Engine
PART NO. 61-0-4
Briggs & Stratton Overhead Valve (OHV) Engine
PART NO. 61-2-0
Easy Car Care
PART NO. 8042

Motorcycle Handbook
PART NO. 9099
Snowmobile Handbook
PART NO. 9124
Small Engine Repair (Up to 20 Hp)
PART NO. 8325

Total Service Series

Automatic Transmissions/Transaxles Diagnosis and Repair
PART NO. 8944
Brake System Diagnosis and Repair
PART NO. 8945
Chevrolet Engine Overhaul Manual
PART NO. 8794
Engine Code Manual
PART NO. 8851
Ford Engine Overhaul Manual
PART NO. 8793
Fuel Injection Diagnosis and Repair
PART NO. 8946

COLLECTOR'S SERIES HARD-COVER MANUALS
Chilton's Collector's Editions are perfect for enthusiasts of vintage or rare cars. These hard-cover manuals contain repair and maintenance information for all major systems that might not be available elsewhere. Included are repair and overhaul procedures using thousands of illustrations. These manuals offer a range of coverage from as far back as 1940 and as recent as 1997, so you don't need an antique car or truck to be a collector.

MULTI-VEHICLE SPANISH LANGUAGE MANUALS
Chilton's Spanish language manuals offer some of our most popular titles in Spanish. Each is as complete and easy to use as the English-language counterpart and offers the same maintenance, repair and overhaul information along with specifications charts and tons of illustrations.

TOTAL SERVICE SERIES / SYSTEM SPECIFIC MANUALS
These innovative books offer repair, maintenance and service procedures for automotive related systems. They cover today's complex vehicles in a user-friendly format, which places even the most difficult automotive topic well within the reach of every Do-It-Yourselfer. Each title covers a specific subject from Brakes and Engine Rebuilding to Fuel Injection Systems, Automatic Transmissions and even Engine Trouble Codes.

For the titles listed, visit your local Chilton® Retailer
For a Catalog, for information, or to order call toll-free: 877-4CHILTON.

 1020 Andrew Drive, Suite 200 • West Chester, PA 19380-4291
www.chiltononline.com